Comparative International Management

The use of comparisons to explain, analyse and understand social and economic phenomena is recognized as a valuable social science tool. This textbook deals with the differences in management and organization between nations and their effects on multinational enterprises.

In comparing management practice across the world, the authors cover themes such as national cultures, diversity and globalization. Students are guided through the key business disciplines, providing a broad introduction to the field and including truly global coverage.

With student- and instructor-friendly resources such as chapter summaries, mini-case scenarios, larger case studies and PowerPoint slides, this book is core reading for students of international business and international management.

Arndt Sorge is Professor Emeritus of Internationalization and Organization at the Social Science Research Center Berlin, Germany, and Honorary Professor at the University of Potsdam.

Niels Noorderhaven is Professor of International Management at Tilburg University, Netherlands.

Carla Koen is Professor of Technology Management and Entrepreneurship at TIAS School for Business and Society, Netherlands.

www.routledge.com/9780415744836

For understanding management differences across cultures, there is no substitute for personal international experience. Academic literature on the subject too often resembles mediaeval scholastic disputes. The editors and authors of the present book have set themselves to inform future practitioners, for which they should be complimented.

Geert Hofstede, Professor Emeritus, Maastricht University, The Netherlands

This is a welcome and well integrated textbook on comparative international management, which is very much needed for degrees and courses in international business. It provides balanced arguments and evidence about the importance of universalistic and particularistic approaches to management across societal boundaries and presents a systematic framework for integrating the considerable literature on comparative management, including studies of organisations in Asia and Africa. It will be particularly useful for students on advanced undergraduate and postgraduate programmes.

Richard Whitley, Professor of Organizational Sociology, Manchester Business School, University of Manchester, UK

Comparative International Management

Second edition

Arndt Sorge, Niels Noorderhaven
and Carla Koen

LONDON AND NEW YORK

First published 2015
by Routledge
2 Park Square, Milton Park, Abingdon, Oxon OX14 4RN

Simultaneously published in the USA and Canada
by Routledge
711 Third Avenue, New York, NY 10017

Routledge is an imprint of the Taylor & Francis Group, an informa business

British Library Cataloguing in Publication Data
A catalogue record for this book is available from the British Library

Library of Congress Cataloging-in-Publication Data
Sorge, Arndt.
Comparative international management / Arndt Sorge, Niels Noorderhaven and Carla Koen. — 2nd edition.
pages cm
Revised edition of Karla Koen's Comparative international management, published by McGraw-Hill Education in 2005.
Includes bibliographical references and index.
1. International business enterprises—Management. 2. Comparative management. 3. Management—Cross-cultural studies. I. Noorderhaven, Niels G. II. Koen, Carla. Comparative international management. III. Title.
HD62.4.S695 2015
658′.049—dc23
2014037781

ISBN: 978-0-415-74482-9 (hbk)
ISBN: 978-0-415-74483-6 (pbk)
ISBN: 978-1-315-79834-9 (ebk)

Typeset in Bembo
by Apex CoVantage, LLC

Printed and bound in the United States of America by Edwards Brothers Malloy
on sustainably sourced paper

Contents

Figures

Tables

Preface

When Carla embarked on this project in 2002, she did not really know what she was getting herself into. She was driven by the sheer lack of teaching material in comparative international management. It was hard, if not impossible, to find material that was accessible for undergraduate and graduate students and that would provide them with a broad and critical view on international business and management.

A truly comparative international textbook, covering as many topics as we have in this book, was a daunting task finished in 2005, when the first edition appeared with McGraw-Hill. Over time, colleagues and students came to appreciate the services that the book has offered, in demanding master courses or very demanding bachelor courses in International Business and Management. But over time, a good textbook has to be updated and adapted to new developments and insights. In 2013, one of Carla's colleagues, Arndt, contacted her to inquire about a second edition. At this time, the book was 'migrating' from McGraw-Hill to Routledge but Carla had too much work to take on a thorough revision for the second edition. Another colleague of both Carla and Arndt, Niels, had also been teaching courses that used the book and was looking forward to a new edition.

So – what do professional colleagues do when there is a need for an important task to be done? They simply do it, although the result may not be rewarded by evaluators, deans and other functionaries that attribute research time. Here is the result. We have tried to keep the core of the book as it was: broad, critical, rooted in a sound research and teaching tradition, rich in material and elaborate in the offer of cases and exercise questions, something for the sophisticated student. We added what was new and important and eliminated a number of things that were not topical any more. But we were also careful to keep substance that we suspected of having become classic. There is more of that than often admitted, in the universities and business schools in which we have come to find ourselves.

Although we distributed writing and revision tasks for chapters, we also looked at each other's chapters and shared responsibility for the whole book, between the main authors. For some specific chapters, we asked other authors, as had also been the practice in the first edition. Much as our authors were not randomly picked from the whole world, we did get an international team together: Carla is Belgian, Niels is Dutch and Arndt is German. The other authors are Turkish and British (Ayse Saka-Helmhout), Albanian and French (Ilir Haxhi), and Dutch (Sjoerd Beugelsdijk). But we share an experience of having worked at Dutch universities, both together and apart.

The greatest debt of gratitude is owed to our past students; with their recognition, criticism and frustrations, they were an indispensable essence in the natural experiment, in teaching and research in different countries that led to this book. In Routledge, we are grateful for the amiable and competent companionship of Terry Clague and Sinead Waldron. The first edition profited from the comments of Ad van Iterson (University of Maastricht), Glenn Morgan (University of Cardiff), Can-Seng Ooi (Copenhagen Business School), and Jan Ulijn (Eindhoven University of Technology).

For the second edition, I, Carla, would like to express my sincere and deepest gratitude to my dearest colleagues Arndt and Niels. Both have put enormous work into this new edition. Without you a new edition would not have seen the light. I can still not believe you have done it. Thank you.

Arndt Sorge, formerly University of Groningen
Niels Noorderhaven, Tilburg University
Carla Koen, TIAS School for Business and Society

About the authors

Arndt Sorge was François Sellier Professor of International Management, University of Groningen, and Director at the Science Centre Berlin for Social Research, 2006–11. He is now Professor emeritus of Internationalization and Organization at the Social Science Research Center Berlin, Germany, and also Honorary Professor at the University of Potsdam. His work involves international comparisons, in the Netherlands, Germany, Britain and France.

Niels Noorderhaven is Professor of International Management and head of the Department of Management at Tilburg University. He has published in major international research journals in the field of management, and his work has attracted over 1,000 ISI citations.

Carla I. Koen is Professor of Technology Management and Entrepreneurship at TIAS School for Business and Society, Tilburg, Netherlands. Carla is member of STW valorization commissions, of the Innovation Board of Taminco, and of the General Board of Antwerp Management School. She is Director of BIS Company.

Other contributors

Ayse Saka-Helmhout is Associate Professor of Strategic Management at the Nijmegen School of Management, Radboud University. Her research focuses on the nature of the relationship between MNEs and their institutional environments in a comparative perspective.

Ilir Haxhi (PhD University of Groningen) is an Assistant Professor of Strategy and Corporate Governance at the Amsterdam Business School, and a visiting professor at Hitotsubashi University. His research interests are in corporate governance, international business and corporate institutional analysis.

Sjoerd Beugelsdijk (PhD Tilburg University) is a full professor in international business at the University of Groningen, the Netherlands. His research interests are in the field of culture, international business, and globalization.

General introduction

Comparative international management deals with differences in management and organization between countries. There is sufficient awareness of the need to study management and organization in an international context. Also, the use of comparison has always been recognized as a valuable tool of social scientific research. Nevertheless, the field of comparative international management is undervalued; few efforts have been made to apply the insights of the field in textbooks. This book is the first of its kind to take this type of comparison seriously.

We respond to older calls from prominent scholars (e.g. Vernon, 1994; Shenkar, 2004) to emphasize the value of comparative work for international business (IB). In 1994 Vernon was already concerned that, 'while comparative national business systems was one of the three core IB areas (the others being international trade and the multinational enterprise), it was the one most at risk of being overrun by US ethnocentrism as well as by high opportunity cost' (cited in Shenkar, 2004: 164). He argued that 'the omission of comparative business and its related components, such as cross-cultural research and comparative management, from the IB agenda is a fundamental error' (2004: 164). 'It amounts to no less than negating the value of local knowledge and assuming no scholarly "liability of foreignness"' (Zaheer, 1995, cited in Shenkar, 2004: 164). In a similar vein, Shenkar (2004: 164) argued that 'the disappearance of the comparative perspective has robbed IB of one of its most important theoretical and methodological bases, and has stripped it of one of its most unique and valuable assets'.

Regrettably, the situation has not improved over time. Reviewing research articles published over a period of 30 years in the journal *Organization Studies*, a journal that has dedicated itself to the study of organizing 'in and between societies' – no less! – Behlül Üsdiken came to the dismal result that cross-national comparison and societal contextualization had declined over time (Üsdiken, 2010). Whilst in the 1980s, 13.3 per cent of the articles had societal contextualization or comparison, in the 1990s it was 9.7 per cent and in the 2000s 6.5 per cent (2010: 729). What was on the rise were more universalistic approaches of various persuasions.

What has this led us to? We have international job markets for research students and professors and substantial mobility of academics, we have international forums and conferences where people meet and discuss amiably in a collegial spirit; like many company policy and public relations statements, academic doctrines and discourse have been influenced by a liberal spirit of openness in globalization. Yet, interest in and knowledge of what actual work, organization and management mean on the ground, has declined. Both academics and managers, too many of them, go to foreign places without understanding what is going on. This is the fertile ground on which management failures and political conflicts cannot but thrive. An illusion of liberal globalization has been entertained on the brittle basis of the English language as a *lingua franca* and the decontextualized use of formal methods.

This book is therefore more urgently needed than ever before. We try to rise to the challenge by studying comparative international management in its broadest sense. We discuss management styles, decision processes, delegation, spans of control, specialization, organizational structure, organizational culture, typical career patterns, corporate governance, production systems, corporate strategy and employment relations. All the chapters use examples from different countries and from different sectors within those countries to bring home a comparative approach. However, the purpose of these examples is not just to serve as an illustration; the acquisition of knowledge of management and organization in different countries and sectors is also one of the objectives of this book. It covers most EU countries, the USA, Japan and other Asian countries, some African countries, and Russia.

The challenge is methodologically demanding. To explain cross-national differences, it is not, for example, particularly useful to compare companies in the automobile industry in Korea with professional service firms in the UK. Nor is it useful to compare the management style of elderly supervisors in Belgium with the actions of young executives in the Netherlands. The entry questions into cross-national differences are: how can they be explained, and are they likely to disappear or will they persist? These questions are at the start of each chapter and are answered in a theoretically informed way, based on cultural and institutional analysis. The book takes a critical approach not only by evaluating critically the different theoretical strands but also by assessing the usefulness of the approaches for non-western, non-capitalist, less-developed countries and countries in transition. This may mean that, in some instances, the book appears intensive and intricate. But when a challenge is demanding, there is no point in a cookbook style.

Plan of the book

The book consists of 11 chapters, and each chapter starts with a learning objectives section and an outline of the chapter, and ends with study questions followed by a recommended further reading list, one or more closing case studies, and a full list of references. Each chapter also includes some real life examples and brief cases related to the topics discussed. These brief studies usually involve the application of the topics discussed in countries in transition such as China and Russia or in less-developed African countries such as Nigeria.

The first chapter sets the scene by introducing the main approaches to comparative international management, together with the 'globalization' debate. As we shall see, this debate has partly been misleading, directing attention away from factual differences, into the direction of a superficial universalistic theme. The cultural and institutional theories, which are introduced in this chapter, are treated in-depth in Chapters 2 to 4. These two theoretical strands form the cornerstone of the explanations of the international management and organization issues that are covered in the subsequent chapters of the book. Whilst Chapters 2 to 4 are broadly relevant and basic, the chapters that follow relate to specific fields of management and organization. Chapter 11 offers a refined approach to a detailed, rather than sweeping, diagnosis of how and why management and organization around the world are coming together or drifting apart, becoming alike or unlike.

Chapter 2 discusses approaches of the more quantitatively comparative variety, to national culture. It shows how national culture shapes organization and management differently in different countries. In order to further stress the influence of national culture at the micro level of the organization, the chapter also includes a section on the popular topic of cross-cultural negotiation. Chapter 3 deals with complementary approaches of the more 'qualitative' variety, which look at culture in greater depth and with an eye for what is specific and particular about cultures.

Complementary to cultural comparisons, we have institutional comparisons. These are discussed in Chapter 4, concentrating on two major European approaches: varieties of capitalism and the business systems approach. In addition, we show how culturalist and institutionalist treatments can conceptually be linked and integrated, using societal analysis. The influence of the national institutional context on the development process of two Asian business systems is shown by comparing the Korean Chaebol and the Taiwanese business system. We also make the first steps to analysing institutional change.

Chapters 5 and 6 concentrate on micro topics: international human resource management issues and corporate governance. These two chapters serve dual purposes. First, they provide the background knowledge that is essential to an understanding of Chapters 7 and 8, which deal with operations and innovation management respectively. Next, they help the reader to understand how the cultural and national institutional approaches that are explained in the previous chapters affect two important areas at the micro level of the organization. In particular, Chapters 5 and 6 explain how nationally specific institutions and national culture shape human resource management and corporate governance in organizations in different countries.

Chapter 7 explores how the societal environment shapes production systems and management in different countries. It concentrates on the major production systems – that is, on mass and flexible production systems, and the forms they take in different countries. Chapter 8 discusses the relationships between the societal environment and national systems of innovation. By means of examples of US, Japanese, German and French innovation systems, it clarifies these relationships.

Chapter 9 concentrates first on explaining the internationalization process of multinational corporations (MNCs). It discusses issues of coordination and control, and of learning. It also deals with the MNCs' responses to cultural and institutional differences. Chapter 10 also analyses the influence of the societal environment on corporate strategy. Since this is a rather new and so far under-researched topic, there is scant literature available. The chapter concentrates on the major existing studies in the field.

Chapter 10 takes us to a more intermediate level of aggregation: regions, clusters of firms and industrial districts. Enterprises not only compete but also cooperate, and they evolved historically significant networks of cooperation in regions. The formation of such networks has a logic in enterprise strategy, but it is also governed by a social nexus and societal settings. Networks and clusters have been a growing focus of attention in international business. From this literature it is clear that different types of network and cluster develop in different national contexts.

Chapter 11 approaches the question of whether differences in cross-national management and organization practices are likely to disappear or to persist in the future. The chapter concentrates on developments in human resource management, employment relations and corporate governance in the two major capitalist models: the Anglo-American and the Rhineland models. We concentrate on these two since, to a greater or lesser extent, the models of most countries – including countries in transition – tend to be variants of these two main models.

One of the problems of the proliferation of sub-fields and approaches is that students and researchers alike are overwhelmed by knowledge in separate niches; they are usually at a loss to combine theories and methods into an integrative treatment. This integration is less a question of dogma than of practice. One has to practise integration at the hand of empirical material. We therefore finish by offering an integrative case in Chapter 12, to enable students to develop an integrated understanding of differences.

References

Shenkar, O. (2004) One more time: international business in a global economy. *Journal of International Business Studies* 35, 161–171.

Üsdiken, B. (2010) Between contending perspectives and logics: organizational studies in Europe. *Organization Studies* 31, 715–735.

Vernon, R. (1994) Contributing to an international business curriculum: an approach from the flank. *Journal of International Business Studies* 25, 215–27.

Zaheer, S. (1995) Overcoming the liability of foreignness. *Academy of Management Journal* 38(2), 341–363.

1 Introduction to the approaches in comparative international management

Learning objectives

By the end of this chapter you will be able to:

- understand the differences between universalistic and particularistic theories
- evaluate the use and usefulness of contingency theory
- assess the explanatory role of culture
- distinguish between emic and etic approaches to cultural analysis
- reflect critically upon the link between institutions and organization and management issues
- appreciate the differences between the two main institutional clusters
- appreciate the complexity of globalization research
- reflect upon the possible consequences of globalization.

Chapter outline

1.1 Introduction to the theory and research literature
1.2 Universalistic theories
The contingency approach
1.3 Particularistic theories
The cultural approach
The institutional approach
1.4 Globalization
1.5 An integrative approach: societal analysis
Study questions
Further reading
Notes
References

1.1 Introduction to the theory and the research literature

Comparative international management is concerned with the study of management and organization in different societal settings. What are societal settings? Societies are larger collectivities of people that, loosely speaking, provide for, and instill in their members, a number of basic orientations and social patterns of dealing with one another. They make not only cooperation between individuals possible, but also allow for individuals to develop an identity and a view of the world which is shared by fellow members of society. The central characteristic of societies is that they provide for, and interrelate, all the aspects of living and working together that human beings require, in order to experience their life and what they do with it, as basically meaningful.

Societies are different from organizations, by largely not being designed rationally and purposefully. Even when they have seemingly powerful heads like kings, dictators or other strong rulers, and although they often claim a very fundamental loyalty and attachment of their members, societies are hard to control. There are two major reasons for this. One reason, applying above all to earlier, pre-modern societies, is that the local autonomy of more local or regional entities, or of clans and kinship groups, is strong. The other reason, applying above all to societies called 'modern', is that these are differentiated into functional spheres that have developed a measure of autonomy: institutions and authorities governing commerce, enterprise behaviour, finance, infrastructure, transport, employment relations, penal law, private life in families or other arrangements, socialization and education of individuals – to name but a few and crude spheres that fall apart into sub-spheres upon closer inspection. Even in such modern societies that are qualified as totalitarian, ruling dictators or central authorities have in practice found it impossible to control everything. How can we classify and order the spheres into which societies are differentiated and which tend to have a life of their own, i.e. a measure of autonomy?

First, all societies have an economy, which is a complex pattern of providing for material subsistence. This includes allocating work roles and specifying the terms and media of exchange of goods and services. Such media of exchange include money, markets, and other trading arrangements and conditions attached to them, but also reciprocal help by neighbours or in larger kinship groups, forced labour or other working arrangements that do not imply the use of money or markets. When we want to emphasize both the economic and the social aspect of such arrangements, we speak of socioeconomic systems.

Second, all societies have a polity, which is a system of deriving binding and sanctioned rules (the legislative part or aspect of the polity), of defining political goals and administrating their implementation (the governmental aspect), and of providing judgment in the case of disputes between individuals or groups (the judicial aspect). Such functions in the polity may be more separate or overlapping. Separation occurs in the modern occidental state, which is one way of giving a basic pattern to the polity. Another is rule by chieftains or, say, rulers in the earlier European Middle Ages, when rulers both governed and made judicial decisions. When we want to emphasize that economic arrangements or decisions are patterned by the polity, or if the economic arrangements influence political structures and processes, we speak of political economy. This is a term for political-economic systems which emphasizes that the polity and the economy are very much inter-related. 'Political economy' is also a term used to designate a set of theories and a field of study. For example, a market order regulated by laws made by the government is a part of both the economy and the polity. The respected classics in economics of different persuasions – Adam Smith, David Ricardo, Karl Marx, Joseph Schumpeter and many others, considered themselves or were in practice political economists.

Third, all societies have a system for providing individuals with the skills and knowledge they require, or aspire to, for life in general and for filling central roles in society. This system includes education and occupational training arrangements, which may be more separate such as in schools or universities; but they may also overlap with the allocation of work roles, such as in learning-by-doing in contact with more experienced practitioners.

It is possible to add more and more refined typologies of systems that we find in societies. We take some of them up in the headings of successive chapters. But across these systems, let us elaborate what is both central for building a societal identity and for interrelating what goes on in a society, across systems. For societal identity is built up by interrelating arrangements across distinct systems or domains, such as those mentioned above, and others which are more specific. This will help us articulate major themes and approaches in the comparison of management and organization. Whilst such themes and approaches have tended to lead a life of their own, they also connect because they come out of a very general analysis of human action.

Humans characteristically create, and relate to, an artificial world of both technical and social, economic and political artefacts. Artefacts are created by humans and they are neither found in nature nor in instinctive dispositions naturally inherent to the species. Without such artefacts, humans would be helpless. Now, artefacts are on the one hand external to humans, as they are supra-individual and have to be taken as given to a large extent by individuals; on the other hand they are internal, because they are represented in the minds of individuals, which is called knowledge (Berger and Luckmann, 1967). Some would say that the only thing we are able to conceptualize as 'real' is our knowledge. It is not only individual knowledge but shared knowledge. More or less at the same time, scholars in sociology and in organization studies analysed the 'interaction' between human actors and what was conceptualized as shared knowledge but is, by the sharing between humans, not only internal but also external: the construction of systems or structures that we necessarily deal with or relate to.

The idea is that human action and artificial systems impinge on one another, reciprocally. We cannot even fully grasp the meaning of individual action without relating it to its shared external references, and we cannot grasp the nature of systems or structures imagined to be shared and external, without referring to what actors have 'in mind'. Such ideas were explained by sociologists such as Anthony Giddens (1986) and Pierre Bourdieu (1986), and organizational scholars such as Karl Weick (1979) or Michel Crozier and Erhard Friedberg (1980). For the particular purpose of international comparison, such basic ideas were developed by Maurice, Sellier and Sylvestre (1986) in an approach called 'societal analysis'.

When we use the term 'society', we therefore do not imply that this is a clearly bounded entity or collectivity at a level of aggregation opposed to individuals. First, most of the historical societies we are aware of have multiple layers and ambiguous boundaries. Even most modern nation states are divided into half-separate identities, demarcated for instance by language or dialect or state boundaries in federal states such as the United States of America, Canada, Australia, Germany, Austria and Switzerland. Spain and the United Kingdom have also become more federal in recent times. Societies may thus have sub-societies. People more or less expect that the various aspects of living and working together are or should be tied together at some place, and if there are different places where this happens, they have often found ways of dealing with this pragmatically, acknowledging different and possibly conflicting authorities and societal entities. In many parts of the world, ethnic and governmental identities diverge and conflict, notably in Africa and also Asia, whilst in Europe, governments have largely made their peace with ethnic diversity within and across nation states. But ambiguity and contestation are still virulent, as can be seen in the cases of Catalonia (in Spain) and Scotland (in the United Kingdom). Further east, parts of Ukraine have recently again become contentious cases. So are other regions in Asia where statehood is divergent from ethnic and cultural identities, which has given rise to conflicts over the years.

The upshot of all this is that we can unravel and explain differences between management and organization in different countries in three major ways, which are connected but also different. The first conceptual and research entry into this world of differences is through the minds of human actors, i.e., we look at what Hofstede called the 'mental programming' of actors and compare this across countries. What actors have in mind and share, is called culture.

As we have seen, humans not only imagine what they share in their mind as something individual but also as external. This means that they conceive of it as something beyond their individual intention or will. And this is behind the other fundamental element: institutions. Institutions are typified patterns of behaviour, with a weaker or stronger normative foundation, which are like 'tools', a bit like in technical work, that we use in order to achieve meaningful results in social communication and every kind of work which implies relating to other people, in an understandable and accepted way.

This allows us to conceptualize culture and institutions as two main major entries into international comparisons, around which theories about international differences have formed and methodologies have been developed. They focus on the two 'poles' of human interaction, shared culture in the minds of actors on the one hand, and institutions as typified regularities conceived to be supra-individual and external on the other hand. The third major entry now is the interrelation of these two: the ongoing reciprocal referencing and formation between actors and institutions. This means that in order to know an actor, we have to look at the institutions the actor has in mind; and when we want to know an institution, we have to look at how actors understand it and practise it. This yields culturalist, institutionalist and interactionist approaches (such as the societal analysis mentioned above) to the study of international differences.

Scholars have gone to great lengths to argue about the relative merits and strengths of these approaches. The point in the present textbook is not to involve the reader in this sort of dispute, and confuse him or her with the intricate quarreling between approaches that it implies. Here, we work by the principle of tolerance between approaches, each of which may perform better for some purposes and worse for others. The separate approaches taken for themselves already require some effort and skill of understanding and practice on their own. Culturalist and institutionalist explanations are themselves differentiated into subtypes. Interactionist theory-building such as societal analysis is even more intricate, often felt to be demanding, and should preferably be engaged after having learned to handle the other two approaches.

Ideally the reader will learn that a picture of international differences and their explanation can never be complete; one should progress from culturalist explanations to institutionalist explanations or vice versa, as the 'root' of differences is never in the minds of actors or in institutions only. A complete or even sufficient explanatory picture can never be based on only one of the approaches. Differences in management and organization never 'ultimately go back to' specific factors. They always go back to bundles of factors that have worked together over a lengthy process in time. Further comparisons make you go on and on. This takes us through interactionist explanations, but it also takes us back to the others.

All this explains the breakdown of the book into chapters. After this introduction, we offer three chapters that go into the specifics of culturalist and institutionalist approaches.

After this conceptual and empirical groundwork, we move on to the specific differences in management and organization fields, in the chapters that follow. The penultimate chapter (11) then ties things together again, dealing with the internationalization or globalization of enterprise, economic and governmental activities that are so widely discussed.

International comparisons deal with the interplay between societal settings on the one hand, and various management and organizational forms and processes on the other. Comparisons always yield both, similarities and differences. It is important to be aware that there are different types of theory and different research designs, which may favour or emphasize either, the search for similarities or the search for differences. Assessing the measure of similarity or diversity is therefore a tricky task, because the outcome depends at least in part on what research design is adopted, and what theoretical foundation this is related to. It is therefore crucial to be open, at all times, to possibilities or biases inherent to concepts and methods, and to consider the possibility of similarities even when differences are obtained, and vice versa. As we shall see in the course of the book, similarities on one account may even be related to differences on another!

Our main theoretical foundation is general organization and management theory, together with related fields in economics, social psychology and sociology, from which organization theory has emerged as a fairly integrated although 'interdisciplinary discipline'. Organization and management theory has explained structures and processes with reference to the following sets of factors:

1 Task environmental characteristics such as organization size; differentiation, variation and innovation of output or demand; the technology of producing products or services;
2 Generic strategies which establish a nexus between management action in different functional, geographical or product-/service-related activities, and which also impinge on task environmental characteristics;
3 Institutional and cultural factors which are not necessarily specific to an organization but rooted in broader settings and arrangements, stretching from the architecture of the law through the political situation to how personalities are formed, by education and parental or other socialization.

Cross-national differences relate more directly to theories working with the third type of factors. These blend into approaches which deal with cross-national diversity. But generic strategies may also go back to societal culture and institutions, as we shall see in later chapters, and even such things as technology which superficially appear to be neutral with respect to culture and institutions, may in fact be influenced by such societal settings.

Given that organization and management are influenced by many factors, the following principle is crucial: if or when we want to find out about how and why organization and management differ between countries, as a first step it is important to eliminate that part of empirical variety which is not due to the operation of cultural and institutional factors. It is a first methodological step, which by no means implies that we should not later, in a more complex reasoning and study, bring back in the first and second factors mentioned above. But the first step is to eliminate that part of empirical variety which is due to the operation of task environmental contingencies (the first set of factors) or generic strategies (the second set of factors).

This consideration leads us to two major sets of theories:

'Universalistic' theories pretend that management and organization are subject to the same universal 'laws' everywhere in the world. An example is the positive relationship between the size of an organization and its degree of internal differentiation, which has been found in many studies. Universalistic theories rely on supposedly fundamental characteristics of human behaviour everywhere. This may be a very ambitious claim, but every science and scholarship rests on such a daring claim. *'Particularistic' theories*, conversely, posit that organization and management in different countries differ fundamentally, and that different explanations are necessary for different countries. This claim is similarly daring, for it rests on the assumption that human societies can be so fundamentally different that what is self-evident or logical in one society, need not to be so in another.

Universalistic theories tend to predict that cross-national differences in management and organization will disappear, as such driving forces as globalization (more and more markets become linked or integrated, 'best practices' are spread world-wide, and international regulation or government is intensified) are important. In this perspective, existing cross-national differences may be seen as temporary disequilibria. The concept of globalization and its consequences are discussed more extensively in the section of this chapter that deals with globalization.

Particularistic theories, on the other hand, tend to predict that cross-national differences in management and organization will persist. They also insist that history matters and national systems of management and organization are path-dependent. The latter means that any change in a human society is influenced by what was previously in that society; changes can be incremental or radical, but even in the latter case such a change can be understood as a reaction to the previous situation, and hence is influenced by it. This implies that culture and institutions may change or be transformed, even radically, but they will always change in ways that are time-and-place specific. Such theorists would for instance say that, even as China has become integrated into the world economy and adopted capitalist management and organization methods, it will nevertheless continue to exhibit the imprint of its thousands of years of history, not least its more recent communist history.

The two alternative theoretical orientations, universalism and particularism, have particular strengths and weaknesses. They should not be seen as mutually exclusive, however, for they usefully complement each other. Most studies from a cultural or institutional perspective started from the insights of universalistic contingency theory, if only to separate cross-national variety from other empirical variety. Hickson et al. (1974: 29) underlined that 'we can only start to attribute features to culture when we have made sure that relations between variables, e.g. between size and degree of specialization, are stable between cultures'. Contingency theory thus permits the researcher to highlight cultural or societal differences by controlling for factors approached as 'more universal'. This means that the researcher makes a cross-national selection of units to be investigated in such a way that they are carefully matched according to such factors. Organization size, degree of dependency, technology or product, and complexity or changeability of the task environment are the variables for which one should control in the selection of units in different societies.

Culturalist and institutionalist approaches should be seen as complementary and can be interrelated in one framework. The ambition in this book is to drive towards the integration of institutional and cultural perspectives. But before getting there, let us first review some universalistic theories which are not directly relevant to the explanation of differences but should be borne in mind because they point to selection criteria, with a view to controlling for non-societal explanatory factors. The discussion also includes a critique of universalistic theory, which points to particularistic theory.

1.2 Universalistic theories

The contingency approach

The contingency approach was developed by the so-called Aston School from the 1960s onwards, and is associated primarily with the names of Hickson and Pugh (see Hickson et al., 1969, 1979). Much of contingency theory research has studied organizational structure, and this tradition is referred to as structural contingency theory. This theory posits that, given similar circumstances, the structure of an organization – that is, the basic patterns of control, coordination and communication – can be expected to be very much the same wherever it is located (Hickson et al., 1974). The theory further posits that, if they are to be successful, organizations need to match organization structure with a series of contingencies inherent to the task environment, as explained above. Probably the most acknowledged account of such standard theory was provided by Mintzberg (1983). Here, we home in on a part of it which neglects such contingency factors as organization size and dependency, but illuminates specific task environmental characteristics that are particularly related to concepts used in international comparisons, not only in the selection and matching of samples, but also leading on to cross-country differences in technology and strategy. Table 1.1 shows the relationship between these particular contingencies and organizational structure.

A mechanistic structure (hierarchical, centralized, formalized) fits a stable environment because a hierarchical approach is efficient for routine operations. Given the routine nature of operations, the management at upper levels of the hierarchy possesses sufficient knowledge and information to make decisions, and this centralized control fosters efficiency. In contrast, the organic structure (participatory, decentralized, unformalized) fits an unstable environment and situations of high task uncertainty. A major source of task uncertainty is innovation, much of which is related to technological and market change or variation. The mechanistic organizational structure is shown to fit an environment with a low rate of market and technological change or variation. Conversely, the organic organizational structure is shown to fit an environment of a high rate of market and technological change.

Table 1.1 Mechanistic and organic organizations

Factors/forms	*Mechanistic*	*Organic*
Environment	Stable	Turbulent
Technology	Mass production	Single product and process production
Size	Large	Small(er)
Dimension/form	*Mechanistic*	*Organic*
Tasks	Narrow, specialized	Broad, enriched
Work description	Precise, procedures	Indicative, results
Decision-making	Centralized, detailed	Decentralized
Hierarchy	Steep, many layers	Flat, few layers

Moreover, each of the contingencies – that is, the environment, technology and size – is argued to affect a particular aspect of structure. This means that change in any of these contingencies will be related to change in the corresponding structure. In this way, the organization moves its structure into alignment with each of these contingencies, so that structure and contingency will fit one another.

Relationships between contingencies and aspects of organization structure in contingency theory are seen as constant in direction but not necessarily in magnitude. For example, in all societies, increases in the size of an organization will bring increasing formalization, but not necessarily the same degree of increase. Contingency theorists posit merely a stable relationship between contingencies and structure across different societies. Hence contingency theory is commensurate with international differences in degree, but not in kind.

The strengths of contingency theory lie in a straightforward argument and a standardized methodology. The various dependent and independent variables are operationalized so that they can be quantified and measured in a precise way (e.g., size equals number of employees). Multivariate analysis of these empirically measurable dimensions, each constructed from scalable variables (64 scales were devised for this purpose), was used to develop a taxonomy (or multidimensional classification) of organizational structures.[1] These strengths gained the contingency approach considerable influence, and for a long time it displaced case study analysis using qualitative research methodology.

The contingency approach, however, also has numerous weak points and blind spots. It has been pointed out that although this theory is able to show the consistency and strength of correlation between the two sets of variables – that is, between contingency variables such as size, or technology and the structural features of an organization – it has never provided an adequate explanation for this (Child and Tayeb, 1981). Are they imperatives or do they merely have the force of implications if a certain threshold is crossed?

In addition, the contingency approach only elucidates properties of formal structure and neglects informal structures (Lane, 1989). The theory focuses only on structure – only on limited aspects of it – and leaves out of the picture the actors involved and the informal interaction between them. It operates at a high level of abstraction and generality. It was argued that contingency theory can only be maintained as a culture-free framework because the actor is left out of the picture (Horvath et al., 1981). However, while formal structures may be remarkably alike across societies, different national actors perceive, interpret or act upon them in very different ways, due to deep-rooted cultural forces.

Contingency theory also seems to suffer from the fact that it evolved from Western traditions of rational design of organizations and from research on organizational populations in mostly Anglo-American institutional settings. A comparative study of 55 manufacturing plants in the USA and 51 plants in the same manufacturing industries in Japan confirms the bias that is inherent in this Western origin and perspective (see Lincoln et al., 1986). The results of this research are consistent with the thrust of much writing on Japanese industrial organization and relations (see e.g. Meyer and Rowan, 1977; Carroll and Huo, 1986). These writings show that the society's distinctive set of highly established and culturally bound action patterns and expectations – culture and institutions – has a particularly strong influence on organizational forms in Japan.

Japanese organizational structures were found to differ from US designs. Compared with those in the USA, Japanese manufacturing organizations have taller hierarchies, less functional specialization and less formal delegation of authority, but more de facto participation in decisions at lower levels in the management hierarchy. These structures are consistent with the internal labour market processes (lifetime employment, seniority-based promotion) that characterize Japanese companies and the general emphasis on groups over individuals as the fundamental units of organization. These findings seem to indicate that organizational theories are more 'culture bound', limited to particular countries or regions in their capacity to explain organizational structure, than contingency theorists maintain.

1.3 Particularistic theories

The cultural approach

Culturalist research is carried out at different levels of analysis. Cross-cultural research takes place at two distinct levels of analysis, those of the individual and of the culture. In comparative management studies, the focus is on the cultural rather than the individual level. Culture is considered to be a background factor, almost synonymous with country. Similar to contingency theory, this research has a macro focus, examining the relationship between culture and organization structure. However, in comparative management research, the concept of culture has also been expanded to include the organizational or corporate level. This research has a micro focus, investigating the similarities and differences in attitudes of managers of different cultures.

Irrespective of the level of analysis, in social science there are two long-standing approaches to understanding the role of culture: (1) the inside perspective of ethnographers, who strive to describe a particular culture in its own terms, and (2) the outside perspective of comparativist researchers, who attempt to describe differences across cultures in terms of a general, external standard. These two approaches were designated the *emic* and the *etic* perspectives, by analogy to two approaches to language: phonemic analysis of the units of meaning, which reveals the unique structure of a particular language, and phonetic analysis of sound, which affords comparisons among languages (Pike, 1967).

The emic and etic perspectives have equally long pedigrees in social science. The emic, or inside, perspective follows in the tradition of psychological studies of folk beliefs (Wundt, 1888) and cultural anthropologists striving to understand culture from 'the native's point of view' (Malinowski, 1922). The etic, or outside, perspective follows in the tradition of behaviourist psychology (Skinner, 1938) and anthropological approaches that link cultural practices to external, antecedent factors, such as economic or ecological conditions (Harris, 1979).

The two perspectives are often at odds. An important reason for this lies in the different constructs, assumptions and research methods that are used by the two approaches (see Table 1.2). Emic accounts describe thoughts and actions primarily in terms of the actors' self-understanding – terms that are often culturally and historically bound. In contrast, etic models describe phenomena in constructs that apply across cultures. Along with differing constructs, emic and etic researchers tend to have differing assumptions about culture. Emic researchers tend to assume that a culture is best understood as an interconnected whole or system, in which each element derives its meaning from its interrelations with other elements, whereas etic researchers are more likely to isolate particular components of culture, and to state hypotheses about their distinct antecedents and consequences.

The approaches also use different research methods.[2] Methods in emic research are more likely to involve sustained, wide-ranging observation of a single cultural group. In classical fieldwork, for example, an ethnographer immerses him or herself in a setting, developing

Table 1.2 Assumptions

Features	*Emic, or inside, view*	*Etic, or outside, view*
Assumptions and goals	Behaviour described as seen from the perspective of cultural insiders, in constructs drawn from their self-understandings Describes the cultural system as a working whole	Behaviour described from a vantage point external to the culture, in constructs that apply equally well to other cultures Describes the ways in which cultural variables fit into general causal models of a particular behaviour
Typical features of methods associated with this view	Observations recorded in a rich qualitative form that avoids imposition of the researchers' constructs Long-standing, wide-ranging observation of one or a few settings	Focus on external, measurable features that can be assessed by parallel procedures at different cultural sites Brief, narrow observation of more than one setting, often a large number of settings
Examples of typical study types	Ethnographic fieldwork; participant observation along with interviews	Comparative experiment treating culture as a quasi-experimental manipulation to assess whether the impact of particular factors varies across cultures

Source: Morris et al. (1999: 783).

relationships with informants and taking social roles (e.g. Geertz, 1983; Kondo, 1990). Emic description can also be pursued in more structured programmes of interview and observation.

Methods in etic research are more likely to involve brief, structured observations of several cultural groups. A key feature of etic methods is that observations are made in a parallel manner across differing settings. For instance, matched samples of employees in many different countries may be surveyed to uncover dimensions of cross-national variation in values and attitudes (e.g. Hofstede, 2001), or they may be assigned to experimental conditions in order to test the moderating influence of the cultural setting on the relationship among other variables (e.g. Earley, 1989).

The divide between the emic and the etic approaches persists in contemporary scholarship on culture: in anthropology, between interpretivists (Geertz, 1976, 1983) and comparativists (Munroe and Munroe, 1991), and in psychology between cultural psychologists (Shweder, 1991) and cross-cultural psychologists (Smith and Bond, 1998). In the literature on international differences in organizations, the divide is manifest in the contrast between classic studies based on fieldwork in a single culture (Rohlen, 1974), as opposed to surveys across many (Hofstede, 2001). Likewise, in the large body of literature on organizational culture, there is a divide between researchers employing ethnographic methods (Gregory, 1983; Van Maanen, 1988) and those who favour comparative survey research (Schneider, 1990).

Given the differences between the two approaches to culture, it is hardly surprising that researchers taking one perspective have generally questioned or ignored the utility of integrating insights from the other tradition. A common tendency is to dismiss insights from the other perspective as based on conceptual or methodological weaknesses. Some scholars, however, recognize that the two are in fact best seen as complementary, and have suggested that researchers should choose between approaches depending on the stage of the research programme. For example, it has been argued that an emic approach serves best in exploratory or theory-building research, whereas an etic approach serves best in testing hypotheses or corroborating theory.

Some scholars (i.e. Berry, 1990) propose a three-stage sequence. In the first stage, initial exploratory research relies on 'imposed-etic' constructs – theoretical concepts and measurement methods that are simply exported from the researcher's home culture. In the second stage, emic insights about the other culture are used to interpret initial findings, with an eye to possible limitations of the original constructs, such as details that are unfamiliar or meaningless outside of the home culture. On this basis, then, the constructs in the model are filtered to eliminate details that cannot be measured with equivalence across cultural settings. The factors that survive this filter – 'derived-etic' constructs – are culture-general dimensions of persons, such as value orientations, or of their environments, such as economic or ecological factors. In the third and final stage, the researcher tests an explanation constructed solely of derived-etic constructs (Morris et al., 1999).

Sequential selection models, such as the one from Berry (1990), have been influential in guiding psychological and organizational researchers in their approaches to culture. Yet these models only begin to explore the synergies between perspectives. Although they address the role of emic insights in refining etic explanations, they say little about how etic insights stimulate emic investigation. In fact, they do not lead to the full integration of both research streams. Thus far, there have been only limited attempts in that direction (i.e. Morris et al., 1999).

The plea for full integration is based on the fact that the different strengths of the two approaches create complementarities. Findings from the two perspectives could challenge each other and stimulate each other's new questions. Moreover, the two kinds of explanation could complement each other in contributing to rich accounts of culture. The emic and etic perspectives each provide only half of the explanation of culture. Because emic studies tap into the explanations held by cultural insiders, the emic perspective leads inherently to an emphasis on the causes of phenomena that are internal and local to the cultures and organizations being studied. Because etic perspectives are attuned to relationships between variables, a functionalist story is more likely to result.

The complexity of the concept of culture, and of the possibilities to carry out research on it, is the reason why we cover major studies in this field of research, and why we treat the methodological problems that are often overlooked, in greater detail. It is essential to understand the ways in which research is, or ought to be, carried out. In Chapters 2 and 3, etic and emic organization culture research are discussed in depth.

The institutional approach

Since the mid-1970s, comparative organizational analysis from an institutionalist perspective has proliferated. Institutionalist analysis also formed a challenge for universalistic theory. Institutionalists in particular criticized the fact that universalists generalize the results of empirical studies based on a population of organizations limited to a single society or family of societies. Institutionalists also argue that such a research approach cannot but lead to finding evidence of convergence.

In contrast, comparative institutional research focuses on comparisons that highlight differences that cannot be attributed to different goals, contexts, environments or strategies of enterprises. 'Intriguing differences are those which arise despite similarities in the factors just mentioned' (Sorge, 2003). As a consequence, institutional analysis has moved 'towards an increasingly explicit insistence upon the maintained diversity and qualitative specificity of social forms in the advanced societies' (Rose, 1985: 66).

Institutionalists differ from culturalists in that they focus on 'wider norms and standards supported or enforced by institutional machineries', as opposed to 'the culturalists' focus on the mind of the individual as the place where differences reside' (Sorge, 2003). When comparing definitions of institutions and culture, however, distinguishing clearly between the two is not always a straightforward matter. A broad and encompassing definition is given by Douglass North, who sees institutions as:

> the humanly devised constraints that structure political, economic and social interaction. They consist of both informal constraints (sanctions, taboos, customs, traditions, and codes of conduct), and formal rules (constitutions, laws, property rights).
> (1991: 97)

Similarly, Scott (1995) points at three types of institutional support:

> The regulative (formal rules and incentives constructed by the state and other empowered agents of the collective good), normative (informal rules associated with values and explicit moral commitments), and cognitive (abstract rules associated with the structure of cognitive distinctions and taken-for-granted understandings).

These definitions suggest that informal and normative institutions and culture are alike – that is, they express customs, traditions, values, and so on. In fact, cultural beliefs are seen as central ingredients of institutions (North, 1995: 49). It is very difficult, therefore, to disentangle the impact of informal and normative institutions from that of culture. In this book, we concentrate on formal institutions as these are less complicated to identify and easier for outsiders to understand; they also lend themselves better to comparative analysis. In a similar way, Whitley (1992: 19), one of the pioneers of institutionalist comparison, has distinguished 'proximate' and 'background' institutions: proximate institutions are more tangible and tend to have a formal expression, whilst background institutions include more deep-seated assumptions.

Similar to cultural analysis, there is thus some variety in the definition of key concepts, measures or methods. Institutional theory has not developed an agreed set of standard variables, nor is it associated with a standard research methodology or even a set of methods. Studies have relied on a variety of techniques, including case analysis, historical analysis, cross-sectional regression, and longitudinal models of various types (Tolbert and Zucker, 1996). But there are some more accepted lists of dimensions to be covered, and of rougher institutional characteristics with shifting operationalizations.

Most European organizational institutional analysis uses qualitative research methods and concentrates on case studies and, to some extent, on (descriptive) statistical analysis. The methodological approach is that of comparing carefully matched pairs in different societies, controlling for such contingency variables describing the task environment and organization context. This method gives a relatively small, non-randomly chosen sample and hence dictates a more qualitative and 'in-depth' study, with attention to detail and thick description.

Institutionalists are interested in the question of how organizations and industrial sectors are influenced by institutionalized rules and institutional environments. Chapter 4 discusses two European institutional approaches that help us to answer this question – the 'business systems approach' and the 'varieties of capitalism' approach. These studies examine the effects of institutions on some organizational entity or process. This is because organizational research is primarily interested in assessing whether and to what extent institutional systems affect individual organizations or collections of organizations.

Institutional analysis emphasizes the fact that different sets of institutions result in divergent organization and management practices, and different advantages and disadvantages for engaging in specific types of activity. Firms can perform some types of activity that allow them to produce some kinds of goods more efficiently than others, because of the institutional support they receive for those activities; the institutions relevant to these activities are not distributed evenly across nations (Streeck, 1992; Whitley, 1999; Maurice and Sorge, 2000; Hall and Soskice, 2001).

1.4 Globalization

The concept of globalization has become extremely popular. The widespread interest in the concept shown by different disciplines has led to different opinions on the contents of the concept and on its consequences. In economics, for example, globalization refers to economic internationalization and the spread of capitalist market relations. In Cox's words: 'The global economy is the system generated by globalizing production and global finance' (1992: 30). Research in this direction usually predicts the increasing influence of integrated and global capital markets upon the domestic context and in most cases points to Americanization as the end result. Globalization has been defined as the production and distribution of products and services of a homogeneous type and quality on a worldwide basis. Simply put: providing the same output to countries everywhere (Levitt, 1983; Rugman and Hodgetts, 2001). Or in Levitt's words: 'The global corporation operates with resolute constancy – at relatively low cost – as if the entire world (or major regions of it) were a single entity; it sells the same things in the same time everywhere' (1983).

Levitt emphasizes that globalization leads to benefits from economies of scale and standardization. This definition of economic globalization implies the need for products that are uniform across countries. For Levitt the global is more present than the local. In this sense, he argues that 'only global companies will achieve long-term success by concentrating on what everyone wants rather than worrying about the details of what everyone thinks they might like' (Levitt, 1983: 1).

A much broader definition of globalization is formulated by writers such as Albrow, for whom globalization refers to 'all those processes by which the peoples of the world are incorporated into a single world society, a global society' (Albrow, 1990: 9). Similarly, Anthony Giddens defines globalization as 'the worldwide interconnection at the cultural, political and economic level resulting from the elimination of communication and trade barriers' (Giddens, 1999). Giddens further states that 'globalization is a process of convergence of cultural, political and economic aspects of life' (1999). Convergence of cultures, tastes, regulations, and the like, is of course an extreme version of homogeneity of products and services.

In a large part of the literature, globalization is interpreted as a multidimensional force that has an impact on different levels of analysis (see e.g. Berger and Dore, 1996; Lane,

2000; Meyer, 2000; Nye and Donahue, 2000). The focus of this literature is on the dynamics of change and on the relationships between global and local. It is recognized that change does not occur everywhere in the same way and at the same rate, and that the particular character of individual societies interacts with the larger-scale general processes of change to produce specific outcomes (Dicken, 1998).

This literature is based on the ideas of many contemporary globalization theorists on the nature of transnational processes (i.e. Hannerz, 1987; Robertson, 1992, 1995, 2001; Garcia Canclini, 1995; Pieterse, 1995; Appadurai, 1996; Tomlinson, 1999). These theorists coin the term 'glocalization' to indicate the interpenetration of the global and the local. They emphasize global heterogeneity and reject the idea that forces emanating from the West in general and the USA in particular are leading to economic, political, institutional and cultural homogeneity. Similar to the more simplistic writings on globalization, however, this research has been unable to provide an answer that is both concrete and general, to the consequences of the dynamics of change and integration.

In general, according to Lane (2000), the divergent opinions on the consequences of globalization in this literature can be summarized in four possible scenarios: (1) convergence towards the Anglo-American neoliberal market system (Dore, 1996; Streeten, 1996; Streeck, 1997); (2) greater specialization of national models in accordance with domestic institutional and cultural characteristics (Vitols, 2001; Sorge, 2003); (3) incremental adaptation of the domestic institutional context in a largely path-dependent manner (Casper, 2000; Whitley, 1994a, b); and (4) hybridization with change in a path-deviant manner (Whitley, 1999; Lane, 2000).

The ideas about the first scenario, convergence of national models, were first systematically articulated in postwar writings about industrial societies.[3] However, while in those days globalization was often interpreted as a process of homogenization or convergence, the postwar writings, while postulating convergence, did not make mention of the concept of globalization. The social sciences of the 1950s and 1960s located the engine of convergence in technology. The core notion was that countries progressed along a common trajectory of technological possibilities. The path of innovation along which they moved was the same for all. They would advance, more or less rapidly, passing through common stages and adopting over time more and more of the same social, political and economic structures.

Starting in the 1970s and 1980s, new research played an important role in undermining the grip of technological explanations within the social sciences. The new research stimulated new lines of speculation on the societal, cultural, political and organizational factors that might explain the differential performance of firms using the same technologies in different national settings. This new research agenda appeared at the end of the 1980s at a time of an apparent weakening of the American economy and triumph of quite different economic institutions and practices in Japan and Germany. These two countries' remarkable postwar growth and prosperity seemed striking demonstrations that economies work in ways quite different from those described by neoclassical economics and US practice. The notion of different forms of capitalism – each type characterized by different institutions, practices, values and politics – began to appear in both scholarly and popular writing (Berger, 1996: 2–9).

The globalization concept became popular at the time of the resurgence of the US economy in the 1990s, and the suggested demise of the German and Japanese models. It is hardly coincidental, then, that some of the most common interpretations of globalization have come to be that the world is becoming more uniform and standardized, through a technological, commercial and cultural synchronization emanating from the West – and, in particular, from the Anglo-American countries (Nederveen Pieterse, 1994). It is clear that the increasing openness of national economies, the swelling volume of funds flowing across national frontiers, and the growing ease of transferring capital and production from one country to another create severe pressures to match others' macro-economic results. Anglo-American capitalism seems to have revived in this context. It is less clear that these pressures do actually work to align diversities generated by different national traditions into an ever more common set of institutions and practices. And, if they do so, that this common set of institutions and practices will necessarily be dominated by the Anglo-American type of capitalism (Berger, 1996: 2–9). More recently, the jolt of the world financial crisis emanating from the heartland of liberal capitalism, after 2007, has severely shaken the faith in financial world capitalism to be a superior model of economic growth in the world. Instead, we now see that a reliance on both public and private indebtedness, as communicating channels, has become increasingly problematic and has stretched the capacities of OECD economies to their limits, holding out the prospect of further crises (Streeck, 2013). If there is one national 'model' that has found renewed interest at this time, it is a North and Central European type coordinated market economy.

We would argue that the varied dimensions of globalization all point to the inherent fluidity, indeterminacy and open-endedness of the concept. And that, when we depart from this point of view, it becomes less obvious to think of globalization in terms of standardization and of uni-directional processes. It is difficult or impossible to conceive of globalization in terms of homogenization, although interdependencies between countries have clearly increased.

The second scenario – increased specialization and sharper accentuation of the domestic system – implies that, under pressure of globalization and integration, 'the domestic' will adapt by specializing more vigorously in what it does best. It is important to distinguish here between two views: 'greater specialization in national industrial profiles' (Vitols, 2001: 360) and development of greater societal specificity (Sorge, 1996). Greater industrial specialization demands that domestic industries will focus more closely than before on the activities in which they have an international competitive advantage. It does not necessarily also imply greater specialization (and, thus, increasing divergence) at the level of the domestic institutions, but incremental improvements in existing institutions as a result of integration. The development of societal specificity, on the other hand, implies both, increasing differences between societies and, as a result, increasing differences in national industrial specialization. In this research, internationalization and universal technical change is argued to trigger development of societal specificity, rather than bringing about convergence between societies (Sorge, 1996: 84). Greater specialization in industrial profiles is seen as inevitable since industries are influenced by the context in which they are embedded.

The third scenario – incremental path-dependent adaptation – focuses on institutions and rules out convergence of one societal system towards the other. The argument is based on the socially constructed nature of institutions, in the sense that they embody shared cultural understandings ('shared cognitions', 'interpretive frames') of the way the world works (Zucker, 1983: 5; Meyer and Rowan, 1991; Scott, 1995: 33). In accordance with the actor–structure logic, emergent and changing institutional forms are argued to be 'isomorphic' with (i.e. compatible, resembling and similar in logic to) existing ones because actors extract causal designations from the world around them and these cause-and-effect understandings inform how they approach new problems (DiMaggio and Powell, 1991: 11; Dobbin, 1994). This means that even when actors set out to redesign institutions, they are constrained in their actions by these embedded cultural and institutional forces.

Finally, hybridization, the fourth scenario, also tends to be a gradual process. In contrast to path-dependent adaptation, however, hybridization implies some change in a path-deviant manner. Hybridization is argued to result from the process of integration into the global system of individual companies. It is argued that subsidiaries, which enjoy a high level of resources and a relatively high degree of autonomy, become embedded in their host countries. This will lead to learning processes and to the adoption of new organizational structures, practices and competences. Organizational learning from host country experience by affiliates will, in integrated transnational corporations (TNCs), initiate organizational learning and hybridization at company level. Such hybrid companies, it is proposed, if they belong to the core companies of a country, may eventually affect the domestic business system (Lane, 2000).

The different opinions on the consequences of global forces define questions for this book. We concentrate on processes of integration – global, regional or local. These effects are not only interesting in their own right. This will help us answer the question of how globalization is taking place, and how it is related to the recreation of societal specificity. If globalization is an ongoing process, then we should be able to identify its elements and consequences. These consequences are addressed throughout the book by tracing the impact of processes of international integration and change upon major interrelated societal spaces and institutional domains. This is important, as changes in the societal context have implications at the corporate firm and industrial level, and also for management and organization at all levels. Chapter 11 winds up this discussion and provides a perspective on the question of which of the aforementioned scenarios are pertinent for the corporate world.

1.5 An integrative approach: societal analysis

Before we split the analysis into culturalism and institutionalism, we started with a more comprehensive framework of actors creating institutions and adopting cultural patterns, and being orientated by institutions and culture in turn. This relationship between actors on the one hand, and culture and institutions on the other, is quite intricate and complex. Scholars speak of 'recursiveness' with respect to the relationship. This means that actors on the one hand 'make' or change institutions and culture, consciously or unconsciously, and on the other, they are orientated by culture and institutions. Recursiveness means that to understand or to explain the disposition of actors, one has to 'go back' to culture and institutions – recursiveness is derived from the Latin word *recurrere* = to run back; and vice versa, to understand and to explain culture and institutions, one has to go back to the disposition of actors.

We also saw that in theory defined as 'duality' theory, the relationship between what is in the mind of actors and what is taken to be external, is particularly tight. They are really like two sides of the same coin. In such theory, there is no causal relation between actors' dispositions and external things, notably institutions; the relation is one of meaning and implication, which has to be reconstructed by interpretation, rather than by an impossible causal analysis. But on the other hand, we saw that there are also theories which speak of actors 'influencing' or causing something considered external to them, and of institutions or culture 'influencing' the behaviour of actors. We can only take notice here that the world of theory we are dealing with, is not consistent. This is a shame, but there is nothing we can do about it; the methodological controversy never goes away.

A further complication, as we saw above, is that the field of institutions is not homogeneous; there is for example the difference between proximate and background institutions. What is more, there is the possibility of tension between these. Proximate institutions, expressed in reasonably clear and articulate norms, may change because actors come to interpret some fundamental background institutions differently or some contingencies happen to have changed. Likewise, as we saw, the world of culture is similarly driven by different types of culture, and we cannot assume that a larger set of cultural values is consistent. Even in a stable society, cultural conflict, not only between different groups but in the personal value set of every individual actor, is an inevitable everyday phenomenon.

All this makes an integrative approach very difficult. Researchers have a habit of casting their theory-building and research within the conventions of a specific and particular approach or theory. This is not helpful to come to grips with very complex real-world phenomena. Such phenomena may be an enterprise, or a sector in a particular country, or a complete nation state or society, even if it is only as large as Luxembourg. You can look at the enterprise, or the sector, or the country, from the points of view of different research methodologies and theories, and they will give different explanations. Some scholars will say that it all comes down to basic values, from which institutionalized practices are derived. Others will say that some fundamental institutions are necessarily inert and give rise to path dependency, from which more specific practices can be derived. Still others will say that organized interests engage in political games which are stable as long as the power of interested parties does not change. And then there are those who say that you can only understand an enterprise, or Luxembourg, from within, studying it like an ethnographer in New Guinea, forgetting about general theory because it is the specific that is of overriding importance. Scholars can do this at great ease, for they do not have to run an establishment in a specific enterprise, or devise a policy for Luxembourg, let alone China.

One could even say that the field of problem-oriented explanation and recommendation, whether it is for the purpose of business and management in a particular enterprise, or reforming an industry in a country, or making policy for a larger country, is littered with failures when a situation was only looked at in the light of only one particular theory. The most spectacular failure was more recently the world financial crisis starting in 2007, which started with the bursting of a bubble that, according to a narrow theory of financial markets integrating all the available information, was not a bubble at all. Others had diagnosed the building of a bubble for about a decade, on the basis of different theories. Ironically, in 2013 both sides won a Nobel Prize in economics.

Against the problems of combining a welter of different theories, putting the limelight on different aspects and being notoriously difficult to combine, we hold out the usefulness of a comparison of theories with an ambition to see where they contradict each other, but also to find out possibilities of combining them. This is not something one can do on the basis of one coherent theory. However, a discussion of theoretical contradictions and complementarities is an important step already, and it is facilitated by the use of human language, in a spirit of empirical realism. Human language, although often disparaged by scientists for being ambiguous and disorderly, by not being built on the foundation of a few axioms only, is eminently geared to pragmatic theoretical evaluation and integration. It is possible to construct an integrative approach, but not by doing theory in the more narrow sense – based on few assumptions leading to deductions which are empirically tested and proven – but in a wider sense: a broadly applicable heuristic which may even go across different methodological foundations (Noorderhaven, 2000).

Our recommendation then is to see what different theories have to say about any situation in a specific enterprise, industry, or country, in comparison with others. One will then find out how they contradict each other or may be combined. The best idea is to go round all the theories offered and see how they perform together or against each other. Very often, an ingenious combination can be found to perform relatively well, once one has seriously decided to take up the challenge of letting the lights of different theories shine on the same real-world situation, from different angles. This can be done throughout the book, as we progress from one theory to another and learn about comparisons in specific functional fields. For trying this out more systematically, we offer an integrative case at the end, in the last chapter. However, teachers and students can also practise an integrative method by collecting material themselves, for further comparative analysis.

Our contention then is that any particular theoretical integration is a very pragmatic affair, which has value only for a specific set of real-world situations. In others, a different combination or weighting of theories will prove to be more suitable. Most of the readers of this book will be interested in combining theories in order to form a well-rounded picture about complex settings with many aspects, in which they will work or which they will encounter.

An integrative approach should embrace two major sorts of recursiveness, in line with the beginning of this chapter:

(1) A cross-referencing between what actors have in mind and the more systemic or structural settings they take for granted: relate more institutionalist explanations to culturalist explanations; sometimes they complement each other, but sometimes they also may compete or contradict each other. More powerful actors by definition have more power in the design or adaptation of regulative institutions, and they may fulfil this role bearing in mind their values, but they may also adapt institutions in an opportunistic way, even going against more widely established values. Note also that value sets are far from consistent, they tend to conflict, and actors that legitimize their action on the basis of values often take a hypocritical posture. For example, dictatorial organizational power is often set up against prevailing values, but on the other hand it is also often accepted on the basis that its exercise leads to results that members or clients of the organization appreciate. Note also that the variance of value sets and institutions, across different behavioural situations, organizational departments, branches of activity or other settings within the same society, may be substantial. This means that one value or institution applies in one department, industry or activity, and a different one in another. The integrative aspect then is that things are different in this way, not by accident but because this is an understood or accepted way of arranging things.

(2) Societies are integrated by a continuous cross-referencing between what we call 'spaces', which are imagined spaces, differentiated and demarcated around a central meaning, purpose or function addressed by actors, within a space. Let us go through major examples of such spaces:

- In a space of organizing, we find a division of labour by distinguishing jobs, occupations and organized sub-units, together with mechanisms of coordination, such as direct supervision, standardization of rules and regulations, standardization of skills and knowledge, mutual adjustment and cultural control (Mintzberg, 1983).

- In a space of competence generation, we have activities geared to educate people, give them occupational training or training on the job, and develop their skills and knowledge in the course of a career, in an enterprise or across enterprises.
- In a space of finance, we see activities and instruments to tap into financial resources (loans, debentures, equity capital), account for results counted in money and distribute the proceeds of the enterprise into salaries, profits and payment of interest and amortization of credit or loans received from banks or other creditors.
- In an industrial space and corporate governance, we have the sectoral or industrial division of labour and the governance of market forms, and the organization of the value chain; we also have mechanisms of establishing relations through value chains and between them, and by organizing relations in business associations and between these and governmental or quasi-governmental bodies.
- In a technical space, we see actors designing and building technical (physical and software) artefacts, standardizing artefacts and routines but also conducting innovation activities to change and develop these.
- In the space of the employment relation, industrial and labour relations, we have organized actors (employer associations, trade unions, management) and individual employees setting up forms of contracting in the employment relation, defining rights and obligations, specifying payment systems and salary levels.

Such spaces are bounded by the meaning, purpose and function of types of action, not by the boundaries of formal organizations, such as firms, universities, chambers of industry and commerce or trade unions. These are institutionalized domains. Spaces typically cross-cut institutionalized domains. Apprenticeship training, for example, happens in the space of competence generation, very often not only in schools or colleges but in firms. Corporate governance, likewise, is arranged and conducted partly by bodies of the state, partly by quasi-public bodies and partly by the statutes of firms. Whitley and Hall and Soskice are not worried about the difference between spaces and institutional domains, but societal analysis is keen on it (Maurice and Sorge, 2000: Introduction). Sociologically it is crucial; institutional domains consist of organizations or authorities which are separate from other organizations and authorities; spaces, however, are never organizationally distinctive or semi-autonomous.

A division into spaces thus emphasizes the need for systemic integration across spaces. Action in one space necessarily evokes requirements and consequences in all the other, complementary, spaces. Take a simple example: occupational education and training happens within a space of competence generation, whether it is done within an enterprise training department, directly at work, or in a professional school or college. How it is done, has implications for work organization, in another space, and also for employment relations (forms of contract, definition of work role, etc.); and how this is financed, takes us into the financial space where, again, different authorities and organizations may come into play. And they may come into play in a controlled way, because actors anticipate implications across spaces, or inadvertently, through actors becoming aware of consequences or requirements in other spaces and taking adaptive action.

In organization theory, the difference between action spaces and institutional domains is inherent to the dialectics of 'loose coupling' (Orton and Weick, 1990): organizations or parts of organizations within institutionalized domains are relatively autonomous in what they do. But spaces, through their more pervasive cross-cutting quality, and because actors continuously have to work out meaningful cross-relations in order to make organizations and other bodies work, tie quasi-autonomous organizational entities together. Although there is a 'de-coupling' of organized entities where delegated autonomy is concerned, action in one space has implications for that in the others. Sometimes, actors know and heed such implications, sometimes they learn about them when they try out courses of action. Loose coupling is dialectical because, although actors tend to be relatively autonomous, what they do has powerful requirements and consequences, such that the action is not 'de-coupled' but tied up with that in other entities.

Our division of chapters after the fourth follows a classification of spaces and related domains. The reader is invited to, at all times, heed the following heuristic, or rule of thumb: relate comparative differences according to one chapter to those reported in others. The classification of spaces is not meant to be dogmatic; one may add more or refine the classification into more specific categories. Now, the important thing is that in principle, arrangements and changes in one space tend to be associated with related changes in all the other spaces. This does not happen automatically but because actors cannot isolate activity within one space from corresponding and 'matching' activities in the others.

Institutionalist writers such as Whitley, and Hall and Soskice, have tried to point out how this happens. Consider a simple example: if an enterprise increased the volume of equity capital (financial space), it became more dependent on providers of equity capital and often the stock market, which often tended to decrease the importance given, in the employment relation space, to bargaining with trade unions and to the collective and stable definition of rights and obligations. This tends to go together, in the industrial space, with focusing on a core business and reducing vertical integration in the value chain. There are also likely to be implications in the spaces of organizing and of competence generation, through the revision of policies for value generation. Again, this is not happening according to the chains of causality that nomothetic theorists have in mind. Through being faced with the practical consequences or requirements of any specific action, actors are led to arrange or rely on corresponding action in other spaces, as something complementary or as a resource. This may happen by anticipation or reaction. It is a world full of both, creative anticipation and poorly reflected reaction, and both are highly pragmatic affairs.

Because of this, there is always aberration from the patterns of relationships suggested by institutionalist varieties of capitalism and business systems theories. Switzerland for example is very clearly a country with the competence generation and organizing characteristics of a coordinated market economy; on the other hand it is like a liberal market economy with regard to finance: enterprises are absolutely flush with equity capital. And there is nothing that supports the opposition between these characteristics, suggested by such institutionalist theories. Furthermore, this is no disfunctional arrangement, as the long-standing success of the Swiss economy has proved. The Swiss seem to have a knack of sucking up huge amounts of money from all over the world and channelling it into equity capital rather than mainly credit finance for non-banks. Similarly, for other parts of the world not well covered by institutionalist theory, we are still far from encompassing and relatively convincing empirical types that explain how and why characteristics across different institutional domains are interdependent. For the moment, we can only refer the reader to tracing the action in linked spaces over time, to reveal how and why under the obtaining historical circumstances actors built institutional arrangements.

We leave the reader with this puzzle, for the moment, but we will provide a way of addressing it which leads to a series of effects. These can eventually be used, as we will show in Chapter 4, to analyse how change occurs, and in Chapter 11, to suggest explanations for phenomena of globalization or internationalization.

Study questions

1 Explain the difference between universalistic and particularistic theories.
2 What are the main arguments of the contingency approach, and how can this approach be reconciled with the cultural and institutional approaches?
3 Explain the differences between the 'emic' and 'etic' approaches to cultural research.
4 Assess under what conditions you would choose one or another type of research.
5 Comment on the compatibility of, and the possibility of integrating the two approaches.
6 Explain the importance of national institutions for management and organization.
7 Explain the broad differences between the liberal and the coordinated institutional cluster.
8 Explain how the concept of globalization could best be defined.

Further reading

Hall, E.T. and Hall, M.R. (1990) *Understanding Cultural Differences.* Yarmouth, USA: Intercultural Press.

The authors offer yet another framework within the emic approach to national culture, elaborating on the concepts of low and high context, and their implications for understanding and communicating with people from different cultural backgrounds.

Hall, P.A. and Soskice, D. (2001) *Varieties of Capitalism.* Oxford: Oxford University Press.

This book offers another framework for carrying out institutional analysis.

Hofstede, G. (2001) *Culture's Consequences* (2nd edn). London: Sage.

This book offers a wide and detailed picture of culture research.

Maurice, M. and Sorge, A. (2000) *Embedding Organizations.* Amsterdam: John Benjamins.

This book offers the latest position, empirical examples and criticism from other points of view, in societal effect research.

Punnett, B.J. and Shenkar, O. (1998) *Handbook for International Management Research.* New Delhi: Beacon Books.

This book deals in an accessible way with research design and methodology for international management research.

Whitley, R. (2007) *Business Systems and Organizational Capabilities: The Institutional Structuring of Competitive Competences.* Oxford: Oxford University Press.

This is the latest position on business systems theory and research, by its leading proponent.

Notes

1 As this complex methodology cannot be explained here, the reader could usefully refer to the articles by Pugh et al. (1963, 1968 and 1969) cited in the References section.
2 The association between perspectives and methods is not absolute, however. Sometimes, in emic investigations of indigenous constructs, data are collected with survey methods and analysed with quantitative techniques. Likewise, ethnographic observation and qualitative data are sometimes used to support arguments from an etic perspective.
3 For postwar writings on the case for convergence see Aron (1962), Kerr et al. (1960) and Bell (1973).

References

Albrow, M. (1990) Introduction, in Albrow, M. and King, E. (eds) *Globalization, Knowledge and Society*. London: Sage.

Amable, B. (2000) Institutional complementarity and diversity of social systems of innovation and production. *Review of Political Economy* 7(4), 645–687.

Appadurai, A. (1996) *Modernity at Large: Cultural Dimensions of Globalization*. Minneapolis, MN: University of Minnesota Press.

Aron, R. (1962) *Dix-Huit Leçons sur la Société Industrielle*. Paris: Gallimard.

Bell, D. (1973) *The Coming of Post-Industrial Society*. New York: Basic Books.

Berger, P.L. and Luckmann, T. (1967) *The Social Construction of Reality. A Treatise in the Sociology of Knowledge*. Harmondsworth: Penguin Books.

Berger, S. (1996) Introduction, in Berger, S. and Dore, R. (eds) *National Diversity and Global Capitalism*. London: Cornell University Press.

Berger, S. and Dore, R. (eds) (1996) *National Diversity and Global Capitalism*. London: Cornell University Press.

Berry, J.W. (1990) Imposed etics, emics, derived etics: their conceptual and operational status in cross-cultural psychology, in Headland, T.N., Pike, K.L. and Harris, M. (eds) *Emic and Etics: the Insider/Outsider Debate*. Newbury Park, CA: Sage, 28–47.

Bourdieu, P. (1986) The forms of capital, in Richardson, J. (ed) *Handbook of Theory and Research for the Sociology of Education*. New York: Greenwood, 46–58.

Carroll, G.L. and Huo, P.Y. (1986) Organizational task and institutional environment in ecological perspective: findings from the local newspaper industry. *American Journal of Sociology* 91, 838–873.

Casper, S. (2000) Institutional adaptiveness, technology policy, and the diffusion of new business models: the case of German biotechnology. *Organization Studies* 21(5), 887–914.

Child, J. (1981) Culture, contingency, and capitalism in the cross-national study of organizations. *Research in Organizational Behavior* 3, 303–356.

Child, J. and Tayeb, M. (1981) Theoretical perspectives in cross-national organizational research. *International Studies of Management and Organization* 10(1), 23–70.

Cox, R.W. (1992) Global perestroika, in Miliband, R. and Panitch, I. (eds) *New World Order? Socialist Register 1992*. London: Merlin.

Crozier, M. and Friedberg, E. (1980) *Actors and Systems*. Chicago, Ill.: University of Chicago Press.

Dicken, P. (1998) *Global Shift: Transforming the World Economy* (3rd edn). London: Sage.

DiMaggio, P. and Powell, W. (1991) Introduction, in Powell, W. and DiMaggio, P. (eds) *The New Institutionalism in Organizational Analysis*. Chicago: University of Chicago Press, 1–40.

Dobbin, F. (1994) *Forging Industrial Policy: the United States, Britain and France in the Railway Age*. New York: Cambridge University Press.

Dore, R. (1996) Convergence in whose interest?, in Berger, S. and Dore, R. (eds) *National Diversity and Global Capitalism*. London: Cornell University Press.

Earley, P.C. (1989) Social loafing and collectivism: a comparison of United States and People's Republic of China. *Administrative Science Quarterly* 34, 565–581.

Garcia Canclini, N. (1995) *Hybrid Cultures: Strategies for Entering and Leaving Modernity*. Minneapolis, MN: University of Minnesota Press.

Geertz, C. (1976) From the native's point of view: on the nature of anthropological understanding, in Basso, K. and Selby, H. (eds) *Meaning in Anthropology*. Albuquerque: University of New Mexico Press, 221–237.

Geertz, C. (1983) *Local Knowledge: Further Essays in Interpretive Anthropology*. New York: Basic Books.

Giddens, A. (1986) *The Constitution of Society*. Berkeley, CA: UCP.

Giddens, A. (1999) *Runaway World: How Globalization is Reshaping our Lives*. London: Profile Books.

Gregory, K. (1983) Native-view paradigms: multiple cultures and culture conflicts in organizations. *Administrative Science Quarterly* 28, 359–376.

Hall, P. and Soskice, D. (2001) *Varieties of Capitalism: the Institutional Foundations of Comparative Advantage.* New York: Oxford University Press.

Hannerz, U. (1987) The world in Creolization. *Africa* 57, 546–559.

Harris, M. (1979) *Cultural Materialism: the Struggle for a Science of Culture.* New York: Vintage.

Hickson, D.J., Pugh, D.S. and Pheysey, D. (1969) Operations technology and organization structure: an empirical reappraisal. *Administrative Science Quarterly* 14, 378–397.

Hickson, D.J., Hinings, C.R., McMillan, C.J. and Schwitter, J.P. (1974) The culture-free context of organization structure: a trinational comparison. *Sociology* 8, 59–80.

Hickson, D.J., McMillan, C.J., Azumi, K. and Horvath, D. (1979) Grounds for comparative organization theory: quicksands or hard core?, in Lammers, C.J. and Hickson, D.J. (eds) *Organizations Alike and Unlike.* London: Routledge & Kegan Paul.

Hofstede, G. (2001) *Culture's Consequences* (2nd edn). London: Sage.

Horvath, D., Azumi, K., Hickson, D.J. and McMillan, C.J. (1981) Bureaucratic structures in cross-national perspective: a study of British, Japanese, and Swedish firms, in Dlugos, G., Weiermair, K. and Dorow, W. (eds) *Management Under Differing Value Systems.* Berlin: Walter de Gruyter.

Kerr, C., Dunlop, J.T., Harbison, F. and Myers, C.A. (1960) *Industrialism and Industrial Man.* Cambridge: Harvard University Press.

Kondo, D.K. (1990) *Crafting Selves: Power, Gender, and Discourses of Identity in the Japanese Workplace.* Chicago: University of Chicago Press.

Lane, C. (1989) *Management and Labour in Europe.* Aldershot: Edward Elgar.

Lane, C. (2000) Globalization and the German model of capitalism – erosion or survival? *British Journal of Sociology* 51(2), 207–234.

Levitt, T. (1983) The globalization of markets. *Harvard Business Review* 61 (May–June), 92–102.

Lincoln, J.R., Hanada, M. and McBride, K. (1986) Organizational structures in Japanese and US manufacturing. *Administrative Science Quarterly* 31, 338–364.

Malinowski, B. (1922) *Argonauts of the Western Pacific.* London: Routledge.

Maurice, M. and Sorge, A. (2000) *Embedding Organizations.* Amsterdam: John Benjamins Publishing.

Maurice, M., Sellier, F. and Silvestre, J.J. (1986) *The Social Foundations of Industrial Power.* Cambridge, MA: MIT Press.

Meyer, J.W. (2000) Globalization: Sources and effects on national states and societies. *International Sociology* 15(2), 233–248.

Meyer, J.W. and Rowan, B. (1977) Institutionalized organizations: formal structure as myth and ceremony. *American Journal of Sociology* 83, 340–363.

Meyer, J.W. and Rowan, B. (1991) Institutionalized organizations: formal structure as myth and ceremony, in Powell, W. and DiMaggio, P. (eds) *The New Institutionalism in Organizational Analysis.* Chicago: University of Chicago Press, 41–62.

Mintzberg, H. (1983) *Structure in Fives: Designing Effective Organizations.* Englewood Cliffs, N.J.: Prentice Hall.

Morris, M.W., Leung, K., Ames, D. and Lickel, B. (1999) Views from inside and outside: integrating emic and etic insights about culture and justice judgement. *Academy of Management Review* 24(4), 781–796.

Munroe, R.L. and Munroe, R.H. (1991) Comparative field studies: methodological issues and future. *HRAF Journal of Comparative Management* 25(1–4), 155.

Nederveen Pieterse, J. (1994) Globalization as hybridization. *International Sociology* 9(2), 161–184.

Noorderhaven, N. (2000) Positivist, hermeneutical and postmodern positions in the comparative management debate, in Maurice, M. and Sorge, A. (eds) *Embedding Organizations.* Amsterdam: John Benjamins, 117–137.

North, D. (1991) Institutions. *Journal of Economic Perspectives* 5(1), 97–112.

North, D. (1995) *Institutions Matter* (mimeo). Seattle: University of Washington.

Nye, J.S. and Donahue, J.D. (2000) *Governance in a Globalizing World.* Washington: Brookings Institution Press.

Orton, J.D. and Weick, K.E. (1990) Loosely coupled systems: a reconceptualization. *Academy of Management Review* 15, 203–223.

Pieterse, J.N. (1995) Globalization as hybridization, in Featherstone, M., Lash, S. and Robertson. R. (eds) *Global Modernities*. London: Sage, 45–68.

Pike, K.L. (1967) *Language in Relation to a United Theory of the Structure of Human Behavior*. The Hague: Mouton.

Pugh, D.S., Hickson, D.J., Hinings, C.R. and Turner, C. (1968) Dimensions of organization structure. *Administrative Science Quarterly* 13(1), 65–105.

Pugh, D.S., Hickson, D.J., Hinings, C.R. and Turner, C. (1969) The context of organization structure. *Administrative Science Quarterly* 14(1), 91–114.

Pugh, D.S., Hickson, D.J., Hinings, C.R., MacDonald, K.M., Turner, C. and Lupton, T. (1963) A conceptual scheme for organizational analysis. *Administrative Science Quarterly* 8(3), 289–315.

Robertson, R. (1992) *Globalization: Social Theory and Global Cultures*. London: Sage.

Robertson, R. (1995) Globalization: time–space and homogeneity–heterogeneity, in Featherstone, M., Lash, S. and Robertson. R. (eds) *Global Modernities*. London: Sage, 24–44.

Robertson, R. (2001) Globalization theory 2000+: major problematics, in Ritzer, G. and Smart, B. (eds) *Handbook of Social Theory*. London: Sage, 458–471.

Rohlen, T. (1974) *For Harmony and Strength: Japanese White-collar Organization in Anthropological Perspective*. Berkeley: University of California Press.

Rose, M. (1985) Universalism, culturalism and the Aix group: promise and problems of a societal approach to economic institutions. *European Sociological Review* 1(1), 65–83.

Rugman, A. and Hodgetts, R. (2001) The end of global strategy. *European Management Journal* 19(4), 333–343.

Schneider, B. (1990) *Organizational Climate and Culture*. San Francisco: Jossey-Bass.

Scott, W.R. (1995) *Institutions and Organizations*. Thousand Oaks, California: Sage.

Scott, W.R. (2001) *Institutions and Organizations*. London: Sage.

Shweder, R.A. (1991) *Thinking Through Culture: Expeditions in Cultural Psychology*. Cambridge, MA: Harvard University Press.

Skinner, B.F. (1938) *The Behavior of Organisms: An Experimental Analysis*. Englewood Cliffs, NJ: Prentice Hall.

Smith, P.B. and Bond, M.H. (1998) *Social Psychology: Across Cultures* (2nd edn). Boston: Allyn & Bacon.

Soskice, D. (1996) *German Technology Policy, Innovation, and National Institutional Frameworks*. Wissenschaftszentrum Berlin, Discussion Paper FS I, 96–319.

Sorge, A. (1996) Societal effects in cross-national organization studies, in Whitley, R. and Kristensen, P.H. (eds) *The Changing European Firm*. London: Routledge.

Sorge, A. (2003) Cross-national differences in human resources and organization, in Harzing, A.-W. and Van Ruisseveldt, J. (eds) *Human Resource Management* (2nd edn). London: Sage.

Soskice, D. (1999) Divergent production regimes: coordinated and uncoordinated market economies in the 1980s and 1990s, in Kitschelt, H., Large, P., Marks, G. and Stephens, J.D. (eds) *Continuity and Change in Contemporary Capitalism*. Cambridge: Cambridge University Press.

Streeck, W. (1992) *Societal Institutions and Economic Performance: Studies of Industrial Relations in Advanced Capitalist Economies*. London: Sage.

Streeck, W. (1996) Lean production in the German automobile industry? A test for convergence theory, in Berger, S. and Dore, R. (eds) *National Diversity and Global Capitalism*. New York: Cornell University Press.

Streeck, W. (1997) German capitalism: does it exist? Can it survive? in Crouch, C. and Streeck, W. (eds) *Political Economy of Modern Capitalism*. London: Sage.

Streeck, W. (2013) *Buying Time: The Delayed Crisis of Capitalism*. New York: Verso.

Streeten, P. (1996) Free and managed trade, in Berger, S. and Dore, R. (eds) *National Diversity and Global Capitalism*. London: Cornell University Press, 353–365.

Tolbert, P.S. and Zucker, L.G. (1996) The institutionalization of institutional theory, in Clegg, S.R., Hardy, C. and Nord, W.R. (eds) *Handbook of Organization Studies*. London: Sage Publications, 175–190.

Tomlinson, J. (1999) *Globalization and Culture.* Chicago, IL: University of Chicago Press.

Van Maanen, J. (1988) *Tales of the Field: on Writing Ethnography.* Chicago: University of Chicago Press.

Vitols, S. (2001) Varieties of corporate governance: comparing Germany and the UK, in Hall, P.A. and Soskice, D. (eds) *Varieties of Capitalism.* Oxford: Oxford University Press.

Weick, K.E. (1979) *The Social Psychology of Organizing.* New York: Addison-Wesley.

Whitley, R. (1992) *European Business Systems: Firms and Markets in Their National Context.* London: Sage Publications.

Whitley, R. (1994a) The internationalization of firms and markets: its significance and institutional structures. *Organization Studies* 1(1), 101–124.

Whitley, R. (1994b) Dominant forms of economic organization in market economies. *Organization Studies* 15(2), 153–182.

Whitley, R. (1999) *Divergent Capitalisms: the Social Structuring and Change of Business Systems.* Oxford: Oxford University Press.

Wundt, W. (1888) Über ziele und wege der volkerpsychologie. *Philosophische Studien* 4.

Zucker, L.G. (1983) Where do institutional patterns come from? Organizations as actors in social systems, in Zucker, L.G. (ed.) *Institutional Patterns and Organizations: Culture and Environment.* Cambridge, MA: Ballinger.

2 National cultures and management – the etic approach

Learning objectives

By the end of this chapter you will be able to:

- define the concept of culture
- distinguish between culture and stereotypes
- understand different views on the origins of national culture
- evaluate the usefulness of the emic and etic approaches to cultural analysis
- understand methodological difficulties in national culture research
- understand and appreciate the strengths and weaknesses of Hofstede's work, Schwarz's work, and the World Values Survey
- relate the three main etic studies of national culture to one another
- recognize the implications of the cultural differences identified by etic studies for management and organization
- understand the differences between culture at the national and at the organizational level
- recognize the implications of cultural differences at the national level for international negotiations.

Chapter outline

2.1 Introduction

Chapter 1 briefly introduced the cultural approach to comparative international management. In this chapter and the next we will discuss this approach in more depth. In doing so, we aim to provide the reader with a balanced view. Too many contributions to cultural management theory are one-sided, arguing for the importance of one particular source of cultural differences (e.g. nationality), and reasoning from one particular theoretical point of view (e.g. 'etic' versus 'emic'). The importance of national differences in culture is undeniable, and we will discuss these differences extensively. There are also other cultural distinctions, however, that may remain unobserved if we continue to look at the nation-state as the main (or sole) source of cultural identity. The reality is that countries have always harboured cultural diversity and are increasingly doing so. The complex influences of cultural differences on management can probably never be understood from only one methodological perspective, hence our discussion of multiple approaches and our emphasis on their complementarity. In particular, we will in this chapter discuss various approaches that fall under the 'etic' perspective, and in Chapter 3 discuss the 'emic' perspective.

However, before going into a description of the contents of these approaches we will discuss the concept of culture. What *is* culture, and what is it *not*? After that we will look at some key methodological issues. The reason for this is that an insight into the methods used in cross-cultural research is of vital importance in understanding the strengths and weaknesses of the various approaches. The distinction between the various approaches to culture is also largely a matter of research methods, and the same can be said of the distinction between cultural and institutional approaches.

Following the section on methodological issues, we will first discuss three large-scale studies representing the etic approach: Geert Hofstede's work, the work of Shalom Schwartz, and the World Values Survey. After that, we will discuss how management and organization in different countries of the world can be better understood on the basis of these studies, and how they help in finding the best way in cross-cultural encounters. In the final part of the chapter we focus on one particular, but very important, aspect of the influences of culture on management, namely international negotiations. International negotiations are of crucial importance to an increasing number of firms, whether in the context of buying or selling across national boundaries, in the context of the formation of an international alliance or joint venture, or in the course of the internal management of a multinational corporation (the subject of Chapter 9).

2.2 What culture is and is not

Defining culture

Anthropologists and pioneering culture researchers Alfred Kroeber and Clyde Kluckhohn collected some 160 definitions of 'culture', which indicates that this is not an easy concept to define. Kroeber and Kluckhohn's own definition aimed to be comprehensive:

> Culture consists of patterns, explicit and implicit, of and for behavior acquired and transmitted by symbols, constituting the distinctive achievements of human groups, including their embodiments in artifacts; the essential core of culture consists of traditional (i.e. historically derived and selected) ideas and especially their attached values; culture systems may, on the one hand, be considered as products of action, and on the other as conditioning elements of further action.
>
> (Kroeber and Kluckhohn, 1952: 181)

This definition indicates that culture consists of patterns of and for behaviour (i.e., pertaining both to what behaviours are and ought to be), as well as ideas and values. It also includes artefacts that embody a culture. For instance, the White House in the United States, as an edifice, can be seen as embodying important elements of the American national political culture. Moreover, Kroeber and Kluckhohn point at the characteristic of culture to both be a product of past human collective action and to be a factor determining future action.

Geert Hofstede defined culture as 'the collective programming of the mind which distinguishes the members of one group or category of people from those of another' (Hofstede, 1991: 5). A number of elements in this definition deserve our attention. First of all, the metaphor of 'programming' indicates that culture is about learned, and not inherited, behaviours, ideas and values (note that Hofstede's definition does not include artefacts). While the 'nature-or-nurture debate' on the relative strength of genetically determined versus learned behaviour continues, culture research clearly focuses on that part of our behavioural repertoire that is not inherited but learned. Furthermore, Hofstede talks about 'collective' programming of the mind, i.e., culture refers to behaviours, ideas and values, shared by a collective. Finally, these behaviours distinguish the members of one group or collective from those of another. This means that culture is about behaviours, etc., that one shares with members of one group or category, but which are different from those of other groups or categories. Hofstede's definition also makes clear that culture can be specific both to a group (i.e., a collective the members of which interact with each other, like an organizational unit) or a category (i.e., a collective the members of which share one or more important characteristics, without necessarily all interacting with each other, like a profession). National culture, the phenomenon we will be focusing on mostly in this chapter, clearly is specific to a collective, rather than a group.

The different elements of a culture can be positioned on a continuum, from the most to the least visible to an observer, and from the highest to the lowest level of awareness of the member of the culture (see Figure 2.1). However, although cultural artefacts may be clearly visible to non-members of a culture, their meaning in many cases remains hidden to these outsiders.

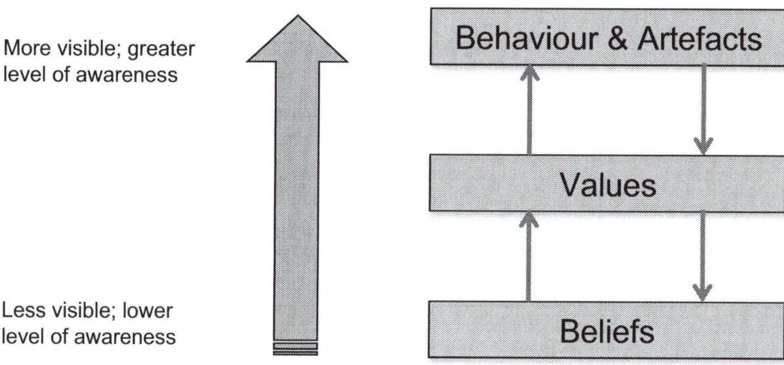

Figure 2.1 Levels of culture.

Adapted from Schein (1984: 4).

Culture and stereotypes

It is important to distinguish culture as we have defined it above from stereotypes. Many studies have looked at how citizens of one country perceive those from another country. For instance, Burns, Myers and Kakabadse (1995) report how managers from five European countries rate themselves and their colleagues from the four other countries on 12 characteristics. The results illustrate that most people tend to see their own culture more positively than outsiders do. For instance, the British managers saw themselves as more trustworthy and hard working than the managers from the other countries saw them. However, the dispersion between self-image and how others see a culture is not equally large for all countries. In the case of France, for instance, the ratings of the French managers themselves and those from their colleagues from other European countries were not very different. A picture arises of French managers as highly educated, reasonably efficient, but not very trustworthy.

How much truth do such perceptions contain? Mostly these are stereotypes, oversimplified images of members of the other groups, not based on much direct experience. Typically, if one has more contact with members from another culture one's perceptions tend to become more nuanced and overall more positive. Both self-images and simplified perceptions of a culture by outsiders may have little basis in reality, however convinced people may be that they contain a core of truth (Chew, 2006). But true or not, stereotypes do have effects. For instance, a study of international joint ventures found that the level of trust one partner has in the other is strongly influenced by both the nationality of the trustor and that of the trustee. The latter effect becomes weaker the more the trustor has experience with the partner, suggesting that experience may indeed substitute first-hand knowledge for stereotypes as a source of trust (Ertug, Cuypers, Noorderhaven and Bensaou, 2013). All the same, we have to assume that both substantive and perceived cultural differences may play a role in international management.

Where does culture come from?

Most of the etic approaches to culture assume explicitly or implicitly that over the ages culture has evolved to help people survive in a particular environment. For instance,

Hofstede (2001: 12) sees forces of nature and forces of man (e.g., war) as important factors moulding the ecology within which a culture evolves. In this view a culture has survival value for the group, it promotes behaviours that are helpful for the group to sustain in its particular environment. In this view culture is an *adaptive system*: it serves to relate a community to its ecological setting (Keesing, 1974). This perspective on culture has a functionalist flavour: cultural characteristics are explained as unintended adaptations of a group or category of people to their environment.

An alternative perspective is what Keesing (1974) calls the *ideational system* view. In this perspective culture consists of behaviours and beliefs that are cumulative creations of the mind. Such a culture, evolving out of ideas responding to other ideas, may help the group to survive, e.g., because it strengthens the coherence of the collectivity. But it may also be at odds with the exigencies of the (natural) environment, and lead to the downfall of the group. A popular example of a culture destroying its natural environment is Easter Island, where the culture of building giant statutes (*moai*) that were transported to their final positions with palm trunks used as rollers, led to the complete de-forestation of the island and impoverishment of the population (Bahn and Flenley, 1992; for a different view, see Rainbird, 2002).

Actually, also in the adaptive system view a culture may very well be detrimental to the survival of a group. Most scholars assume that cultures change only very slowly (e.g., Hofstede, 2001: 34), hence it is perfectly possible that in a rapidly changing environment a culture evolves too slowly. This could be the case for instance if in a period of rapid industrialization old values are maintained that are at odds with the logic of modern employment. The upshot is that independent of the theory of the development of culture that we adhere to, we have to consider that culture can be a positive as well as a negative force in relation to a particular activity or endeavour.

2.3 Methodological dilemmas

As mentioned in the introductory chapter, two main traditions can be distinguished in cross-cultural research: the etic and the emic. We will start with a characterization of both approaches, and then go on to discuss the related subjects of levels of analysis, dimensions and typologies of cultures, boundaries of cultures, and research methods.

Etic versus emic

The comparison of cultures presupposes that there is something to be compared – that each culture is not so unique that any parallel with another culture is meaningless. Throughout the history of the study of culture there has been a dispute between those stressing the unique aspects (the emic approach) and those stressing the comparable aspects (the etic approach). The emic approach emphasizes the need to understand social systems from the inside and through the definitions of their members. It attempts to analyse the internal coherence of single examples and condemns any attempt at classification across cultures as denying the uniqueness of each culture. Because of this emphasis on the unique features of each culture, the approach can also be characterized as 'idiographic'. Pure idiographic research is usually based on qualitative data such as (participant) observation and interviews. Etic research, in contrast, attempts to establish general laws governing large numbers of examples. It looks at the variances and co-variances of variables between cultures (between-society correlations). Because of the emphasis on general laws, this approach can be characterized as 'nomothetic'.

The words 'etic' and 'emic' come from linguistics; they are taken from the terms 'phonetic' and 'phonemic', the distinction between which can be seen as paradigmatic for the major debate within cultural studies. Phonetics is the study of sound and sound changes in human speech. Historically, this branch of science was conceived as a natural science, which tried to uncover the general laws determining human speech sounds. Phonemics, in contrast, is the study of sound units in language that enable speakers to distinguish between meanings. Phonemes differ between languages, and can only be studied within the context of a given language. North Sea Ferries once coined the slogan 'North Sea Ferries, Ferry Good'; however, the pun is only clear to speakers of a language in which the 'f' sound and the 'v' sound distinguish between meanings, like English. In the Dutch language, for instance, the distinction between the 'f' sound and the 'v' sound is not phonemic.

The difference between etic and emic approaches is partly parallel to that between psychological and sociological approaches to culture on the one hand, and anthropological approaches on the other. However, there have also been anthropologists with nomothetic-etic ambitions. This was particularly true of the early generations of anthropologists, like Edward Tyler (1832–1917), who developed a general evolutionary theory of cultural development.[1] All cultures were assumed to progress through a series of stages, from 'primitive' to 'civilized'. It is true that later generations of anthropologists, following in the footsteps of Franz Boas (1858–1942), emphasized that cultures are integrated wholes that need to be studied in detail before any generalization can be made (if it ever can), but more recently, Claude Lévi-Strauss's structural anthropology again sought to identify general regularities. Lévi-Strauss (1908–90), through painstakingly detailed analysis, tried to demonstrate that, at a deeper level, the bewildering variety of cultural phenomena, like kinship systems and myths, can in fact be grouped into a very limited number of basic forms or structures. These structures were seen to reflect the structures of the human unconscious processes that shaped the forms of cultural life (Moore, 1997: 219). Hence, important anthropologists have nourished the ideals of building an objective 'science of society' normally associated with etic approaches. However, since the 1970s, anthropology has 'moved quite rapidly from being a (would-be) science of society to being (once again) one of the humanities, concerned with interpretation and meaning' (Chapman, 1996–97: 4). The consequence is that contemporary anthropological research is predominantly of the emic kind, and hence is fundamentally different from the etic sociological and psychological work. Another consequence, which we will try to avoid here, is that representatives of both perspectives act as if they have nothing to say to each other. We think, in contrast, that it is important for students of comparative international management to familiarize themselves with *both* approaches in order to be able to construct a balanced view of what we know and do not know about cultures and their impact on management.

Research methods

Although the differences between the etic and the emic approach cannot be reduced to issues of method alone (in Chapter 3 we will put forth that at a deeper level there is also a difference in the philosophy of science adhered to, implicitly or explicitly), it is clear that the different foci of the two perspectives do call for divergent research methods, and that these different methods in turn further sharpen the differences between the two perspectives. Etic culture research aims to generalize across the boundaries of individual countries. If a researcher wants to identify dimensions in which cultures differ, he or she has to study a sufficient number of different societies in order to be able to verify the general nature of the proposed dimensions. Hofstede's research, discussed in depth later in this chapter, illustrates this. Hofstede used factor analysis to identify two of his dimensions. In such an analysis, the unit of analysis is the culture. This means that in order to have a sufficient number of observations, many cultures need to be studied.

In large-scale studies, covering many cultures, it is important that observations from the different cultures studied are comparable. For this reason the nomothetic-etic approach has a partiality for standardized instruments, in particular standardized questionnaires. In constructing these instruments one of the main concerns is that the data collected in different societies are indeed comparable. This is the quest for 'equivalence' in etic research. If a particular question is asked of respondents in country A, the same question has to be asked of respondents in country B in order for the answers to be comparable. But what does it mean to ask 'the same' question in different cultures?

Translation into local languages is one aspect of the quest for equivalence. It is standard practice in cross-cultural research to translate a questionnaire into a local language, and then have it 'back-translated' into the original language by a different translator. In this way, inconsistencies between the translated and the original instrument can be identified. However, equivalence issues go beyond translation into different languages. Even if the translation is faithful, the question may have quite different connotations from one country to another. An example is one of the questions used by Hofstede (1980): 'How long do you think you will continue working for this company?' (part of the scale measuring uncertainty avoidance). We may expect that it makes a big difference whether this question was asked of respondents in a country like the USA, with bountiful alternative employment options, or in a country like, say, Peru, with at the time of Hofstede's research far fewer comparable employment possibilities. Hence, differences between answers to the question may partly be due to differences in other context factors than the national culture that is targeted.

With the preference for standardized, equivalent research instruments and large samples, a preference for quantified data becomes inevitable. Quantified data also make it possible to address issues of equivalence post hoc – that is, after the data collection. If we have included in the instrument a number of items that are supposed to measure a particular construct, we can test whether the answers to these items are correlated in all the different societies studied. If this is not the case, this is a sign that the items do not measure the construct in question reliably. Items that do not in all countries studied correlate significantly with the other items measuring the same construct can then be dropped from the further analysis, and in this way the scale is purified. This procedure would be impossible with qualitative data, of course.

Anthropologist Malcolm Chapman (1996–97: 12) notes that the search for equivalence in etic research seems strange from an emic perspective: faced with 'differences in connotation' or 'different divisions and structures of categories', the instinct of a psychologist has been to remove these in order to ask culturally neutral and 'objective' questions. To the anthropologist, by contrast, any 'lack of equivalence' is precisely where research should focus and precisely where objective knowledge must be sought. In other words, from an emic perspective in the quest for equivalence the etic researchers risk throwing out the baby (the 'real' cultural differences) with the bath water ('measurement errors'). Because it focuses on meaning, contemporary anthropologic research by necessity espouses different research methods. It would be futile to try to gauge differences in meaning using large-scale questionnaires. Instead, emic researchers study cultures from within, which involves living within the society being researched for a prolonged period of time, learning the language, engaging in interactions with local people, and so on. The aim is to develop an understanding of the meaning of culturally specific behaviours, symbols and artefacts to the members of the society or group in question. In the words of Clifford Geertz, 'the trick is to figure out what the devil they think they are up to' (Geertz, 1983: 58). The emphasis in the quote from Geertz should be on 'they': in emic culture research the aim is to understand the logic of a culture from within.

The data collected with the 'ethnographic' methods mostly used in emic research are of a rich, qualitative nature, but difficult to compare with those from other studies, because they are also more subjective than the data collected in etic research. If another emic researcher studied the same culture, there is no guarantee that he or she would come up with the same interpretation of meaning. To put it very simply, one could say that data collected in etic research are shallow but reliable, and data collected in emic research rich but less reliable. However, an emic researcher would say, 'What's the use of "reliable" data when they miss the essential point of a culture – that is, its meaning to local people?'

Boundaries of cultures

Another noteworthy problem in cross-cultural research is that the boundaries of the level of analysis cannot always be defined clearly. Within the cross-cultural literature (in particular, in etic studies) the dominant approach has been to equate nations with cultures, and thus to study culture by comparing samples from different countries. However, national boundaries often do not encompass homogeneous societies with a shared culture. Examples are Canada, which has an English- and a French-speaking population with different cultural features; Nigeria, with a Muslim and a Christian population; Germany, with cultural differences between the different states (Bundesländer), and so on. Moreover, the nation-state is essentially a Western invention; elsewhere (e.g. in Africa) the nation-state is relatively young and hardly corresponds to any sense of cultural homogeneity or identity. It is argued, however, that in nations that have existed for some time there are strong forces towards integration (Hofstede, 1991: 12). There is usually a single dominant language, educational system, army, political system, shared mass media, markets, services and national symbols (e.g. flag, sports teams). These can produce substantial sharing of basic values among residents of a nation. This is less the case, of course, in nations with sharp divisions between ethnic groups. Most etic research, however, concentrates on the more homogeneous societies, avoiding this problem but posing limits on the generalizability of the framework. Emic research, in contrast, has traditionally had a tendency to focus on cultural groups that are not defined by national boundaries, like the indigenous peoples of North America, or the Nuer people of the southern Sudan.

To be able to make valid comparisons, research should be based either on representative samples or on more narrow, but carefully 'matched', samples. In order to be representative, a sample should cover (in the right proportions) all the relevant subgroups or categories of people in a society, also taking into account for instance age, gender and occupation or level of education. As a result this strategy calls for large samples. The national samples used in the World Values Survey (to be discussed later in this chapter), for instance, are typically around 1,000 respondents. As for the strategy of matched samples, depending on the nature of the characteristics scholars want to compare, they can compose matched samples of individuals, situations, institutions (such as families) or organizations. An example of the last of these is a study about hierarchy conducted by Tannenbaum, Kavcic,

Rosner, Vianello and Wieser (1974) that covered ten industrial companies, matched for size and product, in each of five countries. When comparing cultural aspects of nations one should try to match for categories such as educational level, socio-economic status, occupation, gender and age group. In addition, there may also be linguistic, regional, tribal, ethnic, religious or caste divisions within nations. We can compare Spanish nurses with Swedish nurses, or Spanish policemen with Swedish policemen; in the case of such narrow samples, however, we have to be careful in interpreting the differences and similarities found. For instance, if differences are found in the values espoused by military personnel in different countries (e.g., Soeters and Recht, 1998) this can reflect value differences between these countries in general, but before drawing any conclusion we will have to ascertain whether the military institutions are functionally equivalent in the nations concerned. If one of the countries has a conscription system and another country a regular (professional) army, there may be a self-selection bias in the second sample that makes it incomparable with the first. A more solid research strategy, if we have to use narrow samples, is to take several samples from different parts of society. With a fourfold sample of Spanish and Swedish nurses and Spanish and Swedish policemen, we can test not only the nationality effect but also the occupation effect (nurses versus policemen) and the possible interaction between the two, which can give clues as to functional equivalence. The quality of the matching of narrow samples can often only be proven ex post facto: if the differences we find between cultures in one sample set are confirmed by those found by others in other matched samples, our matching was adequate (Hofstede, 2001: 23–4).

Levels of analysis

The nomothetic-etic approach presupposes data on a sufficiently large number of cultures and tends to proceed from a study of 'ecological' correlations. The latter are calculated either from mean values of variables for each society or (in the case of categorical variables) from percentages of respondents for a particular score (Hofstede, 2001). Comparative research with an idiographic-emic concern (if statistically inclinated) will express itself in a focus on relations between variables *within* cultures (within-society correlations), followed by a comparison of the patterns found from culture to culture. The within-society indexes are calculated from variables correlated at the individual level. The outcomes can be quite different. Smith (2004: 10) noted that in the work of Shalom Schwartz (discussed later in this chapter), the values 'authority' and 'humility' are negatively correlated within cultures, while cultures in which authority is strongly endorsed also typically approve of humility.

Two common areas of confusion in nomothetic-etic studies concerning the levels-of-analysis problem are the ecological fallacy and the reverse ecological fallacy. The ecological fallacy is committed when conclusions concerning individuals are drawn from higher-level data. The classic example is discussed in Hofstede (2001: 16). In 1930 data, there was a strong correlation ($r = 0.95$) between skin colour and illiteracy across US states: states with a higher percentage of blacks also had higher percentages of illiterates. However, if the same data were analysed at the individual level, across 97 million individuals, the correlation dropped to $r = 0.20$. The ecological fallacy is particularly tempting when data at higher levels of aggregation are available, but individual-level data are not. This is one form of stereotyping.

The reverse ecological fallacy implies that conclusions regarding cultures are drawn from individual-level data. It is committed in the construction of ecological indexes from variables correlated at the individual level. Indexes are, for example, constructed through addition of the scores on two or more questionnaire items. In constructing indexes for the individual level, we ought to make sure that the items correlate across individuals; in constructing indexes for the national level, we ought to make sure that the country mean scores correlate across countries. The reverse ecological fallacy in cross-cultural studies occurs when research compares cultures on indexes created for the individual level (Hofstede, 2001: 16). In other words, within-society correlations are used instead of between-society correlations. One reason the reverse ecological fallacy occurs easily is that studies with data from more than a few societies (more than two or three) are rare, and ecological dimensions can be detected clearly only with data from ten or more societies.

Hofstede (2001: 17) maintains that the reverse ecological fallacy is more than just inadequate data treatment, and that it betrays 'an inadequate research paradigm in which cultures are treated and categorized as if they were individuals'. However, when individual-level questionnaire data are aggregated and analysed at the ecological level, as is the case in nomothetic-etic research, it is unfortunate if the data cannot be interpreted in terms of the individuals who provided the answers in the first place. Culture exists in the minds of people. Hence, one would expect the logic of the culture also to be reflected in the logic of the individual bearers of the culture. For this reason dimensions based on items or questions that do not correlate at the individual level within the cultures studied (as is the case for some of Hofstede's dimensions) are not entirely satisfactory. It would be preferable to construct culture-level scales, which also have good statistical characteristics at the individual level (Maznevski, Gomez, DiStefano, Noorderhaven and Wu, 2002). Research has so far not led to definitive closure on the issue of whether the structure of culture data at the individual and ecological levels is or should be similar (Fischer, Vauclair, Fontaine and Schwartz, 2010).

While less relevant in comparative management research, for the sake of completeness and to emphasize further the levels-of-analysis problem, we discuss here briefly the pan-cultural and individual levels of analysis. Imagine we have a sample that consists of N individuals who belong to n different societies. Pan-cultural analysis pools the data from all N individuals together regardless of the culture they belong to. The pan-cultural analysis, thus, deals with the combined variance from both the ecological and the individual analysis. This makes sense when we try to identify general, not culture-specific, characteristics of individuals. An individual-level analysis is performed on the pooled data for the N individuals after elimination of the culture-level effects. This can be done by deducting from each individual score the culture's mean score on the question, so that the new culture mean becomes 0 and the ecological variance is eliminated. It can also be done by full standardization of the individual scores within each culture, which results in standard scores with a mean (for each question, across the individuals within each country) of 0 and a standard deviation of 1. In both cases, the individual analysis considers precisely that part of the variance in the data that has been eliminated in the ecological analysis. It is a way of pooling the within-culture analyses across all n cultures or units (Leung and Bond, 1989).

It should be obvious by now that the choice of the appropriate level of analysis for the problem at hand is of extreme importance. Briefly, the levels-of-analysis problem in social and behavioural research occurs when conclusions applying to one level have to be drawn from data only available at another level. If the fact that the two levels do not correspond is not recognized and accommodated by the researcher, a cross-level fallacy occurs (Rousseau, 1985). This fallacy can logically go two ways: interpreting data from the social-system level as if they were data about individuals – called the ecological fallacy – and the reverse, as we have just seen, called the reverse ecological fallacy.

To complicate things further, the different levels of analysis interact in a complex way. Most cross-cultural studies, however, tend to concentrate on one level of analysis, neglecting the interplay between different levels. This means, among other things, that the influence of national culture on organizational- and industry-level culture is not often explicitly examined.

Dimensions and typologies

Contemporary comparative cross-cultural research is mainly carried out by scholars who lean towards the nomothetic-etic approach, focusing on the ecological level. An essential step in such research is to operationalize culture. Without operationalization, culture cannot be measured, and measurement is exactly what etic research is about. As yet there is limited agreement on how cultural features are best conceptualized and operationalized in empirical studies. The lack of conceptual and operational consistency in cross-cultural research is expressed most clearly in the fact that different studies have developed different dimensions of national culture.

Dimensions are developed to yield greater cultural understanding and to allow for cross-cultural comparisons. Cross-cultural research focuses on 'values' in order to characterize culture. There are, however, hundreds, perhaps thousands, of values on which societies and other cultural groups could be compared. Some values are relevant in all societies, others are known only in particular societies. Hence, to be able to compare societies effectively, the multitude of cultural values must be organized into a limited number of dimensions. Theorists who address this issue make the assumption that cultural dimensions of values reflect the basic issues or problems that societies must confront in order to regulate human activity (Smith and Schwartz, 1997). For instance, a basic issue in every society is the relationship between those with more and those with less power, and hence values and norms regarding power and authority relations seem to be ubiquitous.

It is clear, however, that while useful tools in explaining cultural behaviour, dimensions have limitations that we ought to acknowledge. It is obvious that any description of culture in a few dimensions cannot do justice to the complexity of the concept and is limiting in the sense that it constrains individuals' perceptions of behaviour in another culture. Moreover, by simplifying the reality of culture into dimensions, we neglect within-country differences, sacrificing completeness. Not surprisingly, dimensions are found to be more beneficial in making comparisons between cultures than in understanding the wide variations of behaviour within a single culture. The existence of so-called cultural paradoxes reveals the limitations in our thinking. For example, based on Hofstede's value dimension uncertainty avoidance, the Japanese have a low tolerance for uncertainty while Americans have a high tolerance. Why then do the Japanese intentionally incorporate ambiguous clauses in their business contracts, which are unusually short, while Americans dot every i, cross every t, and painstakingly spell out every possible contingency (Osland and Bird, 2000: 65)?

Hofstede himself warned against expecting too much of these dimensions and of using them incorrectly. For example, he defended the individualism–collectivism dimension as a useful construct, but went on to say: 'This does not mean, of course, that a country's individualism index score tells all there is to be known about the background and structure of relationship patterns in that country. It is an abstraction that should not be extended beyond its limited area of usefulness' (Hofstede, 1994: xi).

The use of dimensions and/or the simplification of the construct of culture should also be seen against the background of the emic–etic debate. As indicated, an emic perspective looks at a culture from within its boundaries, whereas an etic perspective stands outside and compares two or more cultures. Most cultural approaches in management adopt a between-culture or etic approach. To make between-culture differences more prominent, the etic approach downplays inconsistencies within a culture or, in other words, neglects within-culture differences. Consequently, it could be argued that the dimension approach does not replace in-depth studies of country cultures but, on the contrary, invites them. The most complete, certain and precise understanding of societies would arguably be obtained through a combination of both research approaches. Culture needs to be both observed and measured if we are to take the concept seriously. The combined use of the two research methods would offer the possibility of achieving greater conceptual consistency (i.e. consistency in the features of culture being compared cross-nationally) and equivalence in operational measurement.

Instead of using dimensions, some researchers construct typologies to illustrate differences between countries. A typology describes a number of ideal types, each of which is easy to imagine. The division of regions into the first, second and third worlds is such a typology. The identification of culture areas as ideal types represents a compromise solution between the purely emic position and the extreme etic of the index values. Historically typologies of national culture have been associated with studies of 'national character' which have been criticized for being overly deterministic (Schooler, 1996). However, whereas typologies are easier to understand than dimensions, they are problematic in empirical research. Real cases seldom correspond fully to one single ideal type. Most cases are hybrids, and arbitrary rules have to be made for classifying them as belonging to one of the types. With a dimensions model, such as those from Hofstede, the World Values Survey and the GLOBE study (all are discussed below), cases can always be scored unambiguously. In practice, typologies and dimensional models can be reconciled. On the basis of their dimension scores, cases (countries) can be sorted empirically afterwards into clusters with similar scores. These clusters then form an empirical typology. Hofstede, for example, sorted into 12 clusters more than 50 countries in a study of IBM (see the section on Hofstede, below), on the basis of four dimension scores. In fact, Hofstede uses a kind of typology approach for explaining each of the four dimensions. For every dimension, he describes the two opposite extremes, which can be seen as ideal types. Some of the dimensions are subsequently taken two by two, which creates four ideal types. However, the country scores on the dimensions locate most real cases somewhere in between the extremes (Hofstede, 2001: 28).

Despite all methodological difficulties cross-cultural research has allowed us to make important steps towards understanding cultural differences and their consequences for management and organization. In the remainder of this chapter we will discuss in some detail a number of empirical studies from the etic school of thought (examples from the emic perspective will be discussed in Chapter 3). After that, we will discuss the impact of cultural differences on management and organization and on international negotiations.

2.4 Examples of etic research

To be able to explain cross-cultural differences, nomothetic-etic research has concentrated on identifying dimensions of cultural variation. To identify such dimensions, it is desirable for studies to include as many and as wide a range of cultures as possible. Most extant cross-cultural work has been confined to a small number of cultures, although there are notable exceptions. Two such exceptions are pioneering research projects, which have aimed directly at identifying cultural dimensions of values, namely the projects of Hofstede (1980, 1991, 2001) and Schwartz (1992, 1994, 2008). A third research project that we shall discuss stands out because it is the only one that allows us to trace national culture change over long periods of time: the World Values Survey (Inglehart, 1997; Inglehart and Welzer, 2005).

Geert Hofstede: Five dimensions of work-related values

Overview

Comparative cross-cultural research at the societal or national level gathered significant impetus through the pioneering work of the Dutch scholar Geert Hofstede (1980, 1991, 2001). Hofstede, citing Inkeles and Levinson (1997), suggests that three basic societal problems underlie cultural value dimensions:

1 the relationship to authority;
2 the conception of self, including the individual's concept of masculinity and femininity;
3 primary dilemmas or conflicts, and ways of dealing with them, including the control of aggression and the expression versus inhibition of affect.

One of the most imposing features of Hofstede's original study (1980) is its sheer size. Data were generated from 116,000 questionnaires collected from IBM employees in over 40 countries. Both the size of the sample and the geographic coverage were unprecedented. Since the respondents were all marketing and service employees of a single company, a number of factors could be controlled for. All respondents were doing the same general task (marketing, selling and servicing IBM products) within the same overall company framework. Thus, the technology, job content and many formal procedures were the same. Only the nationalities of the subjects differed. Any variation in attitudes and values would, Hofstede claimed, be related to national cultural differences rather than organizational ones (for a critical view on this claim, see McSweeney, 2002).

'Eclectic analysis' (starting with two single focal items seen as measuring issues of hierarchy and work stress, respectively, and then looking for correlated items) yielded the dimensions of 'power distance' and 'uncertainty avoidance'. Factor analysis of responses to 32 questions about the importance of work goals revealed two additional dimensions of culture: 'individualism–collectivism' and 'masculinity–femininity'. Hofstede defined these dimensions such that they reflect the way members of a society typically cope with each of the 'basic societal problems': power distance to (1), uncertainty avoidance to (3), and both individualism–collectivism and masculinity–femininity to (2) (Hofstede, 2001: 31).

Hofstede's study also allowed for a 'modest' quantitative assessment of cultural change and stability (Hofstede, 2001: 34–6). He did this on the basis of the IBM survey cycles of 1967–69 and 1971–73, through a comparison of answers from respondents in different age brackets. He found that differences in values among respondents of the same national culture but of different ages and/or at different points in time may be due to three different causes: age (maturation), generation and zeitgeist. Age effects simply mean that respondents' values shift as they grow older. Shifts over time are due only to the ageing of the respondents. Generation effects occur for values that were absorbed by the young people of a certain period and accompanied their age cohort over its lifetime. If conditions of life have changed (i.e. due to fast technological change), generations may carry forward different values that they have absorbed in their youth. Zeitgeist effects occur when drastic system-wide changes in conditions cause everyone's values to shift, regardless of age. The changes found within the IBM data are small, which can be taken as an indication that cultural values do not change easily or quickly. This finding could perhaps be an indication of the fact that globalization effects will not lead to cultural convergence in the short or medium term.

Power distance (PDI) describes the extent to which 'the less powerful members of institutions and organizations within a country expect and accept that power is distributed unequally' (Hofstede, 1991: 262). *Uncertainty avoidance* (UAI) describes the extent to which 'the members of a culture feel threatened by uncertain or unknown situations' (Hofstede, 1991: 263). *Individualism versus collectivism* (IDV) describes whether 'the ties between individuals are loose, with everyone being expected to look after himself or herself and his or her immediate family only' (individualism) or whether 'people from birth onwards are integrated into strong, cohesive ingroups, which throughout people's lifetime continue to protect them in exchange for unquestioning loyalty' (collectivism) (Hofstede, 1991: 260–261). *Masculinity versus femininity* (MAS) describes whether 'social gender roles are clearly distinct: men are supposed to be assertive, tough, and focused on material success; women are supposed to be more modest, tender, and concerned with the quality of life' (femininity), or whether 'social gender roles overlap; both men and women are supposed to be modest, tender, and concerned with the quality of life' (Hofstede, 1991: 261–262).

Hofstede later added a fifth dimension to his framework, in response to the work of Bond and colleagues (Chinese Culture Connection, 1987). The IBM studies, which yielded the data from which Hofstede distilled his dimensions, used a questionnaire composed by western minds. The team that first designed it consisted of British, Dutch, French, Norwegian and US members. This exclusively Western input into the research instrument introduced a bias in the sense that the values of non-Western respondents would possibly not be fully expressed by the questionnaire results. In other words, the content validity of the instrument used by Hofstede was limited. Recognizing this bias, Bond decided to introduce a deliberate eastern bias by having Chinese colleagues from Hong Kong and Taiwan prepare an alternative questionnaire. This instrument was subsequently used in a study among university students in 23 countries (20 of which overlapped with those covered by Hofstede's IBM studies). The analysis of the data from this survey revealed four dimensions, three of which showed a certain resemblance to Hofstede's power distance, individualism–collectivism and masculinity–femininity. However, none of the dimensions identified by Bond and colleagues correlated with Hofstede's uncertainty avoidance. Instead another, bipolar, dimension was identified: 'Confucian dynamism', with values at one of the poles reflecting more future-orientated and dynamic values related to the teachings of Confucius, and those at the other pole more past and present-orientated and static (Hofstede, 1991: 166). Hence, the dimension can be seen as distinguishing between more and less dynamic and between future-orientated and past-orientated readings of the work of the Chinese philosopher Confucius (Kong Fu Ze).

Later, Hofstede adopted Confucian dynamism as the fifth dimension in his framework, under the name 'long-term versus short-term orientation'. However, it is important to note that the empirical basis of this fifth dimension is much less robust than that of the other four (Fang, 2003). Both numbers of countries included as the sample sizes in most countries were much smaller in the study in which the fifth dimension was identified than in the IBM studies. Furthermore the respondents in the Chinese culture survey were university students, whereas Hofstede had samples of IBM employees, which were arguably more representative for the working populations of their countries. Recently Hofstede and Minkov (2010) have been able to replicate the long-term versus short-term dimension with data from the World Values Survey. Hence, the confidence in the dimension has increased and we will, following Hofstede, treat long-term versus short-term orientation as an integral part of Hofstede's system of work-related values.

Long-term versus short-term orientation is related to the 'fostering of virtues oriented towards future rewards, in particular perseverance and thrift' (long-term orientation) versus 'the fostering of virtues related to the past and the present, in particular respect for tradition, preservation of 'face', and fulfilling social obligations' (short-term orientation) (Hofstede, 1991: 261–263). An overview of country scores on Hofstede's original four dimensions and on long-term versus short-term orientation can be found in Table 2.1.

Table 2.1 Country scores on Hofstede's dimensions of work-related values

	Power–Distance	*Individualism–Collectivism*	*Masculinity–Femininity*	*Uncertainty–Avoidance*	*Long-term Orientation*
Arab countries	80	38	53	68	
Argentina	49	46	56	86	
Australia	36	90	61	51	31
Austria	11	55	79	70	
Bangladesh*	80	20	55	60	40
Belgium	65	75	54	94	
Brazil	69	38	49	76	65
Bulgaria*	70	30	40	85	
Canada	39	80	52	48	23
Chile	63	23	28	86	
China*	80	20	66	30	118
Colombia	67	13	64	80	
Costa Rica	35	15	21	86	
Czechia*	57	58	57	74	13
Denmark	18	74	16	23	
East Africa	64	27	41	52	25
Ecuador	78	8	63	67	
El Salvador	66	19	40	94	
Estonia*	40	60	30	60	
Finland	33	63	26	59	
France	68	71	43	86	
Germany (West)	35	67	66	65	31
Greece	60	35	57	112	
Guatemala	95	6	37	101	
Hong Kong	68	25	57	29	96

	Power–Distance	*Individualism–Collectivism*	*Masculinity–Femininity*	*Uncertainty–Avoidance*	*Long-term Orientation*
Hungary*	46	80	88	82	50
India	77	48	56	40	61
Indonesia	78	14	46	48	
Iran	58	41	43	59	
Ireland	28	70	68	35	
Israel	13	54	47	81	
Italy	50	76	70	75	
Jamaica	45	39	68	13	
Japan	54	46	95	92	80
Luxembourg*	40	60	50	70	
Malaysia	104	26	50	36	
Malta*	56	59	47	96	
Mexico	81	30	69	82	
Morocco*	70	46	53	68	
Netherlands	38	80	14	53	44
New Zealand	22	79	58	49	30
Norway	31	69	8	50	20
Pakistan	55	14	50	70	0
Panama	95	11	44	86	
Peru	64	16	42	87	
Phillipines	94	32	64	44	19
Poland*	68	60	64	93	32
Portugal	63	27	31	104	
Romania*	90	30	42	90	
Russia*	93	39	36	95	
Singapore	74	20	48	8	48
Slovakia*	104	52	110	51	38
S. Africa (white)	49	65	63	49	
South Korea	60	18	39	85	75
Spain	57	51	42	86	
Surinam*	85	47	37	92	
Sweden	31	71	5	29	33
Switzerland	34	68	70	58	
Taiwan	58	17	45	69	87
Thailand	64	20	34	64	56
Trinidad*	47	16	58	55	
Turkey	66	37	45	85	
UK	35	89	66	35	25
Uruquay	61	36	38	100	
USA	40	91	62	46	29
Venezuela	81	12	73	76	
Vietnam*	70	20	40	30	80
West Africa	77	20	46	54	16
Yugoslavia	76	27	21	88	

Source: Compiled from Exhibits A5.1 and A5.3 (Hofstede 2001: 500, 502). Scores for countries with an asterisk are estimations.

Criticism

As with all studies, Hofstede's has provoked praise as well as criticism. Some criticism has to do with the empirical basis of his study, other criticism concerns methodological issues. We will briefly discuss five main issues: the adequacy of Hofstede's sample, limitations of his research method, the suitability of Hofstede's research instrument, the appropriateness of analysing culture at the level of nations, and the present relevance of the findings given the age of the data.

The issue of the adequacy of the sample should be seen in the light of our discussion of sampling strategies, above. Hofstede argues that it does not matter that samples are atypical 'as long as they are atypical in the same way from one country to another'. He also recognizes that 'multinational corporations have organizational cultures of their own', but argues that 'to the extent that these reduce the variability in the data from one country to another, the remaining variability will be a conservative estimate of the true variability among countries' (Hofstede, 2001: 24). Whether this is true depends on the functional equivalence of the national subsamples. It is not impossible that IBM employees diverged more from the general population in some than in other countries in the sample. This selection bias could be particularly important in comparing industrialized nations with third world countries (McSweeney, 2002).

The second criticism concerns the inherent limitations of the use of the survey method in identifying characteristics of cultures. Hofstede (1980: 18) concedes these limitations, and his general advice is 'to avoid putting all one's eggs into one basket', i.e., don't use only survey methods, but combine these with, e.g., observations or archival data from other sources.

The possibility of bias because of low content validity of the survey instrument (there is no guarantee that all relevant aspects of the cultures investigated are covered by the research instrument) has also been admitted by Hofstede, and partially addressed by including the 'fifth dimension' identified later. More generally the use of the survey instrument in culture research is one of the bones of contention between representatives of the etic and emic approaches. We do not pretend to be able to solve this dispute here, but the spirit in which this book is written is that both approaches, with their own research methods and instruments, can yield complementary insights of importance to issues of comparative international management. However, some fundamental criticism on Hofstede's work coming from the emic perspective pertains to the contents and cross-cultural applicability of some of Hofstede's dimensions, e.g. power distance (d'Iribarne, 1996–97) and long-term versus short-term orientation (Fang, 2003). We will discuss this criticism in some detail in Chapter 3.

Third, questions have been raised about the suitability of the items used to establish the dimensions of culture (Hunt, 1981). Indeed, many of the items Hofstede used to operationalize his dimensions lack face validity (we will return to this issue in our discussion of the work of d'Iribarne in Chapter 3). This is due to the fact that Hofstede's work is an example of 'survey archeology': the IBM studies were never designed to measure national cultures, the interest of the company was more in the area of employee morale. The identification of dimensions of culture was the result of the coincidence of the inclusion of a number of questions concerning personal goals and beliefs, which happened to tap cultural differences, and Hofstede's serendipity and persistence in analysing the data. The problem is that many of the items used by Hofstede at first sight have little connection to the construct measured. For instance, why would a preference for a job that provides training opportunities to improve one's skills or learn new skills be negatively related to individualism? Hofstede's reply could be that the robustness of the findings from the IBM studies depends not so much on the face validity of the items in the instrument used, as in the fact that the dimensions found could be statistically linked to other data sources in an interpretable way (for an extensive overview, see Appendix 6 in Hofstede, 2001). This effectively belies the statement sometimes made that Hofstede's dimensions are statistical artefacts (see, e.g., McSweeney, 2002). All the same, the low face validity of Hofstede's items may be one of the reasons for the slow and hesitant acceptance of Hofstede's work in some parts of the scientific community (see Chapman, 1996–97).

An even more general issue is the question of whether national culture may indeed be expected to exist – that is, whether the country is an appropriate level of analysis for cultures. This is of course a fundamental question, which is relevant to this chapter as a whole, but as the criticism of using the country as the unit of analysis has been most forcefully voiced in the criticism of Hofstede's work we will discuss it here. The nation-state is a relatively recent development; during most of the history of mankind no 'countries' or 'nations' existed. However, once in existence the nation-state can exert a strong influence on the culture of its inhabitants, in particular through the institutionalization of the educational system. As education is one of the two main mechanisms for the transfer and change of culture (the other being the child-rearing practices of parents), it is plausible that as a country has been in existence for long enough, it will have had sufficient influence on the population to enable us to speak of a 'national culture'. The extent to which this is true will of course depend on many factors, like the initial linguistic, ethnic or cultural homogeneity of the population, the pervasiveness and adequacy of national institutions, and so on. But, as Hofstede himself concedes (1991: 12), the nation-state is not always the appropriate level of analysis, as nations may harbour culturally diverse populations, or as members of one particular culture may be spread out over many countries (as, say, in Africa). Moreover, nations sometimes lack stability (McSweeney, 2002). Some fragment into smaller countries, as in the case of the former Yugoslavia. Or nations may merge into new units, as in the case of Hong Kong and mainland China.

One final question, gaining in significance in the years that have passed since the data were collected, is to do with the applicability of Hofstede's findings to the present situation. There are good reasons to assume that cultures change only very slowly, and some research suggests that the relevance of the cultural differences between countries originally found by Hofstede remains undiminished (Steenkamp and Geyskens, 2012). In addition, a 1984 study in 19 European countries replicated Hofstede's dimensions reasonably well (Hoppe, 1990); but the likelihood that all countries in Hofstede's sample will continue to change in the same direction and at the same pace, and that this will be the case in all four (or five) dimensions, seems to be very small. Therefore it seems to be increasingly necessary to obtain new and reliable estimates of the relative positions of countries on Hofstede's dimensions, if the paradigm is to continue to help researchers to make sense of culture (Triandis, 1994).

Shalom Schwartz: seven cultural orientations

Background

Schwartz (1992, 1994, 2008) provides a more recent research of note and a substantive challenge to Hofstede's model in that this work is more theory-driven than Hofstede's work, and it covers a broader diversity of cultures. In recognition of the seminal status of Hofstede's work, Schwartz included in his analysis values suitable for uncovering Hofstede's dimensions, and this serves as a 'check on the replicability of the Hofstede dimensions with a different method of measurement' (Schwartz, 1994). Schwartz's study was originally carried out in 20 countries, but has been expanded continuously and at present covers 75 countries (Schwartz, 2008). Schwartz composed a survey instrument of 56 (57 in some versions) values from the literature. He used two types of matched samples to enable a check on the robustness of the value dimensions generated. The respondents included schoolteachers and university students (as well as some representative country samples), and data was collected from 1988 onwards. The country scores we present in this section are based on both samples (and where one of the samples is missing, on regression estimates of that sample). Schwartz pooled the data from his studies over the years on the basis of the argument that although cultural convergence seems to occur if we look at superficial elements like dress, food and music, basic cultural orientations change only very slowly (Schwartz, 2008: 20). Particulars on how country scores on the seven dimensions were calculated can be found in Schwartz (2008).

Hofstede motivated his value dimensions on the basis of the fundamental societal problems they are associated with. Schwarz does the same, but in his case there is much stronger a priori theorizing (see Schwartz, 2008, for an excellent overview of the development of Schwartz's work). Schwartz also recognizes three basic societal problems, but they are slightly different from Hofstede's:

1 the nature of relations and boundaries between the person and the group;
2 how to make sure people behave in a responsible manner that preserves the social fabric of the group;
3 how to regulate how people treat human and natural resources (Schwartz, 2008: 7).

In Schwartz's view culture is not so much located in the minds of individual people, but in the social environment that confronts them with expectations when individuals enact roles in societal institutions. However, respondents are asked to rate the importance of values as a guiding principle in life, suggesting that Schwartz's instrument measures the extent to which they have internalized the reported values. Schwartz specifies three bipolar dimensions of national culture, which, to some extent, overlap with some of Hofstede's dimensions (Schwartz and Ros, 1995; Smith and Schwartz, 1997; Sagiv and Schwartz, 2000).

Seven cultural orientations

Rather than orthogonal dimensions, Schwartz allows his dimensions to correlate, because he assumes that cultural elements are interdependent. Hence, his theory of culture 'specifies a coherent, integrated system of relations' among seven cultural value orientations that form three correlated bipolar dimensions (Schwartz, 2008: 7). The theoretical structure of Schwartz's value orientations is pictured in Figure 2.2.

In Figure 2.2, values that are on opposite sides of the circle tend to be each other's opposite. A culture that scores high on hierarchy, for instance, is expected to score low on egalitarianism and, to a lesser degree, also on intellectual autonomy and harmony. But a strong emphasis on hierarchy is perfectly compatible with high scores on mastery or embeddedness. This theoretical structure has received considerable empirical support from studies including more than 55,000 respondents in 75 countries over 20 years (Schwartz, 2008: 14). Schwartz's dimensions are described below (source: Schwartz, 2006, 2008).

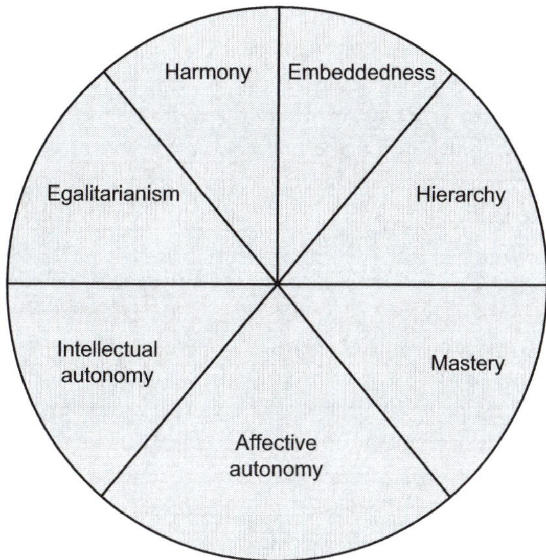

Figure 2.2 Theoretical structure of Schwartz's cultural value orientations.

Source: Adapted from Schwartz (2008).

EMBEDDEDNESS VERSUS AUTONOMY

In embedded cultures, people are viewed as entities embedded in the collectivity, who find meaning in life largely through social relationships. Values such as social order, respect for tradition, security and wisdom are especially important. Embedded cultures emphasize maintaining the status quo and restraining actions or inclinations that might disrupt the solidarity of the group or the traditional order. In autonomy cultures, people are viewed as autonomous, bounded entities who find meaning in their own uniqueness and who are encouraged to express their preferences, feelings and motives. Schwartz distinguishes two types of autonomy: intellectual autonomy and affective autonomy. Intellectual autonomy encourages individuals to pursue their own ideas and intellectual directions independently (important values are curiosity, broadmindedness and creativity); affective autonomy encourages individuals to pursue actively positive experiences for themselves (values include pleasure, and an exciting and varied life). This dimension from Schwartz's model is argued to overlap conceptually to some degree with Hofstede's individualism/collectivism dimension. Both concern the relationship between the individual and the collective, and both contrast an autonomous view of people with an interdependent view. However, while Schwartz's dimension of autonomy/embeddedness strongly contrasts openness to change with maintaining the status quo, individualism/collectivism does not explicitly do so. Rather, Hofstede sees openness to change (modernism) and maintaining the status quo (traditionalism) as consequences of individualism and collectivism, respectively.

HIERARCHY VERSUS EGALITARIANISM

In hierarchical cultures, the unequal distribution of power, roles and resources is seen as legitimate (values include social power, authority, humility and wealth). People are socialized and sanctioned to comply with the obligations and rules attached to their roles. Cultural egalitarianism seeks to induce people to recognize one another as moral equals who share basic interests as human beings. It emphasizes transcendence of selfish interests in favour of voluntary behaviour that promotes the welfare of others (values include equality, social justice, responsibility and honesty). People are socialized to internalize a commitment to voluntary cooperation with others and to feel concern for everyone's welfare. The hierarchy–egalitarianism dimension is said to overlap with Hofstede's power distance. Both are to do with legitimizing social inequality. Power distance refers to the acceptance of inequality by less powerful people. It also expresses their fear of authority. Hofstede sees it as a response to the inevitability of social inequality. Schwartz's hierarchy–egalitarian dimension addresses a different issue: assurance of responsible behaviour that preserves the social fabric. Their capacity to assure responsible behaviour gives hierarchical systems of ascribed roles their legitimacy. Hierarchy does not necessarily entail a preference for distance from authority. Egalitarianism emphasizes the moral equality of individuals, their capacity to internalize commitments to the welfare of others and to cooperate voluntarily with them. These key elements of egalitarianism are absent from the connotations of low power distance (Sagiv and Schwartz, 2000: 421).

MASTERY VERSUS HARMONY

Mastery-orientated cultures encourage active self-assertion in order to master, change and exploit the natural and social environment to attain personal or group goals (values include ambition, success, daring and competence). Harmony-orientated cultures accept the world as it is, trying to comprehend and fit in rather than to change or exploit (values include unity with nature, protecting the environment and world peace). In this view, applying technology to manipulate the environment is problematic and may even be seen as illegitimate. The mastery dimension corresponds to some extent to Hofstede's masculinity dimension. Both emphasize assertiveness and ambition, and both have similar consequences for organizations. However, Hofstede contrasts masculinity with femininity – tenderness, care and concern for others. This implies that masculinity neglects or rejects the interests of others. Schwartz contrasts mastery to harmony – being in tune with others and the environment. Mastery calls for an active, even disruptive, stance, but it does not imply selfishness. Harmony might seem to overlap conceptually with uncertainty avoidance, because both idealize a harmonious order. However, harmony stresses that people and nature can exist together comfortably without the assertion of control. In contrast, uncertainty avoidance emphasizes controlling ambiguity and unpredictability through institutions and beliefs that provide certainty (Sagiv and Schwartz, 2000: 421).

Schwartz's work has some advantages over that of Hofstede, the most important of which are the higher face validity of the items used to operationalize the dimensions, and the measurement characteristics of the scales. On the other hand, culture as measured by Schwartz is broader than the work-related values Hofstede focuses on. This may limit the applicability of Schwartz's framework in the field of comparative international management. Although it has strong theoretical foundations, the usefulness of Schwartz's framework for management and organization has not yet been established to the same extent as that of Hofstede (Steenkamp, 2001).

An overview of country scores on Schwartz's seven dimensions can be found in Table 2.2.

Table 2.2 Country scores on Schwartz's value dimensions

	Harmony	*Embeddedness*	*Hierarchy*	*Mastery*	*Affective autonomy*	*Intellectual autonomy*	*Egalitarianism*
Argentina	3,98	3,52	2,10	3,92	3,73	4,34	4,96
Australia	3,99	3,59	2,29	3,97	3,86	4,35	4,79
Austria	4,31	3,11	1,75	3,92	4,29	4,90	4,89
Belgium	4,35	3,25	1,69	3,84	3,94	4,64	5,20
Bolivia	4,11	4,07	2,66	3,87	2,71	4,34	4,74
Bosnia-Herzegovina	3,88	4,01	1,73	3,79	3,30	4,18	4,66
Brazil	4,03	3,62	2,37	3,93	3,52	4,27	4,89
Bulgaria	4,13	3,87	2,68	4,02	3,47	4,29	4,13
Cameroon	4,19	4,46	2,46	3,60	2,13	3,58	4,68
Canada (Eng.)	3,83	3,46	2,09	4,12	4,00	4,50	4,80
Canada (Fr.)	4,14	3,15	1,87	3,95	4,31	4,81	4,98
Chile	4,33	3,64	2,25	3,78	3,03	4,32	5,06
China	3,78	3,74	3,49	4,41	3,30	4,18	4,23
Colombia	3,66	3,86	2,90	4,03	3,61	4,30	4,69
Costa Rica	4,13	3,49	2,29	4,01	3,49	4,37	4,85
Croatia	4,02	4,00	2,55	4,05	3,92	4,35	4,60
Cyprus	4,01	4,04	1,96	3,95	3,21	3,83	4,85
Czech Republic	4,27	3,59	2,22	3,75	3,49	4,62	4,45
Denmark	4,16	3,19	1,86	3,91	4,30	4,77	5,03
Egypt	3,98	4,45	2,20	3,66	2,50	3,90	4,42
Estonia	4,31	3,81	2,04	3,79	3,36	4,23	4,58
Ethiopia	4,19	4,54	2,33	3,79	2,61	3,94	4,40
Fiji	3,83	4,33	2,58	3,77	3,20	3,85	4,67
Finland	4,34	3,37	1,80	3,66	3,96	4,93	4,90
France	4,21	3,20	2,21	3,72	4,39	5,13	5,05
Georgia	4,09	4,12	2,46	3,73	3,47	4,00	4,66
Germany (East)	4,46	3,16	1,77	4,00	4,28	4,68	4,95
Germany (West)	4,62	3,03	1,87	3,86	4,11	4,99	5,07
Ghana	3,53	4,27	2,68	4,12	2,49	3,89	4,73
Greece	4,40	3,41	1,83	4,25	3,92	4,39	4,84
Hong Kong	3,50	3,76	2,91	4,08	3,20	4,28	4,50
Hungary	4,34	3,60	1,94	3,73	3,63	4,57	4,51
India	3,92	3,97	3,05	4,28	3,48	4,02	4,45
Indonesia	3,82	4,27	2,56	3,84	3,41	3,94	4,32
Iran	3,69	4,18	3,23	3,91	2,97	3,96	4,53
Ireland	3,77	3,41	2,09	4,04	4,05	4,54	4,90
Israel (Jews)	3,28	3,61	2,51	4,02	3,79	4,54	4,77
Israel (Arabs)	3,57	4,09	2,60	4,10	3,37	4,28	4,60
Italy	4,62	3,46	1,60	3,81	3,30	4,91	5,27
Japan	4,21	3,49	2,65	4,06	3,76	4,78	4,36
Jordan	3,67	4,20	2,50	4,20	3,36	4,05	4,40
Latvia	4,46	3,83	1,80	3,75	3,48	4,22	4,32

(*Continued*)

Table 2.2 (Continued)

	Harmony	*Embeddedness*	*Hierarchy*	*Mastery*	*Affective autonomy*	*Intellectual autonomy*	*Egalitarianism*
Macedonia	4,03	3,91	2,72	4,00	3,01	4,24	4,40
Malaysia	3,65	4,35	2,25	3,91	2,98	4,15	4,41
Mexico	4,50	3,90	2,13	3,90	2,83	4,36	4,73
Namibia	3,74	4,04	2,53	4,06	3,29	4,03	4,48
Nepal	4,34	4,18	3,03	4,13	2,99	4,07	4,63
Netherlands	4,05	3,19	1,91	3,97	4,13	4,85	5,03
New Zealand	4,03	3,27	2,27	4,09	4,21	4,65	4,94
Nigeria	3,75	4,41	2,72	3,90	2,54	3,66	4,79
Norway	4,40	3,45	1,49	3,85	3,69	4,68	5,12
Oman	3,71	4,50	2,15	3,83	2,87	3,73	4,49
Pakistan	3,99	4,31	2,44	4,00	3,11	3,76	4,65
Peru	3,71	3,92	2,76	4,08	2,98	4,30	4,84
Philippines	4,04	4,03	2,68	3,76	3,00	3,95	4,59
Poland	3,86	3,86	2,51	3,84	3,32	4,31	4,48
Portugal	4,27	3,43	1,89	4,11	3,62	4,53	5,21
Romania	4,11	3,78	2,00	4,06	3,45	4,61	4,48
Russia	3,90	3,81	2,72	3,96	3,51	4,30	4,38
Senegal	3,58	4,45	2,63	3,74	2,39	3,89	4,92
Serbia	3,96	3,57	1,61	4,03	3,70	4,72	4,44
Singapore	3,76	4,00	2,82	3,88	3,30	3,86	4,60
Slovakia	4,47	3,82	2,00	3,83	2,99	4,29	4,58
Slovenia	4,45	3,71	1,62	3,71	3,72	4,88	4,56
South Africa	3,86	4,03	2,59	3,89	3,48	3,85	4,52
South Korea	3,57	3,68	2,90	4,21	3,46	4,22	4,42
Spain	4,47	3,31	1,84	3,80	3,67	4,99	5,23
Sweden	4,46	3,12	1,83	3,81	4,24	5,09	4,90
Switzerland (French)	4,40	3,04	2,06	3,74	4,33	5,32	5,06
Switzerland (Germ.)	3,94	3,34	2,42	3,97	4,24	4,66	4,92
Taiwan	4,12	3,82	2,69	4,00	3,27	4,36	4,31
Thailand	3,84	4,02	3,23	3,88	3,63	4,02	4,29
Turkey	4,23	3,77	2,97	3,98	3,37	4,45	4,77
Uganda	3,97	4,23	2,99	4,02	2,68	3,80	4,39
Ukraine	3,87	3,93	2,56	3,99	3,49	4,08	4,31
United Kingdom	3,91	3,34	2,33	4,01	4,26	4,62	4,92
United States	3,46	3,67	2,37	4,09	3,87	4,19	4,68
Venezuela	3,99	3,74	2,09	4,01	3,26	4,44	4,77
Yemen	3,70	4,63	2,28	3,79	2,44	3,68	4,73
Zimbabwe	3,62	4,04	2,67	4,19	3,60	3,80	4,30

Source: Email from professor Shalom Schwarz, March 16, 2014.

World Values Survey: national cultures over time

Background

Although Hofstede and, even more so, Schwartz, collected data over protracted time periods, their studies are cross-sectional, meaning that they compare cultures more or less at one point in time. A particularly interesting aspect of the third and last example of an etic study that we discuss, the World Values Survey, is that it allows us to track how national cultures change over time. The World Values Survey (WVS) has been administered four times, in 1990, 1995, 2000 and 2005, and currently the fifth wave is being conducted (2010–14). Moreover, the WVS builds on the work of the European Values Study, initiated in the 1970s at Tilburg University, the Netherlands, and for a limited set of countries there are also data from 1981. Apart from being a repeated study, the WVS also stands out because it is based on representative samples in all the countries included. A lengthy questionnaire is administered by means of face-to-face interviews. By now the WVS has become an enormous project: the 2010–14 data collection effort will comprise 80,000 respondents from 75 countries.[2]

The WVS is like Hofstede's project in that the instrument used is not based on an a priori theory of cultural values. Instead, the original European Values Study that set off the WVS project was inspired by questions regarding the role of religion, in particular the Christian faith, in a unifying Europe. Specifically, the following questions were at the heart of the first European Values Study:[3]

- *Do Europeans share common values?*
- *Are values changing in Europe and, if so, in what directions?*
- *Do Christian values continue to permeate European life and culture?*
- *Is a coherent alternative meaning system replacing that of Christianity?*
- *What are the implications for European unity?*

Consequently, the items in the European Values Survey, and later the WVS, give ample attention to issues of religion, gender roles, family norms and sexual norms. Work-related values play a relatively less important role.

Two dimensions of culture

Although the WVS was not originally intended to identify dimensions of national culture, analysis of the data from the first three waves of the study has led to the identification of two fundamental dimensions of culture change in countries over time. These dimensions are traditional versus rational-secular authority and survival versus self-expression values. As these two dimensions are the result of a factor analysis on a number of selected items, they are orthogonal, i.e., statistically unrelated.

TRADITIONAL VERSUS RATIONAL-SECULAR AUTHORITY

In traditional authority societies God plays an important role in peoples' lives, children are taught to be obedient and maintain the religious faith, citizens have a strong sense of national pride and favour respect for authority, and abortion is regarded to be never justifiable. In rational-secular authority cultures the values are just the opposite. This dimension sets apart values adhered to in pre-industrial societies, where deference to the authority of God, country and family are strongly linked, from those prevalent in industrial societies. The items used to measure the dimension at first sight do not seem conceptually related to each other, but they have been selected deliberately to cover a wide range of topics (Inglehart and Baker, 2000: 23–25). Adherence to traditional values is strongly correlated with a complex of other values, like work centrality, political conservatism, and a whole range of social and religious taboos, among other things.

SURVIVAL VERSUS SELF-EXPRESSION VALUES

Survival values emphasize economic and physical security above other goals, and in cultures scoring high on this dimension people feel threatened by foreigners, by ethnic diversity and by culture change. At the other pole in cultures characterized by self-expression values people are more trusting and tolerant and express higher levels of subjective well being. Some correlates of survival values are importance attached to job security, distinctions made between men and women, and importance attached to teaching children to work hard (Inglehart and Baker, 2000: 25–27). The dimension opposes materialist to postmaterialist values. At the postmaterialist pole values like self-expression, well-being and quality of life are more important than economic and physical security.

Table 2.3 gives an overview of country scores on the two dimensions of the WVS, and Figure 2.3 shows the positioning of cultural clusters on the two dimensions.

Table 2.3 Country scores on the World Values Survey dimensions

	Traditional: secular/ rational authority	*Survival: self-expression*
Albania	0,52	–1,56
Arab world	–1,31	0,15
Argentina	–0,60	0,71
Australia	–0,18	1,96
Belgium	0,50	1,13
Brazil	1,29	0,02
Bulgaria	0,90	–1,23
Canada	–0,16	1,72
Chile	–0,81	–0,08
China	0,79	–1,23
Colombia	–1,71	0,34
Czech Rep	1,07	0,33
Denmark	1,16	1,87
Egypt	–1,64	–0,54
Estonia	1,27	–1,30
Finland	0,68	1,01
France	0,52	0,94
Germany (East)	1,74	0,58
Germany (West)	1,55	1,52
Ghana	–1,94	–0,29
Hong Kong	1,20	–0,98
Hungary	0,79	–0,77
India	–0,54	–0,69

	Traditional: secular/ rational authority	*Survival: self-expression*
Indonesia	−1,07	−0,50
Iran	−1,40	−0,34
Ireland	−0,91	1,18
Italy	0,19	0,85
Japan	1,79	0,37
Luxembourg	0,42	1,13
Malaysia	−0,73	0,09
Mexico	−0,81	0,30
Netherlands	0,84	1,94
New Zealand	0,20	1,78
Nigeria	−1,58	−0,68
Norway	1,31	1,33
Pakistan	−1,39	−0,52
Peru	−1,26	−0,18
Philippines	−1,38	−0,12
Poland	−0,47	−0,41
Portugal	−0,90	0,49
Romania	0,36	−1,26
Russia	0,87	−1,85
Singapore	−0,64	−0,28
Slovakia	0,41	−0,27
Slovenia	0,69	−0,04
South Korea	0,96	−0,64
Spain	−0,37	0,47
Sweden	1,49	1,99
Switzerland	0,82	1,35
Taiwan	0,66	−0,81
Tanzania	−1,84	−0,15
Thailand	−0,64	0,01
Trinidad	−1,83	−0,26
Turkey	−1,13	0,28
UK	0,08	1,24
USA	−0,89	1,62
Uruquay	−0,21	0,48
Venezuela	−1,82	0,35
Zimbabwe	−1,50	−1,36

Source: http://www.worldvaluessurvey.org/wvs.jsp, retrieved on March 15, 2014.

Figure 2.3 shows that the historically Protestant countries tend to have secular-rational and self-expression cultural values. English-speaking traditionally Protestant countries tend to have somewhat more traditional values. The historically communist countries are characterized by secular-rational values (in the communist period the role of religion was marginalized) with a strong emphasis on survival values, which can be understood as a response to the basic uncertainty after the breakdown of the communist systems. Historically Roman Catholic countries are mostly in between these two groups. Asian cultures are split into two clusters: a Confucian-influenced cluster (Japan, China, South Korea and

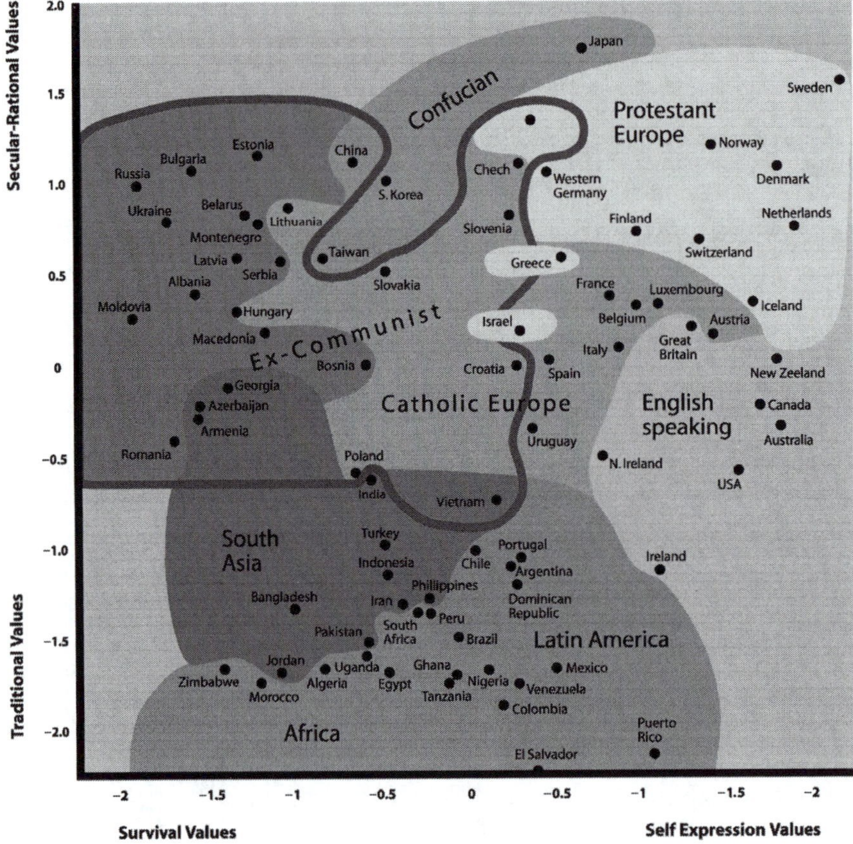

Figure 2.3 Culture clusters in the World Values Survey data.

Source: http://commons.wikimedia.org/wiki/User:Koyos, retrieved 28 March, 2014.

Taiwan) and a more mixed group, with countries as diverse as Muslim Iran, Pakistan and Indonesia, and countries like Vietnam, India and Armenia. Latin America is on the traditional side of the spectrum, but relatively high on self-expression values. African countries, finally, are positioned in the lower-left corner of the graph, and hence are characterized by traditional and survival-oriented values. This is understandable given the still strong role of agriculture in these economies and the low levels of income.

Culture change

As mentioned above, the unique strength of the WVS is that it allows us to track culture change over time. In the view of Inglehart and his co-workers (Inglehart, 1997; Inglehart and Baker, 2000; Inglehart and Welzel, 2005) national culture change is strongly linked to economic development. The shift from traditional to rational-secular authority values is associated with the change from an economy dominated by agriculture to an industrial economy, as well as the increase in income caused by that: 'the shift from an agrarian mode of production to industrial production seems to bring with it a shift from traditional values toward increasing rationalization and secularization' (Inglehart and Baker, 2000: 31). This is understandable as industrialization tends to be accompanied by urbanization and the weakening of formerly tight relationships of religious and worldly authority. This shift from traditional to rational-secular authority values Inglehart calls 'modernization' (Inglehart, 1997). The second trend that the successive waves of the WVS make visible Inglehart (1997) calls 'post-modernization'. This is a shift from an emphasis on survival values to an emphasis on self-expression values. This second shift is associated with the change from an industrial economy to an economy based on services, and typically a further increase in income per capita. The emphasis on other things than those connected with survival in postmodern societies is made possible by the level of wealth and the material security that this affords:

> Postmaterialists are not non-Materialists, still less are they anti-Materialists. The term 'Post-materialist' denotes a set of goals that are emphasized after people have attained material security, and because they have attained material security. Thus, the collapse of security would lead to a gradual shift back toward Materialist priorities.
>
> (Inglehart, 1997: 35)

Although the double trend of modernization and postmodernization typifies culture change in a great number of countries, cultural heritage also plays an important role. Inglehart and Baker (2000) note that for instance countries influenced by Confucianism tend to be more secular than would be expected on the basis of their economic development, while traditionally Roman Catholic cultures tend to be more traditional than expected. Figure 2.4 shows changes in culture over time for a number of countries in the WVS dataset.

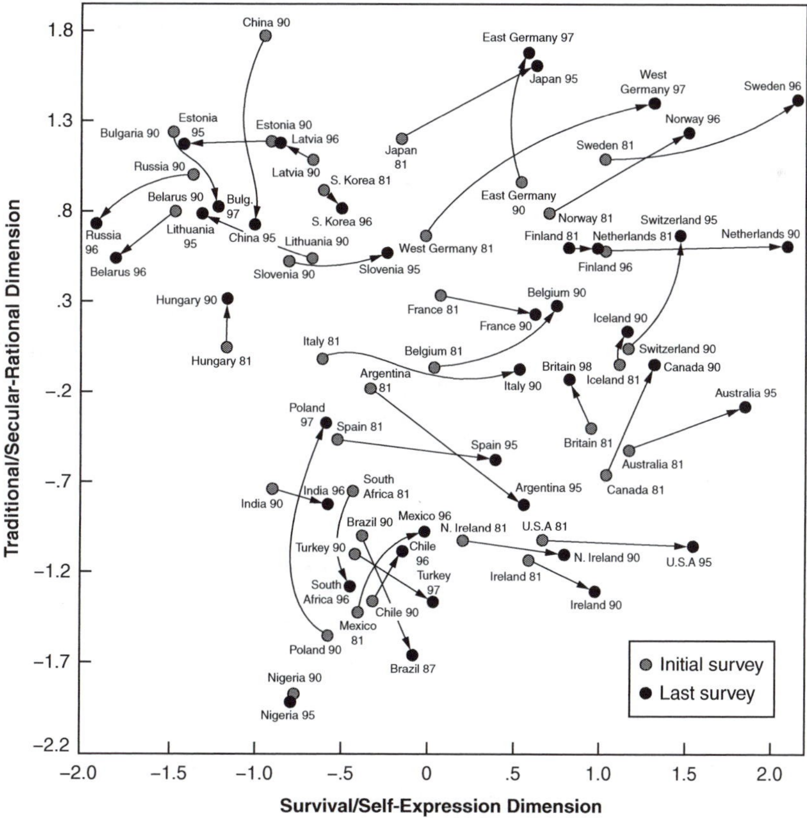

Figure 2.4 Culture change in countries on two dimensions.

Source: Inglehart and Baker (2000: 40).

It is important to note that the modernization and the postmodernization trends are not irreversible. A number of countries (e.g., Brazil, Bulgaria, China) show a shift to more traditional values over time. Other countries (e.g., Belarus, Russia, Estonia) show a shift towards survival values. These counter-trends are likely to have to do with collapses of the political system or severe economic crises (Inglehart and Baker, 2000: 40–42).

Extension

The almost 250 questions asked in the WVS survey of course contain much more information than summarized in the two dimensions discussed above. This means that the WVS data are still a potential goldmine for researchers. An example of this is a study by Minkov and Hofstede (2010), in which they use WVS data to validate Hofstede's long-term versus short-term orientation dimension. The authors were able to find WVS items that were reasonably equivalent to those used to identify the long-term versus short-term orientation dimension, except for 'respect for tradition' (interestingly, although traditional values are one pole of the two dimensions identified in the WVS, none of the items in the WVS survey explicitly asks this question). A dimension based on this set of WVS items correlates strongly with the long-term versus short-term orientation dimension ($r = -0.81$, i.e., the WVS items constitute a reverse measure of Hofstede's long-term versus short-term orientation). Furthermore, the WVS long-term versus short-term dimension correlates with some of the same phenomena as the original dimension. Hence, this study constitutes an independent validation of Hofstede's long-term versus short-term orientation dimension, which is of importance as the empirical basis of this dimension was much weaker than that of the other Hofstede dimensions. However, this statistical evidence does not counter the criticism by Fang (2003), alluded to above. This criticism was based on indigenous knowledge of Chinese culture and philosophy, and will be discussed in Chapter 3.

Minkov (2007) has in a comparable way extracted additional dimensions from the WVS data. While most of these seem to be strongly related to dimensions identified earlier, one of them, 'indulgence versus restraint', seems to constitute a new contribution. In this dimension, '[i]ndulgence stands for a society that allows relatively free gratification of basic and natural human desires related to enjoying life and having fun. Restraint stands for a society that controls gratification of needs and regulates it by means of strict social norms' (Hofstede, 2011: 15). This dimension is weakly correlated with long-term versus short-term orientation. The dimension is related to perceptions of personal control over one's life, the importance attached to freedom of speech, and the importance attached to leisure. These correlations suggest some overlap with the survival versus self-expression values dimension.

2.5 Integration

The multitude of findings from the three main etic studies may give the impression that there is a lack of convergence in the field. However, there may be more closure than meets the eye at first. In Table 2.4 the country scores from the three etic studies discussed above are brought together for a set of overlapping countries, and transformed to form scales from 0 to 100 to make comparison easier.

For 77 countries we have data from at least two of the three major etic studies. The overlap between the WVS and Hofstede's dataset is 57 countries (with the exception of long-term versus short-term orientation, where there are only 35 overlapping countries). Between Hofstede and Schwartz there is an overlap of 51 countries (again with the exception of long-term orientation, where the overlap is only 36 countries). And between the

Table 2.4 Overview of country scores from etic studies

	Tradional-Rational	*Survival-Self-expression*	*Power Distance*	*Uncertainty Avoidance*	*Individualism/ Collectivism*	*Masculinity/ Femininity*	*Long-Term Orientation*	*Harmony*	*Embeddedness*	*Hierarchy*	*Mastery*	*Affective Autonomy*	*Intellectual Autonomy*	*Egalitarianism*
Argentina	28	53	49	86	46	56		52	31	31	40	71	44	73
Australia	47	91	36	51	90	61	31	53	35	40	46	77	44	58
Austria	58	78	11	70	55	79	31	77	5	13	40	96	76	67
Bangladesh	21	23	80	60	20	55	40							
Belgium	64	71	65	94	75	54	38	80	14	10	30	80	61	94
Bosnia	60	30						45	61	12	23	52	34	46
Brazil	19	45	69	76	38	49	65	56	37	44	41	62	40	67
Britain	59	76	35	35	89	66	25	47	19	42	51	94	60	69
Bulgaria	80	9	70	85	30	40		63	53	60	52	59	41	0
Canada			39	48	80	52	23	53	18	25	54	90	62	67
Chile	30	48	63	86	23	28		78	38	38	22	40	43	82
China	81	23	80	30	20	66	118	37	44	100	100	52	34	9
Colombia	10	61	67	80	13	64		28	52	71	53	65	41	49
Costa Rica			35	86	15	21		63	29	40	51	60	45	63
Croatia	53	52						55	61	53	56	79	44	41
Cyprus	37	48						54	63	24	43	48	14	63
Czech Republic	82	54	57	74	58	57	13	74	35	37	19	60	60	28
Denmark	80	89	18	23	74	16	46	66	10	19	38	96	68	79
Dominican Rep	25	53												
Egypt	11	32						52	89	36	7	16	18	25
Estonia	83	17	40	60	60	30		77	49	28	23	54	37	39
Ethiopia	35	36						68	94	42	23	21	21	24
Finland	72	67	33	59	63	26	41	79	21	16	7	81	78	68
France	64	67	68	86	71	43	39	69	11	36	15	100	89	81

(*Continued*)

Table 2.4 (Continued)

	Tradional-Rational	*Survival-Self-expression*	*Power Distance*	*Uncertainty Avoidance*	*Individualism/ Collectivism*	*Masculinity/ Femininity*	*Long-Term Orientation*	*Harmony*	*Embeddedness*	*Hierarchy*	*Mastery*	*Affective Autonomy*	*Intellectual Autonomy*	*Egalitarianism*
Georgia	50	14						60	68	49	16	59	24	46
Germany (East)	87	55						88	8	14	49	95	63	72
Germany (West)	80	55	35	65	67	66	31	100	0	19	32	88	81	82
Ghana	3	38						19	78	60	64	16	18	53
Greece	70	58	60	112	35	57		84	24	17	80	79	47	62
Guatemala	9	41	95	101	6	37								
Hong Kong	81	22	68	29	25	57	96	16	46	71	59	47	40	32
Hungary	61	16	46	82	80	88	50	79	36	23	16	66	57	33
India	38	31	77	40	48	56	61	48	59	78	84	60	25	28
Indonesia	25	33	78	48	14	46		40	78	54	30	57	21	17
Iran	21	34	58	59	41	43		31	72	87	38	37	22	35
Ireland	29	73	28	35	70	68	43	37	24	30	54	85	55	68
Israel	58	53						11	51	54	57	64	48	49
Italy	56	65	50	75	76	70	34	100	27	6	26	52	76	100
Japan	99	58	54	92	46	95	80	69	29	58	57	72	69	20
Jordan	11	20						29	73	51	74	54	27	24
Latvia	69	15						88	50	16	19	60	37	17
Luxembourg	62	71	40	70	60	50								
Macedonia	54	28						56	55	62	49	39	38	24
Malaysia	33	47	104	36	26	50		28	83	38	38	38	33	25
Malta	13	44	56	96	59	47								
Mexico	15	57	81	82	30	69		91	54	32	37	31	45	53
Morocco	11	19	70	68	46	53								
Netherlands	72	90	38	53	80	14	44	57	10	21	46	88	73	79

New Zealand	56	87	22	49	79	58	30	56	15	39	61	92	61	71
Nigeria	13	51						35	86	62	37	18	5	58
Norway	84	76	31	50	69	8	44	84	26	0	31	69	63	87
Pakistan	16	15	55	70	14	50	0	53	80	48	49	43	10	46
Peru	18	46	64	87	16	42		32	56	64	59	38	41	62
Philippines	21	42	94	44	32	64	19	57	63	60	20	38	21	40
Poland	41	31	68	93	60	64	32	43	52	51	30	53	42	31
Portugal	29	56	63	104	27	31	30	74	25	20	63	66	55	95
Romania	44	7	90	90	30	42		62	47	26	57	58	59	31
Russia	78	1	93	95	39	36		46	49	62	44	61	41	22
Singapore	35	38	74	8	20	48	48	36	61	67	35	52	16	41
Slovakia	68	35	104	51	52	110	38	89	49	26	28	38	41	39
Slovenia	75	54						87	43	7	14	70	75	38
South Africa	24	42	49	49	65	63		43	63	55	36	60	16	34
South Korea	79	32	60	85	18	39	75	22	41	71	75	59	37	25
Spain	54	57	57	86	51	42	19	89	18	18	25	68	81	96
Sweden	93	94	31	29	71	5	33	88	6	17	26	93	87	68
Switzerland	72	77	34	58	68	70	40	66	10	38	32	96	81	75
Taiwan	68	26	58	69	17	45	87	63	49	60	49	50	45	16
Thailand	35	45	64	64	20	34	56	42	62	87	35	66	25	14
Trinidad	6	39	47	55	16	58								
Turkey	30	37	66	85	37	45		71	46	74	47	55	50	56
Uganda	16	33						52	75	75	52	24	13	23
Ukraine	74	4						44	56	54	48	60	29	16
Uruguay	46	56	61	100	36	38								
USA	38	82	40	46	91	62	29	13	40	44	61	77	35	48
Venezuela	12	55	81	76	12	73		53	44	30	51	50	49	56
Vietnam	34	50	70	30	20	40	80							
Zimbabwe	14	13						25	63	59	73	65	13	15

WVS and Schwartz 66 countries overlap. If we look at the correlations between the scores of countries on the dimensions identified by the three major etic studies, it becomes clear that there is considerable overlap between a complex of dimensions consisting of traditional versus secular-rational authority, survival versus self-expression values, power distance, individualism-collectivism, embeddedness, hierarchy, affective and intellectual autonomy, and egalitarianism. These value orientations have to do with the relationship between the individual and the collective and with power/authority relations. It is not surprising that the positions that national cultures assume to these fundamental issues are interrelated. Hofstede also observed a strong ($r = -0.67$) negative correlation between power distance and individualism-collectivism (Hofstede, 1980: 221). Both dimensions are related to wealth (Hofstede, 2001: 519). If countries become richer, people can afford to be more individualistic, as they have less need of communities as safety nets. With this increased independence also comes a lower tolerance for power differences. It is striking that Hofstede's uncertainty avoidance and masculinity-femininity are hardly related to any of the other dimensions. They seem to tap into aspects of national cultures that are not well covered by the two other studies.

To visualize the similarities between the three studies, Figure 2.5 plots the 14 dimensions on a two-dimensional plane.[4] The figure shows that the dimensions individualism,

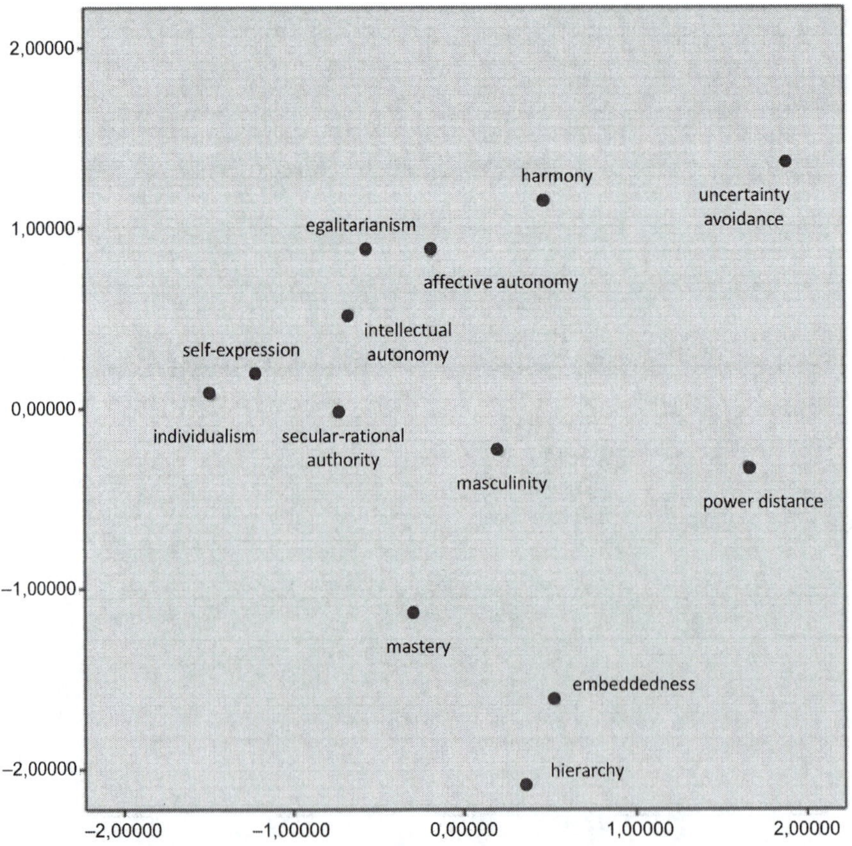

Figure 2.5 Fourteen dimensions of national cultures.

Source: Hofstede (2001); Schwartz (private correspondence); World Values Survey website (http://www.worldvaluessurvey.org/wvs.jsp)

self-expression, secular-rational authority, intellectual and affective autonomy and egalitarianism all cluster in the upper left hand corner. Interestingly, Hofstede's power distance and Schwartz's hierarchy are in different places on the plane, suggesting that they tap into different aspects of national cultures.

A second way of looking at the coherence between the three etic studies is by comparing how countries in the three studies cluster together. The practical implications of cultural clusters can be illustrated through the following example:

> An MNC is establishing a venture in Switzerland. The corporation's directors must determine if management skills will be imported from its subsidiaries in France, Germany or Italy. All three languages are spoken in Switzerland, albeit in different areas. The country clustering suggests that managers be brought from Germany because Switzerland and Germany belong to the same cluster of work values. German managers, therefore, can be expected to be closer to and more familiar with workers' attitudes in Switzerland.
>
> (Ronen and Shenkar, 1985: 447)

Hofstede (2001) reported a hierarchical cluster analysis of 53 countries based on their scores on his four indexes (excluding long-term versus short-term orientation). This analysis yielded 12 cultural clusters. Examples of these statistically derived clusters are the Anglo-Saxon countries (Australia, USA, Canada, Great Britain and New Zealand), the Scandinavian countries plus Finland and the Netherlands, and Japan (forming a cluster all by itself!) (Hofstede, 2001: 62–63). Schwartz (1994) and Schwartz and Ros (1995) conducted multidimensional scaling analyses using nation scores on the seven cultural orientations distinguished by Schwartz. They replicated these analyses with data both from teachers (44 nations) and students (40 nations). The same six culture areas were clearly distinguishable in both analyses: West European, Anglo, East European, Islamic, East Asian and Latin American. Again, Japan was distinctive. The similarity between the Hofstede and Schwartz culture areas is remarkable. Some of the differences doubtless reflect the different sampling of nations – for example, there are hardly any East European nations in Hofstede. The WVS yields slightly different clusters, with separate Protestant and Roman Catholic European groupings, and an ex-communist cluster. This is understandable given the rather different contents of the WVS questionnaire and the different selection of countries sampled. All in all the clustering of countries confirms the idea that national cultures can be seen as Gestalts, i.e., reasonably coherent wholes of mostly corresponding value orientations.

The convergence of many of the values measured in the three studies into two complexes, one power/authority-related and the other individualism-related, could be taken as an indication that the major dimensions of culture-level variation in values have been identified. Moreover, because these studies used data obtained in different ways and from different types of samples, it is apparent that they are relatively robust. There is also evidence that they are relatively stable over time. They emerged both from Hofstede's data, collected nearly 30 years ago, and from much more recent data collected by the WVS group. Moreover, the Schwartz (1994) analysis yielded similar structures of values among samples of rich and of poor nations. This would not be expected if the massive changes that accompany socio-economic development also cause change in the structure of values.

A warning is apposite, however. The dimensions that emerge from these studies are affected by the locations that are sampled. No study has sampled many more than 50 to

70 of the nearly 200 current national entities. Europe, North America and the Pacific Rim are well represented, but African and Arab countries are badly under-represented in all studies. Moreover, the dimensions that emerge are affected by the values included in the survey questionnaires. It is clearly too early to foreclose on the possibility that further theorizing and consideration of values found in indigenous studies will yet point to additional major dimensions (Smith and Schwartz, 1997).

2.6 National culture and organizational culture

As this book focuses on differences between countries that are relevant for international business, the subject of organizational culture is of secondary importance here. Organizational culture distinguishes one organization from another, and the culture of an organization is likely to be influenced by the country context to a certain extent, as we will discuss later in this section. However, inasmuch as this is nothing more than the way in which characteristics of the national culture manifest themselves in individual and group behaviour there is no reason to insert the intermediary level of organizational culture. We will discuss the impact of national culture characteristics on perceptions and behaviours relevant to management and organization in the next section. Here we are concerned with a possible relation between national culture and organizational culture. This issue is important because it has been the subject of a recent debate among cross-cultural researchers.

The context of this debate was a fourth large-scale etic research project, not discussed above: the GLOBE project.[5] The GLOBE project attempted to measure both national and organizational culture with nearly identical sets of questions (see House, Hanges, Javidan, Dorfman and Gupta, 2004). These questions aimed to tap into values at the level of the country, and practices at the level of the organization. However, this attempt failed to identify interpretable organizational cultures that are clearly distinct from those at the societal level, and in the end the researchers merged their findings for practices and values. This failed effort to measure culture at these two levels is instructive, as it shows some of the pitfalls in cross-cultural research.

To assume that characteristics of national cultures influence what is going on in organizations is not the same as to presuppose that organizational culture is actually identical to national culture. But this is in essence what the GLOBE researchers did. They used two virtually identical sets of questions, for some respondents to answer about their country, and for some about their organization. However, there are good reasons to assume that culture dimensions at the level of organizations are different from those at the societal level (Peterson and Castro, 2006). According to Hofstede (2001: 393–394), organizational culture is different from national culture because immersion in a national culture is more intensive and socialization starts at an earlier age (in most cases right from birth, through the childraising practices of the parents). In the case of organizations, members enter at a much more advanced age, when they are less easily influenced. As a result organizational culture has to do less with deeply rooted values than with practices and routines, or, as Hofstede puts it: 'shared perceptions of daily practices' (Hofstede, 2001: 394).

Hofstede, Neuijen, Ohayv and Sanders (1990) came to this conclusion on the basis of a Danish–Dutch study of 20 organizational units. This study surveyed values as well as organizational practices and found the latter to differ significantly between organizational units, while values were more influenced by nationality. Organizational practices reflect the reality within an organization, 'what is' rather than 'what should be' as reflected in values. Hofstede et al. (1990) distinguished between three categories of organizational

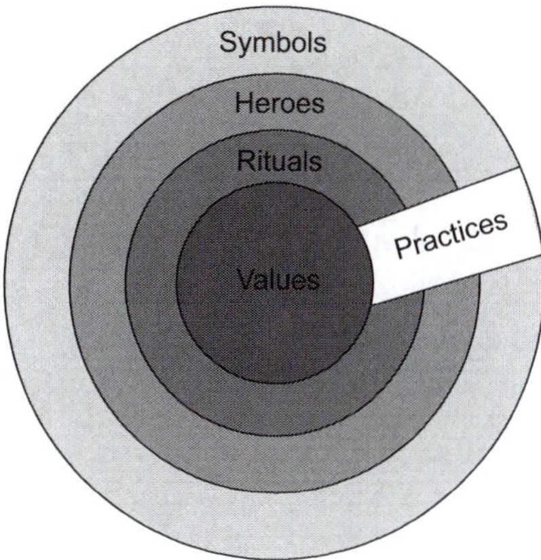

Figure 2.6 Hofstede's onion diagram.

Source: Adapted from Hofstede (1991).

practice: symbols, heroes and rituals, which Hofstede (1991: 64) collectively labels 'practices' in an 'onion diagram' (Figure 2.6). These practices are visible to outsiders and their meaning is interpretable by both insiders and outsiders. The cultural meaning of these phenomena lies in the way they are perceived by organizational members.

Symbols have been put into the outer layer of Figure 2.6 since they represent the most superficial layer. Symbols are words, gestures, pictures or objects that carry a particular meaning, which is only recognized by those who share the culture. The words in a language or jargon belong to this category, as do dress, hairstyles, some brands, like Coca-Cola, and status symbols. Symbols are not unique as they can be copied by others; they are easily developed and old ones may disappear (Hofstede, 1991). *Heroes* are persons, alive or dead, real or imaginary, who possess characteristics that are highly prized in a culture, and who thus serve as models for behaviour. Even fictional or cartoon figures, like Batman in the USA and Asterix in France, can serve as cultural heroes. *Rituals* are collective activities, technically superfluous in reaching desired ends, but which, within a culture, are considered socially essential; they are therefore carried out for their own sake. Ways of greeting and paying respect to others are examples.

Organizational culture and national culture are related. Organizational cultures are mostly nested within national cultures, and even if (as in the case of a multinational company) the organization cuts across national boundaries, what is going on in the various branches and subsidiaries will be influenced not only by the common culture and procedures of the multinational, but also by the local (cultural) environments. Hofstede's study, which had IBM employees in more than 40 countries as respondents, illustrates this. Although these respondents assumedly shared IBM's organizational culture, they also expressed characteristics of their national cultures. As a matter of fact, a multinational context may actually increase the extent to which employees identify with their own national culture (Adler, 1991: 58–59). But any national culture still leaves room for a diversity of organizational cultures (Schneider, Ehrhart and Macey, 2012).

Hofstede (2001: 376–378) speculates on how his dimensions of national culture are likely to be related to organizational cultures. He looks specifically at combinations of power distance and uncertainty avoidance. As we will see in the next section, power distance is related to the role of authority and power in organizations. Uncertainty avoidance is related to the importance of formal rules and procedures. In national cultures characterized by low levels of both power distance and uncertainty avoidance, Hofstede expects relatively informal organizations without strong central authority. In the opposite case the expectation is that organizations will be centralized and bureaucratic.

In the next section we will go deeper into the implications of national culture characteristics for management and organization.

2.7 Implications for management and organization

In this book we are not interested in differences between national cultures for their own sake, but because these differences are linked with divergent ways of organizing and managing firms. In this section we will briefly discuss the links between national culture and management and organization, using the dimensions distinguished by Hofstede as our organizing principle. There is a large literature linking these dimensions to aspects of management and organization, while the findings from Schwartz and the World Values Survey have mainly been linked to societal-level phenomena. We will discuss some of the main findings (based on Hofstede, 2001; Schwartz, 2008; and Inglehart and Baker, 2000).

It is understandable that the power distance dimension is related to the importance and degree of centralization of power. In large power distance cultures power and authority tend to be concentrated at the apex of the organization. There are relatively many supervisors, forming a tall hierarchy, with many layers from the top to the bottom. In large power distance cultures the income inequality between those at the top of the organization and those at the bottom also tends to be bigger. Furthermore the inequality of superiors and subordinates is expressed in status symbols and privileges. Information flows through the hierarchy, i.e., vertically, but much less easily laterally (for instance from one department to the other) where there is no direct hierarchical relationship. In small power distance cultures there is a preference for organizational characteristics that are just the opposite of the picture sketched above. Some of the effects of power distance described above can also be expected for dimensions distinguished by Schwartz and the WVS (but there is little or no data to back this up, so our suppositions in this regard are rather speculative). High embeddedness is, among other things, associated with an emphasis on obedience, fitting this aspect of large power distance organizations, at least as long as the goals set by the powerholders are accepted as collective goals. Equality fits better with the opposite characteristics: flatter organizations and less emphasis on the hierarchy. In traditional cultures obedience to authorities is more self-evident than in secular-rational cultures, where authority needs to be acknowledged by the less powerful.

Uncertainty avoidance is linked to the importance of rules and procedures in organizations, and the importance attached to the formal organizational structure. Expectations with regard to managerial behaviour also differ between strong and weak uncertainty cultures. In strong uncertainty cultures managers are expected to be specialists, involved in operational details, versus generalists, and more focused on strategy in weak uncertainty avoidance cultures. In strong uncertainty avoidance cultures employees are less inclined to change jobs and to go to another employer (one of the questions measuring uncertainty avoidance in Hofstede's original 1980 study pertained to how long the respondent expected to continue to work for IBM). There are no obvious equivalents for uncertainty avoidance in Schwartz's work or in the WVS.

Individualism-collectivism, in contrast, is an aspect of societal culture picked up by all three major etic studies discussed in this chapter. This dimension affects the relationship between the employee and the organization, as well as factors that motivate the employee. In collectivist cultures the relationship between employee and employer is of a moral nature, with the employee being obliged to be loyal to the employer, in return for protection. In individualistic cultures this relationship is more contractual, without moralistic connotations. In individualistic cultures employees are motivated by having the opportunity to be independent in their job, and by varied and exciting work (affective autonomy), whereas in more collectivistic and embedded cultures security is an important motivator. Likewise, in cultures characterized by an emphasis on survival values employees care more about income, while intrinsic interest in the job is more distinctive in cultures emphasizing self-expression values (assuming that payment is above a certain threshold). Egalitarianism is also related, as cultures scoring high on this dimension see cooperative negotiation among members as legitimate. Furthermore individualism is related to how employees prefer to be evaluated and rewarded (on an individual versus a collective basis), and to how decisions are taken: by individual managers or more collectively.

We will refrain from discussing implications of long-term versus short-term orientation on management and organization, as there is too little empirical material. So the final dimension we discuss is masculinity versus femininity. This culture dimension is related, among other things, to work centrality. The work ethos in masculine cultures tends towards 'live in order to work' rather than in feminine cultures where the ethos is more inclined towards 'work in order to live' (Hofstede, 1991). But this dimension is also related to behaviours expected from managers. In more masculine societies managers are expected to be decisive, and to either ignore conflicts or fight to force the solution their way. In more feminine cultures managers are more consensus-seeking, and tend towards compromise and negotiation in case of conflicts. Hofstede (2001) further notes that in masculine cultures employees prefer higher earnings over fewer working hours, and more feminine cultures the opposite. This is reminiscent of the connotations of the survival versus self-expression values dimension, but this dimension is not statistically related to masculinity–femininity.

2.8 National cultures and cross-cultural negotiations

In this final section of the chapter we will discuss from a cross-cultural perspective a very important aspect of doing business across borders, namely international negotiations. Negotiations play an important role in business, as the essential characteristic of economic transactions in a market system is that the parties enter into an agreement of their own free will. In an efficiently functioning market, both parties can also consider alternatives (i.e. there are multiple potential sellers and buyers). In the negotiation process with a particular potential business partner what is at stake is closing a deal that is better than that which could be effected with the most attractive alternative partner. The negotiation process takes place under the shadow of the 'best alternative to negotiated agreement', or BATNA (Lewicki, Litterer, Minton and Saunders, 1994). Each party's BATNA will strongly influence what their minimally acceptable outcome in the negotiation process is. If the other party is not willing to make sufficient concessions, it is better to break off the negotiations and go to the most attractive alternative business partner.

Looking at negotiation processes in a schematic way, two possibilities exist. Either there is an overlap between the parties' 'zones of acceptance' (the set of possible deals they are willing to accept, with the lower limit defined by their BATNAs), or there is no overlap. In the latter case an effective communication process should make this clear to the parties, and the negotiation process will come to an end. The problem is that communication processes are not always straightforward, and this is particularly the case in international negotiations. In the first case (when there is overlap between the parties' zones of acceptance), the ultimate outcome of the negotiation remains indeterminate. The parties may end up with any deal that is acceptable to both, depending on their negotiation skills, the quality and quantity of available information, and the circumstances in which the negotiation takes place. But they may also end up without a deal, simply because the communication process makes them believe that there is *no* overlap between their zones of acceptance. The reason for this is that information is often deliberately misrepresented in negotiations, as negotiators try to get the best deal possible.

Negotiation processes may be ubiquitous in business in general; they are an even more salient characteristic of international business, and levels of complexity and uncertainty in the international arena are also greater. Multinational corporations (MNCs) may negotiate with national governments over the conditions under which they are allowed to invest and to do business in a country. For instance, before Intel Corporation decided to invest in a US$300 million chip plant in Costa Rica it went through a lengthy and complex negotiation process with local political authorities and representatives of institutions (Spar, 1998). Companies may also, however, negotiate with other companies in countries that they seek to enter through exports or licensing, or with a strategic alliance or joint venture. Once active in another country, managers of a company may find themselves engaged in negotiations with local institutions like trade unions or employers' associations. Furthermore, processes *within* MNCs also often have characteristics of negotiation, even if the parties involved are not independent, but parts of the same company. For instance, an MNC's headquarters may find itself negotiating certain policies with a local subsidiary (rather than commanding it to act in a certain way) because it believes local subsidiary managers' views and interests have to be taken into account if good results are to be achieved. Finally, managers of one subsidiary of an MNC may negotiate deals with other subsidiaries without much interference from company headquarters, as is increasingly common in complex 'networked' MNCs (see Chapter 9). In many of these cases, the negotiators and their constituencies (the companies or parts of companies they represent in the negotiation process) are from different cultures. We will now take a quick look at the ways in which cultural differences may influence negotiation processes.

Figure 2.7 shows the elements of an intercultural negotiation process in a schematic form. Each negotiation process takes place within a particular social situation.[6] This means,

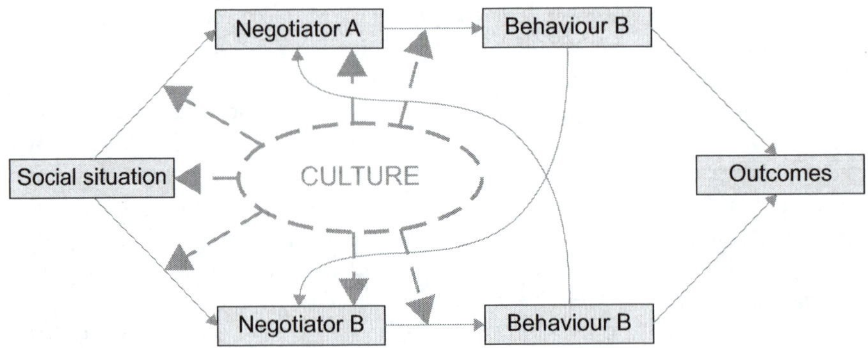

Figure 2.7 Influences of culture on negotiations.

Source: Adapted from Gelfand and Dyer (2000).

for instance, that the negotiators fulfil certain roles (e.g. those of buyer or seller), stand in particular relationships with their constituencies (e.g. as senior manager or as country representative), and may face certain deadlines or other restrictions. These situational factors influence the negotiators, their perception of the situation, their judgment, and their motives and goals. All these factors in turn influence their behaviour in the negotiation process (e.g. more cooperative or more competitive behaviour, the amount of information disclosed, etc.). What makes negotiation processes so complex is the feedback loop from the other party's behaviour to the negotiator's interpretation of the negotiation process. There is a dynamic interplay between one's behaviours, the interpretation of these behaviours by the counterpart, his or her response, and one's own interpretation of the negotiation process (Bazerman and Carroll, 1987). For this reason, negotiation processes always have an element of unpredictability.

Possible cultural influences on international negotiation processes are also indicated in Figure 2.7. Previous research on intercultural negotiation processes has often yielded unclear, or even inconsistent, results. For instance, some researchers find that the extent to which negotiators reciprocate cooperative problem solving behaviour by their counterparts does not differ significantly between cultures. However, in other studies such differences *are* identified, for example that the Japanese are more likely to reciprocate than both Americans and Brazilians (Allerheiligen, Graham and Lin, 1985). This suggests that the influences of culture on negotiations are not very straightforward. This is reflected in Figure 2.7. Cultural influences can work out on (1) the social situation in which the negotiations take place; (2) the way in which this social situation influences the perceptions, judgments, motives, goals, and so on, of the negotiators; (3) directly on these perceptions, and so on; and (4) on the way in which these perceptions and so on influence the behaviour of the negotiators. We will give some examples of each of these.

Gelfand and Dyer (2000) state that the prevalence of types of social situation is likely to differ between cultures. For instance, in more collectivist cultures the negotiator is more likely to be a member of a group, even at the negotiating table, than in more individualistic cultures. Japanese companies are well known for sending large delegations to negotiations with other companies, to the representatives of which the roles of the various Japanese delegates often remain unclear. These authors also expect that in cultures high on Schwartz's mastery dimension negotiators, because they strive for achievement and success, will feel more time pressure during the negotiation than negotiators from cultures orientated towards harmony. The organizational context is also likely to vary with the cultural environment. Organizations from large power distance societies will have more centralized control, with the effect that key negotiations have to be concluded by the top authority (Hofstede and Usunier, 1997).

Culture may also mediate the influence of the social situation on the negotiator. Laboratory experiments show that if negotiators are required to justify their actions to their constituencies after the negotiations, this leads to more cooperative behaviour in terms of ego and cooperative interpretations of the behaviour of the other for collectivists, but to more competitive behaviour and interpretations of the other's behaviour among individualists (Gelfand and Realo, 1999). In large power distance cultures, roles have a stronger influence on negotiation processes and outcomes than in cultures with a smaller power distance (Graham, Mintu and Rodgers, 1994). The social situation is also influenced by personal characteristics of the negotiators. For instance, in many cultures ('ascriptive' cultures, in contrast to 'achievement' cultures) the age of the negotiator is important. If a company sends a very young negotiator to such a country (e.g., Japan) this is likely to be ineffective, and it may even be seen as an insult (Trompenaars and Hampden-Turner, 1997: 109).

Culture also influences directly the perceptions, judgements, motivations, goals, and so on, of negotiators. The negotiation context is not given objectively, but is a cognitive construct of the negotiators, based on the information they receive, but also on their culturally coloured expectations. Individuals use various kinds of 'cognitive heuristics' (subconscious 'rules of thumb') to make sense of ambiguous situations. One way to make sense of a situation is to use metaphors linking the unfamiliar with the familiar. Americans may be more likely to use (competitive) sports metaphors in interpreting negotiation situations, whereas the Japanese would rather be expected to use (more cooperative) family household metaphors (Gelfand and Dyer, 2000). Culture may influence the goals negotiators pursue particularly strongly. Whereas each party will try to get the best outcome of the negotiation process for him or her and his or her constituency, there are also subsidiary goals like the preservation of a good relationship, which may carry more or less weight, depending on the culture. In more collectivist cultures maintaining a good relationship and saving both the 'face' of the negotiation partner and the respect he or she has for ego may be expected to carry relatively more weight. In more masculine (Hofstede) or mastery-orientated (Schwartz) cultures, there will be a strong emphasis on competitive goals ('winning' the negotiation), if necessary at the expense of the relationship (Hofstede and Usunier, 1997; Gelfand and Dyer, 2000).

Case: Who has formal decision rights?

When Honda invested heavily in an extensive relationship with British car manufacturer Rover, workers and managers at the two companies developed very positive working relationships for more than a decade. The partnership intensified after the government sold Rover to British Aerospace (BAe), but as Rover continued to lose money, BAe decided to discard the relationship, abruptly selling Rover to BMW through a secretive deal that caught Honda completely unaware. The Japanese car manufacturer had considered its connection with Rover a long-term one, much like a marriage, and it had shared advanced product and process technology with Rover well beyond its effective contractual ability to protect these assets. Honda's leaders were dumbfounded and outraged that BAe could sell – and to a competitor no less. Yet, while Honda's prized relationship was at the level of the operating company (Rover), the Japanese company had not taken seriously enough the fact that the decision rights over a Rover sale were vested at the parent (BAe) level. From a financial standpoint, the move made sense for BAe, and it was perfectly legal. Yet Honda's cultural blinkers made the sale seem inconceivable, and its disproportionate investment in Rover in effect created a major economic opportunity for BAe. The bottom line: understanding both formal decision rights and cultural assumptions in less familiar settings can be vital.

Excerpt from Sebenius, J.K. (2002) The hidden challenge of cross-border negotiations. *Harvard Business Review* 80(3), 6.

Furthermore, culture may mediate the relationship between a negotiator's psychic state and his or her behaviour in the negotiation. In other words, the same interpretations, goals, and so on, may lead to different behaviours in different cultures. For instance, the norms concerning the display of emotions differ between cultures. Hence, negotiators from different cultures may be equally infuriated by certain kinds of behaviour, but show their anger to a different extent. This, in turn, may lead to inaccurate interpretations by their counterparts of the effects of the negotiation tactics employed. In negotiating with the Japanese a westerner may get the impression that rational arguments carry little weight: they do not seem to be able to change the opinion of the Japanese negotiators. But, as observed by Sebenius (2002: 84), 'in Japan, the negotiating table is not a place for changing minds. Persuasive appeals are not appropriate or effectual'. The reason for this is that the position taken by the Japanese negotiators is very often based on consensus within the constituency. Changing that position is only possible if a new consensus is first reached, which tends to be a highly time-consuming process. National culture also influences the perceived appropriateness of bargaining tactics. In large power distance cultures, for instance, competitive bargaining tactics are seen as less acceptable (Volkema, 2004).

Finally, trust is important in all negotiation processes, but more difficult to build in cross-cultural negotiations (the following is based on Kramer, 2010). Trust is important because it enables the negotiators to enter into integrative bargaining processes. When there is high trust between the negotiators they are more likely to use cooperative or conciliatory influence strategies, while in low trust situations they would fear that such strategies would be exploited by the other party. In cross-cultural settings trust is more difficult to form because of psychological and social factors. Psychologically, all humans are inclined to think in terms of in-groups and out-groups, and trust in members of the in-group tends to be stronger. In cross-cultural negotiations the other party is more likely to be seen as the out-group. Kramer (2010) also discusses three biases that may differ in prevalence or strength between cultures. One of these biases is the zero-sum bias, which makes the negotiator define a situation as a 'you lose, I win' situation, even if in fact both parties could increase their benefits. Another bias is the egocentric bias, which entails that the behaviour of self is seen as more fair than that of others. A third bias is the fundamental attribution error, which means that one is inclined to ascribe the behaviour of others to their dispositions (e.g., if he does not yield to my demands it is because he does not *want* to). Interestingly, all three biases seem to be more manifest in Western negotiators than in Asian negotiators. At the social level, cross-cultural situations seem to strengthen the representation effect, i.e., the negotiator sees himself as defending the interests of the in-group, with a predictable effect that it will be more difficult to come to integrative bargaining. All in all, the difficulty of establishing cross-cultural trust can be expected to make negotiations across cultural boundaries much more difficult than within these boundaries.

As the discussion above illustrates, the influences of culture on negotiation processes are too complex to allow for simple recommendations for managers. But it is clear that managers negotiating across cultures should be aware of the various possible influences depicted in Figure 2.7. This figure may also serve as a warning. Negotiators may be inclined to see the individuals they are dealing with too much as representatives of their culture; but the characteristics of an individual can never be reduced to a cultural stereotype. Rather, negotiators should try to understand the behaviour of their counterparts by also taking into account the wider situation in which the negotiation process is embedded (and which itself may be culturally influenced, as discussed above). Hence, the negotiator should 'along with assessing the person across the table, [figure out] the intricacies of the larger organization behind her' (Sebenius, 2002: 85). Finally, one should never forget that language deficiencies may play an important role in international negotiations. A sense of humour, for instance, can be very difficult to express in a foreign language, especially when one's command of that language is far from perfect. The use of interpreters may help in some respects, but at the same time may introduce yet other difficulties. For instance, if one directly addresses the interpreter rather than one's counterpart, the latter may take this as a sign of disrespect (Mead, 1998: 246). Interpreters may also make mistakes, particularly in translating slang or jokes.

Study questions

1. Explain the differences and similarities between the concepts of culture and stereotypes.
2. Discuss how culture may influence the chances of survival of groups of people in a particular natural environment.
3. Describe the differences between etic and emic culture research.
4. Give an account of possible issues of levels of analysis in culture research.
5. Describe and critically discuss Hofstede's model of culture dimensions.
6. Describe and critically discuss Schwartz's model of culture orientations.
7. Describe and critically discuss the approach of Inglehart and the World Values Survey.
8. Discuss the relative strong and weak points of the work of Hofstede, Schwartz and Inglehart.
9. Compare the concepts of national culture and organizational culture, and explain the differences and similarities.
10. Give examples of how national culture may influence management and organization.
11. Explain how cultural differences may influence negiotiation processes and outcomes.

Further reading

Minkov, M. (2011) *Cultural Differences in a Globalizing World.* Bingley, UK: Emerald.

This book gives a good overview of the main large-scale studies, and then looks for ways to integrate these. Minkov writes in a very readable style, and is not hindered by political correctness.

Hampden-Turner, C. and Trompenaars, F. (2000) *Building Cross-Cultural Competence: How to Create Wealth from Conflicting Values.* Chichester: Wiley.

A good discussion of practical implications of cultural differences, based on six dilemmas, varying from universalism versus particularism to sequential versus synchronous time.

Inglehart, R. and Welzel, C. (2005) *Modernization, Cultural Change, and Democracy: The Human Development Sequence.* Cambridge, UK: Cambridge University Press.

A comprehensive and up-to-date discussion of the findings of the World Values Surveys, with much attention to value change over time.

Case: Leading across cultures at Michelin

Source: based on *Leading Across Cultures at Michelin* (A) and (B), The Case Centre, cases 409-008-1 and 409-009-1.

As Jeff Armstrong, the head of human resources for Michelin's North American operations, left his office, Olivier Chalon reflected on his own leadership style. Olivier was leading a turn-around at a large division of Michelin in Greenville, South Carolina, North America. Jeff had explained the bitter complaints that several of Olivier's colleagues and subordinates had made about his leadership style. The complaints pointed at something deeper than aversion for change. People felt Olivier was arrogant, demoralizing, cold and distant, not making an effort to get to know people at work, unable to motivate people, and lacking people skills. Trained as an engineer at one of France's highly selective and prestigious Grandes Ecoles, Olivier had managed teams in six European countries and had worked in a multicultural environment his entire career. He had a long and successful track record as a talented leader, being able to motivate teams to accomplish great things. His English was fluent and he had 6 years of experience in the UK. Olivier assumed that it would be an easy transition to the US and that he would fit right in. He was just 6 months on the job at Michelin US and Jeff Armstrong made it clear that he had better understand the situation before it damaged the business and his new position would be in jeopardy. Jeff suggested that Olivier meet with a cross-cultural consultant who specialized in helping European managers adapt their leadership style to an American context. Olivier was aware of the differences between different cultural environments but didn't think the US was that different from Europe.

Olivier was hired to turn around the North American division with several plants and 4,000 employees under his management. The business unit was lagging behind competitors and experienced sliding sales and poor financial results. Olivier had to make tough decisions and implement a new strategy, even if it meant upsetting some long-standing managers. The turn-around had the full support of the CEO and president. Headquarters were expecting a turnaround within 2 years. Olivier was under pressure to show results and realized that he would need every member of his team to help him implement the turnaround. He needed to understand what happened fast and find a way to motivate and energize his team.

While talking to the cross-cultural consultant Olivier started to understand that Europeans and Americans had very different approaches towards rewarding and motivating employees. He had been very straightforward with his criticism and relentless when asking for improvement. When he was pleased with people's results he did not show it overtly as he wanted people to push themselves further than before and didn't want to encourage complacency. Olivier had been very direct with feedback and was surprised that he was never challenged. His team members just nodded and didn't push back, which made him believe they were in agreement. While he did not receive much task-related feedback, Olivier was surprised how his American colleagues and subordinates openly talked about their family life, their children at the office and how they would spend their weekend. Sometimes he was introduced to a manager's wife, who stopped by for lunch. But despite his open-door policy, transparency, his frequent walks through the office and informal talks to people, he felt that he did not succeed in really connecting to his colleagues and subordinates.

Little by little Olivier became aware that his leadership style was probably affecting his team. He guessed that he was misreading the cues his colleagues were sending, while they were misreading his. He had been ignorant of the cultural gap between them.

Questions

1 What differences in the American and French culture might be at the root of the difficulties that Olivier Chalon is facing as he implements a new strategy?

2 Once Chalon is aware of how his American staff perceives his management style, what steps do you recommend that he takes in order to improve his relationship with, and the motivation of his team?

Case: The Alcatel-Lucent merger

Written by Niels Noorderhaven on the basis of public materials[7]

On 3 April, 2006, communication solutions providers Alcatel SA from France and Lucent Technologies from the USA signed a merger pact. An earlier attempt in 2001 to merge the companies failed, as Lucent feared that Alcatel, the bigger company of the two, would dominate. This fear was not taken away by the fact that the proposed deal was presented as a merger between equals. In 2006 however, whether because Alcatel was now seen as less dominant, or because the conditions in the industry had worsened enough to make the deal even more necessary than previously, the two companies came together again, and this time they persevered.

Alcatel and Lucent seemed to make a good fit. Alcatel was by far the bigger of the two, with a market capitalization of $21.5 billion, 58,000 employees and sales of $15.9 billion between one-and-a-half and two times as big as Lucent. The companies were natural merger partners, as the French firm was strong in equipment that could make regular telephone lines carry high-speed internet and digital television traffic, while the American company concentrated on wireless technologies and optical networks. In terms of geographical markets, Alcatel did two-thirds of its business in Europe, Latin America, the Middle East and Africa, while Lucent realized two-thirds of its turnover in the United States. The combined company foresaw a 10 per cent cut of the workforce through streamlining and elimination of redundancies.

The merged firm was incorporated in France and headquartered in Paris. The Board was composed of six members of Alcatel's board, six members from Lucent's board, plus two independent directors who had to be Europeans. Lucent top manager Patricia Russo became CEO of the merged entity, and Serge Tchuruk from Alcatel, Chairman of the Board. In the statement announcing the merger, the two top managers said that 'a combined Alcatel and Lucent will be global in scale and have clear leadership in the areas that will define next-generation networks'.[8] At the time of the merger many analysts warned against the cultural difficulties that could be expected in this trans-Atlantic merger, but the two top managers played down these issues: 'I found, and my people found, that there are a lot of similarities' (Patricia Russo); and 'the cultural gap doesn't at all frighten me' (Serge Tchuruk).[9]

All the same, the performance of the merged firm was dismal, with losses posted quarter after quarter in the first 2 years of its existence, write-downs of more than $4.5 billion, and market capitalization cut in half.[10] At least part of this disaster could be attributed to external factors, like the economic crisis and increased competition, among others from China's Huawei. But observers also pointed at culture clashes inside Alcatel-Lucent.

For one, the question was raised how effective Patricia Russo could be in the company's headquarters in Paris, since she did not speak French. The official company language was English, but would that also work in the corridors where the power games were played? To her credit, Russo quickly learned enough French to be able to deliver short speeches, and surprised managers at the Paris headquarters with an unexpectedly collaborative and communicative leadership style. But Russo's reputation as an effective manager had largely been based on her track-record of 'rightsizing' (i.e., doing layoffs) and in the French setting, with strong legal protection of employees and combative unions this was not something that could be repeated easily. The balance of power in Alcatel-Lucent was also different from that in an American firm, with more power lying with Chairman Tchuruk than would have been the case in a US-based company.

The merger between Alcatel and Lucent was also a confrontation of organizational cultures. One of the companies was known to be rigidly hierarchical and centrally controlled, the other as entrepreneurial, flexible and strongly marketing-oriented. However, in contrast with popular stereotypes, it was the US firm that was rigid and hierarchical, and the French one that was flexible and entrepreneurial! This combination made brutal downsizing at the larger of the two, Alcatel, only more difficult. The more so since Alcatel was so strongly decentralized (or out of control?) that no fewer than 20 different accounting systems were used internally. As a result, it took much time to get a clear picture of where precisely profits were bleeding away. In the meantime, each side in the merger was protecting its own turf, leading to clashes of interest that magnified perceived differences.

In the Autumn of 2008 both Russo and Tchuruk stepped down and were succeeded by Ben Verwaayen and Philippe Camus, respectively. Verwaayen previously had been CEO of British Telecom, a company that he had successfully (and mercilessly) turned around. As a Dutchman he was regarded to be culturally neutral. Camus had made his career both in France and the USA, and was said to understand both cultures from the inside. However, when Verwaayen resigned in early 2013, Alcatel-Lucent had gone through a series of restructurings, but without returning to profitability.

Questions

1. What are the differences between the French and the American national cultures (as identified in the etic studies discussed in this chapter) that you consider most relevant for this merger, and why?
2. Explain the difficulties encountered on the basis of the known differences between the two national cultures.
3. Are there also difficulties that you would have expected to occur in the merger on the basis of the differences between the national cultures, but which did not occur?
4. Did you see aspects in the case that cannot satisfactorily be explained on the basis of the differences between the French and the American national cultures (as identified in the etic studies discussed in this chapter)?

Notes

1 The example of the relationship between the child-raising practices and the means of subsistence of a people, discussed above, is based on data collected by this type of anthropologist.
2 http://www.worldvaluessurvey.org/index_html, retrieved on 28 March, 2014.
3 http://www.europeanvaluesstudy.eu/evs/about-evs/history.html, retrieved on 28 March, 2014.
4 The figure is based on factor scores of a factor analysis of the transposed matrix of the 14 dimensions for the 49 countries common to all three etic studies. It is indicative of how strongly the dimensions operationalized in the three studies are related to each other.
5 The reason not to include the GLOBE project in our overview of landmark etic studies is the ongoing controversy regarding the meaning of its findings (see two special sections of the *Journal of International Business Studies*, 2006 issue 1, and 2010 issue 8). Moreover, at the moment still relatively little is known about the impact of the culture dimensions distinguished by GLOBE on management and organization.
6 The discussion in this section is based on Gelfand and Dyer (2000).
7 *Wall Street Journal*, 3 April, 2006; http://online.wsj.com/news/articles/SB114398759746714581, retrieved on 16 July, 2014.

Business Week, 17 June, 2008; http://www.businessweek.com/stories/2008–06–17/alcatel-lucents-troubled-marriage, retrieved on 16 July, 2014.

Business Week, 2 April, 2006; http://www.businessweek.com/stories/2006–04–02/alcatel-and-lucent-a-global-logic, retrieved on 16 July, 2014.

USA Today, 2 September, 2008; http://usatoday30.usatoday.com/tech/products/2008–09–02–4017493346_x.htm, retrieved on 16 July, 2014.

New York Times, 7 February, 2013; http://www.nytimes.com/2013/02/08/technology/ben-verwaayen-alcatel-lucent-chief-resigns.html, retrieved on 16 July, 2014.

8 *Business Week*, 2 April, 2006; http://www.businessweek.com/stories/2006–04–02/alcatel-and-lucent-a-global-logic, retrieved on 16 July, 2014.

9 *Wall Street Journal*, 3 April, 2006; http://online.wsj.com/news/articles/SB114398759746714581, retrieved on 16 July, 2014.

10 *Business Week*, 17 June, 2008; http://www.businessweek.com/stories/2008–06–17/alcatel-lucents-troubled-marriage, retrieved on 16 July, 2014.

References

Adler, N.J. (1991) *International Dimensions of Organizational Behavior* (2nd edn). Boston: PWS-Kent Publishing.

Allerheiligen, R., Graham, J.L. and Lin, C.-Y. (1985) Honesty in interorganizational negotiations in the United States, Japan, and the Republic of China. *Journal of Macromarketing* 5, 4–16.

Bahn, P. and Flenley, J. (1992) *Easter Island, Earth Island*. London: Thames & Hudson.

Bazerman, M.H. and Carroll, J.S. (1987) Negotiator cognition. *Research in Organizational Behavior* 9, 247–288.

Burns, P., Myers, A. and Kakabadse, A. (1995) Are national stereotypes discriminating? *European Management Journal* 13(2), 212–217.

Chapman, M. (1996–1997) Social anthropology, business studies, and cultural issues. *International Studies of Management & Organization* 26(4), 3–29.

Chew, W.L., III (2006) What's in a national stereotype? An introduction to imagology at the threshold of the 21st century. *Language and Intercultural Communication* 6(3–4), 179–187.

Chinese Culture Connection (1987) Chinese values and the search for culture-free dimensions of culture. *Journal of Cross-Cultural Psychology* 18, 143–174.

Ertug, G., Cuypers, I.R.P., Noorderhaven, N.G. and Bensaou, B.M. (2013) Trust between international joint venture partners: effects of home countries. *Journal of International Business Studies* 44, 263–282.

Fang, T. (2003) A critique of Hofstede's fifth national culture dimension. *International Journal of Cross Cultural Management* 3, 347–368.

Fischer, R., Vauclair, C.-M., Fontaine, J.R.J. and Schwartz, S.H. (2010) Are individual-level and country-level structures different? Testing Hofstede's legacy with the Schwartz Value Survey. *Journal of Cross-Cultural Psychology* 41(2), 135–151.

Geertz, C. (1983) *Local Knowledge: Further Essays in Interpretive Anthropology*. New York: Basic Books.

Gelfand, M.J. and Dyer, N. (2000) A cultural perspective on negotiation: progress, pit-falls, and prospects. *Applied Psychology: an International Review* 49, 62–99.

Gelfand, M.J. and Realo, A. (1999) Collectivism and accountability in intergroup negotiations. *Journal of Applied Psychology* 84, 721–736.

Graham, J.L., Mintu, A.T. and Rodgers, W. (1994) Explorations of negotiation behaviors in ten foreign cultures using a model developed in the United States. *Management Science* 40, 70–95.

Grisar, K. (1997) Globalization of work culture: African and European industrial cooperation in Senegal. *Research in the Sociology of Work* 6, 223–246.

Hofstede, G. (1980) *Culture's Consequences*. London: Sage.

Hofstede, G. (1991) *Cultures and Organizations: Software of the Mind*. London: McGraw-Hill.

Hofstede, G. (1994) Foreword, in Kim, U., Triandis, H.C., Kagitcibasi, C., Choi, S.-C. and Yoon, G. (eds) *Individualism and Collectivism: Theory, Method, and Applications*. Thousand Oaks, CA: Sage, ix–xiii.

Hofstede, G. (2001) *Culture's Consequences: Comparing Values, Behaviors, Institutions, and Organizations Across Nations* (2nd edn). Thousand Oaks, CA: Sage.

Hofstede, G. (2011) Dimensionalizing cultures: the Hofstede Model in context. *Online Readings in Psychology and Culture*, 2(1). Online. Available HTTP: <http://dx.doi.org/10.9707/2307–0919.1014>, retrieved on 26 July, 2014.

Hofstede, G. and Minkov, M. (2010) Long-term versus short-term orientation: new perspectives. *Asia Pacific Business Review* 16(4), 493–504.

Hofstede, G. and Usunier, J.-C. (1997) Hofstede's dimensions of culture and their influence on international business negotiations, in Ghauri, P.N. and Usunier, J.-C. (eds) *International Business Negotiations*. Amsterdam: Elsevier-Pergamon, 119–129.

Hofstede, G., Neuijen, B., Ohayv, D.D. and Sanders, G. (1990) Measuring organizational cultures: A qualitative and quantitative study across twenty cases. *Administrative Science Quarterly* 35(2), 286–316.

Hoppe, M.H. (1990) *A Comparative Study of Country Elites*. Unpublished doctoral dissertation, University of North Carolina at Chapel Hill.

House, R.J., Hanges, P.J., Javidan, M., Dorfman, P.W. and Gupta, V. (eds) (2004) *Culture, Leadership, and Organizations; The GLOBE Study of 62 Societies*. Thousand Oaks: Sage.

Hunt, J.W. (1981) Applying American behavioral science: some cross-cultural problems. *Organizational Dynamics* (Summer 1981), 55–61.

Inglehart, R. (1997) *Modernization and Postmodernization: Cultural, Economic and Political Change in 43 Societies*. Princeton: Princeton University Press.

Inglehart, R. and Baker, W.E. (2000) Modernization, cultural change, and the persistence of traditional values. *American Sociological Review* 65(1), 19–51.

Inglehart, R. and Welzer, C. (2005) *Modernization, Cultural Change, and Democracy: The Human Development Sequence*. Cambridge: Cambridge University Press.

Inkeles, A. and Levinson, D.J. (1997) National character: the study of modal personality and sociocultural systems, in Lindzey, G. and Aronson, E. (eds) *Handbook of Social Psychology*, Vol. 4, 418–506. New York: McGraw-Hill (original work published 1954).

d'Iribarne, Ph. (1996–97) The usefulness of an ethnographic approach to the inter- national comparison of organizations. *International Studies of Management and Organization* 26(4), 30–47.

Keesing, R.M. (1974) Theories of culture. *Annual Review of Anthropology* 3, 73–97.

Kramer, R.M. (2010) Trust barriers in cross-cultural negotiations: a social psychological analysis. In Saunders, M.N.K., Skinner, D., Dietz, G., Gillespie, N. and Lewicki, R.J. (eds). *Organizational Trust: A Cultural Perspective*. Cambridge, UK: Cambridge University Press, 182–204.

Kroeber, A.L. and Kluckhohn, C. (1952) *Culture: A Critical Review of Concepts and Definitions*. Boston: Papers of the Peabody Museum of Archaeology & Ethnology 47(1).

Leung, K. and Bond, M. (1989) On the empirical identification of dimensions for cross-cultural comparisons. *Journal of Cross-Cultural Psychology* 20, 133–151.

Lewicki, R.J., Litterer, J.A., Minton, J.W. and Saunders, D.M. (1994) *Negotiation*. New York: McGraw-Hill.

McSweeney, B. (2002) Hofstede's model of national cultural differences and their consequences: a triumph of faith – a failure of analysis. *Human Relations* 55, 89–118.

Maznevski, M.L., DiStefano, J.J., Gomez, C.B., Noorderhaven, N.G. and Wu, P.-C. (2002) Cultural dimensions at the individual level of analysis: the cultural orientations framework. *International Journal of Cross Cultural Management* 2, 275–295.

Mead, R. (1998) *International Management: Cross-cultural Dimensions*. Oxford: Blackwell.

Minkov, M. (2007) *What Makes Us Different and Similar: A New Interpretation of the World Values Survey and Other Cross-Cultural Data*. Sofia: Klasika I Stil.

Minkov, M. and Hofstede, G. (2010) Hofstede's fifth dimension: new evidence from the World Values Survey. *Journal of Cross-Cultural Psychology* 43(1), 3–14.

Minkov, M. and Hofstede, G. (2012) Hofstede's fifth dimension: new evidence from the World Values Survey. *Journal of Cross-Cultural Psychology* 43(1), 3–14.

Moore, J.D. (1997) *Visions of Culture*. Walnut Creek: Altamira Press.

Osland, J.S. and Bird, A. (2000) Beyond sophisticated stereotyping: cultural sense-making in context. *Academy of Management Executive* 14(1), 65–77.

Peterson, M.F. and Castro, S.L. (2006) Measurement metrics at aggregate levels of analysis: implications for organization culture research and the GLOBE project. *The Leadership Quarterly* 17, 506–521.

Rainbird, P. (2002) A message for our future? The Rapa Nui (Easter Island) ecodisaster and Pacific island environments. *World Archaeology*, 33(3), 436–451.

Ronen, S. and Shenkar, O. (1985) Clustering countries on attitudinal dimensions: a review and synthesis. *Academy of Management Review* 10(3), 435–454.

Rousseau, D.M. (1985) Issues of level in organizational research: multi-level and cross-level perspectives. In Cummings, L.L. and Staw, B.M. (eds) *Research in Organizational Behaviour: an Annual Series of Analytical Essays and Critical Reviews* 7, 1–37.

Sagiv, L. and Schwartz, S.H. (2000) A new look at national culture. In Ashkanasy, N., Wilderom, C.P.M. and Peterson, M.F. (eds) *Handbook of Organizational Culture and Climate.* London: Sage, 417–435.

Schein, E.H. (1984) Coming to a new awareness of organizational culture. *Sloan Management Review* 25(2), 3–16.

Schneider, B., Ehrhart, M.G. and Macey, W.H. (2012) Organizational climate and culture. *Annual Review of Psychology* 64, 361–388.

Schooler, C. (1996) Cultural and social-structural explanations of cross-national psychological differences. *Annual Review of Sociology* 22, 323–349.

Schwartz, S.H. (1992) Universals in the content and structure of values: theoretical advances and empirical tests in 20 countries. In Zanna, M. (ed.) *Advances in Experimental Social Psychology*, Vol. 25. New York: Academic Press, 1–66.

Schwartz, S.H. (1994) Beyond individualism and collectivism: new cultural dimensions of values. In Kim, U., Triandis, H.C., Kagitcibasi, C., Choi, S.C. and Yoon, G. (eds) *Individualism and Collectivism: Theory, Method, and Applications.* Newbury Park, CA: Sage, 85–199.

Schwartz, S.H. (2006) A theory of cultural value orientations: explication and applications. *Comparative Sociology* 5, 137–182.

Schwartz, S.H. (2008) *Cultural Value Orientations: Nature and Implications of National Differences.* Moscow: State University – Higher School of Economics Press.

Schwartz, S.H. and Ros, M. (1995) Values in the West: a theoretical and empirical challenge to the individualism–collectivism cultural dimensions. *World Psychology* 1, 91–122.

Sebenius, J.K. (2002) The hidden challenge of cross-border negotiations. *Harvard Business Review* 80(3), 76–85.

Smith, P.B. (2004) Nations, cultures, and individuals: new perspectives and old dilemmas. *Journal of Cross-Cultural Psychology* 35(1), 6–12.

Smith, P.B. and Schwartz, S.H. (1997) Values. In Berry, J.W., Segall, M.H. and Kagitcibasi, C. (eds) *Handbook of Cross-cultural Psychology*, Vol. 3, Social Behavior and Applications. Boston, MA: Allyn & Bacon, 77–118.

Soeters, J. and Recht, R. (1998) Culture and discipline in military academies: an international comparison. *Journal of Political and Military Sociology* 26, 169–189.

Spar, D. (1998) *Attracting High Technology Investment: Intel's Costa Rican Plant.* Foreign Investment Advisory Service Occasional Paper 11. Washington, DC: World Bank.

Steenkamp, J.-B.E.M. (2001) The role of national culture in international marketing research. *International Marketing Review* 18, 30–44.

SteenkampJ.-B.E.M. and Geyskens, I. (2012) Transaction cost economics and the roles of national culture: A test of hypotheses based on Inglehart and Hofstede. *Journal of the Academy of Management Science* 40(2), 252–270.

Tannenbaum, A.S., Kavcic, B., Rosner, M., Vianello, M. and Wieser, G. (1974) *Hierarchy in Organizations.* San Francisco: Jossey-Bass.

Triandis, H.C. (1994) Cross-cultural industrial and organizational psychology. In Triandis, H.C., Dunnette, M.D. and Hough, L.M. (eds) *Handbook of Industrial and Organizational Psychology* (2nd edn), Vol. 4. Palo Alto, CA: Consulting Psychologists Press.

Trompenaars, F. and Hampden-Turner, C. (1997) *Riding the Waves of Culture: Understanding Diversity in Business* (2nd edn). London: Nicholas Brealey.

Volkema, R.J. (2004) Demographic, cultural, and economic predictors of perceived ethicality of negotiation behavior: a nine-country analysis. *Journal of Business Research*, 57(1), 69–78.

3 National cultures and management – the emic approach

Learning objectives

By the end of this chapter you will be able to:

- explain the main criticisms of the etic approach to culture as expressed by emic scholars
- describe the semiotic perspective to culture
- understand hermeneutics as a philosophy of science
- recognize the main features of the ethnographic method of studying culture
- discuss d'Iribarne's approach to the cross-cultural study of management and organization
- describe d'Iribarne's characterization of management and organization in France, the USA and the Netherlands
- understand what indigenous management concepts are, and to give a number of examples
- discuss how etic and emic studies of trust in a cross-cultural context complement each other.

Chapter outline

3.1 Introduction

In Chapter 2 we discussed the distinction between etic and emic studies of culture. In this chapter we will further explore the emic approach, and discuss findings relevant to management and organization.

There seems to be an imbalance in the use of etic and emic approaches to culture in comparative international management. Clearly the etic approaches are better known, among management scholars as well as students. These approaches also come up with quantitative yardsticks for comparing different national cultures, which can be used to operationalize the cultural factor in comparative international research. This is one of the main reasons for the very extensive use of Hofstede's work in management studies, in particular international management. However, there is a danger to this rather one-sided concentration on the etic approach. This is that scholars and practitioners less familiar with the background of the studies will apply the dimension scores uncritically, as if these unproblematically represented the culture of the countries in question. This is also at least partly due to the fact that emic scholars have so far shown far less interest in cross-cultural *management* issues (in contrast with single-culture studies focusing on non-managerial issues). However, the overemphasis on etic approaches, and in particular the quantitative findings, isolated from more qualitative interpretations, leads to reification of the dimensions: what was developed as a tool for interpreting complex phenomena comes to be seen as an inherent aspect of reality. The conceptual lenses developed by Hofstede and other etic scholars can thus become blinders: because we expect to find differences in, for example, power distance, we see them everywhere, and we are likely to miss the many other differences (and similarities) that may also exist. Therefore it is essential that students of comparative international management become familiar with both the etic and the emic approaches, as this will provide them with a more balanced and critical view. To illustrate the pitfalls of too uncritically applying etic findings we consider below the criticism of Hofstede's work of an emic researcher whose work we will examine in some detail in Section 3.3: Philippe d'Iribarne.

The French researcher Philippe d'Iribarne explicitly confronts in his work the findings of etic research with findings from his own emic studies. From his perspective, the limitations of etic research are serious. We will discuss d'Iribarne's criticism of the application of Hofstede's power distance scale in France as an example.

On the basis of his own ethnographic research into French work organizations, d'Iribarne takes issue with Hofstede's finding that French culture would be characterized by a rather large power distance (68, compared with 40 and 38, respectively, for both other countries studied in detail by d'Iribarne, the USA and the Netherlands). This large power distance raises questions for d'Iribarne, for it is higher than that of, for instance, Iran, South Korea, Chile, Turkey or Colombia. It puts France (and Belgium, which in Hofstede's study is closely associated with France) out on a limb as the only non-autocratic nation between the large power distance countries (d'Iribarne, 1996–97). The core of the problem, according to d'Iribarne, is that in Hofstede's power distance dimension the notions of power and hierarchy are conflated. From his own research, as well as from other ethnographic studies of French work organizations, d'Iribarne concludes that 'in the case of France, the notions of hierarchy and power are by no means the same' (1996–97: 36):

> In fact, the existence of a *large symbolic* distance among the various levels of the hierarchy does not in any way mean that the *balance of power* in France particularly favours the upper levels of the hierarchy. One could even say that, to some degree, the existence of a large hierarchical distance tends not to strengthen but rather to limit the power of the bosses.
>
> (1996–97: 37; emphasis in the original)

Looking at how the high score for France was obtained in Hofstede's study, d'Iribarne demonstrates clearly the limitations of questionnaire approaches in general, and Hofstede's instrument in particular. Hofstede's power distance scale is made up of the following three questions:

1 How frequently are employees afraid to express disagreements with their managers?
2 Under which manager would the respondent prefer to work (choosing between descriptions of what can be described as 'autocratic', 'persuasive/paternalistic', 'consultative' and 'democratic' managers (Hofstede 2001: 85)?
3 To which of the above-mentioned four types of manager does the respondent's own manager correspond most closely?

Unsurprisingly, the less often employees are afraid to express disagreement with their managers, the lower the power distance score. But the interpretation of the 'preferred manager' and 'perceived manager' questions is less straightforward. In the 'preferred manager' question, a preference for a consultative manager is associated with a lower score on power distance. But in the 'perceived manager' question, lower scores on power distance are associated with *not* preferring an autocratic manager or a persuasive/paternalistic manager. Note that a preference for a democratic manager is not associated with a lower score on power distance. Hofstede sees this choice as unrealistic, as it is unlikely to be effective in work organizations. He interprets this choice as a 'counterdependent reaction' to a situation of large power distance (Hofstede, 2001: 86). But d'Iribarne notes that the Netherlands scores less hierarchically than the USA with regard to the preferred manager, but more hierarchically than the USA with regard to the perceived manager. In d'Iribarne's own research, the Americans emerged as much more hierarchical than the Dutch, who, among other things, 'vigorously resisted American methods of command, which they judged too authoritarian' (d'Iribarne, 1996–97: 40).

According to d'Iribarne the hierarchical distance in France may be large, but this is mainly symbolic. Hierarchical position does not yield much power to managers, because it actually separates them from their subordinates. Thus, forepersons can be observed stressing the lowly nature of their practical skills, compared with the more theoretical knowledge possessed by engineers, while at the same time they exploit this divergence to keep engineers out of the sphere under their own control (d'Iribarne, 1996–97: 37). Such symbolic hierarchical distance may actually help subordinates to defend their own particular rights and privileges, 'since it traps the superior within an etiquette of propriety that severely limits his or her power' (1996–97: 37). D'Iribarne also quotes a study of Barsoux and Lawrence (1990), in which French respondents agreed less than all other countries in the sample except Italians with the statement 'basically, I will carry out instructions from my supervisor', and agreed more than the respondents from any other country with the statement 'I only follow the instructions of my superiors when my reason is convinced.' These findings do not correspond to a picture of the French culture as emphasizing blind obedience to superiors. Earlier observations of the French sociologist Michel Crozier point in the same direction. Crozier (2010) describes the French culture as a system in which face-to-face authority relations are avoided as much as possible, because the French do not feel comfortable with them. Instead, impersonal rules are employed to regulate relations between those higher and those lower in the hierarchy. 'People on top theoretically have a great deal of power . . . But these powers are not very useful, since people on top can act only in an impersonal way and can in no way interfere with the subordinate strata' (Crozier, 2010: 225).

Hence, emic studies are necessary to complement etic studies. The complementarity between the two approaches can take two forms. Hofstede (1980: 339) concedes that his approach has limitations, and expresses the desirability of complementing his findings with emic descriptions. Thus, emic studies can serve to correct and complement the general picture arising from etic studies. In contrast, d'Iribarne suggests that the opposite order may be called for. In his view questionnaire items correctly representing the dimensions one wishes to measure and compare across cultures can only be formulated after in-depth ethnographic studies have been administered. For instance, referring to Hofstede's uncertainty avoidance, d'Iribarne points out that uncertainty is dealt with in different ways in different countries. In Chinese culture, managerial roles are typically allocated to family members, and this can also be seen as an uncertainty-regulating device, but it is not reflected in Hofstede's operationalization. As a result, Singapore (with a predominantly ethnic Chinese population) could emerge in Hofstede's work as the country with the lowest level of uncertainty avoidance. This could only have been avoided if sufficient fieldwork in different countries had previously revealed the different ways in which societies control uncertainty. Hence emic work should in this view lay the foundation for etic studies.

In this book we assume an agnostic position regarding the primacy of etic and emic studies, but we conclude from the discussion above that knowledge of the emic approach and some of its main findings is essential for an understanding of international comparative management. In the following sections of this chapter we will first discuss a number of methodological issues associated with the emic approach to culture (Section 3.2). After that we will discuss the work of d'Iribarne as an example of an emic scholar focusing specifically on aspects of management (3.3). Subsequently we will look at a number of systems of management and organization from an indigenous perspective, i.e., 'from the inside' of a culture (3.4). To illustrate that many phenomena require a combination of the emic and etic perspective we will in Section 3.5 focus on the issue of trust. It is well known that the general level of trust varies between societies, but it should also be acknowledged that trust does not necessarily mean the same thing in different countries, and may have diverging antecedents and consequences across cultures.

3.2 Methodological background

Whereas most etic studies of culture focus on the values that are held by the inhabitants of a country, emic studies tend to focus on meanings. For example, an etic study could by means of a survey investigate what in the eyes of the average citizen of a country would be appropriate behaviour of a subordinate vis-à-vis his or her superior. From this preference for a particular type of behaviour the researcher then deduces the strength and direction of particular value complexes, like power distance or egalitarianism. An emic study would in a more microscopic way look at the behaviours of the subordinate, and try to reconstruct the meaning attached to these behaviours by the subordinate as well as the superior. Meanings as object of study are less accessible by methods like surveys than values, and as a result the chasm between etic and emic studies to a large extent is also a methodological difference.

An important representative of the emic approach to culture is Clifford Geertz. In Geertz's view the meaning that the people studied attach to certain acts is the proper subject of the study of culture:

> Believing . . . that man is an animal suspended in webs of significance he himself has spun, I take culture to be those webs, and the analysis of it to be therefore not an experimental science in search of law but an interpretive one in search of meaning.
> (Geertz, 1973: 5)

Culture, in Geertz's view, is quintessentially a social phenomena. Though ideational, culture does not exist in the head of individuals, but is public (Geertz, 1973). An idea that would exist only in the mind of an individual, unlike meaning that is shared within a community, would not be able to regulate social life. Such shared meaning is 'consummately social: social in its origins, social in its functions, social in its forms, social in its applications' (1973: 360).

Uncovering the public meanings constituting culture in Geertz's view requires different research methods from those applied in the etic tradition. Geertz uses what he calls 'thick description': detailed description and analysis of particular episodes of social interaction. These episodes are seen as revealing the symbolic structures regulating public life. The point is to find out the meanings that particular actions have for the actors whose actions they are, and, based on this, to draw tentative conclusions about the society in which the actions are embedded. 'The aim is to draw large conclusions from small, but very densely textured facts' (1973: 28).

Because man is a meaning-making animal, in any social setting 'persons are perceived not baldly as such, as mere unadorned members of the human race, but as representatives of certain distinct categories of persons' (1973: 363). For instance, a police officer is not seen as just a random individual, but as a representative of a particular class, viz., the people who have the responsibilities and powers associated with law enforcement. The classes to which people belong are man-made:'they are historically constructed, socially maintained, and individually applied' (1973: 363–364).

The semiotic perspective

The perspective described above can be described as semiotic. Semiotics is the study of signs. A sign is something that refers to, or stands for something else. This relationship between the sign as a physical, visible phenomenon and that to which it refers makes 'meaning'. Thus, a sign consists of two elements: a 'signifier', the form of the sign (e.g., a uniform, a gesture, or particular behaviours), and a 'signified', that to which the signifier refers.

The relationship between signifier and signified is mostly arbitrary, and based on social conventions. For instance, there is no inherent reason to link a handshake to politeness in a particular social situation. This makes it difficult to decipher the meaning of behaviours in a culture that is different from one's own. This difficulty is increased by the fact that cultures are not sets of isolated signs, but systems of signification. This means that any signifier–signified relationship should not be seen separately, but in the light of the other signs that together make up the culture. In a semiotic view social behaviour is a function of the interpretation of a situation in terms of making the link between signifier and signified. Members of a social group 'will act similarly, to the degree that they share the same codes for imputing meaning to the world' (Barley, 1983: 398). An outsider will not be able to make the connection between outwardly arbitrary acts and the meaning that these refer to, and hence cannot interpret these correctly and select the right response.

To make things yet worse, it would be a mistake to think that cultures as systems of signifier–signified relations are fully integrated, seamless wholes (Geertz, 1973: 80). The meaning systems of cultures are often internally inconsistent, contain contradictions and leave open gaps. In such cases the correct behaviours are often even for an insider unclear or contested, making it even harder for an outsider to understand what is going on. One could even wonder how it is possible at all to understand an alien culture. The philosophical and methodological perspective that considers this question is hermeneutics.

Hermeneutics

Above, we have put forth that the difference between etic and emic studies of culture is to some extent a difference between methods, but underlying this difference there is a more fundamental distinction, viz., that between models of scientific explanation. On the one hand there is the tradition of logical empiricism. In this approach valid scientific knowledge is based on statements that are logically true and empirically falsifiable. Science progresses through the empirical cycle. On the basis of earlier studies and logical inferences hypotheses are developed. These hypotheses are subsequently confronted with data, and if they are not refuted they are provisionally accepted as true, and as a contribution to the slowly accumulating body of scientific knowledge.

A good example of this approach in etic culture studies is the work of Shalom Schwartz, discussed in Chapter 2. Schwartz, on the basis of prior work on human values, hypothesized three interrelated bipolar dimensions of culture, designed a questionnaire instrument for measuring these bipolar dimensions, collected data, and was able to empirically reproduce the hypothesized structure of relationships between cultural values (Schwartz, 2008).

Dissatisfaction with this approach in the humanities and biblical studies led to the development of hermeneutics as an alternative to logical empiricism.[1] In the arts, but also in history, the aim is not so much to uncover empirical regularities, as to understand the mindset from which works of art or historical acts were produced. Hence, just like in the semiotic approach to culture discussed in the previous section, the aim is to understand what the creators of the work of art or the historical act 'were up to', the meaning it had to them. The completely objectified, external view of logical empiricism does not lead to this outcome. Instead, the researcher needs to put him- or herself in the shoes of the creator of the phenomenon studied, and imagine the mindset or motivation that could have led to its creation. This is the act of interpretation. The interpretive approach of hermeneutics is applicable to all phenomena that are products of the human mind, so also culture, which in the semiotic perspective consists of socially constructed human systems of meaning.

> Hermeneutics (from the Greek hermeneuein, to explain, to put in words, or translate) refers to the interpretation of phenomena as signs. Interpretation is an act of understanding in which phenomena are taken to be signs referring to a meaning. We try to integrate the signs we aim to interpret into the more or less coherent system of signs that forms our worldview.
>
> (Noorderhaven, 2004: 85)

As an alternative to the empirical cycle of logical empiricism, hermeneutics proposes the hermeneutical circle. In a hermeneutic study of culture the interpreter starts with trying to understand single elements of the culture studied, and on the basis of that gradually constructs an understanding of the culture as a whole. This understanding of the whole is subsequently used to grasp the meaning of other elements, and movement around this circle continues until there is complete understanding.

> Thus the movement of understanding is constantly from the whole to the part and back to the whole. Our task is to expand the unity of the understood meaning centrifugally. The harmony of all the details with the whole is the criterion of correct understanding. The failure to achieve this harmony means that understanding has failed.
>
> (Gadamer, 1999: 291)

Note in the quote above the strong emphasis on harmony, or integration, between all elements of a culture. It is a matter of debate in how far this is tenable in the study of culture. Cultures, as we have stressed above, are often characterized by gaps and contradictions. These would lead to a failure to achieve complete harmony in our understanding between at least some of the elements of a culture and the mental picture of the whole. However, this should then not be seen as a failure of understanding, but rather as an adequate grasp of the tensions and contradictions that characterize a culture at a given point in time. Cultures change, e.g., because of changing living conditions, and are confronted with other cultures through migration and trade. As a matter of fact, instances when different cultural systems clash are especially informative, as then there is a clash of meanings that will bring the taken-for-granted out in the open, both for the inhabitants of the cultures concerned and for the researcher. Hence, although '[c]ultural systems must have a minimal degree of coherence, else we would not call them systems . . . [t]he force of our interpretation cannot rest . . . on the tightness with which they hold together' (Geertz, 1973: 17–18).

In the hermeneutic perspective, understanding products of the human mind that are removed from the interpreter in time, place, or both, is problematic but ultimately possible provided that interpreter and interpreted share some common ground. This can be the case if interpreter and interpreted are joined 'in the depths of tradition' (Gadamer, 1999: 306), i.e., there is understanding based on some degree of cultural overlap or similarity. This would be precarious if one tries to understand a culture that is radically different from one's own. But even then the members of that culture and the researcher share some common ground in that they are all human. Some human traits, like basic emotions, are universal and hence can be understood also across barriers not yet removed. But naturally understanding a culture that is less distant to one's own is overall easier (although the apparent lack of distance may blind one for the more subtle differences that are present).

The hermeneutical procedure for reaching understanding is the dialogue. This can be a 'real' dialogue, between two individuals exchanging ideas. However, in hermeneutics the concept of dialogue is also used when a researcher tries to understand for instance a book. In this case a 'dialogue' takes place between the expectations or early understandings of the reader and the information that becomes available while the book is studied more in depth. The book 'answers' as it were to the queries of the reader, and when there is harmony between the gradually adapting expectations of the reader and every piece of new information dug up from the text, understanding has been reached.

As mentioned, the first engagement with the object to be understood, whether this is a book or a foreign culture, always starts from some expectation or pre-understanding. The hermeneutic philosopher Hans-Georg Gadamer uses the word 'prejudice', but not in the conventional pejorative sense. Such prejudices are in his view necessary pre-judgments without which the hermeneutic circle could not be entered. In the study of cultures such prejudices are akin to the cultural stereotypes that we have discussed in Chapter 2. Stereotypes may contain a kernel of truth (or not), but they have to be put at play in a dialogue for the interpreter to move beyond them and come to a more genuine understanding of the foreign culture. Otherwise, prejudices work as blinders, rather than enablers of understanding. Thus the hermeneutical dialogue requires the willingness to put one's priors and beliefs at risk. If successful, this dialogue leads to a 'fusion of horizons', in that the original worldview of the researcher has been broadened to also encompass the possible meanings of the culture studied. This does not mean 'going native', i.e., buying into the culture studied and adopting its meanings, but rather to acquire the understanding that such meanings, sometimes radically different from those of one's own culture, are in fact possible and even comprehensible.

Case: The Régie Nationale des Eaux du Togo

The Régie Nationale des Eaux du Togo is the national water company of the West African country Togo. Henry (1991) describes how in this company there is a manual of procedures, the Handbook. This book stipulates in the smallest detail the tasks and activities of every employee and in every situation, from the most junior clerk up to the general director. Of course, the job of the lower ranks is described in more detail that those of management. But at all levels the level of detail of the book and the striving for completeness is striking. The book specifies technical tasks as well as management tasks, work processes, prayer times, and rules for leave of work in case of family circumstances. One procedure, procedure 401, even stipulates how the yearly company party needs to be organized:

Procedure 401

(1): The manager of the Social Affairs section is responsible for organizing the party.
(2): He designs the program, selects date and time, and proposes these to the General Manager for approval.
(3): He sees to it that a party tent is erected.
(4): He sees to it that chairs are rented.
(5): He sees to it that tables are set.

(6): He determines the seating order: management, supervisors, and operators.
(7): He chooses the menu.
(8): He selects the presents for the retirees.
(9): He takes care for the music to enliven the party.
(10): He selects a photographer.
(11): He composes a party album.

This overshot codification of task may remind the Western reader of the worst excesses of Taylorism, leading to a complete loss of freedom for workers. Ultimately such a system is believed to lead to alienation and loss of job motivation. However, in a book on African management published by the World Bank (Dia, 1996) the Régie Nationale is mentioned as an example of best practice in Africa. Paradoxically, the handbook increases, rather than unduly restricts, the employees' capacity to act. It frees them of arbitrariness of superiors and allows them to act, also if the boss is not present to make decisions. It also shelters employees from demands from relatives and acquaintances for special treatment. Henry quotes a manager from the Régie who says:

'It rather pleases them [the subordinates] to read this document. It tells each worker that he is taken seriously. If he sees himself in the book he feels more important: "I am the employee, I am the supervisor mentioned". So that makes them feel more important. In my view it motivates them' (Henry, 1991: 455; our translation from French).

Methodological issues

Above, we discussed some aspects of the emic approach to cultures. As we have seen, because this approach focuses on the meanings ascribed to behaviours by members of a culture, rather than the direction and strength of values, it does not fit well with the questionnaire survey method often embraced by etic studies. In this section we will discuss the ethnographic method mostly adopted by emic culture studies.

Ethnography is a 'naturalistic mode of inquiry' (Sharpe, 2004: 307), indicating that unnatural forms of behaviour, like responding to a questionnaire, or even answering questions in a formal interview, are to be avoided. Instead, less obtrusive data collection methods such as (participant and non-participant) observation and informal conversations are privileged in ethnography. Ethnographic studies aim to be holistic, i.e., they have as their goal to describe all relevant aspects of a cultural system, including, e.g., religion, economy, family life, etc. The ambition to be holistic is balanced by the tendency to focus on relatively small, demarcated areas, like a village. Traditionally ethnographers have particularly sought to study small communities that have been subject to no or minimal outside influences, in particular influences from the industrialized West.

Ethnography employed in emic culture studies in the service of international comparative management is relatively rare, and meets its own specific problems. One particular problem pertains to acquiring access.[2] Traditional ethnographers typically studied a small-scale society, and access was not a problem (villagers were commonly not asked for permission to be studied). If the object of study is an internationally operating firm, access does pose problems. Many business firms are not eager to be the object of an emic study, for two reasons. First, such a study occupies the scarce time of managers and employees. Second, business firms operate in competitive markets and have many stakeholders, and the outcomes of an in-depth study might give away strategic information to competitors, or damage the reputation of the firm with important stakeholder groups.

Secondly, the outcomes of an emic study of a firm may be influenced by the identity of the researcher. Every researcher has a number of characteristics, like age or gender, that are likely to influence how members of the organization studied perceive him or her, the extent to which they will open up and the veracity of their answers. This is of course not different from the situation in traditional ethnographies, but typically this potential source of bias is neglected. But since an emic study follows procedures in which many decisions are taken implicitly by the researcher (e.g., where to look, what observations to regard as meaningful enough to give special attention, and who to select as key informants – see below) it is never certain that another researcher studying the same object would come up with the same observations and explanations. A certain degree of subjectivism is inevitable, and this is also the case in etic studies. Only there the subjectivism, pertaining to, e.g., the selection of questionnaire items, is more easily lost sight of because the findings are 'objectified into statistics' (Chapman, Gajewska-De Mattos and Antoniou, 2004: 290).

Particularly in internationally operating organizations, there is another very important aspect of the researcher: his or her nationality. If, in a study of a multinational company, the researcher is of the same nationality as the company's headquarters, employees of subsidiaries abroad may see him or her as a spy. With nationality often also come language abilities. Traditionally, emic researchers take pride in learning the local language, not only to be able to converse with the people studied without the need for an interpreter, but also because the structure of the language is seen as intimately linked to the system of meaning that constitutes the culture. For such a study total immersion is important, and learning a language may take a year or more, making the research very time consuming. Against that background, the practice of conducting international management research in English is understandable, but all the same the possible biases that are introduced in this manner should be faced up to.

Another issue that may introduce bias to ethnographic studies is the selection of key informants. These are rarely randomly drawn from the population. In order to obtain deep access to the organization studied, the emic researcher needs one or more 'friends', organization members who are positively inclined to the researcher and the study. This is a necessary condition, but there is a real danger that the researcher will buy into the views of this 'friend', a danger that becomes bigger if this individual is also involved in the selection of other informants. Again, this potential problem is unavoidable, but it is important that both the researcher and the readers of his or her study are aware of this.

Finally, there is the issue of disclosure. If an emic researcher studies a village or another type of small-scale society there are normally no impediments against publishing the results, but the researcher studying a company from the inside almost always has to strike a deal that includes some restrictions regarding publication. This often leads to one of two compromises: either the results are published with the company's name, but any observations that are deemed to be damaging to the firm's reputation or too revealing to competitors are left out, or the study is made anonymous. In the latter case the researcher has more degrees of freedom (although the company may still put restrictions to publication), but for the reader the findings become somewhat less meaningful and the validity of the study becomes less transparent.

3.3 D'Iribarne: Three logics of culture

In this section we will demonstrate how emic research can contribute to our understanding of international comparative management issues by discussing the work of the French researcher Philippe d'Iribarne, in particular his main work, La Logique de l'Honneur (d'Iribarne, 1989). In defining culture, d'Iribarne (1994) explicitly refers to Geertz: culture for him is essentially a system of references that enables actors to make sense of both the world in which they live and of their own actions.

D'Iribarne calls for an idiographic approach, using ethnographic methodology. Although d'Iribarne gives little detail of his preferred methodology in the book, most elements are clear from some of his other publications (especially d'Iribarne, 1994). In the preface to his book *La Logique de l'Honneur* (1989) d'Iribarne states that he could not be satisfied with the superficial view that would arise from surveys and some interviews with top managers. Instead he chose to concentrate on a very restricted research object: one single plant of an internationally operating company in each of three different countries (France, the USA and the Netherlands). In these plants, direct observations were combined with documents reflecting daily life and with open interviews (d'Iribarne, 1994: 82). These plant-level data were coupled with multiple data sources concerning the countries in which these plants were located. In d'Iribarne's view, it is the political history and culture of a country, and the way in which differences in power are created, maintained and dealt with, that is illuminating (d'Iribarne, 2000).

When looking at descriptions of the political system in a country and its historical developments, the observations at plant level started to resonate with country-level sources about the ways in which individuals relate to collectivities, in which good can be distinguished from bad, legitimate from illegitimate, what is respectable from what is not respectable or what is indifferent (d'Iribarne, 1989: 11–12). In this way the logic governing the phenomena, both at the micro level and at the level of the society, was uncovered. In essence, d'Iribarne's study was a quest for meaning:

> I have made an effort, in each of the localities, to understand the behaviours that could be observed, sometimes odd to the stranger's eye, starting from what gave them meaning to those who adopted those behaviours.
>
> (1989: 14; our translation from French)

This method of trying to comprehend the meaning attributed to behaviour by local actors, in d'Iribarne's view, leads to 'a more certain and precise understanding of the societies under investigation [even if] it does not give the same impression of objectivity' (1996–97: 46). We will now examine d'Iribarne's findings concerning the cultural logics of France, the USA and the Netherlands.

The logics of honour, contract and consensus

In his principal book, Philippe d'Iribarne (d'Iribarne, 1989; summarized briefly in d'Iribarne, 1996–97) reports on a study of three aluminium production units of the French company Péchiney in France, the USA and the Netherlands. The plants were selected to employ the same technology, so that they would be comparable with regard to the main contingency factors. Nevertheless, marked differences between the 'collective lives' within the three plants are noticeable.

France

In France, d'Iribarne observes that the various professional groups are attached to the privileges determined by the particular traditions of each group. These traditions define what individual members of an occupational group should do, and also what they cannot stoop to. The interesting thing is that this definition of what one should and should not do is completely independent from instructions or orders from superiors. Professional pride does not allow an employee to bow to pressure from above, if this goes against the honour of his or her professional group. This emphasis on pride and honour is connected by d'Iribarne to Montesquieu's analysis of French society in the eighteenth century. The influence sphere of each professional group in the organization, from top to bottom, should be respected if managers want to avoid revolt or deceit.

It would be degrading to be 'in the service of' (*au service de*) anybody, in particular, of one's superiors. By contrast, it is honorable to devote oneself to a cause, or to 'give service' (*rendre service*) with magnanimity, at least if one is asked to do so with due ceremony. Under these circumstances, the realization of hierarchical relationships requires a great deal of tact and judgment (1996–97: 32).

D'Iribarne observes large distances between different groups in the French aluminium plant studied. Within and between these groups, like the production workers, the technicians and the managers, different forms of authority apply. The effectiveness of an authority relationship hinges on the honour with which a subordinate can follow instructions. One basis for authority is superior applicable knowledge. In the maintenance department, d'Iribarne observes that the authority of more experienced technicians, with more knowledge, is easily accepted by their subordinates. It is legitimate, and hence not dishonorable, to yield to this type of authority. The authority relation is akin to that between a master and a journeyman in a guild.

Another type of legitimate authority in the French plant studied by d'Iribarne is based on membership of an elite. Higher management is typically trained at one of the Grandes Ecoles. The education they have received there is mostly not applicable in day-to-day practice.

> The young engineers . . . I have often noticed that they were incapable of dealing with a trivial, concrete and ordinary problem. They come with a lot of knowledge, very theoretical and very abstract, no doubt invaluable for their understanding of this or that. I don't want to deny that, but I often got the impression that they were not ready; that they were perplexed to find themselves in the middle of an active life (lower manager).
>
> (1989: 43, our translation from the French)

Nevertheless, these young engineers with all their lack of practical knowledge were accepted as managers – as long as they kept a distance and did not mingle with day-to-day work. Their authority was based on being a graduate from an elite institution, on being elevated in the selective meritocratic system of French top education. Too close supervision of their subordinates, however, would expose their ignorance of practical matters, and thus undermine their authority.

Finally, d'Iribarne also identified a third type of authority relations, but this type was of questionable legitimacy. This is the type of the 'petit chef', the lowest level supervisor who has come up through the ranks of the common workers. The only type of authority such a manager can muster is based on formal position, and this is a dodgy basis. The 'petit chef' is perceived to be the lackey of higher management and a traitor of his own class. As this is not an honorable position, obeying such a person would also be dishonorable. The only way for a 'petit chef' to gain some legitimate authority is to create distance from higher management, to demonstrate that he is *not* a lackey of higher management.

All three types of authority relations demonstrate the discrepancy between power and authority in the French situation, discussed in Section 3.1. The 'petit chef' has formal authority, but little power as this authority is not accepted as legitimate by his subordinates. The highly trained technician has legitimate authority based on elite membership, but little actual power because of a lack of practical knowledge. The authority of the experienced technicians *is* linked to some degree of power, but this power is restricted because ultimately the technician and his subordinates belong to the same group, and the less experienced and knowledgeable members of this group are constantly working to make the gap smaller. Personal relations are in France important to bridge the considerable distances between different groups and layers within the company. A French manager can make someone in a lower position do something that he would normally not regard to be commensurate with his task, by appealing to such a personal relationship. It is acceptable to do something for a specific other, from one's own free will and as a friendly service, which one wouldn't stoop to do if it were an obligation (d'Iribarne, 1989: 107).

USA

In the USA a different logic prevails: the logic of the contract, freely entered into by equals. According to d'Iribarne in the US culture, an organization is seen as 'an interlocking set of contractual relationships', and 'great importance is attached to the decentralization of decision making, to the definition of objectives, and to the rigor of evaluation' (d'Iribarne, 1996–97: 31). The link between the individual employee and the organization, as well as that between the subordinate and the superior, is an agreement specifying what the parties may expect of each other. The employee may expect to be evaluated against explicit criteria that are well known in advance; there should be no room for subjective opinions or feelings from the side of the superior. Hence, on one hand the American manager has more degrees of freedom than his or her French counterpart, as he or she is considered free to set the goals for the employee (who in turn is free to accept or reject these goals, and face the consequences of either option). However, once the superior and subordinate agree on a set of goals, the evaluation criteria the manager can employ are also defined. Explicating the goals against which the subordinate will be evaluated creates a degree of protection for the subordinate who otherwise is vulnerable to much more drastic consequences (including dismissal) than his or her counterpart in France. The discretion of an American supervisor is restricted because he can only make a difference between subordinates if there are objective data showing that one performed better than another, if not, there is always the possibility a grievance is raised. Subordinates also cannot be evaluated against goals that have not explicitly been agreed upon beforehand.

The fact that the contract between supervisor and subordinate specifies the goals that the latter is expected to realize also implies that the way in which these goals are to be reached is largely left to the discretion of the subordinates:

> Our crew is our team, we have to make sure the work gets done. We know what the goals are, and how to best reach them; As long as we stay within certain boundaries I am sure that my manager and the department chief don't care (supervisor).
>
> (d'Iribarne, 1989: 138)

The resulting style of management and organization is linked by d'Iribarne to Tocqueville's description of the 'democratic' relationships between masters and servants in nineteenth-century America. This relationship was fundamentally one between equals, as who was servant at a given point in time could become master, and both parties knew and accepted this. This 'from rags to riches' mythology continues to play an important role in the American mind. Given this view of labour relations as contractual deals between equals, 'selling' one's labour for a salary is perfectly acceptable and does not have the negative connotation it has in France (1989: 131). The image of the relationship between customer and supplier was often used in the interviews: 'that's what they are paid for', and 'that's what I pay them for' (1989: 164).

Hierarchical relations between individuals, based on such contractual agreements, also are not considered problematic in the USA. Whereas in France, face-to-face hierarchical relationships are avoided by making them impersonal through rules and bureaucracy, d'Iribarne notes that in the USA everybody works for a superior. In interviews the phrases 'he works for me' and 'I work for him' returned time and again (1989: 135). One can obey without abasing oneself, because the fundamental equality of everyone is clear (1989: 175–177). This is an example of how a particular type of behaviour can have a very different meaning in one culture than in another.

Relationships between different groups in the plant in the USA were much less problematic than in France. This is true for both vertical and horizontal relationships. For understanding these relationships it is important to note that the notion of freedom, i.e., each party is assumed to enter into a contract on the basis of his or her own free will, is supplemented by an assumption of fairness (1989: 159–160). Fairness plays an important role in two ways. First of all, abuse of a situation of dependence leading to a contract that would be so one-sided that the dignity of and respect for one of the parties would be lost should be avoided. Secondly, contracts are never completely specified, so there are always contingencies that have not been foreseen. In such cases there should be a fair interpretation of the terms of the contract. D'Iribarne notes that freedom and fairness are difficult to reconcile in the practice of American management. Fairness, and the importance of maintaining the other's dignity, also make it mandatory for managers to show interest in the activities of the subordinate. Here we see another example of how an identical act may be interpreted radically different in different cultures: as a sign of suspicion in France, as a sign of genuine concern in the USA.

The Netherlands

In the plant in the Netherlands, d'Iribarne identified yet another cultural logic. Here there were no sharp divisions between occupational groups, each with their own traditions and pride, nor was there strict adherence to agreements. Instead, what struck d'Iribarne was the process of discussion and argument necessary to settle disputes, which were reopened as soon as the conditions of the environment changed. The use of discussion and argumentation, on the basis of factual information, was prevalent both between equals and between superiors and subordinates. To be a manager in Holland means to be a master of argument and persuasion, as the use of severe sanctions is not acceptable. Overt, or even covert, pressure is to be avoided. D'Iribarne's view of Dutch work organizations corresponds very well to what is found in a number of Dutch sources (summarized in Noorderhaven, 2002).

A central position is taken by the concept of consensus. Effective organization in the Netherlands is based on a consensus between all involved. This means that there is also pressure to reach such consensus. This pressure, according to d'Iribarne, is not hard and overt insistence, but a process in which the opinions of those concerned gradually mutually adapt and become aligned (d'Iribarne, 1989: 211). All this takes a lot of communication, because although the Dutch are oversensitive to pressure, they are open to good arguments. Arguments need to be based on or supported by objective facts. Without facts an opinion cannot be maintained: 'at the Dutch side we occasionally sensed a certain level of astonishment about the French capacity of sticking to one's arguments without good grounds' (d'Iribarne, 1989: 217).

The pressure to reach consensus has its good and bad sides. On one hand, unwillingness to engage in consultations (even if these may seem pointless) is frowned upon. Attitudes and behaviours that are seen as detrimental to the consensus are also not appreciated. Differences (e.g., in levels of knowledge, or in opinions) are frequently glossed over, or simply denied. On the other hand, there is no taboo against voicing difference of opinion, as long as this is done in a non-emotional tone, and if accompanied by the willingness to compromise (see also Noorderhaven, Benders and Keizer, 2007). As a result, d'Iribarne notices that from a French perspective the Dutch style is a strange combination of extreme individualism and herd behaviour, of radical independence and subjugation to the group (1989: 208). Nevertheless, a French department head also indicates that he is amazed by the willingness to cooperate that seems to form the basis of all attitudes and behaviours. If the necessity of a change is explained, people are willing to accommodate. 'I'm actually perplexed by the goodwill among the people' (French department head) (d'Iribarne, 1989: 217).

The Dutch style of consensus management is linked by d'Iribarne to the political history of the Netherlands. The origin of Dutch institutions lies in the association of provinces in the Union of Utrecht (1579). In the delicate balance of power between the provinces, lengthy processes of persuasion and mutual accommodation were necessary to reach decisions. Also in more recent times, the cohabitation of the different religious groups (mainly the Protestants and the Catholics) was regulated through the same mechanisms (d'Iribarne, 1996–97: 33). In the United Provinces more freedom of religion and freedom of press existed than in other European countries. In fact, freedom of religion was almost dogmatic for the new Dutch republic (having asserted itself against the Spanish inquisition), and this became a cornerstone of the Dutch political culture and institutions. In dealing with different groups in the society ideological oppositions were taken as immutable givens (d'Iribarne, 1989: 225).

Consequently, Dutch consensus at the societal level is based on a compromise between factions that do not alter their own convictions and principles. More recently the word 'poldermodel' has been coined to refer to this type of societal consensus. The word refers to the polders in the Netherlands, which are protected by dikes. Constructing and maintaining these dikes required joint efforts, obliging representatives of various factions and parties to reach and maintain a general agreement (Noorderhaven et al., 2007). Becker (2001: 471) describes the Dutch culture as one in which 'talking to each other and looking for common solutions is ingrained in everyday life'.

Within the Dutch plant studied by d'Iribarne this was also the case. At the same time, there were observations that seemed to go in the opposite direction. According to a supervisor: 'I have the impression that if one department develops a certain idea, this is a good reason for the others absolutely not to do the same, but something different' (d'Iribarne, 1989: 209). Apparently there is no specific consensus covering the whole plant, in spite of the overall willingness to cooperate noted above. D'Iribarne, although generally positive about the effects of consensus, nevertheless sees this as a mechanism for covering up (rather than resolving) tensions. Hence, anxieties can continue to increase, and according to d'Iribarne are one cause of the high absenteeism and personnel turnover in the Netherlands (1989: 240).

Other observations pertain to a much weaker readiness to be appraised and rewarded (or sanctioned) based on one's individual performance than in the USA. As a matter of fact, many interviewees mentioned the practical impossibility to sanction or dismiss a worker. Generally, individual responsibility if anything went wrong was denied.

> If in [the plant in the USA] there is material damage because of an incident, the maintenance service will only come after a report has been made, who was responsible. They always note who caused the incident and he can be held liable for the mistake. Only after that the repair is done. We have tried to introduce that here, we didn't bring it about (maintenance supervisor)
>
> (d'Iribarne, 1989: 210–211, our translation)

In general there was little respect from subordinates for supervisors or managers in the Dutch plant. Symbolic markers of differences in hierarchy were all but absent. On the other hand, middle management did expect its area of authority to be respected by higher management, a higher manager could not bypass intermediate levels and directly mingle in the work at lower levels. In contrast to what was observed at the French plant, in the Netherlands it was no problem if a production worker was promoted to a supervisory position, such a person's authority would be accepted by his or her former colleagues. A further difference between the Netherlands and France pertains to the role played by emotions. In France a fierce discussion, in which the participants don't hesitate to show their anger, is part of the game (d'Iribarne, 1989: 32). In the Netherlands open display of emotions in work situations is avoided, maybe because this would endanger the consensus.

3.4 Indigenous management practices

D'Iribarne's work on France, the USA and the Netherlands is explicitly comparative, and as such relatively rare in the emic literature. In contrast to this scarcity, there is quite some literature describing particularities of business cultures in different countries in the world. In this section we will very briefly describe some of the specific characteristics of Japan, sub-Saharan Africa and China. Japan is an example of a well-studied society that is markedly different from the West; sub-Saharan Africa is a complex continent that has received far less attention, and serves as an example of how postcolonial conditions have to be taken into account; and China finally shows how an emic perspective can sometimes have to do not only, and maybe even not primarily, with specific fixed emic cultural elements, but more with the dynamic relations between these.

These descriptions of emic elements only serve the purpose of illustration, and are by no way representative of the cultures described. However, they do show that every culture, when looked at in more detail, contains specific elements that are relevant for doing business, and not (sufficiently) captured by the general dimensions identified in etic research.

Japan

The Japanese business culture was one of the first non-Western cultures to be studied by Western researchers. The reason for this were the astonishing economic achievements of the Japanese economy after World War II and the successes of Japanese companies in important world markets like that for automobiles and electronics. This success suggested that other countries could learn from the Japanese approach, and the system of management and organization was seen as one of the keys to understand the Japanese revival (Pascale and Athos, 1981). We will at this place not describe the main 'pillars' of the Japanese management system, like lifetime employment, the seniority system, enterprise unions, just-in-time production, etc. (see, for instance, Aoki and Dore, 1994). Instead we will focus on two emic cultural aspects that seem to be essential for the functioning of the Japanese system: consensus and *amae* ('indulgent dependency').

Consensus

One of the characteristics of management and organization in Japan that strikes many observers is the absence of clearly visible decisions and decision makers. Looking at the Japanese political system, Van Wolferen (1990) spoke about 'the enigma of Japanese power': decisions are made, and the country and its political system do function, but it is often almost impossible to determine who has taken what decision, and when. Many decisions effectively are 'faceless', not only in Japanese politics, but also in the business world. This phenomenon, we think, is caused by the strong preference in the Japanese society for consensus.[3] This preference is signified by the concept of *wa*, referring to 'the avoidance of wanton opposition and the importance of building cooperative, benevolent, and trusting relationships' (Hill, 1995: 124). Striving for *wa* implies that where necessary individual interests are sacrificed if the preservation of group harmony demands this. Conflicts, and even discussions in which differences of opinion are voiced, are a threat to *wa*, and will be avoided if possible. So in Japan it is not only important that the outcomes of decisions are supported by all concerned, but also that the process leading to these decisions does not lead to a loss of harmony. In Japanese organizations two consensus procedures are followed that meet these demands, the informal process of *nemawashi*, and the more formal *ringiseido* process.

The literal translation of *nemawashi* refers to the method of transplanting a tree by first cutting the roots of the tree circumferentially 1 or 2 years before. *Ne* means root, *mawashi* means to go around. The procedure stimulates the tree to form new hair roots, which allows it to survive after the transplantation. In the context of organizational decision making *nemawashi* refers to a process in which affected parties are cautiously sounded and consulted, and in which negotiations are held behind the scenes and not in open fora. Importantly, the *nemawashi* process involves the different parties bilaterally, and in a sequential fashion. This means that any differences of opinion can be addressed in closed meetings, avoiding confrontations in the open that could lead to a loss of face of someone concerned, and a threat to group harmony.

Ringiseido is a more bureaucratic, formalized version of *nemawashi*. In the *ringi* system a formal document (*ringi*) is circulated among all the relevant organization members, often heads of departments. Recipients indicate their approval of the proposal in the document by affixing their *hanko*, personal seal, on the *ringi*. In some cases, the *hanko* is placed upside-down, to indicate rejection, or sideways, to indicate indifference. This does not really alter the process, however, as *ringiseido* is more a procedure to make sure that all parties affected are informed, than to give them a say in the decision. Hence *ringiseido* can be seen as a ritualized process that is not necessarily associated with 'real' consensus. Sometimes the same is said of *nemawashi*, which is seen by some as a masquerade in which hierarchical top-down decision making is dressed up as a consultative consensus process (Kiritani, 1999).

However, this does not do justice to what *nemawashi* means to many organization members in Japanese companies. For the Japanese the consensus reached through *nemawashi* helps avoiding risks, both to the decision maker (because ultimately, there *is* no individual decision) and to the company (because all the information from all those involved has been taken into account). What makes the *nemawashi* process hard to assess for a foreign observer is that in Japan a strong sense of harmony goes hand in hand with strong sense of hierarchy (Ala and Cordeiro, 2000). Superficially the decision may appear to be taken unilaterally by higher managers, but the prolonged groundwork that precedes this final formal decision easily escapes attention.

Amae

Whereas Japanese consensus has both vertical and horizontal aspects, the second emic element that we discuss pertains exclusively to hierarchical relations. As mentioned above, there is a strong sense of hierarchy in Japan. But, like in France, we need to look closer to fully understand what hierarchical relations in Japan mean, and what the implications for power relations really are.

According to Doi (2001) the parent–child relation is the paradigmatic relation after which all other unequal relations are modelled. Doi assumes that subsequent Japanese social bonding, between student and teacher or subordinate and supervisor, is patterned after the primary mother–child experience (Smith and Nomi, 2000: 2). The key to understanding these relations is the concept of *amae*. *Amae* is an indigenous Japanese concept of relatedness (Behrens, 2004: 1) which cannot easily be translated in English, but has been described as 'indulgent dependency' (Smith and Nomi, 2000: 1). One of the problems of understanding an emic concept like *amae* is that approximations in other languages often have (in the case of *amae*) negative connotations that differ from the meaning as perceived by the Japanese.

> Amae has been variously translated into English as playful and babyish behaviour . . ., as whining, sulking, and being spoiled or pampered . . ., and as the British slang word 'mardy'. . . . These English translations, however, have negative connotations that miss its usually positive meaning in Japanese.
>
> (Marshall, Chuong and Aikawa, 2011: 26)

Amae implies that a person who is in a superior position of authority or power, will accept behaviour from a subordinate that is normally seen as inappropriate if his or her relation with the subordinate is close. Understanding this is essential for understanding Japanese hierarchy, because it means that the power of the superior is restricted because of the *amae* that is expected in his or her relationship with (close) subordinates. This also makes clear why after-office-hours drinking parties are important in which members of a section, together with their superior, get drunk. This helps to forge the close social bonds that make the hierarchy function with *amae*, and hence be tolerable.

According to Yoshino and Lifson (1986) a Japanese group, in order to be meaningful, must offer relationships infused with *amae*, and hence must also be vertically structured. Only such groups will receive commitment and identification from their members. It requires from the superior the capability 'to read feelings and to provide carefully balanced doses of support in situations where it is needed' (1986: 180). The contrast with the honourable authority relations d'Iribarne (1989) identified in the French plant he studied is striking.

Africa

Whereas management in Japan and its relation to indigenous cultural characteristics has been studied intensively, management and culture in Africa has only recently begun to receive attention from researchers. Hence, describing management and organization, whether from an etic or an emic perspective, is difficult because of a dire lack of data. The Japanese case is also easier because this country is culturally homogeneous, compared to many other countries. In the case of Africa (even if we restrict ourselves to sub-Saharan Africa, taking the marked differences with the civilizations of North Africa into consideration) we look at a continent with thousands of different languages and ethnic groups. Descriptions of African management and organization consequently tend to start with pointing at the diversity on the continent (to go on and talk about 'African' management all the same, e.g., Ahiauzu, 1986). Notwithstanding these complications, we will briefly describe some emic aspects of African management, as the case of sub-Sahara Africa is an interesting example of hybridization, in this case because of the colonial and post-colonial Western influences.

Nkomo (2011) distinguishes between studies of African management from a Western perspective and writings on indigenous African management.

> the dominant portrayal of 'African' leadership and management in the mainstream literature is one of deficiency rooted in essentialist racial and colonial stereotypes of Africa. On the other hand, the counter narratives . . . often evoke a unique 'African' identity also predicated on essentialism and a recovery of the grandeur of pre-colonial Africa.
>
> (Nkomo, 2011: 370)

Literature that looks at African management and culture from a Western perspective tends to characterize it in a negative way. African leadership, displaying authoritarianism, favouritism and corruption would be an important cause for the underdevelopment of the continent. Jackson (2012: 15) notes that literature on management in developing countries in general, and on management in Africa in particular, 'presents a picture which sees management in these countries as fatalistic, resistant to change, reactive, short-termist, authoritarian, risk-reducing, context dependent, and basing decisions on relationship criteria, rather than universalistic criteria. Such a bleak view of African management is also bolstered by outcomes of etic cross-cultural studies that typically find the few African societies included to score high on power distance and collectivism (e.g., Hofstede, 2001). The cure would be management development, presumably based on received Western management theory. It must be said that much of this literature is based on very thin empirical evidence, mostly just a few countries that somehow are deemed to be representative for the continent. In contrast, in a larger study of fifteen sub-Saharan African countries Jackson (2004) found it difficult to identify a typical 'African' organization.

Even leaving the weak empirical basis for what it is, two additional questions may be asked. Firstly, is the approach to management and organization found in Africa indigenous, in that it is aligned with cultural values of the people? Secondly, is it possible to gauge African culture and management with purely Western measures? Looking at the first question the colonial history of the African continent needs to be taken into account. Colonization and subsequent decolonization 'forced Africans to become actors on a stage they had not set' (Nzelibe, 1986: 10). The British colonial power installed indirect rule, giving some leeway to local chiefs to rule within the confines set by the usurpers. In many regions these chiefs belonged to one particular ethnic group, raising the position of this group vis-à-vis other indigenous groups. This practice stirred up animosity between ethnic groups, which may partly explain favouritism in present-day organizations. In the French colonial system there was a stronger direct hierarchy, in which local bureaucrats trained in French elite institutions played an important role. These local bureaucrats could reach a certain position only at the price of giving up their own culture in favour of that of the colonial power (Richmond and Gestrin, 1998).

As a result, organizations in modern Africa can be seen as 'colonial impositions', not corresponding to indigenous values, and Jackson (2012: 2901) notes that a number of his respondents declared that 'when going to work in the morning they stepped out of their culture, when going back home in the evening they stepped back inside their culture'. According to postcolonial theory the situation is aggravated by the fact that Western representations of non-Western cultures do not only colour how observers from the West see Africa, but also how Africans see themselves, as these representations have been adopted and internalized by the colonized (Said, 1978). This leads to both excess supply of and demand for Western management education and techniques, without much regard to the extent to which these fit local values (Jackson, 2012).

As a reaction to this Western domination, both politically and mentally, a search for indigenous African management philosophy has started. The most consistent observation is that in such a philosophy a sense of community must have a central position. Richmond and Gestrin (1998: 1) in this context cite a Zulu proverb: 'a person is not a person without other people'. An indigenous concept that has been coined to encapsulate this sense of community is *ubuntu*. Although the origins of *ubuntu* are uncertain, it is clear that the concept has been made immensely popular in South Africa by a book published in 1995 by Lovemore Mbigi and Jenny Maree: *Ubuntu, The Spirit of African Transformation Management*. The essence of *ubuntu* is the recognition of and embedding in management of the importance of human interdependence and harmony in human relations (Wanasika, Howell, Littrell and Dorfman, 2011). Much of the literature on *ubuntu* propagates and idealizes the concept, without offering much (or indeed, any) empirical evidence. An example is Mangaliso (2001: 24):

> Ununtu can be defined as humaneness – a pervasive spirit of caring and community, harmony and hospitality, respect and responsiveness – that individuals and groups display for one another.

Mangaliso (2001) describes how the spirit of *ubuntu* can be implemented in management and organization, e.g., in communication style, decision making processes, striking a balance between efficiency and solidarity, social well-being and harmony, adherence to seniority, and respect for traditional religions.

However, to the extent that the spirit of *ubuntu* exists, it tends to be restricted to in-group members like kinsmen (Richmond and Gestrin, 1998). Moreover, Jackson, 2004: 62) found 'little evidence to suggest that [*ubuntu*] has been directly sustained in South Africa or is travelling up the continent'. A concept that seems to be more accurately descriptive of African management, albeit not purely indigenous, is paternalism. Paternalism is a management system in which compliance is sought through 'providing some sort of protection or favour, requiring some kind of conformity or even obedience in return' (Jackson et al., 2008: 413). Central to the concept of paternalism is the metaphor of the parent–child relation, which lends an ethical and affective dimension to unequal relationships that without this could be authoritarian and exploitative (Hernandez, 1975). There is little doubt that paternalism fits well with African cultural values, and paternalistic management was a key finding in Jackson et al.'s (2008) study of Kenyan SMEs.

The other key finding of Jackson et al. (2008) was the prevalence of differences in treatment of members of ingroups and outgroups, and this may indicate that the two approaches of African management, the Western pejorative one and the indigenous, apologetic one, both contain a kernel of truth. In positive cases, paternalism may provide a social environment close to what the proponents of *ubuntu* prescribe. According to a manager in one of the SMEs studied by Jackson et al. (2008: 413): 'The company took me as a family member. They are ready to solve my problems.' This manager, however, belonged to the same ethnic group as the owners of the firm, and others in the company said: 'there is no hope in going up in the organization', and 'the company is not doing enough for its workers'. Although the distinction between 'benevolent' and 'exploitative' paternalism is known from the literature (Aycan, 2006), the strong link with ethnicity might very well be something specific to Africa.

China

The third example of emic cultural concepts focuses on China. The growing importance of China in the world economy has led to a rapid increase in research (Kriz, Gummesson and Quazi, 2014), just as was the case with Japan after the Second World War. Whereas the concept of indigenous cultural concepts was complicated in the case of Africa as a result of postcolonial hybridization, China poses a different type of problem to the (Western) researcher. Emic studies of Chinese culture and management have not led to the identification of strikingly novel cultural concepts. Yet according to Tsui (2006) using an etic approach to management in China engenders entails the danger of missing the truly important management or organization issues in the Chinese context.

Jia, You and Du (2012) mention three specifically Chinese concepts: market transition, network capitalism and *guanxi*, and of these the first two are economic institutional conditions rather than cultural concepts. Below we will first discuss the preeminent Chinese management-related cultural concept: *guanxi*, or the use of networks of personal relations in business. After that we will go into what according to some is the most essential characteristic of Chinese culture, and what makes it so elusive to Western cultural studies, viz., the capability of the Chinese mind to combine apparent opposites, symbolized by the *Yin-Yang* philosophy.

Guanxi

In publications on management culture in China, the concept of *guanxi* is hardly ever absent. Although the word *guanxi* is relatively new in the Chinese language, the practice is very old (Kriz et al., 2014). The essence of *guanxi* is the interpersonal, rather than institutional nature of bonds in China. Getting something done in China depends not on the formal order but on who you know, and how that person sees his or her obligation to you (Tian, 2007: 50). The value of personal relations to open doors may be universal, but in the case of China it is of extraordinary importance.

> guanxi can be said to go to the heart of Chinese interpersonal relationships because the key concepts of *guanxi* – *renqing* (favours) and *li shang wang lai* (a favour deserves

> a return favour) – are intertwined as *bao* (harmony), which is the central tenet of Chinese interpersonal relationships
>
> (Kriz et al., 2014: 32)

Whereas we have seen that harmony (*wa*) is strongly connected to group consensus in Japan, in China for preservation of harmony the exigency of fulfilling one's role in personal relations is key. Not every personal relation is equally strong or important, though. Zhang and Zhang (2006: 381) distinguish three concentric layers of *guanxi*: obligatory or familial relations (*qinqing guanxi*), reciprocal relations (*renqing guanxi*) and utilitarian relations (*jiaoyi guanxi*). These types of *guanxi* are obviously of different strength. The weaker the tie, the more quickly a favour should be repaid. In the case of familial relations reciprocity is long-term and non-specific. With utilitarian relations, in contrast, favours must be returned quickly and specifically. Moreover, in these relations one is obliged to both the go-between and to the new tie (Bian, 1997). This indicates that building up a *guanxi* network is a costly (and time consuming) process.

Guanxi brings many benefits to individuals, and through the *guanxi* relations of key managers, also to firms. With the increasing dynamism and uncertainty in the present-day Chinese society, the importance of *guanxi* networks also escalates. They help firms secure necessary inputs and maintain legitimacy. Both horizontal relations, with suppliers, customers and competitors and vertical relations, with government authorities, play a role (Park and Luo, 2001). However, *guanxi* also has its downsides. As mentioned above, building up and maintaining a *guanxi* network consumes time and resources (ibid.). Moreover, the need to rely on established relations for realizing transactions is likely to lead to suboptimal exchange outcomes (Kriz et al., 2014). The partners one is connected to or can reach indirectly through the *guanxi* network are not necessarily the best ones for a given deal. Most seriously, although there is a debate on whether this should be seen as part of the *guanxi* concept, the emphasis on personal relations to get something done can easily slip into corruption in the form of kickbacks or nepotism. Such practices are also referred to as 'the back door' (*zouhoumen*) (Kriz et al., 2014: 33). Use of personal relations is something else than corruption, however, one can give rise to or accommodate the other.

For foreigners doing business in China understanding the concept and practice of *guanxi* clearly is critical. A non-initiated businessman might easily misunderstand the magnitude and nature of the network of obligations he or she enters into, and lose face or make his or her business partners lose face. Knowing the extent to which a relationship is ruled by *guanxi*-based obligations is also necessary to gauge whether strong contractual protection is necessary, or whether a deal can be based on trust.

Yin-Yang

Although the nuances of *guanxi* are difficult to grasp for non-Chinese, a more fundamental problem is that the Chinese culture seems to defy unambiguous characterization. Fang and Faure (2011) use the concepts of *Yin* and *Yang* in this connection. In the Chinese tradition *yin* and *yang* refer to the dual cosmic energies, in which yin stands for female energy and yang for male energy. These are associated with polarities between water and fire, dark and light, and passivity and activity. However, these values or concepts are not simply opposites, but they contain the seeds of each other, and together form a changing unity. Hence, where in Western thought something can be referred to as dark or light, in the *yin-yang* philosophy it can just as well be dark and light. In the same vein old and new cultural values, that often seem contradictory to the outsider, can co-exist in China.

Faure and Fang (2008) describe a number of such paradoxical Chinese values. For instance, these authors acknowledge the importance of *guanxi*, also in modern China, but they also describe how at the same time the emphasis on professional competence is increasing. This means that having *guanxi* is no longer sufficient. A firm or manager who has *guanxi*, but is lacking in abilities, will nevertheless lose out. The other way around, having no *guanxi* is no longer an insurmountable obstacle for young people who want to develop their professional career.

Another paradox discussed by Faure and Fang (2008) is that between preservation of face and directness. The authors note that the concern for keeping face is universal, but that it is particularly salient in the Chinese culture. However, as the economy develops and people become more affluent, the desire for self-expression also becomes stronger (as reflected in Inglehart's work, discussed in Chapter 2). The result is an openness and assertiveness that seems to be difficult to reconcile with face-saving behaviour. However, note that for present-day urban Chinese this is not impossible:

> [they manage] to conjugate two imperatives: face preservation on the one hand and self-expression on the other hand, without opposing them on a unique continuum.
> (Faure and Fang, 2008: 199)

Another striking paradox is that between the traditional collectivist orientation towards the family and modern individualism. Collectivism in China is different from that in Japan, having the family as the target of identification rather than the firm. However, this traditional Chinese type of collectivism, which is linked to a strong respect for one's elders and paternal authority, it's put to the test by an economic realty in which sons and daughters frequently earn much more than their parents. 'It is often not the father but rather a junior member of the family who pays the bill when the family goes out dining' (Faure and Fang, 2008: 200). The decline of the family as the nucleus of society is further illustrated by the increasing number of childless marriages in present-day China, whereas not bearing a child was considered to be 'the biggest moral crime' in traditional Chinese culture (Faure and Fang, 2008: 200).

A final paradox we mention here is that between long-term and short-term orientation. As discussed in Chapter 2, China is the quintessential long-term oriented culture according to Hofstede (2007), the culture on which this dimension (previously termed 'Confucian dynamism') is based. But Faure and Fang (2008) note that a change in time perspective is occurring in China, with an increasing emphasis on quick results. Moreover, the Chinese orientation towards time has always been ambivalent. On the one hand, Chinese traditionally did not regard time to be money, and the very long-term perspective in which events were seen is exemplified by Mao Zedong's response, when asked about the French revolution: 'The French revolution happened in 1789. It is still too early to tell' (quoted in Faure and Fang, 2008: 204). But on the other hand Chinese business people have always been weak in planning, and often intend on cashing out quickly. It is also for this reason that Fang (2003: 355) considers Hofstede's dimension of long-term versus short-term orientation to be fundamentally flawed, as this dimension is based on opposing elements from Confucius' teachings, while according to Fang 'each Confucian value has its bright and dark sides and involves constructive and destructive qualities'. *Yin-yang*, in effect.

The Chinese example shows that appraising culture change in a society in transition like China as consisting of simple shifts on established cultural dimensions, like individualism-collectivism or long-term versus short-term orientation, may be misleading. Instead, Faure and Fang (2008) note that behaviours associated with both the old and the new value orientations co-exist, and evocation of these value orientations is strongly context-dependent. This intermingling of values and behaviours associated with both old and new orientations, makes seemingly opposed orientations exist simultaneously. In the specific case of China this may actually be a constant, rather than a passing effect of transition, as 'China seems to have never given up its single most important cultural characteristic, the ability to manage paradoxes' (Faure and Fang, 2008: 194).

From this brief discussion of some emic insights into management in Japan, Africa and China a few conclusions can be drawn. First of all, attention to specific emic cultural concepts can help us understand management and organization in its societal context. This is exemplified by the concept of *amae*. Secondly, it may in many cases be difficult to distinguish indigenous values from imported values, especially in the wake of colonialism. The discussion of African management as seen from a Western perspective, in contrast to an indigenous perspective, illustrates this. Moreover, the African context, and specifically the literature on *ubuntu*, suggests that uncritically adopting a purportedly emic concept may be just as counterproductive as forcing etic concepts upon an indigenous value system. Finally, the Chinese case shows that a quickly changing economic context may make traditional emic concepts (e.g., *guanxi*) not less, but arguably even more relevant.

In the next section we will look at one particular phenomenon, trust, and discuss how this can be studied from an etic perspective, an emic perspective, and a combination of the two.

3.5 Trust as an etic-emic phenomenon

Trust is an important social phenomenon, which has been shown to influence important outcomes at the level of the society, the level of organizations, and the level of individuals (see, e.g., Knack and Keefer, 1997; Filbeck and Preece, 2003; and Colquitt, Scott and LePine, 2007, respectively). In this section we will look at trust from an etic and from an emic perspective, and demonstrate that both approaches are necessary to fully understand trust in a cross-cultural perspective.

Etic

An enormous amount of work on trust in an international context has been performed from an etic perspective. We will focus here on one stream of literature, which looks at the general propensity to trust in different societies. The World Values Survey (discussed in Chapter 2) includes a question on 'generalized trust' (i.e., not trust in a specific other, or a specific organization or institution): 'Generally speaking, would you say that most people can be trusted, or that you can't be too careful in dealing with people?' Uslaner (2002) has shown that this type of trust (which he calls 'moralistic trust') does not depend on particular experiences with specific others, but is something that is learned early in life. For this reason, we see generalized, or moralistic trust as strongly linked to the culture of a society.

This type of trust is 'extremely stable over time' (Hofstede, 2001: 34): inhabitants of some countries tend to have low trust in others, and inhabitants of other countries high trust, and the differences remain stable over time (Uslaner, 2002). Generalized trust seems to be deeply rooted in the social constitution of a society, and is related, among other things, to social distances between citizens (Bjørnskov, 2006). This macro-level phenomenon also has effects on the level of individual choice behaviour, as inhabitants from high-trust cultures are more cooperative and trusting than inhabitants from low-trust cultures. In a study of international joint ventures Ertug, Cuypers, Noorderhaven and Bensaou (2013) show that home country generalized trust also has an effect in these collaborations. Representatives from high-trust cultures also tend to have more trust in their joint venture partners, keeping everything else constant.

However, this is only part of the story, because not only the level of trust may differ systematically across borders, but this is likely to be also true of the meaning of the concept of trust, and the way in which trust is built up in a relationship (Zaheer and Zaheer, 2006). We will now give two examples of emic studies of trust in business relations.

Emic

Emic cross-cultural trust research is scarce, and this literature suffers from the drawback that conclusions can be drawn only for the culture(s) that is (are) included in the study. By way of example we will look at two emic studies, one of *maquiladoras* (mostly US-owned manufacturing operations in free trade zones in Mexico), and one of business relationships between German and Chinese firms.

In her study of maquiladoras, Lindsley (1999) looked, among other things, at behaviours of supervisors that according to the Mexican employees induced or destroyed trust. Trust-inducing behaviours included protecting the other's honour, offering help, and asking for help. Trust destroying behaviours were, among other things, directly expressing disagreement, directly expressing a negative evaluation, and telling someone what to do. Looking at these factors inducing/destroying interpersonal trust a quite different picture arises compared with the ten behaviours Butler (1991) identified with supervisor trust building in a North American context: supervisor availability, competence, consistency, discreteness, fairness, integrity, loyalty, openness, promise fulfilment and receptivity. It is clear that supervision relationships at the US–Mexican interface can easily go wrong. Management in this context, if destruction of trust is to be avoided, needs to be more indirect than is the custom in North America, as exemplified in an interview with a Mexican manager:

> When I have to discipline an employee, I start off by talking about the person's place in the corporation and what they are there for . . . what their role is in the plant. Then I talk to them about what they need to do. It is important not to hurt the employee, because once you do – [he shrugged, as if to say, 'It's the end'].
>
> (Lindsley, 1999: 24)

The second example pertains to managers in Sino-German joint ventures (Muethel and Hoegl, 2012). This study looked at aspects of trust that were deemed important by German and Chinese managers, but these directly suggest trust-building behaviours, of course. Some aspects were found to be important in both cultures: dependability (fulfilling agreements in the absence of control), credibility (authenticity in communication) and honesty (truthful presentation of facts). Nevertheless, even in these shared components of trust there were slight differences between the Germans and the Chinese, with the German managers more strongly emphasizing cognitive aspects, and the Chinese managers also emphasizing emotional aspects.

But there were also aspects that one nationality did see as important to trust, and the other nationality did not. The Germans emphasized openness (delivering information in a forthcoming manner) and reliability (taking one's task seriously) as important for trust. The Chinese, in contrast, emphasized two different elements, shared understanding and morality. Whereas shared understanding for the Germans meant interpreting a business situation in the same way, for the Chinese it has a deeper, and more emotionally charged connotation:

> Shared understanding is an emotion. For example, when talking with X about the project, I did not have a positive sentiment that we would be able to effortlessly complete the task together. And X did not understand and was not even willing to understand why I suggested addressing the task in a certain way. (Chinese)
>
> (Muethel and Hoegl, 2012: 428)

Morality, finally, for the Chinese, referred to subordinating one's individual interests to the group's interests: 'morality is whether a person is willing to sacrifice himself for others' well-being' (Muethel and Hoegl, 2012: 428). For the Germans morality referred to universal values, and was less relevant to specific relationships between individuals.

These few examples from etic and emic studies of trust in a cross-cultural context suggest that while we can get some way with etic research, in-depth emic studies can offer specifics about trust and trust building in particular societies that promise to lead to more managerially relevant advise. All in all, this brief analysis supports the view that etic and emic research needs to be combined to be able to the get the fullest possible understanding of international comparative management issues.

3.6 Conclusions

This chapter has looked at culture from an emic perspective, and is complementary to Chapter 2. We have discussed the necessity of adding an emic perspective to the study of international comparative management. Etic approaches help us to get the big picture, but the meaning of the differences found in etic studies can only be identified with emic research. Emic research differs from etic research in its focus (a single culture, or a few cultures, versus a larger number of cultures), but also in the methods used. Emic research mostly uses 'thick description': a focus on micro-level interactions that are described in great detail, and from which conclusions can be drawn regarding the larger culture in which these interactions are embedded. The perspective is often semiotic, i.e., phenomena are not taken at face value, but behaviours have a symbolic function, they refer to shared systems of signification that help members of a culture impute meaning to the world.

In terms of philosophy of science the approach is closer to hermeneutics than to logical-empirical positivism. This perspective denies the possibility of a 'view from nowhere'; every interpreter inevitably has pre-understandings that colour his or her interpretation of the social system studied. Such pre-understandings are no handicap, but rather a condition for achieving an understanding of the social system. The method used in emic research is mostly that of ethnography. Ethnographic international management research has a number of characteristics and encounters a number of specific problems that need to be dealt with. These issues have to do with, among other things, getting access to companies, securing permission to publish results, selection of key informants, and issues related to the identity of the researcher.

As an example of emic comparative international management research the work of Philippe d'Iribarne has been discussed. D'Iribarne shows how in otherwise comparable production plants in France, the USA and the Netherlands different logics prevail in the interactions between employees and managers, and that these logics are linked to the cultural and institutional heritages of the three countries.

This chapter has also discussed a number of indigenous management practices and emic concepts, focusing on Japan, Africa and China. This discussion shows that indigenous concepts are important to understand cultural influences on management and organization in a particular country. But it also demonstrates that studies that try to identify emic concepts can easily oversimplify and overgeneralize. Moreover, although some of the research seeks to reach back to a past in which the indigenous culture studied was still 'pure' and uncontaminated by Western (management) culture, the reality is complex, and different influences are next to impossible to disentangle. Especially in emerging economies the situation is made more complex because of the fast rate of change, which may make indigenous concepts at the same time both more and less relevant.

Finally, we have focused on the issue of trust in a cross-cultural context, and briefly discussed the outcomes of some etic and some emic studies. This exploration reinforces the main message of this chapter and the previous one: for a good understanding of culture and international comparative management a combination of insights from etic and emic research is direly needed.

Study questions

1 What is the main criticism of d'Iribarne of Hofstede's work? Can this criticism be generalized to other etic studies? Explain your answer.
2 Why would a questionnaire study not be an effective research approach from a semiotic perspective on culture?
3 How does Philippe d'Iribarne explain differences in management and organization between comparable plants in different countries?
4 What are the main features of management and organization in France, the USA and the Netherlands according to d'Iribarne?
5 Why is an emic approach necessary to identify indigenous management concepts?
6 Please give examples of indigenous management concepts from Japan, China, and Africa.
7 Explain trust in a cross-cultural context from both an etic and an emic perspective.

Further reading

Ferrin, D.L. and Gillespie, N. (2010) Trust differences across national-societal cultures: Much to do, or much ado about nothing? In Saunders, M.N.K., Skinner, D., Dietz, G., Gillespie, N. and Lewicki, R.J. (eds) *Organizational Trust: A Cultural Perspective*. Cambridge, UK: Cambridge University Press, 42–86.

Ferrin and Gillespie give a comprehensive overview of cross-cultural trust studies. Although written for an academic audience this review article is not too difficult to read.

D'Iribarne, P. with Henry, A. (2007) *Successful Companies in the Developing World: Managing in Synergy With Cultures*. Paris: Agence Française de Développement.

Most of the work of Alain Henry and Philippe d'Iribarne on Third World countries has only been published in French. This is a selection of their writings translated into English.

Jack, G., Zhu, Y., Barney, J., Brannen, M.Y., Prichard, C. Singh, K. and Whetten, D. (2013) Refining, reinforcing and reimagining universal and indigenous theory development in international management. *Journal of Management Inquiry* 22(2), 148–164.

This article, based on an Academy of Management symposium, offers the view of five leading scholars on the relationship between etic and emic studies.

Jackson, T. (2004) *Management and Change in Africa: A Cross-Cultural Perspective.* London: Routledge.

Terence Jackson has been involved in studying management in Africa for many years, and this book summarizes the main findings. Contains case studies of management in Nigeria, Cameroon, Kenya and South Africa.

Case: Management of phosphate mining in Senegal

Source: Grisar (1997) and general information on Senegalese phosphate mining and processing.

The Senegalese mining industry is dominated by phosphate mining, and phosphate-related exports are a major currency earner for the country. In 1994 a merger between the Compagnie Senegalaise des Phosphates de Taiba (CSPT) and the Industries Chimiques du Senegal (ICS) made CSPT/ICS the dominant player in the regional phosphate mining and processing industry. The CSPT, on which this case focuses, was founded in 1957 with French capital and imported technology. It started production and export in 1960, the year of Senegal's independence. In 1975 the Senegalese state took a 50 per cent interest in the company's shareholdings. In 1980 the process of 'Senegalization' of the management of the company took a new turn when the first Senegalese exploitation manager took over, and for the first time in history the company had more Senegalese than French managers (27 versus 16). During the 1980s, labour relations and relationships with the unions gradually deteriorated. Concurrently, the company suffered from declining productivity until its absorption by ICS. A superficial reading of the history of the firm might conclude from the simultaneity of Senegalization and decline that the Senegalese managers were less capable than their French predecessors. However, such an attribution would be too easy. Closer inspection shows that the Senegalese managers were trained by the French, and practised the same management style as the French. But, paradoxically, what was effective when practised by the French did not work for their Senegalese successors. Senegalese employees, looking back at the period when the French managed the company, expressed positive sentiments (quoted in Grisar, 1997: 235):

> 'We used to be like a big family in former times.'
> 'Before, we were all equal.'
> 'You were respected for good work and efforts no matter what position in the hierarchy you had.'

The perception of equality voiced in these quotes is surprising, as during French rule there was a very clear-cut hierarchy, the French being the bosses and the Senegalese the subordinates. When interviewing Senegalese workers about the conduct of the former French and the present Senegalese managers, Grisar (1997: 238) made the striking observation that 'Senegalese managers lost respect among workers for the same behaviour for which the French had been respected.' Apparently what was acceptable, or even laudable when coming from the French, was interpreted very differently when coming from fellow countrymen. According to Grisar the key to understanding this paradox is the isolation of the French expatriates in Senegalese society, and their ignorance of caste and class differences and affiliations, which normally determine an individual's status in Senegalese society. Because the French were in a special position, outside the fabric of the networks of society, Senegalese subordinates tended to accept their decisions as impartial. The same decisions taken by Senegalese managers, in contrast, were often explained on the basis of the social relationships (or lack of such) between superior and subordinate. Hence the acceptability of managerial decisions depended on the motives ascribed to the manager taking the decisions, with systematically different (social) motives being ascribed to fellow Senegalese and the French.

Questions

1. To what extent can the relative failure of Senegalese management at CSPT be explained by the positions of France and Senegal in Hofstede's five dimensions of culture (see Figure 2.6)?
2. What would you recommend the management of CSPT/ICS do in order to improve the effectiveness of its management?

Case: Americans negotiating a contract in China

Based on EECH Case: Cross-Cultural Negotiation. Americans negotiating a contract in China. Reference number 405-066-1.

Upon arrival at the headquarters of his company in Alabama from 2 months of negotiations in Shanghai, Scott Jones looked back at the tiresome negotiations and the many difficulties which had ultimately led him and his team to pull out of the process. Scott's company had hoped to establish a Joint Venture (JV) with a Chinese state-owned vehicle component company. They wanted to outsource some of the production to China to reduce costs. Before flying to China, Scott and his team prepared thoroughly. They inquired about the Chinese company, the production facilities, product quality and production costs. They knew exactly which information they needed in order to make a mutually satisfactory and fair proposal.

His Chinese counterpart, Sung Wang, and his team had also done their homework thoroughly. They had made inquiries about the US Company, and felt they had a good understanding of the company's overall business philosophy, corporate culture, the people running the company and the sophisticated production technology. They were keen to get to know the company and hoped to enter a long-term partnership built on mutual trust, enabling them to learn from the technological know-how of the Americans.

Scott was informed that the Chinese were tough negotiators but when looking back he didn't find them to be. He believed the Chinese played unfair games and tried to cheat wherever possible. He did feel impressed by the reception they received upon arrival in Shanghai. A delegation was waiting for them at the airport and a huge banner across the company's gate was put up to welcome them. They had meetings with many people from the Chinese company but also with local government officials. In the evenings they had one banquet after another.

The warm welcome and the many organized dinners did not stop Scott and his team becoming increasingly annoyed about the absence of a schedule and agenda. They were completely ignorant as to what would happen the next day and this went on for days. Scott's boss called him every day to see where they were with the negotiations. Each time he had to tell him they hadn't started yet. Scott and his team began to push the Chinese for a schedule and to start the negotiations. The Chinese counterpart didn't quite understand how the Americans could be so ignorant as to not know that the Chinese counterpart didn't have the detailed schedule of the meetings. Their bosses decided this. By openly showing their annoyance and asking questions about the agenda, the Americans made the Chinese lose face.

Meanwhile, during this informal stage, in a casual way, the Chinese were asking business case-related information, which Scott and his team answered openly in order to maintain good ambiance. The Chinese, however, didn't respond to similar questions from Scott and his team. Instead they changed the conversation to various subjects such as the 'long-established' friendship between China and America. Scott felt the Chinese were deceiving him and didn't see how he could trust them. Sung, on the other hand, thought the Americans were rather naïve with being overly honest. In a business negotiation, you need to be strategic and not reveal everything. It puts you in a weak position.

Finally, after more than a week, the first real business meeting was scheduled with the CEO, Mr. Chen. Scott rehearsed his presentation carefully, as Chen was much higher in rank than him and probably 20 years older. To his surprise, for the whole meeting, the matter of the contract wasn't touched. Mr. Chen talked about the Chinese civilization and the promising Chinese business environment. Chen stressed the importance of reaching an agreement during the meeting on the general principles between both partners and refused to talk about the details of a contract. He talked about the importance of mutual understanding, goodwill, trust, long-term relationships, the importance for the Chinese side to learn from the technological knowledge of the American company. Not quite understanding what the general principles really meant, Scott went along with it and said yes to everything, but also mentioned the American interests. Then a communiqué was drafted and Scott noticed that his company's interests were only marginally mentioned in the document while the Chinese interests were spelled out in detail. He didn't comment in order to keep good relations and reckoned it was just a legally non-binding statement of intentions. Much later in the negotiations however Scott realized the importance of this document for the Chinese. They kept referring to it whenever he refused to make further concessions. Each time the Chinese counterpart reproached him that he didn't understand the spirit of those general principles and warned him not to endanger the mutual understanding. Scott just couldn't understand how the Chinese managed to make the link between the details of the contract they were trying to draft and the ineffective general principles.

The Chinese, in turn, didn't understand Scott's attitude. After all he had agreed upon the general principles, which represented the foundation of the relationship. They didn't see how they could trust someone who ignored general principles, which are based on trust. Generally, the Chinese felt quite offended about Scott and his team's shortsightedness and ignorance. They had made enormous efforts to welcome the Americans, given them the chance to talk to people with high rank and influence, which increases one's own status and opens doors. All the Americans could think of was their business presentation. In addition, the American CEO did not bother to fly over to discuss the general principles with the CEO of the Chinese company, which is the most important part of the negotiations. For the Chinese this was a sign of disrespect and insincerity, but in order not to disturb the atmosphere they hadn't mentioned it.

As the negotiations pursued, Scott and his team tried to go swiftly through all the details, looking at all the issues and facts in a logical order. Whenever Scott and his team thought they were making progress, the Chinese had to double check with their superiors and even government and party officials. Scott felt the Chinese were using delays to put them under pressure. The Chinese team felt offended by the fact that the Americans didn't seem to understand they often needed approval not only from superiors but also from government officials and this takes time. The Chinese could not discuss this openly as it makes them lose face. They had expected the American team to understand that negotiating teams in China don't have the same autonomy as the Americans. Moreover, the Chinese didn't see the use of discussing the details of a contract before they got to know the people they were going to do business with. For them the general principles were of greater importance, as the details of a contract would need to be adjusted to reality as it unfolded. In order to be able to adapt the details to reality, mutual understanding is needed, which didn't seem to develop.

At some point during the negotiations Scott was encouraged by the Chinese counterpart to take senior officials of the local planning approval commission out for a luxurious dinner. Building up good connections would shorten the application process for the planning permission for the building of a plant from several months to just a couple of weeks. Scott was shocked by this suggestion. It sounded like corruption to him. Aside from his personal feelings, it was his company's strict policy not to engage in this type of activity. The Chinese couldn't understand why Scott didn't follow their advice. Taking people to dinner is about building relationships and achieving a balance between the favours you receive and do. People in China feel morally obliged to return favours, which for them seems like a much smoother and flexible process than having to rely on contracts and courts. If you go to court, all parties involved lose face.

What frustrated Scott most, however, was that the Chinese counterpart never gave a definite answer. The Chinese often re-opened subjects which Scott thought had been settled, and a lot was 'subject to approval'. The Chinese never responded with a 'no'. They mentioned 'it would be difficult', or 'as long as. . .'. Scott and his team realized after a while that these expressions in fact meant no. The Chinese considered reality too complex to be divided into yes and no. They have a holistic approach and didn't see how one could analyse things easily, like the Americans proudly do. To analyse means to take apart. How can one take things apart that are connected? As a result of this perception, negotiations for the Chinese team were a circular, iterative process whereby one can revisit issues.

Despite all the difficulties and misunderstandings the negotiation teams did finally manage to set the day for the formal signature. Scott's CEO planned to fly in for this event. The Americans were very enthusiastic and especially eager to go home after this tiresome period. At the last minute, however, Sung approached the American team with a few 'little points', which his superiors wanted to reconsider. For Scott and his team these 'little points' were absolutely fundamental and unacceptable. Scott was enraged and called Sung a dishonest game player. Scott and his team decided the deal was off and the next day they flew home. Sung thought it was very unfortunate. It is common tactical behaviour to try to score some final points at the very end when your negotiation partner is tired and eager to return home. Sung didn't expect full agreement to his proposal. A minor concession would have demonstrated his negotiation skills to his superiors. Sung didn't see how they could possibly do business even in the future with people who behave in such a way.

Questions

1. What are the different approaches both parties take to business negotiations?
2. What are the mistakes both parties have committed in this cross-cultural negotiation process and what could they have done better?
3. Can you explain the different approaches and mistakes on the basis of etic and emic research into the American and Chinese national cultures?

Notes

1 The following text is based on Noorderhaven (2004).
2 In the text below we follow Chapman, Gajewska-De Mattos and Antiniou (2004).
3 The following paragraphs are based on Noorderhaven, Benders and Keizer (2007).

References

Ahiauzu, A.I. (1986). The African thought-system and the work behavior of the African industrial man. *International Studies of Management & Organization* 16(2), 37–58.

Ala, M. and Cordeiro, W.P. (2000) Can we learn management techniques from the Japanese ringi process? *Business Forum* 24, 22–25.

Aoki, M. and Dore, R. (eds) (1994) *The Japanese Firm: The Sources of Competitive Strength.* Oxford: Oxford University Press.

Aycan, Z. (2006) Paternalism: towards conceptual refinement and operationalization. In Kim, U., Yang, K.S. and Hwang, K.K. (eds) *Indigenous and Cultural Psychology: Understanding People in Context.* New York: Springer, 445–466.

Barley, S.R. (1983) Semiotics and the study of occupational and organizational cultures. *Administrative Science Quarterly* 28(3), 393–413.

Barsoux, J.-L. and Lawrence, P.A. (1990) *Management in France.* London: Cassell.

Becker, U. (2001) 'Miracle' by consensus? Consensualism and dominance in Dutch employment development. *Economic and Industrial Democracy* 22(4), 453–483.

Behrens, K.Y. (2004) A multifaceted view of the concept of amae: reconsidering the indigenous Japanese concept of relatedness. *Human Development* 47, 1–27.

Bian, Y. (1997) Bringing strong ties back in: indirect ties, network bridges and job searches in China. *American Sociological Review* 62(3), 366–385.

Bjørnskov, C. (2006) Determinants of generalized trust: a cross-country comparison. *Public Choice* 130, 1–21.

Butler, J.K. (1991) Toward understanding and measuring conditions of trust: evolution of a conditions of trust inventory. *Journal of Management* 17, 643–666.

Chapman, M., Gajewska-De Mattos, H. and Antoniou, C. (2004) The ethnographic international business researcher: misfit or trailblazer? In Marschan-Piekkari, R. and Welch, C. (eds) *Handbook of Qualitative Research Methods for International Business*, Cheltenham, UK and Northhampton, MA: Edward Elgar, 287–305.

Colquitt, J.A., Scott, B.A. and LePine, J.A. (2007) Trust, trustworthiness, and trust propensity: a meta-analytic test of their unique relationships with risk taking and job performance. *Journal of Applied Psychology* 92, 909–927.

Crozier, M. (2010) *The Bureaucratic Phenomenon*, New Brunswick, NJ: Transaction Publishers (originally published in 1964 by the University of Chicago Press).

Dia, M. (1996) *Africa's Management in the 1990s and Beyond: Reconciling Indigenous and Transplanted Institutions.* Washington, DC: The World Bank.

Doi, T. (2001) *The Anatomy of Dependence.* New York: Kodansha America.

Ertug, G., Cuypers, I.R.P., Noorderhaven, N.G. and Bensaou, B.M. (2013) Trust between international joint venture partners: effects of home countries. *Journal of International Business Studies* 44, 263–282.

Fang, T. (2003) A critique of Hofstede's fifth national culture dimension. *International Journal of Cross Cultural Management* 3(3), 347–368.

Fang, T. and Faure, G.O. (2011) Chinese communication characteristics: a yin yang perspective. *International Journal of Intercultural Relations* 35, 320–333.

Faure, G.O. and Fang, T. (2008) Changing Chinese values: keeping up with paradoxes. *International Business Review* 17, 194–207.

Filbeck, G. and Preece, D. (2003) Fortune's best 100 companies to work for in America: do they work for their shareholders? *Journal of Business Finance & Accounting* 30, 771–797.

Gadamer, H.-G. (1999) *Truth and Method* (second revised edition). Translation revised by J. Weinsheimer and D.G. Marshall. New York: Continuum.

Geertz, C. (1973) *The Interpretation of Cultures.* New York: Basic Books.

Grisar, K. (1997) Globalization of work culture: African and European industrial cooperation in Senegal. *Research in the Sociology of Work* 6, 223–246.

Henry, A. (1991) Vers on modèle du management africain. *Cahiers d'Études Africaines* 124(31–4), 447–473.

Hernandez, E.-M. (1975) Afrique: l'Actualité de modèle paternaliste. *Revue Française de Gestion* 128, 98–106.

Hill, C.W.L. (1995) National institutional structures, transaction cost economizing and competitive advantage: the case of Japan. *Organization Science* 6, 119–131.

Hofstede, G. (1980) *Culture's Consequences.* London: Sage.

Hofstede, G. (1991) *Cultures and Organizations: Software of the Mind.* London: McGraw-Hill.

Hofstede, G. (2001) *Culture's Consequences: Comparing Values, Behaviors, Institutions, and Organizations Across Nations* (2nd edn). Thousand Oaks, CA: Sage.

Hofstede, G. (2007) Asian management in the 21st century. *Asia Pacific Journal of Management* 24, 411–420.

d'Iribarne, P. (1989) *La Logique de l'Honneur: Gestion des Entreprises et Traditions Nationales.* Paris: Éditions du Seuil.

d'Iribarne,P. (1994) The honour principle in the 'bureaucratic phenomenon'. *Organization Studies* 15(1), 81–97.

d'Iribarne, P. (1996–97) The usefulness of an ethnographic approach to the international comparison of organizations. *International Studies of Management and Organization* 26(4), 30–47.

d'Iribarne, P. (2000) Management et cultures politiques. *Revue Française de Gestion* 128, 70–75.

Jackson, T. (2004) *Management and Change in Africa: A Cross-Cultural Perspective.* London: Routledge.

Jackson, T. (2012) Cross-cultural management and the informal economy in sub-Saharan Africa: implications for organization, employment and skills development. *The International Journal of Human Resource Management* 23(14), 2901–2916.

Jackson, T., Amaeshi, K. and Yavuz, S. (2008) Untangling African indigenous management: multiple influences on the success of SMEs in Kenya. *Journal of World Business* 43, 400–416.

Jia, L., You, S. and Du, Y. (2012) Chinese context and theoretical contributions to management and organization research: a three-decade review. *Management and Organization Review* 8(1), 173–209.

Kiritani, E. (1999) Creating group consensus. *Journal of Japanese Trade & Industry* 18, 26–27.

Knack, S. and Keefer, P. (1997) Does social capital have an economic payoff? A cross-country investigation. *Quarterly Journal of Economics* 112, 1251–1288.

Kriz, A., Gummesson, E. and Quazi, A. (2014) Methodology meets culture: relational and guanxi-oriented research in China. *International Journal of Cross Cultural Management* 14(1), 27–46.

Li, P.P., Leung, K., Chen, C.C. and Luo, J.-D. (2012) Indigenous research on Chinese management: *what* and *how*. *Management and Organization Review* 8(1), 7–24.

Lindsley, S.L. (1999) Communication and 'the Mexican way': stability and trust as core symbols in maquiladoras. *Western Journal of Communication* 63(1), 1–31.

Mangaliso, M.P. (2001) Building competitive advantage from *ubuntu*: management lessons from South Africa. *Academy of Management Executive* 15(3), 23–33.

Marshall, T.C., Chuong, K. and Aikawa, A. (2011) Day-to-day experiences of amae in Japanese romantic relationships. *Asian Journal of Social Psychology* 14, 26–35.

Muethel, M. and Hoegl, M. (2012) The influence of social institutions on managers' concept of trust: implications for trust-building in Sino-German relationships. *Journal of World Business* 47, 420–434.

Nkomo, S.M. (2011) A postcolonial *and* anti-colonial reading of 'African' leadership and management in organization studies: tensions, contradictions and possibilities. *Organization* 18(3), 365–386.

Noorderhaven, N.G. (2002) De grenzen van de Nederlandse bedrijfscultuur. In Batenburg, R., Van der Lippe, T. and Van den Heuvel, N. (eds) *Met het Oog op de Toekomst van de Arbeid*. Den Haag: Elsevier Bedrijfsinformatie, 77–89.

Noorderhaven, N.G. (2004) Hermeneutic methodology and international business research. In Marschan-Piekkari, R. and Welch, C. (eds) *Handbook of Qualitative Research Methods for International Business*. Cheltenham, UK and Northhampton, MA: Edward Elgar, 84–104.

Noorderhaven, N.G., Benders, J. and Keizer, A.B. (2007) Comprehensiveness versus pragmatism: consensus at the Japanese-Dutch interface. *Journal of Management Studies* 44(8), 1349–1370.

Nzelibe, C.O. (1986) The evolution of African management thought. *International Studies of Management & Organization* 16(2), 6–16.

Park, S.H. and Luo, Y. (2001) Guanxi and organizational dynamics: organizational networking in Chinese firms. *Strategic Management Journal* 22(5), 455–477.

Pascale, R.T. and Athos, A. (1981) *The Art of Japanese Management*. New York: Warner.

Richmond, Y. and Gestrin, P. (1998) *Into Africa: Intercultural Insights*. Yarmouth, ME: Intercultural Press.

Said, E. (1978) *Orientalism*. New York: Vintage Books.

Schwartz, S.H. (2008) *Cultural Value Orientations: Nature and Implications of National Differences*. Moscow: State University/Higher School of Economics Press.

Sharpe, D.R. (2004) The relevance of ethnography to international business research. In Marschan-Piekkari, R. and Welch, C. (eds) *Handbook of Qualitative Research Methods for International Business*. Cheltenham, UK and Northhampton, MA: Edward Elgar, 306–323.

Smith, H.W. and Nomi, T. (2000) Is amae the key to understanding Japanese culture? *Electronic Journal of Sociology* 5(1), 1–14.

Tian, X. (2007) *Managing International Business in China*. Cambridge, UK: Cambridge University Press.

Tsui, A.S. (2006) Contextualization in Chinese management research. *Management and Organization Review* 2(1), 1–13.

Uslaner, E.M. (2002) *The Moral Foundations of Trust*. New York: Cambridge University Press.

Van Wolferen, K. (1990) *The Enigma of Japanese Power: People and Politics in a Stateless Nation*. New York: Vintage Books.

Wanasika, I., Howell, J.P., Littrell, R. and Dorfman, P. (2011) Managerial leadership and culture in sub-Saharan Africa. *Journal of World Business* 46(2), 234–241.

Yoshino, M.Y. and Lifson, T.B. (1986) *The Invisible Link: Japan's Sogo Sosha and the Organization of Trade*. Cambridge, MA: MIT Press.

Zaheer, S. and Zaheer, A. (2006) Trust across borders. *Journal of International Business Studies* 37, 21–29.

Zhang, Y. and Zhang, Z. (2006) Guanxi and organizational dynamics in China: a link between individual and organizational levels. *Journal of Business Ethics* 67(4), 375–392.

4 Institutional diversity and management

Learning objectives

By the end of this chapter you will be able to:

- understand what comparative institutional research is about
- explain the major differences between the three main European institutional approaches – varieties of capitalism, business systems and societal analysis
- understand the relationship between culture and the national institutional environment
- reflect critically upon the explanatory power of societal and institutionalist analysis
- assess the value of institutional typologies
- use approaches to analyse globalization pressures.

Chapter outline

4.1 Institutional analysis: what and why?

It is central to be well aware of what institutions are, in the sense of organization studies and of political economy. Institutions are not organized entities or collectivities (such as the Royal National Lifeboat Institution in Great Britain). As explained in the first chapter, there are institutions in a softer and in a harder sense, and there are proximate and background institutions. Do at all times make sure that you understand the differences and know which type of institution is being addressed. Soft institutions are more pliable, open to negotiation between contracting or interacting people or corporations. Hard institutions consist of binding norms about patterns of behaviour and regularities. Proximate institutions are tangible and concrete; they can be defined, either in writing or less formally. Background institutions are 'in the back of people's minds' and less tangible, but they may very well be fundamental. And whatever the adjective added is, an institution is a behavioural regularity, including mental behaviour, which suggests what to think or do under which circumstances, and which is attributed a meaning under the circumstances in question. Do note that what is written in law texts or company regulations need not be hard institutions; depending on the country and other contextual situations, soft institutions which are not written down may be much more important.

Note also that soft background institutions are very close to cultural values, discussed in the previous two chapters, which also shows that they may very well be fundamental. The difference is that, as behavioural regularities, institutions always imply an action situation: which behaviour is to occur in which situation between which participants. Emic cultural analysis then is particularly suited to operate next to soft institutions, whilst etic cultural analysis best operates next to hard institutions that are also proximate.

Empirical institutional research on organizations has shown that corporations are at all times influenced by contextual variables. Contextual variables not only provide corporations with constraints (i.e. certain levels of (technical) training; capital constraints, etc.) but also with opportunities (i.e. the provision of sufficient risk capital, tax-free loans, subsidies etc.). Institutional theory therefore insists that institutions have two sides, implying a limitation of behaviour and a facilitation of behaviour. Rather like in cultural analysis, we have within the institutional camp several approaches developed to analyse how societal institutions influence organizational forms (usually) in capitalist economies. Sections 4.2 and 4.4 of this chapter discuss the features of the two main institutionalist approaches used in comparative organization and management studies and in comparative political economy: the 'varieties of capitalism' (VoC) and the 'business systems' (BSys) approach. We then show the institutional diversity in countries, to the extent that it has been researched more systematically.

In order not to separate culturalist and institutionalist studies too much, we then show how they can be integrated through the 'societal effect' approach. All the approaches mentioned have made major contributions to the study of management and organization in market economies and beyond. They compare institutional systems across two or more societies, and they explain what they mean for organizations, management and industrial structure. They emphasize the importance of history, attending to when and how developments occurred.

The BSys approach, which is discussed in Section 4.2, was developed by Whitley (1990, 1992a) and is a manifestation of the idea that organization and management institutions cluster into types with their own distinctive logic, and that more national patterns consist of combinations of business system types. Whitley's use of the national business system concept is to explain why different countries have evolved different sets of institutions to coordinate economic activities which are only superficially similar from one country to another (Casson and Lundan, 1999).

In most approaches in sociology, economics, and organization and management studies, which accept the idea that organization (in a broad sense) – including corporate governance, the market-hierarchy choice and firms' internal organization – is strongly influenced by the national context, economic organization has entered the picture slightly later. The main point of interest in most of these studies is to understand two things: 1) why prima facie similar firms in different countries do things differently; 2) how a firm's international competitiveness, whether it is a multinational enterprise or not, is nationally conditioned (e.g. see Kogut, 1991, 1993; Lundvall, 1992). In the VoC and BSys approaches, however, economic organization occupies a prominent place.

The complexity of BSys research may be illustrated by the brief explanation of Whitley's empirical research on the South Korean and Taiwanese business systems in Section 4.4. It is widely acknowledged that Asian firms behave very differently from those in Western countries, and that these differences are connected to distinctive features of dominant societal institutions (Whitley, 1999). Besides the success of these specific business systems, with the rise first of Japan and then of Taiwan, South Korea, Singapore, Thailand, Malaysia, India and China – sometimes qualified as the Asian Tigers – there is also the fact that we are living in an international or 'globalized' business world, which makes it important to place them on a comparative map.

The SE approach, which is discussed in Section 4.5 to facilitate integration of culturalist and institutionalist perspectives, has been developed by Maurice and Brossard (1976); Maurice et al. (1976/1986); Maurice et al. (1980); and Sorge and Warner (1986). The most recent statement and discussion is found in Maurice and Sorge (eds., 2000).

If the nature of actors, including organizations, and their modes of acting are constituted and constrained by institutions, and if institutions are interpreted and practised by actors, how can these actors change the very institutions in which they are embedded? Much of the scholarly attention to change tends to look at the formation of new institutional forms and associated changes in industries and individual organizations. For we have to see both, the action of actors and the constitution of values and institutions, as paradoxical: as actors are propelled by values and institutions to devise strategies and implement these in practice, they not only reproduce these values and institutions but deliberately or unwittingly work for changes, in the very values and institutions in which they are embedded. Therefore, institutional change implies the 'de-institutionalization' of existing forms and their replacement by new arrangements that, in time, undergo institutionalization (Scott, 2001). A discussion of this topic is especially relevant to an understanding of the consequences of internationalization and globalization (see the first and the very last chapters). As globalization involves institutional change, we should have a sound concept for it. This is developed in Section 4.6.

4.2 Varieties of capitalism

The analysis of varieties of capitalism, through VoC approaches, arose from political economy and organization studies, and it is shared by political science, economics and sociology. Whilst this necessarily by-passed the socialist or communist world of the cold war period, now the world consists of more or less capitalist economies and societies, with the exception of North Korea and, probably increasingly less, Cuba. So, the fact that capitalism is subject to great institutional variation has become ever more striking, and by that token the salience of VoC but also the diversity of the varieties, between the USA and the mixed economy of China – capitalism managed by the Communist Party, as it were.

Different versions of institutional analysis have developed different typologies on the basis of linkages between social institutions (i.e. Hall and Soskice, 2001; Whitley, 1999; Amable, 2000). Two major ideal types that are identified in all the typologies are the liberal market, or 'Anglo-American', and the coordinated market economies (see Table 4.1).[1]

The first ideal type is said to be dominant in the Anglo-American cluster of countries, including the USA, the UK, Ireland, Australia, New Zealand and Canada. It is characterized by:

- a financial system that imposes relatively short-term horizons on companies, but at the same time allows high risk-taking;
- an industrial relations system in a deregulated labour market that discourages effective employee representation within companies – hence, weak unions – but that facilitates unilateral control by top management;
- an education and training system that emphasizes general education and discourages long-term initial vocational training, but encourages subsequent bit-by-bit skill acquisition, especially for those with sufficient general education;
- an inter-company system that imposes strong competition requirements and, hence, limits possible cooperation between companies.

Table 4.1 Institutional typology

National institutions	*Liberal cluster*	*Coordinated cluster*	
	Anglo-American	Northern Europe + Germany	Japan
Business organization and coordination	Weak	Strong and well-organized at the industry level	Strong and well-organized at the group level
Relations between institutions and actors	Arm's length; short-term; low trust	Long-term; high trust	
Financial institutions	Market	Banks and market	Banks
Education and training system for lower-level workers	Ineffective	Effective	
Unions	Weak	Important role	
Career patterns of managers	Between firms	Within firms	
Labour market	Flexible; deregulated	Regulated	

Coordinated market economies include most northern European economies (the Netherlands, Scandinavian economies, Germany, Switzerland, Austria) and Japan. The model is characterized by:

- a financial system that allows the long-term financing of companies;
- an industrial relations system in which unions play an important part and that allows cooperative industrial relations within the company and coordinated wage bargaining across companies;
- an education and training system that encourages serious initial vocational training of young people, and in which organized business and/or individual companies are closely involved;
- an inter-company system that enables substantial technology and standard-setting cooperation to take place between companies.

The coordinated market economy family has two quite distinct sub-branches. These sub-branches are defined by the way in which business is organized: whether the primary unit of business coordination is the industry (or part of an industry); or whether the primary unit of business coordination is across industry grouping of companies.

Industry-coordinated (or northern European) market economies

In these economies, which include Germany, the primary locus for coordination of activities between companies with respect to technology transfer, initial training, industrial relations, and so on, is at the industry level. Coordination across industries usually takes place via industry bodies, rather than individual firms.

Group-coordinated market economies

In Japan, the primary locus of inter-company coordination takes place within across-industry groupings of large companies, to which the great majority of very large companies belong. These groupings include companies from each major industry, with relatively little product-market overlap between the companies in any one group. Many smaller supplier companies have close and exclusive relations with a larger company, and, hence, fall within the sphere of influence of the relevant group.

As suggested, the different social institutional features of different constellations help us to explain differences in international competitiveness. The Anglo-American model is argued to foster product market strategies that emphasize competition over prices, accompanied by more radical forms of innovation. The coordinated market economies' model pushes manufacturers towards a product-market strategy that emphasizes high-quality products and incremental innovation (Hall and Soskice, 2001).

Liberal market economies and coordinated market economies are not the only type of advanced economy, however. France is an example of a different type of economy: in France, the state still plays a much more important role in the coordination of large companies than it does in other countries. Some advanced economies do not fall easily into any type. To make the typology more generally applicable, developing countries and/or countries in transition should be taken into account. But this is still a challenge for research work in progress. Similar to cultural analysis, until now, institutional analysis has largely concentrated on advanced (and usually western) economies.

From the 1990s onwards, as recessions in Germany and Japan set in, some scholars predicted the erosion and convergence of the 'Rhineland model' (coordinated market economies) towards Anglo-American capitalism. On the other hand, the world financial crisis after 2007 has refocused interest on the German variant of capitalism. And the USA institutional order survived this world crisis only because the increasing governmental debt of the liberal capitalist USA was financed by the – Communist – government of China, in return for the sustained and considerable increase of Chinese exports to the USA and most other countries. Opportunity makes strange bedfellows, as can be seen, and it makes actors ride rough-shod over VoC and also BSys concepts; they are too tidy to take proper account of the jungle of national socio-economic orders, but they are still a good point of departure. Probably the best and most readable recent analysis of VoC from a political economy perspective is Becker (2009).

4.3 The business systems approach

The BSys approach was developed by Richard Whitley on the basis of his research into East Asian organizations and their institutional contexts (Whitley, 1990, 1991). The approach is particularly useful by a more fine-grained differentiation of institutional orders, not only in the European and North American parts of the world but also in Asia. The concept of a business system is conceived by Whitley (1992b: 125) as 'particular ways of organizing, controlling and directing business enterprises that become established as the dominant forms of business organization in different societies'. This not only includes institutions within organizations but also market orders (for capital, labour and traded goods or commodities markets) and governmental regulation.

The main features of business systems that the approach seeks to explain are:

- the nature of firms as economic actors, including the extent to which firms dominate the economy and how they share risk;
- the nature of authoritative coordination and control systems within firms, including the types of authority exercised, and the extent of differentiation and decentralization; and
- the nature of market organization, including the extent of interdependence among firms and the role of competitive versus cooperative ties.

(Whitley, 1992b: 129–30)

Unique systems are argued to arise 'wherever key associated institutions are both mutually reinforcing and distinctive from other ones' (Whitley, 1999: 44). In this sense, nation states often develop distinctive business systems because 'state actions determine the effectiveness and role of formal institutions in governing many important aspects of economic coordination' (Whitley, 1999: 44).

The core argument of the approach is that:

> differences in societal institutions encourage particular kinds of economic organization and discourage other ones through structuring the ways that collective actors are

> constituted, cooperate, and compete for resources and legitimacy, including the standards used to evaluate their performance and behavior.
>
> (Whitley, 1999: 27)

The BSys approach is most often used to understand cross-national differences; but the national level is not the only level at which business systems can be analysed. It is true that in general, the institutions that help us explain business systems (i.e. the financial system, the educational and training system) are regulated at the level of the nation. This does not necessarily need to be the case, though. It could well be that, for example, regional institutions (such as EU-level institutions), and broad cultural norms and values are distinct from national ones and exert considerable influence in the economic sphere. In such cases, Whitley expects distinctive kinds of economic organization to become established at the regional level. This is especially so if national agencies and institutions are less effective in coordinating activities and implementing policies.

Business system features are argued to be general and long term in nature, implying that they do not change very rapidly or in response to the behaviour of individual firms. Moreover, the approach assumes that business systems interact with the institutional environment but that the pattern of interaction is seen as a co-evolutionary process that is strongly path-dependent. Path-dependency allows for, at best, incremental change. But change is argued to be dependent on the cohesiveness and integration of institutional frameworks and business systems. It is assumed that where major institutions are strongly interdependent, and business systems are highly integrated and cohesive, change is unlikely to occur unless there are significant changes in the institutional framework, i.e. a quasi-revolution. In contrast, where institutions are more differentiated and their interdependence weaker, business system characteristics and particular institutions may undergo change without leading to a radical departure from established patterns. Thus, the strongly interdependent nature of institutions in postwar Japan is argued to have resulted in the Japanese business system being much more integrated than its Anglo-American counterparts, and as a result, more difficult to change.

Main features of business systems

The first step in BSys research is to describe the basic features of business systems and their interconnections. Whitley (1999: 33) suggests that differences in the nature of relationships between five broad kinds of economic actors are particularly important in contrasting business systems:

1 providers and users of capital
2 customers and suppliers
3 competitors
4 firms in different sectors
5 employers and different kinds of employee.

These vary in both the extent of organizational integration and whether this is achieved primarily through ownership-based hierarchies, formal arrangements, personal obligations or informal commitments, and so on. The relationships between these categories of actors

Table 4.2 Key characteristics of business systems

Ownership coordination
Primary means of ownership control (direct, alliance, market contracting)
Extent of ownership integration of production chains
Extent of ownership integration of sectors
Non-ownership coordination
Extent of alliance coordination of production chains
Extent of collaboration between competitors
Extent of alliance coordination of sectors
Employment relations and work management
Employer–employee interdependence
Delegation to, and trust of, employees (Taylorism, task performance discretion, task organization discretion)

Source: Whitley (1999: 34).

that make up a business system are also reflected in the primary features that Whitley (1999) accords to business systems (see Table 4.2).

Institutional typology

The connections between these dimensions, or characteristics, of business systems suggest that a limited number of combinations of business system characteristics are likely to remain established over historical periods, because contradictions between them can be expected to generate conflicts between social groupings and prevalent institutional arrangements. For example, business systems based on market types of ownership relations are unlikely to be supportive of long-term risk sharing between suppliers and customers, or employers and employees, because portfolio owners usually prefer liquidity to lock-in (Whitley, 1999: 41).

On the basis of these connections, Whitley (1999: 41–44) identifies six major ideal types of business systems. He distinguishes four types of market economies in terms of their degree of ownership-based coordination of economic activities, and the extent of non-ownership or alliance form of organizational integration.

First, there are those where both forms are low, so that the overall levels of coordination are limited. These are termed fragmented business systems. Fragmented business systems are dominated by small owner-controlled firms engaged in adversarial competition with each other, and short-term market contracting with suppliers and customers. Employment relations are also short term and dominated by 'efficient' external labour markets. Short-term results-orientation abounds and, along with this, a pronounced flexibility to convert the firm from one product or service to another. The most useful example of such a low-commitment economy is Hong Kong.

Second, coordinated industrial district business systems combine relatively low levels of ownership integration – and thus are dominated by small firms – with more extensive inter-firm integration and cooperation, and stronger links across sectors. Economic coordination is more geared to long-term perspectives, and cooperation, commitment and flexibility are emphasized in the sphere of work relations and management. Examples are postwar Italian industrial districts and similar regional districts (see Chapter 10 for more examples) in European countries.

Third, compartmentalized business systems are dominated by large firms, which integrate activities between sectors and in the industrial chain, also through shareholdings, but exhibit low levels of cooperation between firms and business partners. Moreover, in both commodity and labour markets more adversarial competition or confrontation abounds. Owner control is exercised at arm's length, through financial markets and shareholding. Firms are islands of authoritative control in a sea of market competition, as in the stereotypical Anglo-American economy.

Finally, Whitley distinguishes between three types of business system that combine relatively large units of ownership coordination with extensive alliances and collaboration between them. The three types are further differentiated by owner-control type, size of firm, and extent of alliance integration between firms and within them.

State-organized business systems are dominated by large firms that are dependent on state coordination and support to integrate production chains and activities in different sectors. These business systems differ in their ownership patterns. Families and partners in these economies are typically able to retain direct control over large firms. They are called state organized because the state subsidizes their growth, and thus dominates economic development and guides firms' behaviour. Prominent examples are France in Europe and Korea in Asia.

Collaborative business systems, on the other hand, exhibit more collective organization and cooperation within sectors (through industrial, employer and employee association, and quasi-government of the economic order by semi-private organizations such as chambers), but less ownership integration of activities in technologically and market-unrelated sectors. Ownership control of these large firms is typically alliance in nature; they develop a greater degree of employer–employee interdependence and trust of skilled workers than employers in compartmentalized and state-organized business systems. Prominent examples are to be found in western continental Europe, in German-speaking countries, and also in Scandinavia.

Highly coordinated business systems are also dominated by alliance forms of owner control and have extensive alliances between larger companies, which are usually conglomerates, and a differentiated chain of suppliers. Employer–employee interdependence is high, and a large part of the workforce is integrated into the enterprise in a more stable way. Japan is the most prominent example of this type of system.

Whitley's typology is not the only one that has been developed within the institutional literature, but in organization studies in Europe it is the most frequently used and most differentiated one. Such typologies, whether founded in VoC or Bsys approaches, are very crude tools that help us to sketch broadly the differences between, say, Korea and Japan, but that are unable to capture the more specific differences. BSys is more refined than VoC, but also in the case of VoC, a typology does not easily explain why a particular country develops a specific type of business system at a particular time. To this extent, theory building is limited. Typologies are useful, though, in forcing us to identify linkages between different institutional domains (Sorge, 2004).

Background versus proximate institutions

In considering the key social institutions that influence the sorts of business system that become established in different market economies, and the ways in which they vary, Whitley (1992a: 19) distinguishes between more basic, or 'background' institutions and 'proximate' institutions. 'Proximate' means tangible, concrete and specific. Background institutions refer to more fundamental social norms and legal rules, such as property rights,

Table 4.3 Key institutional features structuring business systems

Proximate institutions
The state
Dominance of the state and its willingness to share risks with private owners
State antagonism to collective intermediaries
Extent of formal regulation of markets
Financial system
Capital market or credit-based
Skill development and control system
Strength of public training system and of state–employer–union collaboration
Strength of independent trade unions
Strength of labour organizations based on certified expertise
Centralization of bargaining
Background institutions
Trust and authority relations
Reliability of formal institutions governing trust relations
Predominance of paternalist authority relations
Importance of communal norms governing authority relations

Source: adapted from Whitley (1999: 48).

that structure general patterns of trust, cooperation, identity and subordination in a society (see Table 4.3).

Background institutions are reproduced through the family, religious organizations and the education and training system, and they exhibit considerable continuity. They are crucial because they structure exchange relationships between business partners and between employers and employees. They also affect the development of collective identities and prevalent modes of eliciting compliance and commitment within authority systems. Variations in these institutions result in significant differences in the governance structures of firms, the ways in which they deal with each other and other organizations, and prevalent patterns of work organization, control and employment. For example, how trust is granted and guaranteed in an economy especially affects the level of inter-firm cooperation and the tendency to delegate control over resources. Another example is the impact of a society's level of individualism or collectivism. Individualistic societies such as the USA and the UK tend to have 'regulatory' states, a preference for formal, contractual regulation of social relationships, and market-based employment and skill development systems.

Proximate institutions are more directly involved in the economic system. They are often a product of the industrialization process and frequently develop with the formation of the modern state (see Table 4.3). Proximate social institutions affect forms of business organization and, in turn, become influenced by long-established and successful business systems. While there is no doubt about the existence of these causal relationships, the overemphasis of the BSys approach on 'thick' description is not matched by equally meticulous efforts at spelling out and theorizing the causal relationships between the relevant variables (Foss, 1999). This is perhaps due to the fact that the approach is 'aggregative and is not rooted in any spelled-out theory of individual behavior' (Foss, 1999: 4). The neglect of the actor within the framework is a lost opportunity to explain (institutional) change and institutionalization. As is explained in more detail below, the SE approach surpasses this problem by using structuration theory (Giddens, 1986) or the 'actor–structure' argument.[2]

Major societal institutions

The BSys approach, just as VoC, concentrates on a fixed number of dominant societal institutions that help to explain the variations between the business systems in different countries. The framework of a priori defined institutions and business system features helps the researcher to focus his/her analysis and probably contributes to the widespread use of the framework.

According to Whitley, the crucial institutional arrangements, which guide and constrain the nature of ownership relations, inter-firm connections and employment relations are argued to be those governing access to critical resources, especially labour and capital. In particular, these institutions are the state, the financial system, and the skill development and control systems (Table 4.3). Particularly important aspects of the state are its dominance of the economy, its encouragement of intermediary economic associations and its formal regulation of markets. The crucial aspect with regard to the financial system concerns the processes by which capital is made available and priced (see Chapter 6 for an extended explanation of this topic). A central distinction is made between capital-market-based and credit- or bank-based financial systems. In the former, resources are allocated through competition in capital markets, whereas in the latter they are allocated by the state or by financial institutions. In terms of the skill development and control systems, important factors are, first, the types of skill produced by education and training systems, and the extent to which employers, trades unions, and the state are involved in developing and managing such systems. This area also concerns the organization and control of labour markets, in particular the strength and organization of independent trade unions and the coordination of bargaining (see Chapter 5 for a discussion of this topic).

Connections between dominant institutions and business system features

The argument about the importance of major societal institutions, in defining a logic which explains how and why features of business systems 'come together', i.e. are coherent and complementary, can be detailed by a discussion of this logic for each type of system[3]:

Fragmented business systems

Fragmented business systems, then, develop within an institutional context that is characterized by low trust, unreliable formal institutions, difficult-to-share risks, and an at best neutral and at worst predatory state.

Coordinated industrial districts

Coordinated industrial districts develop and continue to be reproduced in an institutional context in which both formal and informal institutions limit opportunism and provide an infrastructure for collaboration to occur. Local governments, banks and training organizations typically work with potentially strong forms of local labour representation to restrict adversarial, price-based competition in favour of high-quality, innovative strategies based on highly skilled and flexible labour. There are various forms of market regulation at the local level. Firm size is limited by strong preferences for direct control by 'artisanal' entrepreneurs.

Compartmentalized business systems

Compartmentalized business systems develop in arm's length institutional contexts with large and highly liquid markets in financial assets and unregulated labour markets with a highly mobile workforce. States are regulatory rather than developmental. Compartmentalized business systems are also associated with weakly developed skills training and control systems. Practical manual worker skills are not highly valued, and training in them is typically governed by ad hoc arrangements with little or no central coordination. Unions may be influential at times but are usually organized around occupational skills rather than industries, and bargaining is decentralized. The relatively impoverished institutional infrastructure in the societies in which compartmentalized business systems develop is argued to restrict organizational integration between ownership units and leads to a strong reliance on ownership-based authority relations for coordinating economic activities.

State-organized business systems

State-organized business systems develop in a dirigiste environment, where the state dominates economic decision-making and tightly controls intermediary associations. Unions are weak and/or state controlled, and bargaining is decentralized – where it takes place at all as an institutionalized activity. Coordination in general is great and is centralized by the state. Firms and their owners are highly dependent on state agencies and officials. As a result, they delegate little to employees and find it difficult to develop long-term commitment with business partners or competitors.

Collaborative and highly coordinated business systems

Collaborative and highly coordinated business systems develop in collaborative institutional contexts that encourage and support cooperation between collective actors. The state performs a coordinating role and encourages the development of intermediary associations for mobilizing support and implementing collective policy decisions. Markets are typically quite regulated in these societies, limiting the mobility of skilled workers and the price-based allocation of capital through impersonal market competition. These kinds of business system are more likely to develop in economies with credit-based financial systems in which the providers of capital are strongly interconnected with its users and cannot easily exit when conditions change. Corporatist wage bargaining arrangements, based on strong unions, often lead to considerable employer–employee collaboration. Labour systems in these economies are often organized around public training systems in which strong sector or enterprise unions cooperate with employers. These systems encourage investment in high levels of skills, which are cumulative (built up in successive courses over working life) and linked to organizational positions. Moreover, trust in the efficacy of formal institutions governing exchange relations and agreements encourages joint commitments between the bulk of the workforce and management to enterprise development.

The differences between collaborative and highly coordinated business systems are argued to result from variations in the extent of institutional pluralism, especially regarding the institutions that govern the organization and control of labour power, and the concomitant dominance of the state's coordinating role. Highly coordinated business systems are more likely to develop in societies where the state dominates the coordination of economic development and the regulation of markets. Collaborative business systems are likely to develop in societies where banks, industry associations and similar organizations perform coordinating functions independently of state guidance.

Second, and probably more important in separating the two business systems, are the autonomy and influence of unions and other forms of labour representation in policy-making. Collaborative business systems develop when unions are strong at the national and sector level. Strong unions at the national level limit the capacity of state–business coalitions to coordinate and integrate economic development and restructuring on a significant scale. In particular, strong sector-based unions, involved in national policy networks, limit state coordination of economic changes across sectors. Additionally, powerful national unions, coupled with strong public training systems, limit worker dependence on particular employees, which, in turn, restricts the extent of organizational integration of manual workers within firms. However, centralized bargaining, collaboration in the management of training systems, and other factors, encourage greater integration of the bulk of the workforce in many firms in continental Europe – certainly more than in the Anglo-American economies. Societies, such as Japan, that develop highly coordinated business systems have less strong unions at the national and sector level. Japan has company-based unions, which do not form a strong counterweight against state dominance of economic coordination. Japan has limited public training systems. Training is organized at the company level, resulting in high employer–employee interdependence.

A systematic taxonomy on business systems

Whitley's typology resulted from a compilation and synthesis of many studies, but there had not been any attempt at the definition of standard operationalizations of the concepts, such that country characteristics could be 'measured' against a scale in a transparent way. Table 4.4 shows the key institutional features Whitley had defined, for deriving characteristics of business systems types. Whitley's method had been one of qualifying central results from a diverse array of many studies with different methodologies. More recently, however, Jasper Hotho has tried to derive a more systematically tested taxonomy on the basis of standard data collected in the OECD and in the World Competitiveness Report (World Economic Forum, 2000, 2011). Data were subjected to a fuzzy set analysis, which can deal with qualitative data, and these had been derived mainly from statistics in the OECD and World Economic Forum data series.

It has to be said that many of the measures adopted are not quite what Whitley had in mind when he came up with his analysis. To this extent, what Hotho (2014) produced does not have the very same empirical foundation and, by this token, conceptual implications. But it is the most systematic and transparent attempt to 'test' Whitley's ideas about how characteristics cluster into systems in such a way that the clustering is both meaningful, reflecting a functional logic that constitutes the coherence of the system, and statistically corroborated.

Any kind of comparative study is plagued by the trade-off between validity of operationalizations and representativeness of data. Whitley had opted for valid observations although findings were very complex and they came from different sorts of studies, but they were shrewdly synthesized. Representativeness of data was not an issue that Whitley

Table 4.4 Matching clusters and business system types

Institutional features	*Cluster 1 2000*	*Cluster 1 2011*	*Compartmentalized business systems*	*Cluster 2 2000*	*Cluster 2 2011*	*Collaborative business systems*	*Cluster 3 2000*	*Cluster 3 2011*	*State organized business systems*	*Cluster 4 2000*	*Cluster 4 2011*	*Cluster 5 2011*	*Coordinated industrial districts*
The state													
Strength of state coordination	Low	Low	**Low**	Considerable	Limited	**Considerable**	High	High	**High**	Low	Low	High	**Considerable locally**
Incorporation of intermediaries	Some	High	**Low**	High	Considerable	**High**	Low	Low	**Low**	Considerable	High	High	**Considerable locally**
Extent of market regulation	Low	Low	**Low**	High	Some	**High**	High	High	**High**	Low	Low	High	**Considerable locally**
Financial system													
Capital market or credit based	Capital market	Capital market	**Capital market**	Credit	Credit	**Credit**	Credit	Mixed	**Credit**	Capital market	Credit	Credit	**Some local bank risk-sharing**
Skill development and control													
Strength of public training system	High	Considerable	**Low**	Low	Low	**High**	High	Considerable	**Limited**	High	High	High	**High**
Union strength	Limited	Limited	**Low to some**	Some	Some	**High**	Low	Low	**Low**	High	High	Considerable	**High**
Centralization of bargaining	Low	Low	**Low**	High	High	**High**	Limited	Limited	**Low**	High	High	High	**Low**
Trust and authority													
Trust in formal institutions	Considerable	High	**High**	Limited	Considerable	**High**	Low	Low	**Limited**	High	High	Low	**Some**
Paternalist authority	Limited	Low	**Low**	Some	Limited	**Low**	High	High	**High**	Low	Low	High	**Variable**

sought to address or resolve systematically. Hotho now shifted the emphasis from validity to representativeness. This means that he compromised on Whitley's concepts, and he introduced variables and operationalizations that were not always wholly what Whitley had had in mind. However, this methodological design did allow a transparent 'test'.

Here is the list of variables that Hotho had collected from the mentioned sources, which can be compared to the list of key institutional features as defined by Whitley, in Table 4.3 above:

- State dominance (in economic governance and policy)
- Prevalence of clusters (the regional clustering of firms in an industry)
- Burden of regulation (as experienced by firms)
- Market capitalization to credit (as a source of enterprise finance)
- Strength of the education system
- Union density (the share of union members in the work force)
- Centralization of bargaining (about wages and other work conditions)
- Trust (between people in general)
- Paternalism (the obligation of more highly placed individuals to look after those for whom they are responsible).

Uncomfortably, the clustering was not quite the same in 2000 as in 2011; apparently, business systems are not immune to an economic and institutional change, which does call into question the argument about institutional stability. This is what we would expect; it does slightly upset any current taxonomy of systems, but we cannot expect institutional change to be absent, although it casts a doubt on the pertinence of any typology or taxonomy. However, the changes only concern a few countries (Ireland, Spain and Italy). Let us look at the clustering that emerged more recently, in 2011, in Table 4.5. The main deviation from Whitley is that the collaborative business system type has lost its Nordic European countries, which now emerge as a separate cluster. But that tallies with BSys concepts; the literature had already indicated that modern institutions in collaborative systems had been informed by different interests: in the Nordic countries, it was the social democratic parties in government and the trade union movement that marked the construction of the welfare

Table 4.5 Cluster membership 2011

Cluster 1	*Cluster 2*	*Cluster 3*	*Cluster 4*	*Cluster 5*
Canada	Germany	Czech Republic	Finland	Italy
United Kingdom	Austria	Portugal	Denmark	
Australia	Belgium	Slovakia	Sweden	
Switzerland	Ireland	South Korea		
Luxembourg	Netherlands	Poland		
Japan		Spain		
USA		Hungary		
New Zealand		Turkey		
		Greece		
		Mexico		

Source: Hotho (2014: 684).

state and socio-economic coordination, whilst in Western and Central Europe, it was the business federations and associations working with 'people's parties' in government, such as Christian Democrats, or together with unions and social democrats during economically precarious periods after the two world wars. Now 'forgotten' but historically significant, what was called 'corporatism' in political economy (devolution of economic governance from the state to organized interests) also owed a push to fascist governments in Austria, Italy, Spain and Portugal, to National Socialism in Germany and the countries under German-Austrian occupation in World War II. Such diverse influences gave different institutional imprints, but more collaborative systems resulted in the two types now distinguished by Hotho. In Table 4.5, these are therefore called Collaborative Nordic and Collaborative Central/Western E.

There are also deviations between Whitley's characterizations and Hotho's, such as for the strength of a public training system, which should be high in collaborative business systems according to Hotho but comes out low in Hotho's cluster 2. This is due to problems of getting the appropriate data in countries like Austria and Germany, where so many actors and collectivities share in the costs of training that it is impossible to get an aggregate figure without a more comprehensive investigation. In more school-bound systems such as in Sweden or France, however, the institutional concentration of training makes it easier to get an aggregate figure that does not leave out a particular cost. In this respect, Whitley's characterization is not misleading.

Table 4.5 shows the lists of countries belonging to each of the clusters derived by Hotho, for 2011. There are some deviations from what Whitley had suggested: the presence of Japan, Switzerland and Luxembourg in cluster 1, and of Ireland in cluster 2. Most likely, again, measurements which refute Whitley's ideas about associations between characteristics along key features, such as Switzerland's high capital finance, and imperfections in the operationalizations chosen explain the deviations.

On the whole and with a pinch of salt, therefore, BSys concepts are confirmed, despite somewhat different variables and operationalizations. Note that due to the reliance of Hotho's analysis on OECD data, non-OECD countries dropped out of this BSys analysis, which made large parts of Asia disappear, except for South Korea and Japan; hence, there is no fragmented business system type in the analysis in Table 4.5. But we will make up for this later in the chapter, in focussing on a BSys comparison of South Korea and Taiwan.

Also, the perceptive reader will be able to use, by now, BSys concepts as defined above, to analyse countries not yet included in systematic comparisons. For instance, China can be imagined as a combination of a State-regulated business system, due to central management of the economy and publicly owned commercial enterprises, with the fragmented type well established already for Hong Kong.

Based on Hotho's analysis, we can now add that collaborative business systems have to be divided into two sub-types: The European Nordic and the Western/Central variant. Roughly speaking, in the Nordic variant, collaboration has developed more around the trade unions and social democratic governments, forming new institutions and policies in collaboration with concentrated industrial groups. Sweden post-1937 is the classic case, with highly concentrated capital ownership and highly centralized trade unions. In the Western/Central European variant, employers' and industrial organizations and chambers of industry and commerce were more influential, but links with the state and unions, notably during economically catastrophic periods after world wars, were again crucial. Here, Austria is the classical case of a type found in the German language countries including Switzerland, although Hotho located it in

Table 4.6 Rough country scores on the dimensions of the four ideal types

	Liberal	*Statist*	*Corporatist*	*Meso-communitarian*
Australia	H	I	L	L
Austria	L	H	VH	L
Belgium	L	I	I	L
Canada	H	I	L	L
Denmark	L	I	H	L
Finland	I	I	H	L
France	L	H	L	L
Germany	I	I	H	L
Ireland	I	I	L	L
Italy	L	H	L	L
Japan	L	I	L	H
Netherlands	I	H	H	L
New Zealand	H	L	L	L
Norway	L	H	VH	L
Spain	I	H	L	L
Sweden	L	I	H	L
Switzerland	I	I	H	L
UK	H	I	L	L
USA	VH	L	L	L

the Anglo-American cluster. Switzerland is another case of opportunity making strange bedfellows, with its combination of Germanic employment and organizational systems with abundant liberal financialism.

As pointed out, typologies and taxonomies very much depend on the kind of data taken into consideration. Whilst the types derived by Whitley and Hotho are more based on business and management information, scholars in political economy following Hall and Soskice have derived types based on data and other information in taxation, public finance, employment relations, economic policies and control of the economy. From a very careful analysis of such taxonomies and information, Becker (2009) derived a synthesis of varieties of capitalism which made an important point: The distinction between control by markets and collective control of markets needs to be refined, because of distinctions in who exercises control There are clear differences between types of control exercised by (1) the state, (2) organized associations of business and labour, and (3) communities of enterprises across industries established by ownership or other dependence relations. The latter type of control is called meso-communitarian by Becker and it is exemplified by Asian examples such as keiretsu and chaebol. In addition, we have a type which the same as liberal market economies in VoC. Furthermore, Becker showed that to some extent these types exist in all the countries but to different extents, so that they can be considered dimensions of a country's variety of capitalism – with a slant towards political economy. In Table 4.6, you can see the result of a treatment which is too complex to explain here but detailed in Becker (2009); it consists of rough country scores on the dimensions of liberal, statist, corporatist and meso-communitarian varieties of capitalism (H = high, VH = very high, L= low, I= intermediate). You can see or work out to which extent the characterization and grouping of countries is similar to that in Hotho's analysis. If the analysis had had more

Asian countries, we would presumably have seen higher scores on the meso-communitarian dimension in Table 4.6, but also more statism; such an Asian picture is shown more vividly by what follows.

The following section on Taiwan and South Korea is an exemplary exercise in how to use BSys concepts creatively, not as an orthodox categorization with fixed types, but as an array of key concepts that can be used in a historically institutionalist analysis, to explain the niceties of systems. This shows how specific systems arise even, in broadly similar larger types such as state dominated systems in East Asia. As the 'proof of the pudding is in the eating', so the proof of BSys theory is in the historical unravelling, using available categories, to find out about the logic of national paths of development.

Conclusions

To sum up, differences in economic organization or business systems arise from contrasting processeses of industrialization and were shaped by social and political structures evolving during periods of industrialization. Variations in political arrangements and policies, and in the institutions governing the allocation and use of capital, have major effects on the extent and direction (vertical/horizontal) of organizational integration. Equally, the ways that skills are developed, certified and controlled exert significant influence on prevalent employment relations and work systems, as do the dominant norms governing trust and authority relationships.

All these institutional arrangements, in addition, affect the management of production and market risks, and they structure the ways that dominant firms are organized and controlled in market economies. And this is, in turn, linked to the sorts of competitive strategy they pursue. There will be more on this in successive chapters.

4.4 Business systems research applied to Taiwan and South Korea[4]

As discussed, the BSys approach argues that different dominant institutions encourage and constrain the development of distinctive and effective ways of organizing economic activities. Of course there are deviant patterns from the dominant one, but these can easily be identified. For instance, while there are some large capital-intensive firms in Taiwan, these are either state owned, or controlled and supported (such as Formosa Plastics), and do not reflect the dominant pattern of specialized, family businesses interconnected through elaborate personal networks. The focus here is on forms of business organization in South Korea (henceforth referred to as Korea) and Taiwan that compete effectively in the world markets. The analysis of the business systems features deals with the situation in the 1980s and 1990s. The dominant institutions that together help to explain these features, and how they do so, are also discussed briefly. The intention is to help you understand how to apply the business systems approach in detail and also in less well-known business systems.

The major distinguishing features of the postwar business systems in Korea and Taiwan are summarized in Table 4.7. These features were established between 1960 and 1990, and remained largely unchanged in the 1990s. Some features are quite similar in both business systems, particularly those concerned with employment relations and ownership control. There are, however, significant differences between the two; these are to do with firm size, ownership integration and horizontal linkages in particular.

Table 4.7 The postwar business systems of Korea and Taiwan

Business system features	*Korea*	*Taiwan*
Ownership coordination		
Owner control	direct	direct
Ownership vertical integration	high	low except in intermediate sector
Ownership horizontal integration	high	high in business groups, low elsewhere
Non-ownership coordination		
Alliance-based vertical integration	low	low
Alliance-based horizontal integration	low	limited
Competitor collaboration	low	low
Employment relations and work management		
Employer–employee interdependence	low except for some managers	low except for personal connections
Worker discretion	low	low

The Korean business system

Ownership relations

The Korean economy is dominated by very large family-owned and controlled conglomerate enterprises called Chaebol (well-known examples are Hyundai, Daewoo and Samsung). These large firms have driven industrialization in Korea since the 1952–54 war, under the strongly directive and coordinating influence of the authoritarian state. They dominate many manufacturing industries (i.e. the heavy and chemical industries), as well as significant parts of the service sector – in particular, the construction industry, transport services, insurance and related financial services. Moreover, seven large general trading companies, which are members of the largest ten Chaebol, have come to dominate Korea's export trade.

The Chaebol remain largely family owned and controlled, despite their rapid growth and state pressure to sell shares on the stock market. In the large Chaebol most of family holdings are indirect in the sense that owner control is exercised through a number of core companies rather than direct family ownership in all firms. The smaller Chaebol are more directly dominated by family owners. The continuance of high levels of family ownership despite the rapid expansion and large size of these conglomerates was facilitated by most of their expansion being funded by state-subsidized debt, which did not dilute family shareholdings. Family ownership continues to mean largely family control and direction, with most of the leading posts held by family members and/or trusted colleagues from the same region or high school as the founding entrepreneur. Family ownership also continues to imply strong central control over decision-making. This high level of direct owner control is implemented by substantial central staff offices that intervene extensively in subsidiary affairs. These offices typically deal with financial, personnel and planning matters, including internal auditing and investment advice, and some have as many as 250 staff. The high level of centralized decision-making encouraged considerable integration of economic activities, as capital, technology and personnel could be centrally allocated and moved between subsidiaries. The Chaebol are in fact managed as cohesive economic entities with a unified group culture focused on the owner.

These strong owner-controlled large groups of firms are highly diversified, both vertically and horizontally. Most are vertically strongly integrated, with many individual Chaebol business unit members themselves being vertically integrated, and the network of firms even more so. Horizontal diversification is considerable, with the average Chaebol operating in five different manufacturing industries. For example, Samsung's 55 firms were active in textiles, electronics, fibre optics, detergents, petrochemicals, ship building, property development, construction, insurance, mass media, healthcare and higher education in the early 1990s.

The Chaebol have grown extremely fast since the 1950s, with high growth at the expense of profitability. Detailed analysis of the Chaebol suggests that the objective of the firms of the large Chaebol is not to maximize profits but to maximize sales. Ownership rights are held for control purposes more than for income, and, as indicated, growth has been financed by state-provided and subsidized credit, rather than from retained profits.

Non-ownership coordination

The large size and self-sufficiency of the Korean Chaebol mean that they exhibit low interdependence with suppliers and customers, and are able to dominate small and medium-sized firms. Typically, their relationships with subcontractors are predatory. Core firms are able to increase their working capital by squeezing the subcontractors associated with the Chaebol. The Chaebol pass recessionary shocks on to subcontractors or even merge with them if it suits their plans.

Relations between the Chaebol, and between ownership units in general, tend to be adversarial in Korea, with considerable reluctance to cooperate over joint projects. New industries in particular are often the site of intense competition for dominance, and the major driving force behind many new investments often appears to be corporate rivalry for the leading position in them. In general, markets are not organized around the long-term mutual obligations that characterize the postwar Japanese economy, but rather are characterized by predominantly short-term, single-transaction relationships. These sometimes develop from personal contacts, as when subcontracting firms are set up by ex-employees. Where cooperation does occur between firms, direct personal ties between chief executives are usually crucial to reaching agreements. Alliance-based modes of integration, then, are weak in the postwar Korean business system.

The high degree of competition between the leading Chaebol, which has been fuelled by the state's policy of selecting entrants to new industries and opportunities on the basis of competitive success, has severely limited the development of independent sector-based organizations in Korea. There have been few, if any, industry-wide autonomous associations or other bodies promoting cooperation between firms and collectively lobbying the state. In the 1980s and 1990s, however, the umbrella organization, the Federation of Korean Industries, together with a few other associations, attempted to diverge from this and publicly influence state policies.

Employment policies and labour management

In most Chaebol the level of employer–employee commitment is limited for manual workers. Although seniority does appear to be important in affecting wage rates, and employers do provide accommodation and other fringe benefits in the newer capital-intensive industries, Korean firms are reluctant to make the sorts of long-term commitment to their workforce that many large Japanese firms do. Mobility between firms, both enforced and voluntary, has been considerably greater for manual workers – and some non-manual – than is common in the large-firm sector in Japan. Annual turnover rates of between 52 and 72 per cent were quite usual in the 1970s in Korea and were especially high in manufacturing. Leading firms in Korea sometimes poach skilled workers from competitors rather than invest in training programmes. Firms that are characterized by low turnover rates tend to lock in workers through high levels of overtime pay rather than workers feeling committed to them. White-collar employees are more favoured and tend to remain with large employers more often, not least because their pay and conditions are usually substantially better than they could obtain by moving.

The centralized and personal nature of authority relations in the Chaebol is accompanied by a largely authoritarian, not to say militaristic, management style. The Korean management style is characterized by top-down decision-making, enforcement of vertical hierarchical relationships, low levels of consultation with subordinates, and low levels of trust, both horizontally and vertically. Superiors tend to be seen as remote and uninterested in subordinates' concerns or their ability to contribute more than obedience. This authoritarian management style encourages close supervision of task performance. In order to facilitate supervision, the physical layout of offices is arranged in a specific way and tasks are usually described carefully. Because of the importance of personal authority in the Korean Chaebol, jobs and responsibilities are determined more by supervisors' wishes than by formal rules. Moreover, strong supervision of task performance is allied to considerable role specialization for manual workers. Unskilled workers continue to carry out relatively narrow tasks without much movement between jobs and skill categories. Non-manual workers, in contrast, do appear to be moved between tasks and sections, and sometimes develop more varied skills, in the larger and more diversified Chaebol. Managers in particular are often transferred across subsidiaries and have more fluid roles and responsibilities.

Institutional influences on the Korean business system

The dominant institutions stem from both pre-industrial Korean society and the period of Japanese colonial rule, as well as the Korean war and the post-1961 period of military-supported rule (Table 4.8). The dominant and risk-sharing nature of the Korean state can be traced back to the period between 1392 and 1910, when Korea was ruled by the Yi, or Chosun dynasty. This dynasty entrenched Confucianism as the official ideology. This ideology is based on the idea that the stability of society is based on unequal relationships between people. The Confucian heritage in Korea helps to explain the population's respect for hierarchy. During the Yi period, political power was highly centralized by the administrative elite, who claimed moral superiority over the population on the basis of examination successes. The elite were awarded official posts by the king, and access to examinations for the leading posts was restricted to those of aristocratic status. In addition, because the possibility of obtaining a state office was always present for the Korean aristocracy, they were discouraged from developing non-official corporate interest groups at the local level. Military institutions had little prestige in the Confucian-dominated political culture; Korea also lacked a strong commercial class, and this class was subjected to strict surveillance. In pre-industrial Korea, successful merchants were considered to be potential threats to the official elite, by manifesting an alternative basis of prestige and power to the official examinations, potentially constituting an independent source of power. The private

Table 4.8 Dominant institutional influences on the postwar Korean business system

The state
Dominant and risk sharing
Antagonistic to independent collective intermediaries
Strong formal and informal state regulation of markets
Financial system
State-dominated, credit-based financial system
Skill development and control system
Weak public training system; no collaboration with unions
State-controlled official unions
Weak occupational associations
Little institutionalized bargaining
Trust and authority
Low trust in informal institutions and procedures
Patriarchal authority relations

accumulation of wealth was officially regarded as an indicator of corruption. Hence, traders were considered to be exploiters and pedlars were organized into a state-controlled guild to be used for political control of any threats to the established order.

The 35 years of Japanese rule (1910 until approximately 1945) and the subsequent US occupation of Korea intensified some of the features of the pre-industrial political system, such as its high level of centralization. Among other things, the Japanese developed a formal administrative apparatus that enabled the state to control rural communities directly, without needing the local elites, and thus enhanced the centre's power over society as a whole. But much of this so-called 'modernization' of Korean society by the Japanese retained crucial elements of the earlier patrimonial system, notably the capricious and unpredictable behaviour of the executive. During the colonial period, indigenous enterprises experienced as much insecurity and instability as during the Yi period, encouraging further the dependence on close family ties among top managers and the intensive cultivation of personal connections with the governing elite. Indeed, as well as inhibiting the development of new indigenous political institutions, the Japanese occupation also prevented the growth of an independent Korean entrepreneurial elite and technical strata. Koreans were systematically excluded from middle- and senior-ranked posts in both the state bureaucracy and in privately owned businesses that were dominated by the Japanese. The few indigenous firms that did develop and survive were mostly in the textile and food-processing industries, and were heavily dependent on their toleration by the colonial administration. The bulk of the productive land, manufacturing and industrial enterprises was owned and managed by the Japanese, and the forced industrialization of Korea in the 1930s and 1940s was directed almost entirely towards supporting Japanese military expansion in mainland Asia. The Japanese did, however, provide a model of how industrial enterprises and banks could be organized, and they did develop the physical and social infrastructure necessary for an industrial economy, albeit one designed to support the colonial power.

When Korea recovered its independence in 1948, many of the traditional patterns recurred, especially the dependence on the centre. This dependence grew even more in the 1950s after land reform weakened the landlord class and rural elites. Particularly important, too, was the virtual giving-away of the formerly Japanese-owned businesses between 1947 and 1957 to favoured businessmen. These firms formed the basis of many of the leading Chaebol. The high level of business dependence on the state, and especially on personal relations with the chief political executive and/or bureaucratic elite, intensified further after the 1961 military coup led by Park Chong-hui. Initially, Park brought the richest men together in an anti-corruption campaign and charged them with illicit profiteering. After realizing that this would merely prevent the economy from developing, and that it was not popular, the military regime released the major business leaders and much of their property in exchange for paying fines in the form of establishing new enterprises and cooperating with the state in its ambitious industrialization plans.

The one exception to this return of expropriated property was the banking system, which was used systematically to direct investment, reward exports and other achievements desired by the state, and to punish inefficiency and/or political opposition. Thus, rather like in Japan, the Korean state limited the flow of cheap credit and, in particular, access to foreign loans and technology, to the fast-growing Chaebol in favour of its developmental priorities, first in light manufacturing exports and later, in the 1970s, in the heavy and chemical industries. The direct financial risks for the Chaebol-owning families were, therefore, limited since they did not need to find the capital themselves to dilute their control by selling shares on the stock market. However, the political risks were quite high, either for failing to meet state targets or for not supporting the regime. Big business in Korea was, and remains, highly dependent on the state and especially the president and his close advisers for access to subsidized credit and the means to expand. In return for these resources, the Chaebol diversified into heavy industry in the 1970s to fulfil state priorities, and they funded the political campaign of the ruling party. This high level of dependence, together with the traditional devaluation of formal legal institutions, engendered a low degree of trust in formal institutions and procedures. Trust, cooperation and loyalty in Korea remain largely based on groups constituted by predominantly ascriptive criteria and/or shared collective experiences.

The difficulty of establishing long-term trust relations outside kinship or similar groupings, inhibits the delegation of control to non-family managers in the Chaebol, and this is reinforced by the importance of personal superior–subordinate relationships. Moreover, given the pervasive insecurity of the entrepreneur in Korean society, and the lack of institutional mechanisms for generating trust and loyalty beyond the lineage, or similar personally based groupings, long-term obligations and alliances between firms are also difficult to develop and maintain. Enterprise and economic growth has therefore been managed internally by Chaebol owners rather than through extensive networks and business groups as in Japan. The overweening power of the central state likewise prevented the establishment of powerful intermediary institutions to coordinate economic activities within and between sectors.

In addition to providing cheap credit, the state reduced the risks for the Chaebol by controlling and restricting trade unions, and by limiting real wage increases. For political and economic reasons, the military regime maintained considerable control over the organized labour movement in Korea and often intervened in strikes and other industrial disputes. The weakness of the trade unions has meant that Chaebol owners have not had to gain the cooperation of workers or make long-term commitments. The plentiful availability of relatively cheap labour until the mid-1980s, due to population growth and emigration from the land to the major cities, also limited real wage growth and the need to gain workers' commitment to enterprise goals.

The general prestige of educational qualifications and their perceived necessity for high-status white-collar jobs have led to high levels of investment in general education, both public and private. However, whereas general academic qualifications enjoy great prestige in Korea, technical education is of relatively low status and limited in provision. Hence, managers were one of the least scarce resources, whereas skilled and experienced workers were most scarce. Moreover, the difficulty of establishing reliable long-term trust relationships and collective commitments beyond kinship and similar groupings prevented the generation of 'Japanese-style' employment policies in the Chaebol. Hence, as suggested, turnover among manual workers is great, as is the reliance on external labour markets for scarce skills.

The Taiwanese business system

Ownership relations

Taiwan developed a large state-owned enterprise sector that dominates the capital-intensive, upstream industries together with a large number of small and medium-sized family-owned and controlled firms dominating the export trade in consumer goods. The production of intermediate goods tends to be more dominated by larger enterprises, often exercising quasi-monopoly control and also forming more diversified business groups. These groups are usually under common ownership, although this may be shared between a number of business partners who have established highly personal trust relationships with one another.

From the early 1950s onwards, Taiwan has had one of the biggest public enterprise sectors outside the communist bloc and Sub-Saharan Africa. Indeed, the only Asian countries with a comparable public-sector contribution to capital investment were India and Burma. In 1980 the Taiwanese Ministry of Economic Affairs owned firms in the power, petroleum, mining, aluminium, phosphates, alkali, sugar, chemicals, fertilizers, petrochemicals, steel, shipbuilding, engineering and machinery industries, while the Ministry of Finance owned four banks and eight insurance companies. These public enterprises were very large by comparison with privately owned ones and often dominated, if not monopolized, their sectors. Thus, the state has retained ownership and control of the 'commanding heights' of the economy in Taiwan, especially the upstream capital-intensive sectors. Despite enormous differences and conflicts originating in World War II, between the Kuomintang government that 'fled' to Taiwan on the one hand, and the Communist (Maoist) government that was established in mainland China after a ferocious civil war, the government of the economy thus became less radically different between Taiwan and mainland China than might be assumed: publicly owned enterprises played an important role.

Privately owned Taiwanese businesses follow the traditional pattern of the Chinese family firms that dominate many Asian economies. Most are limited in size, relatively specialized in particular industries, concentrated in light manufacturing industry and commerce, and embedded in highly flexible networks of suppliers, subcontractors and customers. When successful, they often engage in opportunistic, unrelated diversification. Most networks between family firms are not particularly stable or long-lived, except where they are based on strong personal ties of mutual obligation and support. Private firms in Taiwan are nearly all owned and controlled by families, as indeed are most Chinese businesses throughout Southeast Asia. Owners are highly involved in the running of their firms, and there are strong connections between ownership and the direction of economic activities. As in many family firms in other economies, authority in Taiwanese companies is highly centralized and personal, with little emphasis on formalized rules. In diversified firms, subsidiaries are coordinated through personal relationships and family domination of multiple top-management positions, rather than by systematic planning or joint activities. This emphasis on family ownership and control means that dominant goals are focused on the acquisition and growth of family wealth rather than on the growth of the firm as a separate entity. The pursuit of large size, irrespective of profitability, is not usually the dominant objective in these firms, especially if it could lead to the loss of personal control or to being considered a threat by the ruling party's interests.

Vertical integration is weak in most of these firms and they are rarely self-sufficient in terms of combining the management of key processes and activities in one organization. Instead, they are usually highly interdependent with other enterprises for inputs and for distributing their outputs, and they form fluid subcontracting networks. This interdependence is not usually accompanied by a willingness to share long-term risks with suppliers and buyers, however. More restricted and limited connections are preferred. Some Taiwanese business groups do exhibit a greater degree of backward integration in the production of intermediary goods, but this is much less than in Korea or many Western firms.

Diversification of a horizontal nature is more widespread in private Taiwanese firms, especially those forming business groups of associated companies. While by no means all successful firms develop into highly diversified business groups (including some of the largest), those that do diversify tend to move into a variety of sectors in a seemingly ad hoc and idiosyncratic way, often as the result of personal requests or obligations. A common pattern of expansion for leading Taiwanese business groups is to establish a dominant presence – quasi-monopolistic in many cases – in a particular sector supplying export-orientated firms, and then to set up a number of quite separate and unrelated businesses to be run by the patriarch's sons and other male relatives. Ownership-based diversification is quite considerable in the intermediate sector, but less so in the capital-intensive state sector or the small-firm-dominated export sector.

Non-ownership coordination

The specialization and interdependence of Taiwanese family businesses mean that they have to rely on each other to obtain inputs for their products and services, and to distribute and market them. Thus multiple market connections between firms are crucial to their operation. These are not necessarily long term or based on mutual obligations. Rather, inter-firm links are often managed in such a way as to reduce risks, and in this way commitments to other economic actors are restricted. Exchange partners may, then, be numerous and selected on the basis of their personal reputations for competence and reliability, but do not usually form networks of long-term trust and reciprocal loyalty. Market relations can change rapidly and are quite fluid, and flexibility is emphasized over long-term risk sharing. Indeed, when the Taiwanese state tried to encourage the formation of Japanese-style subcontracting arrangements, it failed. Equally, attempts to establish trading companies as long-term coordinating agencies in Taiwan have been less successful than in Korea.

Business partnerships, on the other hand, often do involve long-term reciprocal commitments, and they can lead to the development of elaborate networks of personal obligations that structure strategic decisions and new ventures. Where significant resources are involved and firms need to undertake activities jointly, connections are highly personal and dependent on trust between the owners. Without high levels of personal trust, such partnerships cannot be formed successfully in Taiwan and, as a result, many medium-sized firms do not grow into large enterprises because they are unable to find partners they can rely on. In general, the extent of systematic, stable, vertical and horizontal integration of economic activities through alliances and long-term partnerships is limited in Taiwan. Partnerships based on personal connections and trust, on the other hand, seem easier to develop and to be more sustained than in Korea.

Sectoral cooperation is also limited by this concern with personal control, as well as being restricted by the state's intolerance of independent intermediary organizations. Moreover, the survival strategies of Taiwanese small and medium-sized enterprises are to seize opportunities, take full advantage of them and then leave the industry; the result is frequent entry and exit of Taiwanese enterprises, making stable associations of industry-specific associations difficult to maintain. Collective organization and joint action by competitors are therefore lacking in Taiwan.

Employment policies and labour management

Long-term employment commitments and seniority-based promotion practices tend to be reserved for those workers with whom the owning family has personal obligation ties, while previously unknown staff hired though impersonal channels neither expect nor receive such commitments. In particular, young, female, semi-skilled, non-family workers in the light manufacturing export sector are expected to stay only for a short time and are rarely trained for more demanding posts.

The intensely familial nature of these businesses restricts senior managerial posts to family members or those who have family-type connections to the owner. Thus, many skilled workers and managers prefer to leave and start their own businesses once they have acquired business skills and some capital. This is especially so in the labour-intensive export sector, where subcontracting is widespread. Both the general cultural preference for personal business ownership over employment, and the unwillingness to trust non-family subordinates on the part of the employers, limit the scope and length of employer–employee commitments in the Chinese family business, where obligations are restricted to close personal connections.

The importance of personal relationships and authority in Chinese family businesses means that the formal specification of roles and positions is less important than in most Western societies. Equally, jobs and skills are not rigidly defined and separated by formal procedures, but rather are fairly broad and flexible. Many managers in Taiwanese groups hold multiple positions, are rarely restricted to a single specialized role, and their responsibilities are liable to be changed suddenly at the behest of the owner.

The strong commitment to patriarchal relationships in the workplace, and in society as a whole, means that superior–subordinate relationships are quite remote and distant, particularly those between the owner-manager and the employees without a familial connection with management. Much as in the Korean situation, paternalism implies a lack of confidence in the abilities and commitment of staff, so that close supervision of work performance is a feature of Taiwanese firms, as is considerable personal discretion in how authority is exercised, especially at the top of the enterprise.

Institutional influences on the Taiwanese business system

Some of the institutional features of Korean society can be found in Taiwan, but there are also significant differences, which have resulted in a different kind of business system. The dominant institutions in Taiwan during its industrialization combine some features from pre-industrial society – such as the strong identification with, and loyalty to, the family – with a number of quite distinctive features resulting from Japanese colonialism and the imposition of the Kuomintang (KMT) rule after the war (Table 4.9). Perhaps the most important feature of Taiwan's industrialization since the end of Japanese colonialism in 1945 has been the large-scale movement of the Chinese nationalist government and its followers to Taiwan in 1949 following its defeat in the civil war by the communists. This take-over of Taiwan by Chiang Kai-shek and the KMT not only effectively created a new state but also established a major division in its population between the 6 million or so Taiwanese and the 1 to 2 million 'mainlanders', which had major consequences for the organization and control of economic activities.

In particular, it resulted in a highly authoritarian state, which excluded most Taiwanese from the state bureaucracy and political leadership and from the management of the large publicly owned industrial sector. This domination of Taiwanese society by outsiders continued the pattern established by the Japanese occupation (from 1895 until 1945), in which the indigenous population learnt to obey and fear their rulers and to develop economic activities within the context and framework established by an external power. The lack of trust between the KMT and its mainlander followers and the Taiwanese, together with the military objective of retaking control of mainland China, which justified the continuance of martial law and the authoritarian state – at least in the eyes of the leadership – resulted in the state maintaining ownership of the larger, upstream and capital-intensive sector of the economy. In addition, many state officials and leading KMT politicians continued to regard the establishment of large privately owned concentrations of economic resources with considerable suspicion and considered them a potential threat

Table 4.9 Dominant institutional influences on the postwar Taiwanese business system

The state
Dominating state controlled by mainlanders; commitment to state-led development with little risk sharing with Taiwanese firms
Antagonistic to independent collective intermediaries
Strong state control of upstream capital-intensive sectors, agriculture and new industries; low control of small firms in export sector

Financial system
State-directed, credit-based financial system; limited state control of informal curb market in SME sector

Skill development and control system
Stronger state technical training system for technicians and engineers than elsewhere in East Asia
State-controlled and repressed labour organizations
Weak occupational associations
Little institutionalized bargaining
Trust and authority
Low trust in formal institutions and procedures
Patriarchal authority relations

to their power. Hence they were reluctant either to privatize state enterprises or to encourage large Taiwanese firms to develop independently from the state. State ownership extended to the banks and the bulk of the formal financial sector, and enabled the regime to provide jobs for its followers.

But this also encouraged the development of the small-firm Taiwanese-dominated export sector. However, the KMT domination of the economy was different from that of the military-backed regime in Korea, in that it concentrated more on state ownership and control of tariffs, import licences, and so on, than on direct control over the flow of credit to privately owned firms. Although the formal banking system in Taiwan has been owned and controlled by the state since the Second World War, the regime has not used this control to direct the flow of capital to favoured private firms pursuing state priorities. Rather, it has been more concerned to prevent the growth of the large Taiwanese enterprises that had close links with major banks. In general, the banks themselves prefer to lend to the state enterprises and the largest privately owned firms, which have good mainlander connections, since the risks are lower. Banks function more as branches of the bureaucracy than as risk-sharing supporters of industry. As a result, the bulk of firms in the Taiwanese-dominated export-orientated sector rely more on the informal market and capital from family and friends for growth than on the formal banking system. This is especially true for smaller and newer enterprises, which have little or no collateral to support their applications for bank loans. Consequently, informal, personal networks of trust and support are crucial to firms' survival and growth in Taiwan, and the development of large-scale capital-intensive industries is difficult without strong state support.

The regime's antagonism to large privately owned enterprises that are independent of the state has prevented long-term collaboration between the state and large-scale private interests. Instead, the private Taiwanese-dominated part of the economy has largely been treated with official disdain, and relations between state officials and Taiwanese businessmen are often described as 'cool' and 'distant', in contrast to those between officials and the leaders of publicly owned enterprises. As a result, the degree of direct dependence on the state of most Taiwanese businesses is limited, and the state has found it difficult to gain the cooperation of firms in a particular sector when it has wanted to achieve a specific objective through collaboration. The large number of small firms in most sectors, and the traditional distrust of the regime and its agents, exacerbate this.

Moreover, the traditional Chinese leaders' concern with limiting the power of private wealth holders, exacerbated by the ethnic divide between the Taiwanese and the mainlanders, was expressed most strongly in the conflict over the liberalization of the economy and movement to a more export-orientated policy at the end of the 1950s. However, more for political reasons than for economic ones, coupled with strong US pressure, Chiang Kai-shek (first president of Taiwan and Kuomintang leader in the Chinese civil war) supported the reform group in 1958, and Taiwan adopted a more liberal, though still state-dominated, approach to economic management. This boosted the largely Taiwanese-owned export-orientated sector, and confirmed the distinctive division of the political and economic system between mainlanders and Taiwanese. The former dominated the military, the political system, the bureaucracy and the state enterprises, while the latter concentrated on building up family businesses in export-focused light manufacturing and commerce. Although this division became attenuated in the 1980s as the proportion of mainlanders declined and economic growth increased the regime's security, it remains a distinctive feature of Taiwan's society and has had major consequences for the business system that has become established.

As in Korea, the Confucian emphasis on education has resulted in high rates of private and public investment in education. However, the exclusion of the Taiwanese from leading positions in the bureaucracy has meant that the private sector has been more attractive to college graduates than might be expected. The public education system in Taiwan has produced large numbers of engineers over the past 30 years, and the appeal of technical subjects such as electrical and electronic engineering seems to have been greater than in Korea. This has not been accompanied, however, by the development of strong craft-based skills accredited by public institutions. Employers' use of technical skills has not, then, been constrained by specialized, publicly certified and standardized practical competences, but remains largely determined by individual firms' organization of tasks and on-the-job training. Consequently, the education and training system develops certified technical skills without standardizing jobs around them or institutionalizing highly specialized roles within firms. Although university education remains highly prized and competition to enter universities is high, traditional literary qualifications and official positions are not as highly regarded as in traditional Chinese society. State control over the labour movement has been strongly enforced, as in Korea.

As in Korea, too, unions and occupational associations have had little impact on skill development and standardization, and they have not affected the way work is organized and controlled in firms. The KMT maintained firm control over unions for political as well as economic reasons, and the right to strike was prohibited under martial law. State control over, and repression of, trade unions meant that business owners have not had to formalize employment procedures, nor to elicit long-term commitment from employees, especially those to whom personal obligations are not due. In addition, the combination of the strong preference for family entrepreneurship, close rural–urban linkages, and the relatively decentralized nature of industrial development throughout much of Taiwan has restricted the development of large concentrations of urban workers wholly dependent on employment. This, in turn, has limited the formulation of a self-assured working-class movement that could exert pressure on employers and the state. Furthermore, the predominance of small to medium-sized family-controlled businesses, in which traditional conceptions of paternalistic management remained important, has inhibited the growth of unions. The significance of personal relationships, and foundations of trust in Taiwanese society, limit the establishment of formal collective organizations representing workers' interests in favour of personal obligations and commitments. Skill-based occupational identities and organizations are, similarly, unimportant in Taiwan.

Conclusions

Internationalization, growth and institutional developments have not, then, constituted such strong and discontinuous changes as to lead to major shifts in dominant forms of economic organization in Korea and Taiwan.

While the democratization of the Korean and Taiwanese states has reduced the extent of authoritarian direction of economic development and firms' policies in recent years, the state remains the dominant collective agent of economic decision-making in these economies.

Moreover, the lack of strong intermediary organizations in both countries remains, as does the limited extent of collaboration between competitors over such issues as training, bargaining and technological development. Risk sharing continues to be largely absent beyond personal ties in Korea and Taiwan.

Finally, democratization in both countries does not yet seem to have developed such discontinuities with the recent past as to generate major changes in business-system features.

The reader will appreciate that although we are dealing with East Asian countries, influenced by Confucianism and the associated values, and the countries were strongly influenced by periods of Chinese or Japanese rule, and Taiwan has for some time rivalled with the People's Republic of China for being the legitimate Chinese state, including a seat on the Security Council of the United Nations, remarkably different national business systems have come about, which are also different from the current order of the People's Republic of China: in the latter country, the main export industries are partly state-owned and partly private, family ownership of industrial groups has lost its role, and a state run by the Communist Party has retained a very strong role in the economy.

4.5 Integrating approaches

SE analysis is not a theory in the conventional sense but an 'approach' that is open to further development. Unlike the business systems (BSys) approach, which focuses on an a priori fixed set of institutions, the SE approach works with a classification of spaces, mentioned in the introductory chapter, which is filled by institutions that may change over time; it is less specific on institutions. The SE approach offers a balance between structure, action and actor-centric elements. As is explained more extensively below, the attention for the actor or agency means that the approach is better able to explain change than the BSys approach.

Note that the notion of actor as used in SE analysis is not confined to the 'individual subject'. It can equally well be applied to categories and groups of actors (i.e. organized occupational categories, unions, and other collective actors), in an enterprise and across enterprises in an industry or the whole economy.

One thing that SE analysis shares with BSys and VoC concepts, is the idea that structures and events in distinct domains, in SE parlance the spaces, are not independent but always inter-linked. Thus, when work organization changes, this will entail concomitant or subsequent changes in the other spaces. The idea of a correspondence between characteristics across institutional domains is also quite strong in VoC and Bsys. Also, a lot of the evidence for Whitley's and Hall and Soskice's writings, to the extent that it refers to employment, organizational and management systems in Britain, France and Germany, was based on evidence form SE research.

But SE theorizing has a strong dose of dialectical and paradoxical reasoning, meaning that institutionalized practices in the different spaces not only change over time; but they change in a way which upsets existing institutional correspondences in creative and surprising ways, although (note that the dialectics and the paradox come in here!) the core of previous arrangements and their logic always persists. The continued presence of the core of a logic, combined with institutional change, is called the non-identical reproduction of institutions: Even under radical change, an underlying logic is reproduced; it may sometimes be 'watered down' but it may also be sharpened. At such moments, background institutions or values may matter a lot.

Now, many readers and reputed scholars absolutely abhor the idea of dialectics and paradox. However, it imposes itself empirically, rather than being the obsession of French and German thinkers. Let us consider a number of stylized examples.

The societies, economies and polities of the former Tsarist Empire, which became Soviet Russia in 1917 and a less socialist Russian republic after 1992, has gone through some of history's most radical institutional transformations. Yet, a problem already mentioned by Karl Marx is the poor and fuzzy separation and integration of political and economic bodies and functions in what he called the 'Asian mode of production'. Also, the vertical social inequality, between an upper crust of 'oligarchs' and people below, between the absolutely filthy rich and the hard pressed, defeats any West European imagination, even though the latter is quite used to capitalist modes of operation. Has socialism been an unremarkable and brief interlude of some 80 years? SE analysis says that even in revolutionary change, actors always of necessity fall back on some institutional logic and some values; even in a revolution, human actors search for values and institutional orientations which are familiar and have a chance of being accepted, even if working that out is a very bloody and unpredictable affair.

Look at China in a similar way. From imperial rule it has gone via a feeble republic through a civil war linked with Japanese occupation, to first Maoist Communism, and unparalleled bloodshed in the 'great leap forward', to a mixed economy under Communist Party management. Yet, the seeking of harmony and working things through *guang-xi* (networks of related or well acquainted people) has never lost its importance. Also, note that when Max Weber at the beginning of the twentieth century wrote on the differences between occidental and oriental societies, he observed that Chinese cities were very different from Central European ones: whilst in China people came under the affiliation and jurisdiction of their place of birth and family location, in Europe it was their place of legitimate residence and citizenship. In present-day China, despite the massive changes that have taken place towards supposed universalism, we still find the practice of hu-kou, meaning that rights and entitlements are governed by the place of origin, rather than the place of work.

France is another country which has featured prominent revolutions. Philippe d'Iribarne (mentioned in Chapter 3) suggested that never mind the numerous revolutions, basic social gradations (such as the difference between 'vassals' and 'lackeys' in the pre-1789 kingdom) and aspirations (to become a 'vassal' in large and preferably public organizations and move up the scale) have been unchanging. Even industrial apprentices see themselves as engaged in career steps to something that is distinctive. Michel Crozier suggested that increasing institutional rigidity and inertia of necessity leads to a revolution every now and then. The whole cycle of phases of revolution, institutional re-orientation, rigidity and inertia is itself almost institutionalized! This is a perennial point of discussion and soul-searching in France.

And then we have a country like Germany which has gone through revolutions bestowed upon it 'from above' – the Bismarckian change towards a more integrated government and a parliament more equally elected than in any other country in Europe except for Switzerland at the time – or from the outside, such as in the changes wrought by Napoleon after 1803, and under Allied military occupation after 1945. Change from the outside or above almost appears like an institutional pattern itself. Yet, throughout the vicissitudes and vacillations of the Kaiser, the republic, the Führer, Communism in the East, and postwar democracy, Germany seems to have thrived on the meticulous rule of law even when law was perverted, a link between 'theory' and 'practice' in education and training, and between conceptualization and execution in organizations. Another continuity is the strength of voluntary associations as intermediaries between governments and the people.

In SE analysis, actors thus reproduce values and institutions because otherwise meaningful action is impossible. They also drive towards institutional change, deliberately or unwittingly. Actors always have different interests, and the pursuit of their specific interests brings out their own and specific conceptions of what they want to change and what they want to keep. However, their interests are a result of socialization into roles, which brings in values and institutionalized competences. Furthermore, they are guided by opportunism, which means considering legitimate institutional patterns, alliances with other interests and institutionally structured opportunities. Even in revolutions, actors have to refer to background institutions and to some extent proximate ones, in order to mobilize followers and potential allies into concerted action.

A major characteristic of SE research then is that it aims to relate organizations to the institutional and cultural systems of the surrounding society, and thus attempts to overcome the split between institutionalism and culturalism. SE thus addresses a weakness of etic cultural analysis, which tends towards methodological individualism, using value surveys that target individuals to explain systemic characteristics. It also addresses a weakness of institutional analysis, which neglects the individual in favour of system characteristics. Faced, for example, with organizational outcomes in Japan, compared with other societies, institutional analysis (such as the BSsys approach) would play down the role of Japanese culture to the extent that this refers to individual mental programmes and general socialization processes. Institutionalists would argue that the specificity of Japanese practices resides in a different construction of professional careers, labour markets (life-long employment), payment systems and industrial relations, or, in other words, in system characteristics. They would argue that, if Europeans and Americans were to be transplanted into a Japanese-type context, they would reproduce or generate the same organizational patterns (Sorge, 2004). They ignore the question of why Japanese institutions developed in Japan in the first place and not in Europe or the USA. Cultural analysis would argue the opposite – that is, it would stress the importance of mental programmes as opposed to system features in explaining organizational outcomes. The aim of societal analysis is to capture the interrelationship between all these influences and their effect on organization. That makes it less straightforward, more complicated, but also more integrative with regard to an array of approaches that would otherwise co-exist without working out linkages that are eminently useful.

Actor–structure relationship

One of the major theoretical features of the SE approach is the aim to contextualize phenomena, i.e. to look at them in their respective contexts. This is linked with the emphasis on the reciprocal constitution of actors and structures. The approach thus draws on structuration theory (Giddens, 1986: Chapter 4), which has made the point that individual behaviour and social structure are reciprocally constituted: it is impossible to imagine a normative regularity, instituted to be more or less binding, as not being kept in place by acting individuals. Likewise, individuals do not make behavioural choices without regard for norms (Sorge, 2004). It is precisely by recognizing that actors (individuals and organizations) are able to influence institutions (i.e. laws, rules, systems) and processes that SE analysis is able to inject dynamics into BSys analysis. The SE approach argues that actor–space interaction patterns do not necessarily reproduce something that remains unchanged. Actors have the ability to innovate practices, which reduces the inertia usually implied by institutions.

Since actors are embedded in social structures and institutions, they replicate some more abstract qualities of practices – Whitley's background institutions – even as they innovate them. Furthermore, structural properties and rules of the game tend to load the individual 'choices' that actors make in a specific way, if only for opportunistic reasons of feasibility. Actors tend to see particular 'choices' as generally favourable, and develop a specific 'programming of the mind', mentioned by the culturalists. The dynamics in this way link both elements of stability and change within 'non-identical reproduction'. In other words, since individuals or organizations live by, use, accept or are familiar with existing rules, laws, regulations, and so on, they will, almost unconsciously and automatically, base themselves on the existing and the 'known' to innovate or introduce change. As a consequence, change will usually be incremental (non-identical reproduction) rather than revolutionary. And when it is revolutionary, as we could see in the stylized examples above, incremental adaptation to previously existing institutions or structures will invariably creep in, for otherwise the coherence that actors need will be lost.

The interactive relationship between actor and spaces may be marked by both correspondence, or complementarity, and opposition: faced, for example, with hierarchical organization patterns, the actors may learn to internalize corresponding assumptions and find them legitimate. They may also develop a dislike for them, and attempt to evade them while trying at the same time to comply with them. This means that expressed value preferences and manifest behaviour may both converge and diverge (Sorge, 2004). This is the entry into an important phenomenon: social action necessarily generates a diversity of values, institutions and more mundane practices of all sorts. The consequence is that even in the most homogeneous society, values and institutional patterns are not uniform but diverge, often radically, between types of enterprises, industries and situations.

The SE approach distinguishes two levels of change, one more abstract and the other more concrete. Concrete practices, arrangements and actor predispositions change over time. However, since new practices are linked to existing logics of action, they will take on a specific form that is in accordance with the existing societal identity. In other words, new practices will be moulded by the existing societal institutions while existing societal institutions remain visible in the specific form that changes take on. Actors and institutions thus have a historical dimension. The 'construction of actors' (their knowledge, values and predispositions) and the 'construction of institutions' shape the actors' identity and the nature of specific institutions. Recognition of this historical nature enables the approach to take account of the dynamics of change. Historical analysis is used to identify influences extending from specific events in the past, whether it is the personal biography of human beings, the history of organizations or other collectivities, or the history of states and entire societies.

Important points:

- There is an interactive relationship between actor, structure and process.
- This relationship can be characterized by correspondence and opposition, and can produce institutional change.
- Relevant actors and spaces should be empirically determined and not theoretically fixed.

Institution as a process and a structure

Let us go back to the spaces of action already introduced in the first chapter, and go a bit further in their analysis. Each of these spaces can be subdivided into a structure and a process aspect. The structural aspect refers to the 'stocks' and properties that characterize the composition of an aggregate of people or of a system. The process refers to the changes that occur with regard to a space, over a certain period of time. Structures and processes are related reciprocally. A process – for instance, labour market mobility between enterprises – has a clear structure, being de-composed into relative shares of types of labour differentiated by age, experience, specialism, education and training, and other salient variables. Inversely, a structure is characterized by processes since a structure is never entirely stable. The identity of the structure over time is not limited to those elements that remain stable over a period of time; it also includes a relatively stable pattern of changes.

The organizational space has structures, such as formal and informal organization structures, of both hierarchical and functional kinds. The process side is characterized by primary and secondary transformation processes, which transform inputs into outputs.

The **competence generation space** has, on the structure side, professional structures, the apparatus (schools, instructors, teaching methods, etc.) dedicated to training, and the educational system of a society, both inside and outside enterprises. On the process side, there are personnel flows across stages of education, training and socialization more generally. The latter includes job changes, since even a succession of jobs without a manifest training purpose has a socialization effect.

The **industrial space** includes, on the structure side, the subdivision of an economy into sectors and industries, and the subdivision of industries into enterprises of different types (differentiated according to size, age, dependence, etc.). The construction of the value generation chain (vertical and horizontal integration or differentiation over organized units and enterprises) is a part of this. On the process side, there are transactions of commodities and goods between industries and sectors, including ideas and information, rather in the manner of an input–output table. There are also processes that involve the leaving and entering of enterprises in industries.

The **employment relations space** has structures such as organizations, contractual, informal and statutory rules, which govern processes in the transaction of labour power. Professional structures are also a structural aspect, since they affect the supply of and demand for labour. Such professional structures also form part of the competence generation space, which is close to the employment space.

In the **technical space**, we have the structural features of physical artefacts, of their mode of development, design and employment, and the processes of information and of knowledge and experience flows. These flows constitute and change technology. Innovation comes under the process aspect of the technical space, being concerned with changes to structures of technical experience and knowledge.

As indicated, the SE approach does not aim to define a rigid de-composition of the society and the economy into subsystems. Proponents of this approach do not think that classifications, such as those offered by the BSys approach or VoC, should become a quasi-orthodoxy. Instead, they stress the relationships between events, arrangements, structures and processes, across any classification. This means that it is essential to explore the societal aspect of any social, economic and political phenomenon with which we are concerned. Societal analysis is concerned with lateral, reciprocal relationships between any subdivided components of reality. Briefly, this means that what happens in a specific space has to be explained with reference to a set of cross-relationships with as many other spaces as possible.

Institutional interdependence

The reciprocal constitution of actors and spaces, and the cross-referencing of institutions across spaces, were conceived to bear regard to a phenomenon mentioned by all the institutionalist perspectives discussed: interdependence between arrangements in different spaces and institutional domains. Because of this interdependence, we have correspondences (linkages which appear meaningful) across the boundaries of spaces and domains. For example, capital market and labour market arrangements are complementary. The short-term view, which capital finance implies, goes hand in hand with short-term labour contracts.

Action spaces are interlinked in such a way that they condition each other reciprocally, thus safeguarding the 'coherence' between the spaces. This means that specific patterns of work organization and enterprise structures are linked with specific patterns of human resource generation, of industrial and sectoral structures, and of employment relations. What happens in one space has implications for what happens in the others.

Societal effects are therefore not what they are often construed to be, the effect of characteristics at the 'societal level' upon characteristics at 'lower' levels. Instead, they are conceived to originate from the reciprocal constitution of spaces. The distinctiveness of a particular society, and what is called societal identity, lies in the features that a historically specific type of reciprocal constitution has brought about.

Important point: Spaces and institutional domains are complementary. The implication of this is that change in one space will affect the other spaces.

Societal analysis is open to further development, through rearrangement of spaces and reconsideration of societal specificity over time. The openness of the approach will allow us to use it to examine whether the notions of globalization (which is discussed in Chapter 1) and convergence (discussed in the concluding chapter) are useful and relevant perceptions of reality. The rhetoric of globalization is usually based on the analysis of financial flows, commercial exchanges, supranational government and multinational enterprises. The SE approach could widen the debate by including an analysis of the context in which globalization forces are active, highlighting the diversity of both predispositions and reactions from actors at national or local levels.

This would mean that a certain priority would be given to the 'local', which serves as a basis for revealing the 'global'. The notion of 'societal' will then need to be reformulated, making it no longer necessarily associated solely with national spaces (that is, spaces enclosed by the boundaries of the nation-state). The analytical dialectic that characterizes the approach allows for forging links between the forms of sectoral, regional, national, supranational and international regulation to which the actors active in the different spaces contribute.

Important point: The fact that relevant spaces and actors have to be empirically identified and are not a priori fixed, combined with the analytical dialectic of the SE approach, implies that it can be used to examine globalization effects in management and organization.

4.6 Institutional change

One last topic in this chapter is institutional change. Most versions of institutional analysis are static and have a limited view of change, as if it happened from one type of institutional set to another. This is a result of the basic assumption that institutions are stable over time and difficult to change. In reality, however, we observe that institutions do change, both incrementally and in a revolutionary way. The literature points to many causes of institutional change. Three general types of pressure towards institutional change, which are relevant in the context of this book, are functional, political and social (Oliver, 1992).

Causes of institutional change

Functional pressures

Functional pressures are those that arise from perceived problems in performance levels associated with institutionalized practices. For example, the Japanese keiretsu have been questioned as a consequence of the generally deteriorating performance of keiretsu members. Worsening performance leads to a loss of legitimacy. Reduced legitimacy, in turn, allows increased consideration of reform or change. Another example is 'financialization': treating all manner of assets as potentially financial ones which can be traded in financial markets, combined with the global integration of markets, has for a number of years changed the 'costs of capital' calculation of firms, to the advantage of equity capital and stock exchanges. This has meant a shift from the credit financing of investment, over to equity.

Political pressures

Political pressures result from shifts in interests or underlying power distributions that provided support for existing institutional arrangements. Scott et al. (2000), for example, show how the long-term reduction in membership of the American Medical Association, associated with the rise of speciality associations, resulted in the weakening and fragmentation of physician power and, as a consequence, a reduction in professional control over the healthcare field. Internationally, after the collapse of the Bretton Woods agreement about fixed exchange rates, fluctuating currencies led to world-wide industrial restructuring.

Social pressures

Social pressures are associated with differentiation of groups, and the existence of heterogeneous divergent or discordant beliefs, interests and practices. When particular social pressures gain strength, this can stimulate institutional change. Consider, for example, how pressures from an initially small group of environmentalists has gained widespread interest and put increased pressure on governments to enforce cleaner technology by law.

Theorizing institutional change

One of the questions we wish to examine in this book is whether internationalization and globalization pressures lead to institutional and organizational change. The literature has debated four possible change scenarios:

1. Convergence towards a neoliberal market system dominated by Anglo-American institutions (liberal market economies in VoC, compartmentalized business systems in BSys analysis).
2. Greater specialization of national institutions in accordance with domestic institutional and cultural characteristics.
3. Incremental adaptation of the domestic institutional context in a largely path-dependent manner.
4. Hybridization of institutions.

These four scenarios were explained in the introductory chapter. In this section we will examine which of these four scenarios have theoretical support.

In our explanation of the SE approach, we suggested that if we want to be able to explain institutional change, we must examine institutions not only as a property or state of an existing social order, but also as a process. By looking at 'spaces' with structures and processes, we also look at dynamics. As suggested, the structural aspect of the space refers to the properties of a system, while the process refers to the changes that occur with regard to a system.

The dialectical relationships between the actor and structures and institutions implies that systemic characteristics are reproduced in a non-identical way. The pattern of actor–structure interactions and the ability of the actor to innovate practices, means that the inertia, which is usually connected with institutions, is only relative. However, since new practices are linked to existing logics of action they will take on a specific form, one which is in accordance with an existing societal identity. The latter implies that convergence of one institutional setting to another, as proposed in scenario 1 above, can only be very limited since convergence would imply a shift away from an existing logic and identity.

Moreover, even if at the national level, international (or global) pressures would stimulate developments in the direction of convergence (e.g. convergence of regulations and laws), this does not necessarily mean that convergence would take place at the micro level (the firm level). While external conditions (market and institutional) shape the opportunities and constraints faced by firms, the logic of goal formation and decision-making within organizations requires one to look inside at the internal constitution of the firm (Cyert and March, 1963, cited in Jackson, 1997: 5). The diverging interests and bargaining processes between potential stakeholders within the firm impose constraints on the goals and the capacities of the business firm to adapt to changes in its environment.[5] We can thus explain the deviations in the behaviour of German and Japanese firms from the profit-maximization model (e.g. the inclination to pursue high growth, the stickiness of corporate employment, and the high level of firm-specific investments) in terms of different internal coalitions among the stakeholders of those German and Japanese firms that strive to preserve acquired rights.

In addition to the principle of reciprocal constitution of actors and social structures there is the principle of the interactive constitution of structures and institutions with regard to each other. Structures and institutions are inter-linked and thus safeguard the 'coherence' of the overall order (Maurice, 2000). This principle of coherence is related to the notion of complementary institutions (Amable, 2000) and what North (1994) calls the 'institutional matrix', a framework of interconnected institutions that, together, make up the rules of the economy. Several institutions in different spaces reinforce each other so that they form a coherent and stable, but not everlasting, structure. The concept of complementary institutions is based on multi-lateral reinforcement mechanisms between institutional arrangements: each one, by its existence, permits or facilitates the existence of the others.

Complementary institutions make one another more or less efficient according to their respective characteristics. Specifically, the influence of one institution is reinforced when the other complementary institution is present. For instance, the set of incentives to the firm defined by the German and Japanese bank-based system makes long-term employment possible and efficient, which in return reinforces the efficiency of the bank-based system.

The complementary character is fundamental for defining the coherence and the pattern of evolution of a societal system. The coherence of a societal system results from complementarity between specific institutional arrangements (i.e. a certain pattern of industrial specialization, a certain type of innovation, certain specific characteristics of the labour force in terms of skills or adaptability, a structure of wage differentials, etc.). Institutional complementarity also involves that change in one element of the system may have consequences well beyond the area concerned and threaten a certain pattern of complementarity. The effects of financial liberalization, for example, may not only be a decrease in the intermediation margin and a cheaper cost of capital as, one assumes, is intended. The introduction of more competition in the financial system is also argued to threaten the stability of long-term relationships (Allen and Gale, 1997; Amable, 2000).

The argument is that the decrease in intermediation margins may reduce the investment projects-monitoring capacity of intermediaries, which will lead them to reorientate their lending policy towards projects where monitoring matters less or is less intensive – for instance, short-term projects. Moreover, the increase in competition in financial intermediation in general is argued to promote arm's-length finance and undermine relationship banking (Amable, 2000). The consequence of these arguments would be that globalization pressures (i.e. financial liberalization and integration of capital markets) would lead to hybridization or change in a path-deviant manner in systems where institutional complementarities with relationship banking are important (i.e. Japan and Germany). Rather like the scenario of incremental path-dependent adaptation, hybridization implies gradual change. In contrast to path-dependent adaptation, however, hybridization implies change in a path-deviant manner.

The notion of complementarity also implies, however, that change in one element of the system would lead to instability of the system. For instance, a decentralized financial system and arm's-length relationships with centralized labour market institutions would generate contradictory incentives and constraints, making the system unstable and less efficient. The actor–system dynamic, though, could be assumed to prevent the development of such contradictions. However, even if there were to be a temporary disequilibrium, one could assume that the actor–structure dialectic would, in any case, be able to push the system to the next equilibrium defined by, but non-identical to, the previous one.

In view of the actor–structure dialectic, the next equilibrium could not be reached in a wholly path-deviant way. For the link with established knowledge, values and predispositions implies continuity of the path. The combination of the notion of complementarity with the actor–structure dialectic would provide theoretical support for the scenarios of greater specialization in accordance with existing values and institutions, and incremental change. Finally, the notion of complementarity also helps to explain that the same institution (i.e. regulation or law) may affect outcomes differently depending on the other institutions.

4.7 Conclusions

As regards institutional dynamics, then:

- Institutions are a state of an existing order as well as a process.
- There is a dialectical relationship between actors and institutions, structures and processes.
- The economic logic of institutional dynamics is specified by social forces.
- The complementary character of institutions has implications for the pattern of institutional change.
- Any institutional order features internal diversity and contradictions, which makes actors not only adapt to but generate change.

This section presented a framework for the analysis of change, and it leaves open a variety of specific findings and interpretations. In Chapter 11, we examine how it can help us explain recent and contemporary developments in management and organization.

Study questions

1. Provide a brief outline of the main differences and/or similarities between the 'varieties of capitalism', 'societal effect' and 'business systems' approaches.
2. What is methodological individualism?
3. A major aim of the SE approach is to contextualize phenomena.
   (a) Explain what this means and how the approach goes about theorizing this aim.
   (b) Explain how contextualization can help the approach to overcome the gap between culturalism and institutionalism.
4. Explain how the notion of 'space', as it is used within the societal effect approach, is more extensive than the concept of an institutional domain.
5. Explain the differences between the concept of background institutions, as it is used in the BSys approach, and national culture.
6. Assess whether and how the approaches in this chapter can help you to understand differences between organizations in different countries.
7. Explain why it is important to use 'matched' samples in comparative analysis.
8. Assess whether typologies, such as the one developed within the BSys approach, are useful analytical tools.
9. Explain how the SE approach is able to account for change as well as the type of change it accounts for.
10. Explain why the BSys framework is a static as opposed to a dynamic approach.
11. Explain how, despite the dynamic nature of the SE approach, there is a static aspect to the approach.
12. Explain whether and how both the BSys and the SE approaches recognize and are able to incorporate globalization pressures within their framework.
13. Explain whether and how institutional interconnectedness can hamper convergence despite globalization pressures.

Further reading

Becker, U. (2009) *Open Varieties of Capitalism: Continuity, Change and Performances.* London: Palgrave Macmillan.

This is probably the most complete and readable synthesis of VoC studies, including recent analysis by the author himself, from a political economy perspective.

Foss, J.N. (1999) The challenge of business systems and the challenge to business systems. *International Studies of Management and Organization* 29(2), 9–24.

Critical article reflecting on the weaknesses of business systems research and how economics can help to overcome them (and vice versa), pointing to ways in which business systems research offers opportunities to enhance economics research.

Hall, P.A. and Soskice, D. (2001) *Varieties of Capitalism.* Oxford: Oxford University Press.

This book offers the first and authoritative statement of the VoC approach.

Maurice, M. and Sorge, A. (2000) *Embedding Organizations.* Amsterdam: John Benjamins.

This is the latest position in and empirical examples from SE research.

Whitley, R. (2007) *Business Systems and Organizational Capabilities: The Institutional Structuring of Competitive Competences.* Oxford: Oxford University Press.

This is the most recent and evolved statement about business systems theory and research.

Case: The Japanese keiretsu[6]

The existence and functioning of interorganizational groups or corporate groups has long been a focus of economic research on Japan. This is unsurprising since the basic structure of Japanese business consists of business groups, the so-called keiretsu. There are two main kinds of corporate grouping in Japan. The best known of these are the horizontal or financial keiretsu, or groups of firms organized around a large bank. While member firms may buy and sell to each other, the glue that holds the group together is argued to be mutual stock-holding and bank loans to members, supplemented by personnel exchanges and meetings between the presidents or leaders of the organizations belonging to the groups. In short, these organizations are linked primarily by finances rather than products.

The bank at the core of a financial keiretsu, called the 'main bank', does much more than simply make loans available. It is also the central clearing house for information about group companies and coordinator of group activities. It monitors the performance of its group, holds equity in most of the major companies, and provides management assistance when it deems this necessary. In the worst case, if one of the group's firms is in serious trouble, the main bank is expected to step in both with financial assistance and with a whole new management team selected from among the bank's executives.

Three of the six financial keiretsu (Mitsui, Mitsubishi and Sumitomo) are direct descendants of the famous pre-Second World War zaibatsu (financial cliques), while the remaining three (Fuyo, Sanwa and Dai-Ichi Kangyo) have less direct links to earlier organizations. The connections in all three, however, are definitely both historical and financial. In contrast to the zaibatsu, however – which were controlled by a single family, usually through a central holding company – the contemporary keiretsu are horizontally structured groupings. Stockholding and influence move in both directions between pairs of firms, although loans and personnel are likely to come mainly from the commercial banks and the insurance companies within the group and to go to the others. The driving force behind the re-establishment of the major prewar zaibatsu and the formation of the new groups was a combination of weak stock markets in Japan after the war, the stagnant share prices of major Japanese companies and the resulting vulnerability to take-over threats. In this situation, cross-shareholdings and dependence on group financial institutions formed a protection mechanism. (See Chapter 6 for an in-depth explanation of the financial aspects.) In addition, between the 1950s and 1970s, the government made it difficult for business to raise the funds it needed from any source other than the banking system, and at the same time encouraged the city banks to lend to important industries. It rewrote the law to make it legal for the banks to own stocks in their clients (contrary to the Antimonopoly Law that was put in place by the US occupation right after the Second World War). Moreover, because the government wanted to control the limited flows of capital in the economy, the Ministry of Finance (MoF) also devised strict regulations to make sure that the stock market would not mature and rival the banks. Thus the government helped to build and shape the new bank-led keiretsu and the banks became the source of funds for postwar industry. This primacy remained essentially unchallenged until the late 1980s.

Until the late 1970s, the structural paradigm for the zaibatsu descendants as well as for the new groups was based on the concept of 'one firm in each major industrial sector'. Hence, aside from a large bank, the nucleus of the keiretsu would also include a trading company and a major manufacturer. There would also be a trust bank, a life insurance firm and a non-life firm, so that, together with the bank and the trading company (which provides trade credit), most of the group's financial needs could be met internally. Then there would ideally be one key company in each important industrial sector, including chemicals, construction, steel, electricals, cement, paper, glass, oil, autos, shipping, warehousing and non-ferrous metals. When a sector became prominent, all keiretsu would jump into it, whether there was room for six major firms or not. The result was intense competition, much more than in the prewar days when the zaibatsu could privately carve up markets among a few strong players and close everyone else out. After the Second World War, the government – more specifically, the Ministry of International Trade and Industry (MITI) – decided on the industries to be developed. As a result, the growth of certain sectors would be assured and all the keiretsu wanted to be part of it.

However, while the big six financial keiretsu did not simply drift together, they were not assembled according to some master plan formulated by the government. The MITI prepared the ground that allowed the 'big six' to emerge, then nurtured their core companies, steered them, and protected them from outside competition until the 1970s. The actual formation of the keiretsu and much of their activities were left up to the groups and the individual companies. By the 1970s, the big six had achieved the government's goals of building up Japan's heavy industries to internationally competitive levels. By the 1980s, as calls were going up around the world for Japan to open up to free competition, the keiretsu no longer needed protection, although the vestiges of it remained for years in many sectors, and some are still intact today.

A second major type of inter-firm collaboration is the vertically structured group, or vertical keiretsu. There are two types of vertical keiretsu: production keiretsu, in which a myriad of parts suppliers and assemblers put together products for a single end-product manufacturer, such as in the auto (i.e. Toyota) or electronics industries; and distribution keiretsu, in which a single firm, usually a manufacturer, moves products out to market through a network of wholesalers and retailers that depend on the parent firm for goods. Most manufacturers have both types of keiretsu.

Production and distribution keiretsu exist in almost every industry in Japan, from oil to cosmetics to advertising to broadcasting. Hence, Japan has dozens of these large independent groups or vertical keiretsu. Stockholding in these groups is more pyramidal than in financial keiretsu, strengthening control in the core firm. Hence, the structure consists of vertical relationships rather than horizontal, which is characteristic of the financial keiretsu. The goods and services produced by the group are often complementary, but they need not be. Moreover, the core company has the best-known name, and may or may not lend this to other members of the group. It owns the largest shareholdings in other group companies and is also the most likely source of personnel or technical assistance to other group members, particularly those just beneath it in the group pyramid.

Otherwise, enterprise groups differ considerably. In some groups, such as the Hitachi Group, member firms have moved into a broad range of businesses, such as construction, consumer electronics and financial services. Other groups consist of related companies that produce the same kinds of product as the core firms. For example, Victor Co. of Japan, Ltd, the developer of the VHS format for videocassette recorders, and today mainly a manufacturer of that type of product as well as audio equipment, is 50.8 per cent owned by Matsushita Electric Industrial Co., Ltd, which is best known to consumers for its Panasonic and Quasar lines of consumer electronics products.

While not centred around a bank, some large enterprise groups have significant holdings in financial services firms. For example, Toyota is the largest individual stockholder, at 40.6 per cent, in Chiyoda Fire & Marine Insurance Co., Ltd, Japan's tenth largest non-life insurance firm. In addition to being the largest lender to Nissan Fire & Marine Insurance Co., Ltd, Japan's 12th largest firm, Nissan Motor Co., Ltd, has a 7.3 per cent stake in the company, making it the second largest shareholder.

In general, as noted above, the flow of financial and other resources is mostly one-way in all the enterprise groups. The list of 20 largest stockholders in Matsushita Electric Industrial does not include JVC or much other representation from the Matsushita Group. Only one firm, Matsushita Electric Works Co., Ltd, ranks 19th, holding 1.1 per cent of the stock. However, until his death in 1989, Konosuke Matsushita, the group's founder, ranked eighth, holding 2.1 per cent of the shares. This illustrates another characteristic of such groups and one that distinguishes them from financial keiretsu: one family or individual may hold substantial power. The fact that firms belonging to groups organized around independent firms are usually much younger than companies associated with zaibatsu or their descendants explains why company founders still play leading roles in some relatively independent companies such as Sony.

Some of the core firms of the leading independent groups, however, are themselves members of the financial keiretsu, at least in name. Toyota is an example of such a firm, officially a member of the Mitsui keiretsu, but operating at the periphery of group affairs. The companies to which they are linked may or may not belong to the same financial keiretsu. For example, despite Toyota's position as the largest stockholder in Chiyoda Fire & Marine Insurance, the insurer belongs to the inner circle of the Fuyo Group. Nissan Fire & Marine Insurance is part of the Dai-Ichi Group. Moreover, some companies, while strongly associated with financial keiretsu, have their own enterprise groups. For example, Mitsubishi Heavy Industries, Ltd, which plays a major role in the Mitsubishi financial keiretsu, has dozens of firms under it. And, to make things even more complex, there are a few very large companies that claim allegiance to more than one group. Hitachi is the best-known example of a firm that considers itself above the keiretsu and boldly flies the flag of three different groups.

In short, financial keiretsu and enterprise groups may be related in several ways. In some situations, the leading members of financial keiretsu themselves are at the core of other, distinct large groups of firms, a sort of circle within a circle. In others, industrial firms are more independent, with some group members linked to a financial keiretsu (intersecting circles) or two or more financial keiretsu (one circle intersecting with two other circles) or with no strong ties at all. Even where the circles intersect, members of enterprise groups often have a high degree of independence from other members of the financial keiretsu.

Consequently, while, as suggested in the above, there is competition between the member firms of the different keiretsu, there is also cooperation. In general, one of the most striking characteristics of Japan's industrial organization is the predominance of stable, long-term inter-firm relationships, which are non-exclusive. For example, Matsushita, the largest consumer electronics products and robotics manufacturer in Japan, sells its component-inserting machine to its rivals, contributing to their high productivity. Another example is Nikon, a firm that dominates the lithography market. Although Nikon is a core member of the Mitsubishi Group, it maintains long-term relationships with firms outside it. Similarly, Toyota has advised its suppliers, even firms of which Toyota is the largest shareholder, to do business with other manufacturers, even if they are Toyota's rivals. As a result, many members of the Toyota suppliers' association also belong to another car manufacturer's association, such as Nissan, Mazda or Mitsubishi.

The long-term relationships are based on trust and reciprocity. Even when a long-term relationship ends at some point, there is sufficient confidence, trust and loyalty between partners to avoid the leaking of trade secrets. Finally, the keiretsu structure expresses the dislike of major Japanese firms for dealing with 'independent' subcontractors. In fact, in the subcontracting pyramid, Japanese manufacturers effectively control their subcontractors. It is quite common, for example, for Japanese manufacturers to instruct the subcontractor to invest in new equipment. Over time, this brings the parent firm all the advantages of state-of-the-art production equipment with little or none of the cost. In addition to arranging for equipment investment by their affiliated suppliers, the parent companies can push their subcontractors to work extra hours, deliver parts at the parent's convenience (part of the famous just-in-time (JIT) system, which is explained further in Chapter 7), and accept payment when the parent's cash flow permits. Most important, the parent firm tells the supplier how much it will pay for the parts. In addition, the parent firm adjusts these prices – always downwards – at least twice a year and usually by at least 5 to 10 per cent each time. In fact, subcontractors are treated as 'shock absorbers' by the manufacturing firms. In crisis situations, price cuts are passed on to the smallest bottom-level subcontractors. Often these do not survive the hard times since they do not have much of a profit margin to work with in the first place.

Questions

1. According to Whitley's framework, ownership coordination is one of the features of a business system. The concept of ownership coordination consists of owner control, ownership vertical integration and ownership horizontal integration. Use the information in this case to describe these features for the dominant business system in Japan – that is, for the keiretsu.
2. The second major feature of a business system is the degree of non-ownership coordination. Non-ownership coordination consists of alliance-based vertical integration, alliance-based horizontal integration and competitor collaboration. Use the information in this case to describe these features for the Japanese keiretsu.
3. Discuss the institutions that help explain the development of the characteristics of the Japanese business system that you were asked to describe in Questions 1 and 2.
4. Explain the main differences and similarities of the patterns of ownership and non-ownership coordination between the Japanese keiretsu and the Korean chaebol.

Notes

1 The following section is based on Hall and Soskice (2001).

2 For an explanation of the link between dominant institutions and business system features see Whitley (1999: 54–59).

3 The following explanation of the institutional context of different business system types draws on Whitley (1999: 59–64).

4 The explanation of these two business systems is based on Whitley's research (1999: Chapters 6 and 7). For a more detailed elaboration see the original text, as well as Whitley (1992a).

5 This view is consistent with Aoki's definition of the firm (1988: 33, cited in Jackson, 1997: 5), which is characterized 'as a field of bargaining among the firm-specific resource-holders including the body of employees, rather than simply as a bundle of individual exchange relationships supplemented by the existence of marketable residual claims (equity). There does not seem to exist a single objective of the firm such as the maximization of residual (profits); rather, the firm internalized a bargaining process in which the conflicting objectives of firm-specific resource-holders are brought in equilibrium with a framework of the co-operative relations.'

6 This case study is based on the following sources: Teranishi (1994), Ostrom (1990), Miyashita and Russell, (1994) and Miwa (1996).

References

Allen, F. and Gale, D. (1997) Financial markets, intermediaries and intertemporal smoothing. *Journal of Political Economy* 105, 523–546.

Amable, B. (2000) Institutional complementarity and diversity of social systems of innovation and production. *Review of International Political Economy* 7(4), 645–687.

Aoki, M. (1988) *Information, Incentives, and Bargaining in the Japanese Economy*. Cambridge: Cambridge University Press.

Becker, U. (2009) *Open Varieties of Capitalism. Continuity, Change and Performances*. London: Palgrave Macmillan.

Boyer, R. (1996) *Elements for an Institutional Approach to Economics*. Mimeo, Paris: CEPREMAP.

Casson, M. and Lundan, S.M. (1999) Explaining international differences in economic institutions. *International Studies of Management and Organization* 29(2), 25–42.

Cyert, M. and March, J.G. (1963) *A Behavioral Theory of the Firm*. Englewood Cliffs, NJ: Prentice-Hall.

Foss, N.J. (1999) Preface: perspectives on business systems. *International Studies of Management and Organization* 29(2), 3–8.

Freeman, R. (2000) Single peaked vs diversified capitalism: the relation between economic institutions and outcomes. *NBER Working Paper* No. 7556.

Giddens, A. (1986) *The Constitution of Society*. Berkeley, CA: UCP.

Hall, P.A. and Soskice, D. (2001) *Varieties of Capitalism*. Oxford: Oxford University Press.

Hotho, J. (2014) From typology to taxonomy: a configurational analysis of business systems and their explanatory power. *Organization Studies* 35, 671–702.

Jackson, G. (1997) *Corporate Governance in Germany and Japan: Development Within National and International Contexts*. Mimeo, Max-Planck-Institut für Gesellschaftsforschung, Cologne.

Knight, J. (1992) *Institutions and Social Conflict*. Cambridge: Cambridge University Press.

Kogut, B. (1991) Country capabilities and permeability of borders. *Strategic Management Journal* 12, 33–47.

Kogut, B. (ed.) (1993) *Country Competitiveness: Technology and the Organizing of Work*. Oxford: Oxford University Press.

Lundvall, B.-A. (1992) *National Systems of Innovation*. London: Pinter.

Maurice, M. (2000) The paradoxes of societal analysis: a review of the past and prospects for the future. In Maurice, M. and Sorge, A. (eds) *Embedding Organizations*. Amsterdam: John Benjamins Publishing.

Maurice, M. and Brossard, M. (1976) Is there a universal model of organization structure? *International Journal of Management and Organization* 6, 11–45.

Maurice, M. and Sorge, A. (2000) *Embedding Organizations*. Amsterdam: John Benjamins Publishing.

Maurice, M., Sellier, F. and Silvestre, J.-J. (1982) *Politique d' Education et Organisation Industrielle en France et en Allemagne*. Paris: Presses Universitaires de France.

Maurice, M., Sellier, F. and Silvestre, J.-J. (1976/1986) *The Social Foundation of Industrial Power: A Comparison of France and Germany*. Cambridge, MA: MIT Press.

Maurice, M., Sorge, A. and Warner, M. (1980) Societal differences in organizing manufacturing units: a comparison of France, West Germany and Great Britain. *Organization Studies* 1, 59–86.

Mintzberg, H. (1983) *Structure in Fives: Designing Effective Organizations*. Englewood Cliffs, N.J.: Prentice-Hall.

Miwa, Y. (1996) *Firms and Industrial Organization in Japan*. New York: New York University Press.

Miyashita, K. and Russell, D. (1994) *Keiretsu: Inside the Hidden Japanese Conglomerates*. New York: McGraw-Hill.

Müller, F. (1994) Societal effect, organizational effect and globalization. *Organization Studies* 15(3), 407–428.

North, D. (1994) *Institutions Matter*. Mimeo, Washington: Washington University.

Oliver, C. (1992) The antecedents of deinstitutionalization. *Organization Studies* 13(4), 563–588.

Ostrom, D. (1990) Keiretsu and other large corporate groups in Japan. *Japan Economic Institute Report* No. 2A.

Scott, W.R. (2001) *Institutions and Organizations*. London: Sage.

Scott, W.R., Ruef, M., Mendel, P.J. and Caronna, C.A. (2000) *Institutional Change and Healthcare Organizations: from Professional Dominance to Managed Care*. Chicago: University of Chicago Press.

Sorge, A. (1991) Strategic fit and the societal effect: interpreting cross-national comparisons of technology, organization and human resources. *Organization Studies* 12(2), 161–190.

Sorge, A. (2004) Cross-national differences in human resources and organization. In Harzing A.-W. and Ruysseveldt, J. van (eds), *International Human Resource Management: An Integrated Approach* (second revised edition). London: Sage, 117–140.

Sorge, A. and Warner, M. (1986) *Comparative Factory Organization: An Anglo-German Comparison of Management and Manpower in Manufacturing*. Aldershot: Gower.

Soskice, D. (1991) The institutional infrastructure for international competitiveness: a comparative analysis of the UK and Germany. In Atkinson, A.B. and Brunetta, R. (eds) *Economics for the New Europe*. London: Macmillan.

Soskice, D. (1994) Innovation strategies of companies: a comparative institutional approach of some cross-country differences. In Zapf, W. and Dierkens, M. (eds) *Institutionenvergleich und Institutionendynamik*. Berlin: Sigma.

Teranishi, J. (1994) Loan syndication in war-time Japan and the origins of the main bank system. In Aoki, M. and Patrick, H. (eds) *The Japanese Main Bank System*. Oxford: Clarendon Press.

Whitley, R. (1990) Eastern Asian enterprise structures and comparative analysis of forms of business organization. *Organization Studies* 11(1), 47–74.

Whitley, R. (1991) The social construction of business systems in East Asia. *Organization Studies* 12(1), 1–28.

Whitley, R. (1992a) *European Business Systems: Firms and Markets in their National Context*. London: Sage.

Whitley, R. (1992b) The social construction of organizations and markets: the comparative analysis of business recipes. In Reed, M. and Hughes, M. (eds) *Rethinking Organizations: New Directions in Organization Theory and Analysis*. Newbury Park, CA: Sage, 120–143.

Whitley, R. (1999) *Divergent Capitalisms: the Social Structuring and Change of Business Systems*. Oxford: Oxford University Press.

World Economic Forum (2000) *The Global Competitiveness Report 2000*. New York: Oxford University Press.

World Economic Forum (2011) *The Global Competitiveness Report 2011–12*. Versoix, Switzerland: SRO-Kundig.

5 Managing resources: human resource management

Ayse Saka-Helmhout

Learning objectives

By the end of this chapter you will be able to:

- understand differences in human resource management practices between countries
- provide a societal explanation for the diversity in human resource practices between countries
- reflect on the differences in human resource systems between advanced and newly developed nations
- analyse the impact of elements of comparative human resource management on firm structure
- analyse the effects of international competition and globalization on human resource management systems.

Chapter outline

5.1 Introduction

Developments in international human resource management (HRM) have come a long way since the 1980s when the literature dealt predominantly with the transplantation of the 'superior' Japanese model. The early accounts were constructed by US scholars. Adopting an implicit managerialist approach, they focused on how HRM could benefit shareholders (Boxall and Purcell, 2003). Their assumption was that employees and managers have a great deal of freedom in determining the design and implementation of HR practices and policies, which led to prescriptive notions of 'more successful' HRM models. This highly ethnocentric approach overlooks contextual differences across countries in terms of the knowledge of societies, languages, concepts, values and culture. It was assumed that factors across contexts are stable, hence HRM practices in one country can be generalized to other settings, constituting a universalistic approach to understanding HRM. The advocacy of universalism is driven by the idea that firms are better off if they identify and adopt 'best practice' in the way they manage people (Boxall and Purcell, 2000).

In an effort to contextualize HRM practices, there has been a proliferation of a comparative perspective on HRM since the 1990s. By contrast to the 'best practice' school, comparative human resource management (CHRM) advocates a 'best fit'. In other words, HR strategy will be more effective when it is appropriately integrated with its specific organizational and environmental context. Enthusiasts of this school aim to explain the variations in HRM practices by a multitude of environmental forces. Drawing on the cultural (e.g. Laurent 1986), institutional (e.g. Ferner, 1997), or the societal analysis perspectives (Maurice et al. 1980), outlined in Chapter 1, scholars have aimed to discuss the importance of interaction of HR practices with the larger social, legal, and political contexts. The European view is, in particular, noteworthy in its emphasis on the importance of context. Researchers in Europe underscore the significance of balancing the interests of multiple stakeholders such as employees, unions, and governments. For instance, it has been shown that HRM practices vary across countries as organizations aim to attain and maintain external credibility through adherence to institutional structures, rules and norms at the national level (e.g. Gooderham et al., 1999). Nationally idiosyncratic institutional pressures such as the scrutiny of labour unions, whose strength and attitudes towards management vary, can constrain employees from determining their own HRM systems. What makes this European perspective distinct are four antecedents (Brewster, 2007), leading to different HRM models (e.g. Brewster and Bournois, 1991; Sparrow and Hiltrop, 1994):

- i less focus on individualism (widespread feeling that businesses need to be controlled and employees need to be treated in a socially responsible way),
- ii the role of the state (higher level of legislative requirements on pay and conditions of work, social security provision, and state involvement in training, job creation and transition),
- iii the role of trade unions and consultation (considerable legally backed power to employee representatives), and
- iv patterns of ownership (interlocking shareholdings and close involvement in the management of corporations hence long-term outlook to development).

CHRM advocates an interaction between HR strategies, business strategy and HR practice and their engagement with an external environment (Budhwar and Debrah, 2001).

The evaluation of these interactions requires an investigation of conditions at the level of the nation state and the level of the firm. This chapter aims to illustrate diversity in HRM by focusing on practices in the USA, the UK, Sweden, Japan, Germany, and the Netherlands. These countries have not been chosen at random. Aside from the last two, they represent the major types of industrial relations and human resource systems worldwide (Begin 1997). The Netherlands is added as an example of a European country where companies use a hybrid human resource system, with features of both the Anglo-American and the German type. China is added in the form of a case study to extend the analysis to the evolution of human resource systems in nations in transition.

While stressing the cultural, institutional, or societal influences, the chapter does not deny the ability of actors to change, innovate or borrow designs from other human resource practices, thus reducing the inertia that has traditionally been attributed to institutions. Although actors may import practices that fit the existing societal logic, increasing number of studies demonstrate actors' willingness and ability to challenge, reinterpret, or circumvent institutions (Streeck and Thelen, 2005; Hall and Thelen, 2009). For instance, the German wage bargaining has accommodated a cost competition-driven model of wage regulation (Hassel, 2007), and its employee relations have gradually built in more numerical flexibility and individualization of contracts (Tüselmann, 2001). Similarly, the Japanese HRM system has experienced changes due to pressure from increased competition and recession. However, significant path-shifting or equilibrium-breaking behaviour, leading to full-fledged shift from one HR system to another is highly unlikely due to general inefficiencies created by noncomplementary institutions (Hancké et al., 2007). Actors are simply conditioned by past institutions and underlying complementarities between institutions (Hall, 2007). Consequently, any explanation of change must incorporate constraints by external institutions; especially in the form of previous human resource policies, which exercise inertial forces, management values as shaped by norms accepted in the society, legal constraints and unions' bargaining agendas.

This needs to be heeded, in particular, when we look at the dates of figures from research and other information in this chapter, but also others. Many students and teachers alike tend to think that new figures and information are always better than older figures and information. Generally applied, this argument is a treacherous fallacy and obscures a grasp of what is important not only in HRM arrangements but most of all here: culture and institutions imply an amount of inertia which may appear frustrating to change enthusiasts but is the order of the day, anywhere. Often, publicist rhetoric points to change, but in larger populations of organizations and above all societal practices, the facts point to inertia or continuity. In Chapter 4, we explained how conceptually to tackle the relation between continuity and change. Here, we start with the most recent comparative analysis of HRM changes over time in European countries, conducted by researchers in CRANET, a network of comparative research centred at Cranfield University in the UK.

In summarizing their comparison over time, here is what the authors found:

> The accepted wisdom is that individuals and organizations have . . . to adapt to ever changing contextual conditions. . . . However, CRANET's results seem to be in striking contrast to such a dictum. In the area of European HRM, stability and little change seem to be not the exception but rather the rule. To be sure, this does not mean that everything stays exactly the same. Yet, very often even in the areas where one might expect change . . . the data remain unclear or even point in the opposite direction.
>
> (Mayrhofer and Brewster, 2005: 52)

The bits of sentences not quoted here are those in which the authors were more expressive and scathing e.g. about the 'change frenzy' of academics. The authors further summarize tendencies by saying that 'directional convergence' can be demonstrated to some extent, which means that arrangements in different countries move in 'the same direction'; but 'final convergence', which is what convergence means in the more rigorous mathematical sense (a curve approaching a straight line, usually in infinity) does not happen. In other words, and broadly speaking, although countries may appear to be moving in a similar direction, the differences between them remain in place. This is, in short, what we explained in Section 4.6. And this is also what would come out if we did a systematic comparison involving e.g. China or any other country reputed to have more remarkable change during a period.

Regrettably, more meticulous international comparisons, looking at practices at both the macro and the micro level and what they actually mean, rather than staying at a statistical surface, have become rarer over time. There were references showing as much, in the beginning of our general introduction. The consequence is that to give a vivid picture of practices and their meanings, older information is inevitable. Where possible, we will indicate what relative changes must be taken into account. But the general caveat holds: the comparative picture hardly changes, although specific secular or cyclical tendencies can be identified as having influenced practices in various countries. A tendency established for the Netherlands but also likely to happen in other countries is the following: in a time of liberalization during the 1990s and at the beginning of the millennium, large enterprises above all recognized and promoted the individualization of contracts and the individual expression of interests rather than collective representation through enterprise councils and trade unions. But as they promoted such HRM policies, they also became aware of problems of equitably rewarding efforts across groups, departmental or other dividing lines; these problems could jeopardize commitment. Thus, the pendulum could swing back to more collective consultation and bargaining to control the individualization that had taken place (Goodijk and Sorge, 2005). The most recent development along such lines is that the employers, the trade union federation and the government in Germany together are moving, at the time of writing, to bring back a principle by law, of 'one establishment – one collective agreement'. This is to go against problems arising from the spread of occupational rather than general unionism, in such cases as railway drivers and conductors, and cockpit and cabin staff in airlines.

We draw on Gospel's (1992) broad typology to compare different HRM systems across countries. We focus on two HRM dimensions: (1) work structure (i.e. the way work is organized), and (2) employment relations (i.e. the arrangements governing such aspects of employment as recruitment, promotion, job tenure and the reward of employees). An understanding of these two dimensions is also essential to grasping the details of the concept of institutional advantage, which, in the context of this chapter, is the link between human resource systems and industrial competitiveness. This link is explained extensively in Chapter 7.

Gospel's third dimension is industrial relations (i.e. the representational aspirations of employees and the voice systems that may exist, such as joint consultation, employee involvement practices, works councils and collective bargaining). This is nowadays often included under employment relations. It is a societal factor that influences HRM systems. Similarly, institutional arrangements such as the national education and training systems, and labour market policy, are also shown to be prominent societal influences. These various societal elements are shaped by the historical and the immediate settings in which they are embedded; they are intrinsically interconnected such that they form a whole. This societal logic also serves as the binding glue of the HRM components that guides their functioning. For example, in Germany, high employment stability is imposed on firms through collective agreements, codetermination and legislation. Firms are thus forced to adjust through the internal labour market by redeployment. As a consequence, employment protection encourages employer investment in training and long-term HR development. Moreover, shaped and reproduced in a non-identical way by the societal setting, HR systems, in turn, influence organization structures (as explained in the following section) and, as indicated, in firm performance.

The organization of the chapter is as follows: as indicated, the next section discusses various aspects of work relationships. Sections 5.3 and 5.4 deal with the second dimension of Gospel's typology; specifically, Section 5.3 explains the differences in the hiring, and dismissal and promotion procedures in the aforementioned countries, while Section 5.4 focuses on differences in industrial relations, explaining the variations in collective bargaining and co-determination in pay systems. Section 5.5 provides a summary of the chapter, emphasizing the link between societal and HR practices.

5.2 Work structure

This section discusses various aspects of work structuring. It compares job classification, design and coordination, and functional specialization in the US, the UK, Sweden, Japan, Germany and the Netherlands. These HRM aspects are shown to be influenced essentially by the national education and vocational training system, and by the national system of industrial relationships. For example, the relative emphasis on general versus specialist education impacts on the scope of the job, the centralization as well as stratification of the workforce, and the relative reliance on bureaucratic procedures. Equally important is the relative amount of practical and technical training. This is negatively related to the segmentation of labour into impoverished jobs. Technical and scientific education is likely to be more specialized, leading to shorter hierarchies, more consensual decision-making and less bureaucracy (Hage, 2000). At the end of the first and second subsections, we provide a summary in the form of tables (Tables 5.1 and 5.2). The Netherlands is not included since its model lies somewhere on the continuum between the German and the Anglo-American ones.

Work classification, design and coordination

The traditional job design practices of large US firms differentiate jobs into hundreds of discrete titles, carry out systematic job evaluations to ascertain the scope and depth of job responsibilities, record these in great detail in formal job descriptions, and make them the basis of compensation decisions. A powerful historical force behind the preoccupation of US firms with formal job design and classification has been the scientific management movement, which, in Taylor's teachings, saw the minute analysis and delineation of job duties, and the elimination of worker discretion as critical elements in the rationalization of production and the transfer of control to management. In the USA, vocational education in schools has been accorded a low status and offered only narrow training to workers. Hence workers were not flexible in taking on a broader range of tasks in times of change, nor were they capable of participating in more complex business decisions. Taken together, job classifications came to be defined in terms of plant hierarchy in which gradations were based on income and working conditions.

In US factories, work is controlled through the direct supervision of foremen, who in the typical factory do not perform manufacturing operations. Foremen and industrial engineers, rather than engineers, are relied upon to find and resolve problems. The low degree of worker autonomy in the USA is partly explained by the virtual absence of vocational education, apprenticeship, training in craft skills relevant to manufacture, and job-related training for foremen and technicians, in the European tradition (Lawrence, 1996). The 'Cook's tour' traineeship, or rapid succession of assignments, is very common in US organizations. This can be related to the deregulated nature of most labour law, which creates an extremely active labour market. The active labour market, in turn, makes employers less willing to invest in training and retraining. Furthermore, the financial system creates a host of incentives to develop short-term business strategies, since most US companies view stockholders as their primary stakeholders. Investment in human capital, to say nothing of investments in efforts to transform the labour–management relationship, offers only long-term returns. Moreover, since they are in many regards qualitative, these returns are hard to measure (Turner et al., 2001). Since many managers' salaries are tied to financial performance on a quarterly basis they are often unwilling to invest in long-term qualitative improvements.

The numerous job classifications have, however, created strong property ownership of jobs, and thus have 'hinder[ed] . . . flexible and fluid job assignments' (Aoki, 1990: 52). During the 1990s, as many US manufacturing firms adopted innovative work practices (i.e. some of the flexible work system features), the number of job classifications declined, as job designs became less specialized both horizontally and vertically. Moreover, as manufacturing organizations move towards relying more on work teams, they are also beginning to place a higher priority on worker training. However, the investment still lags substantially behind that in Japan and Germany, and the strategies being used do not sufficiently promote flexible employment systems. For example, formal differences between production and maintenance work remain. In general, it has been argued that Taylorism that combines high levels of job fragmentation, managerial control over task performance and work organization, and strong manager–worker separation (Whitley, 1999) have been difficult to override (Begin, 1997).

Similar to the situation in the USA, UK manufacturing work systems are characterized by many vertically and horizontally specialized jobs, and factories are staffed by low-skilled production workers doing repetitive tasks with little authority. Skilled craft workers in UK factories have a low division of labour with a high degree of discretion. The crafts created job territories, so that there is a high degree of job demarcation among crafts, and between the crafts and the production jobs (Lane, 1989). Similar to the USA, the UK has neither the German vocational training system nor the Japanese firm-level training system to prepare individuals for work. In comparison with their counterparts in the USA, however, UK production workers have had a higher degree of control over job design, task allocation and manning practices through a strong shop-steward system (Lane, 1989: 154; Lorenz, 1992: 463–464). Taylorism is less diffused in the UK due to the absence of shop-floor control by managers. The anomaly of the UK system is that work is controlled neither by the standardization of skills as in Germany (this form is incompatible with unskilled workers) nor by standardization of process as in the USA (which is compatible with unskilled workers) (Begin, 1997: 119). At best, there is a weak form of standardization of process control, an outcome in part caused by the low level of technical training of supervisors and managers, which reduces their ability to systematically manage the production process (Lane, 1989: 154–155). UK first-line supervisors, unlike those in Germany, stand above the work group as supervisors and are not part of the work group;

in many firms they must relate to the work group through shop stewards (Dore, cited in Begin, 1997: 119).

As with the situation in the USA, the highly segmented internal labour market in the UK limits functional flexibility and work reorganization since employee job rights are tied to job definitions. Though in recent times, efforts to broaden out jobs have increased, the occupational demarcation of UK factory workers remains a fact (e.g. Hotho et al., 2014). Most of the attempts to change have aimed to increase functional flexibility by expanding the range of tasks within jobs, rather than through multiskilling (Cross, cited in Begin, 1997: 120). Neither management nor unions have really embraced work redesign: management because of the perceived threat to their autonomy, and unions because they had other priorities, namely pay, job security and involvement in management decision-making.

Sweden has been a pioneer in developing autonomous work teams at companies like Volvo and Saab (see Chapter 7). The advanced state of Swedish technology in some sectors has permitted the development of more flexible job designs. Job design and task assignments are to a striking degree the prerogatives of the production team. Workers enjoy autonomy in job performance and the allocation of specific tasks (Lincoln, 1993). The development of this type of work organization in Sweden should be understood against the background of sharpened demands on the product market, labour shortage and consequent improved prospects for union influence (Berggren, 1992). The tight labour market, combined with high and rising rates of short- and long-term absenteeism, was of great concern to the business community, the government and the unions, and furnished the motivation for a growing number of projects in the 1980s aimed at changing work organization. The excellent education system, which delivers a well-trained labour force, enabled the development of flexible job designs and worker autonomy. The Swedish education system does encourage limited on-the-job training. In addition, it is well integrated with employing organizations. Educational reform in the early 1970s eliminated a separate vocational education system, and 2- or 4-year vocational programmes were integrated into the school system. By the early 1990s, vocational routes were 3 years in length (Begin, 1997).

The 'modernized' plants (i.e. in the car industry) contrast sharply with the many traditional plants (i.e. in the metal sector) that are still using the old Taylorist job design principles, or that are only in the early phase of changing job designs. Thus, many workers on assembly lines have jobs that are specialized both horizontally and vertically as on assembly lines in the USA and the UK. In fact, the diffusion of the Swedish 'socio-technical' system (see Chapter 7) has not been high, and production jobs are not being changed enough to draw upon or expand worker knowledge. In many factories, job enlargement is often limited to providing workers with multiple skills to improve functional flexibility, but the work organization is otherwise unchanged (Kjellberg, 1992). However, unlike in the USA, where job analysis and evaluation mechanisms form the core of job control unionism, in Sweden job descriptions are used, if at all, primarily for determining relative wage differentials among different types of job (Begin, 1997: 204).

Finally, in general, Swedish employers also have a great deal of flexibility in moving workers among different kinds of job, including jobs in different geographical areas, as long as the movement of a worker to a less skilled job does not reduce the worker's income. Rather like Japanese practice, employee transfer is a major device for adjusting workforces. Seniority is not a determinant of transfer. Workers have a right to work and to income protection if a restructuring of jobs happens, but not to a specific type of work. Thus Swedish employers have more flexibility in moving workers among different types of job than their counterparts in the USA or the UK, but less flexibility in reducing the level of the workforce, the primary means used by US and UK employers to balance production levels and employment.

Job classifications are kept simple and broad in Japanese firms, with most factory production workers, for example, falling within a single classification. Job descriptions, if they exist at all, are typically short and couched in vague terms. Detailed job titles, formal job descriptions, and job-related criteria for pay and advancement have been conspicuously absent from Japanese employment practices, whereas job rotation and extensive cross-training are the rule (Lincoln, 1993). Extensive on-the-job training is used to train workers through 'learning by doing', while off-the-job training is used to supplement this process with systematic and codified knowledge about the firm, industry and functions of which employees are in charge (Morishima, 1995). The employee development systems require employees at all levels to acquire experience over time in different aspects of the business (Nishida and Redding, 1992). For instance, Womack et al.'s (1991) study of the automotive industry found that new production workers in Japanese plants received about 370 to 380 hours of training in their first year; comparable figures for European and US plants were 173 and 46 hours, respectively.

The segregation between management and workers in Japan is not as pronounced as that in the US or the UK (Lincoln and Kalleberg, 1990). For example, Japanese foremen are working members of the team who can fill in for absentees and coordinate the team. However, rather like the case in Sweden, production teams and job rotation are central features of Japanese factory organization. However, in contrast to Swedish workers, Japanese workers experience little freedom in determining how production tasks are to be performed. A refined set of work specifications is usually provided by the company's industrial engineers. Workers do have input into job design, but the criteria against which all refinements are made are rigorous industrial engineering standards. The use of job evaluation is quite limited in Japanese factories. It is used primarily in fixing wage levels rather than job duties since the tasks performed by individual workers are neither fixed nor permanent.

The simple and broad job designs in Japan are related to Japanese collective bargaining contracts and other legal instruments used in this society. These are phrased in very flexible and general language. Japanese unions, particularly in the tumultuous formative period of Japanese labour relations (the 1920s and 1930s), have certainly, at times, shown strong resistance to the exercise of arbitrary supervisory authority. In general, however, they have not challenged the prerogative of management to set the criteria for job design and labour allocation, so long as employment security guarantees have been preserved (Lincoln, 1993). Moreover, the extreme flexibility with which Japanese companies rotate, retrain and transfer workers is also very much an adaptation to the constraints imposed by permanent employment and seniority wage systems. In sharp contrast with US and UK norms, these systems set severe limits on a company's flexibility to terminate the contracts of employees whose particular skills and specialities are no longer in demand. Lifetime employment and seniority wage systems are two institutions in which postwar Japanese unions have had a considerable stake and they have fought hard to defend them. Japanese unions have also been active partners in the development and diffusion of joint consultation committees, quality circle programmes and other participatory workplace arrangements. Activities such as team-level sharing have strengthened knowledge-creation capabilities (Fruin, 1997), and have created a 'sense of belonging, involvement and participation' (Liker et al., 1999: 11). Strong cultural arguments have also been made for the low level of job or occupation consciousness in Japan. It is proposed that there are deep-seated differences in the social-structural attachments of Japanese and western people. Westerners identify with their occupational positions and roles, and only secondarily with the organizations and groups in which those positions and roles are embedded. In contrast, the Japanese are argued to link themselves first to groups and only secondarily to functional positions within them (Lincoln, 1993).

Worker flexibility and permeable boundaries, due to 'all-round' training and a strongly developed internal labour market are also evident in Germany. Germany is known for its highly developed system of vocational education and training (VET), sustained by the long history of its craft sector, and diffused throughout not only industry but also virtually all the sectors of employment. It provides nationally standardized courses for manual, technical and clerical-administrative occupations, from apprenticeship level up to master craftsman and/or engineer. It thus offers career ladders and ensures homogeneity of competence and orientation at various hierarchical levels. Financing is a joint effort by employers and the state, and the coverage of both theoretical (at school) and practical aspects of VET results in broadly based skills and competencies. Unions are involved in course design in a consultative manner (Lane, 1992).

There is no union control over the allocation of tasks, and job classifications are broad and receptive to change through a variety of informal and formal negotiation processes in Germany (Thelen, 1991). A strong craft tradition, underpinned by an extensive apprenticeship system, has thrived and bolstered policies to obtain versatile workers that can also be retrained more easily. The extensive training (some would say overtraining), of German workers explains their polyvalence. Work has also been less specialized horizontally due to the existence of polyvalent workers capable of carrying out a wide range of tasks.

The control of work is achieved via the standardization of skills through extensive training rather than by the standardization of processes, which is the method commonly used in the USA and the UK. The fact that first-line supervisors are considered to be 'technical experts' rather than direct controllers of the work process is an indication of a standardization of skills approach to work coordination (Lane, 1989: 150). As a consequence of this type of standardization, workers have a high degree of control in carrying out work tasks and the jobs are not specialized vertically (Begin, 1997). Together with their foreman, workers exercise greater discretion than their European counterparts in terms of how jobs are carried out, referring to 'craft' judgement and making informal arrangements (Lane, 1989).

While German work systems never adopted the highly vertically and horizontally specialized jobs typical of the USA and the UK, neither did they approach the much less vertically and horizontally specialized Japanese work systems. Japanese work systems show a greater degree of task sharing, with workers alternating between assembly line and non-assembly line work, and job enrichment through involvement in so-called 'indirect' activities (i.e. materials preparation, quality control, maintenance, scheduling, etc.).

US and German unions pursue very different goals in terms of work organization, but, in both cases, plant-level bargaining is key, and the primary channels for negotiation and conflict resolution are legalistic. In this respect, a distinction has been made between the contractually based rights of US unions and the constitutionally anchored rights of their German counterparts. The key difference is that, in Germany, works councils negotiate over work organization on the basis of a set of stable shop-floor rights, whereas in the USA negotiations over work organization are inextricably linked to negotiations over labour's core rights in the plant. The character of labour's shop-floor rights reflects Germany's general pattern of regulation through a broad and flexible framework (*Rahmenbedingungen*) that structures relationships between actors in the market without dictating outcomes directly. This contrasts sharply with the US pattern of shop-floor relationships premised on detailed contracts, which are themselves, in turn, embedded in a broader system of state regulation resting on a 'tangled web of statute and precedent' (Thelen, 1991: 52). Specifically, the US system has a multitude of rules and no overarching framework, while the German system has a broad but clearly articulated framework, which contains a coordinated set of general rules (Thelen, 1991).

In the Netherlands, there is a tendency to formalize rules and to specialize work roles. Consequently, job classification and design are more detailed and dedicated than in Germany. Production and services are more rationalized, so that division of labour, segmentation or organizational subunits and specialization of work roles prevail. The apprentice system has dwindled over the years, apprenticeship figures are substantially lower than in Germany, and apprenticeships are predominantly served by those who have not succeeded in gaining entry into 'proper' secondary, and subsequent vocational or university, education (Sorge, 1992). In addition, in contrast with Germany, the practice of mixing normal work experience with further education and training is not widespread. Generally, education is concentrated in the period before sustained work activity.

In the USA and the UK, the more rigid division of labour also means deficient communication and more disputes, and hence more time spent on resolving labour disputes and grievances. In the Netherlands, however, this is not the case. Within Dutch companies there is a strong emphasis on consensus, negotiation and consultation between employees, top management and shareholders. This emphasis is institutionalized by a number of laws. In managing a large corporation, the executive board has to consult and cooperate, on the one hand, with the employees' representatives (the works council) and, on the other hand, with the supervisory board on all major decisions. The shareholders then evaluate the outcomes of this careful balancing act once a year (Heijltjes et al., 1996).

Dutch industrial relations at national and industry levels are interlinked with company- and plant-level relationships in a way that is similar to the German system (Sorge, 1992). Dutch labour organizations have a tradition of broad unionism. The relationship between companies and unions is mainly indirect. The Enterprise Council mostly handles matters that are related to work and working conditions in companies. The labour unions' main focus is on working out collective labour agreements, *Collectieve Arbeidsovereenkomsten* (CAOs). CAOs are legally established series of agreements, which result from bargaining sessions between labour and management (Iterson and Olie, 1992). In order to determine these CAOs job classifications are needed.

Functional specialization

Institutional arrangements like management education and vocational training have been found to be the most prominent societal influences on the degree of functional specialization. In this sense, generalist management education can be related to functional specialization; while a more specialist management education enhances functional agglomeration. Furthermore, vocational training with more specialization on offer, some of which is specific to a branch of industry or type of work, leads to a more specialist management orientation. At the same time, the degree of functional specialization in a country is strongly related to the career management policies of firms. Generalist education, combined with formal business school training and the competitive labour market for executive manpower, relates to high functional specialization in US companies. The USA has a thriving market for further management development, epitomized by its business schools, which attract students from all over the world to obtain an MBA (Finegold and Keltner, 2001). The US generalist education, on the other hand, has implications for management behaviour and careers. It goes hand in hand with a conscious professionalism; it facilitates an 'arm's-length' approach, and enhances the standing of forecasting, planning, marketing and control activities. It legitimizes mobility between both functions and companies in personal careers, and stresses the importance of the overall view at the top. The US view is that there are general principles of management that have validity across a range of operations and branches of industry.

Similar to the US situation, the UK business organization is highly departmentalized, with different functional areas. Also like the USA, the UK is characterized by a national culture of generalist, as opposed to specialist, managers (Lehrer and Darbishire, 1999). And like the USA but unlike Germany, employees who have had a specialist education, such as engineers, are employed as technical specialists, 'whose assumed lack of wider knowledge and social skills makes them ineligible for promotion to top management posts' (Lane, 1989). In the UK context, a degree in accounting was held to be an ideal qualification for a top management position. Generally, it was argued that the promotion to top-level posts of 'gifted amateurs' was a uniquely UK phenomenon. As in the USA, too, from the 1960s onwards in the UK, business schools were established, and these provide a general

Table 5.1 Work relationships

	Job design	*Societal determinant*
USA	Highly specialized jobs Formal job descriptions Systematic job evaluations Direct supervision of foremen Standardized processes	Job control unionism Low status/narrow vocational training Deregulated labour market Market finance
UK	Highly specialized jobs except for craft workers Shop steward system Absence of shop-floor control	A type of job-control unionism Low level of vocational training Deregulated labour market Market finance
Japan	Broad job classifications Refined job specifications Job rotation and cross-training No fixed or permanent tasks Limited job evaluation	Unions – employment security Collective bargaining Contracts in flexible/general language Lifetime employment Seniority wage system
Germany	Broad job classifications All-round training Standardization of skills No job specifications High degree of discretion for workers	High-quality vocational training Nationally standardized courses Apprenticeship system Unions – employment security
Sweden		
In the modernized plants	Flexible job design Autonomous production team	Tight labour market union influence
In the traditional plants	Taylorist job design No systematic control employee transfers possible	Excellent education system integrated with employing organizations Limited on-the-job training

management education at a high level (Lane, 1989). Today, the 'gifted amateurs' and the specialists who want to advance, have an MBA.

Like in Germany, Swedish management is characterized by specialist education with a high level of technical training. The qualifications of Swedish managers are overwhelmingly in three subjects: engineering, economics and law (in that order of frequency). Production managers and managers in technical functions have engineering qualifications. Commercial managers usually have a degree in economics. Personnel managers are a mixed bunch; the traditional qualification is a law degree, as in Germany, but many have an economics qualification. Unlike in Germany but similar to the case in the UK, there is in Sweden a relative absence of managers with a doctorate.

From the 1960s onwards, there seems to have been some change in the pattern of qualifications among heads of companies in Sweden. Sweden's traditional strength was in engineering, and most of the big-name companies were engineering firms. In the past, the great majority of these firms had an engineer as managing director. In fact, if one takes an overview of all ranks, not just the top ones, engineers still predominate in Swedish industry. However, at the top, it is generally agreed that there has been change; since the 1960s there has been a tendency to appoint as managing director people with a sales or marketing background, who also tend to have an economics background (Lawrence and Spybey, 1986). From the mid-1980s, there has been a new development, going beyond the move from managing directors qualified in engineering or economics. Indeed, the current fashion seems to be to appoint as managing director someone who is strongly profit-orientated and alert to business opportunities, rather than being simply production- or market-orientated. This development is by no means a widespread one and refers merely to the top manager's state of mind rather than to his qualifications and training.

Finally, unlike the case in the Anglo-American countries, the Swedish universities and related institutions do not engage in continuing education activities for managers, and general management degrees are not widespread. Only two higher educational institutes train senior and middle management in both functional areas of management and general management (Begin, 1997).

The Japanese propensity to reject Western habits of organizing around functional specialities is not confined to job design. Narrow specialization is likewise typical neither of organizational subunits nor of management careers. Japanese companies rarely have the array of specialist staff departments – finance, planning, law, and so on – found in US firms (Lincoln, 1993). The generalist thrust of Japanese education, and the relative absence of formal business school training for Japanese managers, which in the USA produces large numbers of functional specialists committed to a professional career in marketing, finance or accounting, has been a factor in the low specialization of the Japanese company (Lincoln, 1993). In the unitary system of Japan, the state focuses on the provision of academic education, leaving firms to organize their own technical training. The Japanese education system produces highly disciplined and literate school, college and university graduates, who have faced severe competition in achieving entry into the higher-ranking schools and universities. Their selection by leading companies is on the basis of the rank of their school and/or university, their academic achievements and their character. Japanese factories screen for talented generalists fresh out of school and invest heavily in training them for a wide array of responsibilities. High-school graduates are recruited for technical and clerical work, university graduates for technical and administrative work. The technical training and education received by Japanese employees is entirely firm specific. The employee development system requires employees at all levels to acquire, over time, experience in different aspects of the business (Nishida and Redding, 1992).

As in the case of production jobs, another factor in the low specialization of management occupations is the premium the Japanese firm places on a flexible, multiskilled workforce that can be redeployed. The traditional assumption that managers will spend their entire careers within the firm and that higher positions are filled through internal promotion and reassignment plays a major role in this respect. Effective top management is said to demand long experience across a range of specialities and divisions within a single organization. Management-track employees in manufacturing industries typically begin their careers with a stint on the production line, undergoing the same training that production workers receive. The US pattern of terminating surplus employees in a declining speciality and recruiting to a growing one experienced people from outside has simply not been an option for Japanese companies (Lincoln, 1993).

Unlike in Japan, the USA and the UK, in Germany, the generalist approach to education and skill formation has not received institutionalized recognition, and additional qualifications that are highly rewarded are either a doctorate in science or engineering or, alternatively, an apprenticeship earlier on in the career (Lane, 1992). Germany has traditionally exemplified a specialist approach in management education, with an emphasis on specific knowledge and skills, especially technical ones. Most German managers in manufacturing were trained as engineers, and more than a few have passed through apprenticeship training too. It is worth mentioning that, in Germany, first degrees in subjects such as engineering encompass management education as a part of the course, which is part of the more general tendency for technical courses to be broader-based than they are in many competitor countries (Warner and Campbell, 1993).

More traditionally, German managers will have identified themselves in specialist terms as, for instance, an export salesman, a production controller, a design engineer, a research chemist, and so on, rather than using the general label 'manager' (Lawrence, 1991). This specialism also enhances the integrity of particular functions, and careers are formed within functions. Specialism is also apparent in the German organizational format, with companies being agglomerations of functions, coordinated by a 'thin layer' of general management at the top. Over time, with internationalization and in multinational enterprises, the term manager has come to be used more frequently.

The more rigid division between functions is also evident in the Netherlands. Management, design, development, planning and other 'indirect' functions will be more separate from direct work, and concentrated into specific departments or at specific levels (Sorge, 1992). The educational background of Dutch managers shows a strong patterning according to the subjects studied; the three traditional subjects for people entering commercial or industrial management are law, economics and engineering (Lawrence, 1991). In addition, there has been a significant increase in the study of management itself as a university subject, and a vast increase in its popularity. In this respect the Netherlands has much in common with US generalism. However, Dutch higher vocational education (where courses are, as its name suggests, more vocational), with a greater degree of specialism on offer, resembles the German specialism approach. Furthermore, the expectation that new recruits will go into a particular function, learn it through experience and demonstrate their abilities in it has much in common with the situation in Germany. In a certain way, functional specialization does fit the Dutch highly stratified education and training system. Although equality may be a strong value in the Netherlands, the Dutch education system is marked by a high level of differentiation, not only along confessional lines or through state affiliation, but also according to educational level. However, virtually every different level of education guarantees a sound standard of knowledge and skill in employees, whatever the institution the student graduated from.

Table 5.2 Work relationships: management

	Functional specialization	*Societal determinant*
USA/UK	high	Generalist management education, i.e. sales/marketingbackground Formal business school training Competitive labour market for executive manpower External career paths
Sweden	low	Specialist management education e.g. engineering/economics/law Limited formal business school training
Japan	low	Generalist management education Firm-specific technical training Absence of formal business school training Internal career paths
Germany	low	Specialist management education e.g. engineering/science Limited formal business school training Internal career paths

Organizational hierarchy and spans of control[1]

Research that focuses on the interrelationships between the social fields (i.e. the interaction of people at work, work characteristics of jobs, education, training and industrial relations) is able to explain the more detailed differences in organization shape and structure between countries in carefully matched pair comparisons (Maurice et al., 1980). These differences are played down or ignored by general theories of organizing of different types.

Societal effect research found organizations divided into roughly similar categories of employees, arranged in a hierarchical manner. It seems that a basic division of labour between 'staff' (that is, those doing white-collar and management tasks) and 'works' (that is, blue-collar workers), between 'control' and 'execution', is an indispensable feature of the capitalist enterprise. Further horizontal division of labour developed with the increasing complexity of the capitalist enterprise (Lane, 1989: 40). These common structural features are illustrated in Figure 5.1.

Most importantly, research into societal effects found that the size of each category, relative to other categories, differed significantly between the societies. These differences in organization configurations were shown to arise because of the joint emergence of different work structuring and coordination, and qualification and career systems (Maurice et al., 1980). The societal effect took place primarily by way of the latter two systems. Two of the countries that are discussed in this chapter – the UK and Germany – were also examined in societal effects research and are elaborated upon here by way of example.

The differences between German and UK manufacturing units in the division of labour and in the allocation of tasks to positions are expressed in the following detailed features (see Figure 5.2).

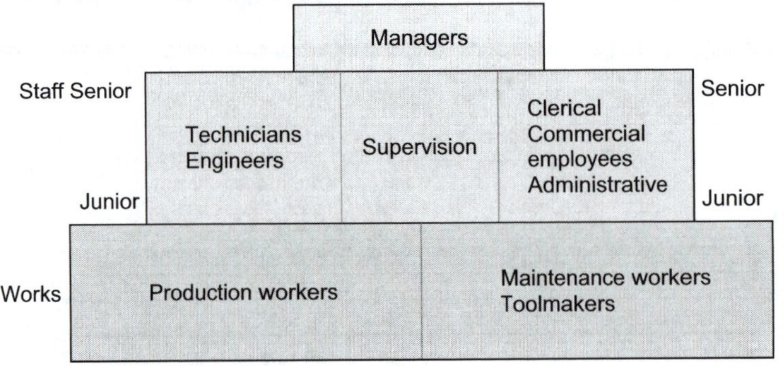

Figure 5.1 A basic organizational configuration.

Source: Maurice et al. (1980: 67).

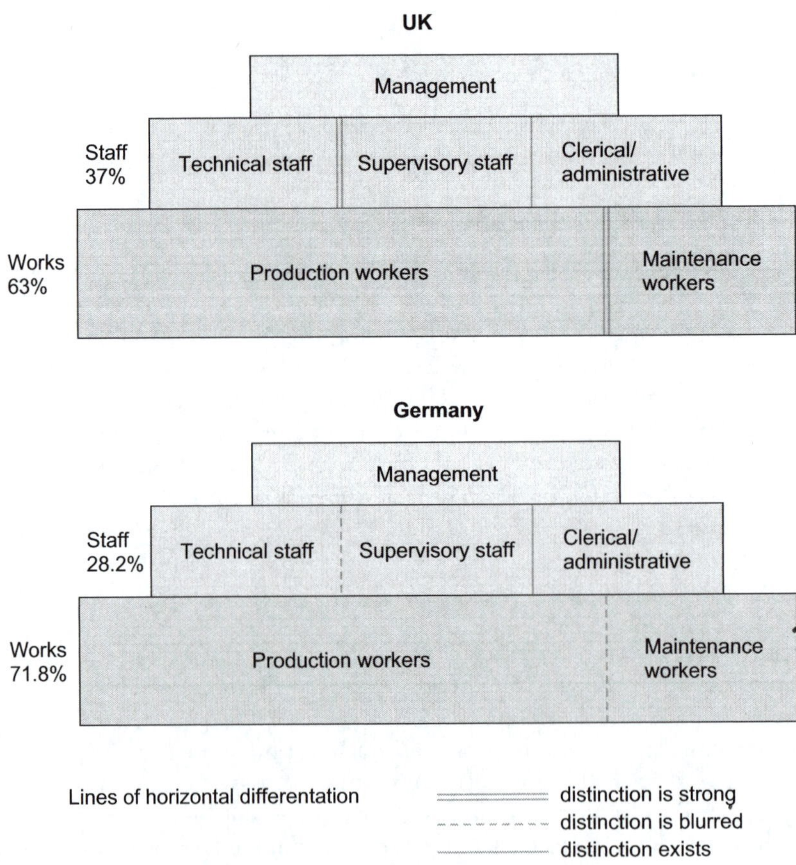

Figure 5.2 National organizational configurations.

Source: Lane (1989: 47).

1 The relation of 'works' to 'staff' differs significantly between Germany and the UK. Germany has the highest 'works' component, reaching an average of 71.8 per cent of all employees. In the UK organizations take an intermediate position with an average of 63 per cent of 'works'.
2 With respect to the ratio of supervisory staff (foremen) to 'works', German enterprises have the lowest ratio and the UK again occupy a rather intermediate position.
3 If all managerial/supervisory staff (i.e. all staff positions with authority over other employees) are considered in relation to the 'works' component, UK business organizations have the fewest, while German organizations occupy an intermediate position. This result is due to the fact that in German enterprises there is no strong distinction between those in supervisory/managerial positions and those with 'technical staff' status. Consequently, many of those in authority positions are, at the same time, technical experts. In the UK, in contrast, this distinction is strong and technical experts are rarely found in supervisory/managerial positions.
4 The ratio of technical staff to 'works' was found to be lowest in Germany (an average of 12.8 per cent) and medium–high in the UK (21 per cent).

These differences between countries remain broadly the same today despite the pervasive tendencies for having more indirect workers (staff). In a replication of Maurice et al.'s (1980) study, Brumana and Delmestri (2012) find that German organizations have still lower job and functional differentiation than Anglo-American organizations. Even after the 2008 financial crisis, French, US, German, and Italian firms are reported as maintaining their organizational and human resource systems.

The qualification and career systems thus have an effect on the organizational configuration in different countries. Employment relations also play a role: Among German manual workers, both skilled and semi-skilled, a high proportion have a relatively high level of skill, have received 'all-round' training and demonstrate a capacity for self-motivation. They do not exercise union control over the allocation of tasks but are consulted through the works councils. Consequently they can be utilized flexibly, with operators rotating between the jobs in the plant, and the distinction between maintenance and production is blurred. In addition, German workers carry out technical and supervisory tasks themselves. Hence, separate technical staff have a less prominent role on the German shop floor.

In UK enterprises, worker autonomy in work structuring is less, and direction from staff departments more entrenched. The lesser degree of autonomy among manual workers is partly explained by generally lower levels of skill, both on the part of the workers themselves and the foremen directing them. In the UK, the craft unions have retained a degree of control over labour recruitment and deployment. The practice of job demarcation has maintained a division of labour both between maintenance workers and operators, and between the various maintenance crafts, although union representatives have become less rigid or less responsible in this. Worker flexibility, due to training methods, is not as developed as in Germany. The supervision needed in UK manufacturing units, combined with the poor flexibility of UK workers and job demarcation practices, explains why UK organizations have a lower works-to-staff ratio than German ones.

Inevitably, these different modes of work structuring have repercussions for task allocation at other levels of the hierarchy, and they affect horizontal differentiation and integration at all levels. They are also reflected in the shapes of organizational hierarchy and spans of control, or the number of subordinates responsible to a manager. A narrow span exists when this number is small, and a wide span denotes the opposite.[2] In this respect, the shape of German organizational structures is generally said to be flat, with wide spans of control, particularly at the supervisory level. German business organizations manage with a relatively low overall staffing level because of the way jobs are designed and supervised. Organizational boundaries, and formal and hierarchical coordination mechanisms are softened and complemented by informal and professional modes of coordination (Sorge, 1991).

The UK organizational structure is more hierarchical and, generally, the spans of control are significantly narrower than in German enterprises. However, although the ratio of staff to works and the ratio of supervisory labour to works are greater in the UK than in Germany, the ratio of managerial/supervisory staff taken together is lower. Thus, spans of control must get wider as we ascend the management hierarchy in UK units.

In addition, the different kinds and degrees of competence, and the resulting role of the foreman in the UK and German business organizations, also have widespread repercussions for organizational structure. Indeed, the wide scope of the German foreman's (Meister) competence is often linked with the fact that there are fewer managerial/supervisory staff in German firms than there are in the UK ones. The higher degree of technical competence of both supervisory and line management in Germany is both a reflection of the training received and a consequence of the relatively frequent mobility from 'skilled worker' status to technical and supervisory staff. German foremen must possess a foreman's certificate (Meisterbrief), which indicates the successful passing of an examination, awarded after attendance of a 2-year (part-time) training course, which teaches mainly technical competence. This technical competence is passed on to workers via foremen in their role as teachers of apprentices.

UK foremen, in contrast, rarely receive such formal technical training. If they receive any training it prepares them mainly for their supervisory role. In the UK, there exists a relatively high proportion of staff without any formal qualifications, even among technical staff. Hence, whereas the UK foreman has mainly supervisory duties, and has to refer technical matters either to higher managerial or technical staff, the German Meister is competent to take on both supervisory/administrative and technical tasks. He performs the combined roles of the UK foreman and superintendent (found only in larger UK firms) and is, in his degree of qualification and in his duties closer to the latter than the former. The German Meister differs from the UK superintendent in his greater degree of shop-floor experience, which affords him a better understanding of, and thus a better level of communication with, the workers (Sorge and Warner, 1986: 101).

The similarities between the UK and US institutional arrangements could lead us to assume similar organizational configurations. Indeed, in spite of many famous cases of innovation, and countless quality and employee involvement programmes, the US workplace remains significantly hierarchical and authoritarian (Wever, 2001). Similar to the case in the UK, the taller organization with narrow spans of control in the USA can be explained by the virtual absence of vocational education, apprenticeship, training in craft skills relevant to manufacture, and job-related training for foremen and technicians. The generally lower level of skills, both on the part of the workers themselves and the managers directing them, results in a reduced degree of worker autonomy. As Ferner et al. (2004) argue, US companies tend to be more centralized, standardized, and formalized in their management of human resources than other nationalities, including the UK. An illustration is offered by Thory (2008) who reports strong US parent company intervention in the recruitment, pay, and employee communications in their operations in Scotland.

Since, to our knowledge, no research has been done on this topic in Swedish companies, it is impossible to provide hard facts. However, in view of the features explained above it would probably not be far-fetched to assume that Swedish operations resemble German ones. But in general, it has been less of a challenge for Swedish firms to adopt US practices, such as performance-related pay, as the 'democratic' management style and openness of communication has promoted learning of practices from other countries (Hayden and Edwards, 2001).

The professional background and ethos of Dutch management shows, in a way, a middle position between the German-style specialism and 'cult of engineering', and the Anglo-American generalism and 'cult of short-term financial responsibility' (Sorge, 1992). Also, in terms of hierarchical structure, the Dutch organization takes an intermediate position. Production and services are more rationalized, so that division of labour, segmentation or organizational subunits, and specialization of work roles prevail. This breeds a bureaucratic structure of formalization and hierarchical intensity. However, employees are more skilled and greater worker autonomy is typical in Dutch companies. Hence, spans of control are less narrow compared to those in the USA, and bear a closer resemblance to those in the German organization.

A finely layered status and authority pyramid with narrow spans of control is highly characteristic of Japanese organization. The structure of the Japanese firm's authority and status hierarchy is distinctive in a number of important respects. Moreover, along with low degrees of job fragmentation and functional specialism, it is widely regarded as a factor contributing to the cohesion and loyalty for which the Japanese firm is renowned (Lincoln, 1993). For one thing, Japanese organizations decouple status ranking and job responsibility to a striking extent. Whereas shifts in status within US companies typically involve changes in job responsibility as well, Japanese status systems are more closely analogous to civil service, military and even academic ranking systems in the USA – that is to say, an upward move is a reward for merit, experience and seniority, but does not necessarily entail a change in responsibility or an increase in management authority. Although Japanese organizations have a large number of hierarchical layers, a common observation is that they often show advanced decentralization of decision-making, an aspect often referred to as employee participation or involvement. Involvement by blue-collar workers through such means as quality control circles and team production, and greater involvement of middle- to low-level managers in firms' strategic decision-making are often cited as examples of the decentralization of decision-making (Morishima, 1995).

5.3 Employment relations

Recruitment of qualified people to fill job vacancies is a significant issue in CHRM for the simple reason that a mismatch between jobs and people could dramatically reduce the effectiveness of other human resource functions (Huo et al., 2002), and a failed expatriate assignment can result in waste of resources for the manager and the MNE in question. Given its implications for organizational performance, recruitment has to be understood and analysed as a strategic act with long-term consequences.

The methodology of personnel selection has never been uniform around the world. Moreover, whether a specific personnel selection practice should be adopted universally remains an unresolved issue. However, given the crucial role played by this personnel function, especially in managing a multinational workforce, understanding the similarities and dissimilarities of existing practices in different nations ought to be the first step taken by human resource managers and researchers. This section, therefore, considers some of the core characteristics of the recruiting system in the countries under discussion. First, we answer the question of whether significant differences exist among nations in terms of

Table 5.3 Employment relationships

	Recruitment and selection criteria	*External recruitment versus promotion*
USA	Ability match – technical work experience	External recruitment for all levels Limited promotion possibilities
UK	Word-of-mouth application form interview	External – for lower end Internal/external – for management Limited promotion possibilities
Sweden	Wide scale of sophisticated techniques	External recruitment for all levels Internal/external – for management
Japan	Personal interview ability match – personal potential to do a good job	External recruitment for low-status jobs Internal labour market includes new graduates Internal career paths
Germany	Personal interview Application form references specialist knowledge and experience	External recruitment for apprentices and management trainees Internal career paths
Netherlands	Personal interview Application form references specialist knowledge and experience Aptitude test	External recruitment for apprentices and management trainees Internal career paths

commonly used recruitment and selection methods. Next, we focus on the alternative of external recruitment versus promotion. In this sub-section, we provide a table that offers a summary of these issues (Table 5.3). Lastly, we outline dismissal procedures in the specific countries.

Recruitment and selection methods

Even in the most democratic organizations, personnel selection criteria are rarely set by a consensus generation process; more likely, they are the result of trial and error over the years, bound by legal requirements, and subject to many other institutional constraints (Huo et al., 2002). Recruitment practices are complex and difficult to comprehend through the filter of written studies. The diversity of practices is such that the same concepts may cover different realities. For example, what does 'interview' or 'CV analysis' mean for German, Japanese, Dutch or US organizations? Also, the recruitment methods used to hire a manual worker, a technician, a 'technical manager' and a 'top manager' will differ (Dany and Torchy, 1994). While recruitment and selection covers a wide array of subjects, this section will concentrate on the leading features in the selected countries.

In the USA, the selection criteria tend to focus on what is relevant to the job and predictive of future performance (Aycan, 2005). The most commonly used criteria include education, past experiences, personality traits, and cognitive skills (Huo et al., 2002; Aycan, 2005). As indicated, the generalist thrust of US education and formal business school training for managers together produce large numbers of functional specialists committed to a professional career in marketing, finance, accounting or organization. Most US companies are not willing to invest in training and the US-style competitive labour market for manpower is grounded in the belief that talented employees can be effective across a range of corporate cultures and business settings. These factors clarify the special emphasis on a person's ability to perform the technical requirements of the job and their proven work experience in a similar job. Moreover, the fact that demonstrated ability counts for more than academic credentials relates to the influence of the decentralized educational system in the USA. The decentralization of the US educational system implies that the quality of some educational programmes is highly variable compared with those of other nations.

Most UK management does not pay recruitment and selection the attention they deserve, and does not make use of many of the techniques and procedures available. In recruitment, they continue to place a great deal of reliance on word of mouth. In selection, they place near-total reliance on the application form to pre-select, and also on the interview, supported by references, to make the final decision. In the UK, and the USA, recommendations are used as a final check, whereas they may be heavily relied upon in south-eastern European countries (Sinha, 1997). Testing and assessment centres, let alone some of the more recent developments such as the use of biodata, are conspicuous by their absence. Significantly, too, all groups are affected from the bottom to the very top of the organization. Indeed, contrary to what might be expected, testing in particular is even less in evidence in the case of managers than it is in other groups (Watson, cited in Begin, 1997: 128).

Intensively used recruitment methods in Sweden (and in all Scandinavian countries) are references, interview panel data and biodata. Psychometric testing, aptitude tests and assessment centres are also used, but to a lesser extent. The determination of recruitment and selection policies is decentralized and is done most of the time at site level and not at national level. Line managers are very much involved in the management of recruitment and selection where the human resource department is supportive of line management (Dany and Torchy, 1994).

The selection means that stand out as those most commonly used in Japan are personal interview, a person's ability to get along well with others already working at the firm, and a person's *potential* to do a good job, even if that person is not great at it when s/he first starts. Another interesting finding is that Japan places relatively little emphasis on a person's ability to perform the technical requirements of the job. This is related to the fact that the Japanese state focuses only on the provision of academic education, leaving firms to organize their own technical training. As we saw above, Japanese factories screen for talented generalists fresh out of school, and invest heavily in training them for a wide array of responsibilities. Hence, the important selection criteria used by Japanese firms revolve around 'trainability' or the ability to learn, rather than the ability to execute tasks and duties (Huo et al., 2002).

The heavy emphasis placed by Japanese companies on a person's potential and his/her ability to get along with others may be traced to the lifetime employment system (Huo et al., 2002). As noted by some researchers (e.g. Pucik, 1984), large Japanese organizations usually conduct recruitment and selection on an annual basis and tend to hire a cohort of fresh school graduates annually in April rather than conduct recruitment throughout the year as vacancies arise. This phenomenon reflects the importance of harmonious human relationships in Japan, since people from the same schools would find it easier to develop a smooth interpersonal relationship within a team due to their common educational backgrounds (Huo et al., 2002).

Since a large internal labour market operates in Germany and the Netherlands, recruitment mainly takes place at entry-level positions, rendering extensive selection methods less essential (Heijltjes et al., 1996). German companies emphasize the application form, interview panel and references as recruitment methods. Recruitment is on the basis of specialist knowledge and experience, especially in technical areas. German companies regard university graduates as good abstract thinkers, but prefer recruiting from among the more practically educated graduates from the senior technical colleges and the MBAs specializing in management because they are considered to be better prepared for jobs as specialists (Scholz, 1996). As mentioned above, since the German system of initial vocational training is standardized, it is less important to test the technical knowledge of those employees who hold such a qualification.

Dutch firms emphasize the three methods that are used by German companies and add to these the aptitude test. This result can be related to the fact that virtually every different level of education guarantees the sound standards of knowledge and skills of employees, whatever institution the student graduated from. If you were to ask Dutch personnel managers engaged in recruitment what they look for, you would be given a mix of generalist and specialist factors (Lawrence, 1991). Certainly the latter do not predominate, even for technical jobs, in the way that they do in accounts given by German HR managers. In the Dutch case, personal qualities, communication skills and variations on the theme of being flexible all figure. Assessment centres, which are considered to be among the more valid techniques, are not used widely for recruitment purposes, except in the Netherlands (Dany and Torchy, 1994). This might be explained by the Dutch perception that the vocational education system is inadequately matched to the demand side of the labour market. An assessment centre is, then, a valid technique for testing the skills in which the company is interested.

External recruitment versus promotion

Does the organization want to recruit poorly qualified people and develop them through vocational training? Does it want to recruit highly qualified people, assuming that they are best qualified to improve organizational performance? Decisions between an external recruitment policy, on one hand, and a policy relying on internal promotion, on the other, can potentially have a substantial social impact (Dany and Torchy, 1994). Indeed, the choice that is made affects the nature of the employer–employee relationship, the social climate and the innovative ability of the organization, while the choice itself is affected by the flexibility of the labour market.

The deregulated nature of most labour law in the USA creates an extremely active external labour market. Hence, US firms are more likely to hire, at all levels of the organization, from the external labour market. Job hopping by employees, particularly skilled or managerial employees, is generally viewed positively by society as the means for an individual to improve his or her prospects more quickly, as long as this is done in moderation. Numerous private employment agencies that facilitate the operation of the external labour market are not restricted or regulated by law and they, to some extent, make up for relatively low government expenditure on labour market services and training (Begin, 1997). Moreover, the generalist education and predominantly financial orientation among top managers (Aguilera and Jackson, 2003) and the more diversified nature of US firms makes movement between firms, and even between industries, relatively easy.

The USA has consistently applied the concept of shareholder value. Company law, stock market regulations and take-over rules are all orientated to the defence of shareholder interests. Inter alia, this implies that managers of publicly owned companies focus more intensively on investors' benefits by striving to reward them with the most attractive rate of return on their capital possible. Short-termism and a risk-prone attitude must also be cited as key features of US management, perhaps best illustrated by executives' recurrent obsession with the next quarter's results rather than the long-term health of the organization (Schlie and Warner, 2000). Hence, since investment in human capital offers only long-term returns, US managers are not usually willing to invest in training and internal promotion.

The external labour market in the UK is active at all levels of the organization. There seems, however, to be a tendency to recruit more heavily at the low end of the skill range and to rely to a greater extent on internal promotions and transfers to fill higher skilled and management positions. The recruiting of top managers has been reported to be balanced between an internal and external recruitment pattern, neither recruiting externally as much as the Scandinavian countries and France, nor promoting internally as much as countries like Germany and Japan. Many of the best UK companies promote managers from within, but the external labour market for managers is very active and most managers choose to move up by taking better jobs with different firms rather than by long-term service with one firm. As a result, and in a similar way to US managers, UK managers focus more on short-term results that will improve their external marketability rather than on long-term business goals (Begin, 1997).

In open labour markets such as the UK, vacancies are likely to be filled externally (Aguilera and Jackson, 2003). Similar to the situation in the USA, it is easy to hire and fire instantly. Managers are expected to job-hop across firms to progress their careers. The internal labour market is highly segmented, with employees having little opportunity to work themselves up; thus there is a low ceiling for careers in factory-type environments. Unskilled or semi-skilled operators cannot usually move into the craft maintenance occupations because they are given little training, and because recruitment and assignment are controlled by the craft unions. Nor do such workers have much leverage in the external labour market to improve their position, due to their lack of technical skills. The growing subcontracting of skilled work has further limited the internal promotional opportunities of core workers (Lane, 1989).

Promotion through the supervisory route is also limited. In Germany technically trained supervisors are promoted up the organization, thus enhancing the technical knowledge of higher managers. These often hold PhD degrees in engineering or chemistry (Aguilera and Jackson, 2003). First-line supervisors in the UK rarely move beyond that level, and the technical specialists who are in the technostructure of UK organizations remain there, for the most part, throughout their careers. Many of these technical specialists were promoted from skilled crafts in the works without further technical training; thus the limited technical backgrounds of the skilled crafts are carried upwards in the technostructure.

Employers in Swedish firms have a major influence over who gets promoted; seniority is not a major determinant. Promotion-from-within policies are not uncommon in Swedish organizations. For managerial personnel, the incidence of such a policy is highly variable across organizations. Most supervisors are promoted internally from the general workforce. However, the promotion of supervisors into higher management positions is most unusual because most middle managers are recruited externally (Faxen and Lundgren, 1988). For management, Sweden is one of the least likely countries in Europe to use succession plans to regularize internal promotions. Moreover, middle managers tend to be functional specialists and are not exposed to other functions by being rotated through promotions to other functional areas (Begin, 1997).

The hierarchy in Japanese firms is constructed almost exclusively on the basis of career paths that are internal to the organization. As a result, any links with the external labour market are confined to a certain number of low-status jobs, while access to the higher levels, or to managerial or supervisory positions, cannot be gained through external mobility. This detachment from the external labour market tends to channel actors towards internal strategies (promotion) and to create a 'balkanized' labour market (Nohara, 1999). The internal labour market organization of the Japanese firm includes recruitment of new graduates into entry-level positions after an intensive screening process, subjecting them to intensive on-the-job training in skills and values that are heavily firm-specific (Lincoln, 1993). University graduates constitute a more or less undifferentiated population of recruits from which, after a period of between 10 and 15 years, the new generation of senior managers will be selected. In other words, the entire population of new recruits is treated as a single reservoir of human resources from which specific resources are gradually extracted (Nohara, 1999). Not having any immediately useful skills, all these new recruits undergo the same occupational and organizational apprenticeship. Their skills develop during a long process of socialization: the new recruits begin by exploring technically limited tasks carrying little responsibility, gradually extending their sphere of competence by moving on to related tasks. As noted by a number of researchers, one of the most important implications of long-term employment practices in Japan is their ability to encourage firms to invest in intra-firm training (Morishima, 1995). It is argued that, since employers are not likely to lose their investment in human capital, they are motivated to provide in-house training to their workers more intensively than otherwise.

In recent years, however, the rapid technological change in some industries has called into question the effectiveness of in-house training, which is a linchpin of the entire system. The demands of new technologies are not well met through an experience-based system of skill formation. Increasing competition in product markets requires breakthrough innovations more than incremental adjustments in product developments. The incremental adjustments, which have been regarded as a competitive advantage for Japan's manufacturing industries, are consistent with in-house training, while the breakthrough innovations are compatible with more flexible personnel policies based on external labour markets (Thelen and Kume, 1999).

In Germany and the Netherlands, where mobility between companies is also fairly low, the internal search is more prominent than recruitment from external sources. This implies that the recruitment function is less important than in countries with prominent external recruitment. In both countries, promotion into supervisory or managerial positions, although dependent on further formally certified training, is rendered more likely by loyalty to a given firm and, thus, pursued in internal labour markets.

In the Netherlands, frequent changes in career paths are generally regarded as a sign of disloyalty and even ingratitude. Larger Dutch firms are inclined to promote positions internally and fill most positions in this way, including those on the executive board. However, this promotion occurs at a slow rate. Mobility between sectors is even more insignificant. In particular, mobility from public service to business, or vice versa, is more the exception than the rule, although some exchange of managers occurs with respect to the Ministries of Economic Affairs and Finance, as well as government agricultural departments. Mobility between large companies, notably the multinational firms and the smaller Dutch firms, is equally rare. In this respect it looks as if a distinct labour market circuit exists (Iterson and Olie, 1992). This supports employers and employees to invest in company-specific training and skills.

Internal labour markets force and enable firms to invest in long-term human resource development (Streeck, 1991). The German training regime obliges employers to train more workers and afford them broader skills than required by immediate product or labour market pressures. German firms train large numbers of apprentices and retain most of them on completion of their training. Although such training is not firm-specific, its broad and flexible nature nevertheless makes it a valuable resource that large firms are anxious to retain. Further flexibility is acquired by more informal and firm-specific upgrading of training (Weiterbildung), which greatly increased in volume during the 1980s, and by works councils' support for the flexible utilization of core labour (Lane, 1992). Rather like the Japanese human resource system, however, the German system of in-company training and internal promotion does not fit with radical innovation industries. Hence, Germany experiences the same problems with radical innovation. On the other hand, it has been distinctive for combining new techniques with more traditional ones. Since the mid-1990s, the German government has been supporting the development of small entrepreneurial technology firms. For instance, Casper (2000) shows that Germany's new technology policies have built on existing institutional incentives and rigidities such as its skills development system amongst establishing new institutions such as 'public venture capital' to promote radical innovation in biotechnology.

Dismissal procedures

US firms have substantial freedom in adjusting the size of their manufacturing labour forces due to the absence of employment security programmes (except for job control mechanisms) and the absence of restrictions on their ability to reduce workforces using a number of staffing policies. Indeed, US manufacturing firms evolved employment policies that gave them great freedom to move employees into and out of organizations, thus using the external labour market to regulate the allocation of workers among jobs. At the same time, many manufacturing firms developed staffing policies, often in the collective bargaining process, that limited their ability to flexibly allocate employees within firms in accordance with need (Begin, 1997). Employees higher up in the organization – the managers, professionals and technical employees paid by salary – often enjoy an implicit type of job security, but this security was undermined substantially in the late 1990s under a new social contract.

US employers have successfully fended off union efforts at both state and federal levels to restrict their freedom to lay off employees. Currently, there are no substantial limits except for a 60-day federal notice requirement for plant closures or layoffs in firms with 100 or more employees. Moreover, firms do not have to justify layoffs with an economic analysis acceptable to a government agency. Neither do they have to negotiate with unions their decisions to close plants; they only have to negotiate the effects on workers (Begin, 1997: 94).

> Job cuts continue to make headlines in the United States. . . . In the first half of 2001, American firms announced around 770,000 layoffs, as many as in any full year during the 1990s. . . . The axe was often wielded with little thought for long-term strategy. Or at least it seemed that way to those who were laid off – and more crucially, to those left behind, whose morale plunged. Generous early-retirement packages tempted many of the experienced employees that firms would, on reflection, have preferred to keep; and, conversely, missed many of those they would happily have lost. When the economy rebounded more quickly than expected, firms had to resume hiring, and those that had cut most aggressively found it harder to recruit[3]

Similar to US firms, UK companies also have a great deal of freedom from legal or social limits on reducing the size of their labour forces or dismissing individuals. The layoff of employees is a major strategy used by employers to adapt to changes in demand; indeed, it is generally believed that it is easier and less expensive to lay off a worker in the UK than in any other European country (Anderton and Mayhew, 1994: 37). Unskilled workers are highly interchangeable with the external labour market. Unless an employee has been with a firm more than 2 years, he/she can be laid off without any legal or financial obligation. Employers must give notice of layoffs (redundancies) to the Department of Employment, and must consult with the unions. Usually, firms will reach agreement with the unions on who is to be laid off (Begin, 1997).

In Sweden, layoffs are considered a last resort rather than a primary adjustment strategy, due to government policy that substantially restricts layoffs. However, in times of severe economic duress, firms lay off many employees (Begin, 1997). The Security of Employment Act 1974 established strong statutory employment security for Swedish employees, which impacted on the substantial flexibility that Swedish employers previously enjoyed to lay off, deploy and dismiss employees. Now employees are considered to be hired indefinitely unless there are 'reasonable grounds' for dismissal. Previously, employment security was provided by mobility in the external labour market, which was enhanced by government programmes (Martin, cited in Begin, 1997). Under the provisions of the act noted above, the ability of employers to dismiss workers either for poor work performance or because of shortage of work is severely restricted. In addition, older workers (over 45) have special 'layoff protection'. It is difficult for an employer to adjust a workforce in relation to market needs unless it can be established by a thorough investigation that transfers to other duties are not appropriate. Both notice and transfer obligations have been expanded by bargaining agreements. Before any workers can be laid off, primary negotiations with the unions affected under the Codetermination Act must take place, a time-consuming process that could involve several levels of negotiation. Employees also have input to potential layoff decisions through their participation on boards of directors. In the final analysis, the employer, after having given the unions an opportunity to affect the outcome, has the right to determine the scope and organization of operations. In a ranking of nations as to whether the obstacles to the termination of employment contracts were 'insignificant, minor, serious, or fundamental', Sweden, together with Japan and the Netherlands, was given a 'serious' ranking; Germany was given a 'fundamental' ranking (Begin, 1997: 213).

As already indicated, an important feature of Japanese human resource management is lifetime employment. An important implication of the Japanese lifetime employment system is not to discharge or lay off core employees except in very unusual circumstances. Lifetime employment is not a contract, rather it is a morally charged way of thinking on the part of both employer and employee. Once a person enters an organization, he devotes himself to it and stays until he retires at 60. After this age, there typically exists a secondary job market of firms and positions of 'old-age employment'. A person will avoid moving from organization to organization in primary employment until 60 years of age. The organization, on the other hand, will take care of him throughout his working life and will not terminate his employment lightly. When profits decline, a company will take many measures to reduce its costs, including the curtailing of dividends and bonuses of top management, but it will retain its employees for as long as possible. This is in contrast to US corporations, which tend to lay off employees to keep the dividend rate high, and increase the value of stock options for top managers even while laying off employees (Kono and Clegg, 2001). It is important to mention, however, that the Japanese lifetime employment system does not apply and never has applied to all employees. It omits temporary workers, subcontractors, seasonal workers, part-timers and dispatched employees. The system applies only to larger companies, and the definition of lifetime employment refers to core employees' long-term training and employment within the enterprise group or keiretsu. It does not state that they never leave their particular companies, either for another company within the keiretsu or to pursue a career at another company (Ornatowski, 1998).

A misconception about lifetime employment is that the staffing level is never reduced. After the oil crisis and following the recession in the 1990s many companies reduced the size of their workforces, but this was done on a phased basis rather than through sudden redundancies or layoffs (Kono and Clegg, 2001). This is undoubtedly linked to the nature of corporate governance in Japan, which is less subject to short-term financial discipline and tends to put off radical restructuring of industrial activities and to avoid taking drastic measures if at all possible (Nohara, 1999). Moreover, in order to avoid the need to discharge employees because the jobs they do have become redundant, employees' skills are updated to meet the organization's new requirements. However, series of economic stagnations have cast doubt on the sustainability of lifetime employment practice. A survey by Nikkei Research in 2002 showed that over half of 800 firms surveyed could no longer sustain this practice. The business world has been riddled by job cuts, a prominent one of which was Matsushita cutting 8,000 jobs through voluntary layoffs in 2002. This became a turning point in Japanese industrial relations (Moriguchi and Ono, 2006).

In spite of pressures for change, the practice of lifetime employment persists in an adapted form. First, Japanese employment security is firmly grounded in legal precedents set by Japanese courts, which has made it almost impossible for employers to dismiss or lay off their regular-status employees without the employees' or their unions' consent. Second, both long-term employment and employment security have been explicit policies of the Japanese government. Third, among the bargaining areas of Japanese enterprise unions, wage increases have always been considered in tandem with the protection of employment security for the firm's permanent workforce. Wage issues have always been relegated to second place relative to employment security and, when employment security has been threatened, Japanese enterprise unions engaged in tough and often violent negotiations (Morishima, 1995). Moreover, lifetime employment is an important part of Japanese management practices as a whole because it reduces the commitment problems associated with firm-based private-sector training. Lifetime employment provides incentives for workers to stay with the company that trains them; in turn, this makes it safe for the firm to invest heavily in skills without fear of workers leaving and taking these skills to other firms (Thelen and Kume, 1999). While, as indicated, lifetime employment, combined with internal promotion ladders and continuous in-company training, hampers radical innovation, it is an essential ingredient of the cooperative relationship between producers and suppliers working on a high-quality and just-in-time basis.

Similar to the situation in Sweden and Japan, in general, German manufacturing firms do not have a great degree of flexibility in adjusting the size of their workforces through layoffs, subcontracting, or transfers or loans to other firms, although these policies have become more widespread more recently. In international comparisons, Germany is generally believed to have the most extensive restrictions on layoffs and dismissals (Büchtemann, 1993: 274). Layoffs are costly, complex, restricted by law as to required notice, and essentially must meet a 'just cause' test. Moreover, high employment stability is imposed on firms through collective agreements, codetermination and legislation. While there are no formal laws stipulating long-term employment, German labour has used its power on supervisory boards, as well as its formal consultative rights under codetermination law over training, work organization and hiring, to demand unlimited employment (Casper, 2000). The employment relationship, which has evolved under the influence of legislation on the rights and obligations of workers within the enterprise during the postwar period, has given workers high de facto employment security (Lane, 1989).

For a major employee dislocation like a plant closure, the German regulations contained in the Dismissal Protection Act 1951 (amended in 1969) are among the most comprehensive among advanced nations. According to the original intention of this Act, the purpose is to legally prohibit dismissals that are not motivated by good reasons (Eger, 2004). Approximately 80 per cent of those workers with permanent employment contracts are protected by its provisions. The works council and the regional government must be notified 12 months prior to the final decision to close a plant. The notice to the works council of a staff reduction must include the reason for the layoffs, the number of workers affected and the planned duration of the layoff. The firm and the works council then discuss options for minimizing layoffs. The law requires employers to make every reasonable effort to prevent layoffs through such mechanisms as retraining, work sharing and reassignment (Büchtemann, 1993: 276).

A significant feature of the relationship between management and unions in the Netherlands is the commitment to employee security. Massive layoffs, such as those that occur in the USA and the UK in order to adjust the labour force to the changing demands of industry, are not tolerated. In some ways, this commitment resembles the German and Japanese employment system. Traditionally Dutch people do not like to fire employees for two reasons: first, it involves making judgements about people as individuals and violating corporate security expectations; second, it is expensive – firing managers is legally and procedurally complicated, and it costs a lot in compensation.

However, attitudes to mobility have softened (Lawrence, 1991). A management philosophy termed Management en Arbeid Nieuwe Stijl (MANS) brought a widespread Dutch feeling of 'no-nonsense management' into practice and was a reaction to the human relationship management style of the 1960s. At that time unprofitable companies were subsidized, unions had more power, employees who performed poorly were not dismissed or demoted, and employees were given more time to discuss and participate in corporate policy. MANS emphasized output goals, the needs of the customer, flexible operations, just-in-time inventory, total quality control and doing more with less manpower. In this climate, layoffs became drastic and widespread (Wiersma and van den Berg, 1998).

Fuelled by globalization, economic competition has increased dramatically. Companies now need to have greater control over their staffing needs. In recent years, a number of large firms have been forced to downsize and therefore make drastic cuts to their workforces. As a result, employee outplacement has become a prevalent human resource management activity. Where this used to be an activity that was contracted out to specialized agencies, now it takes up a significant amount of the personnel officer's job. This relates to the Dutch emphasis on care for personnel (Heijltjes, 1995). Because it is still difficult to terminate full-time staff in the Netherlands, companies increasingly use temporary personnel, on contracts with the company itself or via recruitment by a manpower agency. Although the interests of employees are increasingly being protected, permanent employment is also being systematically undermined (Wiersma and van den Berg, 1998). Dutch employers have effectively increased the flexibility of labour use through introducing new types of working time, subcontracting production or services, and using temporary labour from employment agencies. This has led to a multiplication of the types of employment relationship and contractual forms (Guest, 2004).

5.4 Compensation and benefits

Managing international compensation and benefits successfully requires knowledge of the mechanics of compensation, such as employment and taxation law, customs, environment and the employment practices of foreign countries (Dowling et al., 1999). Yet, with all of this in mind, the three primary objectives of international compensation plans are no different from a domestic-only plan to attract, retain and motivate employees to achieve competitive advantage (Lowe et al., 2002). The loyalty and commitment of employees can be elicited in several ways. This section will cover wage systems as well as performance-related pay in the selected countries. Table 5.3 offers an overview of the details discussed in this section.

Pay systems, collective bargaining and co-determination[4]

The bargaining system in the USA is one of the most decentralized in the world: single employer and single union at local level. Labour contract negotiations are at plant level rather than company level. US companies are autonomous in the matter of the remuneration they offer. Most of them are not unionized and, in any case, the preservation of the managerial prerogative is always a priority. Personnel departments frequently take the initiative in matters of salary data, industry and regional variations, pay relativities and remuneration trends (Lawrence, 1996). This is facilitated by a weak industrial relations system and the common absence of representatives of organized labour telling management what workers want. Companies consult salary data (on industry averages or on the local average) prior to deciding how and where to position workers.

The difference between compensation for a CEO and the average plant worker in the USA is the greatest among advanced nations. The average US CEO is paid 160 times as much as the average plant worker, compared to 10 to 20 times in Japan (Tsurumi, 1992: 15). Moreover, many firms offer top executives a number of different 'perks' (perquisites), including executive dining rooms, cars, stock options, fancy offices and travel on corporate jets. At lower levels of the organization, managers and professionals are offered many perks not available to white- and blue-collar employees, such as special parking privileges and dining rooms. Most blue-collar workers are still not paid salaries, but are paid on an hourly basis (Begin, 1997). The majority of US states have minimum-wage laws or wage boards that fix minimum wage rates industry by industry.

In the USA, benefits are frequently a competitive weapon. Companies attract and retain employees with the quality of the benefits they offer. Benefits administration has to be good, and companies put much creative energy into the development of benefits. On a rank ordering of OECD states by social funding of pensions, healthcare, unemployment insurance and the like, the USA is second to last. As a consequence, the well-being of workers depends on market earnings and employer-provided benefits more in the USA than in most other countries. Taxes and cash transfers are less redistributed than in other countries. US decentralized wage setting, with rent sharing between prosperous firms and their workers, and limited provision of social wages, puts the country at the top of the developed world in terms of wage inequality (Rogers, 1995). Furthermore, the system of equity finance and frequent profit reporting has led to an attempt to enhance profits by squeezing wages (Lawrence, 1996). Consequently, by the 1990s, labour contract discussions centred on benefits, the new battleground, rather than on wages where any gain would be small.

In the UK, during the 1980s, under successive Conservative governments, an emphasis on collective bargaining as the most effective method of determining pay and conditions was abandoned, based on the view that unions were responsible for wage 'stickiness' in response to changes in supply and demand, which was undermining the performance of the economy (Sisson, 1989: 25–26). Since the UK labour market was already essentially unregulated by statute law, and instead covered by the 'custom and practice' of and in collective agreements, the nation's strategy for achieving greater flexibility was to weaken the power of one of the major players. A unique feature of the UK bargaining system is, in the absence of a legal framework setting the rights and obligations of the parties, the emergence of the workplace as the focus of problem solving under collective bargaining. The shop steward system evolved after the Second World War, and has been described as giving workers direct and substantial authority over decisions relevant to their work group, including pay determination and a broad range of benefits. The written labour agreements are only the tip of the iceberg, since informal custom and practice comprise the bulk of agreements between labour and management at the workplace (Begin, 1997: 140).

The rewards system in the UK has always been closely tied to the operation of the labour market due to the absence of government restrictions on pay determination. Moreover, in the 1980s, whatever restrictions there had been were weakened. Minimum wages have become essentially non-existent. Around 75 per cent of UK workers are paid a fixed wage per hour, shift, week, month or year, with no provision for individual performance. Local work group negotiations between lower management and shop stewards often add supplements to cover seniority, dirtiness of work, complexity of work, safety, and work away from the plant site. The number and size of these additions to pay often vary across work groups within plants, which can make worker transfer across groups with varying payment difficult. Even in the days when multi-employer bargaining was more common, wage settlements were often added at the firm level, and further local shop steward negotiations shaped the final economic package. Except for the work group variations over which they have little control, and which probably account for a relatively small amount of the pay package, top firm managers maintain strong control over wage increases, even with the substantial decentralization of pay determination to divisions of corporations (Brown and Walsh, cited in Begin, 1997: 143).

Salary differences between manual workers and managers in the UK are not as high as in the USA, but are greater than those in Germany (Lane, 1989: 130) and Sweden. Payment systems for non-manual workers in the UK are based on monthly salaries, and merit pay of some type is usually available, while manual workers are paid on an hourly or weekly basis. The number of single-status payment systems introduced for blue- and white-collar workers has been very limited.

Even more than in Germany, worker governance through unions and codetermination has been substantial in Sweden. The Swedish codetermination system, however, has not been as extensive and it is provided by unions at the firm/plant level and not by statutory works councils as in Germany. The Swedish Codetermination Act, one of the major legislative initiatives of the Swedish union confederations during the 1970s, provided for labour–management negotiations over pay and other terms and conditions of employment, which culminated in a contract requiring agreement of the parties. The organization of Swedish employers in a strong coalition through the SAF – the sole peak employer association – contributed to the subsequent development of centralized wage negotiations in Sweden.

Up until the early 1990s, negotiations between the SAF and the LO, the Swedish blue-collar trade union federation, traditionally followed a pattern that involved three stages. At the highest level, there were centralized negotiations between the SAF and LO, which had established the 'basic agreement', a sort of employment relations constitution by contract. No SAF member could agree to pay less than the agreed settlement. The mid-level of negotiations took place between industry employers' associations and the LO to develop agreements responsive to industry-level conditions. Issues such as the type of wage payment (hourly, salary, piece rates, profit sharing), overtime pay, shift pay, the definition of normal working hours, and compensation when no work is available, are discussed at this level. Finally, at the third level, individual companies negotiated with local unions on issues specific to the company. Throughout the negotiations, the parties preferred to manage their negotiations without significant government intervention, an outcome that no doubt derived from the substantial political power of the unions.

One similarity with Germany is in the unionization of management, although the unions are different in Sweden. A total of 90 per cent of the supervisors and 70 per cent of the mid-level managers are in unions, so their salaries are determined by collective bargaining. Hence, the shift from manufacturing to service employment in Sweden did not result in a decline in union membership, as in the USA. Instead it resulted in some tension among those unions that represent the different occupational groups of employees: the LO, the blue-collar employees; TCO, the white-collar employees; and the SACO/SR, the professional employees. As the structure of the labour market has shifted to more white-collar and professional employees, power has shifted from the manual unions to the highly unionized white-collar and professional groups.

Consequently, whereas, since the Second World War, the centralized wage determination process was controlled by the manufacturing industries through the LO/SAF agreements, from the 1970s service workers and public employee unions were no longer accepting of the blue-collar control of wage settlements. Employers operating the export market also preferred the flexibility provided by decentralized negotiations in adapting to international competition, including the flexibility to compete within Sweden for highly qualified workers in the very tight labour market. As a result, there was growing 'informal' decentralization of bargaining, and a large gap developed between the centralized LO/SAF wage agreements and what was actually agreed to at many work sites (the 'wage drift'). More recently, wage bargaining has become more firm based, as the SAF refused, from 1991, to participate in peak negotiations with the LO. The metal industry had withdrawn from centralized negotiations in 1983.

For blue-collar workers, collectively determined pay is primarily job based and somewhat seniority and skill based, too. For white-collar workers, collective bargaining determines the pot to be distributed, but wage increases are determined individually within the context of a job structure outlined by a job evaluation scheme. The salaries for low- and mid-level managers are negotiated by unions, in much the same way as for white-collar workers, although starting salaries are subject to individual negotiations.

Seniority-based pay and promotion is a familiar feature of the Japanese reward structure. The Japanese Ministry of Labour's definition of seniority-based pay and promotion is 'a system or practice which emphasizes number of years of service or age and educational background in determining pay and promotion'. This does not mean that seniority measured by the number of years with the company is the only means to determine pay, but rather it is a primary means. Even in companies that use a seniority-based pay and promotion system, there has always been a fair amount of competition among same-year entrants to the company. Informal evaluation of individual performance begins soon after new employees enter the company, even though they are treated equally in terms of pay and promotion for a number of years (Ornatowski, 1998). Since the 1960s, the Japanese system has been premised not so much on pure seniority wages but on job capability and skill-based wages (Thelen and Kume, 1999). In the Japanese job capability wage system, wage development reflects the accumulation of experience by a worker over the course of his/her career in the firm, as skills are acquired through on-the-job and in-house training.

The Japanese skill-grade system, using a set of very detailed criteria, assesses each employee according to what he/she is capable of performing, not what he/she actually performs. In this system, employee capabilities are considered to be formed on the basis of cumulative on-the-job experience and internal training, and, therefore, strongly related to their tenure. Behind the strong positive correlation between tenure and average pay, individual differences exist in the levels of achievement of skill development, and they are exactly what the skill-grade system is intended to measure. On the surface, the skill-grade system is quite close to the system of skill-based pay or pay-for-knowledge that has become increasingly popular in Western countries. The literature suggests, however, that, assisted by very broadly designed job classifications, there is a much larger number of skills to be learned in a Japanese skill grade relative to those of a skill grade in a US workplace. The skill-grade pay system encourages learning over the long term during one's career. Since there are, on average, seven to eight skill grades for an employee's occupational category, and advancement to a certain skill grade is required as a precondition for promotion to managerial positions, this system provides incentives for promotion. Thus skill-grade pay offers a strong incentive for Japanese employees to learn and improve their skills (Morishima, 1995).

With very few exceptions (e.g. All Japan Seamen's Union), Japanese unions are enterprise unions, each representing the employees of a different firm. The enterprise union organizes both blue- and white-collar employees. The fact that a single union represents employees in diverse occupational groups within a common firm has been a significant force for standardizing working conditions, payment levels and systems across occupational boundaries. The enterprise union is considerably more dependent on the company than the typical craft or industrial union. This connection places limits on how far the union is willing to push the company in a labour–management dispute, and it fosters an impulse on the union's part to identify with company goals (Lincoln, 1993). Observers of Japanese industrial relations, while acknowledging the structural dependence of enterprise unions on Japanese firms, none the less see Japanese unions bargaining hard on wage, benefit and job security issues. Unions can be credited with the rapid postwar rise of aggregate wage levels in the Japanese economy, and with many of the distinctive institutions of the Japanese employment system (permanent employment, seniority wages, etc.) (Lincoln, 1993).

In the early postwar period, unions fought to preserve a guarantee of wages based on workers' minimal living costs: living wages (Seikatsu-kyu). The idea was to guarantee wages at a time when high inflation was damaging Japanese workers' ability to keep up with high costs. The system became the basis for seniority-based wages and promotion and, together with the lifetime employment system, was viewed by management as a way to secure labour peace and retain skilled workers. From the unions' viewpoint, on the other hand, lifetime employment and seniority wages were ways to stave off management's tendency to lay workers off in order to adjust labour costs and to beat the threat of an inflated cost of living. At the same time, to achieve flexibility in labour costs and provide lifetime employment to the core workforce, management limited lifetime employment to a core group, created a separate group of temporary workers it could lay off easily, instituted twice-yearly bonuses based on the company's financial results, varied workers' overtime hours and squeezed suppliers in times of recession to adjust overall system labour costs (Ornatowski, 1998).

In the 1980s and 1990s, a number of factors, both internal and external to large firms, have contributed to increasing pressure for change in the seniority system. A major internal factor is the gradual long-term deterioration of returns. This factor, in turn, can be explained by the overwhelming emphasis on market share rather than profitability by the large firms, itself made possible by relatively tolerant, long-term-orientated shareholders. Falling profits can also be explained by a rising percentage of employees in white-collar jobs with much slower productivity growth than blue-collar workers. In addition, with baby boomers reaching middle age, the number of older workers has increased, contributing to steadily rising labour costs under traditional seniority-based wages. An excess of middle-aged and older workers was more easily tolerated when the economy was growing fast and profit margins were higher. This has not been the case in recent years. The productivity of such excess staff has become a major issue (Ornatowski, 1998: 78–79). The second aspect of seniority is promotion. You generally do not overtake your senior in your own company. The ageing of the population results in what may be called a 'jam effect' (Dirks et al., 2000: 531). It has become difficult for companies to generate the kind of opportunities for advancement within firms that in the past justified seniority-based wage increases. This problem has become even more acute in recent years, which have been marked by corporate retrenchment rather than expansion (Thelen and Kume, 1999: 484). Finally, attitudes among younger employees are much more attuned to the principle of equal opportunity, which is implied by a performance-based pay system. Younger employees are increasingly less tolerant of the principle of equality of results and patiently waiting for the promotion implied by the traditional seniority system (Ornatowski, 1998: 79).

A major external factor is the maturing of the Japanese economy, in terms of both lower growth rates and growth of the service sector, and the end of the catch-up economy. Enterprises have increasingly invested in subsidiaries in lower wage countries, such as Korea and increasingly China. Further economic growth is increasingly dependent on internal technical innovation, a move to higher-value-added products, and major cuts in government regulation. The result is a simultaneous pressure on firms, both to develop more high-value-added products through innovation and to shift more of the manufacture of their lower-value-added products out of Japan, as evidenced by the reluctance to outsource R&D and the emphasis on shifting production to China (Ernst, 2006). Another external factor is the decline in large Japanese companies' international competitive position. Large Japanese firms are in fierce competition with both Western firms in high-value-added products on technological grounds and price, and in lower-value-added products with firms in Korea and Taiwan. In the higher-value-added sectors, in which large Japanese manufacturing companies compete, high-quality production of standardized products in mass quantities, or even large varieties of quality products in smaller lots, is no longer sufficient. Rather, large firms increasingly need to develop unique or highly innovative products that cannot easily be copied and continually move up the value-added chain with new innovations. They also need to develop entirely new technologies more often and more quickly. Performance-based wages, rather than seniority wages, help by motivating the more innovative workers and forcing the 'slackers' to either improve their performance or risk lower pay and demotion. Moreover, performance-based wages are also argued to help companies hire the mid-career specialists necessary to develop new technologies or enter new fields. Large companies, therefore, see seniority-based wages as in need of revision (Ornatowski, 1998: 80) (see discussion under performance-related pay).

Wage bargaining in Germany is characterized by a negotiation structure focussing on industries, which, due to union pressure, emerged after the war and was aimed at pursuing a 'solidaristic wage policy' that averaged out 'market power among the different groups of the working class' (Streeck, 1984: 14). These centralized negotiations are usually conducted external to the firm, between unions and employers' associations. The result is that wage negotiations are simply structured and well coordinated nationally since they rarely involve more than one union (Streeck, 1984: 24). Union members are organized regardless of their skill and occupation, and thus are industry unions; craft unions are few, except for airline pilots and cabin staff, and for train drivers, which have become more forceful recently (Streeck, 1984: 5). The employer associations are also structured by industry, and negotiations are usually conducted on a regional level by industry. A decentralization of the bargaining structure has been a continuous trend in Germany, with works councils assuming more influence over negotiations so as to better match bargaining outcomes to the economic performance of firms, although centralized negotiations are still prevalent. Pressure on matching bargaining outcomes to firm-level needs has come from the employers' associations (Begin, 1997: 181).

An examination of pay in the German context has to distinguish between employees covered and not covered by collective agreements. Exempt are all those employees that earn significantly more than the highest base salary prescribed by the collective bargaining agreement. Collective bargaining agreements in Germany set a relatively high minimum wage and ensure an adequate basic compensation. In contrast, variable compensation is not generally fulfilled, as effective wages are not much higher than the collectively set ones. Individual bonuses for employees covered by agreements are relatively small. But companies have more freedom with regard to pay for exempt employees. Exempt pay is normally the exclusive province of senior management. However, although exempt pay is little affected by collective bargaining, remuneration decisions for this group of employees are constrained by codetermination. Even if there is no formal system in pay determination, the works council has an influence on exempt remuneration (Müller, 1999a). However, trends have indicated a decline in the number of German companies affected by works councils, for some time. As Grahl and Teague (2004) show, trade unions find it difficult to establish works councils in small 'new economy' firms as those in the IT and biotechnology fields, but also for small firms in outsourced services, in building and in catering. The growing importance of small firms outside the classical industries has contributed to undermining the country's mandatory system of employee voice.

Since around 90 per cent of all German employees are covered by a collective bargaining agreement, increases in wages take place every 12 to 15 months. The average wage increases negotiated outside the firm are then tailored to the profitability of individual firms by the works councils, creating a wage drift that varies by industry and region. However, the size of the wage drift has not been the problem that it has been in other countries like Sweden. Although, unlike Sweden, an egalitarian pay system has not been given the priority of German unions, in international comparison the wage differentials across occupations and industries are not high, and the differences between white- and blue-collar workers have been declining. There is a current trend to pay blue-collar workers monthly salaries and to otherwise equalize the employment conditions of blue-collar workers with those of white-collar workers. Some general framework agreements in industries where technological change has blurred the lines between white- and blue-collar workers have provided for a common pay structure (Begin, 1997).

More than in Germany, wage negotiations in the Netherlands are centralized and take place between the employers' associations and trade unions, with the government playing an active part. However, the persistently high level of national/industry-wide bargaining in the Netherlands has been argued to mask greater scope and flexibility for adjusting these at firm level (Visser, 1992: 351). Company-level agreements are argued to affect approximately one-third of employees. In the case of large firms, in particular, independent agreements are arrived at. The legally prescribed collective-bargaining process between trade unions and employers' associations usually results in (industry- or company-specific) collective labour agreements (CAO, or *Collectieve Arbeidsovereenkomst*). About 700 of these CAOs (at industry level or at company level) are concluded each year. These agreements deal with wages, but also with vocational training and early retirement procedures. They function as minimum standards that apply to entire industries (Heijltjes et al., 1996). The rather centralized system of labour relations traditionally produces salary systems that are more concerned with a reasonable distribution of income than with the creation of performance-related incentives (van Dijk and Punch, 1993).

The Dutch government, employers and employees also consider their societal responsibility for decreasing unemployment and industrial disability. This leads to greater protection of employment security, for those employees that perform less well. Pay is therefore more often tied to tenure than to performance (Heijltjes et al., 1996). Moreover, many Dutch companies feel that providing employees with additional education, so that they keep abreast of the latest developments, is a significant motivator. This explanation fits well with a cultural emphasis on education and on people's desire to be fully conversant with all aspects of one's chosen occupation. Designing jobs to fit people is another type of intrinsic reward that is valued highly in the Netherlands. This means increasing task variety and flexibility, and having a whole piece of work to complete. In addition, employees are educated to understand how their job fits into the bigger picture (Wiersma and van den Berg, 1998).

This discussion needs to be weighed against the general decline in union membership at different rates in different parts of the world. In almost all OECD countries, union membership is on the decline. In the USA, the UK, Germany and Japan, unions' share of the workforce has dropped steadily to about half its level in 1980 (*The Economist*, 6 April 2013). New recruits at Scania, a Swedish vehicle manufacturer, question the need to join the union. These pressures are significant effects on the way in which unions organize themselves and engage with governments and businesses. Very recently, in IG Metall, the German metalworkers' union, membership has, however, been increasing. The reasons lie in a mixture of industrial resurgence and recruitment and services that this union has been implementing.

Performance-related pay

Human resource management prescriptions tend to favour performance-related over job- or person-based pay systems. The reason for its popularity among managers is that performance-related pay is perceived to increase financial flexibility, to undermine collective bargaining, to strengthen the role of the line manager and to enhance employee commitment to the organization (Müller, 1999b). By motivating individual workers to be more efficient at work, incentive schemes are expected to improve impersonal relationships, raise job satisfaction, lower absenteeism and waste of intermediate material or capital (Bryson et al., 2013).

With the exception of piece rates and similar incentive systems, historically there has been an insignificant relationship between individual, group and organizational performance, and employee pay in the USA. Piece-rate systems in plants were popular earlier in the century, but they have declined substantially in recent years, primarily because manufacturing systems have changed. Nowadays, individual merit pay is based on subjective performance evaluations. Rather than objective indicators of performance, like the number of pieces produced, cost savings or profits are used widely. A survey of Fortune 1000 firms indicated that 96 per cent used merit pay, 31 per cent using it for all employees. The introduction of performance-related reward systems in the USA was stimulated by the decentralized nature of industrial relations, the short-term orientation of US business and the need to quickly realize a significant return on investment. Profit sharing is used widely, although it is by no means a universal practice. A survey of Fortune 500 firms indicated that 60 per cent covered some employees with a profit-sharing plan, with 15 per cent covering all employees (Begin, 1997: 104).

From the 1980s onwards, there has been an increasing interest in pay-for-performance programmes in the UK, although manual workers usually remained untouched by the changes that took place; only a third of manual workers were rewarded with merit pay of some type (Kessler, 1994: 471). Another survey indicated that only a quarter of firms had merit programmes for manual workers, compared to 40 per cent for managers, and one-third for clerical/administrative staff. So the major diffusion of these programmes has been to non-manual staff. These programmes have primarily been based on individual merit pay derived from indicators of financial performance at the individual, subfirm or firm level. Individual and collective bonus payments have declined (Begin, 1997). More common in the UK have been profit-sharing schemes, including employee share ownership based on profits. Aided by government regulations, by 1990, 55 per cent of private-sector firms had some type of share ownership programme (one-third, compared to 23 per cent in 1984 and 13 per cent in 1980) and/or profit-sharing programme (40 per cent of the firms) (Millward et al., 1992: 262–263). The adoption of these schemes, as is demonstrated by, for instance, CEE countries, tends to be driven by decentralized firm-level bargaining and weak level of unionization (e.g. Poutsma et al., 2014).

As jobs in Sweden have become less specialized in industry, there has been a shift from piece rates towards group incentives, although there appears to be some employer resistance to abandoning piece rates. The use of piece rates in Sweden was very significant compared to their use in other countries, in part because the LO has also been a strong advocate of piece rates in the context of job designs called Taylorist. As we shall see in Chapter 7, this is strange in a strictly Taylorist perspective, because Taylor had advocated wage determination independent of the individual will and achievement of the worker. While the use of piece rates has been declining, employers are starting to individualize wage payments to a greater extent through pay-for-performance and profit-sharing or gain-sharing plans, with payments from these sources added to the centrally agreed-upon base increases. The movement towards more flexible pay patterns is illustrated by the degree of diffusion of pay-for-performance systems. In a 1991 survey, 55 per cent of the workers questioned received some type of payment for performance, 27 per cent received fixed pay, while only 17 per cent were compensated by some form of piece rate. Information from SAF membership surveys indicates a somewhat higher degree of flexible compensation, with two-thirds of the employees of SAF members receiving supplements from such compensation programmes as profit sharing or payment by results, although payment by results is much more popular, with over half of Swedish firms using this type of compensation. The use of pay for performance for managerial staff, according to one survey, is the lowest in Europe with only 13 per cent of employer respondents indicating that they use such a system (Begin, 1997: 229–230).

The influence of the recession and the emphasis on the creation of new technological resources in Japan has led to attempts to renew incentive mechanisms, particularly the wage system, long considered excessively rigid and ill suited to the new competitive conditions. Up to the late 1980s, almost all white-collar managers and administrative employees were paid on the basis of their skill levels. Consequently, there was little variation in managers' pay from year to year. This began to change in the early 1990s, when firms started to introduce reward arrangements based on individual performance levels (Morishima, 1995). Since then, attempts have been made to put in place a new system – albeit one that takes a wide range of different forms – that combines greater flexibility with increased competition. It must be noted, however, that the Japanese notion of merit or performance differs from the Western focus on work results, and includes communication skills, cooperativeness and sense of responsibility.

The emerging consensus among larger companies seems to be that, while lifetime employment will be retained, seniority-based pay and promotion will generally be phased out (Ornatowski, 1998). Some firms have already introduced 'nenposei', a lump-sum salary that is renegotiated annually and depends to a large extent on individual performance. In line with the 1997 Japanese Commercial Code, firms have been granting stock options as compensation to top management and employees. Nearly 350 firms adopted option-based compensation plans between 1997 and 2001 (Kato et al., 2005). Performance-related pay has the advantage of fluctuating, both upwards and downwards, in accordance with individual results, and of individualizing to a large extent the remuneration of each employee. Such strengthening of incentive mechanisms is intended to encourage autonomy and individual creativity, particularly among white-collar workers, whose productivity is considered rather mediocre, even if this development means sacrificing some of the benefits of cooperation (Nohara, 1999).

Moves to reform the wage structure, though typically coded as part of the same managerial offensive that has put long-term employment at risk, are frequently part of a strategy to preserve long-term employment. Patterns of resilience and change are closely interwoven. Technological developments in the past decade have outstripped the skills of experienced workers, and the need to fill the gap has unleashed fierce competition among firms for promising young workers, not so much because of the relatively lower wages that they can be paid but because of their adaptability to new technology. Hence, abolishing seniority wages appears to be less a neoliberal strategy against labour than it is a mechanism for achieving advantage against other firms in competition for the best new recruits. If reforms of the wage system have in part been motivated by the attempt to achieve advantage in competition with other firms over the most desirable young workers, the reforms have also reflected a desire to make it less costly for firms to retain older workers. In other words, such reforms are seen as necessary to maintain the stability of long-term employment. Many specialists argue that the introduction of new performance-based wages will help management to retain younger but highly skilled workers with higher wages (Thelen and Kume, 1999). However, performance-based pay and mid-career hiring are far from being modal practices. That these HR innovations are diffusing slowly in Japan can be attributed to huge sunk costs in the traditional system, which is built on complex interdependencies between micro and macro institutions, and to the historical success of the system's enterprise-orientated incentives (Jacoby, 1995). The successive financial crises have raised concerns and have led to incremental changes that may eventually produce a qualitative transformation. However, Japan is nowhere near that point, yet.

Pay for performance has had a mixed history in Germany. In the classical metalworking industries, pay for performance (time needed to do a job compared to the time planned) has been a dominant and long-lasting form of remuneration, which also fitted with the relative autonomy of the skilled worker. In this respect, Germany has been the leader in payment by results for workers, and the union has supported this. But managers have been least likely among the different staff categories to be subject to performance-related pay. It appears that against the background of a long-standing tradition of profit sharing as part of managerial remuneration, the use of formal performance-related pay schemes has not found much acceptance (Begin, 1997). Moreover, because unilateral decision-making is limited, German firms cannot easily create strong performance incentives for management. As a result, performance rewards tend to be targeted at groups rather than at individuals (Casper, 2000). For the top management of joint-stock companies, however, bonuses have gained a more important position as part of total compensation, although in the wake of the 1991 and 2007+ crises, doubts have come in about the fit between enterprise long-run well-being and the incentives that came into fashion in the 1990s, notably the stock-market oriented rewards criteria for top management.

The comparatively high uptake for some employee groups is a reflection of particular collective agreements. The collective agreement for the metal industry, for example, includes provisions for appraisal-linked pay increases (Filella and Hegewisch, 1994: 102). In the past, although extrinsic rewards were less popular in Germany, organizations had already used differential rewards and effort bonuses (*Leistungszulage*) to reward good performance on the shop floor. These were paid, on the recommendation of foremen, to around 10 per cent of the workforce. The rating system was transparent. Works councils participate in working out the system, and unions have their own REFA (Association for Work Study) expert to help them work with such a system.

From the 1990s onwards, it appears that the ideology of individual performance-related pay has had more impact on German managers. Some firms attempted to link pay more to performance by introducing analytical job evaluation for those exempt, by changing fixed bonuses into variable ones, and by linking merit increases and bonuses to an appraisal scheme. For instance, in 1996, Daimler-Benz and Deutsche Bank decided to offer stock-based incentives to their managers. These adoptions were enabled by firms' exposure to high-status institutional environments, and experience with other contested practices (Sanders and Tuschke, 2007). Works councils, however, remain critical of performance-related pay and sometimes prevent its introduction (Müller, 1999b: 135).

Because performance-related pay implies a stimulus of competition between employees to achieve the best performance, which is further enhanced by the knowledge that if the performance criteria are not met the employees can be fired, this reward system is also hard to implement in the Netherlands. The underlying assumptions are in conflict with Dutch business culture, where a consensus orientation prevails (Heijltjes et al., 1996). However, changes in industrial relations and human resource management are also gradually unfolding in the Netherlands. Whereas, previously, negotiations occurred on a national level and applied to all companies and employees in a particular industry (Collectieve Arbeidsovereenkomst), they are now occurring more within individual corporations. The firm has been rehabilitated as the central theatre of labour relations, although the extent and effect of this trend towards greater decentralization differs between economic sectors (Visser, 1992). The sectors that are subject to intense international competition, such as chemicals and consumer electronics, exhibit the most advanced changes in employee relations. These changes afford greater flexibility and more variation across companies in terms of compensation practices. In these companies, the professional personnel managers and the works council play the dominant role in determining working conditions and personnel policy (not the employers' associations or trade unions). In sectors that operate within more stable markets and/or more domestically orientated markets – like building and construction, and retailing – it is unlikely that the traditional labour relations system, characterized by collective bargaining between the employers' associations and trade unions, will change dramatically in the short term. Additionally, little change is likely to occur in the collective and subsidized sectors where union membership is at its highest (Heijltjes et al., 1996).

However, for some, the trend towards pay for performance in the international sector indicates that extrinsic rewards will play a greater role in motivating employees in the Netherlands in the future. Furthermore, Dutch companies changed in that they started competing in terms of differentiation rather than conformity (Wiersma and van den Berg, 1998). This emergent individualism has been accompanied by a franker interest in remuneration. Stock option schemes have become more widespread for senior executives, and fringe benefits more acceptable and more sought after at other levels (Lawrence, 1991).

Case: Human resource management in China

There have been great changes taking place in China, not only in the macroeconomic sphere, but also at enterprise level. The reforms introduced in the 1980s set the scene, but in the 1990s management–labour relations, employment and human resources moved closer to external models. In September 1997, in particular, approval of the faster reform of state enterprises by the Chinese Communist Party seemed to play a major role in the change process (*The Economist*, 'No job, no house, no welfare', 28 May 1998). Nevertheless, in some ways, institutional and organizational inertia continues to hamper the shift from the older practices, especially in the larger state-owned enterprises (SOEs). What has emerged has been called 'human resource management with Chinese characteristics' (Warner, 1997: 41). Indeed, the imperfect or partial transformation from the old to a newer system of management–labour relations is evidence of specificity rather than universalism.

Until the second half of the 1970s, the Chinese Ministry of Labour exercised tight control over labour allocation. Workers and staff were assigned to particular jobs in a unit for life by the local labour bureau, with an overall quota set by the Ministry of Labour. Neither workers nor enterprises had any say in the allocation process, but had to accept whatever jobs or manpower were given. The recruitment function was practically non-existent in a state enterprise. This system resulted in the mismatching of talents and jobs, and a misallocation of labour resources in SOEs. Moreover, as a result, there was no labour market to speak of in China. From the end of the 1970s, however, the labour control system loosened up somewhat. The reforms in the 1980s and 1990s introduced further change vis-à-vis past hiring practices, and meant a shift from central allocation to marketization of the labour force, with the emergence of a nascent labour market. The legacy of the past cannot easily be dispensed with, however.

The quality of China's labour force is significantly lower than that of other industrialized countries. Recognizing the importance of worker education and industrial training, the reform programmes launched from 1979 onwards emphasized training for technical staff. However, training for management has been carried out with equal vigour. It has been recognized that training a core of managers is the key to successful implementation of the nation's modernization programmes. This view is in great contrast to that of the Cultural Revolution years (1966–76), during which management as a subject of study was abolished by the 35 institutions that offered a programme modelled after the Soviet Union. Nowadays, managers are trained both by the enterprises themselves, as well as by universities and finance/economics colleges. Management courses place a strong emphasis on quantitative methods such as production engineering, operations research and statistics. Qualitative courses such as human resource management, marketing and skill development, on the other hand, are rather weak (Mee-Kau Nyaw, 1995).

A linchpin of the state-owned industrial sector was China's 'iron rice bowl' employment system, which promised job security and cradle-to-grave welfare coverage. Aside from job security, and egalitarian but low wages and limited bonuses, the system provided workers with heavily subsidized services such as low-cost housing, food and transportation, free medical treatment, retirement pensions, childcare, and so on. This practice of a low basic wage with many subsidies is unique to China – a paradox that has yet to be resolved. Indeed, this social support system drains substantial resources from the enterprises, and over the years has become a great burden on them (Mee-Kau Nyaw, 1995).

Since the mid-1980s, Chinese enterprises have slowly begun to abandon the lifetime employment part of the system. After 1986, Chinese enterprises introduced fixed-period labour contracts for new employees. The 1994 labour law extended the phasing-out of the entire system to a wide range of SOEs. However, until the mid-1990s, layoffs of redundant workers were uncommon as there was strong 'unofficial' opposition from the state security unit for fear of social unrest if workers were thrown out of their jobs. From the late 1990s, in those parts of the country where the state economy weighs heaviest, such as Changchun, in China's industrial northeast, being laid off has become a daily threat. Moreover, the city governments in this part of China also announced an end to subsidized housing (*The Economist*, 'No job, no house, no welfare' 28 May 1998). 'China is trying to set up a social-security system to take over the welfare role once played by the enterprises.' (*The Economist*, 'Urban discontent', 13 June 2002).

The 'iron rice bowl' in state enterprises had co-existed with an egalitarian wage payment system involving a flat reward structure for much of the time. Basic wages were low and fixed according to national scales, and incentive bonuses were developed at plant level but within limits again set by the government. Both wages and bonuses were unrelated to the performance of enterprises. Moreover, lack of proper job evaluation meant that wage levels were more or less arbitrarily determined by state bureaucrats for all Chinese SOEs (Mee-Kau Nyaw, 1995). Recognition of the arbitrariness of the wage system, and of the fact that its overwhelmingly egalitarian nature seriously reduced the initiative and motivation of good workers, resulted in the national abandonment of the old wage grade system. From the mid-1990s onwards, the new 'post plus skills' (gangji gonzi zhi) system, with age, position and skill determining the basic wage, has been widely adopted (Warner, 1997). Moreover, the government also lifted the bonus limits to give enterprise management the ability to reward the good and diligent, and to punish the unproductive. This was to enhance the motivation of workers and technical staff, but in order to have any effect income differences had to increase.

For a long time the promotion system in Chinese SOEs has been based on the seniority of workers and staff rather than on performance. In addition, *guangxi* (or 'connections') is another major factor in determining who should be promoted. Workers and staff with special ties to the superiors in power, either through family connections or via the formation of special cliques, usually get promoted over others lacking these connections. These types of practice have denied many capable workers and staff the chance of promotion to higher ranks. Furthermore, a manager can also be said to be 'sitting on an iron chair' while enjoying an 'iron rice bowl' (i.e. he can be promoted to senior ranks but cannot be demoted regardless of capability or performance). This has resulted in a phenomenon of too many high-ranking officials with too few rank-and-file staff, and there is overstaffing with too few staff actually performing work. Since the end of the 1970s, governmental reform programmes have tried to rectify such practices. However, there are a number of obstacles that make it difficult to implement change:

1. low wages make senior management staff unwilling to step down from their positions, as to do so would imply that they would lose many privileges
2. the lack of a rigorous performance appraisal system
3. the lack of regulation that can be implemented and enforced.

From the 1980s onwards, however, there have been indications that promotion is increasingly being based on ability (Mee-kau Nyaw, 1995). Finally, the role of the Chinese trade unions – in the form of the All China Federation of Trade Unions (ACFTU) – in management–labour relations is also changing. In China, the trade unions play a supportive rather than an adversarial role. The unions have not been bargaining freely or negotiating wage levels, as is normally the case in western countries. The ACFTU was assigned two functions: top-down transmission, mobilization of workers for production on behalf of the state and, by bottom-up transmission, protection of workers' rights and interests. Formally at least, trade unions were supposed to implement the details of resolutions passed by enterprise-level Workers' Congresses (the nominally representative workplace mechanism of the ACFTU). In reality, however, the Workers' Congresses themselves had no power to make decisions that were binding on the factory director. Hence managerial authority, together with the power of the party committees, prevailed in enterprise management. In the everyday work of the enterprise, union officials were expected to look after the ongoing welfare needs of their members (Warner, 1997). With much greater emphasis now being placed on economic efficiency, the status of the trade union in the enterprise hierarchy is expected to improve, leading to a more active form of worker participation (Mee-Kau Nyaw, 1995). In reality, however, the government is frightened that at some point the ACFTU will, 'break up into independent unions that might actually speak up for the workers' (*The Economist*, 'Getting organized, with western help', 29 November 2001).

Questions

1 Compare the changes in features of the Chinese human resource management system with the Anglo-American and Japanese systems. What are the differences and/or similarities?
2 How would you link the changes that have happened in the Chinese human resource system to Chinese societal and historical features?
3 In what way can the changes help to increase productivity in the SOEs? What would you recommend as further changes that are feasible in view of the societal features?
4 What does the case tell you about the change in the education of workers and white-collar employees, and how will this affect the organization structure in the SOEs? What would the organizational structure have been before the changes and why?

5.5 Conclusions

International comparative research on the major human resource systems shows that the meaning, importance and composition of human resource techniques are related to the societal settings of each country. Countries with similar institutions and cultures develop similar human resource systems. The Anglo-American cluster has developed an entirely different human resource model from that of the Rhineland cluster. However, the clusters also differ greatly internally. The Anglo-American cluster, with its focus on short-term results, its highly developed external labour markets, generalist management education, low level of vocational training, and arm's-length industrial relations system, is characterized by a high degree of vertical and horizontal specialization, instant hiring and firing policies, promotion between firms, and poor in-company training. The Rhineland cluster, on the other hand, with its long-term view, its less extensive external labour market, specialist management education, excellent vocational routes, and close employment relations system, focuses on extensive in-company training, long-term employment contracts and internal promotion possibilities, and is characterized by low vertical and horizontal specialization. The Dutch case shows that a hybrid societal environment produces a hybrid human resource model – that is, a model that has features of both the German and the Anglo-American models. The Dutch case also shows that internationally orientated industries exploit the hybrid character and, as a result, increased resilience of national institutions far more than the domestic sectors.

This chapter also emphasizes that the roles that separate human resource elements play should not be considered in isolation. The interdependent relationships among the elements of human resource systems are accepted and legitimated by the parties involved, despite recurrent conflict between the parties. Long-term employment in Japan and Germany will not easily be abandoned as it supports the internal promotion ladders and intensive training commitment of companies, which in turn explain worker commitment and functional flexibility. The latter are necessary for the development of organizational capabilities to generate and put into production innovation, as we shall see in the next chapters. Similarly, unstable and/or competitive employment in US and UK companies help to explain the absence of serious in-company training efforts and the lesser degree of internal promotion opportunities, both of which in turn explain reduced worker commitment and a high degree of functional specialization. HRM thus contribute to different patterns of economic change: in coordinated and cooperative business systems, change occurs more by the transformation of enterprises and their products and processes, in compartmentalized business systems more by sectoral and industrial shifts.

The institutionalization of human resource systems, however, does not imply that they are impossible to change, but rather that change does not happen overnight. There is an interplay between management choices and the constraints upon these choices. The general idea is that some threat to firm survival and prosperity must be perceived by the management in order to initiate the process of change. Management next evaluates the constraints upon change (implied by the societal context) and examines the elements of the human resource system that are most conducive to change. To the extent that firms are constrained in their choices, management will opt for the most efficient solution from a set of possibilities. In this way, as a business system evolves, the link between specific choices and specific constraints, becomes tighter. For instance, in Japan, a few large employers have made the choice to modify the rules regarding seniority-based pay, but not regarding lifetime employment. The trend away from seniority-based pay, however, appears to be rather slow and cautious overall. Lifetime employment is retained not only because it is a protected right, but also because of the heightened dependence on stable and predictable relationships with labour at the plant level, in the context of tightly coupled production networks and the demands of producing high quality just-in-time. The evolution of human resource features in the countries discussed reveals a mixed picture of cautious and slow change as a result of the resilience and continuity of the relevant societal context.

Over time, it is striking that both the research literature and surveyed higher managers in large enterprises seem to have become fascinated with a more normative HRM concept proposed in the USA since about 40 years ago, featuring a more active or more pro-active stance in recruiting and developing human resources, appreciative of their productive role rather than the cost factor. This ethos has at least propagandistically spread to various countries. All the time, it was not clear what practical significance it had acquired in the USA, a country particularly torn between opposed traditions of personnel management, between trade union influence and the protection of acquired rights in the older industrial regions and new liberal personnel management in the new ones, between the normative rhetoric of HRM and everyday practice. In a more recent survey of leading managers in the USA, Japan and Germany, Pudelko (2005) showed a programmatic 'partial convergence to a hybrid model'; the author found these ideas curiously but factually orientated towards German practices, although the managers considered these least inspiring. This demonstrates the tension between normatively inspired views of the world on the one hand, and what factually happens on the other. Much as the author welcomes a tendency for HRM in different countries to learn from one another, he draws the conclusion that 'research should seek more insights regarding the knowledge of managers about foreign management models, their perception of these models and how these perceptions are generated' (Pudelko, 2005: 2045). It is in this spirit, of an unending quest to go beyond what is the rhetoric of both researchers and managers, that this chapter was written.

Study questions

1. What are the differences between Anglo-American and German work relationships? Explain these differences on the basis of the institutional approach.
2. Explain the differences in employment relationships between the Anglo-American and German models. Use institutional theory in your explanation.

3 Discuss the working of hybrid human resource models.
4 What have been the major changes in the Japanese human resource system? Explain the pressures that have induced these changes.
5 We have studied the human resource management models of the USA, the UK, Sweden, Germany, Japan and the Netherlands. Explain on the basis of institutional theory in which of these countries pay for performance is generally used and in which of them it is not well accepted. Differentiate between workers and different levels of management.
6 Examine whether, under pressure from globalization, human resource systems will converge towards one 'best' model.
7 Explain, in general, which elements of the societal environment and which human resource management practices are interdependent with firms' organization structure. Apply your argument to structure in Germany and the USA.

Further reading

Ferner, A. and Quintanilla, J. (1998) Multinationals, national business systems and HRM: the enduring influence of national identity or a process of 'Anglo-Saxonization'. *The International Journal of Human Resource Management* 9(4), 710–731.

Article discussing the 'nationality effect' in the management of human resources by multinational companies (MNCs). The article assesses the elements of the national environments that are most likely to influence MNC behaviour. It explores the tensions arising between the requirements of 'globalized' operations and the characteristics MNCs have adopted from their home environments.

Kogut, B. (1993) *Country Competitiveness: Technology and the Organizing of Work*. Oxford: Oxford University Press.

Though written at the beginning of the 1990s, this book remains an excellent example of how the societal has an impact upon the organizing principles of work in different countries. The book adds a further step and analyses the implications for firm performance of diversity and changes in the principles by which work is organized.

Moore, L.F. and Devereaux Jennings, P. (1995) *Human Resource Management on the Pacific Rim: Institutions, Practices, and Attitudes*. Berlin: Walter de Gruyter.

Excellent book on human resource practices in 11 Pacific Rim countries: Australia, Canada, Hong Kong, Japan, New Zealand, China, South Korea, Singapore, Taiwan, Thailand and the USA.

Sorge, A. (1991) Strategic fit and the societal effect: interpreting cross-national comparisons of technology, organization and human resources. *Organization Studies* 12(2), 161–90.

The article analyses the reciprocal relationship between societal differences in organizing and generating human resources, and business strategies and performance. The argument implies that economies and societies develop Ricardian comparative advantage on the basis of institutionalized organization and human resource patterns.

Case: Human resource management among Korean affiliates in the Dutch consumer industry[5]

During the 1990s, many Korean companies established logistics locations in the Netherlands. The Korean multinationals were attracted by the Dutch tax system (which was beneficial to foreign companies), the broad knowledge of the English language and the openness of Dutch society. Despite these advantages, however, all Korean companies experienced difficulties as a result of societal differences, and some closed their Dutch plants after just a few years. Korean managers suggested that cultural differences, combined with the differences in laws and regulations, and especially the unwritten rules, made it extremely difficult to manage their Dutch sales and distribution plants.

Similarly, Dutch managers pointed to societal differences that made it difficult for them to work in Korean subsidiaries. Dutch managers experienced the relationship with their Korean superiors as tiring in the sense that they had to explain to them time and again 'the Dutch way of working'. 'This requires patience and perseverance,' a Dutch manager comments. In the following we will take a closer look at the difficulties that Korean and Dutch managers experience in working together in Korean subsidiaries in the Netherlands.

A major area in which difficulties were experienced was in human resource management. Korean human resource management policies are quite different from Dutch ones, and Korean managers admit that they often have a hard time understanding and accepting these differences. The problems had already started during the recruitment phase. Korean managers asked candidates about their medical history, sexual preferences, and so on. In fact, some candidates were turned down for giving 'undesirable' answers to such questions. These questions are part of standard recruiting practices in Korea; hence it was quite normal for Korean managers to ask them and to turn down candidates when undesirable answers were given. Such questions are, however, illegal in the Netherlands and candidates could take companies to court when discriminated against on the basis of their answers to them.

Further, Korean management mentioned that they could not understand why companies did not have access to employees' medical files in the Netherlands. In fact, Dutch 'sickness' laws in general were not understood. In the Netherlands, an independent doctor needs to be appointed and has to verify the ability of employees to work when illness is reported. Korean management found it upsetting when the doctor, after declaring that an employee was not fit enough to work, refused to explain the employee's physical condition. Moreover, Korean management never really understood why employees could stay home because they had a cold! 'Korean employees will come to work until they are truly unable to do so,' Korean managers argued. Korean views with respect to Dutch illness laws and the like are such that they distrust Dutch employees who call in sick too often.

Initially, some Korean companies had a hard time recruiting and retaining good employees because of their reputation as bad employers. This image was caused partly by Korean human resource practices. For example, some Korean firms dismissed employees without (according to Dutch standards) an acceptable reason. Moreover, some Korean companies maintained a policy of hiring employees on short-term contracts (3 weeks) so that they could dismiss them whenever necessary. In Korea, employees can be dismissed when, at the end of a day's work, they have been unable to meet that day's goal or haven't performed as they were expected to. Against this background, a Korean manager said that he couldn't understand the lack of loyalty of Dutch employees. The manager complained about high employee turnover and the fact that employees did not hesitate to switch jobs when they got a better offer.

Korean management was usually experienced as quite authoritarian in their dealings with employees. 'Especially, in the beginning', a Dutch manager states, 'Korean management would call their subordinates by clicking their fingers and pointing at the doors of their offices.' The Dutch manager had a hard time explaining to them that this attitude was considered rude in the Netherlands. Moreover, employee evaluations were an annual event. Korean management keeps a list of all the comments and criticisms they have and then present them all at once during the yearly evaluation. Dutch employees, who hadn't received any criticism or comments throughout the year, felt completely overwhelmed. During the initial phases of most Korean companies in the Netherlands, in particular, they experienced high turnover rates of local managers and employees as a result of these differences in behaviour and perception. 'The only way to avoid frustration and to be able to work together,' argued a Dutch manager, 'is to be aware of each other's customs and practices.'

Another problematic point proved to be working hours. Dutch employees generally work from 9 am until 5 pm. In Korea, employees will work until the job is done, regardless of the time. Initially, this difference led to serious misunderstandings. Particularly when companies were in the start-up phase, Korean expatriate managers worked long hours and expected the same from their Dutch personnel; 12-hour days and working until around 10 pm was considered normal and was, in fact, expected by Korean management. Dutch employees, in contrast, saw this as extreme overtime. Dutch staff had to constantly explain what were considered 'normal' working hours in the Netherlands, as well as Dutch expectations about work in order for Korean management to understand employee behaviour. In such cases, a question much asked by Korean management was 'But why can't they do this for the company?'

In the Netherlands, there is also a clear distinction between functions; jobs are clearly described in terms of functions, and employees are reluctant to perform any job outside those descriptions. In Korea, people are assigned to a department and can be employed in any job in that department, from cleaning to book-keeping. Hence, Korean management, wanting to reorganize jobs between employees or assign extra tasks outside the regular functional duties of an employee, experienced difficulties.

Furthermore, in Korea 'the boss is the boss'. He can do anything he pleases. He can order people to do certain tasks at any time of day and they will usually work until they are finished. He can hire and fire whenever he feels it essential. Initially, Korean expatriate managers expected the same to hold for managing a workforce in the Netherlands and were quite surprised about the laws and regulations that prevented them from acting in this way. The importance attached to the hierarchical ranking is demonstrated in yet another way: when top management from Korea visits the Dutch subsidiaries, the Korean managers of the subsidiaries seem quite submissive to their superiors from Korea; they would only speak and comment when specifically asked to.

Moreover, Korean management does not accept criticism; it is considered an attack on their honour, or face. Criticism was something Korean managers had to get used to in the Netherlands, as Dutch employees tend to be more critical and direct than Korean staff. Nevertheless, even when they made a mistake and were criticized for it, Korean management would not apologize. Apologizing to subordinates is akin to admitting that you are wrong, and leads to loss of face for Koreans. A Dutch manager once came in to work to find a present on his desk, telling him implicitly that the Korean manager had made a mistake. Honour and face are important in Korean management.

Moreover, Koreans take a long time to build trust. 'It takes years before they trust their Dutch managers and delegate some [more] important tasks to them,' one Dutch manager commented. It also takes time and trust before Korean management will listen to the ideas of Dutch managers and adopt them in the organization. What often happens is that when, initially, Korean management doesn't trust the Dutch managers, they carry out the tasks that are considered important themselves. Here are some examples.

One of the Korean companies under investigation mainly assembles computers, according to the customer's specifications. A Dutch manager is in charge of acquiring the parts to assemble these computers. In the beginning, however, Korean managers who had more information on new projects ordered the parts without informing the Dutch manager. Parts would be delivered, and the Dutch manager had no idea where they came from or who ordered them.

A Korean operations manager has a good overview of the production lines from his office. In the beginning, every time he saw something that he believed should be organized differently, he came down from his office and started to interfere with the procedure on the production line. He would tell the workers what to do, and when and how to make changes. The Dutch manager responsible for the production lines and production line workers was not consulted. The Korean manager didn't feel it was inappropriate to interfere with production directly, without telling or consulting the production manager. The Dutch production manager would sometimes come back to the factory floor and find his line completely reorganized. Indeed, at one point, the Dutch manager commented 'Well, I think I'll leave now, since my job can be done without me anyway.'

Korean managers tend to distribute tasks as problems occur. They focus on one goal that is important at the time and disregard all the other tasks in progress. However, when the task they have asked to be performed first is almost finished, they start enquiring as to why the other projects are falling behind. It is argued that Korean managers have a rather short-term focus and are essentially occupied with ad hoc project management.

Dutch employees also experience communication as a considerable barrier to smooth relationships between the Koreans and the Dutch. Korean managers often have a limited working knowledge of English. However, language is not the only obstacle. In addition, the way in which Korean management communicates is different from the Dutch way. While the Dutch are direct and open to all staff, Korean managers tend to consult each other and make decisions without informing the Dutch employees. A Dutch manager recalls a case when potential customers and business partners were informed of certain decisions while he wasn't. This was a most embarrassing experience for him. Korean management, on the other hand, said the Dutch were extremely direct in their communication and did not accept orders. The Dutch complained that Korean management would order something rather than request it.

Moreover, when Korean managers have complaints about performance or when problems occur, Korean management will never confront their Dutch managers in a direct way. The Korean manager assigned to confront the local manager will first walk around a bit, then ask how things are going and talk about various other subjects, while trying to approach the problem. A Dutch manager comments, 'By now, I recognize the "walk" and behaviour of Korean management when they are assigned to talk to you about a problem, and I ask what their problem is and how I can help.'

In the Netherlands, a company with over 50 employees is obliged by law to install a works council (*ondernemingsraad*), in which employees are informed of, evaluate and comment on certain company decisions. Initially, Korean management experienced the concept as a threat to the company and, in some companies, tried to stop employees from introducing this organization. Korean management said they could not understand why their company needed a works council since everything was fine. Korean management failed to understand, even after several attempts from Dutch management to explain, that a works council is meant to involve employees in decision-making and will not, as in Korea, result in violent strikes. Korean management next hired a consulting firm to inform them of the laws and regulations with respect to works councils and to ascertain the necessity for them, as they didn't trust their employees. Finally, when a Dutch manager, who had a trusting relationship with his Korean superior, accepted the role of president of the company's works council, his Korean manager felt betrayed, and asked him time and again how he could do this to the company.

In general, it was admitted by both Korean and local managers that the first 5 years of operation were difficult, and characterized by underperformance due to the difficulties stemming from differences in practices and customs, lack of trust, and so on. It was argued by both sides that improvement of the situation depends very much on willingness on the part of foreign management to delegate functions to local employees, and to adapt to local customs and practices.

Questions

1 Sketch briefly the main problems experienced by Korean managers in their Dutch subsidiaries. Identify, on the basis of these problems, some Korean societal features.
2 Explain in which EU countries Korean companies would experience similar problems.
3 Can we transfer ideas on the Korean-Dutch differences to other potential problems of Japanese or Chinese management in European subsidiaries?
4 Explain in which countries of the EU they would avoid more problems than in others.
5 Evaluate whether Korean companies would fit into the Japanese societal environment. If they would, how can you explain that virtually no Korean group has important subsidiaries in Japan?
6 Assess which of the Korean human resource practices could be applied in the US context.

Notes

1 This section largely draws on Maurice et al. (1980) and further ideas in Lane (1989: Chapter 2).
2 A narrow span exists when this number is small, and a wide span denotes the opposite.
3 *The Economist* (12 July 2001).
4 We are indebted to Begin (1997: Chapter 6) for the information in this section.
5 This case study is based on original research in eight Korean subsidiaries in the Netherlands, and on interviews in Korea carried out in the first half of 2003, by Bas A. Daamen. Interviews were obtained from both Korean and Dutch management. I am grateful to Bas for letting me use the original material from his interviews. For reasons of confidentiality, names of companies and persons are not mentioned.

References

Adler, N.J. (1984) Understanding the ways of understanding: cross-cultural management methodology reviewed. In Farmer, R.N. (ed.) *Advances in International Comparative Management, vol. 1*. Greenwich, CT: JAI Press, 31–67.

Aguilera, R.V. and Jackson, G. (2003) The cross-national diversity of corporate governance: dimensions and determinants, *Academy of Management Review* 28, 447–465.

Anderton, B. and Mayhew, K. (1994) A comparative analysis of the UK labour market. In Barrell, R. (ed.) *The UK Labour Market: Comparative Aspects and Institutional Developments*. Cambridge: Cambridge University Press, 15–50.

Aoki, M. (1989) The nature of the Japanese firms as a nexus of employment and financial contracts: an overview. *Journal of the Japanese and International Economies* 3, 333–366.

Aoki, M. (1990) Towards an economic model of the Japanese firm. *Journal of Economic Literature* 28, 1–27.

Aycan, Z. (2005) The interplay between cultural and institutional/ structural contingencies in human resource management practices. *International Journal of Human Resource Management* 16, 1083–1119.

Begin, J.P. (1997) *Dynamic Human Resource Systems: Cross-National Comparisons*. Berlin: Walter de Gruyter.

Berggren, C. (1992) *Alternatives to Lean Production*. Ithaca: ILR Press.

Boxall, P. and Purcell, J. (2000) Strategic human resource management: where have we come from and where should we be going? *International Journal of Management Reviews* 2, 183–203.

Boxall, P. and Purcell, J. (2003) *Strategy and Human Resource Management*. New York: Palgrave.

Brewster, C. (2007) Comparative HRM: European views and perspectives. *International Journal of Human Resource Management* 18, 769–787.

Brewster, C. and Bournois, F. (1991) A European perspective on human resource management. *Personnel Review* 20, 4–13.

Brumana, M. and Delmestri, G. (2012) Divergent glocalization in a multinational enterprise: institutional-bound strategic change in European and US subsidiaries facing the late-2000 recession. *Journal of Strategy and Management* 5, 124–153.

Bryson, A., Freeman, R.B., Lucifora, C., Pelizzari, M. and Perotin, V. (2013) Paying for performance: incentive pay schemes and employees' financial participation. In Boeri, T., Lucifora, C. and Murphy, K.J. (eds) *Executive Remuneration and Employee Performance-Related Pay: A Transatlantic Perspective.* Oxford: Oxford University Press, 123–279.

Büchtemann, C. (ed.) (1993) *Employment Security and Labor Market Behavior.* Ithaca, NY: ILR Press, Cornell University.

Budhwar, P.S. and Debrah, Y. (2001) Rethinking comparative and cross-national human resource management research. *International Journal of Human Resource Management* 12, 497–515.

Casper, S. (2000) Institutional adaptiveness, technology policy, and the diffusion of new business models: the case of German biotechnology. *Organization Studies* 21(5), 887–914.

Dany, F. and Torchy, V. (1994) Recruitment and selection in Europe: policies, practices and methods. In Brewster, C. and Hegewisch, A. (eds) *Policy and Practice in European Human Resource Management.* London: Routledge, 68–88.

Dirks, D., Hemmert, M., Legewie, J., Meyer-Ohle, H. and Waldenberger, F. (2000) The Japanese employment system in transition. *International Business Review* 9, 525–553.

Dore, R. (1989) Where we are now? Musings of an evolutionist. *Work, Employment and Society* 3, 425–446.

Dowling, P.J., Welch, D.E. and Schuler, R.S. (1999) *International Human Resource Management: Managing People in a Multinational Context.* Cincinnati, OH: SouthWest.

Eger, T. (2004) Opportunistic termination of employment contracts and legal protection against dismissal in Germany and the USA. *International Review of Law and Economics* 23, 381–403.

Ernst, D. (2006) Searching for a new role in East Asian Regionalization: Japanese production networks in the electronics industry. In Katzenstein, P.J. and Shiraishi, T. (eds) *Beyond Japan: The Dynamics of East Asian Regionalism.* New York: Cornell University Press, 161–187.

Faxen, K. and Lundgren, H. (1988) Sweden. In Roomkin, M. (ed.) *Managers as Employees: An International Comparison of the Changing Character of Managerial Employment.* New York: Oxford University Press, 150–172.

Ferner, A. (1997). Country-of-origin effects and HRM in multinational companies. *Human Resource Management Journal* 7, 19–37.

Ferner, A., Almond, P., Clark, I., Colling, T., Edwards, T., Holden, L., and Muller-Camen, M. (2004) Dynamics of central control and subsidiary autonomy in the management of human resources: case study evidence from US MNCs in the UK. *Organization Studies* 25, 363–391.

Filella, J. and Hegewisch, A. (1994) European experiments with pay and benefits policies. In Brewster, C. and Hegewisch, A. (eds) *Policy and Practice in European Human Resource Management.* London: Routledge, 89–106.

Finegold, D. and Keltner, B. (2001) Institutional effects on skill creation and management development in the US and Germany. In Wever, K.S. (ed.) *Labor, Business and Change in Germany and the US.* Michigan: Upjohn Institute for Employment Research, 55–92.

Fruin, W.M. (1997) *Knowledge Works: Managing Intellectual Capital at Toshiba.* Oxford: Oxford University Press.

Gooderham, P.G., Nordhaug, O. and Ringdal. K. (1999) Institutional and rational determinants of organizational practices: human resource management in European firms. *Administrative Science Quarterly* 44, 507–531.

Goodijk, R. and Sorge, A. (2005) *Maatwerk in Overleg. Kiezen Voor Passende Overlegvormen: Ervaringen in Grote Nederlandse Bedrijven.* Assen: Van Gorcum.

Gospel, H.F. (1992) *Markets, Firms, and the Management of Labor.* Cambridge: Cambridge University Press.

Grahl, J. and Teague, P. (2004) The German model in danger. *Industrial Relations Journal* 35, 557–573.

Guest, D. (2004) Flexible employment, contracts, the psychological contract and employee outcomes: an analysis and review of the evidence. *International Journal of Management Reviews* 5/6, 1–19.

Hage, J. (2000) Path dependencies of education systems and the division of labour within organizations: formalizing the societal effects perspective. In Maurice, M. and Sorge, A. (eds) *Embedding Organizations: Societal Analysis of Actors, Organizations and Socio-economic Context*, Vol. 4, Amsterdam: John Benjamins.

Hall, P.A. (2007) The evolution of varieties of capitalism in Europe. In Hancke, B., Rhodes, M. and Thatcher, M. (eds) *Beyond Varieties of Capitalism: Conflict, Contradictions and Complementarities in the European Economy*. Oxford: Oxford University Press, 39–88.

Hall P.A. and Thelen, K. (2009) Institutional change in varieties of capitalism. *Socio-Economic Review* 7, 7–34.

Hancké, B., Rhodes, M. and Thatcher, M. (2007) Introduction: beyond varieties of capitalism. In Hancké, B., Rhodes, M., and Thatcher, M. (eds) *Beyond Varieties of Capitalism. Conflict, Contradictions and Complementarities in the European Economy*. Oxford: Oxford University Press, 3–38.

Hassel, A. (2007) What does business want? Labour market reforms in CMEs and its problems. In Hancké, B., Rhodes, M. and Thatcher, M. (eds) *Beyond Varieties of Capitalism. Conflict, Contradictions and Complementarities in the European Economy*. Oxford: Oxford University Press, 253–277.

Hayden, A. and Edwards, T. (2001) The erosion of the country of origin effect: a case study of a Swedish multinational company. *Relations Industrielles/Industrial Relations* 56, 116–140.

Heijltjes, M. (1995) *Organizational Fit or Failure: Competitive Environments, Generic and Specic Strategies in Great Britain and the Netherlands*. Maastricht: Universitaire Pers Maastricht.

Heijltjes, M., van Witteloostuijn, A. and van Diepen, S. (1996) The Dutch business system and human resource management. In Clark, T. (ed.) *European Human Resource Management*. London: Blackwell, 156–184.

Hofstede, G. (1980) *Culture's Consequences*. London: Sage.

Hotho, J., Saka-Helmhout, A. and F. Becker-Ritterspach (2014) Bringing context and structure back into situated learning. *Management Learning* 45, 57–80.

Huo, P.Y., Huang, H.J. and Napier, N.K. (2002) Divergence or convergence: a cross-national comparison of personnel selection practices. *Human Resource Management* 41(1), 31–44.

Iterson, A. and Olie, R. (1992) European business systems: the Dutch case. In Whitley, R. (ed.) *European Business Systems*. Newbury Park: Sage, 98–115.

Jacoby, S.M. (1995) Recent organizational developments in Japan. *British Journal of Industrial Relations* 23(4), 645–650.

Kahn-Freund, O. (1979) *Labour Relations: Heritage and Adjustment*. New York: Oxford University Press.

Kato, H.K., Lemmon, M., Luo, M. and Schallheim, J. (2005) An empirical examination of the costs and benefits of executive stock options: Evidence from Japan. *Journal of Financial Economics* 78, 435–461.

Kessler, I. (1994) Performance pay. In Sisson, K. (ed.) *Personnel Management*. Oxford: Basil Blackwell, 465–494.

Kjellberg, A. (1992) Sweden: can the model survive? In Ferner, A. and Hyman, R. (eds) *Industrial Relations in the New Europe*. Oxford: Basil Blackwell, 88–142.

Kono, T. and Clegg, S. (2001) *Trends in Japanese Management*. Houndsmills, Basingstoke: Palgrave.

Lane, C. (1989) *Management and Labor in Europe*. Aldershot: Gower.

Lane, C. (1992) European business systems: Britain and Germany compared. In Whitley, R. (ed.) *European Business Systems, Firms and Markets in their National Contexts*. Newbury Park: Sage, 64–97.

Laurent, A. (1983) The cultural diversity of western conceptions of management. *International Studies of Management and Organization* 1/2, 75–96.

Laurent, A. (1986) The cross-cultural puzzle of international human resource management. *Human Resource Management* 25, 91–102.

Lawrence, P. (1991) *Management in the Netherlands*. Oxford: Oxford University Press.

Lawrence, P. (1996) *Management in the USA*. London: Sage.

Lawrence, P. and Spybey, T. (1986) *Management and Society in Sweden*. London: Routledge.

Lehrer, M. and Darbishire, O. (1999) Comparative managerial learning in Germany and Britain, in Quack, S., Morgan, G. and Whitley, R. (eds) *National Capitalisms, Global Competition, and Economic Performance*. Amsterdam: John Benjamins.

Liker, J.K., Fruin, W.M. and Adler, P.S. (1999) *Remade in America: Transplanting and Transforming Japanese Management Systems*. New York: Oxford University Press.

Lincoln, J.R. (1993) *Work Organization in Japan and the United States.* Oxford: Oxford University Press, 54–74.

Lincoln, J.R. and Kalleberg, A.L. (1990) *Culture, Control and Commitment: A Study of Work Organisation and Work Attitudes in the United States and Japan.* Cambridge, New York: Cambridge University Press.

Lorenz, E. (1992) Trust and the flexible firm: international comparisons. *Industrial Relations* 31(3), 455–472.

Lowe, K.B., Milliman, J., De Cieri, H. and Dowling, P.J. (2002) International compensation practices: a ten-country comparative analysis. *Human Resource Management* 41(1), 45–66.

Martin, A. (1995) The Swedish model: demise or reconfiguration. In Locke, R., Kochan, T. and Piore, M. (eds) *Employment Relations in a Changing World Economy.* Cambridge, MA: MIT Press.

Maurice, M., Sorge, A. and Warner, M. (1980) Societal differences in organizing manufacturing units: a comparison of France, West Germany, and Great Britain. *Organization Studies* 1(1), 59–86.

Mayrhofer, W. and Brewster, C., (2005) European human resource management: researching developments over time. *Management Revue* 16(1), 36–62.

Mee-Kau Nyaw (1995) Human resource management in the People's Republic of China. In Moore, L.F. and Devereaux Jennings, P. (eds) *Human Resource Management on the Pacific Rim.* Berlin: Walter de Gruyter.

Millward, N., Stevens, M., Smart, D. and Hawes, W. (1992) *Workplace Industrial Relations in Transition.* Aldershot: Dartmouth.

Moriguchi, C. and Ono, H. (2006) Japanese lifetime employment: a century's perspective. In M. Blomström and S. LaCroix (eds) *Institutional Change in Japan: Why It Happens, Why It Doesn't.* Abingdon: Routledge, 152–176.

Morishima, M. (1995) Embedding HRM in a social context. *British Journal of Industrial Relations* 33(4), 617–637.

Mroczkowski, T. and Hanaoka, M. (1997) Effective rightsizing strategies: is there a convergence of employment practices? *Academy of Management Executive* 11(2), 57–67.

Müller, M. (1999a) Unitarism, pluralism, and human resource management in Germany. *Management International Review* 3(Special Issue), 125–144.

Müller, M. (1999b) Human resource management under institutional constraints: the case of Germany. *British Academy of Management* 10, 31–44.

Nishida, J.M. and Redding, S.G. (1992) Firm development and diversification strategies as products of economic cultures: the Japanese and Hong Kong textile industries. In Whitley, R. (ed.) *European Business Systems, Firms and Markets in their National Contexts.* Newbury Park: Sage, 241–267.

Nohara, H. (1999) Human resource management in Japanese firms undergoing transition. In Dirks, D., Huchet, J.-F. and Ribault, T. (eds) *Japanese Management in the Low Growth Era.* Berlin: Springer, 243–262.

Ornatowski, G.K. (1998) The end of Japanese-style human resource management? *Sloan Management Review* 39(3), 73–84.

Poutsma, E., Ligthart, P.E.M. and Moerel, H. (2014) Multinational enterprises: Comparing performance-related pay between companies in Eastern and Western Europe. Working Paper, Radboud University.

Pucik, V. (1984) White collar human resource management in large Japanese manufacturing firms. *Human Resource Management* 23, 257–276.

Pudelko, M. (2005) Cross-national learning from best practice and the convergence–divergence debate in HRM. *International Journal of Human Resource Management* 16(11), 2045–2074.

Purcell, J. (1993) The challenges of human resource management for industrial relations research and practice. *International Journal of Human Resource Management* 4, 511–527.

Rogers, L. (1995) Labour markets and employment relations in transition: the case of German unification. *Employee Relations* 17(1), 24.

Rosenzweig, P.M. and Nohria, N. (1994) Influences on human resource management practices in multinational corporations. *Journal of International Business Studies* 25, 229–251.

Sanders, W.M.G. and Tuschke, A. (2007) The adoption of institutionally contested organizational practices: the emergence of stock option pay in Germany. *Academy of Management Journal* 50, 33–55.

Schlie, E.H. and Warner, M. (2000) The 'Americanization' of German management. *Journal of General Management* (Spring), 33–49.

Scholz, C. (1996) Human resource management in Germany, in Clark, T. (ed.) *European Human Resource Management.* Oxford: Blackwell, 118–155.

Sisson, K. (ed.) (1989) *Personnel Management in the UK.* Oxford: Basil Blackwell.

Smith, P.B. (1992) Organizational behaviour and national cultures. *British Journal of Management* 3, 39–51.

Sinha, J.B.P. (1997) 'A cultural perspective on organizational behaviour in India', in P.C. Earley and M. Erez (eds) *New Perspectives on International Industrial/Organizational Psychology.* San Francisco, CA: The New Lexington Press, 53–75.

Sorge, A. (1991) Strategic fit and the societal effect: interpreting cross-national comparisons of technology, organization and human resource. *Organization Studies* 12(2), 161–190.

Sorge, A. (1992) Human resource management in the Netherlands. *Employee Relations* 14(4), 71–84.

Sorge, A. and Warner, M. (1986) *Comparative Factory Organization: An Anglo-German Comparison of Management and Manpower in Manufacturing.* Aldershot: Gower.

Sparrow, P. and Hiltrop, J.M. (1994) *European Human Resource Management in Transition.* Hemel Hempstead: Prentice Hall.

Streeck, W. (1984) *Industrial Relations in West Germany: A Case Study of the Car Industry.* London: Heinemann.

Streeck, W. (1989) Skills and the limits of neo-liberalism: the enterprise of the future as a place of learning. *Work, Employment and Society* 3(1), 83–104.

Streeck, W. (1991) On the institutional conditions of diversified quality production. In Matzner, E. and Streeck, W. (eds) *Beyond Keynesianism.* Aldershot: Elgar, 21–61.

Streeck W and Thelen K (2005). *Beyond Continuity: Explorations in the Dynamics of Advanced Political Economies.* Oxford: Oxford University Press.

The Economist (2001) The jobs challenge: how to reduce labour costs without doing more harm than good remains top of the agenda in America's boardrooms. *The Economist* 12 July 2001, downloaded 9 July 2014.

The Economist (2013) Unions are in trouble, but some are learning new tricks from the bosses. *The Economist*, 6 April 2013, downloaded 8 July 2014.

Thelen, K. (1991) *Union of Parts: Labor Politics in Postwar Germany.* London: Cornell University Press.

Thelen, K. and Kume, I. (1999) The effects of globalization on labor revisited: lessons from Germany and Japan. *Politics and Society* 27(4), 477–505.

Thory, K. (2008) The internationalization of HRM through reverse transfer: two case studies of French multinationals in Scotland. *Human Resource Management Journal* 18, 54–71.

Tsurumi, Y. (1992) If Americans were Chinese . . . *Pacific Basin Quarterly* 19(Fall), 13–19.

Turner, L., Wever, K.S. and Fichter, M. (2001) Perils of the high and low roads. In Wever, K.S. (ed.) *Labor, Business and Change in Germany and the United States.* Kalamazoo: W.E. Upjohn Institute, 123–156.

Tüselmann, H.-J. (2001) The new German model of employee relations. Flexible collectivism or Anglo-Saxonisation? *International Journal of Manpower* 22, 544–559.

van Dijk, N. and Punch, M. (1993) Open doors, closed circles: management and organization in the Netherlands. In Hickson, D.J. (ed.) *Management in Western Europe.* Berlin: Walter de Gruyter, 167–190.

Visser, J. (1992) The Netherlands: the end of an era and the end of a system. In Ferner, A. and Hyman, R. (eds) *Industrial Relations in the New Europe.* Oxford: Blackwell.

Warner, M. (1997) Management–labour relations in the new Chinese economy. *Human Resource Management* 7(4), 30–43.

Warner, M. and Campbell, A. (1993) German management. In Hickson, D. (ed.) *Management in Western Europe.* Berlin: Walter de Gruyter, 89–108.

Wever, K. (2001) Mutual learning with trade-offs. In Wever, K. (ed.) *Labor, Business, and Change in Germany and the United States.* Kalamazoo: W.E. Upjohn Institute, 1–16.

Whitley, R. (1999) *Divergent Capitalisms: The Social Structuring and Change of Business Systems.* Oxford: Oxford University Press.

Wiersma, U.J. and van den Berg, P.T. (1998) Influences and trends in human resource practices in the Netherlands. *Employee Relations* 21(1), 63–79.

Womack, J., Jones, D. and Roos, D. (1991) *The Machine that Changed the World.* New York: Harper Perennial.

6 Comparative corporate governance

Ilir Haxhi

Learning objectives

By the end of this chapter you will be able to:

- grasp the concept of corporate governance
- contrast the differences between alternative models of corporate governance and more particularly the shareholder versus stakeholder model
- provide a societal explanation for the differences between these corporate governance models
- evaluate the position of the Japanese model of corporate governance vis-à-vis the shareholder and stakeholder models
- understand the European difficulties in developing one unified European model of corporate governance
- understand how corporate governance is practised in the BRIC countries
- assess the differences between corporate governance issues in large, small and medium-sized companies
- recognize the cultural and institutional influences on the worldwide diffusion of codes of corporate governance
- reflect on the effects of globalization and contextual drivers to convergence or divergence of corporate governance systems.

Chapter outline

6.1 Introduction

The question of how the governance of enterprises, including the governance of markets for shares in enterprises, should be arranged is as old as the market economy and capitalism itself. Reforms have been stimulated by scandals, through the ages. More recently, corporate scandals such as Ahold in the Netherlands, Enron in the US, Parmalat in Italy or Maxwell in the UK imposed a critical discussion on the way public corporations are directed and controlled. More dramatic scandals could have been revealed from other countries, if they had had more open discussion and an investigative press.

The literature on corporate governance, which originated in the USA and the UK, was initially concerned with a fairly narrow set of issues such as how shareholders can monitor and motivate management to act in their interests (the agency problem) or how to improve 'shareholder value' through increasing share price (Vitols, 2001). Effective corporate governance was all about: (1) the ability of owners to monitor and, when required, intervene in the operations of management, and (2) the vigour of the market for corporate control, which should vest the monitoring task in those owners most capable of carrying it out.

From the mid-1990s onwards, corporate governance has become a fiercely debated topic in the comparative management and international business literature. While this literature has aimed to grasp the existence of international variations in corporate governance and explain the impact of these differences on the competitive performance of firms, less consensus exists on a single unifying definition of corporate governance. Scholars and practitioners of corporate governance give the term a large variety of definitions. For example, social scientists and economists define corporate governance as 'the institutions that influence how business corporations allocate resources and returns' (O'Sullivan, 2000) or as 'an institutional framework in which the integrity of the transaction is decided' (Williamson, 1996). For corporate managers, capital providers, and policy-makers, corporate governance is considered as a system of rules and institutions that determines the control and direction of the corporation and that defines relations among the corporation's primary participants (Aguilera and Jackson, 2003). These definitions focus not only on the formal rules and institutions of governance, but also on the informal practices that evolve in the absence or weakness of formal rules. They incorporate both the internal structure of the corporation and its external context, including capital market and government policies (Haxhi and Aguilera, 2014).

This literature distinguishes between two dichotomous models of corporate governance for which different terms are used interchangeably in the literature:

1 The shareholder, outsider or market-based model, also called the Anglo-American model, which is characterized by strong shareholder rights, single powerful CEO and protection of minority shareholders, prevails mainly in Australia, Canada, the US and the UK. Here the maximization of 'shareholder value' is the primary goal of the firm and shareholders enjoy strong formalized links with top management.
2 The stakeholder, insider or bank-based model, also called the Rhineland model, which is characterized by weaker shareholder rights, consensus leadership, and concentrated ownership, prevails in most of the European continent, Latin America and Japan. A variety of firm constituencies – including employees, suppliers and customers, and the communities companies are located in – have a say in the firm, and the interests of all of them are balanced in management decision-making (e.g. Aoki, 1999; Gregory and Simmelkjaer, 2002; Shleifer and Vishny, 1997).

The term *market-based* refers to the fact that, within the system, the financial needs of firms are fulfilled through the capital markets, while the *outsider* means that the locus of corporate control and monitoring resides in the disciplines of capital markets. The model presumes that information flows are relatively good and that the regulatory system requires ample disclosure of information, enforces strict trading rules and allows a market in corporate control (via hostile takeover) to flourish. The model is based on liquid stock markets and diversification of portfolios (see Table 6.1) and has a dispersed share ownership (e.g., Coffee, 1999; La Porta et al., 1998).

The contrasting stakeholder, or insider, model is in part a misleading term because interests of the wider community are certainly not insider interests. It relies on the representation of diverse interests on the board of directors, which is expected to play a strong monitoring and disciplining role with regard to management. Management discipline via securities markets is weak in this model. There is concentrated shareholding, with cross-holdings among companies being fairly common. Another feature of the insider or

Table 6.1 Differences between the 'shareholder' and 'stakeholder' models

Shareholder model
• Financial needs of firms fulfilled through the market
• Locus of corporate control and monitoring resides in the disciplines of the market
• Assumption of perfect information flows
• Effective regulatory system
• Model is based on liquid stock markets and diversification of portfolios
Stakeholder model
• Financial needs of firms are fulfilled through bank finance
• Monitoring and control function resides in the dual-board system
• Concentrated shareholding and thus illiquid markets
• Regulators often allow for asymmetric information flows
• Rights of minority shareholders are not always protected effectively

stakeholder model is that securities regulators often permit asymmetric information and are not overly concerned about the rights of minority shareholders. The term bank-based refers to the fact that firms generally turn to banks rather than capital markets for finance (see Table 6.1). In the stakeholder model, the large publicly traded corporations are run by control groups or blockholders with substantial equity interests in the firm (e.g., Del Brio et al., 2006).

In addition, the comparative management literature often treats corporate governance as a facet of the broader debate about the evolution of the different models of capitalism. In this context, scholars claim that one or the other corporate governance model is economically superior and that, over time, we should observe convergence towards this model of 'best practice'. A considerable controversy has emerged among corporate governance scholars regarding an inevitable global convergence towards the shareholder value maximization model as the normative ideal type (Aguilera and Jackson, 2010). A key debate exists on three fronts. First, several scholars argue that cross-national patterns of governance are converging towards the Anglo-American, shareholder-centred model (e.g. Coffee, 1999; Hansmann and Kraakman, 2001). A second set of scholars suggest the 'hybridization' perspective, where economic institutions are capable of change and transnational practices are adapted to fit local institutional contexts (Djelic, 1998). As a result, such adaptation leads to increasing hybridization rather than to a global convergence to one ideal model. Finally, a third body of researchers, has advanced compelling arguments against convergence by demonstrating that powerful path dependencies can arise out of adaptive sunk costs, network externalities, or endowment effects (Bebchuk and Roe, 1999).

For a number of reasons, comparative corporate governance debates often take place within the contours of the cultural–institutional or societal approach used in this book. First, corporate governance issues can fruitfully be examined within the framework of this approach as it helps to explain the differences among countries, as governance structures and systems are a product of societal and institutional contexts. Divergent paths resulted in multiple governance forms and practices. The 'institutional clusters' concept of coordinated market economies (CMEs) and liberal market economies (LMEs), which are discussed in Chapter 4, provide a framework for this.

Moreover, the corporate governance regime itself is perceived as an institution, which helps to explain the comparative institutional advantage of firms. Indeed, some firms appear to view differences in corporate governance as an untapped source of competitive advantage. As part of their efforts of value creation, they adopt structures and mechanisms from different governance systems. For example, Ford Motor Company has adopted extensive cross-ownership relationships through equity holdings, acquisitions, alliances and research consortia, practices common in the Japanese keiretsu. German firms such as Daimler-Benz, Deutsche Telecom and Hoechst have altered their financial disclosure practices to gain access to American financial markets (Rubach and Sebora, 1998).

Since institutionalists and the societal approach stress the embeddedness of national institutions and 'complementarities' between institutions, alternative responses to internationalizing capital markets, other than convergence, appear possible (Haxhi et al., 2013). Companies may respond very differently to similar sorts of pressure, and distinct sets of 'best practice' contingent on the national context may emerge. This argument is discussed in Chapter 7.

The current chapter applies this approach by examining the interaction between corporate governance aspects in large, small and medium-sized firms and national institutions in different countries, in the context of internationalizing capital markets. The focus here is on the impact of formal institutions on the corporate governance aspect, without playing down the impact of informal institutions. Since governance institutions are embedded in the societal framework, cultural effects are reflected in the choice of formal institutions. For instance, the lower a country value on the uncertainty avoidance dimension of Hofstede (2001), the more it will be market-orientated. Capital market investments entail risks, which risk-averse nations would arguably want to avoid as much as possible.

The next section relates the discussion Anglo-American to the institutional approach through an analysis of the major corporate governance features influencing postwar company decision-making in advanced economies. At the same time, these features together make up the broad definition of corporate governance used here:

- the structure of ownership of companies
- the relationship between management and the various stakeholders in a company
- the structure of management or top management institutions (i.e. unitary or two-tier boards), and
- the method of bringing about corporate restructuring.

The in-depth explanation of the two main models is followed by an analysis of the Japanese model of corporate governance, which is argued to be similar to the Rhineland model. The subsequent section explores the continental European models, which are variants of the two main models. The analysis shows that variations among the advanced and transition economies in these corporate governance features stem from differences in key societal institutions, such as governmental regulation, the character of the financial system, corporate law, and cultural values. Next, we offer an overview of the models of corporate governance in BRIC countries and more specifically, we discuss in the form of case studies, Russian and Chinese models of corporate governance.

The fourth section deals with the worldwide diffusion of codes of corporate governance, which are instruments of self-regulation, defining best practices with respect to boards, management, supervision, disclosure and auditing (Aguilera and Cuervo-Cazurra, 2004). We discuss the main drivers of diffusion of codes and their characteristics across countries. Codes show similarities related to their objectives, which improve the quality of companies' governance and increase the accountability of companies to shareholders while maximizing shareholder or stakeholder values (Aguilera and Cuervo-Cazurra, 2004; Haxhi, 2010). Further on, the discussion on the worldwide diffusion of codes is complemented with a broad view on a possible convergence or divergence of corporate governance best practices (Haxhi and Aguilera, 2012).

Finally, the closing case, dealing with the Ahold scandal, should be seen in the light of the link between corporate governance and corporate social responsibility (CSR). The movement for more responsive corporate governance seeks to ensure that managers act in the best interests of their shareholders. While there are many questions with respect to whether and how companies should be responsible in society, the focal point here is whether there is a new meaning for CSR that is consistent both with the greater need for corporate responsiveness to employees and communities, and with the greater demands from investors for performance. The chapter concludes with the major strengths and weaknesses of the two main corporate governance models. At the same time, a summary is provided of the discussion on the direction of change in the two main models.

6.2 Major capitalist models of corporate governance

While there is a range of different modes of corporate governance systems in advanced economies, as indicated, two offer clear and distinctly different characteristics: the shareholder, or outsider, model (also referred to as the 'Anglo-American') and the stakeholder, or insider, model (referred to as the Rhineland model). The first is dominant in the Anglo-American cluster, including the US, the UK, Ireland, Australia and Canada. Rhineland capitalism is attributed to Germany, Japan and continental European countries.

However, the distinction between the two systems does not express the variations that exist between the systems classified as 'insider'. Each of the continental European systems has some elements of the outsider system. For example, the Netherlands, Sweden and Switzerland, three countries considered to have insider systems, have a relatively large number of domestic listed companies and a high stock market capitalization (see below). Classifying Germany and Japan as examples of the insider system is also rather problematic. Both might have some similar mechanisms of corporate control, but their dissimilarities are even greater. The corporate governance systems of continental Europe and Japan could perhaps best be positioned somewhere on a continuum between the Anglo-American model with its strong emphasis on shareholder value, and the Rhineland model with its attention to broader societal needs.

This section illustrates how difficult it is to generalize about corporate governance systems. Recent changes in corporate governance aspects are highlighted throughout the section, which concludes with a case on BRIC countries, to illustrate the problems that countries in transition experience in setting up a reliable corporate governance system.

The Anglo-American model

Capital markets and regulation

Aguilera and Jackson (2003) stylize the Anglo-American model in terms of financing through equity, dispersed ownership, active markets for corporate control and flexible labour markets, and the stakeholder or continental model in terms of long-term debt finance, ownership by large block-holders, weak markets for corporate control and rigid labour markets. Anglo-American corporate governance places the emphasis on equity finance for business. This means that companies issue shares or bonds rather than relying on bank loans for fulfilling their financial needs. Capital markets tend to be large and regulated in a manner favourable to trading in equities. Large, diversified and efficiently functioning stock markets are argued to develop when supported by complementary institutions, such as the legal protection of small shareholders and maximum limits on the shareholdings of financial institutions (Roe, 1994). These are typically institutions that are characteristic of the Anglo-American model.

As in most countries, and akin to the Rhineland model of finance, small firms in the US and the UK rely on bank lending to make investments. The large firm model in Germany and Japan, on the other hand, is said to be converging towards the Anglo-American model. As will become clear later on in this section, the main differences between the two models are found in the medium-sized firm segment.

The structure of ownership

In the Anglo-American model, companies do not generally hold each other's stocks. In other words, unlike in Germany and Japan, one does not find extensive cross-shareholding.

Table 6.2 Structure of ownership in some countries like UK/US/Germany/NL or France (2007) in %

	US	*EU*	*UK*	*Germany*	*France*	*Netherlands*	*Italy*
Individual investors/ Households		14	12.8	13	7	4	27
Foreign Investors		37	40	21	41	70	14
Public Sector		5	0.1	2	10		10
Private Financial enterprises: Banks & other		5	44.4*	24*	29*	9*	23*
Private Financial enterprises: Collective investment		22					
Private non-financial companies		17	2.7	40	13		26
Not Identified						17	
Year of collection		*2007*	*2006*	*2007*	*2007*	*2007*	*2006*

* = combined value of Private Financial enterprises (PFE): Banks & other and PFE: Collective investment

Source: FESE (2007) http://www.fese.eu/_lib/files/Share_Ownership_Survey_2007_Final.pdf

Also, unlike the case in Germany and Japan, financial institutions rarely hold stock issued by their customer companies for longer periods, except in certain cases such as venture capital firms. For the US, the latter can be explained by the fact that US banks were prevented by legislation from holding large stakes in industrial companies. Ownership of shares is largely in the hands of private funds (e.g. 44.4 per cent in the UK), whose focus is on relatively short-term return on capital, rather than longer-term market share issues. The major investors in the UK and the US – investment funds, pensions funds and (to a certain extent) insurance companies – take a 'portfolio' approach to risk management by taking small stakes in a large number of companies. The types of investor more likely to take large strategic shareholdings – enterprises, the public sector and banks – account for a minority of the shareholdings. In sum, the Anglo-American system is characterized by dispersed ownership by share price orientated financial institutions (Vitols, 2001).

The relationship between stakeholders and management

Anglo-American corporate governance is characterized by arm's-length relationships between all the stakeholders and management. Neither investors nor employees, nor the local communities within which firms invest, have any close links with companies. As banks provide a relatively small share of business finance, the links between banks and companies are not strong either. Consequently, the US and other Anglo-American countries depend heavily on active markets for corporate control.

Institutional investors in the US and the UK continue to view the corporate governance problem as one of assuring that the corporation is managed in the best interests of shareholders. For Americans, corporate governance is about shareholders controlling managers for purposes of shareholder value (managerial fiduciary duty); for many Europeans, it is more about society controlling corporations for the purpose of social and economic long term sustainability (Haxhi and Aguilera, 2014). In addition, company law, stock market regulations and rules all originated in defence of shareholder interests. The conventional proposition of the Anglo-American model is that a company has only one responsibility, both morally and legally: to maximize the value of the shares of those who have invested in it (Friedman, 1962). Corporate board members and executives are 'fiduciaries' under the law – agents solely of the shareholders. But in fulfilling their responsibility to the investors, according to this view, boards and executives also indirectly fulfil their responsibility to the rest of society – to other 'stakeholders' such as their employees, members of their community and fellow citizens – because they help to ensure that society's productive assets are allocated to the most efficient uses.

Optimistic advocates of corporate social responsibility argue that what is good for a company's shareholders over the long term is also good for its other stakeholders over the long term. That is, if one looks far enough into the future, all interests converge: all stakeholders have an interest in a strong economy, well-paid employees, a healthy and clean environment and a peaceful society. However, fuzzy long terms are no match for hard-nosed short terms. Capital markets are notoriously impatient, and are becoming less patient all the time. Most of today's institutional investors have no particular interests in a 'long term' that extends much beyond the next quarter, if that long (Reich, 1998).

While the relationship between investor and company can be seen as a 'cultural' feature of the system of corporate governance, it originates from and is supported by regulatory policies that are shaped by interest groups (Woolcock, 1996). For example, the combined effect of bankruptcy laws and insider trading legislation contributes to explaining the absence of relationship banking[1] (see the following pages for an explanation) and of closer relations between shareholders and the management of companies in the Anglo-American model (OECD, 1998).

Company law and the structure of top management institutions

Company law is based on a unitary board system, which is seen as most efficient because it avoids fragmentation of responsibility. Board composition, in both the US and the UK, tends to reflect a preference for outside directors or non-executive directors (NEDs). In the UK and to a lesser extent in the US, boardroom scenery was dominated by executive directors; however, the role of NEDs became paramount following the issuance of several codes of corporate governance such as the UK Combined Code (2003, see www.ecgi.org) and the Sarbanes-Oxley (SOX) Act in 2002 in the US. For example, the UK Higgs Review in 2003 strengthened the independence requirement, through measures such as the unequivocal separation of roles of the chief executive and the chairman, and a board composed by at least 50 per cent NEDs, excluding the chairman. In addition, the SOX Act covers a vast amount of behavioural issues that tie in with managerial and director conduct. Amongst other elements, it encompasses elements like the erecting of the Public Company Accounting Oversight Board, Auditor Independence, Corporate Responsibility, Enhanced Financial Disclosures, Analyst Conflicts of Interest, and Corporate Fraud Accountability, which addresses the penalization of knowingly obstructing judicial actions against oneself or one's firm. It is effective for all US firms that are publicly traded, and concerns foreign corporations listed at US indices as well.

Consequently, NEDs who are currently in the majority are seen as a countervailing power against the dominant influence on the board, whether of the management or of the shareholders. Hence, in states where the shareholders have a limited impact on decision-making, NEDs will be seen as a check on the overwhelming influence of the management.

This is the case in the US and the UK, where due to the wide distribution of share ownership, management was able to exercise a dominant influence. The appointment of NEDs is a favourite instrument for the institutional investor to use to bend the company's policies without assuming responsibility for the actual management decision.

The existence of the joint chief executive officer (CEO)–chairman of the board blurs the separation between management and oversight functions in many companies. While there are no legal rules related to this issue, in the UK separation is highly recommended and often practised by large companies. In the US, in contrast, CEOs still often chair the board. And although CEOs can neither hire nor fire directors, they often choose the nominating committee for the directors, or even indirectly nominate the directors themselves (Lightfood, 1992). The US unitary board system could, in fact, be seen as an expression of the CEO-dominated system. The typical leadership role is for the CEO who, after a period of consultation with other managers, makes major decisions unilaterally and takes sole responsibility for these decisions.

Consensus and the institution of employee representation

Another clear distinction between the Anglo-American and continental European corporate governance is on the issue of statutory employee representation. In contrast to most of continental Europe – especially Germany, which has laws requiring parity co-decision-making in supervisory boards and works councils – in the Anglo-American model there are no legal provisions for employee representatives on company boards. However, the UK's membership of the European Union has not stopped its government and business from continuing to oppose statutory requirements on employee participation. Underlying the opposition to any form of employee participation in the UK is a legacy of confrontational attitudes to industrial relations, especially during the 1970s, compared to the more consensual approach in Germany (see Chapters 5 and 7 for an extended explanation of this topic).

More fundamentally, however, there is a deep-seated difference between the free market philosophy of the Anglo-American model and different forms of 'social market economy' in continental Europe. The predominant view in UK industry and government circles is that increased social provision and efforts to seek consensus are costs that undermine competitiveness and thus general economic prosperity. For many continental Europeans social provision and consensus are seen as prerequisites of stable (long-term) economic growth. The conviction that cooperative forms of industrial relationship are not possible in the UK continues to shape employers' approaches (Woolcock, 1996).

Corporate restructuring

As indicated, the takeover mechanism is at the heart of the Anglo-American open-market model for corporate governance. Any party can bid for the control rights of a listed company by accumulating a large enough ownership stake. Takeovers are commonly viewed as playing two related roles.

1 First, the threat of takeover may contribute to efficient management by making managers concentrate on maximizing shareholder value, rather than on pursuing their own personal objectives (an example of potential principal–agent problems).
2 Second, in the event of managerial failure, takeovers allow poor management to be replaced with good management.

In general, takeovers are not the normal form of corporate control. The US and the UK are the exception rather than the rule in this regard. The UK accounts for the bulk of mergers and acquisitions within the European Union (EU). The use of takeovers in corporate restructuring follows, among other things, from the size and regulation of the capital markets, defensive and strategic considerations, tax motives, empire building and the pursuit of monopoly power (Shleifer and Vishny, 1997).

The legitimacy of the takeover option has militated against enterprise growth from small to medium size (Lane, 1994) and has thus contributed to the creation of a polarized industrial structure in both the UK and the US. Small family-owned companies choose to remain small because if they grow they will be forced to go to the stock market to obtain funding and will not only lose control of the company but will also face the threat of take-overs. Hence, in comparison with Germany, in the Anglo-American world there is a low incidence of medium-sized companies.

The Rhineland model

Capital markets and regulation

In general, the Rhineland form of corporate governance relies more on debt finance by banks. All banks are universal – that is, by law, they can engage in the full range of commercial and investment banking services. Moreover, banks can often adopt a longer-term focus, partly because they know that German firms may credibly offer sustained commitments to employees and other stakeholders in the firm, and can often closely monitor the status of their investments through their seats on the supervisory board or by means of direct contracts (Casper, 2000). Despite the recent expansion of capital markets, Germany remains a bank-centred financial system.[2] The majority of German firms continue to rely on banks and retained earnings to finance investments.

Small and medium-sized enterprise (SME) owners have been criticized for avoiding listing in order to prevent any dilution of their control and for their unwillingness to reveal profitability. Such SMEs have not made much use of share capital as a means of meeting their growing financing needs, despite reforms aimed at making it easier for them to do so (the 1986 introduction of a 'second market', or *geregelter Markt,* and the 1994 Law on Small Public Companies, or *Gesetz über kleine Aktiengesellschaften*).

Case: Grohe AG[3]

The disadvantages of being listed from the point of view of small and medium-sized family-owned firms

Friedrich Grohe AG & Co. KG, which was founded in 1911, manufactures sanitation products that range from single taps to electronic water management systems. In 1991, the favourable market situation induced the family to make the company public, both to gain access to funds for growth and to enable the family owners to cash in some of their shares on attractive terms. At the launch, Friedrich Grohe AG floated 1.3 million non-voting shares to the public, with the Grohe family holding all of the remaining 1.7 million ordinary shares. Members of the Grohe family also filled all the seats on the supervisory board. But in the late 1990s, with the stock trading at disappointing levels, the Grohe family decided to delist and go private again. The reasons given were as follows:

- to avoid ongoing listing costs
- to prevent a possible hostile takeover by a competitor
- to achieve greater flexibility from operating as a different legal corporate entity, and
- the family's unwillingness to raise equity at the low prices commanded by its stock.

As the company's major shareholder, the Grohe family considered that their firm belonged to an industry that investors considered 'boring and unattractive'. As a result, they felt that the company was in the undesirable position of being unable to attract further capital through share offerings, while they were at the same time constrained by the 'inflexible legal duties' of a listed stock corporation.

But the next chapter in the history is again different. As so often happens when there is no central figure to carry on the entrepreneurship and the family cannot agree or they lose interest in the firm, Grohe was sold to a private equity investor in 1998. Such investors tend to be different from the 'patient capital' ownership more familiar in family capitalism. As family members 'cashed in' on their ownership by selling, the private equity investor who had acquired the firm with 'leveraged' funds, was compelled to earn sufficient return on the investment. And they did this by implementing a cost-cutting operation. This led to some conflict with the union and the works council, and it was argued to jeopardize the position of the firm as a market leader in quality. Grohe did, however, succeed in maintaining such a position, and it set up production facilities in China. The end of the story is that Grohe was in 2013 bought up by Lixil, a Japanese group. Back to 'Rhineland capitalism', which oddly enough includes Japan. But it was not an owner-managed firm any more.

Questions

1 Trace the links between insider interests, patient capital, employment relations and quality manufacturing!
2 Give reasons why it might not be an accident that Grohe finished up in the ownership of a Japanese group.

The SMEs argue that there remain barriers to listing. For example, banks must be involved in the first segment of trading (i.e., issuing shares). As the banks are concerned about their reputation they are thought to be careful about dealing with new entrepreneurs. In contrast to the situation in the US or the UK, therefore, it is difficult for young entrepreneurs to raise equity capital. This is seen as an impediment to the growth of young dynamic companies in fast-moving technology or services sectors (Vitols and Woolcock, 1997). Another consequence is that capital markets tend to be smaller and to have fewer public companies than in the UK and the US. Even during the stock market boom of 1999–2000, it was clear that the activity included only a handful of companies in certain industries (Schaede, 2000). In the meantime, the stock market created for smaller joint-stock enterprises in Germany had collapsed in the wake of the bursting of the 'dotcom' bubble in 2001.

From the late 1990s, a handful of large German companies increasingly turned to the global capital markets for funding. In order to gain access to the liquid US capital markets, German firms had to adopt US accounting standards. The German accounting system adopts a long-term view and is investment- rather than trading-orientated – profit figures and asset values tend to be understated. Furthermore, it allows for building up 'hidden reserves', also due to the traditional German emphasis on exercising 'commercial caution'. Overall, the adoption of US accounting standards by some large German firms means that they are more in line with international practices and that the transparency of their published accounts has improved significantly (Schlie and Warner, 2000).

The transparency of accounts, or increased information disclosure, in turn, is positively related to corporate social responsibility. Providing increased disclosures is arguably responsive to the needs of several stakeholders. Firms that engage in socially responsive activities are said to provide more informative and/or extensive disclosures than do companies that are less focused on advancing social goals (Gelb and Strawser, 2001). In addition, it has been found that socially responsible firms are more likely to provide this increased disclosure through better investor relations. Investor relations, however, have only recently become important in the German model of corporate governance, as it is essentially a bank-based model. Whilst the importance of new international or American accounting standards has remained strong, the fashion to list at the New York stock exchange has, however, subsided.

The structure of ownership

Owner–company relations in the 'large firm' Rhineland model are most often characterized by one or more large shareholders with a strategic motivation for ownership. The types of investor likely to have strategic interests – enterprises, banks and the public sector – hold the majority of shares. Enterprises generally pursue strategic business interests. The state generally pursues a public goal. The large German banks have tended to view their shareholdings as a mechanism for protecting their loans and strengthening their business relationships with companies rather than as a direct source of income (Vitols, 2001). From the end of the 1990s onwards, large banks have reduced the size of most of their equity stakes in non-financial companies in order to reduce risk exposure and the likelihood of having to bail out a client. These changes in the 'large firm' financial model accelerated in the 1990s as a result of financial internationalization and the efforts of the German financial and industrial community to transform Frankfurt into an international financial centre. It could, in fact, be argued that the German financial model is increasingly becoming two distinct (though intertwined) models: a finance and corporate governance model for the small and medium-sized companies (the *Mittelstand*) and a different model for the large firms (Deeg, 1997). The German *Mittelstand* firms are usually family-owned, but are sometimes also tied by shareholdings to larger firms.

The ownership types having smaller shareholdings – investment funds, pension funds/insurance companies and households – account for only 35 per cent of total shareholdings of the large German companies. The Rhineland system is, then, characterized by concentrated ownership by actors pursuing a mix of financial and strategic goals (Vitols, 2001). Hence, despite the tendency for the German 'large firm' financial model to adopt features of the Anglo-American model of finance, at least one critical distinction remains: the majority of the large German firms continue to have stable, long-term shareholding, protecting firms from the short-termism of Anglo-American capitalism.

The relationship between stakeholders and management

The relationship between the company and all the stakeholders – investors, employees and local communities – tends to be closer than is the case with Anglo-American corporate governance. Consistent with CSR views, the German stakeholder model implies that, by law, management must pursue actions that bear regard to a broad class of stakeholders rather than those that serve only to maximize shareholder interests. This casts the corporation as a social entity where firms are not only driven by shareholder value maximization (Aguilera and Jackson, 2003). Moreover, the German model emphasizes long-term relationships built upon trust. Banks in particular have retained relatively close links with companies through their role as shareholders in their own right, through their role as proxies for smaller shareholders[4] through participation in supervisory boards and by fulfilling the role of 'lender of last resort' during crises. The latter implies that when problems arise, the normal practice is for the stakeholders to voice concern and for changes in management to take place, rather than stakeholder 'exit' and a change in ownership. This enables implicit contractual relationships to develop between management and the stakeholders, and means that take-overs or changes in ownership are not the norm for corporate restructuring. The structure of regulation and practice tends to favour such long-term commitment to companies. For many years, Germany had subjected its stock exchanges to a 'gentleman's agreement' that supposedly kept bankers and executives from trading on special information. In short, this model advocates social efficiency of the economy through trust relationships and long-term contractual associations between the firm and stakeholders as well as inter-firm cooperation and employees' participation.

From the end of the 1990s onwards, however, the relationships between some of the large German firms and the stakeholders have weakened. Against the German tradition of social responsibility, several companies have adopted a cruder form of capitalism by rigorously shifting production away from Germany to lower-cost countries, despite rear-guard action by their 'social partners' in the supervisory board. Moreover, in some large firms, corporate performance is increasingly being measured in terms of share price, thus adopting the Anglo-American shareholder value concept. Having opted for an emphasis on 'shareholder value' over 'stakeholder welfare', the subsequent step large firms made was the introduction of performance-related pay schemes for executives, to ensure that managerial incentives are sufficiently aligned with shareholder interests (Schlie and Warner, 2000). One can also observe an increase in the number of firms listed at the stock exchange; a trend explained by the fiercer global competition and the need to reach a certain size in order to effectively compete against other MNEs (Deeg, 1997). German banks have also begun to lose their traditional position in large firms such as the Deutsche Bank which was transformed into an investment bank, generating a higher income through the continuous buying and selling of companies more in line with an Anglo-American model. In addition, changes in taxation have encouraged the selling of protective cross of shares, which corporate owners of cross-holdings promptly did. However, another change happened after the 2007 financial crisis; since then, political parties and employers have been re-discovering the productive 'virtues' of the 'social market economy'.

Company law and the structure of top management institutions

The clearest manifestation of employee rights in large German companies is the dual company board system, with an executive (*Vorstand*) and a supervisory board (*Aufsichtsrat*). The supervisory board is mainly in charge of the selection, appointment or dismissal, and the supervision of the *Vorstand*. Its task is mainly that of supervising the functioning of the company. The supervisory board contains bank representatives and employee representatives. Half of the members of the supervisory board of very large joint-stock companies are chosen by shareholders and the other half are elected by workers. Since the supervisory board appoints the management board members, workers can indirectly influence management. The obligatory supervisory board system applies only to stock corporations (*Aktiengesellschaft*, or AG) and companies with limited liability (*Gesellschaft mit beschränkter Haftung*) and more than 500 employees.[5] While there are no supervisory boards in smaller firms, they often have advisory boards (*Beirat*) which also have representatives of one or more banks.

The management board is clearly separated from the supervisory board. The management board has a chair, generally considered to be 'first among equals'. Major decisions or proposals to the supervisory board are reached through consensus. The individual appointment of top managers by the supervisory board reduces the dependency of individual members on the chair/speaker (Vitols, 2001).

Consensus and the institutions of employee representation

As indicated, employees in large German companies enjoy strong 'voice' thanks to corporatist bargaining and codetermination. Every plant with at least five regular employees is entitled under the Works Constitution Act 1972 (*Betriebsverfassungsgesetz*) to elect a works council. This works council has the right to negotiate key issues with management, including the hiring of new employees, the introduction of new technology, use of overtime and short-working time, and, in the case of mass redundancies, the negotiation of social plans (*Sozialpläne*) covering redeployment, severance payments and early retirement.

As indicated, employee representatives are also included on German supervisory boards under the 1976 Codetermination Act (*Mitbestimmungsgesetz*), which applies to almost all companies with 2000 or more employees. This law makes the following key provisions.

- Employee representatives are to comprise half of the supervisory board representatives, and shareholder representatives the other half. Shareholders, however, elect the chairperson, who holds the casting vote in cases of 'deadlock' between shareholder and employee blocs.
- The number of supervisory board seats total 12 in the case of companies with between 2000 and 10,000 employees, 16 in the case of companies with between 10,000 and 20,000 employees, and 20 in the case of companies with more than 20,000 employees.
- In the case of companies with between 2000 and 20,000 employees, two employee representatives can be union functionaries (i.e. non-employees); in the case of companies with more than 20,000 employees, three may be union functionaries.

In practice there is typically a close overlap between codetermination at board level and plant level; the head employee representative on the supervisory board is typically a leading works council member (Vitols, 2001).

Consensus has a higher priority than in the Anglo-American system, both within society and within the company. Within the economy as a whole, consensus is supported by the social market economy; within the company it is supported by solidarity in the shape of moderate wage and skill differentials, and institutions such as works councils (Woolcock, 1996).

Corporate restructuring

The German financial system and the greater protection from hostile take-over it affords help to explain the survival of many small and medium-sized companies in Germany. The *Mittelstand* model is based on close, long-term relationships between the many regional cooperative and municipal banks and firms to which banks provide not only long-term finance, but also an increasing number of non-financial business services – notably business consulting to their clients. The close relationship of these banks with local industry is demonstrated by the fact that their boards are typically composed of local industrialists (Sabel et al., 1987). This not only provides a close connection between industry and banking, but also forges horizontal links between SMEs in a region. Moreover, the guaranteed financial support enables SMEs to grow into medium-sized firms more easily than is the case for their UK and US counterparts.

As indicated, the use of takeovers in corporate restructuring has been the exception rather than the rule in the Rhineland model. Hostile takeovers were prevented from occurring through legal safeguards and the high degree of concentration of corporate control (in terms of bank ownership and/or voting rights). Groups of banks have acted as 'crisis cartels' to assist in the restructuring of traditional industries or to rescue ailing giants (Lane, 1994). When companies begin to run into difficulties it is the major shareholders, usually the banks, that step in to coordinate a rescue. Rather than sell up to a predatory holding company, which would probably realize the value of assets 'locked up' in the financial statements, the German approach is to seek to preserve as much as possible.

From the end of the 1990s, however, like their Anglo-American counterparts, large German companies have started to use domestic and foreign takeovers to restructure. For example, in 1997, Krupp-Hoesch, a German steel conglomerate, launched a hostile takeover bid for its local rival Thyssen, which provoked an outbreak of public opposition from politicians, union representatives, the media and employees, as well as the management of the target company. The leader of the IG Metall union, Klaus Zwickel, accused Krupp management of using 'wild west' methods, and Chancellor Helmut Kohl urged both parties to find a 'prudent solution' based on careful consideration of their 'social responsibility'. In April 1999, as part of a shake-up in the German telecommunications industry, Mannesman staged a domestic takeover of rival O.tel.o. and, in May 1999, launched a bid for the UK mobile phone provider Orange.

Other examples can be found in the car industry, and in the chemical and life sciences. The question arises as to whether the Rhineland model is, indeed, adopting elements of the Anglo-American system in response to increasing and new forms of competition. On the surface, it seems that this is happening. When looking at the details, one will find that most if not all of these takeovers failed or ended in a 'voluntary' merger. Hence, while the large firm model has been changing and seems slowly to be adapting to increased global competition, the embeddedness of the model explains that its deep-rooted features are preserved and remain visible through the changes.

The Japanese model of corporate governance

Capital markets and regulation

Rather like the Rhineland model, the Japanese model is characterized by corporate reliance on bank lending or on retained earnings. In contrast to the German banks, Japanese banks were not universal banks; until the Financial System Reform Act was introduced in 1993, there was a clear separation between commercial banks (specializing in deposits and loans) and securities firms (in charge of securities underwriting and dealing).

From the late 1980s onwards, large Japanese firms have shown high levels of self-finance and increased use of securities markets (at home and abroad). From that time onwards, the large city banks, which used to concentrate on providing loans to large firms, were forced to actively seek new borrowers and started to channel funds into the smaller firms. Until 1985, Japan's small and medium-sized firms had to rely on their local banks, which did not have sufficient resources. From the late 1980s onwards, the small and medium-sized firms have, thus, found borrowing restrictions easing. From the 1990s onwards, the crisis in the financial sector under the recession forced banks to become more selective in their lending habits. Smaller firms in particular have been hit hardest by these changes. Unable to go to the bond markets and restricted in their bank borrowing, these firms face hard times.

Also rather like the German situation, in Japan the corporate governance and finance models seem to be moving towards a hybrid model, where the traditional bank model continues to be used in the small and medium-sized firms, while the large firms incorporate elements of the Anglo-American model. We cannot speak of convergence towards the Anglo-American model or divergence from it. However, due to international pressure from foreign investors, more attention is given to adapting towards a more Anglo-American system which is more outsider-shareholder focused, thus providing more transparency (Yoshikawa et al., 2007).

The structure of ownership

The majority of shares of major corporations in Japan are held by stable shareholders, which include other corporations in the same business group, major creditors and major customers/suppliers connected through interlocking directorships, cross-holding of shares and inter-firm relations. These shareholders hold shares primarily to maintain their relationships rather than for financial gain. Governance is largely external and in the hands of the banks, but employees have a relatively strong voice as part of rather informal arrangements between labour and management (Jackson and Moerke, 2005). As part of a network, Japanese managers are highly committed to their company and develop informal business relationships to achieve consensus through vertical and horizontal decision-making.

For example, in 1990, Mitsubishi Corporation owned 1.6 per cent of Mitsubishi Heavy Industries, which, in turn, owned 3.2 per cent of Mitsubishi Corporation. Although these cross-holdings are usually small on a bilateral basis, between 10 and 25 per cent of all the outstanding shares of group members are generally held within the keiretsu (corporate group) itself.

Banks and insurance companies often number among the major shareholders of their main large clients. While Japanese banks were prohibited by law from holding more than 5 per cent of the outstanding stock of any other firm, the main bank could mobilize shareholdings by the group-affiliated trust bank, insurance company, trading company and other firms for reasons of concerted voting or to protect a customer firm from hostile takeover. Banks thus also allow large firms to have a long-term strategy.

The bank crisis and the need for Japanese banks to boost their capital-to-assets ratios at the end of the 1990s forced banks to sell some of their shareholdings. The banks did not, however, sell shares of companies in which they held a larger amount of the companies' stocks than any other bank, being their 'main bank'. Hence, like German firms, Japanese companies can invest while not having to worry about short-term profits for reasons of stock market performance.

Similar to the German *Mittelstand*, Japanese SMEs are also usually family owned and, if listed on the stock market, are tied to larger companies, thus providing them with stable shareholdings. However, due to a durable crisis since 1997 and regulatory changes, stable shareholdings and reciprocal shareholdings dropped. Some of the shares were redistributed to new stable shareholders, mostly acquired by foreign and domestic arm's-length investors (Yoshikawa et al., 2007).

Another pressure on the Japanese capital market was the increase of foreign ownership, performance-oriented expectations and social and political pressures. Because of this more shareholder-orientated approach, the new foreign investors can pressure Japanese firms to restructure their operations in the case of poor performance. Thus, the structural reforms, revision of Japan's regulation and government policies promoted corporate restructuring and increased the FDI in Japan through mergers and acquisitions.

The relationship between stakeholders and management

Rather like in Germany, relationships between stakeholders and management in large, small and medium-sized Japanese companies are close. Relationships are especially close between a company and its 'main bank'. The relationship between a main bank and its customer can be viewed as a particularly intense manifestation of relationship banking. The main bank not only positions one of its employees as a board member, when requested it also seconds bank officers to customer clients as full-time employees. The main bank also plays the leading role in monitoring and substantial intervention.

The most powerful safeguard in the Japanese corporate governance system is the ability of one or more equity-owning stakeholders to intervene directly and explicitly in the affairs of another company when this is required in order to correct a problem. Such assistance can be as modest as helping a troubled company generate new sales, or as dramatic as injecting new capital, restructuring assets and replacing top management. As in Germany, such intervention is typically led by a company's main bank, usually to remedy non-performance in the face of impending financial distress. Unlike in Germany, however, intervention in Japan is by no means limited to banks. Although less common, major industrial stakeholders will sometimes take quick, decisive steps to supplant an important supplier's or customer's autonomy with temporary de facto administrative control when non-performance becomes imminent (Kester, 1996).

The stability of cross-shareholding patterns in Japan could be seen as an indication of the fact that, as in Germany, Japanese capital markets will tend to remain relatively illiquid and will continue to be prevented from playing an active role in corporate control in the foreseeable future. Unlike in Germany, however, as a result of the morally hazardous behaviour[6] of banks during the stock market boom, the Japanese banks' monitoring abilities have been called into question. Moreover, the banks' diminished control over the supply of capital to the large firm segment and the practice of zaiteku[7] has greatly reduced both the ability of the banks to undertake corrective action and to perform their corporate control function effectively. As a consequence, and given the continuing importance of major aspects of the traditional model, one option could be the strengthening of the role of the board of directors and the introduction of a legislative requirement for outside directors to occupy a certain number of seats on the board (Koen, 2001).

Company law and the structure of top management institutions

Like the Anglo-American model, Japanese corporate law is based on the unitary board system. Though outwardly similar in some respects, Japanese boards differ from those of most Anglo-American companies in numerous ways. The Japanese Commercial Code stipulates that a shareholders' meeting elects directors and makes decisions about 'fundamental changes' to the company, such as a merger, a sale of all the firm's assets and amendments to the firm's charter. There must be at least three directors. The board elects representative directors, the Japanese counterparts of US and UK executives. There must be at least one representative director. Representative directors are managers, and they run the company.

In reality, the board of directors in a typical large Japanese company consists of about 20 to 25 directors, most of whom are at least 50 years old. However, unlike normal practice in Anglo-American economies, it is rare to find independent outside directors on Japanese boards. Japanese company law does not require outside directors. Instead, virtually all Japanese directors are inside managing directors chosen from the ranks of top management itself. Although, formally, shareholders are supposed to elect (usually unanimously) directors at annual meetings, the majority are nominated by management itself. Indeed, most members of the board are appointed as a reward, near the end of their careers, and regard the position as an honour rather than an opportunity to contribute (Williams, 2000). Major share-owning stakeholders in a Japanese company often obtain indirect representation through former executives that assume positions on the boards of companies with which their former employers do business. Typically, an executive from a share-owning corporation, bank or other financial institution who is well into his career (most often in his mid-fifties) will be 'retired' from his first job and start a 'second career' as a director of the associated company in question. In some instances, mid-career executive transfers become permanent when the transferred executive rises relatively quickly to the position of managing director (Lightfood, 1992).

Any control over the president in the past came from the banks; however, now these are much weakened by their own severe problems, any controls largely come from the president's predecessors: they are normally appointed, frequently for life, as advisers (soudan-yaku) or senior advisers (meiyo-yaku), who generally have to be consulted on all major decisions (Williams, 2000). Moreover, instead of outside directors, Japanese company law requires kansayaku, often (somewhat misleadingly) translated as 'statutory auditors'. These are elected at the shareholders' meeting and do not have to be accountants or other professionals. A statutory auditor is responsible for overseeing the activities of management. This is understood to include the legality of management's activities. The statute requires collaboration between accounting auditors and statutory auditors.

Consensus and the institutions of employee representation

Japanese company law prescribes a one-tier board system. Employee participation, or codetermination, has not been adopted; however, the enterprise-based unions provide employees with an opportunity for internal participation. Employees are important constituencies in Japan, promoted for loyalty, social compatibility and performance (Tricker, 2009); however, the labour market is almost completely closed. Employees can exercise voice through 'the extensive use of joint labour-management consultation' (Jackson and Moerke, 2005: 352), which is then 'written into collective agreements as basis for firm decision making' (Aguilera and Jackson, 2003: 455). A traditional and frequent statement is that Japanese companies are run in the best interests of employees and not in the interests of shareholders. The strong emphasis on employee retention is also evident when looking at employee competence formation. Employees enjoy frequent in-house and cross-functional training, which is essentially firm specific, as employee turnover is not expected. Thus a common phenomenon is that when a Japanese company is facing financial distress, management will cut dividends before it starts firing employees. In fact, lifetime employment, compensation tied to seniority and company-by-company labour unions are often singled out as the distinctive characteristics of Japanese companies, and have functioned to keep employee supremacy alive (Kanda, 1998).

Corporate restructuring

Again rather like in Germany, as a consequence of stable shareholding patterns, a hostile take-over is very difficult to implement and rarely happens in Japan. Also rather like in Germany, mergers and rescue operations to aid financially troubled firms are generally set up by the main bank. In addition, past research suggests that the Japanese government has also been closely involved in the corporate governance process by initiating mergers and persuading banks to set up rescue operations. Hence, despite the fact that the government is not a shareholder, it has intervened substantially in corporate governance issues.

In short, following the 2008 financial crisis, we can denote three major changes in Japanese corporate governance. First, the governmental intervention has become more important, for example, when it comes to the initiative for corporate restructuring and providing loan guarantees for traditional Japanese firms. Second, the role of the bank is considered for redesigning the corporate finance and governance, as the bank is expected to be an important monitor for the traditional Japanese firm, which takes more explicit contracts with clients. Finally, inside ownership has developed, which means that corporate and employee holding of equity is considered as an alternative to public and bank ownership.

6.3 Corporate governance systems in Western Europe

As indicated above, continental European models of corporate governance are situated in-between the Rhineland and Anglo-American models. Due to the implementation of EU directives and requirements of the financial markets, changes have been introduced in the corporate governance systems of EU countries. Changes have excluded the central part of internal company life and structure, mainly as a consequence of member states' reluctance to modify the internal company structure, which is often based on balances of influence and power. These matters deal with core rules in the governance debate, such as: the structure of the board, and the corporate control market, especially the regulation of take-overs and protection against them the rules on groups of companies, and the protection of minority shareholders (Wymeersch, 1998).

Hence, while change and harmonization efforts have taken place in European corporate governance, differences in policy practice and philosophy have frustrated efforts to agree on a number of measures, hampering the development of a common system of European corporate governance. Comparative statistics help here to provide a clear picture of the diversity in corporate governance and finance practices that exists in Europe.

Capital markets and regulation

All European states have their own stock exchanges. In order to measure the significance of the stock exchange phenomenon in the different economies of Europe several yardsticks are used. The traditional yardstick is the relationship between market capitalization[8] and GDP (Table 6.3). Market capitalization is assumed to be related to GDP because a larger economy would normally produce larger firms and hence a higher capitalization.

Table 6.3 Market capitalization of the main OECD countries (2012)

Market	*Market capitalization** *(bn US$)*	*GDP (bn US$)*	*Market capitalization in % of GDP*
Italy	480.5	2014.7	23.85
Austria	106	394.7	26.86
Portugal	65.5	212.3	30.87
Germany	1486.3	3428.1	43.36
Norway	252.9	499.7	50.62
Ireland	109	210.8	51.72
Japan	3681	5959.7	61.76
Belgium	300.1	483.3	62.09
Finland	158.7	247.5	64.10
France	1823.3	2612.9	69.78
Denmark	224.9	314.9	71.41
Spain	995.1	1323	75.22
Netherlands	651	770.6	84.49
Sweden	560.5	523.8	107.01
Canada	2016.1	1821.4	110.69
US	18668.3	16244.6	114.92
UK	3019.5	2471.8	122.16
Luxembourg	70.3	55.2	127.48
Switzerland	1079	631.2	170.96

* Market capitalization (also known as market value) is the share price times the number of shares outstanding. Listed domestic companies are the domestically incorporated companies listed on the country's stock exchanges at the end of the year. Listed companies do not include investment companies, mutual funds, or other collective investment vehicles.

Source: World Bank (2012) http://data.worldbank.org/indicator/NY.GDP.MKTP.CD

Table 6.3 rates several European states, Canada, Japan and the US according to their relative involvement in the securities (bonds and shares) business in 2012. It is apparent that five states show a higher than average intensity in the use of the securities markets. Switzerland, with 170.96 per cent of GDP, has the highest capitalization; while Italy with 23.85 per cent of GDP the lowest market capitalization. Similar disparities are shown for Switzerland, Sweden, the Netherlands and Luxembourg. All of these are states in which the securities business has experienced the strongest development. These states are also most concerned with market organization, regulation of the securities business and financing in general. This evidence partly suggests that the Netherlands, Sweden, Luxembourg and Switzerland exhibit a tendency to shift from the insider model of corporate control to the outsider model, in which corporate control is left to the markets.

At the opposite end of the spectrum, Austria, Italy, Portugal and Germany are the states in which capital markets play a less important role in comparison to their relative economic weight. This also means that the industry in these states is mainly supported by financing means other than securities financing, and that securities financing has not been widely practised in two-thirds of Europe. The latter figures are the more striking as these states contain some of the larger European firms.

The number of shares available on a market also illustrates its importance. In this respect, Table 6.3 once again confirms that, in 2012, the Rhineland countries were still less market orientated than the Anglo-American model. The US and the UK markets show the highest capitalization ratio (except Luxemburg and Switzerland). The higher ratio of Japan in comparison with Germany indicates that large Japanese firms are turning more to the securities markets for financing than are large German firms.

The structure of ownership

An analysis of the patterns of share ownership can be carried out on macro figures and yields information on the amount of capital shares held by the different classes of securities holder, such as physical persons, institutional investors, and so on (Table 6.4).

Table 6.4 Ownership structure of the EU countries

Old indicators	*Dispersed ownership*	*Dominant ownership*	*Family owned*	*Foreign owned*	*Cooperative*	*Government owned*
FESE indicator	Individual investors	Collective investment	Private non-financial firms	Foreign investors	Private financial firms	Public sector
Austria		28.5	23.5	30.6	33.7	4.9
Belgium	19.5		20.2	38.7	18.7	2.9
Denmark		7.0	30.7	30.2	19.9	0.8
Finland				61.6		
France	6.7	20.2	13.1	41.1	27.5	10.3
Germany			39.3	21.3	24.2	1.9
UK	12.8		2.7	40.0	44.4	0.1
Italy	26.6	13.8	26.6	13.9	23.2	9.7
Netherlands		12.5		71.0	8.9	
Norway		5.6		40.8	6.7	30.5
Spain	20.1		25.4	36.8	17.6	0.2
Sweden	15.8		9.4	38.0	27.0	7.8

Note: (empty fields represent missing data)

Source: FESE (2007) http://www.fese.eu/_lib/files/Share_Ownership_Survey_2007_Final.pdf

Explanation of FESE indicators in Table 6.4, see also FESE (2007)

Individual investors: households

Collective investment: insurance and pension funds, investment companies, mutual funds

Private non-financial firms: limited companies, private organizations and trusts

Private financial firms: banks and savings banks, bond-issuing mortgage companies

Public sector: central and local governments, companies owned by governments (incl. banks and post)

Looking at Table 6.4, it appears that there are clear differences between nations, giving the impression of strong national effects. For example, as already indicated, dispersed ownership is common in the UK and (to a lesser extent) in the Netherlands, but rare or non-existent in the rest of Europe. Foreign ownership is predominant in the Netherlands and Finland but much less frequent in Germany and Italy. Government ownership is common in Spain and France, but not in the Netherlands and Finland. These differences in ownership structure can largely be explained by history and were dealt with in the analysis of Chapter 4.

Ownership structures in French corporations to some extent depart from a path-dependent evolution. French corporations used to be characterized by a large share of government ownership. This was partly a consequence of nationalization after the Second World War and by the Mitterrand government in the early 1980s. It also reflected the French tradition of government intervention. Large-scale privatization, in recent times, explains why the large share of government ownership in France has been reversed. Another interesting feature of French ownership structure is the role played by holding companies originally established by industrial companies to overcome financing constraints, which also helps to explain the frequency of cross-holdings and dominant minority ownership.

The high degree of government ownership in Austria dates back to nationalization of property that was technically German, a major drive of industrialization of Austria being due to the government of Germany; Austria was part of Germany in 1938–45. Italy is notable for the extent of state ownership, which dates back to industrial reconstruction after the Second World War. State ownership of some large Norwegian energy companies (Norsk Hydro, Statoil) may be explained by a combination of German occupation, nationalism and inadequate domestic finance.

In Belgium, the strategy of attracting foreign direct investment from the USA in particular became a national economic strategy after the Second World War; this helps to explain the high frequency of foreign ownership. Spain has a large number of multinational companies, which in part reflects a conscious policy to attract foreign direct investment initiated by the Franco government. A high frequency of family and cooperative ownership in Denmark is partly attributable to the small size of the average company and a relative factor advantage in agricultural products. Sweden's share of minority ownership is partly a consequence of the German-style industrialization in which banks and large entrepreneurs played a major role. In Germany banks played an active role in the industrialization process and financial institutions continue to exercise dominant minority control over many large companies, although founding families have often continued to exercise some control (by large shareholdings) even in joint-stock companies. The Netherlands is said to have been influenced by its proximity to the UK, which may have increased the frequency of dispersed ownership (Pedersen and Thomsen, 1997).

The relationship between stakeholders and management

In general, relationships between companies and stakeholders tend to be closer in continental Europe than in the UK and the US. In continental Europe, while there is increasing attention to shareholder value, the stakeholder model, with its attention to wider social concerns, is still prevalent. In most European countries, relationships between banks and companies have not been as close as in Germany and Japan. Banks do provide finance to companies but generally do not perform the same role as in the Rhineland model. Moreover, the relatively close relationships, based on trust, between banks and companies have become harder to maintain. EU legislation has limited bank holdings in all EU countries. International capital adequacy rules agreed under the auspices of the Bank for International Settlements (BIS) and largely incorporated into the EU through the EU's Capital Adequacy Directive, have increased the costs of bank equity holdings. Deregulation has resulted in increased competition among banks as well as between banks and other financial institutions (Pedersen and Thomsen, 1997).

Company law and the structure of top management institutions[9]

The unitary-board system

In most EU member states, listed companies are obliged by statute to organize a board of directors. Most European company laws have adopted the unitary board structure, which is the exclusive board structure in the UK, Belgium (except for banks), Denmark, Greece, Ireland, Luxembourg, Spain, Italy, Sweden and Switzerland. Board members are formally elected by a general meeting of shareholders, which also determines the number of seats on the board. In all systems, the main sources of influence on the appointment of directors come from the chairman of the board, or CEO, often supported by the full board. Only in France and Belgium do shareholders have an influence on appointments. For France and Belgium, institutional investors are also mentioned as having a significant influence on board nomination: one can probably identify these 'institutional investors' as 'holding companies', in which case the finding would be comparable to that for Germany. In each case, the larger or largest shareholder has a significant influence on the nomination of board members (Wymeersch, 1998: 1090).

In the systems where shareholders have an overwhelming influence, independent directors are seen as instrumental in balancing shareholder influence in favour of other shareholders. Independent directors can only exercise 'balancing' power, keeping in check the overwhelming influence of the dominant shareholder without being able to actively direct the firm's policy. The dominant shareholder will not easily surrender this influence – except on a de facto basis – particularly as this would reduce the value of his shares. Therefore, it has been more difficult to impose independent directors on continental European schemes than in a system with wide share ownership, such as that of the US and the UK.

Case: Parmalat – The failure of Italy's corporate and market regulation

Million of dollars worth of Parmalat bonds were sold to an estimated 100,000 unwitting mom-and-pop investors before that company's 24 December bankruptcy. 'Italians feel betrayed,' says Rosarios Trefiletti, president of Federconsumatori, a Rome-based consumers' group that's filing suits and staging noisy demonstrations. 'We Italian investors get no help at all from the government,' laments Vincenzo Nieri, a retired manager of a Bristol-Myers Squibb unit in Milan. 'Nobody has ever taken the initiative to protect investors.' Meanwhile, Berlusconi and Co. have willfully overlooked the need for stiff penalties for accounting irregularities. . . . Berlusconi's government, by contrast, essentially decriminalized most kinds of fraudulent accounting in 2001 by making it a mere misdemeanor instead of a felony. The law should be revised – but only some factions of Berlusconi's coalition agree. That hardly sends the right signal to Italy Inc. Moreover, little of the government debate on financial market reform has focused on key issues like the need for more independent board members and an autonomous audit committee. Crony boards are flourishing in Italy. Parmalat had one – stacked with family and friends of boss Calisto Tanzi. Italy urgently needs to extend the law giving minority shareholders the right to choose independent board members. It now covers only privatized former state-owned companies.[10]

The dual-board system

In some jurisdictions, companies are directed by a 'supervisory' and a 'managing' board together; there are both optional and compulsory two-tier board systems. Membership of employees, here called 'codetermination', is usually placed at the level of the supervisory board.

Systems with an optional two-tier board system, not necessarily linked to co-determination, can be found in Finland, in France and in smaller firms in the Netherlands. Two-tier boards without obligatory worker representation are compulsory for Portuguese companies. This structure is also found in Italy, where the managing board is headed by a *collegio sindacale*, whose powers and influence are, however, considerably less than those of the traditional supervisory board. Belgium is often wrongly classified among those systems with a two-tier board. This is a consequence of banking law, which recognizes the use of two-tier boards in credit institutions. No other companies may, technically, introduce a two-tiered board. Aside from Germany's large companies, the two-tier board with compulsory worker representation is also found in large Dutch and Austrian firms.

Finland has introduced an optional regime: companies opting for a one-tier board should provide for the designation of a board of three members to be elected by the general meeting of shareholders. However, the charter can stipulate for a minority of board members to be appointed by a different method (i.e. by the employees). Larger companies must appoint a 'managing director' to act within the limits of his assignment by the board of directors. Larger companies may provide for a two-tier system: the supervisory board must be composed of at least five members, elected by the general meeting or in a different way, allowing for employee representation. Although there is no compulsory system of employee representation, there is a widespread practice of organizing voluntary representation: 300 companies are reported to have voluntarily introduced this type of industrial democracy.

In France, too, a two-tier system may be introduced by charter provision in a public company limited by shares (*Société Anonyme*, SA). However, this is found in only about 12 per cent of French companies (Williams, 2000). The members of the management board, called *directoire*, are appointed by the supervisory board. The number of its members varies from one to five, or seven if the company is listed. The president is also appointed by the supervisory board. Members of the supervisory board cannot be members of the *directoire*. The supervisory board is appointed by the shareholders. It is composed of three to 12 members, to be increased to 24 in the case of a merger. In general, French companies are directed by the *Président Directeur Général* (PDG), who is both chairman of the board and CEO. The possibility of challenges to the PDG is limited by the culture of the French corporate establishment, in which a very large number are graduates of a very small number of *écoles supérieures* (elite schools mostly separate from the universities), and there are numerous interlocking directorships and shareholdings: it is not hard for the PDG to handpick those he or she believes will support him or her (Williams, 2000).

Since 1971, Dutch company law has prescribed the 'structure regime' to be adopted by large corporations. The regime applies to firms that meet the following three conditions during a 3-year period:

- outstanding capital (issued capital and reserves) of at least 12 million euros according to the balance sheet
- a works council
- at least 100 employees of the company and its dependent companies employed in the Netherlands.

When these criteria are met, the 'large' company is legally obliged to establish a supervisory board. Each of the members of this board is appointed by the board itself (called co-optation). The general meeting of shareholders and the works council is allowed to object to candidates if they believe they are not qualified, or if they judge the composition of the board to be inappropriate. Moreover, the general meeting of shareholders, the works council and the managing board is allowed to recommend candidates for appointment to the supervisory board. These recommendations are binding.

The supervisory board (*raad van commissarissen*) of the structure corporations is legally endowed with a number of compulsory powers that, under the normal regime, are allotted to the general meeting of shareholders. Thus the structure regime transfers some major competencies from the shareholders to the supervisory board. These competencies include the right to appoint and dismiss members of the managing board (*raad van bestuur*) and to adopt the annual accounts. Furthermore, a number of major managerial decisions are compulsory, subject to approval by the supervisory board. These include the issue of shares, investment plans and company restructuring.

Companies that do not meet the aforementioned criteria for large companies are legally allowed to voluntarily opt for the structure regime by including this in their articles of association. This is only possible if they have a works council in the company. Certain types of 'large' company may request exemption from the application of the structure regime. This is granted to international concerns that have their principal headquarters in the Netherlands, function merely as management companies, and employ the majority of their employees outside the Netherlands. The Dutch subsidiaries that meet the criteria for 'large' company are then subject to a milder regime, which implies that they must have a supervisory board. However, this milder regime means that the supervisory board is not given the right to appoint and dismiss members of the managing board or to adopt the annual accounts. If a parent company, which has its principal seat in the Netherlands, is fully or partly subject to the structure regime, its subsidiary is exempt from the regime.[11]

Austria has maintained the German approach, dating back to the 1937 German law. A two-tier board is compulsory, with at least one person at management level (*Vorstand*) acting on his own responsibility. At the supervisory level, there should be at least three members. Members are elected by the general meeting, but one-third may be appointed – or revoked – by specific shareholders, such as the holders of a class of shares. The number varies according to the size of the capital.

Belgian law recognized the two-tier board, but only in the field of credit institutions. In Belgium, banks may (in practice, they are urged to) introduce a two-tier board. In major

Belgian banks, the board of directors acts as a supervisory board; it deals with general policy issues and is in charge of overseeing the management board's actual banking. Initially, the rules governing the composition of the board served to isolate the bank's actual management from the influence of the controlling shareholders, with the aim of ensuring that the bank was run in its own interests, rather than the interests of its controlling or referee shareholders. In the early 1990s, shareholders took over the reins of power. The objective is no longer to reduce the influence of the dominant shareholder, nor to avoid the bank functioning in the exclusive interests of its shareholders. Instead, the rule aims to exclude undesirable shareholders.

Technically, the Italian *società per azione* is also characterized by the presence of two levels of 'boards'. The larger companies are managed by a board of directors – the *consiglio di amministrazione* – composed of inside and outside directors. This board often elects an internal managing board, the *comitato esecutivo*. In addition, Italian law provides for a surveillance body, the *collegio sindacale*, composed of members elected by the general meeting and in charge of supervising the activities of all company organs, including the general meeting. Italian legal writers do not consider this board to be comparable to the German supervisory board. Instead, they classify the Italian system as belonging to the unitary board system.

Consensus and the institutions of employee representation

In some of these jurisdictions, the presence of labour representatives or other stakeholders at board level has been introduced. Boards with employee representation are, first and foremost, a German–Austrian–Dutch phenomenon. However, in the 1970s, employee representation was introduced in several other European states, either as part of the unitary board's functioning or, more usually, in the two-tier structure. Apart from mandated codetermination, most states have voluntary systems of co-decision-making at board level, based either on employer-organized co-decision-making or on collective labour agreements. These evolutions are not very well documented and have not been investigated in detail (Wymeersch, 1998).

In addition to representation at board level, employees may be able to influence decision-making through their participation in other bodies, most frequently the 'enterprise council'. These are parallel bodies that are mandatory for all larger organizations whether they are engaged in business or not. These bodies are mostly not involved in corporate decision-making, but are restricted to employment conditions, including layoffs and plant closures. At the European level, a 'European Works Council' has become compulsory for all larger undertakings or groups of undertakings with at least 1000 employees within the EU, of which there are at least 150 employees in two or more member states. In the UK, however, this system continues to be opposed by employers. The fear is that the introduction of the Works Council would be a step towards employee representation at board level.

The institution of employee representation

One-tier board systems and employee representation

Employee representation is obligatory in the one-board system in Denmark, Sweden, Luxembourg and France, and, as just explained, optional in Finland.

In Denmark, the Companies Act provides that half the number of the members of the boards elected by the shareholders, or by the other parties entitled to appoint directors, will be elected by employees, with a minimum of two. Companies and groups (parents and subsidiaries) located in Denmark and with at least 35 employees are subject to this regime, which is applicable to the parent companies.

In the 1977 Codetermination Act, Sweden introduced a system of compulsory co-determination with respect to all companies – of SA or cooperative type – that employ more than 25 people: two labour representatives must be appointed to the board. If there are more than 1000 employees, three members of the board must be designated. However, since representatives are reportedly reluctant to intervene in the board's decision-making, participation is essentially regarded as serving informational purposes only.

In France, there is a threefold system of voluntary codetermination within the unitary board. Codetermination had long been opposed both by employers and employees, the unions refusing to be involved with running the firm. Gradually the idea began to gain momentum, though, and in 1982 a form of compulsory representation was introduced to public-sector firms, followed in 1986 by an optional minority codetermination system in the private sector. A 1994 law rendered the system compulsory for privatized state enterprises. The system of codetermination was introduced in all firms with an enterprise council: two representatives of this council take part on the board, as observers and without votes. Their influence is actually very limited: the decisions are made by the directors in a preliminary meeting. This type of codetermination decision-making has been referred to as 'a mockery'.

Another system of codetermination in France is based on a voluntary scheme; this can be introduced by the general meeting by way of a charter amendment. Representatives of employees of the firm – numbering between two and four, and occupying a maximum of one-third of the board seats – are elected by their peers, not by the general meeting. They take part in the meetings of the board in the same position as the other directors. In practice, however, board meetings are often split into two parts, with the representatives invited to the formal part. Hence the system is reportedly not very effective, especially as a result of the fear that the representatives might divulge information. Also, the directors fear that co-decision-making will increase the union's power. The number of companies that have opted to adopt this regime is unknown, but is probably rather small.

France has introduced a more elaborate system of codetermination for its privatized public sector, including firms that are majority owned by the French state. Apart from representatives of the state and expert members (both one-third), one-third of members of the supervisory board or of the management board are representatives of the employees. In general, employee representatives on French boards are relatively rare.

In Switzerland, although the law does not call for employee participation at board level, some companies have voluntarily introduced codetermination. Examples are Nestlé and the retail distributors Migros and Co-op.

In Ireland, the Worker Participation (State Enterprises) Act 1977 introduced board-level employee participation at a selected number of state-owned enterprises employing 43,700 employees. Members are appointed by the minister competent for the state firm in question, and are nominated either by the union or by a percentage of the employees (a minimum of 15 per cent). In addition, only employees of the firm may be appointed. The system has not been extended to the private sector, although proposals have been made to that purpose.

In Italian business firms, employees are not represented at the board level. The Italian union tradition is based on confrontation not on *co-gestione*. In Belgium there is no labour representation at board level. In some state-owned firms there may be limited representation of labour (e.g. in the national railway company, where three members are nominated by the unions and elected by the employees). Belgian (unitary) boards usually comprise internal managers, representatives of large shareholders, and independent out-siders. In Spain, there is no legally imposed system of codetermination, but it can be continued on a voluntary basis. The latter is the case in state-owned enterprises.

Two-tier board systems and employee representation

The Dutch system of labour representation is based on the consensus between the two traditional production factors: capital and labour. Labour representation at the level of the supervisory board is indirect and based on co-optation of members of the board who, without being labour representatives, enjoy the confidence of the employees. Therefore, members of the supervisory board do not represent labour interests, but have to take care of 'the interests of the company and its related enterprises' as a whole.

Austria has introduced employee representation more or less along German patterns: at the level of the supervisory board in large companies, one-third of the members should be employee representatives. These are appointed for an indefinite time period by the works council or, in larger firms, by the central works council, and chosen from among their members. Union influence is reported to be strong.

As indicated, there is no legally imposed system of codetermination in the two-tier system in Portugal.

Corporate restructuring

As with issues concerning the structure of boards, the corporate control market (especially in terms of the regulation of takeovers and protection against them) has escaped European harmonization and is still determined nationally. Diverging features of share ownership and related regulations explain, to a large extent, the relatively wide diversity in the way the corporate control market is organized and functions. While public take-overs and comparable transactions are common in the UK, they occur less frequently in continental European countries (Table 6.5a).

Company restructuring in most continental European countries takes place by negotiated measures rather than directly as a consequence of market transactions. The frequency and importance of mergers and acquisitions in Europe illustrate this (Table 6.5b). In all states there is an active 'private' market for corporate assets and corporate control. In terms of the number of transactions, about half those taking place worldwide involve European companies, whether on the buying or the selling side. This 'private' market for corporate assets and control runs through the communication channels of the large accounting firms and investment banks that operate across Europe. The transactions mostly, if not exclusively, relate to privately owned firms, including subsidiaries and divisions of listed companies. Both in terms of the number of transactions and turnover, the mergers and acquisitions market largely exceeds the more visible markets for public takeover bids (Wymeersch, 1998).

Table 6.5a Information on mergers and acquisitions. Target country by volume – global private equity deals

	2011	*2012*	*2013*
US	3.935	4.382	3.895
UK	641	724	792
France	543	572	404
India	332	339	356
Germany	312	358	336
Canada	262	297	305
Spain	179	157	185
China	360	226	175
Italy	111	131	173
Russia	61	89	159
Israel	96	113	150
Japan	105	110	146
Netherlands	130	111	129
Sweden	151	143	106
Finland	88	77	104
Brazil	61	91	82
Switzerland	48	45	70
Australia	69	81	67
Bulgaria	3	34	64
Denmark	41	57	60

Source: http://www.mandaportal.com/getattachment/8ff3c7f7-7179-45a4-8109-2246d640ddac/Global,-FY-2013
Raw data: http://www.bvd.co.uk/zephyrreport/GlobalFY2013.xls

Table 6.5b Information on mergers and acquisitions. Target country by volume – Western Europe deals

	2011	*2012*	*2013*
UK	5.854	6.262	6.517
Spain	2.276	2.27	2.26
France	1.772	1.773	1.739
Germany	1.396	1.589	1.733
Finland	1.561	1.482	1.47
Sweden	1.251	1.384	1.4
Netherlands	2.161	1.281	1.38
Italy	1.148	1.344	1.165
Turkey	754	564	870
Norway	808	792	822
Denmark	441	487	563
Switzerland	387	385	465
Belgium	368	388	449
Ireland	228	231	237
Austria	161	150	183
Portugal	214	214	162
Luxembourg	108	106	129
Cyprus	87	114	108
Greece	46	63	70
Gibraltar	13	11	18

Source: http://www.mandaportal.com/getattachment/8ff3c7f7-7179-45a4-8109-2246d640ddac/Global,-FY-2013
Raw data: http://www.bvd.co.uk/zephyrreport/GlobalFY2013.xls

6.4 Corporate governance in BRIC countries

BRIC has come into fashion as a term for Brazil, Russia, India and China. The reason for the grouping is highly pragmatic: they are all countries with very large populations (about 150 million in Russia, 200 million in Brazil and well over a billion in China and India); they were becoming increasingly important by opening up to world trade, becoming more liberal capitalist, economic growth and investing in other countries, in roughly the same period. But in most other respects they are quite dissimilar. Never mind the pragmatic grouping, these countries are more recent industrializers and they merit attention, because of their size and increasing importance in the world economy. Because they are institutionally and culturally dissimilar (Hofstede, 2001), they will be dealt with individually. More recently, the Republic of South Africa appears to have managed to join the club, so that it became BRICS. We do not consider it here, although it is an economically important country in Africa, because its economic institutions are not that divergent from liberal market economies.

Brazil

The Brazilian model of corporate governance is characterized by a high concentration of ownership (41 per cent on average for the biggest shareholder and 61 per cent of the equity capital for the top five shareholders), with a large number of family-owned firms and business groups, relatively small corporate boards with a limited number of independent directors and a majority (about 75 per cent) of outside directors nominated by controlling shareholders (Black et al., 2010; Brugni et al., 2013). This often causes conflicts among controlling and majority shareholders, with a lack of transparency since many firms do not provide financial statements and lack an audit committee (Caixe and Kreuter, 2013). As a substitute, the Brazilian legislation authorizes an independent fiscal board to investigate financial reporting by firms; however, its efficacy remains questionable (Black et al., 2010). Since the 1990s, due to a large-scale privatization program, government ownership has considerably declined.

In the light of new economic development, the Brazilian Institute of Corporate Governance has recommend new standards aiming to increase the quality of disclosed financial information by publicly held firms, differentiated in three segments: Novo Mercado (118 firms), Level 1 (16 firms) and Level 2 (38 firms). For example, included in these rules is the obligatory separation of the chairman and the CEO; however, only 40 per cent of companies listed on the Bovespa (Sao Paolo Stock Exchange) are included in the special listing segments for corporate governance (Brugni et al., 2013). Thus, in a comparative perspective, the Brazilian model of corporate governance is positioned in-between the shareholder and stakeholder models, sharing characteristics of both models, resulting sometimes in conflicting situations such as the case of fewer independent directors mostly nominated by controlling shareholders.

Russia

After the collapse of the Soviet Union in 1991 and the election of Boris Yeltsin as president, corporate managers soon became de facto owners as a result of the Russian government's privatization program. One objective of privatization, launched in 1993, was to place shares of formerly state-owned enterprises into the hands of managers, other employees and all

Russian citizens. By the time the privatization process ended in 1994, many enterprise managers had become majority or large shareholders in their firms, accumulating shares at nominal cost from other employees and the public. Many managers utilized their powerful positions to engage in self-enriching practices such as asset stripping and setting up false subsidiaries through which they channelled cash and valuable assets. Owner-managers, in addition, often crushed the rights of other shareholders by not holding shareholder meetings, deleting names from stock registers and other crude practices (McCarthy and Puffer, 2002). Not only the ownership became concentrated at the company, but also the aggregated level since the Russian assets are controlled by a group of 'oligarchs' (e.g. about 40 per cent of the Russian industry belongs to 22 largest business groups, Lazareva et al., 2009).

Banks were able to keep some control over the financial accounts of enterprises through legislation that required all enterprises to hold their accounts in a single bank, and allowed banks to intervene in decisions on how to divide up enterprise profits between consumption and investment funds. The enforcement of such measures was, however, haphazard (Litwack, 1995). Moreover, the vast majority of Russian banks did not participate actively in the privatization process. Minor participation in enterprise privatization was followed by the banks' minor involvement in corporate governance. In addition, inflation led to the popularity of short-term lending, making unnecessary and cost-ineffective any monitoring of the borrower's performance (Belyanova and Rozinsky, 1995). Industrial management control thus remained unchallenged by the banks.

Major exceptions to this general picture of the Russian bank sector are the so-called 'hard-currency islands' – banks specializing in hard-currency operations (including hard-currency-denominated loans), with Russian exporters as their main customers. This small group of 'export-sector banks' (ESBs) has tended to overcome the Russian banks' general inability to interfere in corporate governance. The specialization of these banks in hard-currency operations, supported by their larger-than-average size and lending capacity, has determined their capacity to exercise control over the industrial enterprises.

In general, it could be argued that ineffective and conflicting laws, lack of enforcement and a limited infrastructure for protecting shareholders' rights help to explain Russia's dysfunctional corporate governance system in the aftermath of the privatization process. A major example is Russian company law. This law, though defining a two-tier structure for corporate governance boards, promoted a governance structure that was strongly dominated by major shareholders. The law did not allow outsiders who did not represent the interests of the major shareholders on to the board of directors. Neither did it automatically allow representatives of insiders, such as managers or workers, on to the board unless they were also significant shareholders or their legal representatives. A shareholders' meeting directly appoints a president and a management board head from the members of a board of directors. The auditing committee, as a supervisory board, is also appointed directly by shareholders.

One damaging result of the enormous power of the owner-managers and the consequent malpractice was that the prospect of attracting investment to Russian enterprises had all but vanished. Indeed, the implications of the privatization process in Russia virtually blocked equity market development. On the one hand, managers and employees are expected to be very conservative shareholders, reluctant to sell their shares; on the other hand, industrial shares are not as attractive as some others to potential buyers because of the low dividends they offer and the virtual impossibility of obtaining large blocks of shares. The equity market, therefore, tends to be thin and incapable of providing adequate control mechanisms (Belyanova and Rozinsky, 1995).

The 1998 economic crisis, which had a very adverse effect on Russian corporate life, made large Soviet companies aware of the fact that effective corporate governance is a crucial underpinning to business success. With the election of Vladimir Putin at the turn of the decade, and Putin's law-and-order platform, which included steps to stabilize the economy and crack down on crime (including destructive business activities), Russia chose to move forward with reform of the corporate governance system. The subsequent development of institutions to support effective corporate governance was a joint effort of Putin's team and private business groups, who shared this objective. This business–government collaboration resulted in new legislation and keener enforcement, as well as a developing culture of more openness and responsibility. The combined result of these developments, together with the need to attract investment capital, as well as the prospect of benefiting more from public listing than from private plundering, motivated enterprises, among other things to:

- operate in a way that benefits all shareholders to maintain a focus on long-term financial returns;
- disclose to shareholders, and the appropriate regulatory and international bodies, accurate, consolidated and timely information;
- use internationally accepted standards and accounting principles verified by an independent, qualified audit;
- disclose their ultimate ownership structure, including beneficial share ownership by executive officers, board members and any group holding more than 5 per cent;
- to have a board of directors that is elected by and accountable to the shareholders, and that includes qualified non-executive directors.

In 2002, the Russian Stock Exchange issued the Corporate Code of Conduct, recommending best practices, not enforceable by law; however, companies that did not follow the code, lost their eligibility for an A1 listing (considered the most prestigious type of listing) on the Russian Stock Exchange (Puffer and McCarthy, 2003). Nevertheless, complying with the new Code of Conduct revealed to be challenging since the established formal rules may conflict with current informal norms and practices in Russia.

Although the independent directors aim for minimizing conflicts of interests while monitoring managers, their role in Russian boards is different (Berezinets et al., 2011). Directors are formally independent, but in reality have close ties with the management or the controlling shareholder, who largely nominate them, therefore, less likely to be fully independent (Buck, 2003).

Therefore, due to the mass privatization process, which was driven more by speed than oriented to quality, Russian capital markets are considered to have underdeveloped financial institutions, weakly protected private property rights and high country risks for foreigners (Buck, 2003). While there is still a long way to go to improve corporate governance practices in Russian business, compared with the situation in the past, it could be argued that progress has been made due to gradual development and growth of Russian capital markets that leads to getting closer to the primary goals of privatization: promoting the openness of company information disclosure and liquid capital markets as a means of disciplining the actions of enterprise decision-makers (Buck, 2003). Yet the country continues to score relatively low on various related measures. The World Bank (2013) ranks Russia 111th out of 189 countries in terms of the ease of doing business. The KPMG (2013) report concludes that business continues to be impeded by bureaucracy in the government system, its internationally noncompliant property rights legislation, the inconsistent application of laws and regulations, and a lack of transparency.

India

There has been a clear move in India to develop the corporate market to attract FDI, which is slowly increasing shareholder diversity in some companies. Even though the Indian legal system provides one of the best systems of investor protection in the world, the reality is different due to slow courts and corruption. Much of the corporate sector displays relationship-based informal control and governance mechanisms, inhibiting financing and keeping the cost of capital at high levels, even though India has a developed banking sector (Chakrabarti, Megginson and Yadav, 2007). There is significant pyramiding and tunnelling among Indian business groups due to concentrated ownership and family control; however, most of the corporate governance issues are in fact common in Asia and in other BRIC countries.

The Indian market regulator, the Securities and Exchange Board of India (SEBI), recently issued a consultative paper on the 'Review of Corporate Governance,' calling for: the splitting of the roles of chairman and chief executive, disclosure of the reasons for an independent director's resignation from office, a limit on the term of appointment of independent directors, and greater involvement of institutional investors. Making radical changes seek to ensure the implementation of these corporate governance recommendations including:

- the appointment of independent directors by minority shareholders;
- independent directors to receive compulsory training and pass examinations; and
- the adoption of a principle-based approach for certain principles.

Although the proposals emerges from the Anglo-American model, in some instances they introduce new initiatives, and the adoption of certain UK-based concepts such as 'comply-or-explain' should be expected to be adopted cautiously, given the radical nature of certain proposals. New regulatory institutions may be needed, strengthening the existing institutions and hybrid approaches adopted in Anglo-American countries.

China[12]

From 1978 onwards, the Chinese government embarked on an ambitious program of economic reform. One of the most important creations was that of the firm as an independent business entity. Under the central planning regime, China's industrial and commercial enterprises were not autonomous but were workshops and production units with no independent decision-making power. The central plan replaced the function of the market, and the conditions for the existence of a firm (as understood in market economies) were absent. All means of production were nominally owned by the state; contracts and market transactions were not needed for organizing production activities.

The workshop and production units within the central input–output planning matrix have been replaced by business enterprises with independent legal status. The emergence of the company as a basic economic entity was accompanied by a process of financial reform that has turned the newly created or reorganized state-owned banks into the primary providers of finance for Chinese enterprises, replacing the old system of state budgetary grants. Most working capital needs of state-owned enterprises (SOEs) are met through bank lending. The banks were encouraged to use economic criteria for evaluating loan applications on the basis of market demand for the enterprises' output, the availability of raw materials and the profitability of investments. The transformation of the Chinese banking system into a truly commercial one, however, is proving an extremely slow process. Some party officials have been reluctant to increase the independence of the central bank and of other banks because officials have been exploiting the banks to finance their own needs. The Chinese government also continues to use the banks to siphon surplus funds from private enterprises to subsidize the losses of state enterprises. Moreover, the political upheaval and mass unemployment involved in making the banks themselves efficient further contribute to slowing the pace of progress. Hence, while banks are technically more independent, in practice they are to a large extent still acting as cashiers for the state and can hardly play a useful role in corporate governance.

From the mid-1980s onwards, when grass-roots efforts to develop China's capital markets began spontaneously, shareholding companies were formed. To raise funds, state and collective enterprises issued various forms of shares and bonds, and informal securities trading could be found in most major Chinese cities. China's first securities and brokerage company was established in Shenzhen in 1987. In the following year, securities companies were set up in every province under the auspices of the local branches of China's central bank. By 1991, China's two official stock exchanges in Shanghai and Shenzhen were ready for full operation. Approval for a company to obtain listing on these markets, however, is determined by the government on the basis of an annual quota broken down to each province and ministry. The listing of a company is thus usually decided not on its commercial merit but for political and sectional reasons. Just like the state banking system, which supports SOEs through the debt market, the securities market in China is essentially a state securities market, conceived and operated primarily to support corporatized SOEs.

Chinese-listed companies are in the main partially privatized SOEs. That is, their major shareholder is the state in its various forms, including other SOEs. The high degree of concentrated state ownership has restricted the capacity of China's equity market to perform a financial disciplinary role in the corporate governance of listed firms. Because of the high rate of saving and the very limited range of investment instruments available in China, individual investors in the stock market have from the beginning exhibited a highly speculative tendency with a very short investment horizon. In July 2013, China's State council published ten guidelines for financial market restructuring, focusing on the legalization of privately run banks and the regulation of private lending. In China commercial loans can only be obtained from state-owned banks, thus it is tough for private entrepreneurs and SMEs to get a loan, since these state-owned banks favour lending to government firms (Tsai, 2004). High demand for finance in the private sector provides opportunities for illegal private fundraisers, while the legal private 'lenders' are basically situated in a grey area (Zou and Adams, 2008). Since listing on the Chinese capital market is mostly a political process, the market is also described as a state securities market and is missing its disciplinary role (Zou, Pang and Zhu, 2012).

Chen et al. (2009) argue that there are four main types of ownership control in Chinese listed companies:

- state asset management bureaus (SAMBs)
- SOEs affiliated to the central government (SOECGs)
- SOEs affiliated to the local government (SOELGs), and
- private investors.

SAMBs are shareholding institutions that have been established by the state to manage state assets. They normally invest in listed companies by owning the state shares and sometimes the legal person shares. SOECGs are generally big or nation-wide companies and are subjected to strict monitoring under the central government and the National Audit Office. Unlike SAMBs, the chairmen selection process is strict as the officials are chosen for their political ability. The main difference between SOECGs and SOELGs is that latter are controlled by a local government. The companies that they usually invest in are SOE spin-offs and they are the largest group of controlling shareholders of companies. Private investors can be both private companies and individuals. A dominant investor will typically become the CEO or chairman of the company. Agency problems will not steam for the dominant investor, but they will concern the minority shareholders. As private companies are not subjected to state monitoring, the dominant investor has the power to expropriate the income and assets of the company away from the minority shareholders (Chen et al. 2009).

Despite its majority ownership, the state does not exercise effective control over its companies. Control of China's companies rests primarily with the insider management and their party–ministerial associates. The Chinese government, together with the party organization, exercise influence through, for example, recruitment policy. For listed companies with the state as a majority shareholder, the pool for appointment to the positions of chief executive, most senior managers and a high proportion of the directors on the company board is restricted and subject to government influence or direct intervention. Moreover, many company executives may still have an affiliation to their previous state organization (Wymeersch, 1998).

Companies operating under the country's company law have a two-tier board. The board of directors is essentially made up of executive directors. There are few independent directors in Chinese companies. Although it is mandatory for at least one third of the board of directors be formed of independent directors, the issue is that these directors are appointed by majority shareholders so they generally do not contradict their intentions or actions. In addition to the board of directors, Chinese companies also have a supervisory board. This board is small in size and usually has labour union and major shareholder representatives. However, it only has a loosely defined monitoring role over the board of directors and managers, and has not so far played any effective governance role. The interests of employees are safeguarded primarily by party representatives in consultation with the controlling shareholder, which is usually the state. Trade unions in China are organized hierarchically and led by the All China Federation of Trade Unions, which is the world's largest trade union with more than 190 million members. Companies with more than 25 trade union members have to set up a board, but in practice, the role of trade unions is often limited to social functions, such as events and outings.

While there has been progress in developing accounting standards, China is still a long way from achieving the degree of effectiveness and independence required for the Anglo-American model to work. It is widely believed that false accounting and financial misreporting are pervasive among Chinese SOEs and companies. However, as in other transition economies, a company's reputation for integrity and performance is often not required in order to raise capital in the stock exchange. Indeed, the unpredictable movements generated by market manipulation may, in fact, at times be applauded by some investors, who hope to profit from such speculative waves and are eager to follow the 'winners'.

Many of the shortcomings in the actual practice of corporate governance in China derive from weaknesses in the policy and institutional environment, and from peculiar cultural and political governance traditions. For example, collusion among insiders, and lack of transparency and disclosure to outsiders on the actual performance and workings of the firms have been explained as a consequence of the tradition of insiders versus outsiders with a built-in convention of secrecy among insiders. Family or clan members, as 'insiders', are expected to bear collective responsibility for promoting and safeguarding the interests of the unit. The interests of outsiders are either secondary or irrelevant. Safeguarding the interests of the unit involves maintaining confidentiality on internal affairs, and disclosures are regarded as a betrayal of the unit's interests. Also important is the impact of political governance on corporate governance. Since the Chinese system of political government itself lacks accountability and transparency, it is difficult, and perhaps incongruous, for corporate governance to be effective and institutionalized. Moreover, the market-orientated legal system, and the corporate and securities law framework in China has only been developed over the past two decades and is still relatively rudimentary and untested in many aspects.

6.5 Codes of corporate governance

A wave of corporate scandals at the end of the 1980s promoted the emergence of codes of corporate governance as a new mode of regulating corporate governance practices, primarily in the UK and the US. Codes are a set of best practices designed to address deficiencies in the formal contracts and institutions by suggesting prescriptions on the preferred role and composition of the board of directors, relationships with shareholders and top management, auditing and information disclosure, and the remuneration and dismissal of directors (Haxhi and Aguilera, 2012).

By the end of April 2014, 91 countries worldwide had created at least one code (ECGI, 2014). Several studies in many countries show that the content of codes has a direct influence on firm corporate governance practices as they are considered a benchmark and regulatory tool. Although corporations are the ultimate implementers of codes, executives, directors, shareholders, proxy advisors, rating agencies and all the other stakeholders as well as public policy and regulators care about codes because they provide a metric to guide and assess governance behaviour.

Codes can be distinguished from other modes of regulation in that they are formally non-binding, issued by committees of experts, flexible in their application, built on the market mechanism for evaluation of deviations and evolutionary in nature (Haxhi and van Ees, 2010). Their voluntary and self-regulatory nature is exemplified in the widely used 'comply-or-explain' principle, which entails that while compliance with code provisions is voluntary, the disclosure of non-compliance is mandatory (Wymeersch, 2005). The practice of regulating corporate governance through formally non-binding codes or the comply-or-explain principle is supposed to be the same throughout all the EU countries; however, the meaning of this regulatory mechanism differs substantially across countries. In the Netherlands and Germany, for example, the comply-or-explain principle is amended by law, and firms have to explain non-compliance with the code's provisions (Haxhi and van Manen, 2010). In the UK, meanwhile, the stock exchange forces code implementation (MacNeil and Li, 2006).

In short, regulating corporate governance through codes is seen as a process, where soft-law, e.g., codes, are favoured over hard law. Compliance studies in several countries find that codes have an effect on the structure and functioning of the board of directors (Alves and Mendez, 2004), reduce the agency cost of managerial entrenchment and enhance board oversight (Dedman, 2002), and positively impact the stock price, since markets react positively to announcements of compliance (Goncharov et al., 2006). However, unlike hard-law regulation, e.g., Sarbanes-Oxley Act of 2002 in the US, codes do not entail strict compliance (Haxhi and Aguilera, 2012).

Codes and their convergence

The current literature on corporate governance is unclear whether we are moving towards convergence in governance practices. It is essential to move the debate beyond the convergence versus divergence discussion and pay more attention to the national culture and institutions, and transnational issuers of codes as drivers of convergence. There are several transnational entities enabling the diffusion of codes, such as the World Bank or the OECD (Aguilera and Cuervo-Cazurra, 2009), which by promoting a common set of practices may indirectly be contributing to the achievement of convergence; not toward a particular model but a more general global model. In addition, Reid (2003) sees internationalization forces such as globalization, market liberalization, foreign investors, and recommendations on global best practices by transnational organizations as facilitators of this confluence.

Moreover, with respect to the national cultures, Haxhi and van Ees (2010) find that the cultural values that reflect societal norms and beliefs about the integration of individuals with groups, the distribution of power, and the tolerance for uncertainty affect the issuance of codes and the identity of the issuers. Individualist cultures (Hofstede, 2001) have a stronger tendency to develop codes. In cultures with high power differences, there is a higher probability that the first issuers are from the government, directors, and professional associations; while in the opposite case, the stock exchange and investors are more likely to initiate the first code.

Furthermore, as a response to the 2008 financial crisis, a new hard law regulation saw the light in the US. The financial crisis also prompted the US Congress to expand the federal government's involvement in corporate governance. Whereas the Sarbanes-Oxley Act regulated the composition and responsibilities of audit committees, the Dodd-Frank Act (The Dodd-Frank Wall Street Reform and Consumer Protection Act, signed into law on 21 July, 2010) requires a broad range of financial institutions to have a risk committee as well. The risk committee will be responsible for overseeing the firm's risk management practices, and the committee must have at least one risk management expert having experience with similar firms. The Federal Reserve is empowered to decide how many independent directors must serve on the committee. The Act includes a number of broad executive compensation reforms that are not limited to financial institutions, including a requirement that US public companies provide shareholders with a non-binding say-on-pay vote. The SEC is also required to instruct the stock exchanges to adopt new listing standards imposing enhanced independence requirements for board compensation committees. It will be interesting to see how other countries will react to these new rules enacted in the US (Haxhi and Aguilera, 2012).

The global integration of product and capital markets is leading to worldwide changes in corporate governance. However, to date there is no clear evidence that such an observable evolution would constitute actual convergence; these changes are a direct search for greater efficiency in governance system and improved legitimacy in financial markets (Haxhi and Aguilera, 2012). Local institutions, culture and politics can impede these governance changes or initiate 'hybrid' practices (Yoshikawa, Tsui-Auch, and McGuire, 2007).

Case: The Ahold scandal

As the post-Enron wave of corporate scandals washed over the US, a common response in Europe was: it couldn't happen here. Far from having the world's best-policed markets, many European politicians claimed, the US suffered uniquely from a lethal combination of greedy and overpaid bosses, conflicted auditors and investment bankers, reliance on accounting rules not principles, and an obsession with quarterly profit numbers.

As more sensible European regulators recognize, this smugness was never justified: it is only necessary to recall scandals such as Vivendi, ABB, Elan and EM.TV. But Europe's claim of immunity from corporate sleaze was blown out of the water by the revelations that Royal Ahold of the Netherlands, the world's third-biggest food retailer, overstated its profits for 2001–02 by as much as $500m. Its chief executive and chief financial officer have both quit.

It is true that Ahold's accounting deficiencies mainly involved American subsidiaries that it bought in a decade-long acquisition binge though they also stretched to Argentina and Scandinavia. But the company's Amsterdam-based auditors, Deloitte & Touche, failed to pick the problems up in 2001, even though worries about Ahold's accounts were widely expressed in the markets. Ahold's board, far from questioning the chief executive closely, tamely extended his term for up to 7 years as recently as last spring. The Dutch market regulator admitted that it had no powers of discipline over faulty auditing.

What about the relative numbers of restatements? Because America's GAAP accounting system relies on thousands of pages of rules, it is more vulnerable to manipulation than Europe's more principles-based approach. Wall Street's excesses of the 1990s were also more egregious than Europe's. But given the largely non-existent regulation of auditors and the poor corporate governance prevalent in much of Europe, a more plausible conclusion is that Europe has had fewer accounting scandals than America mainly because nobody has seriously looked for them, not because they are not there.

This is not to say that Europe should adopt Sarbanes-Oxley. That hastily drafted law was designed for America's very different system; it precludes the two-tier boards that are common in Europe, for example. Many of the law's rules on managers and boards seem unduly intrusive even for America. But statutory, independent regulation of auditors, as prescribed by Sarbanes-Oxley, makes sense everywhere. So do rules to stop accounting firms doing consulting work for audit clients; and it is also worth considering mandatory rotation of auditors (Deloitte had audited Ahold for 15 years). However, it is little use taking this welcome step towards tougher accounting standards, which the Europeans are urging on America in the interests of global harmonization, if there is nobody to oversee the rules. Yet the European Federation of Accountants admits that, in six EU countries, there is in effect no enforcement at all.

Bad apples and oranges

After Enron and WorldCom were followed by the bankruptcy and criminal conviction of Andersen, which had audited both companies, the remaining Big Four hinted that Andersen had been an exceptional case: a rotten apple amid a barrel of good ones. Andersen does seem to have been peculiarly culpable. Yet most of the other firms have now also been tarnished by scandal in the past year or so: KPMG over Xerox, PricewaterhouseCoopers over Tyco, Deloitte over Adelphia, for example. As companies such as Ahold go global, they run into countless national regulators and supervisors – and it is the weakest link that is always most likely to prove their (and their investors') undoing. The right response is to adopt the strongest, not the laxest, auditing regime possible. This means both enforcement of international accounting standards and tough regulation of auditors.

Questions

1 What explains the occurrence of the Ahold scandal?
2 Should the Ahold case be seen as a failure of the (Dutch) two-tier board system? Please explain your opinion of this issue.
3 The US$500 million overstatement was due primarily to Ahold's US subsidiaries. Would you, therefore, argue that Ahold is less a European problem than yet another US accounting failure?
4 Would the Ahold scandal occur typically in 'global' corporations or could a similar situation arise in companies operating in only one nation?

6.6 Conclusions

The comparative analysis of corporate governance systems and of their institutional–cultural roots is not only useful in its own right but also for building an understanding of the impact these systems might have on competitive advantage of national industries. The comparative analysis in this chapter shows that history, politics and societal traditions shape the development of financial and corporate governance institutions. They are bound up with more economic forces. The lesson to be learned is that financial and corporate governance reforms must adapt to the unique history and social–political structure of a country. Less advanced and transitional countries cannot blindly follow the financial and corporate governance reforms of other countries.

This chapter also shows that both the Anglo-American and the Rhineland models of corporate governance have their strengths and weaknesses, which help to explain their divergent impact on industrial competitiveness (see Table 6.6). Major strengths of the Anglo-American system of corporate governance include efficiency, flexibility, and responsiveness in financial markets, and high rates of corporate profit. More explicitly, the Anglo-American system is good at re-allocating capital among sectors, funding emerging fields, shifting resources out of 'unprofitable' industries, and achieving high private returns each period, as measured by higher corporate returns (Porter, 1997). Major weaknesses of the system stem essentially from two of its features: the unitary board system and its short-termism. The unitary board system, while allowing for efficient decision-making by management, impedes effective monitoring of management performance. The election of outside directors (which happens on a voluntary basis in the UK), the use of proxy voting mechanisms, and, as in recent times, the development of shareholder advisory committees have emerged in the Anglo-American system as preferred techniques for solving many of these control problems. When these governance techniques fail, corporate control becomes entirely dependent on the market.

Theoretically, the threat of a hostile takeover should ensure that assets are controlled by those best able to manage them, and in the US and UK, with their well-developed markets for corporate control, a hostile takeover is the ultimate check on management. When shareholders fail to take an interest in the governance of a company, or when their governance proves ineffective, low-quality managers are able to remain in power or management's allegiance to the shareholder may falter. In either of these cases, a company's share price should drift lower so as to form a gap between the stock's actual price and its potential value. If the gap between a company's market value and its perceived potential value were to grow large enough, a takeover would ensure that control over the company's assets eventually goes to those who can earn a higher return on those assets (Lightfood, 1992).

Moreover, the unitary board system, combined with the threat of takeover, helps to explain the difficulty of the Anglo-American system with aligning the interests of private investors and corporations with those of society as a whole, including employees, suppliers and local communities. Indeed, the market for corporate control often disregards its effects on both human and social capital. Short-term capital is also argued to contribute to impeding the creation of the organizational competencies necessary for firms competing in sectors characterized by incremental innovation (Streeck, 1992). In other words, the system fails to encourage sufficient investment to secure competitive positions in existing business. It also induces investments in the wrong forms. It heavily favours acquisitions, which involve assets that can easily be valued, over internal development projects that are more difficult to value and that constitute a drag on current earnings (Porter, 1997). It is interesting to note that this regulation does not speak at all to the practice of codes, which are based on the idea that 'not one size fits all.' Also, the 2001 and 2007 crises showed that a lot of the profitability and even financial market data were manipulated. Notably in the US, court cases are still pending at the time of writing this.

Major strengths of the Rhineland model are that it encourages investment to upgrade capabilities and productivity in existing fields; it also encourages internal diversification into related fields – the kind of diversification that builds on and extends corporate strengths. The Rhineland model comes closer to optimizing long-term private and social returns. The focus on long-term corporate position – encouraged by an ownership structure and governance process that, together, incorporate the interests of employees, suppliers, customers and the local community – allows the German economy to utilize more successfully the social benefits of private investment (Porter, 1997: 12–13).

Downsides of the Rhineland model, however, are the tendency to over-invest in capacity, to produce too many products, and to maintain unprofitable businesses. Moreover, the stable, long-term relationships between banks and firms are increasingly seen as inhibiting the formation and growth of firms in new sectors. As indicated above, the long-term stable shareholder relationships typical of the Rhineland model impede the development of a large, liquid capital market. A large capital market is critical for risk capital or venture capital providers, as it creates a viable 'exit option' via initial public offering (IPO) and mergers or acquisitions (Casper, 1999). Without this exit option, it is difficult for venture capitalists to diversify risks across several investments and to create a viable refinancing mechanism.

The comparison in this chapter reveals the fact that there is no such a thing as a 'perfect' or the 'best' system. While, at present, the majority view is that the shareholder model will prevail due to the increasing dominance of institutional investors on international capital markets (Lazonick and O'Sullivan, 2000), the intense and ongoing competition between the Anglo-American and the Rhineland models in Europe provides evidence to the contrary. The impact of this competition provides few signs of change in the UK and only small step-changes, incorporating some elements of the Anglo-American model into the 'large firm' Rhineland model. Since national forms of corporate governance are embedded in established 'practices' and 'regulatory policies', change in one area does not involve a change in the entire system.

The example of Germany shows modifications of the existing approach to corporate governance that accommodates the new circumstances. Root-and-branch change is not found, and there is not even a consensus on the need for change, let alone a consensus on what that change should be. The attractiveness of an overall corporate governance model very much rests, not only on efficient financial markets, but also on macroeconomic performance. Here, we currently have contradictory information: the Anglo-American countries have stuck to national systems but also relied heavily on governmental bailout of technically bankrupt enterprises and governmental debt. The world growth leader, China, has combined government influence and ownership, and management of the currency exchange rate, with the adoption of capitalist forms and practices. The European countries to come best out of the crisis with a strong export surplus, Sweden and Germany, have adopted some Anglo-American practices but they also revitalize their own traditions.

Table 6.6 The Anglo-Saxon and Rhineland models of corporate governance: major weaknesses and strengths

	Anglo-Saxon model	*Rhineland model*
Major strengths	• good reallocation of capital between sectors • funding of emerging fields • shifting resources out of 'unprofitable' industries • high rates of profit • efficient decision-making by management	• encourages investment to upgrade capabilities and internal diversification in related fields • utilizes the social benefits of private investments more successfully • effective monitoring
Major weaknesses	• stemming from board system ineffective monitoring • plus threat of take-over no incentives to invest in organizational capabilities • favours acquisitions instead of internal development projects	• stemming from stable bank ties • tendency to over-invest in capacity • tendency to produce too many products • tendency to maintain unprofitable business • tendency to impede the development of liquid capital markets and, as a result, • tendency to inhibit the development and growth of firms in new sectors

Study questions

1. Explain the main differences between the 'shareholder' and the 'stakeholder' models of corporate governance.
2. What is the broad definition of corporate governance?
3. What do you understand by 'effective corporate governance'?
4. Explain how the German accounting system differs from the US one.
5. Explain the main differences between the Anglo-American and the Rhineland model of corporate governance.
6. What is meant by the terms 'exit' and 'voice' in the governance area?
7. What are the main strong and weak points of the Japanese system of corporate governance?
8. Explain why the take-over option of the Anglo-American model of corporate governance has militated against enterprise growth from small to medium size.
9. Is the German model converging towards the Anglo-American model of corporate governance? Give reasons for your argument.
10. Would it be economically beneficial for the German model to converge towards the Anglo-American model?
11. Explain the effects of globalization forces on corporate governance systems.

Further reading

Aoki, M. and Kim, H.-K. (1995) *Corporate Governance in Transitional Economies*. Washington, DC: World Bank.

An interesting book paying special attention to insider control, the possible role of banks in corporate governance, and the desirability of taking a comparative analytic approach to finding solutions.

Hopt, K.J., Kanda, H., Roe, M.J., Wymeersch, E. and Prigge, S. (1998) *Comparative Corporate Governance: The State of the Art and Emerging Research*. Oxford: Oxford University Press.

An interesting book that explains a wide range of corporate governance topics in different countries.

Jürgens, U., Naumann, K. and Rupp, J. (2000) Shareholder value in an adverse environment: the German case. *Economy and Society* 29(1), 54–79.

This article provides an interesting analysis of the ability of the German corporate governance system to change in the direction of shareholder value.

Rasheed, A. and Yoshikawa, T. (2012) *Convergence of Corporate Governance: Promise and Prospects*. Basingstoke: Palgrave Macmillan.

Sheard, P. (1998) Japanese corporate governance in comparative perspective. *Journal of Japanese Trade and Industry* 1, 7–11.

This article offers a brief but critical comparative analysis of the Japanese and Anglo-American systems of corporate governance.

Zhuang, J., Edwards, D. and Capulong, V.A. (2001) *Corporate Governance and Finance in East Asia: a Study of Indonesia, Republic of Korea, Malaysia, Philippines, and Thailand*. Manila, Philippines: Asian Development Bank.

Notes

1 Bankruptcy regulation militates against relationship banking in that any bank that intervenes in order to assist a customer in difficulties is likely to have its seniority as a debtor reduced. These laws are based on the principle that creditors of any bankrupt company should be treated equally, but the effect of this is to provide a fairly powerful disincentive to active intervention. Insider trading

legislation militates against active institutional shareholders, because if they obtain price-sensitive information as a result of involvement in a company they cannot trade without infringing insider trading legislation. As a consequence, corporate restructuring occurs through takeovers, as shareholders are tempted to accept bid premia and sell or 'exit' rather than become actively involved in the rescue by 'voicing' concern about the performance of management.

2 For an extended overview of the measures that have been taken to make the capital markets more attractive in Germany, see Schaede (2000).

3 This case draws on Nowak (2001).

4 German banks have the ability to exercise proxy votes at the shareholders' meetings of the AGs on behalf of shareholders who have deposited their shares with the banks for safekeeping.

5 See Baums (1994) for an elaborate explanation of the composition and functioning of the supervisory board.

6 Japanese banks were not selective in lending money and lent to dubious companies. Morally hazardous behaviour is behaviour without an appropriate level of care.

7 Zaiteku means profit-seeking financial activity by the corporate treasury departments of large Japanese companies, which has resulted in an uncoupling of financial policies and financial executive decisions from overall corporate strategy.

8 Market capitalization, also called market value, is the number of shares in existence multiplied by the share price.

9 Extracts from 'Italy needs a renaissance in corporate and market regulation', *Business Week*, 2 February 2004.

10 The Dutch law on works councils requires firms with 35 employees or more to install a works council.

11 Under the normal regime, the establishment of a supervisory board is optional. In such a case, the members of the supervisory board are appointed by the general meeting of shareholders. The latter is endowed with considerably more power than it would be under the structure regime since it retains a number of important decision rights.

12 The majority of the information in this case is based on Tam (2002), Eu (1996) and Lin (2001).

References

Aguilera, R.V. and Cuervo-Cazurra, A. (2004) Codes of good governance worldwide: what is the trigger? *Organization Studies* 25(3), 415–443.

Aguilera, R.V. and Cuervo-Cazurra, A. (2009) Codes of good governance. *Corporate Governance: An International Review* 17(3), 376–387.

Aguilera, R.V. and Jackson, G. (2003) The cross-national diversity of corporate governance: dimensions and determinants. *Academy of Management Review* 28(3), 447–465.

Aguilera, R.V. and Jackson, G. (2010) Comparative and international corporate governance. *Annals of the Academy of Management* 4, 485–556.

Alves, C. and Mendes. V. (2004) Corporate governance policy and company performance: the Portuguese cases. *Corporate Governance: An International Review* 12(3), 290–301.

Aoki, M. (1999) Convergence and diversity in corporate governance regimes and capital markets. Law and Economics Conference, Evoluon Conference Center, Eindhoven.

Baums, T. (1994) The German banking system and its impact on corporate finance and governance. In Aoki, M. and Patrick, H. (eds) *The Japanese Main Bank System*. Oxford: Clarendon Press.

Bebchuk, L.A. and Roe, M.J. (1999) A theory of path dependence in corporate ownership and governance. *Stanford Law Review* 52(1), 127–170.

Belyanova, E. and Rozinsky, I. (1995) Evolution of commercial banking in Russia and the implications for corporate governance. In Aoki, M. and Hyung-Ki Kim (eds) *Corporate Governance in Transitional Economies*. Washington, DC: World Bank, 185–214.

Berezinets I., Ilina Y. and Muravyev I. (2011) *EERC Project No 09–528*. Graduate School of Management, SPBU.

Black, B.S., Garvalho, A.G. and Gorga, E. (2010) Corporate governance in Brazil. *Emerging Martket Reiew* 11, 21–38.

Brugni, T., Bortolon, P.M., de Almeida, J. and Paris, P.S.K. (2013) Corporate governance: a panoramic view of Brazilian boards of directors. *International Journal of Disclosure and Governance* 10(4), 402–421.

Buck, T. (2003) Modern Russian corporate governance: convergent forces or product of Russia's history. *Journal of World Business* 38(1), 299–313.

Caixe, D.F., and Krauter, E. (2013) The influence of the ownership and control structure on corporate market value in Brazil. *Revista Contabilidade & Finanças* 24(62), 142–153.

Casper, S. (1999) *High Technology Governance and Institutional Approaches*. WZB discussion paper FS I 99–307. Berlin: Wissenschaftszentrum für Sozialforschung Berlin.

Casper, S. (2000) Institutional adaptiveness, technology policy, and the diffusion of new business models: the case of German biotechnology. *Organization Studies* 21(5), 887–914.

15 Extracts from 'Ahold Out' © The Economist Newspaper Limited, London (March 1st 2003).

Chakrabarti, R., Megginson, M.W. and Yadav, P.K. (2007) Corporate governance in India. CFR working paper, No. 08–02 Provided in Cooperation with: Centre for Financial Research (CFR), University of Cologne, Germany.

Chen, G., Firth, M. and Xu, L. (2009) Does the type of ownership matter? Evidence from China's listed companies. *Journal of Banking & Finance* 33, 171–181.

Clarkson, M.B.E. (1995) A stakeholder framework for analyzing and evaluating corporate social performance. *Academy of Management Review* 20(1), 92–117.

Coffee J.C. (1999) The future as history: the prospects for global convergence in corporate governance and its implications. *Northwest University Law Review* 641, 644–645.

Dedman, E. (2002) The Cadbury committee recommendations on corporate governance – A review of compliance and performance impacts. *International Journal of Management Review* 4(4), 335–352.

Deeg, R. (1997) Banks and industrial finance in the 1990s. *Industry and Innovation* 4(1), 53–73.

Del Brio, E.B., Maia-Ramires, E. and Perote, J. (2006) Corporate governance mechanisms and their impact on firm value. *Corporate Ownership and Control*, 4(1), 25–36.

Djelic, M.-L. (1998) *Exporting the American model: The Post-war Transformation of European Business*. Oxford: Oxford University Press.

European Corporate Governance Institute (ECGI) (2014). www.ecgi.org

Eu, D. (1996) Financial reforms and corporate governance in China. *Columbia Journal of Transnational Law* 34(2), 469–502.

Friedman, M. (1962) *Capitalism and Freedom*. Chicago, IL: University of Chicago Press.

Gelb, D.S. and Strawser, J.A. (2001) Corporate social responsibility and financial disclosures: an alternative explanation for increased disclosure. *Journal of Business Ethics* 33, 1–13.

Goncharov, I., Werner, J.R. and Zimmermann, J. (2006) Does compliance with the German corporate governance code have an impact on stock valuation? An empirical analysis. *Corporate Governance: An International Review* 14(5), 432–445.

Gregory, J.H. and Simmelkjaer, T.R. (2002) *Comparative Study of Corporate Governance Codes Relevant to the European Union and Its Member States*. New York: Weil, Gotshal and Manges LLP.

Hansmann, H. and Kraakman, R. (2001) The end of history for corporate law. *Georgetown Law Journal* 89, 439.

Haxhi, I. (2010) Institutional contextuality of business best practices: the persistent cross-national diversity in the creation of corporate governance codes. PhD dissertation, University of Groningen Press: Groningen, the Netherlands.

Haxhi, I. and Aguilera, R.V. (2012) Are codes fostering convergence in corporate governance? An institutional perspective. In Rasheed, A. and Yoshikawa, T. (eds) *Convergence of Corporate Governance: Promise and Prospects*. Basingstoke: Palgrave Macmillan.

Haxhi I. and Aguilera, R.V. (2014) Corporate governance through codes. In Cooper, C. (ed.) *Wiley Encyclopedia of Management* (3rd edn), Vol. 6: *International Management*. Oxford: Wiley-Blackwell.

Haxhi, I. and van Ees, H. (2010) Explaining diversity in the worldwide diffusion of codes of good governance. *Journal of International Business Studies* 41(4), 710–726.

Haxhi, I., and van Manen, J. (2010) Nationale cultuur en de wereldwijde verspreiding van corporate governancecodes. *Goed Bestuur*, 3.

Haxhi I., van Ees, H. and Sorge A. (2013) A political perspective on business elites and institutional embeddedness in the UK code-issuing process. *Corporate Governance: An International Review* 21(6), 535–546.

Hofstede, G.H. (2001) *Culture's consequences: Comparing values, behaviors, institutions, and organizations across nations* (2nd edn). Thousand Oaks, CA: Sage.

Hughes, A. (1990) Industrial concentration and the small business sector in the UK: the 1980s in historical perspective. Working Paper No. 5, Small Business Research Center, University of Cambridge (August).

International Monetary Fund (2012) *Russian Federation – Concluding Statement for the 2012. Article IV Consultation Mission.* Retrieved from: http://www.imf.org/external/np/ms/2012/061312.html

Jackson, G. and Moerke, A. (2005) continuity and change in corporate Governance: comparing Germany and Japan. *Corporate Governance: An International Review* 13(3): 351–361.

Kanda, H. (1998) Notes on corporate governance in Japan. In Hopt, K.J., Kanda, H., Roe, M.J., Wymeersch, E. and Prigge, S. (eds) *Comparative Corporate Governance.* Oxford: Oxford University Press.

Kester, W.C. (1996) American and Japanese corporate governance: convergence to best practice. In Berger, S. and Dore, R. (eds) *National Diversity and Global Capitalism.* London: Cornell University Press.

Koen, C. (2001) *The Japanese Main Bank Model: Convergence or Hybridisation?* Mimeo Tilburg: Tilburg University.

KPMG (2013) *Doing Business in Russia: Your Roadmap to Successful Investments.* Retrieved from:http://www.kpmg.com/RU/en/IssuesAndInsights/ArticlesPublications/Documents/Tax_2e.pdf

Lane, C. (1994) European business systems: Britain and Germany compared. In Whitley, R. (ed.) *European Business Systems.* London: Sage.

La Porta, R., Lopez-de-Silanes, F., Shleifer, A., and Vishny, W.R. (1998) Law and finance. *Journal of Political Economy*, 106(6), 1131–1155.

Lazareva, O., Rachinsky, A., and Stepanov, S. (2009) A survey of corporate governance in Russia. In *Corporate Governance in Transition Economies.* New York: Springer US, 315–349.

Lazonick, W. and O'Sullivan, M. (2000) Maximizing shareholder value: a new ideology for corporate governance. *Economy and Society* 29(February), 13–35.

Lightfood, R.W. (1992) Note on corporate governance systems: the United States, Japan, and Germany. *Harvard Business School Note 9–292–012*, Harvard: Harvard Business School Publications.

Lin, C. (2001) Corporatisation and corporate governance in China's economic transition. *Economics of Planning* 34, 5–35.

Litwack, J.M. (1995) Corporate governance, banks, and fiscal reform in Russia. In Aoki, M. and Hyung-Ki, K. (eds) *Corporate Governance in Transitional Economies.* Washington, DC: World Bank, 99–120.

MacNeil, I., and Li, X. (2006) Comply or explain: market discipline and non-compliance with the Combined Code. *Corporate Governance: An International Journal* 14(5), 486–496.

McCarthy, D.J. and Puffer, S.M. (2002) Russia's corporate governance scorecard in the Enron era. *Organizational Dynamics* 31(1), 19–34.

Moerland, P.W. 1995. Alternative disciplinary mechanisms in different corporate systems, *Journal of Economic Behavior & Organization*, 26, 17–34.

Nowak, E. (2001) Recent developments in German capital markets and corporate governance. *Journal of Applied Corporate Governance* 14(3), 35–48.

OECD (1998) *Tendances des Marches de Capiteaux no. 69* (February). Paris: OECD.

O'Sullivan M. (2000) Corporate governance and globalisation, 570 ANNALS, AAPSS 153, 154.

Pedersen, T. and Thomsen, S. (1997) European patterns of corporate ownership: a twelve-country study. *Journal of International Business Studies* 4, 759–778.

Porter, M. (1990) *The Competitive Advantage of Nations.* New York: Free Press.

Porter, M.E. (1997) Capital choices: changing the way America invests in industry. In Chew, D.H. (ed.) *Studies in International Corporate Finance and Governance Systems.* Oxford: Oxford University Press, 5–17.

Puffer, S.M. and McCarthy, D.J. (2003) The emergence of corporate governance in Russia. *Journal of World Business* 38(4), 284–298.

Reich, R.B. (1998) The new meaning of corporate social responsibility. *California Management Review* 40(2), 8–17.

Reid, S.A. (2003) The internationalization of corporate governance codes of conduct. *Business Law Review*, 233.

Roe, M.J. (1994) Some differences in corporate governance in Germany, Japan, and America. In Baums, T., Buxman, T. and Hopt, K.J. (eds) *Institutional Investors and Corporate Governance*. Berlin: Walter de Gruyter.

Rubach, M.J. and Sebora, T.C. (1998) Comparative corporate governance: competitive implications of an emerging convergence. *Journal of World Business* 33(2), 167–184.

Sabel, C., Herrigel, G., Deeg, R. and Kazis, R. (1987) Regional prosperities compared: Massachusetts and Baden-Württemberg in the 1980s. Discussion paper of the Research Unit Labour Market and Employment, Wissenschaftszentrum für Sozialforschung Berlin.

Schaede, U. (2000) The German financial system in 2000. *Harvard Business School Case Study 9–700–135*. Boston: Harvard Business School Publishing.

Shleifer A. and Vishny R.W. (1997) A survey of corporate governance. *Journal of Finance* 52(2), 737–783.

Schlie, E.H. and Warner, M. (2000) The 'Americanization' of German management. *Journal of General Management* 25(3), 33–49.

Seibert, U. (1997) Kontrolle und Transparenz im Unternehmensbereich (KonTraG): der Referenten-Entwurf zur Aktienrechtsnovelle. *Zeitschrift für Wirtschaftsund Bankrecht* 51(January), 1–48.

Streeck, W. (1992) On the institutional conditions of diversified quality production. In Streek, W. (ed.) *Social Institutions and Economic Performance*. London: Sage, 21–61.

Tam, O.K. (2002) Ethical issues in the evolution of corporate governance in China. *Journal of Business Ethics* 37, 303–320.

Tricker, B. (2009). *Corporate Governance: Principles, Policies, and Practices*. Oxford: Oxford University Press.

Tsai, K.S. (2004). *Back-Alley Banking: Private Entreprenuers in China.* Cornell University Press.

Vitols, S. (2001) Varieties of corporate governance: comparing Germany and the UK. In Hall. P.A. and Soskice, D. (eds) *Varieties of Capitalism*. Oxford: Oxford University Press.

Vitols, S. and Woolcock, S. (1997) Developments in the German and British corporate governance systems. Discussion paper, Workshop on Corporate Governance in Britain and Germany, Berlin, WZB.

Williams, A. (2000) Developments in corporate governance around the world. *Benefits & Compensation International* June, 3–9.

Williamson, E.O. (1996) *The Mechanism of Governance 11*, Oxford University Press.

Wood, D.J. (1991) Corporate social performance revisited. *Academy of Management Review* 16(4), 691–718.

Woolcock, S. (1996) Competition among forms of corporate governance in the European community: the case of Britain. In Berger, S. and Dore, R.(eds) *National Diversity and Global Capitalism*. London: Cornell University Press.

World Bank (2013) *Doing Business 2014: Understanding Regulations for Small and Medium-Size Enterprises.* Washington, DC: World Bank Group. License: Creative Commons Attribution CC BY 3.0.

Wymeersch, E. (1998) A status report on corporate governance rules and practices in some continental European states. In Hopt, K.J., Kanda, H., Roe, M.J., Wymeersch, E. and Prigge, S. (eds) *Comparative Corporate Governance*. Oxford: Oxford University Press.

Wymeersch, E. (2005) Implementation of corporate governance codes. In Hopt, K.J., Wymeersch, E., Kanda, H. and Baum, H. (eds) *Corporate Governance in Context: Corporations, States and Markets in Europe, Japan, and the US*. Oxford: Oxford University Press.

Yoshikawa, T., Tsui-Auch, L.S. and McGuire, J. (2007) Corporate governance reform as institutional innovation: the case of Japan. *Organization Science* 18(6), 973–988.

Zou, H. and Adams, M.B., (2008) Corporate ownership, equity risk and returns in People's Republic of China. *Journal of Business Studies*, 39, 1149–1168.

Zou, X.P., Pang, Y.X. and Zhu, H.L. (2012) The study between shadow banking and financial fragility in China: an empirical analysis based on the co-integration test and error correction model. *Quality & Quantity*, 1–8.

7 Managing resources: operations management

Learning objectives

By the end of this chapter you will be able to:

- understand the origin of the main production models
- explain the main differences between different operations systems
- critically assess the advantages and disadvantages of these models
- reflect on the societal effect of production systems and production management
- link human resource management and corporate governance to modes of production
- understand the concept of fit in the context of production models and operations management
- assess the possibilities of applying different production models within divergent societal contexts.

Chapter outline

7.1 Introduction

Most, if not all, textbooks on international business and management, leave out production management or operations management, as it is now called, to take account of value creation outside the narrower area of industrial production. This is strange, and it might reflect the illusions of a period in which strategy, finance, corporate governance and R&D were central and 'deindustrialization' and 'post-industrial' society were stylish. Nowadays, many older and former industrial countries are waking up from such illusions. Most of you will also have noticed that there are substantial differences in production systems and methods of production management between countries. This makes it necessary to give attention to such differences. A failure to understand them will lead to serious problems in multinational enterprises and in cross-national business dealings. We therefore deal with variations in patterns of work organization and control across societies.

While the superior efficiency of some production models has often been emphasized, it is now increasingly acknowledged that in order to be effective, there has to be some degree of fit between the production system and the societal environment (see e.g. Streeck, 1991). Hence there is, for instance, a large and successful population of medium-sized investment goods engineering firms in Germany, which were given less attention during the heyday of financialism but are coming back into the limelight after the 2007 economic crisis. In the UK and France, either large batch producers or defence, electronics and specialized 'high-tech' manufacturers are more competitive on a world scale (Sorge and Maurice, 1990). It had been argued that while Taylorism, or scientific-management, principles were once thought to represent the only efficient way of structuring work activities, they are now seen as historically and societally contingent patterns of work organization that depended on a number of circumstantial factors to become established in the USA, and that by no means dominated industrial organization in Europe. It is also apparent that Fordist production systems have had many variants and have not always proved as effective as some adherents claimed (Whitley, 1999: 88). Similarly, more recent modes of production, such as Japanese Toyotism, Swedish Uddevallaism and German diversified quality production – which are explained below – developed in specific societal contexts and, when applied elsewhere, had to be adapted to different societal circumstances.

Different operations systems are characterized by contrasting ways of work organization, organization structure, skill and knowledge requirements in jobs, methods of educating and training employees of all kinds, working careers, remuneration systems and employment relations. The societal context in which production systems develop explains why some production systems are characterized by quite different patterns in these fields and contribute to maintaining them. It can be seen that such patterns are specific to a certain society, prevailing without regard for different industrial goals and contexts (nature of products, production technology, size of units, dependence, regional location) (Sorge and Maurice, 1990: 142). Differences between US and German skills and practices, and managerial identities, for instance, reflect variations in labour market institutions, and educational and industrial relations systems, as well as general conceptions of professional expertise and status.

Drawing on societal differences, this chapter compares and contrasts the key differences in major production systems and management across four capitalist societies, and suggests how we might explain the prevalence or relative absence of particular kinds of production system. Such systems are very manifold, can to some extent be combined, and systems in real life are always intermediate expressions or combinations between stylized more ideal types. Here, we simplify the picture a bit by concentrating on more stylized types, in order to show how particular societal constellations encourage the development and reproduction of distinctive kinds of work organization and control. This chapter discusses the USA, Japan and Germany above all because their prevalent modes of operations management lend themselves better to a stylized treatment, against the background of distinctive institutions, and they have also been shown, with an emphasis varying according to period fashions, as examples of good practice.

Taylorism and Fordism developed within the US societal context and spread to Europe. Toyotism from Japan and diversified quality production from Germany were inspired by the flexible production of high-quality products. 'Flexibility' here means adjustment to customer-specific requirements, instead of production of standardized products or services. With the dissolution of the Taylorist–Fordist production systems of the older industrial countries of Europe and North America in the 1980s and 1990s, these flexible models were seen as the future production models. But at the same time, it could be seen that more standardized production moved to newly industrializing countries, so that it is safe to say that the share of different operations management models probably did not change very much in a world-wide perspective. It would be too easy to dismiss Taylorism and Fordism as purely historical because we do not see much of them around e.g. Europe any more. We would see more of them if we cared to look into the places in which our clothing is made in, for example, Bangladesh, or our electronic entertainment and communication equipment in a variety of Asian countries. And in Europe and North America, in the call centres that have spread in direct marketing and customer service systems, Taylorism has seen a revival.

The next section explains the key characteristics of production systems. This discussion is targeted at readers without a background in operations management or the sociology of work. Readers who know about production systems can immediately turn to the subsequent section. This provides an explanation of the connections between the features of the production systems that are described in the first section and the societal contexts in which these systems developed.

7.2 Characteristics and types of production system

Taylorism, or scientific management[1] (1890–1911)

At the turn of the nineteenth century, a US engineer and former worker called Frederick Taylor undertook the first systematic steps towards what he called scientific management. His ideas have remained highly influential up to the present day – albeit often in a vulgarized or adapted form – and they merit closer examination (Lane, 1989: 140). Based on his long experience as a worker, first-line supervisor and manager, Taylor made a distinction between what he termed the 'first-class man' and the 'average man'. In Taylor's view, a first-class man is highly motivated and pushes forward with his work rather than wasting time or restricting output. Ideally such men should be selected for the appropriate task and supported by management through financial incentives. In Taylor's experience, restriction of output was the norm in the many workshops he had encountered and he described the phenomenon as 'soldiering' (Sheldrake, 1996: 15). Taylor's response to these problems was the application of what he termed a 'systematic and scientific time study', breaking each job down into simple, basic elements and working out precisely what kinds of body movement were required by able workers to execute individual tasks in the shortest possible time without increasing the intensity of labour. Timings of the basic elements were then placed on file and, with appropriate weightings built in, used as the means to construct standard times for various jobs (ibid.). There was an extensive control of all aspects of production, including tooling, machines, materials, methods and job design, thus replacing worker knowledge by the expertise of experts controlling the worker (Sheldrake, 1996: 16).

'Central to Taylor's system was the desire to rationalize and standardize production techniques in the interests of the economy, efficiency and mutual prosperity' (Sheldrake, 1996: 23). Such concepts were also the epitomy of the 'American system of manufacture', thus called by its inventor Eli Whitney before Taylor. This took off in the manufacture of army rifles in Springfield, Ill., during the American Civil War: the practice of making standardized rifle parts was pioneered, thus eliminating the time and labour consuming 'adaptive machining' to make parts fit together, in assembling the rifle.

The technical setting of Taylor's writings is in 'metal-cutting', i.e. the turning, milling and grinding of metallic parts, which has been central in mechanical and parts of electrical engineering. But by analogy, it can be transferred to other work and operations. As Lane explains, Taylor's advocacy (though not invention) of the principle of maximum decomposition of work tasks implied the minimization of skill requirements – deskilling – in the resulting manual tasks, and it introduced two new kinds of division of labour. The first, and most insidious, is the separation of mental labour (or conception, planning of labour) from manual labour (or execution, doing); the second is the divorce of direct from indirect labour, i.e. the production tasks from those of setting up, preparation and maintenance (Lane, 1989: 141).

Taylor summed all of this up in three central principles:

1 the substitution of a science for the individual judgement of the workers;
2 the scientific selection and development of the worker, after each has been studied, taught and trained – instead of allowing the workers to select themselves in a haphazard way; and
3 the intimate cooperation of the management with the workers, so that they do the work together in accordance with the scientific laws that have been developed, instead of leaving the solution of each problem in the hands of the individual worker.

(Sheldrake, 1996: 18)

Taylorism claimed that expert knowledge of the technical means of production, coupled with time study and financial incentives, could substantially improve efficiency levels. Tayloristic forms of production management have gained huge increases in productivity, achieved, both directly and indirectly through enhanced control over the labour process. Taylor was aware that the greater the level of technical complexity, the greater the need for managerial control and the less autonomy required for the individual worker. Ironically, the greatest publicity has been given not to Taylor's management of the interface between complex technology and the worker, but to a situation of low technical complexity, in which the required competence of the worker is limited to brute strength and stamina (Sheldrake, 1996: 19).

Taylor's view of industrial work was combined with particular assumptions about human psychology and a particular approach to incentives (Sheldrake, 1996: 22). He argued that the goals of the worker had to be brought into line with the goals of the enterprise. This problem was to be solved by gearing the worker's wage to his production output through a system of incentive wages. Taylor believed in the natural laziness of workers and recommended close supervision throughout the work. Control of work is, of course, made easier by the fact that tasks are simple and contain no indeterminate 'mental labour' requirements. Secondly, Taylor postulated that individuals would be willing to work in this way if their pay was made to rise with the amount of effort they invested. Taylor thus propagated an exclusive emphasis on extrinsic rewards and speed, which implied a high degree of toleration of monotonous and meaningless activity (Lane, 1989: 141).

Taylorism spread from the USA all over the industrialized and industrializing world, and was widely accepted by European management from the 1930s onwards. However, the world-wide diffusion of Taylorism has not always entailed the adoption of all its elements and frequently involved a merging with elements of other management philosophies and/or techniques of work organization to suit specific national traditions or economic conditions (Lane, 1989: 142). A legitimate definition of Taylorism, therefore, should be precise and should include its main features in order to avoid confusion and dispute about the true nature of the system. The following criteria are widely accepted as a working definition of Taylorism:

- a high degree of decomposition of labour
- a low degree of worker discretion
- close task surveillance
- a minimum-interaction employment relationship, based only on the cash nexus.

Diffusion of Taylorism was aided by the internationalization of technology – which was usually accompanied by American management techniques, and by the spread of multinational companies (Lane, 1989: 144–145). Important to the widespread acceptance of Taylorism was the emergence of vast mass markets for industrial goods, in the more advanced industrial countries, from the 1930s onwards. The principles of Taylorism are, of course, particularly adapted to the production of large quantities of standardized and relatively cheap goods by special-purpose machinery (Lane, 1989: 145). However, often practices are called Taylorist although Taylor advocated something different; payment by results (bonus for completing a job faster than planned) is not Taylorist because Taylor advocated an 'objectively' fixed wage. Furthermore, full Scientific Management has never penetrated European societies to the same extent it did in the USA. It had to interact with, and adapt to, enterprise strategies (between customization, or adaptation to customer requirements, and standardization), managerial culture, industrial relations systems and, above all, the human resources of the labour force and the expectations of both managers and workers that resulted from them (Lane, 1989: 145; Wood, 1982).

Fordism, or mass production in assembly lines

Taylorist concepts had focused on the production of parts. That had left out the rationalization of the assembly of parts into a complex and complete product. Around 1914, Henry Ford's adaptation of Taylor's ideas to the assembly operations further intensified and spread the decomposition of labour and control over the speed of operations, which became dictated by a new machine. The machine was the mechanized assembly line, which mechanically moved the core of the car on a track, along which specialized workers mounted or inserted specific further parts at successive workstations, so that at the end of the line a finished car could roll off. Ford's system thus had mass production in the assembly, using special-purpose machinery and predominantly unskilled labour. This again had a logic of standardization and speed reduction, relying on economies of scale, capital intensity and labour productivity through routinization of decomposited jobs.

This new type of mass production reduced training and competence requirements for direct workers. Higher levels of production also made it more attractive to produce parts in-house instead of depending on external suppliers. There is, however, a downside to this approach. Lower levels of training of workers and routinization also invite greater opportunities for human error. The complexity of the production process increases as more items are manufactured in-house. To prevent errors from paralysing the entire operation, extra reserves are stockpiled that function as buffers between various departments. Similarly, parts from outside suppliers are stored to ensure a consistently available inventory of suitable quality (Dankbaar, 1995). When the number of extras and variants of cars increase, e.g. for reasons of marketing, the complexity and diseconomy of the system increases by leaps and bounds, with stores running over and highly specialized workers standing idle when they do not have to mount their specific part.

However, Ford was able to dominate what soon became the world's largest industry by becoming the first to master the principles of mass production, which made productivity increase immensely. 'Rather, it was the complete and consistent interchangeability of parts and the simplicity of attaching them to each other. These were the manufacturing innovations that made the assembly line possible' (Womack, Jones and Roos, 1991: 27).

Box 7.1 The main characteristics of craft production

- A workforce that is highly skilled in understanding the design of parts, machine set-up and operation, and fitting (putting together parts to form a sub-assembly). Most workers progressed through an apprenticeship or vocational school to a full set of craft skills. Many could hope to run their own machine shops, becoming self-employed contractors to assembler firms.
- Organizations that are decentralized and mostly have one location. The system is coordinated by an owner/entrepreneur in direct contact with everyone involved: customers, employers and suppliers.
- The use of general-purpose machine tools to perform drilling, grinding and other operations on metal and wood.
- A low production volume of products made in small batches, often according to customer-specific requirements or design specifications.

> The key to interchangeable parts, as we saw, lay in designing new tools that could cut hardened metal and stamp sheet steel with absolute precision. But the key to inexpensive interchangeable parts would be found in tools that could do this job at high volume with low or no set-up costs between pieces. That is, for a machine to do something to a piece of metal, someone must put the metal in the machine, then someone may need to adjust the machine. In the craft-production system – where a single machine could do many tasks but required lots of adjustment – this was the skilled machinist's job.
>
> (Womack, Jones and Roos, 1991: 35–36)

> Ford dramatically reduced set-up time by making machines that could do only one task a time. Then his engineers perfected simple jigs and fixtures for holding the work piece in this dedicated machine. The unskilled worker could simply snap the piece in place and push a button or pull a lever for the machine to perform the required task. This meant the machine could be loaded and unloaded by an employee with 5 minutes' training. In addition, Ford could place his machines in a sequence so that each manufacturing step led immediately to the next. . . . Because set-up times were reduced from minutes – or even hours – to seconds, Ford could get much higher volume from the same number of machines. Even more important, the engineers also found a way to machine many parts at once. The only penalty with this system was inflexibility. Changing these dedicated machines to do a new task was time-consuming and expensive.
>
> (Womack, Jones and Roos, 1991: 36)

As indicated, these dedicated machines allowed Ford to eliminate the skilled fitters who had always formed the bulk of every assembler's labour force. In fact, what had been a handicraft form of production was transformed into a series of divided, repetitive tasks marked by extremely restricted autonomy and great physical burden. Indeed, Ford not only perfected the interchangeable part, he perfected the interchangeable worker. Ford took Taylor's division of labour to its ultimate extreme. The skilled fitter in a craft production plant of 1908 had gathered all the necessary parts, obtained tools from the tool room, repaired them if necessary, performed the complex fitting and assembly job for the entire vehicle, then checked over his work before sending the completed vehicle to the shipping department.

> In stark contrast, the assembler on Ford's mass-production line had only one task – to put two nuts on two bolts or perhaps to attach one wheel to each car. He didn't order parts, procure his tools, repair his equipment, inspect for quality, or even understand what the workers on either side of him were doing.
>
> (Womack, Jones and Roos, 1991: 31)

> Someone, of course, did have to think about how all the parts came together and just what each assembler should do. This was the task for a newly created professional, the industrial engineer. Similarly, someone had to arrange for the delivery of parts to the line, usually a production engineer who designed conveyor belts or chutes to do the job. Housecleaning workers were sent around periodically to clean up work areas, and skilled repairmen circulated to refurbish the assemblers' tools. Yet another specialist checked quality. Work that was not done properly was not discovered until the end of the assembly line, where another group of workers was called into play – the rework men, who retained many of the fitters' skills.
>
> (Womack, Jones and Roos, 1991: 31)

> With this separation of labor, the assembler required only a few minutes of training. Moreover, he was relentlessly disciplined by the pace of the line, which speeded up the slow and slowed down the speedy. The foreman – formerly the head of a whole area of the factory with wide-ranging duties and responsibilities, but now reduced to a semiskilled checker – could spot immediately any slacking off or failure to perform

the assigned task. As a result, the workers on the line were as replaceable as the parts on the car.

(Womack, Jones and Roos, 1991: 31–32)

In this atmosphere, Ford took it as a given that his workers wouldn't volunteer any information on operating conditions – for example, that a tool was malfunctioning – much less suggest ways to improve the process. These functions fell respectively to the foreman and the industrial engineer, who reported their findings and suggestions to higher levels of management for action. So were born the battalions of narrowly skilled indirect workers – the repairman, the quality inspector, the housekeeper, and the rework specialist, in addition to the foreman and the industrial engineer. These workers hardly existed in craft production. . . . However, indirect workers became ever more prominent in Fordist, mass-production factories as the introduction of automation over the years gradually reduced the need for assemblers.

(Womack, Jones and Roos, 1991: 32)

Ford was dividing labor not only in the factory, but also in the engineering shop. Industrial engineers took their places next to the manufacturing engineers who designed the critical production machinery. They were joined by product engineers, who designed and engineered the car itself. But these specialists were only the beginning. Some industrial engineers specialized in assembly operations, others in the operation of the dedicated machines making individual parts. Some manufacturing engineers specialized in the design of assembly hardware, others designed the specific machines for each special part. Some product engineers specialized in engines, others in bodies, and still others in suspensions or electrical systems.

(Womack, Jones and Roos, 1991: 32)

These original "knowledge workers" – individuals who manipulated ideas and information but rarely touched an actual car or even entered a factory – replaced the skilled machine-shop owners and the old-fashioned factory foremen of the earlier craft era. Those worker-managers had done it all – contracted with assembler, designed the part, developed a machine to make it, and, in many cases, supervised the operation of the machine in the workshop. The fundamental mission of these new specialists, by contrast, was to design tasks, parts, and tools that could be handled by the unskilled workers who made up the bulk of the new motor-vehicle industry work force.

(Womack, Jones and Roos, 1991: 32–33)

In this system, the shop-floor worker had no assured career path, except perhaps to foreman. But the newly emerging professional engineers had a direct climb up the career ladder. Unlike the skilled craftsman, however, their career paths didn't lead toward ownership of a business. Nor did they lie within a single company, as Ford probably hoped. Rather, they would advance within their profession – from young engineer-trainee to senior engineer, who, by now possessing the entire body of knowledge of the profession, was in charge of coordinating engineers at lower levels. Reaching the pinnacle of the engineering profession often meant hopping from company to company over the course of one's working life.

(Womack, Jones and Roos, 1991: 32–33)

Flexible production

During the 1970s, the Western industrial world was characterized by a revolt against Taylorism and degrading work in mass production. However, it wasn't until the first half of the 1980s that the debate on new forms of production and work organization took a more dramatic turn in most advanced economies. The new developments in the organization of production in advanced societies not only called into question Taylorist practices of work organization but also presented a more comprehensive new industrial strategy in which a new approach to product markets had coalesced with the emergence of more sophisticated production technology and new forms of utilizing labour power (Piore and Sabel, 1984 as in Lane, 1989: 67). This new model of industrial production organization was called flexible specialization or flexible production. The new model seemed to be able to attain superior competitiveness in world markets through the sophisticated application of information technology, a diversified product range, and non-price-competitive marketing strategies, combining all these with high wages, skilled labour and a flexible, non-Taylorist organization of work.

The new strategy was a reaction to worldwide economic changes, which rendered problematic the old form of industrial development – mass production of standardized goods with the use of special-purpose machines and semi-skilled labour. As indicated, such production requires large and stable markets and, during the 1970s, various economic developments combined to undermine this stability. The most important of these was a shift in the international division of labour and world trade. The emergence of industrial economies in low-wage East and Southeast Asian and Latin American countries, which produced standardized goods cheaper than the advanced industrial countries, has forced the latter to reconsider their role in the international division of labour and to look for alternative markets. The production of specialized/ customized and/or high-quality goods, particularly producer goods, suggested itself as a new strategy. This also applied to home markets, where the demand for standardized goods was often saturated and where the development of more sophisticated tastes required more individualized goods as well as more frequent changes in product.

This changeover to a new market strategy was facilitated and stimulated – by the emergence of new technology (Lane, 1989: 164). Micro-electronics was one of the technical innovations to gain momentum in the 1970s, and the use of upgraded micro-electronic applications has become particularly widespread since the late 1970s. Since then, micro-electronic circuits have become increasingly integrated, information-processing time has been reduced, and the price of switching functions has fallen proportionally. Improved computer performance has led to the incorporation of computers in equipment, installations and machinery in order to expand, improve and accelerate processing capacity (Sorge, 1995: 270). Computerized equipment made production more flexible as it made possible the frequent conversion of machinery and its adaptation to the production of small batches and/or individual customized products at relatively low costs. It also made possible instant adjustments of machinery to changing market demands – hence the term 'flexible specialization' or 'flexible production' to characterize the new form of production. The computer-controlled machinery not only facilitated the production of specialized goods at greater speed but also at a higher degree of precision and thus to higher quality standards. In fact, products of a craft type could be produced at a similar speed and price as were standardized mass goods. Further advantages flowing from the new technology are that the shorter production runs commit less capital, and that its flexible nature, making the enterprise less dependent on large and stable markets, renders investment in machinery a less precarious matter.

In order to be able to analyse the alternative manufacturing policies that were enabled by the new technology three variables are important: the degree to which products are standardized, the type of competition they try to meet, and the volume of output. The first two factors appear to be closely related in that standardized products are generally sold in price-competitive markets, whereas customized products tend to be quality-competitive. This suggests a distinction between standardized price-competitive and customized quality-competitive production, on the one hand, and low- and high-volume production on the other. Crossing the two dimensions generates four alternative product or manufacturing strategies (as depicted in Figure 7.1), two of which – the low-volume production of customized quality-competitive goods ('craft' production) and the high-volume production of standardized price-competitive goods ('Fordist' production) – were quite conventional. With some simplification one could say that before the advent of micro-electronic technology, these would have been the only production patterns possible.

This simple picture, however, became considerably more complicated as a result of technical change. Among other things, new technology seemed to have lowered the break-even point of mass production, both enabling traditional mass producers to survive with shorter production runs and making it easier for artisanal low-volume producers to achieve economies of scale and enter mass-type markets. At the same time, the capacity of the new technology for fast and inexpensive retooling seemed to have made it attractive for small component producers dependent on large assemblers to differentiate their product range and move into an advanced form of craft production, so as to reduce their exposure to price fluctuations and monopsonistic demand (one buyer and many sellers).

The most important impact of the new technology on manufacturing strategy, however, seemed to be that it had created a new option for firms in the form of high-volume production of customized quality-competitive goods. In many manufacturing sectors, microelectronic circuitry in new machine control and planning systems had eroded the traditional distinction between mass and specialist production. The high flexibility of

Differentiation of output

Volume of output	Small Standardized Competitive prices	Large Customized Competitive quality
Small	Specialized component parts	Craft production
Large	Mass production ('Fordism')	Diversified quality production

Figure 7.1 Categorization of work systems.

Adapted from Sorge (1995).

micro-electronic equipment, and the ease and speed with which it can be reprogrammed enabled firms to introduce a hitherto unknown degree of product variety, as well as product quality. The result was a restructuring of mass production in the mould of customized quality production, with central features of the latter being blended into the former and with small-batch production of highly specific goods becoming enveloped in the large-batch production of basic components or models. This pattern was what came to be called diversified quality production. It can be approached by firms through two different paths of industrial restructuring: by craft producers extending their production volume without sacrificing their high-quality standards and customized product design, or by mass producers moving upmarket by upgrading their products' design and quality, and by increasing their product variety, in an attempt to escape from the pressures of price competition or from shrinking mass markets.

Flexible specialization or production also implied a new way of deploying labour. The operation of the more complex technology, and the frequent changes required, were more satisfactorily accomplished by the utilization of skilled labour and the organization of work along occupational lines. The Taylorist strategy of designing high-specialization/low-discretion jobs or work roles was replaced by seeking more overlap between specialisms and flexibility of deployment, linked with the exercise of 'craft' judgement and skill. Thus, polyvalency of skill was given particular emphasis in the new form of worker deployment. Workers were assigned more encompassing work tasks and enriched jobs, and they enjoyed greater autonomy and responsibility. By referring to Table 1.1 in Chapter 1, you will see that this is what basic organization theory would predict: a change from a more mechanistic organization to a more organic one, in line with the environmental and strategic changes mentioned above.

During the 1980s, when flexible specialization was in its developmental phase, scholars were already debating the feasibility of adopting these new technologies, and the new form of work organization they implied in all advanced societies. Some argued that only societies with a surviving craft tradition (i.e. a tradition relying on skilled, all-round workers, operating in a high-trust environment, free from detailed or continuous management control) would be able to successfully adopt the new form of work organization. They identified such remnants of a craft tradition in Germany, Italy and Japan, and saw the new production concept emerging mainly in these societies. In the USA and France, in contrast, they suggested, the extinction of this tradition, and the extant forms of union and state control, respectively, militate against the adoption of the strategy of flexible specialization (Piore and Sabel, 1984).

Flexible operations systems, whether they are in manufacturing or services, have been promoted on the basis of two main secular developments. One is the shift to more differentiated markets and innovation, which means a shift from mature products for which demand has started to decline, to new and more customized ones, and with the 'migration' of mass production activities to newly industrializing countries.

The other development consists of pressures on employers to 'humanize' work, meaning less monotony, less work stress and physical exertion, and increasing intrinsic challenges to workers, by job and work role enrichment, and by the formation of work teams and groups with a greater amount of autonomy in allocating specific tasks in the group or team. Such pressures were either presented directly by 'labour supply', i.e. through the preferences of people in taking up employment and positions; mainly in western Europe, despite international migration, it became more and more difficult to find suitably committed and able people to fill routine and stressful jobs. This was so, as could be expected, during the period of full employment until the 1970s which has been called 'the thirty glorious years' (*les trente glorieuses*) in France. Furthermore, owing to full employment, trade unions and local interest representatives of workers had become stronger, both in collective bargaining over wages and other conditions and politically.

This had led to major movements of 'job redesign'. One, the most extensive and long-lasting one, was the German 'work humanization programme' starting in the 1970s, involving governmental research, development and subsidies for experiments, in conjunction with organized employers and trade unions. This gave a boost to the wide-spread introduction of job-enriching, team-orientated and less hierarchically heavy forms of work organization and management, and it happened in many industries, from automobile manufacturing through electrical engineering industries down to the processing of forms in administrative functions in governmental and commercial services.

However, the most spectacular and symbolically visible movement happened in Sweden, where both the labour market background (full employment and wage increases) and the political circumstances were eminently in evidence: post-war Sweden was more or less run by a social democratic government, which was in turn run by a singularly centralized trade union movement pushing for wage equalization. Extensive job-redesign was the result. This led to a model stylized as *uddevallaism*, after an automobile manufacturing factory at Uddevalla in which it was pioneered.

The goal of this project was to organize production in tune with the requirements of a younger generation. Initial efforts at robotization were designed to eliminate the most tedious and dangerous tasks. Modifications were made to the principles of the assembly line – for instance, through experiments with semi-autonomous groups. Without doubt, it was in Sweden that this work was developed most resolutely and systematically (Boyer and Durand, 1997).

The Swedish car manufacturer Volvo was searching for an approach that differed from the international mainstream in that it intended to create a 'human' workplace. By the late 1980s, new solutions had materialized in a number of new facilities, with Volvo's Uddevalla plant being the prototype of the Swedish 'experiment in humanistic manufacturing' (Berggren, 1992: vii). The Uddevalla project began in 1985, the year in which Volvo was the world's most profitable car manufacturer. 'Sweden was in a period of intensive economic expansion, during which labour shortages were acute. At the same time, an extensive debate was taking place about repetitive strain injuries (RSIs) in industrial jobs. More broadly, there was renewed general interest in the reform of working life' (Berggren, 1992: 12). While different sections of the auto industry launched projects for change, Uddevalla had the most comprehensive and consistent ambitions. Small autonomous teams build complete cars (in ergonomically correct positions) in work cycles lasting several hours (a traditional assembly line has short work cycles, often lasting only minutes). The plant attracted wide public interest as an example of the most fundamental attempt so far to solve the problems of the auto industry: the inexorable rhythm of the line (with no opportunity to vary the pace), the overwhelming monotony and repetitiveness of the work, the heavy physical strain, the lack of free movement, and the difficulty of gaining a sense of purpose and meaning in the fragmented work process (ibid.).

The novelty of 'Uddevallaism' was that it combined small-scale assembly with a largely automated materials-handling process, a computer-integrated information system, a comprehensive development of new assembly tools, and significant new forms of vocational training (Berggren, 1992: 13). The plant's practices embodied a radical shift away from line assembly. Prominent and inspiring as the concept was, in its specific form it was not long-lasting. Today, it is more of a historical reminiscence than an established practice. What happened? First, the Swedish model of wage equalization and macro-economic management more or less broke down in 1990. The reason was that white-collar and managers' unions, separate from the main LO union confederation, bargained against wage equalization, which led to wage-price spirals and an excessive tax burden. Second, and partly as a reaction to the latter, Sweden entered the European Union and 'exported' a lot of large-scale manufacturing activities to other countries with lower wages. Well-known IKEA furniture, for example, despite the branded stylization of Swedish equality and comradeship at work, was increasingly manufactured in Eastern Europe, where Communist regimes could still guarantee low wages and capital costs for capitalist entrepreneurs. It is still mostly produced in Eastern Europe, adorned with the symbols of Swedish culture.

On a less spectacular level, however, flexible operations systems have profoundly taken root in both manufacturing and services. In car assembly, above all in the up-market segment, semi-autonomous teams have become the state of the art in the automobile industry. In various industries, operator responsibility for quality checks has become widespread. 'Empowerment' of ordinary workers and employees has become a buzzword but also a part of reality, meaning delegation of responsibilities. That may also mean increasing work pressure, which is not what the promoters of work humanization on the union side had had in mind. As flexible operations models became more common, they also lost a bit of their humanist tinge, which made the business logic of flexibility come out more strongly: augment yield in diversified quality operations, reduce stocks and inventories and work in progress, respond to marketing opportunities more rapidly and smoothly, reduce direct and (increasingly also) indirect labour costs, reduce labour turnover, improve the reliability of the organization through better communication. To this extent, flexible operations systems have come to overlap the features of the organizational model we come to next.

Lean production[2]

The widespread popularity of, as well as the many misconceptions regarding, lean production explain the amount of attention that is paid to the concept in this chapter. Forced by societal circumstances, Japanese producers were experimenting with flexible production techniques from the 1950s onwards. It all began when Eiji Toyoda, a young Japanese engineer from the Toyoda family, and Taiichi Ohno, his production genius, after a visit to a US Ford plant, realized that mass Fordist production could never work in Japan. The problems facing the Toyota company were as follows.

1. The domestic market was tiny and demanded a wide range of vehicles – luxury cars for government officials, large trucks to carry goods to market, small trucks for Japan's small farmers, and small cars suitable for Japan's crowded cities and high energy prices.
2. The native Japanese work force, as Toyota and other firms soon learned, was no longer willing to be treated as a variable cost or as interchangeable parts. What was more, the new labor laws introduced by the American occupation greatly strengthened the position of workers in negotiating more favourable conditions of employment. Management's right to lay off employees was severely restricted, and the bargaining position of company unions representing all employees was greatly reinforced. The company unions used their strength to represent everyone, eliminating the distinction between blue- and white-collar workers, and secured a share of company profits in the form of bonus payments in addition to basic pay. Furthermore, in Japan there were no

> "guest workers" (temporary immigrants) willing to put up with sub-standard working conditions in return for high pay, or ethnic minorities. In the West, by contrast, these individuals had formed the core of the work force in most mass-production companies.
>
> 3 The war-ravaged Japanese economy was starved for capital and for foreign exchange, meaning that massive purchases of the latest Western production technology were quite impossible.
>
> 4 The outside world was full of huge motor-vehicle producers who were anxious to establish operations in Japan and ready to defend their established markets against Japanese exports.
>
> (Womack, Jones and Roos, 1991: 49–50)

In order to become a full-range car producer with a variety of new models, Taiichi Ohno realized that neither Ford's tools and methods nor its craft production methods were suitable. He needed a new approach. From this tentative beginning was born what Toyota came to call the Toyota Production System and, ultimately, lean production. An important example, which demonstrates some lean production techniques, concerns the production of the different metal parts of a car from sheet steel. Mass producers of cars start with a large roll of sheet steel. They run this sheet through an automated 'blanking' press to produce a stack of blanks slightly larger than the final part they want. They then insert the blanks in massive stamping presses containing matched upper and lower dies. When these dies are pushed together under thousands of pounds of pressure, the two-dimensional blank takes the three-dimensional shape of a car fender or a truck door as it moves through a series of presses.

> The problem with this second method, from Ohno's perspective, was the minimum scale required for economical operation. The massive and expensive Western press lines were designed to operate at about twelve strokes per minute, three shifts a day, to make a million or more of a given part in a year. Yet, in the early days, Toyota's entire production was a few thousand vehicles a year.
>
> (Womack, Jones and Roos, 1991: 52)

'The dies could be changed so that same press line could make many parts, but doing so presented major difficulties' (Womack, Jones and Roos, 1991: 52). In order to avoid these problems, die changes were assigned to specialists. Die changes were undertaken methodically, and typically required a full day to go from the last part with the old dies to the first acceptable part from the new ones. Western manufacturers, selling a large enough volume, found that they could often 'dedicate' a set of presses to a specific part and stamp these parts for months, or even years, without changing dies.

Toyota's budget, however, was unable to finance the hundreds of stamping presses needed to make all the parts needed for the car and truck bodies. Its capital budget dictated that practically the entire car be stamped from a few press lines. This gave rise to the idea of developing simple die-change techniques and to change dies frequently – every 2 to 3 hours versus 2 to 3 months – using rollers to move dies in and out of position, and simple adjustment mechanisms. 'Because the new techniques were easy to master and production workers were idle during the die changes, Ohno hit upon the idea of letting production workers perform the die changes as well' (Womack, Jones and Roos, 1991: 52). After endless experiments, from the late 1940s onwards, Ohno eventually perfected his technique for quick changes. By the late 1950s, he had reduced the time required to change dies from a day to an astonishing 3 minutes and eliminated the need for die-change specialists. In the process he made an unexpected discovery – it actually cost less per part to make small batches of stampings than to run off enormous lots.

> There were two reasons for this phenomenon. Making small batches eliminated the carrying cost of the huge inventories of finished parts that mass-production systems required. Even more important, making only a few parts before assembling them into a car caused stamping mistakes to show up almost instantly. The consequences of this latter discovery were enormous. It made those in the stamping shop much more concerned about quality, and it eliminated the waste of large numbers of defective parts – which had to be repaired at great expense, or even discarded – that were discovered only long after manufacture.
>
> (Womack, Jones and Roos, 1991: 53)

However, while Toyota made having small or zero inventories a priority and thus chose to concentrate on small-batch manufacturing, the objective was still similar to that of mass production: to produce the highest possible cumulative volume of each product. Long total runs were (and are) decisive for the careful preparation of the manufacture of each part; standardizing tools, methods and operations; streamlining suppliers; and developing the just-in-time (JIT) flow. The Toyota system is the antithesis of large-batch manufacturing, very much reducing the number of identical pieces made in one production run with the same tools, dies and programme. Flexibility is a matter of switching quickly between a number of models or parts, implying retooling from model A to model B. The high frequency of such switching in the Toyota system has also meant that 'resetting work' could itself be standardized and intensified. It has become part of the highly rationalized system of high volume production. The Toyota system's flexibility has therefore been argued to represent an extension of the sphere of influence of scientific management (Berggren, 1992: 28–29).

In contrast to large-batch mass production, however, in order to make the small-batch system work – a system that ideally produced 2 hours or less of inventory – an extremely skilled and highly motivated workforce was needed. See Table 7.1 for a contrast between mass and lean production. If workers failed to anticipate problems before they occurred, and didn't take the initiative to devise solutions, the work of the whole factory could easily grind to a halt. Holding back knowledge and effort – repeatedly noted by industrial sociologists as a salient feature of all mass-production systems – would swiftly lead to disaster in Toyota. As indicated, labour conditions had changed in Japan after the Second World War; strong unions combined with severe restrictions on the ability of company owners to fire workers led to protracted negotiations between unions and owners at many plants, including Toyota. These negotiations resulted in the development of a compromise that, to a large extent, remains the formula for labour relations in the Japanese auto industry today. Specifically, employees were granted lifetime employment and seniority pay, and often received access to company facilities such as housing, recreation, and so forth (see Chapter 5 for a full explanation). In return, the company expected that most employees would remain with the company for their entire working lives. The employees also agreed to be flexible in work assignments and active in promoting the interests of the company by initiating improvements rather than merely responding to problems.

Table 7.1 Lean and mass production systems compared

	Lean system	*Mass system*
Type of production	Small-batch flexible mass production	Large-batch mass production
Complexity	Low • elimination of waste in structure • fewer functional hierarchical levels	High • allows complex and redundant structure • more hierarchical levels and more differentiated divisions
Formalization	Low • emphasis on teamwork • flexible job responsibilities • encourages multiple job skills and expertise	High • communication and decision-making is based on strict vertical individual command chain • discourages participation from lower-level employees or lateral-level co-workers
Centralization	Low • lateral communication is encouraged and decisions are made collectively on a team basis • encourages participation from lower-level employees and lateral-level co-workers	High • communication and decision-making is based on strict vertical individual command chain • discourages participation from lower-level employees or lateral-level co-workers
Problem-solving attitude	Proactive • workers actively search for problems • workers are trained to tackle problems	Reactive • workers wait passively for problems to happen • workers are trained to pass rather than to tackle problems

Source: adapted from Zhiang Lin and Chun Hui (1999).

This new approach to human capital allowed Toyota to eliminate other types of waste (muda) that characterized mass production (wasted effort, materials and time). At Toyota it was thought that assembly workers – instead of performing one or two simple tasks, repetitively as in mass production – could probably do most of the functions of the Fordist specialists and do them much better because of their direct acquaintance with conditions on the line. Toyota started to group workers in teams with a team leader rather than a foreman. 'The teams were given a set of assembly steps, their piece of the line, and told to work together on how best to perform the necessary operations. The team leader would do assembly tasks as well as coordinate the team, and, in particular, would fill in for any absent worker – concepts unheard of in mass-production plants' (Womack, Jones and Roos, 1991: 56). The team was also given the job of housekeeping, minor tool repair and quality checking. Finally, once the teams were running smoothly, time was set aside periodically for them to suggest ways of improving the process. This continuous, incremental improvement process (kaizen) took place in collaboration with the industrial engineers, who were still present but in much smaller numbers than in the mass-production plants (ibid.).

In striking contrast to the mass-production plant (where stopping the line was the responsibility of the senior line manager), to eliminate the passing on of errors until the end of the line, in the Toyota plant a cord was placed above every workstation and workers were instructed to stop the whole assembly line immediately if a problem emerged that they couldn't fix. Then, the whole team would come over to work on the problem. It was reasoned that the mass-production practice of simply passing on errors in order to keep the line running caused errors to multiply endlessly. Because problems would not be discovered until the very end of the line, a large number of similarly defective vehicles would have been built before the problem was discovered.

In American mass-production plants, problems tended to be treated as random events. The idea was to repair each error and hope that it didn't recur. Toyota, however, instituted a system of problem-solving, which taught production workers to systematically trace every error back to its ultimate cause, then to devise a fix, so that it would not occur again. After a while the result was that the line practically never stopped, the amount of rework needed before shipment fell continually and the quality of the shipped cars improved steadily. This was for the simple reason that quality inspection, no matter how diligent, simply cannot detect all the defects that can be assembled into complex vehicles. A major strength of the lean production system is the lean supply chain. The task of a final assembly plant, which assembles the major components into a complete vehicle, accounts for only 15 per cent of the total manufacturing process.

> The bulk of the process involves engineering and fabricating more than 10,000 discrete parts and assembling these into perhaps 100 major components – engines, transmissions, steering gears, suspensions, and so forth. Coordinating this process so that everything comes together at the right time with high quality and low cost has been a continuing challenge to the final assembler firms in the auto industry.
>
> (Womack, Jones and Roos, 1991: 58)

While Ford's initial answer to this problem was complete vertical integration, after the Second World War, the company disintegrated to 50 per cent. The world's mass-production assemblers ended up adopting widely varying degrees of formal integration, ranging from about 25 per cent in-house production at smaller specialist firms (i.e. Porsche and Saab) to 70 per cent at General Motors. The central engineering staffs of mass-production assemblers such as Ford and GM designed most of the parts needed in a vehicle and the component systems they comprised. A number of suppliers – whether formally part of the assembler firm or independent businesses – were given the drawings and were asked for bids on a given number of parts. Among all the outside firms and internal divisions that were asked to bid, the lowest bidder got the business. In general, success depended on price, quality and delivery reliability, and the car makers often switched business between firms at relatively short notice.

At Toyota, it was found that the real question was not the make-or-buy decisions that occasioned so much debate in mass-production firms, but rather how the assembler and the suppliers could work together smoothly to reduce costs and improve quality, whatever formal, legal relationship they might have. The solution to this problem was found in taking a new, lean production approach to components supply. The first step was to organize suppliers into functional tiers. First-tier suppliers were responsible for working as an integral part of the product-development team in developing a new product – for instance, a steering, braking or electrical system that would work in harmony with the other systems. Toyota stimulated cooperation among its first-tier suppliers in order to improve the design process.

> Because each supplier, for the most part, specialized in one type of component and did not compete in that respect with other suppliers in the group, sharing information was comfortable and mutually beneficial. Then, each first-tier supplier formed a second tier of suppliers under itself. Companies in the second tier were assigned the job of fabricating individual parts. These suppliers were manufacturing specialists, usually without much expertise in product engineering but with strong backgrounds in process engineering and plant operations.
>
> (Womack, Jones and Roos, 1991: 60–61)

Second-tier suppliers were also grouped into supplier associations to exchange information on advances in manufacturing techniques.

Such a high degree of cooperation and information sharing cannot be obtained through marketplace relationships, and Toyota did not wish to vertically integrate its suppliers into a single, large bureaucracy. 'Instead, Toyota spun its in-house supply operations off into quasi-independent first-tier supplier companies in which Toyota retained a fraction of the equity and developed similar relationships with other suppliers who had been completely independent. As the process proceeded, Toyota's first-tier suppliers acquired much of the rest of the equity in each other' (Womack, Jones and Roos, 1991: 61). Toyota also encouraged its suppliers to perform work for other assemblers, and for firms in other industries, because outside business almost always generated higher profit margins. Toyota also shared personnel with its supplier-group firms in two ways. 'It would lend them personnel to deal with workload surges, and it would transfer senior managers not in line for top positions at Toyota to senior positions in supplier firms' (Womack, Jones and Roos, 1991: 61).

Case: Japanese production practices in China[3]

China has become an increasingly important destination for Japanese foreign direct investment. China is second only to the USA as a location for Japanese overseas investment. Moreover, Japan is the second largest inward investor to China, behind the quasi-overseas Hong Kong and Taiwan. The question to be answered in this context is to what extent Japanese production management techniques have been transferred to Japanese plants in China. The societal arguments of similarities in the social relationships of work tend to indicate that the 'process of Japanization' should be much easier in Asia than in Western countries.

In order to evaluate this question, 20 Japanese manufacturing plants based in China were investigated. Of the 20 plants, 12 were located in Guangdong Province and four each in Nantong and Tianjin. Categorized by industry, there were eight chemical-related plants, seven consumer-electrical, four apparel and one machining (auto parts) factory. Japanese investors held majority share ownership in over half the plants. The average age of the plants was a little over 5 years, with the oldest 14 years old and the youngest only 1 year old. The primary objective for 13 of the Japanese firms setting up manufacturing operations in China was to take advantage of cheap land, labour and raw material costs. This was especially evident in Guangdong Province. In five cases, proximity to Hong Kong was a major objective and, in four, it was access to China's growing market.

In half of the cases, the Chinese partner was a government agency and/or a state-owned enterprise. For the Chinese partners the transfer of hard technology and modern 'capitalist' management systems was of primary importance. In three cases, the Chinese managers also considered employment opportunities and stimulation of international competitiveness as being important in cooperating with the Japanese.

The plants generally had only a few (three to six) Japanese personnel members on site. There were two exceptions to this: one where a plant had 150 Japanese and over 3000 local staff making precision electronic goods and CD drives, and another employing over 8000 locals and about 70–80 Hong Kong and Japanese staff, which made earphones, speakers and similar audio products. Both these product lines required a reasonably high degree of technical support in order to ensure such processes as quality management and machine maintenance. At least one more firm also required such high-level quality assurance, but this was achieved by other means. With respect to production technology, it was found that, in half the cases, most of the machinery was imported from Japan. In general, the plants in China had more or less the same physical sort of factories as would be found in Japan, though sometimes on a smaller scale.

With respect to production and inventory management, however, there were significant differences between plants in China and those in Japan. In Japan, production varies according to consumer demand. At its most sophisticated, JIT production allows output to correspond to final demand through a system of pulling production through the factory, significantly reducing the need for inventories. In addition, the ultimate in lean arrangements allows multi-skilled workers to work on a range of products in short runs so as to rapidly match market demands, leading to mixed production, which has been regarded as a key feature of JIT.

In eight Chinese plants, there was no variation at all in production output over a year. These firms included five chemical and three electronics plants, the latter being two component suppliers to Japan and one electronics multinational producing facsimile machines for export. Among these plants, only two held very low levels of stock of finished goods on-site. This reflects highly predictable production output rather than the achievement of JIT production. The other 12 firms coped with fluctuations in product demand primarily through traditional techniques of either producing for stock or varying working time. Five plants, mainly labour-intensive apparel, leather products and electronics manufacturers coped with variations in product demand by using overtime work. The other seven firms, including leather goods producers, three chemical firms and two electronics plants (making laser pitches and stereos), employed temporary workers at peak times. Other plants tried to maintain steady production, sometimes despite seasonal variations in demand. Thus, stocks were accumulated either to maximize machine utilization or in order to preserve regularity in plant operations, large variations in activity being seen as disruptive to work routines.

Another aspect of Japanese production techniques – that is, frequent and fast changes in production runs, requiring workers to have knowledge of various types of product – was also applied only marginally. While all 20 firms had some kind of variation in their product lines over time, this was usually limited to workers having no more than one product change a day or three a week. Moreover, these changes in products usually had minimal impact on line workers' jobs. In chemical production, changeovers took much longer than in, say, electronics, resulting in production-line stoppages of hours at a time. Consequently, the notions of flexible and mixed production were not really applied, the costs of 'retooling' far outweighing any benefits from lower stockholding.

Chinese employees pointed to Japanese workers' excessive attention to detail. Such detail included ascertaining and reducing rejection rates from individuals and machines, regulating 'wasted time' from toilet breaks down to machine set-ups, as well as frequent management meetings to review and plan. Japanese management, on the other hand, was frustrated by the lack of urgency or seriousness that the Chinese workers applied to this 'attention to detail'; a reflection of the apparent Chinese lack of interest in Japanese efforts towards continuous improvement.

Japanese firms are also well known for the quality of their products, brought about in large part by the efforts of shop-floor workers, whether this involvement is voluntary or coerced, or a combination of the two. What is seen as distinctive about Japanese quality management is the organization of shop-floor employees so that they are involved in continuous quality control and quality improvement. In China, all 20 firms were submitted to the strict quality management measures being introduced by the Japanese. However, quality control was in the hands of Japanese experts, and involved multiple checking, goods inward and outward checks, and checks at various stages of production. Moreover, the Japanese concern with quality was backed with incentive pay schemes that took account of rejects attributed to individual workers. Thus, strong pressure from material incentives was placed on workers to conform to quality standards, with hardly any inculcation of quality consciousness among Chinese workers. In two firms, the work group rather than the individual was held accountable for quality targets, so that the group's bonus was dependent on each individual's performance. Thus, on the whole, there was little evidence that sufficient concern was given to incorporating workers' intrinsic motivation towards developing a consciousness of quality.

Questions

1 What does the case tell you about the transferability of Japanese production techniques to China?
2 Explain how, if at all, the Japanese firms adapted their techniques to the Chinese environment?
3 Assess how far differences between Japan and China related to culture, institutions, and the task environment and company strategy, play a role in the case.

Finally, to coordinate the flow of parts within the supply system on a day-to-day basis, the famous just-in-time (JIT) system, known as kanban at Toyota, was developed. The idea behind it was to simply convert a vast group of suppliers and parts plants into one large 'machine', like Ford's plant, by dictating that parts would only be produced at each step to supply the immediate demand of the next step; the mechanism was the containers carrying parts to the next step. As each container was used up, it was sent back to the previous step, and this became the automatic signal to make more parts. This simple idea was enormously difficult to implement as it eliminated practically all inventories and meant that when one small part of the vast production system failed, the whole system came to a standstill (Womack, Jones and Roos, 1991: 62).

While lean production represents a major advance in productivity, work pressure didn't seem to have changed much from the classical Fordist system. Although the routineness of work had been reduced, the rhythm and pace of the work on the assembly line is more inexorable under the Japanese management system than it was before. Off-line jobs, such as those in subassembly (the senior workers' favourite positions, in which a personal work pace was possible) have been outsourced or are geared strictly to the main line by means of JIT control. Idle time is squeezed out of each workstation through the application of kaizen techniques, while work pressure has been intensified and staffing drastically reduced in the name of eliminating all 'waste' (muda) (Berggren, 1992: 5–6). The combined JIT and quality pressure (zero defects) of the modern 'Japanized' lines demand a high degree of mental concentration on work that is still very standardized. Acquiescent unions and highly dependent workers who submit to the relentless demands explain that, until the late 1980s, Japanese auto makers had never had to confront and change the character of the work itself (Berggren, 1992: 6).

From the early 1990s onwards, as the Japanese labour market pool has declined in size, criticism of the industrial conditions, the long working hours and the trying physical environment have become widespread. Manufacturing firms have been encountering mounting recruitment difficulties, and there has been a soaring turnover among newly hired employees. It seemed, then, that the prescription of some (i.e. Womack, Jones and Roos, 1991) that the West must adopt the Japanese production system was at odds with the debate in Japan in the 1990s. In fact, many of the demands raised in the Japanese debate were strikingly similar to the goals of the Swedish work reforms, which were applied from the mid-1980s onwards (see below) and, more generally, to the European human-centred concept of work reform.

7.3 Operations systems and the societal environment[4]

From the 1980s onwards, there has been wide acceptance of the argument that production systems cannot operate in isolation from the rest of the society. They originate and can only be maintained with the support of institutions and culture that are societal, rather than only organizational. The emergence and stability of production systems are dependent on their compatibility with society-wide social relations: employment relations, competence formation, and in fact most of the other societal spaces mentioned in Chapters 1 and 4. Clearly, the skills of workers have to be acquired either within schools and training institutes or on the job within the firm. The pay system and the nature of the hierarchy within the firm are influenced by the style of employment relations and the stratification of competencies and rewards in society. Conceptions about fairness necessarily interfere with the internal management and influence income differentials across skill levels, firms or regions. Even the organization of capital markets must be considered. Some mass-production and continuous process industries require such a vast amount of capital that the very characteristics of financial intermediation play an important role in the viability of any production system. The state or corporatist associations and organizations delivers some general preconditions for productive efficiency to prosper: clear rules of the game concerning property rights, but also labour law, international trade, access to knowledge, and so on. We could call this complementarity between private management tools and their embeddedness into more general, society-wide relationships a societal system of production.

A societal system of production is a complex configuration of inter-linked institutions: the internal structure of the firm along with the society's industrial relations, the training system, the relationships with competing firms, their suppliers and distributors, the structure of capital markets, the nature of state intervention and conceptions of social justice (Boyer and Hollingsworth, 1997: 2). Given these complementarities at each period and for a given society, there exist a limited number of such societal systems of production. A society may indeed have more than one societal system of production; Italy has become famous for being divided into three societal systems of production: large and concentrated firms in the North, a dependent state-subsidized economy in the *mezzogiorno* (south of Rome, more or less), and the 'third Italy' of networked and regionally clustered small and medium-sized firms. On the other hand, one generally imposes its flavour, constraints and opportunities on other production systems. This is the dominant societal system of production. This is tuned to the core societal institutions concerning employment, finance and state intervention, and it is more involved with an international regime. While there is considerable variability in the way production is organized within a particular society, that variability generally exists within the broad parameters of a single societal system of production (Boyer and Hollingsworth, 1997).

Before going further, it is important to see that any coherent societal system of production, even if it is very coherent indeed, by necessity generates a dialectical internal variety. Consider the stylized case of mass production car manufacturing. As explained, this works with dedicated machinery, specifically and often individually developed and made for a particular machining, welding, assembly, painting etc. problem. Developing and making this sort of machinery now requires the very opposite of the characteristics of mass production: skilled and responsible shop-floor workers working together with planning and development engineers, and indeed often becoming engineers in their career; organic work organization rather than a mechanistic one; and other features of the more artisanal workshop as opposed to the large factory floor. There cannot be any mass production without more artisanal machine tool, transfer line, robot etc. manufacturers. This opposition is dialectical because it is not just accidental, but one requires the opposite to be able to exist – the usual combination of opposite logics: conflict and tension between the governing principles, but complementarity of the principles at the same time.

The following discussion includes the institutional configurations of the societal systems of mass and flexible production. Lean production and diversified quality production are included as examples or variants of flexible production. Then, we have the institutional configuration of the US societal system of production, one that has, historically, been embedded in a societal system of mass standardized production. Largely for this reason its economic actors find it difficult to mimic the practices and performance of their Japanese and German competitors. This demonstrates how a society's societal system of production limits its capacity to compete in certain industrial sectors, but enhances its competitiveness in others.

Mass standardized societal systems of production

Not just any country could have a mass standardized production system as its dominant form of production. For such a social system to be dominant, firms have to be embedded in a particular environment, one with a particular type of employment relations system, education system and financial markets, one in which a market mentality is very pervasive, and the dominant institutional arrangements for coordinating a society's economy tend to be markets, corporate hierarchies and a state that leaves a whole range of things unregulated although – note again the dialectical counterpoint – it is very strict and fierce about some things, such as tax evasion in the USA. Firms that successfully employ a mass-production strategy have to use specific types of machinery – that is, special-purpose machines – and relate in particular ways to other firms in the manufacturing process. Firms engaged in mass standardized production require large, stable and relatively well-defined markets for products that are essentially low in their rate of technological change (see Table 7.2).

Table 7.2 A typology of societal systems of production

Variables	*Mass standardized production*	*Flexible production*
Work skills	Narrowly defined and very specific in nature	Well-trained, highly flexible and broadly skilled workforce
Institutional training facilities	Public education emphasizing low level of skills	Greater likelihood of strong apprenticeship programmes linking vocational training and firms
Investment in work skills by firm	Low	High
Labour–management relations	Low trust between labour and management; poor communication and hierarchical in nature	Relatively high degree of trust
Industrial relations	Conflictual labour–management relations	High social peace between labour and management
Internal labour market	Rigid	Flexible
Work security	Relatively poor security	Long-term employment, relatively high job security
Relationship with other firms	Highly conflictual, rather impoverished institutional environment	
Collective action	Trade associations poorly developed and where in existence are lacking in power to discipline members	
Modes of capital formation	Capital markets well developed; equities are highly liquid	
Anti-trust legislation	Designed to weaken cartels and various forms of collective action	
Type of civil society in which firms are embedded	Weakly developed	Highly developed
Degree of pervasiveness of market mentality of society	High	Low

Source: adapted from Hollingsworth (1997: 274–275).

> Because specific purpose machines are geared to relatively stable markets for those that buy them, firms either engaged in backward integration or were in a strategic position to force their suppliers to invest in complementary supplies and equipment. Once firms announced their need for specific types of parts, suppliers had to produce at very low costs or lose their business. Over time, those firms that excelled in mass production tended to develop a hierarchical system of management, to adopt strategies of deskilling their employees, to install single-purpose, highly specialized machinery, and to engage in arm's-length dealings with suppliers and distributors based primarily on price. In the long run, the more a firm produced some standardized output, the more rigid the production process became – e.g. the more difficult it was for the firm to produce anything that deviated from the programmed capacity of its special purpose machines. On the other hand, such firms were extraordinarily flexible in dealing with the external labor market. As employees in firms engaged in standardized production had relatively low levels of skill, one worker could easily be exchanged for another. Management had little incentive to engage in long-term contracts with their workers or to invest in the skills of their employees.
>
> (Hollingsworth, 1997: 269)

> As mass production was been developed in the USA, it should come as no surprise that historians found that US schools were historically integrated into a societal system of mass standardized production and that the education system was vocationalized. In such a system, schools for most of the labor force tended to emphasize the qualities and personality traits essential for performing semi-skilled tasks: punctuality, obedience, regular and orderly work habits.
>
> (ibid.: 270)

> Hogan argues that schools in a social system of mass production provide skills that are less technical than social and are less concerned with developing cognitive skills and judgments than attitudes and behavior appropriate to mass production organizations and their labor process.
>
> (ibid.: 271)

> Because labor markets in such a system were segmented, however, educational systems also tended to be segmented, but intricately linked with one another. Thus, such a system also had some schools for well-to-do children that emphasized student participation and less direct supervision by teachers and administrators.
>
> (ibid.: 270)

Where societal systems of mass standardized production have been highly institutionalized, such as in the USA, the financial markets have also been highly developed. Large firms in such a system – in comparison with those in other societies – have tended to expand from retained earnings or to raise capital from the bond or equity markets, but less frequently from bank loans.

> Once financial markets become highly institutionalized, securities become increasingly liquid. And the owners of such securities tend to sell their assets when they believe their investments are not properly managed. Since management embedded in such a system tends to be evaluated very much by the current price and earnings of

> the stocks and bonds of their companies, it has a high incentive to maximize short-term considerations at the expense of long-term strategy.
>
> (Hollingsworth, 1997: 271)

See Chapter 6 for an extended explanation of such strategic and corporate governance aspects, and recall the basics of VoC and BSys institutionalist approaches in Chapter 4.

> [The] short-term horizon limits the development of long-term stable relations between employers and employees – a prerequisite for a highly skilled and broadly trained workforce. Instead, the short-term maximization of profits means that firms in a societal system of mass standardized production tend to be quick to lay off workers during an economic downturn, thus being heavily dependent on a lowly and narrowly skilled workforce.
>
> (Hollingsworth, 1997: 271)

Societal systems of flexible production

Flexible production makes use of more easily convertible resources, so that a system of production can flexibly adapt to different and shifting market demands. It relates to an ever-changing range of goods with customized designs to appeal to specialized tastes (Hollingsworth, 1997: 272). Similar to the argument for mass production, not all countries can have flexible production as their dominant societal form of production. Moreover, because the institutional arrangements of each social system of flexible production depend on complementary arrangements in other spaces and domains, they are not easily transferable from one society to another.[5] Societies with societal systems of flexible production tend to have most, if not all, of the following characteristics, all of which are mutually reinforcing (see also Table 7.2):

- An employment relation and a competence generation system that promote continuous learning, broad skills, work-force participation in production decision-making, being perceived by employees to be fair and just.
- Less hierarchical and less compartmentalized arrangements within firms, thus enhancing communication and flexibility.
- A rigorous education and training system for labor and management, both within and outside firms.
- Well-developed institutional arrangements to facilitate cooperation among competitors.
- Long-term stable relationships with high levels of communication and trust, of producers with both suppliers and customers.
- A system of financing that permits firms to engage in long-term strategic planning, limiting dependence on volatile stock markets.

(ibid.: 277)

In contrast to mass standardized production, flexible production requires workers to have high levels of skills, who can implement and adapt plans and instructions according to a professional understanding. This means that there is not the close work supervision that firms in mass production have. Because of the need to adapt production strategies quickly, management must be able to depend on employees to assume initiative, to integrate an analysis of tasks with execution, and to interpret guidelines independently to come up with solutions considered sensible.

> A key indicator for the development of such a system of flexible production in a society is its employment and industrial relations system. For workers with transferable skills that are useful not in an individual firm and on a wider market require some form of assurance that they will not be dismissed from their jobs. Job security is also necessary in the interest of employers, in order to have sufficient incentives to make long-term investments in developing the skills of their workers.
>
> (ibid.: 272–273)

Firms with flexible production are usually more specialized and less vertically integrated than those in mass production. As a result, such firms must be in close technical contact with other firms. To employ technologies of flexible production effectively, management must be willing

> to cooperate and have trusting relationships with their competitors – to some extent at least – suppliers, customers, and workers. But the degree to which these trust relationships can exist depends on the institutional and the cultural environment in which firms are embedded. Firms in flexible production are embedded in institutions that promote long-term cooperation between labor and capital, and between firms and suppliers. Markets are less impersonal and behaviour in them more limited by trust-based norms. The collective organization of both employers and workers facilitates cooperation among competitors.
>
> (ibid.: 273)

> The economic importance of such institutional arrangements for rich and long-term relationships between labor and capital, and among suppliers, customers, competitors, governments, universities, and/or banks is that they link economic actors enjoying and producing high levels of mutual trust. They also combine different knowledge bases with greater ease, such as mechanics and electronics. The ability to combine knowledge bases is important when technology and knowledge become very complex and change rapidly.
>
> (ibid.: 273)

For a societal system of flexible production to thrive, firms must be embedded in a community, region or country in which many other firms share similar forms of production. Firms that adhere to the principles of such a societal system of production over long periods of time tend to do so either because of communitarian obligations or institutional constraints.

> For a social system to sustain itself, firms must invest in a variety of redundant capacities. Redundant capacities are not used at all times but available at exactly the moment they are needed. Such redundancies are only in reserve if firms are embedded in associative organizations, or when the state requires such investments. Firms acting voluntarily and primarily from a sense of a highly rational calculation of their investment needs are unlikely to develop such redundant capacities. Firms in flexible production require a workforce that is broadly and highly skilled, and capable of shifting

> from one task to another and of constantly learning new skills. Broad competence implies an element of redundancy by itself. . . . But firms that are excessively rational in assessing their needs for skills are likely to proceed very cautiously in their skill investments; in such firms, accountants and cost benefit analysis are likely to insist that only those investments be made that will yield predictable rates of return in the short term.
>
> (ibid.: 276)

In a world of rapidly changing technologies and product markets, firms that invest only in those skills for which there is a demonstrated need are likely to find they have skills shortages. Under market and technical change, excessively rational economic thinking along the principles inherent in a social system of mass production may well result in poor economic performance. Thus, firms in flexible production require excess or redundant investments in work skills, and can sustain this over time if they are embedded in a social system that has highly developed collective forms of behaviour, encouraging a long-term perspective.

> Another redundant investment – one that is complementary – involves efforts to generate social peace. High quality and flexible production persist if there is social peace between labor and management. The maintenance of peace is costly, and it is impossible for cost analysts to demonstrate how much investment is needed in order to maintain a high level of social peace. Thus, just as highly rational managers are tempted to invest less in skills than will be needed over the longer term, so also they tend to underinvest in those things that lead to social peace. But for a firm to have a sufficient supply of social peace when needed, it must be willing to incur high investments in social peace when it does not appear to need it. In this sense, investment in and cultivation of social peace create a redundant resource which is exposed to the typical hazards of excessive rationality and short-term opportunism.
>
> (ibid.: 277)

> Investment in such redundant capacities (transferable skills and social peace) requires long-term employment relationships. While firms may develop such capacities voluntarily and for themselves, such individualistic voluntarism is less effective and less common than when it is socially imposed by compulsory arrangements, which imply institutionalized obligations. Social systems of mass standardized production represent a social order based on contractual exchanges between utility-maximizing individuals, and most firms in such systems underinvest in the skills of their workers and in social peace. Social systems of flexible production require cooperative relations and communitarian obligations among firms, which make available collective inputs that firms would not enjoy or produce based purely on a rational calculation of a firm's short-term economic interests.
>
> (ibid.: 277)

The societal system of lean production

As explained in the first section of this chapter, Japanese lean production involves a small-batch flexible mass-production system and, hence, is based on flexible production techniques. As a consequence, most of the societal features that support the development of flexible production as the dominant societal system (mentioned in Table 7.2) also support the development of lean production systems. One of the most important features of the Japanese societal system of production, from which many have been derived and which contributes to the development of flexible production systems, is the distinctiveness of Japan's capital markets (Hollingsworth, 1997: 279). As discussed at length in Chapter 6, Japanese firms have long been dependent on outside financiers for capital, such as the main banks and the large firms and banks of the major financial groups. These relationships are strengthened by cross-ownership and interlocking directorships. This kind of mutual stockholding obviously diversifies risk and buffers firms from the uncertainties of labour and product markets (ibid.).

> The extensive cross-company pattern of stock ownership in Japan is an important reason why Japanese firms can forsake short-term profit maximization in favor of a strategy of long-term goals. This is very much in contrast with the pressures on American managers to maximize short-term gains. Moreover, the patterns of inter-corporate stockholding also encourages many long-term business relationships in Japan, which in turn reinforce ties of interdependence, exchange relations, and reciprocal trust among firms.
>
> (ibid.: 280)

These kinds of relationship have also led to low transaction costs among firms, high reliability of goods supplied from one firm to another and close coordination of delivery schedule. 'Because Japanese trade associations are highly developed and span a variety of suppliers, buyers, and related industries, they too have played an important role in developing cooperation among competing and complementary firms, as well as in facilitating the clustering of industries' (ibid.: 283).

'Having the option to develop long-term strategies, large Japanese firms have had the ability to develop the kind of long-term relations with their employees, on which investment in worker training and flexible specialization are built' (ibid.: 280). Inter-corporate ties explain that many large firms – particularly in steel, shipbuilding and other heavy industries – have been able to shift employees to other companies within their industrial group during economic downturns rather than dismissing the workers altogether. Moreover, firms with long-term job security have the capacity to implement a seniority-based wage and promotion system, which in turn, promotes employee motivation and identification with the company. Long-term job security also enables the implementation of a system of job rotation (in work teams) and flexible job assignments, and intensive in-firm instruction and on-the-job training. In addition, however, lifetime employment combined with seniority pay, involves a high degree of employee dependence on the firm. Indeed, since all large firms recruit externally only for positions at the bottom of the job hierarchy and train their specialists for better jobs through on-the-job training and job rotation, there is no further possibility of advancement outside that firm (Dohse et al., 1989). The unitary school system in Japan (see Chapter 5 for an explanation), with its poorly developed system for providing practical or vocational training, explains that Japanese firms offer this type of training. And, because of the existence of long-term job security, employees and unions accept that training is highly firm-specific and not very generalizable to other organizations. This, of course, further increases inflexibility in the external labour market.

The Japanese employment relations system being characterized by company unions, these constitute a much more advantageous arena of negotiations for management than industrial or general unions which recruit members more widely. The ties of company unions to the individual company make them much more strongly dependent on market success, and hence the productivity and cost structure of their firm. As a consequence, the scope of labour union demands is restricted; conflictual goals with respect to working conditions are avoided in favour of positions that can be of benefit to both sides. This pacification function, which is inherent in the structure of the company union, was stabilized in the 1950s through destruction of the militant unions. The intensive labour struggles of the 1950s were a decisive phase in the constitution of the current Japanese system of employment relations. In the course of this conflict, Japanese firms succeeded, in particular in the automobile industry, in destroying the militant postwar unions, which had an industry-wide orientation, and firing union representatives. As can be seen, it was not all peace and harmony to start with; the establishment of a mainly company union system happened under the application of a physical violence against unions approaching civil war, in some firms. In this way, Japanese automobile industry firms were able to prevent from the outset the development of a strong labour union movement, to particularize the interest representation of employees into plant or company unions, and to considerably limit the scope of labour union demands.

Any discussion of the Japanese institutional configuration would be incomplete without mention of the Japanese state.

> The Japanese state has been closely involved in industrial development – though its role is somewhat less pronounced today. The Japanese state has developed many forms of protection to keep out foreign competition, it has fostered an environment for cooperation among fierce competitors, it has channelled subsidies into targeted areas of research and development, and has encouraged and helped firms to mobilize internal resources. Moreover, for many years, it adopted a set of macro-economic policies designed to fuel economic growth with a yen that was under-valued compared to the dollar.
>
> (ibid.: 282–283)

The German societal system of diversified quality production

While Japan shows an example of diversified quality *mass* production, the German societal system promotes another variant of flexible production: diversified quality *medium and small-scale* production. While there are other forms of societal systems of flexible production (e.g. in parts of northern Italy or western Denmark), the Japanese and German systems stand out because they have been conducive to high and continued investment in human resources in large firms.

> Streeck and others have suggested that there is some similarity in the social systems of flexible production of West Germany and Japan, including a high degree of social peace, a workforce that is highly and broadly trained, a flexible labor market within firms, a relatively high level of worker autonomy, a financial system with close ties between large firms and banks, a high degree of stable and long-term relationships between assemblers and their suppliers: overall, a system of production for high quality products. Despite similarity in these characteristics, there are major differences in the social systems of production in the two countries.
>
> (Hollingsworth, 1997: 288)

Whilst some authors have emphasized these similarities, there are also substantial differences.

> In Germany, industrial unions are highly developed, whereas in Japan the emphasis has been on company unions. In Germany, both labor and business are politically well-entrenched at most political levels, whereas this is not at all the case with labor in Japan. And in Germany, there is nothing resembling the keiretsu structure which is so prevalent among large Japanese firms. Moreover, the Germans tend to focus on the upscale, high-cost segments of many markets, whereas the Japanese – with their emphasis on large market share of various products – have been more concerned with competitively priced high-quality products. In Germany, the institutional arrangements underlying the rich development of skills depend on corporatist associations (of firms in an industry or in handicraft trades), which historically have strongly supported and sponsored vocational training. Vocational education has long been important as a precondition for access to certain sectors of the labor market in Germany, and it has very much been governed by associations to which governmental regulation of education and training has been devolved. That has assured education and training linking theory and practice, according to general rather than firm-specific standards. Japan, however, has had a much more limited public vocational training program, so that the state has run schools and universities and enterprises have run training.
>
> (ibid.: 288)

> This type of long-term relationship between firms and banks has encouraged firms to be much more immune to the short-run fluctuations of the price of equities than their competitors in the US and to take a long-term perspective concerning their industry needs. This capacity on the part of management has meant that German firms have had more incentive to engage in the long-term development of products and have been less likely to lay off workers during a modest economic downturn, as has so often been the case with their American competitors who have been more constrained by short-term fluctuations in the financial markets.
>
> (ibid.: 285)

However, unlike Japan, in Germany there is no keiretsu structure, which means that during economic downturns, temporarily redundant workers cannot be placed within friendly companies. What Germany does have, on the other hand, is a system of short-time working supported by the federal agency of labour, which allows firms to keep workers employed in cyclical down-turns. This was highlighted more recently, after the financial crisis of 2007+, as one of the main moderators of a cyclical decline in employment.

> Unlike Japan, another set of institutional arrangements, which contribute to long-term strategic thinking within German companies, is the country's employment relations system. This system is shaped by the highly developed employer and business associations in conjunction with the trade unions. Peak association bargaining, mediated by the state, has not only played an important role in shaping distributional issues, but has also played a role of great importance in influencing the quality and international competitiveness of German firms. It has thus not only played an important role

in shaping distributional issues but also in influencing the quality and international competitiveness of German products.

(ibid.: 286)

In contrast to Japan, German trade unions, organized by industry or sector, have relatively encompassing and centralized organizational structures (see Chapter 5 for a more complete explanation of this topic). This has been maintained despite a current of decentralization of wage bargaining after 1990.

> Unions are responsible for collective bargaining and participation – through policies of codetermination – in corporate boardrooms, while elected work councils participate in defining working conditions inside firms and ensuring that protection laws are obeyed by management. Collectively, these arrangements have been instrumental in reducing conflict between labor and management, and in enhancing flexible production inside firms.
>
> (ibid.: 286)

> The job security enjoyed by labor, under codetermination policies, has encouraged firms to invest in the long-term training of their labor force. When management has realized that it cannot easily dismiss workers in the event of economic adversity, it has had an incentive to engage in the investment of employees with skills high and broad enough to adjust to complex and rapidly changing technologies and unstable markets. And in Germany, the rigidity imposed by strongly organized industrial unionism and works councils has encouraged firms to invest in more skills and social peace than management would otherwise have invested under flexible external market conditions, a process which has directly contributed to a diversified quality, flexible social system of production – the key to Germany's high level of competitiveness in the world economy.
>
> (ibid.: 286–287)

Moreover, the lack of employer freedom in hiring and firing has largely been counteracted by the fact that unions and works councils support a flexible deployment in qualitative terms. The move to greater functional flexibility in labour deployment is not regarded as a threat to union power as unions are neither organized along craft lines nor do they support demarcation between crafts.

The new technology involved in flexible production also requires that management possess the necessary technical skill to assess the feasibility of investing in this technology, as well as the ability to understand the implications for the organization of work, for manpower requirements and for training needs. The engineering and technical educational background of many German managers (see Chapter 5) explains their high level of managerial technical competence.

> Managers of many German firms found the system quite distasteful. They would like to have followed the practices of their American colleagues in the face of stiff international competitiveness by cutting wages and reducing the size of the workforce. Yet, because they were constrained by the system of codetermination (regulated at the plant level by the Works Constitution Act of 1972 and at the enterprise level by the

> Works Constitutions Act of 1952, superseded in 1976) which resulted in a high wage system, German firms were forced – with little choice – to become engineering and highly skills intensive, with diversified and high quality producers. With the rigidities that firms faced in dealing with job protection and high wages for their workers, it was highly rational for management to invest more in the training of their workforce than they would have been inclined to do were they simply following market signals. Almost unintentionally, German firms were pushed to develop one of the world's most skilled labor forces.
>
> (ibid.: 287)

This author emphasized the 'push' from the union side a lot, and he underlines an important factor. On the other hand, outside the automobile industry and in the heartland of investment goods manufacturing, it has also been clear that an influential faction in German entrepreneurship and management has always appreciated the importance of a stable stock of skilled and experienced workers, notably at a time when customization of products and innovation were called for. As works councils and unions and management learned to work together, either side has also learned to appreciate the respectively other side for its contribution to achieving its own goals. This was demonstrated most markedly in the success of the Volkswagen Group: this is simultaneously probably the most codetermined, or co-managed, enterprise in Germany, and a world leader in competitiveness and quality in the medium and higher segments, together with Toyota.

The case of Sweden resembles Germany where diversified quality production is concerned, although its vocational training is more centred on schools. But it is similarly influenced by the union movement and general regulation and norms. In many respects the societal data on Scandinavian economies are closely related to those on Germany: the

Table 7.3 Models of flexible production organization

Swedish model	*German model*	*Japanese model*
Semi-skilled workers with high initial training (quasi-apprenticeship)	Skilled workers deployed on direct production jobs after full apprenticeship	Semi-skilled workers with generally high starting qualification
Work totally uncoupled from the production cycle	Work (partially) uncoupled from the production cycle	Work tied to the production cycle
Holistic tasks with long work cycles (>1 hour)	Job enlargement with work cycles below 1 hour	Highly repetitive work; cycle times around 1 minute on the assembly lines, around 5 minutes in the machining areas where multimachine work is the norm
Homogenous groups	Mixed teams of 'specialists'	Homogenous groups
High partial autonomy for teams through process layout	Little partial autonomy for team through automation and module production	No partial autonomy for the teams through JIT design
De-hierarchization with elected speaker and self-regulation of group affairs	Controversial role of group speaker/leader and of degree of self-regulation	Strong hierarchical structures, group leader appointed by management, no group self-regulation

Source: Jürgens (1995: 204).

role and importance of strong unions, the range of issues covered by collective bargaining, inclusion of the need for competitiveness in employment negotiations, widespread acceptance of technical change as a means of promoting better standards of living and maintaining employment levels, and the significance accorded to quality and product differentiation. Although the Uddevalla site was closed down as far as complete assembly of cars in autonomous groups is concerned, semi-autonomous groups have spread to other industries and countries as an influential principle of work design. In Germany, Audi was a leading innovator of semi-autonomous groups replacing assembly lines, in the middle of the 1980s in final assembly. This has set a new standard of flexible production in the high quality car segment. Flexible production, although not proposed in the ambitious form of Uddevalla any more, has become more widespread but also more differentiated into different forms. It has come to include semi-autonomous groups, operator responsibility for checking quality and other measures in favour of 'responsible autonomy'. This has greatly reduced the importance of Taylorism, but again, it has to be stressed that the more Taylorist industries or branches of industry have emigrated to newly industrialized countries. Also, a lot of work impoverished by segmentation has in the older industrialized countries simply vanished over time, replaced as it was by automated machinery such as robots.

At the same time, however, services have become subject to a new form of quasi-Taylorism, and the most prominent one is work in call centres, for direct marketing and customer service activities. But again, it is also true that such new forms have not meant the end of national differences. In a comparison of call centre work in the USA and Germany, Doellgast (2012) showed that the differences we have become used to, between more Taylorist production in the USA and flexible production in Germany, again came out. The lesson is that 'new technology', new systems or new concepts proclaimed as a new state of the art, are further developed and implemented in practice, to continue rather than do away with the differences we have come to know.

Short-termism and institutional inertia: the difficult transition in the USA

As Taylorism and Fordism were developed within the US societal system of production, US manufacturers have had a hard time shifting to flexible production. The ability of the USA to move towards a societal system of flexible production is argued to be limited by its prevailing practices of industrial relations, its education system and its financial markets – or, in short, by the constraints of its past societal system of production (Hollingsworth, 1997: 292).

> And while these types of incentive and skill systems have become quite widespread in the core of the Japanese and German economies, in the United States manufacturing employment has tended to be much more job-specific, workers have been less broadly trained, internal labor markets have been much more rigid, and employers have had much less incentive to invest in their workers' skill development. Because the US has one of the world's most flexible external job markets, it has been much easier for American workers to leave jobs for other firms than is the case in countries where workers have long-term job security.
>
> (ibid.: 292)

Unsurprisingly, this has provided a disincentive for US employers to invest in worker training.

A reorganization of the productive apparatus from mass to flexible production requires a management committed to technological innovation, confident to forge ahead, and competent both to acquire the right type of equipment, and to put it into operation and maintain it without too much disruption of the production process. Such an approach, however, requires a high level of technical expertise among management and support staff at all levels, which is not sufficiently present in US manufacturing companies.

To some extent this flies in the face of popularized images of the USA being associated with innovativeness and flexibility. To be sure, as we mentioned earlier on in the chapter, any institutionalized system features dialectical counterpoints, so that we can always find the opposite of one more dominant institutional regime in other segments of the economy and society. The USA has highly versatile and flexible biotechnology, electronics and software enterprises. But it has been characteristic that some industries have, with increasing liberalization of world trade notably after 1970, 'left' not only the USA but also countries in Europe, so that personal computers and other end-user information technology equipment, including television and radio sets, which were previously manufactured 'at home', nowadays mainly come from Asian countries. With technical progress, notably automation of standardized manufacturing tasks, international trade and the division of labour between countries, deindustrialization and automation have reduced the number of industries still present in the USA, so that this country has been running a sizeable trade balance deficit for many years now. It has lost market shares precisely where diversified quality production regimes such as in Germany and Sweden have gained, although these lost jobs in older industries even more: in high value-added (quality and luxury) car manufacturing and in a range of investment goods manufacturing industries and services that is very broad and differentiated, including all kinds of production machinery from bread-making to machine tools, and equipment in different sorts of public and private infrastructure.

> The American industrial relations system is shaped in large part by the weakly developed business associations and trade unions. The large size and complexity of the American economy, combined with the racial, ethnic, and religious diversity of the working class have created substantial heterogeneity of interests among both labor and capital, making it difficult for each to engage in collective action. And the weak capacity of both capital and labor to organize collectively has placed severe limits on the ability of the United States to move more rapidly in developing a social system of flexible production.
>
> (ibid.: 292)

> Countries with firms tightly integrated into highly institutionalized systems of business associations (e.g., Germany and Japan) have rather rigid external labor markets but flexible internal labor markets, needed for flexible production. The United States, with weak associative structures, tends to have more flexible external labor markets but more rigid internal labor markets.
>
> (ibid.: 292–293)

This is what follows from the difference between liberal and coordinated economies, or compartmentalized and collaborative business systems (see Chapter 4).

> The capital markets in the United States have also placed constraints on the development of broad employee skills by encouraging firms to engage in short-term

> maximization of profits. In the United States, the equity markets were highly institutionalized by the end of World War I, and managers of large firms have subsequently had low dependence on commercial banks for financing. . . . However, the Clayton Antitrust Act of 1914 made interlocking directorships among large banks and trusts illegal. Moreover, it also forbade a corporation to acquire the stock of another if the acquisition reduced competition in the industry. In the longer term, the Clayton Act tended to reduce the ability of investment banks and firms to carry out a long-term strategy of promoting a community of interests among firms either in the same or in complementary industries. In addition, the American government in 1933 forced a sharp separation between commercial and investment banking. From that point on, investment banks lost much of their access to capital. As a consequence, American nonfinancial corporations became dependent for raising capital on liquid financial markets rather than on banks. Increasingly, corporate managers became dependent on the whims and strategies of stockholders and bond owners. This resulted in an emphasis on a short-term horizon for large firms which has limited the capacity of American management to develop long-term stable relations between employers and their employees – a prerequisite for a highly skilled and broadly trained work force and a flexible or diversified quality social system of production.
>
> (ibid.: 293)

This is a good example of how factors in different spaces and institutional domains come to work together and become interdependent, to form a dominant societal system of production. Again, this in no way precludes opposite characteristics being the rule in specific segments. Indeed, Boeing does have a long-term orientation, it is not noticeably less flexible in production than Airbus, and it is subsidized by public contracts and R&D funding. It is dependent on the capital market but also on government support. But it is not in the centre of dominant institutions, although parts of its operations systems and employment relations characteristics are reminiscent of collaborative business systems.

In the meantime, the USA had of course abolished the separation of investment banking from credit banking, and it has become commonplace in many countries for companies to buy back their own shares. This can be interpreted as a further sharpening of the liberal economic profile that the USA had already acquired, since institutional controls standing in the way of free markets were further reduced, whilst institutional controls to make financial markets work according to the principles of open, contestable and anonymous markets were strengthened. In a way, the USA has become even more American. Despite the crisis of 2007+, this tendency has on the one hand not abated: the US economy has become more dependent on the resources that it has traditionally been strong in: natural resources – nowadays explored by the 'fracking' of shale oil and gas to such an extent that the energy independence of the USA can be envisaged – and accumulation of capital; in addition there is importation of capital, notably for financing an increased governmental indebtedness which, so far, appears to be unstoppable. Reliance on the money-creating effects of increasing prices of assets, from homes to values of share capital, appears to have come back after the world financial crisis. The publicized importance of human resources is also important; in the high-tech industries the country has increasingly relied on the importing and cultivation of highly educated labour, mainly from Asia. But this targeted highly visible industries that have less employment. The mass of employed people remains mainly located in routine, poorly paid jobs still reminiscent of the heritage of Taylorism.

7.4 Comparative work organization characteristics

Everything discussed so far leads to the question: can we offer a systematic comparison of how work organization affects the job characteristics of individual employees? It would be very nice to show representative data on the immediate organizational environment that workers are subject to. Such information reflects how workers are controlled and managed, and it informs on the measure and kind of responsibility they can develop in their work role. Regrettably we do not have comparable and representative data for this, on a world scale or across continents. But we do have some reliable information for some European countries. The European Union has a centre for the study of working conditions, and this has compared conditions in the European Survey of Working Conditions. An analysis of such data informs on societal operations systems at different levels of work, from ordinary workers up to managers. Furthermore, there are data on all kinds of industries and occupations. The data are not strictly representative but care had been taken to select reasonably matching organizations in all the countries. You will remember from earlier chapters that the matching of units across countries is important to control for differences due to size of organizations and type of industry, in order to 'isolate' and zoom in on differences due to values or national institutional characteristics. The data leave out the complexities of management systems and the financial management, employment relations, product portfolios and market orientations of enterprises. But a view of organizational characteristics of jobs is something valuable in itself.

The types of work systems were classified by the authors of the study we here refer to (Arundel et al., 2007), into the following:

- Discretionary learning
- Lean production
- Taylorist organization
- Traditional organization.

Lean production and Taylorist organization are familiar enough from this chapter. Discretionary learning is less stylized as a concept; it means that workers, as they get to learn and master a job, are given discretion or a measure of autonomy over time, in a piecemeal way. This happens typically in rather bureaucratic organizations without rigid controls that instil a measure of responsibility in workers. This would typically happen in the police or in banks. Traditional organization is also less stylized and a wide term; it means that workers have a job not well specified and controlled by elaborate rules and technical facilities but are led or managed in a more personal way, relying on direct supervision by superiors who are close the job that they supervise. This would often happen in e.g. retail or car repair shops.

Table 7.4 shows findings about shares of job traits related to work systems in 15 EU countries. They were collected from 8081 salaried employees in the 15 European countries mentioned. Here is how the authors described the main tendencies in inter-country differences:

> The discretionary learning form of work organization is most prevalent in the Netherlands, the Nordic countries and to a lesser extent Germany and Austria, while it is the least prevalent in Ireland and the southern European nations. The lean model is most in evidence in the UK, Ireland and Spain and to a lesser extent in France, while

Table 7.4 National differences in forms of work organization

	Per cent of employees by country in each organizational class				
	Discretionary learning	*Lean production*	*Taylorist organization*	*Traditional organization*	*Total*
Belgium	38.9	25.1	13.9	22.1	100.0
Denmark	60.0	21.9	6.8	11.3	100.0
Germany	44.3	19.6	14.3	21.9	100.0
Greece	18.7	25.6	28.0	27.7	100.0
Italy	30.0	23.6	20.9	25.4	100.0
Spain	20.1	38.8	18.5	22.5	100.0
France	38.0	33.3	11.1	17.7	100.0
Ireland	24.0	37.8	20.7	17.6	100.0
Luxembourg	42.8	25.4	11.9	20.0	100.0
Netherlands	64.0	17.2	5.3	13.5	100.0
Portugal	26.1	28.1	23.0	22.8	100.0
UK	34.8	40.6	10.9	13.7	100.0
Finland	47.8	27.6	12.5	12.1	100.0
Sweden	52.6	18.5	7.1	21.7	100.0
Austria	47.5	21.5	13.1	18.0	100.0
EU-15	39.1	28.2	13.6	19.1	100.0

Source: Third Working Condition survey. European Foundation for the Improvement of Living and Working Conditions.

> it is little developed in the Nordic countries or in Austria, Germany, and the Netherlands. The Taylorist form of organization shows almost the reverse trend compared to the discretionary learning forms, being most frequent in the southern European nations and in Ireland, and Italy. Finally, the traditional form of work organization is most prevalent in Greece and Italy and to a lesser extent in Germany, Sweden, Belgium, Spain and Portugal.
>
> (Arundel et al., 2007: 1188–89)

The authors then go on statistically to isolate 'national effects' from the more structural effects (strength of particular industries and enterprise size classes in the data). A national effect reflects the influence that an employee's country of residence and work has on the type of work organization she or he is subject to. Here is what the authors summarize: 'the large differences in the prevalence of different forms of work organization are not due to national differences in the distribution of firm size, industry and occupation. Instead, unexplained national factors that could be due to historically inherited management-worker relations or attitudes to organizational innovation strongly influence national differences in the use of different sets of organizational practices' (Arundel et al., 2007: 1190). This is as detailed as a comparative picture of operations management systems for many countries can get.

As the reader may be aware, a comparative picture on a world scale would conjure up much more intricate problems of comparability, and of standardizing valid characteristics of systems. Especially outside Europe and North America, we find operations systems which are strikingly 'modern' in some industries or sectors of employment, while they are much more 'traditional' in others. And in between, there are highly original but also confusingly eclectic amalgamations of more traditional and more modern traits. The literature has often described and discussed mixtures of traits from different operations systems under the theoretical concept of hybridization. This term was derived from the Latin 'hybrida' = mixture of races by cross-breeding. The phenomenon is very common when types of organization are transferred from one country to another; this invariably implies 'cross-breeding'. Since operations systems always imply an ensemble of the more technical features (equipment, software, operating instructions) and the more social-organizational and human resources features, the more technical aspects are often more internationally standardized whilst the more social-organizational and the human resource aspects are more nationally diverse. Thus each of the more stylized types put forward in this chapter, and any other type such as the 'traditional' and the 'discretionary learning' types mentioned above, are in point of fact nationally idiosyncratic by inevitable hybridization.

It is therefore important to cross-reference writings on operations management types with those on human resource management types, such as in Chapter 4 of this book. A splendid example concerns a case described and discussed in Becker-Ritterspach (2009), a study of car manufacturers in India. One of them, Daimler-Benz with headquarters in Germany, had started a production plant in India, making cars also produced in or for other countries in the world. It used a type of production called 'CKD (completely knocked-down) kit production'. This is not a term from the world of boxing matches but means that cars are assembled from a kit of discrete parts and sub-assemblies sent to the manufacturing site which, thereby, is mainly an assembly site. The manufacturing operation is therefore rather lean since all the parts production is 'outside', in this case mostly outside India. Lean production is a fairly modern operations type, as we saw.

But on the other hand, you can imagine that quality production in the luxury segment of the car market implies high standards, which brings in the question of how to achieve and maintain them. Daimler-Benz in this case learned by experience that guaranteeing the quality that Mercedes buyers expected meant a particular effort of human resources cultivation, including motivation and a personalized form of management. And this in turn brought in the social-organizational characteristics of management in India: paternalist authority and support of workers by paternal managers, refined status distinctions and other cultural and institutional patterns well known and respected in India. A very traditional form of organizing people and of HRM was thus combined with a very modern operations system.

This recombination of what is specific for one country with what is an international state of the art, and of what is traditional with what is very modern (in this case lean production) is intriguing, and it may be much more frequent than the mind trained to differentiate between the modern and the traditional is enabled to conceive. Yet, it is very important indeed in newly industrialized countries or what is often called 'emerging markets'. The nasty aspect of this phenomenon of hybridization by way of recombination is that it muddies clear differences between operations systems, it adds to the differentiation of national sub-types under the generic types, and the muddying typically creeps in from the human resources and socio-organizational end of operations systems, as Becker-Ritterspach (2009) had demonstrated. As lean production had unmistakably Japanese roots, so its transfer to other countries implies a translation and adaptation into the cultural and institutional worlds of a new country, which makes it difficult to use universal operations management types. They may be a first point of departure, but as we move into the details of the real world, we have to devote increasing attention to understanding the specificities of national or, indeed, more disaggregated types. This then is one central lesson of this chapter: whenever someone expounds a new type of organization and management on a world scale, be distrustful of ambitious generalizations and concentrate on finding out how and why new concepts and practices are being adapted to new locations, often changing their nature in due course.

7.5 Conclusions

Different societal conditions give rise to different operations patterns. It seems that markets and hierarchies work well when firms are embedded in a societal environment impoverished by collective forms of economic coordination. However, institutionally impoverished economies that rely on markets and hierarchies for the governance of economic activities (such as the USA and the UK) do not necessarily perform better than societies where economic behaviour is more socially regulated (Streeck, 1991).

> the Japanese and German cases demonstrate that diversified quality forms of production work best when they are embedded in an environment with institutional arrangements which promote cooperation between producers and suppliers, and among competitors, especially an environment which facilitates the exchange of information among competitors. It requires firms to engage in collective behavior far in excess to what is needed for markets and hierarchies to function effectively and in excess of what single firms are likely to develop for themselves. Flexible and diversified quality production systems function best when they are embedded in an institutional environment with rich multilateral or collective dimensions: cooperative action on the part of competitors, rich training centers for workers and managers, and financial institutions willing to provide capital on a long-term basis.
>
> (Hollingsworth, 1997: 295)

Hence, it could be argued that a repertory of social institutions that exceeds the neoclassical minimum may in specific conditions make a positive contribution to competitive market performance (Streeck, 1991). This may not be true in every comparison of individual enterprises, but it does appear to work in comparisons of societal systems of production.

> Because of the low levels of skill of American labor in most manufacturing sectors and because American management has tended to be recruited from marketing, financial, and legal rather than engineering and production backgrounds, American manufacturing firms have been less successful in improving upon products once developed than their Japanese and German competitors. And because American consumers are less demanding of product quality than the Japanese and Germans, American firms – particularly in the consumer goods industries – have been more competitive in the production of low-cost standardized products which can be mass marketed and easily discarded. Also, in contrast to the German and Japanese, the Americans – particularly in many manufacturing industries – have been more willing to compromise on design, quality, and service and to compete in terms of price.
>
> (Hollingsworth, 1997: 296)

> Relationships among producers and suppliers in the United States have been more opportunistic and based more on hard-nosed bargaining over prices than in Japan and Germany. This kind of intense bargaining over price has also had an adverse effect on the Americans' ability to sustain product quality and to achieve a high level of competitiveness in global markets. There are industries in which the technology is not very complex and does not change, and, given the large size of the American market, mass standardized production is still effective in such industrial sectors. For example, paper products, breakfast cereals, soft drinks, bug sprays, floor wax, deodorants, soaps, shaving cream, and hundreds of other products remain symbolic of the familiar hierarchical form of corporate America.
>
> (ibid.: 296)

However, Germany and Japan, like all other countries, have firms that compete and perform well in some industrialized sectors, but not very well in others. 'By focusing attention on Japan, Germany, and the United States, it becomes quite obvious that why countries succeed in certain sectors depends less on such classic factor endowments as climate, natural resources, and land than on their national traditions, values, institutional arrangements, quality of labor and management, and the nature of capital markets' (ibid.: 283).

The crowded living conditions and tight space constraints throughout Japan have stimulated the Japanese to produce compact, portable, quiet and multifunctional products. 'They have excelled in producing compact cars and trucks, small consumer electronic equipment (TV sets, copiers, radios, and video sets), motorcycles, machine tools, watches and clocks, and a number of business related products such as small computers, fans, pumps, and tools' (Hollingsworth, 1997: 283). 'Even though the Japanese have been enormously successful in improving upon existing products, they have been less successful in developing new products – primarily because of their particular institutional configuration. Their educational system emphasizes rote learning rather than creative synthesis or critical analysis. Their universities are structured to facilitate consensus decision-making and group conformity' (ibid.: 284). The overall weakness of Japanese universities as research institutions is an important reason why the Japanese have lagged behind in industries involving chemistry and biotechnology, and other fields heavily dependent on basic science (see Chapter 8 for a discussion of this issue).

The German institutional landscape also helps to explain why Germany has excelled in competing in the production of machine tools, automobiles and chemical products, as well as in many industrial products in investment goods industries where clients are either knowledgeable engineers or firms, or where clients require more customized and adapted solutions.

> They have been especially successful in applying the latest microelectronic technology to the production of traditional products and to new production processes. On the other hand, the Germans have been less competitive in many newer industries, e.g., computers, semiconductors, and consumer electronics. In other words, the Germans have placed less emphasis on developing entirely new technologies and industries than in applying the latest technologies to the production of more traditional products. And it is the specific type of German industrial relations system (high job security, the high levels of qualification, and continuous training of German workers) which is conducive to the rapid diffusion of the latest technology to the production of more traditional but high quality products. In addition the strong engineering and technical

> background of senior management, the high levels of skill of the workforce, and a strong consumer demand for high-precision manufacturing processes have contributed to the development of various manufacturing sectors with very high quality products.
>
> (ibid.: 289–290)

There is more on this, in the following chapter on national innovation systems. But even then, a caveat is in order, especially if an author is as historically well-grounded as Hollingsworth. Guess in which country the electric dynamo, synthetic production of ammoniac fertilizer, the four-stroke car engine, the first electronic computer (working with valves rather than transistors), the first experimental television set, the first ballistic missile, the first helicopter, and the first fighter propelled by a jet engine saw the light of day! It was in Germany. This country was apparently better at radical innovation in the past.

As explained in Chapter 5, Sweden is different from Germany and Japan in that it had both a large traditional Taylorist industry as well as modern flexible production in some sectors (such as the car industry). The fact that the Swedish societal environment is relatively similar to that of Germany explains that some Swedish sectors (such as the car and truck industries, and the machinery industry) could shift to flexible production. Traditional production methods and low-skilled workers were used in the traditional industries, which successfully exploit Sweden's main raw material resources: wood and iron ore. Much of this manufacturing has, however, moved abroad, notably with Sweden's entry into the European Union.

We can see that operations systems tend to fit into national patterns of culture and institutions described and discussed in Chapters 2–4. At this point, it is possible to say that e.g. most coordinated market economies, or all collaborative business systems, have had diversified quality production systems emerging. On the other hand, liberal market economies or compartmentalized business systems have appeared to drift in the direction of Taylorized production systems. But e.g. state dominated business systems, which are represented across different parts of the world, have operations systems not well compared to state dominated systems in European countries. However, the state dominated business systems in Europe are more in evidence in southern Europe, and these have a tendency for both more traditional work systems and Taylorism side by side, as we saw. State influence, or the overlapping of government and entrepreneurship, appears more widespread in more recently industrialized countries. In countries as different as Egypt and China, modern enterprises are very much controlled or even owned by the government. Yet the industries that such countries have developed can vary a lot, between, say, the garments manufacturing in Bangladesh and the automobile and electronics manufacturing in Korea. Operations systems are expected to differ accordingly.

The upshot is that a lot of more detailed research would have to be done in detail, to establish a credible link of institutional orders with operations systems. But it is not too hazardous to suggest a link between the cultural dimension of power distance mentioned in Chapter 2 on the one hand, and state domination on the other, and that this will also be reflected in the more hierarchical relations within operations systems. An uncertainty avoidance culture appears to be linked with more Taylorist countries in the south of Europe, in a plausible way: uncertainty avoiders will turn this disposition to good use in devising Taylorist work systems. On the other hand, the USA are low on uncertainty avoidance, which shows in liberal entrepreneurship, but they have also invented and spread

Taylorism, avoiding uncertainty in the sphere of work. This shows again how complicated the picture may be and that we must avoid undifferentiated generalization.

We do not want to belabour the point of dialectical reasoning too much, but you can see that it is useful here, too: Imagine what an uncertainty-avoiding entrepreneur American style would do, in opening a mass market with more standardized products and services: Internally, he or she may be guided by the logic of competition through cost leadership via economies of scale and the segmentation of work systems and jobs, to go for Taylorism. This means cultivating a different culture internally, different from the risk-taking in finance, research and development and corporate governance. The same applies to national diversity of operations systems: to have Taylorist and Fordist production systems, you need specialized makers of highly customized machinery and installations; the latter cultivate operations systems with the opposite characteristics of their clients! The implication is that industrial differentiation will breed diversity of institutionalized practices. The same applies in more recent industries: automated mass manufacturing and automated services such as retail banking or internet services rely on more other enterprises devising customized software, which are the opposite where work systems are concerned. It is the same story all over again, as with mass producers and machine tools.

Now, imagine what happens when the car producers and their equipment makers are in the same country: the contrast between their operations systems will weaken societal institutions. Then, imagine what happens when car makers are in one country and their equipment makers in another: in this case, industrial differentiation will overlap with, and potentially aggravate, societal effects!

Thus, our best bet is to look at enterprise strategies and product and service markets as modifying the link between culture and institutions on the one hand, and operations systems on the other. This can turn a link between culture and operations systems on its head, in a manner of speaking, which is what dialectics means in simple terms that can be traced empirically. But beware that such complex relations are, most likely, far from deterministic. They may change over time historically, which notably Hollingsworth demonstrated for the USA. They do not allow pinpointing fixed 'independent variables' separate from 'variables to be explained', either. Sometimes, product market situations evolving may explain a lot, sometimes it may be employment relations and human resources, and sometimes, it may be a conjunction of markets and employment and human resource situations that lead to operations systems. Again, we have to summarize a lot of the research presented as boiling down to historical constellations in societies. These are matching characteristics of economic opportunities, interests of powerful actors, governmental regulation, enterprise strategies, and institutions in employment and competence generation systems, HRM and finance.

Study questions

1. Which societal features could help to explain why Taylorism and Fordism developed in the USA?
2. Why do you think Toyotism, or lean production, developed in Japan long before flexible production was recognized in the West?
3. Explain how lean supply chain management fits the societal features of Japan and of Germany.
4. Explain the links between human resource management systems and corporate governance modes to mass production, and to the lean and flexible modes of production.

5 Explain why lean production could be more difficult to implement in the USA.
6 Explain the main differences between mass and flexible production systems, and link these differences in features to the differences in the societal institutions that are needed to develop these models.
7 Explain which type of operations systems we would have to expect in China, a country which combined state domination with new capitalism and has become a major international competitor in final consumption goods, mass markets and notably consumer electronics.
8 Australia is a leading exporter of uranium, coal and other 'extracted' commodities. Russia is also a major exporter of extracted commodities (notably gas and oil). In some ways they will therefore have comparable operations. But what about the expected design of operations systems in comparison?
9 Explain whether, in your opinion, convergence can occur in the areas of production systems and production management. Consider the role of the international division of labour as you do, i.e. the tendency for societies to specialize in industries and market segments.

Further reading

Delbridge, R. (1998) *Life on the Line in Contemporary Manufacturing: the Workplace Experience of Lean Production and the 'Japanese' Model.* Oxford: Oxford University Press.

The book provides us with a sophisticated story of the actual work process on the assembly lines in two UK factories: a Japanese-owned television assembly plant and a European-owned automotive parts supplier. Through detailed ethnographic accounts, it convincingly dispels many myths about the humanization of factory life and the innovatory potential of Japanese investment in the West.

Sorge, A. (1991) Strategic fit and the societal effect: interpreting cross-national comparisons of technology, organization and human resources. *Organization Studies* 12(2), 161–190.

A summary of societal effect studies relating operations systems to both, enterprise strategies and societal institutions and culture.

Fujimoto, T. (1999) *The Evolution of a Manufacturing System at Toyota.* Oxford: Oxford University Press.

Excellent book describing how, in the early 1990s, Toyota had to change its assembly lines to make them more worker-friendly.

Taylor, B. (1999) Japanese management style in China? Production practices in Japanese manufacturing plants. *New Technology, Work and Employment* 14(2), 129–142.

Through an examination of 20 Japanese-owned manufacturing plants in China, this article questions the usefulness of identifying Japanese competitive success as being associated with specific Japanese production management techniques.

Case: Manufacturing machine tools in Germany and France[6]

Machine tools are machines that bring tools to bear on raw material or pieces, to give the object a particular shape devised by a design drawing. There are turning machines (lathes), milling, drilling, grinding, forming and many other types of machines. Generating shapes according to very precise standards or which are complex, is a process which requires highly engineered and controlled machines. The machine tool industry caters for nearly all the industries that make 'discrete' products consisting of several parts, rather than 'integral' products from oil to yoghurt.

Machine tool producers in all countries are distinctive, compared to other industrial sectors, for an absence of very large firms, an often rather artisanal mode of production, strong continuity from workers' to technicians' and engineers' jobs, training backgrounds and contents, and required skills and knowledge (Sorge and Maurice, 1990: 144). Since these sectoral patterns correspond to societal patterns in Germany, it is an industry in which Germany has held a very strong position since the beginning of the twentieth century. It has also held this position reasonably well under the Japanese onslaught from the mid-1970s.

Surprisingly, contrary to the characteristics that apply in the French societal context, and in general far removed from the prevailing industrial norm, which is associated with continuous process production regimes and a hierarchical culture, the French machine tool industry had even more customized development and production, smaller production runs, much smaller average plant and enterprise sizes, more skilled craft workers and fewer semi-skilled workers, and fewer engineers than the German one. The German machine tool firms had many more unskilled workers and fewer craft workers because they concentrate on larger batch sizes. The much larger share of engineers in the German industry can be explained by the greater effort that goes into product development and design, as well as by larger batch size production. Despite the more artisanal approach to machine tool production, however, the French industry experienced a more severe sectoral crisis after the mid-1970s than the German one. The question is whether functional equivalence (of operations systems and societal production models) or its obverse, affinity between societal and sectoral regimes applies in this particular industry (ibid.: 145). Qualitatively, the differences between the two sectors can be summarized as follows.

1 The industry in France was less export-oriented and its exports were concentrated on specific markets: Eastern Europe and Africa. The German industry exported more and exports were more evenly spread across destinations.
2 Producers in Germany specialized more systematically with regard to specific metal-working processes and machine types, such as lathes, milling, drilling, grinding, honing/lapping, stamping, presses, forging etc.
3 French manufacturers had a larger product range, combining on average more machining processes in their product spectrum.
4 French firms more frequently made machines to order, customizing according to the requirements of individual clients. This is related to the fact that they also made special-purpose machines more frequently, which are customized almost by definition, such as in the automobile industry.
5 The German firms made more universal machines, with modular modifications and additions, selling more frequently by catalogue and producing for stocks.
6 Production batches were larger in the German firms, and production planning and systematization efforts more pronounced.
7 Plant and enterprise sizes were much higher in Germany, on average twice as large as in France (ibid.: 146).

By all accounts, the professional careers of workers and works management and supervision, on the one hand, and design and development, on the other, are generally more separated in France, and the geographical distance between head office/development functions and production is sometimes greater in France (ibid.: 147). This finding is in accordance with the general institutional and cultural or societal patterns in France. Here, we have a finding which is in greater accord with previously conducted general Franco-German comparisons; these had shown greater continuity of working careers in Germany, starting from basic education and training processes, from production into higher technical functions (ibid.).

There are also important differences in the way the two machine tool industries are embedded in their respective economies and societal settings. In Germany, it enjoys numerous and close relationships with technical universities. The production engineering and machine tool departments enjoy high standing, draw good students, are quite generously staffed, and maintain close collaboration with firms in development projects (ibid.: 147).

In France, the opposite applies on many counts. Departments of production engineering and machine tools have low prestige in the leading engineering schools (*grandes écoles*). There is less contract research and development for the machine tool industry, and overall research and teaching staff in production engineering departments is much smaller. The industry is not backed up by an academic establishment as large and reputed as in Germany, and the cross-fertilization between the two is much less in evidence (ibid.: 148).

In France, mechanical engineering plays an inferior role and occupies a vulnerable competitive position. It is easy to understand, then, that other industrial sectors are more important clients for the French machine tool industry than mechanical engineering. Domestically, French machine tool makers have been confronted with a clientele that is prone to segment workflow hierarchically and laterally to a greater extent, and which goes for single-purpose automation and, therefore, tailor-made installations. This favours concepts of machines which are not strong on the professional autonomy and responsibility of machine tool setter-operators (ibid.: 149).

Hence, the French machine tool industry has come to specialize in customer-specific single-purpose machines, the production of which necessitates craft-dominated artisanal work processes. At the same time, however, the societal environment imposed segmented career and organization structure patterns on the industry. The contrary applies in Germany; this country's machine tool makers confront more firms which emphasize less organizational differentiation of workflow, requiring flexible but standard machine tools and favouring the socialization and use of professionally autonomous setter-operators (ibid.). Consequently, German machine tool enterprises and plants are much larger than French ones; work processes are characterized by less artisanal principles in production but, as a result of societal influences, also by less overall lateral and hierarchical segmentation of work careers and functions.

Machine tool making firms in France are almost the inverse of the norm structures that apply in their clientele. A manufacturing industry dominated by large batch or mass production firms and large concerns will be congenial to manufacturers of customized machine tools, which have a market strategy and personnel structure that is opposed to that of their clients. A manufacturing industry in which small-batch production of investment goods for more differentiated markets is more typical, as in Germany, will go together with a machine tool industry that makes more flexible but standard machines, and hence has a market orientation, production systems and personnel structure of a more industrial kind, i.e. closer to that of its clients (ibid.: 149–150).

During the immediate postwar period and until the early 1970s, the French machine tool industry outpaced its German counterpart. During this period there was no evidence of a technological gap between the two countries. If anything, the French industry had benefited from its close relations with the aerospace client industry which is strong in France, for an earlier adoption of NC (numerical control) systems which had largely been pioneered by the aerospace and armaments industries, first in the United States and then in Britain and France. This innovation, the bases for which were laid during the 1950s, at first led to piece-meal changes of machine tool technology and a slow progression of NC machine sales and utilization (ibid.: 153).[7] The new technique of that time required substantial development of organizational, personnel and planning capacities for programming machines largely away from the shop floor, and for de-bugging and running in job and batch specific machining programmes. It was therefore a technique more fitting for manufacturers with the capacity and will to install substantial planning groups, i.e. larger enterprises and firms in 'elite' industries (ibid.: 153). The requirements of this NC technology were one of the reasons why French machine tool producers outpaced their German counterparts at that time. When automated machines for larger batches are in demand in the domestic market, alongside the development of a slowly increasing number of advanced NC machines for industries such as aerospace, it seems that a 'French' type of societal environment is favourable.

This situation changed significantly after the mid-1970s. A worldwide crisis in machine tools started to develop just at that time, for slower growth of disposable income and of goods markets reduced the need for additions to single-purpose automation and investment goods on the whole (ibid.: 153). While both Germany and France were hit by this crisis, it came at a different time for each, and was dealt with differently in the two countries. But it is significant that from roughly 1977 onwards, CNC machines that improved on the earlier NC generations and became attractive for a wider clientele beyond the original core of NC users, started to be sold more widely (ibid.: 155).

CNC was more quickly, more early and more widely seen in Germany as offering the potential for an original improvement on previous NC techniques, and was more in tune with the work organization and human resource patterns (see Chapter 5) of large parts of the clientele of German machine tool producers. It would appear that German machine tool users jumped on CNC machines more quickly since they saw them as breaking with the previous cumbersome division of labour between planning, programming and machine operation (ibid.: 155).[8] The distinctive factor is, as was shown in previous comparisons, the professional continuity and propinquity between worker, technician and engineering occupations in Germany, and the professional discontinuity and distance in France, regarding status, education, remuneration and careers (ibid.: 158).

The perpetuation of professional and organizational structures therefore does not simply happen in response to the evolution of techniques or markets; it also predisposes enterprises to go for particular variants of new techniques and explore particular markets which have an affinity with these structures (ibid.: 158). German machine tool producers were already previously more prepared to manufacture universal, non-dedicated machines which can be operated flexibly, and they continued along this way by entering more systematically the market for universal CNC machines with operating flexibility, made in batches. Domestic user concepts stressing flexibility in universal machines thus went hand in hand with a more industrialized machine tool industry which produced catalogue machines on a larger scale (ibid.: 163–164).

It can be seen that the German industry explored new markets more quickly because its own structure and user expectations prepared it better for entering the new markets for CNC machines (ibid.: 163–164). The German industry could apparently better afford backward integration into CNC system design and manufacture, since it had much larger firm and plant sizes, which provided for better opportunities to spread overhead and development costs on the basis of greater economies of scale and larger development departments (ibid.: 164). Another important element in the explanation is that despite individually greater backward integration into CNC system design and manufacture, there was also greater cooperation between makers of machines, and between them and electronics firms, software houses, non-industrial research and development institutes and users of machines. Intensive collaboration alleviated problems with which individually operating firms are confronted. However, not only the extent of cooperation is important. Also, the better status of production engineering within German industry and academia vis-à-vis other specialisms, and the higher status of machine tool firms vis-à-vis other reputed industrial manufacturers must be considered (ibid.: 164).

Throughout the discussion of the German machine tool industry, it became clear that it has been closer in its profile to user industries, intertwined craft and higher engineering functions, brought artisanal and research and development work closer to each other, put manufacturers into more intimate collaboration with reputed and technologically advanced institutions outside the industry, bridged the gap between mechanical and electronic and software engineering more comfortably (ibid.: 168). The German machine tool industry was favoured by the fact that institutionalized social structures and relations are conducive to bridging gaps between artisanal and industrial systems of production, between practices in small and large firms, between craft and technological professions, between 'noble' and less noble branches of engineering (ibid.: 168).

It conforms with the more general argument: In this specific industrial case, the German firms do better, because their existing markets and their less artisanal profile in operations prepared them better for achieving a fit with the requirements existing for the industrialized development and manufacture of CNC machines to capture new markets for an innovation (ibid.: 166–167). The opposite story emerges as we summarize the findings for French machine tool makers. These opened up new markets through CNC less quickly and to a lesser extent. They were already previously less present in these markets but more successful in dedicated customized machines requiring less flexibility of operation, installed with users in 'high-tech' industries, larger companies or plants with longer production runs.

The French industry entered the crisis later, and its reaction was negatively prejudiced through this later start but also through its orientation towards market segments and user interests different from those that provided latent new demand for CNC machines. Furthermore, collaboration between makers to share professionally novel (electronic and software) development efforts was much more difficult to get off the ground, which was all the more serious in an industry characterized much more than the German one by small firm and plant sizes, enjoying less status vis-à-vis other industries and being more cut off from non-industrial research and development institutes and prestigious higher engineering schools (ibid.: 164–165).

Because of these interconnected disadvantages, the backward integration of machine tool makers into CNC systems and software development got stuck in the beginning. However, the industry was not only less prepared to explore new export markets, this being a disadvantage inherited from its industrial history, but was also less able to tap the new domestic markets that became more profitable in the drive towards differentiated quality production. Hence, the emerging markets were more captured by the foreign, notably Japanese, competitors. But it is again also true that demand for CNC machines was, in France, slower to take off and assert itself in a wider scale as it did in Germany (ibid.: 165). As already suggested, this has something to do with the structure of the industry in France, which has previously been weaker in investment goods manufacturing in mechanical engineering but stronger in precisely those sectors where flexible universal machines were much less required than dedicated purpose-specific machinery.

Questions

1 Explain the relationships between organizational patterns and societal features in the German and French machine tool industries.
2 Identify the link between the human resource practices and inter-organizational relationships in the French and German machine tool industries and the rest of the domestic industry.
3 Explain comparative advantage in the French and German machine tool sectors on the basis of human resources, organization patterns and the embeddedness of firms in the societal structure.
4 Explain the concept of 'fit' in the context of the French and German machine tool industry. In what sense can 'fit' help to explain the competitiveness described in this case?

Notes

1 This section is based mainly on Sheldrake (1996), Chapter 2 and Lane (1989), Chapter 6.
2 Unless indicated otherwise, this section draws on Womack et al. (1991). Extracts are reprinted with the permission of Rawson Associates/Scribner, an imprint of Simon and Schuster Adult Publishing Group, from Womak, J.P., Jones, D.T. and Roos, D. (1990) *The Machine That Changed The World*. Copyright ©1990 by James P Womak, Daniel T Jones, Daniel Roos, and Donna Sammons Carpenter.
3 This case is based on Taylor (1999).
4 Unless indicated otherwise, this section is based on Hollingsworth (1997).
5 Historically, however, there were always examples of flexible production in societies where a social system of mass standardized production was dominant, and examples of standardized production occurred in societies in which flexible production was most common.
6 This case draws essentially on Sorge and Maurice (1990) and Sorge (1991).
7 NC systems are the earliest forms of machine, using computerized machine tools. They became current in the early 1950s and were dominant until the mid-1970s. The operations of machine tools were determined and controlled first by an electronic plug-board and later by a simple computer. In this early form the sequence of operations that the machine was meant to perform was contained on a paper or magnetic tape. The computer was separate from the machine tool and usually not on the shop floor at all. To change the operations of the machine tool – previously a complex and costly task – one now simply had to change the tape.
8 Computer numerically controlled machines operate along the same lines as NC machines but with a more advanced form of computer. The new micro-computer was built into the machine itself and had a 'dialogue' video display unit and keyboard. Thus, the process could be monitored and machines be adjusted while production is under way. Alternations dictated by production conditions at a given time could thus be taken into consideration on the spot. The need for human intervention directly with the machine, by handling levers, was reduced still further. The more sophisticated computer allows the production of more complex and sophisticated parts with ever greater precision.

References

Arundel, A., Lorenz, E., Lundvall, B.-A. and Valeyre, A. (2007) How Europe's economies learn. A comparison of work organization and innovation mode for the EU-15. *Industrial and Corporate Change* 16, 1175–1210.

Becker-Ritterspach, F. (2009) *Hybridization of MNE Subsidiaries: The Automotive Sector in India. Houndmills.* Basingstoke, Hampshire: Palgrave Macmillan.

Berggren, C. (1992) *Alternatives to Lean Production.* New York: ILR Press.

Boyer, R. and Durand, J.P. (1997) *After Fordism.* London: Macmillan.

Boyer, R. and Hollingsworth, R. (1997) The variety of institutional arrangements and their complementarity in modern economies. In Hollingsworth, J.R. and Boyer, R. (eds) *Contemporary Capitalism.* Cambridge: Cambridge University Press.

Dankbaar, B. (1995) The crisis of Fordism: restructuring in the automobile industry. In Van Ruysseveldt, J., Huiskamp, R. and Van Hoof, J. (eds) *Comparative Industrial and Employment Relations.* London: Sage, 293–314.

Doellgast, V. (2012) *Disintegrating Democracy at Work. Labor Unions and the Future of Good Jobs in the Service Economy.* Ithaca NY: ILR Press.

Dohse, K., Jürgens, U. and Malsch, T. (1989) From 'Fordism' to 'Toyotism'? The social organization of the labor process in the Japanese automobile industry. *East Asia* 5.

Hollingsworth, R. (1997) Continuities and changes in social systems of production: the cases of Japan, Germany, and the United States. In Hollingsworth, J.R. and Boyer, R. (eds) *Contemporary Capitalism: the Embeddedness of Institutions.* Cambridge: Cambridge University Press, 265–310.

Jürgens, U. (1995) Group work and the reception of Uddevalla in the German car industry. In Sandberg, A. (ed.) *Enriching Production.* Aldershot: Avebury, 199–213.

Lane, C. (1989) *Management and Labour in Europe.* Aldershot: Edward Elgar.

Lin, Z. and Hui, C. (1999) Should lean replace mass organizations systems? A comparative examination from a management coordination perspective. *Journal of Business Studies* 30(1), 45–80.

Piore, M.J. and Sabel, C. (1984) *The Second Industrial Divide.* New York: Basic Books.

Sheldrake, J. (1996) *Management Theory.* London: International Thomson Business Press.

Sorge, A. (1991) Strategic fit and the societal effect: interpreting cross-national comparisons of technology, organization and human resources. *Organization Studies* 12(2), 161–190.

Sorge, A. (1995) New technologies, organizational change and employment practices. In Van Ruysseveldt, J., Huiskamp, R. and Van Hoof, J. (eds) *Comparative Industrial and Employment Relations.* London: Sage, 266–314.

Sorge, A. and Maurice, M. (1990) The societal effect in strategies and competitiveness of machine tool manufacturers in France and West Germany. *International Journal of Human Resource Management* 1, 141–172.

Streeck, W. (1984) Guaranteed employment, flexible manpower use, and cooperative manpower management: a trend towards convergence. In Shigeyoshi, T. (ed.) *Industrial Relations in Transition.* Tokyo: University of Tokyo Press.

Streeck, W. (1991) On the institutional conditions of diversified quality production. In Matzner, E. and Streeck, W. (ed.) *Beyond Keynesianism: The Socio-Economics of Production and Full Employment.* Aldershot: Edward Elgar, 21–61.

Taylor, B. (1999) Japanese management style in China? Production practices in Japanese manufacturing plants. *New Technology, Work and Employment* 14, 2.

Whitley, R. (1999) *Divergent Capitalisms: The Social Structuring and Change of Business Systems.* New York: Oxford University Press.

Womack, J.P., Jones, D.T. and Roos, D. (1991) *The Machine that Changed the World.* New York: HarperCollins.

Wood, S. (ed.) (1982) *The Degradation of Work? Skill, Deskilling and the Labour Process.* London: Hutchinson.

8 Managing resources: national innovation systems

Learning objectives

By the end of this chapter you will be able to:

- appreciate the difference between incremental and more radical types of innovation
- explore the link between the 'techno-economic paradigm' shift and dramatic change in national institutions
- identify the major institutions involved in innovation processes
- assess the role of these different institutions in innovative systems
- compare and explain the differences in the main features of the innovation systems of the USA, Asia, Germany and France
- explain how these divergences help to understand differences in national innovation trajectories

Chapter outline

8.1 Introduction

Problems of economic growth in the advanced industrial nations and thinking about how to modernize other economies have induced research and policies concerned with supporting the technical innovative competence of national firms. The enhanced technical sophistication of firms from Japan and then Korea, Taiwan, China and other newly industrializing countries (NICs) has broadened the range of nations whose firms are competitive in fields that used to be the preserve of only a few, and has led other nations, who today have a weak manufacturing sector, to wonder how they might emulate the performance of the successful NICs (Nelson and Rosenberg, 1993: 3). Against this background, a recent body of scholarship has underscored the importance of the national institutional context as an explanation for differences in national patterns of innovation (e.g. Dosi et al., 1990; Lundvall, 1992; Kogut, 1993; Nelson, 1993). From this perspective, technological development is rooted in the skills, capabilities and knowledge that accumulate over time in the national innovation system. Country-specific technological paths are argued to be shaped by the other ingredients of business systems (see Chapter 4) that influence the accumulation and diffusion of knowledge required for industrial innovation.

Institutional perspectives highlight two ways in which the national institutional context shapes specific country patterns of innovation. First, they show how the societal institutions that support industrial innovation vary cross-nationally. For example, the policies and practices of a nation's universities and government research institutes are shaped to a large extent by that nation's singular historical development and socio-economic structures. Universities and research institutes provide knowledge and human capital to firms in technology-driven industries. As a consequence, the features of these institutions influence the technological performance of a country's firms (Ergas, 1987; Porter, 1990; Nelson, 1993).

Second, the national context influences the institutional arrangements and behavioural patterns of firms themselves. For example, the organization of work and patterns of communication within and between firms, or between firms and universities, reflects broader societal characteristics that have been imprinted on firms and institutionalized over time (Kogut, 1991; Powell and DiMaggio, 1991). Such institutionalized arrangements are particularly important in emerging science-based technologies, such as biotechnology, in which the relative success of different countries will depend on the successful coordination of scientific infrastructure and industrial capabilities (Dosi et al., 1990).

This chapter draws on these institutional arguments to explain how the national institutional environments of different countries shape nationally specific innovation patterns. Before that, it provides some background information on the existing types of innovation, in Section 8.2. In Section 8.3, it offers a brief discussion of the major institutions that can be involved in innovation processes. Sections 8.4 to 8.7 discuss the dominant features of the innovation systems of the USA, Asian countries, Germany and France. This discussion should enable the reader to understand the link between the nationally specific institutional features and technological trajectories of these countries. As a result of this discussion, you will become aware of the importance of 'location' to successful innovation (Porter and Stern, 2002). Innovation-centred organizations are not only driven by input costs, tax incentives, subsidies or even wage rates for scientists and engineers; they also depend on locational advantages – rooted in, for example, special relationships with local universities and companies, preferential access to local institutions, and so on. To some extent, firms not only move to where such locational advantages are but help to bring them about, in networks including other firms, R&D and governmental bodies (see Chapter 10).

8.2 Technical and technological advancement[1]

Although 'innovation' may happen in a great deal of fields such as politics, education, urban planning, enterprise organization, the construction of the value chain etc., this chapter deals with technical and technological innovation more specifically. This is the innovation around all manner of technical artefacts, i.e. tools, machines but also designs, programmes, user manuals and operating procedures and instructions. 'Technical' is derived from the Greek word *techne*, meaning skill or ruse, in this case the skill of using and improving such artefacts. 'Technology', by adding the -ology suffix, reminds us that there are words, theories and other forms of articulate knowledge, to explain the workings of technical artefacts and their grounding in natural science. A lot of technical advance has rested, and still does, on experiential trying-out or experimentation; this emphasizes the skills association in 'technical'. This association is also evoked by the term 'engineering'. 'Technological' on the other hand evokes the fact that engineers, in collaboration with scientists, have worked towards systematically formalized and tested theories of how and why artefacts work in the way they do, they have together sought to expand and exploit the natural science foundation that is potentially useful for the design and development of improved artefacts. Innovation thus comes through improvement of formal knowledge but also use and improvement of skills, which is also knowledge but 'embodied knowledge', i.e. not written down somewhere. It would be dangerous to neglect this; competitive advantages of individuals, firms, sectors and countries not only rest on formalized knowledge (in patents, handbooks, libraries and archives) but very much in technical skills, which include the ability to use, retrieve, select and combine tangible knowledge.

The point about innovation systems is that, behind every act or instance of improving technical artefacts and technologies, there are institutions and cultural predispositions in education, training, working careers and all the other societal spaces mentioned in the earlier chapters. That makes it appropriate to speak of, not only systems but national systems. In order to be able to understand the innovation process and national innovation systems, one has to have some notion of the types of technical and technological development that occur in the modern world. This section provides a brief overview of existing types of technical change. The taxonomy of innovations, which is discussed below, is based on empirical work. It distinguishes between:

- incremental innovation
- radical innovation
- disruptive innovation
- sustaining innovation
- high and low technology
- new technology systems, and
- changes of techno-economic paradigms.

Incremental versus radical innovations

Incremental innovations are small-step innovations that occur more or less continuously in any industry or service activity, although at differing rates in different industries and different countries, depending on a combination of demand pressures, socio-cultural factors, technological opportunities and trajectories. They may often occur not so much as the result of any deliberate research and development activity, but as the outcome of inventions and improvements suggested by engineers and others directly engaged in the production process, or as a result of initiatives and proposals by users. They are frequently associated with the scaling-up of plant and equipment, and quality improvements to products and services for a variety of specific applications. Although their combined effect is extremely important in the growth of productivity, no single incremental innovation has dramatic effects, and they may sometimes pass unnoticed and unrecorded. On the other hand, through such organizational innovations as 'continuous improvement' documentation, they may be objectified.

Radical innovations are discontinuous events and have in recent times usually been the result of a deliberate research and development activity in enterprises and/or universities and government laboratories. There is, for example, no way in which nylon could have emerged from improving the production process in rayon plants or the woollen industry. Radical innovations are unevenly distributed over sectors and over time, and whenever they occur, they are important as a potential springboard for new markets, and for the surges of new investment associated with economic booms. On the other hand, they may also upset workers and firms active in products or processes made superfluous by a radical innovation.

They may often involve a combined product, process and organizational innovation. Over a period of decades, radical innovations, such as nylon or the contraceptive pill, may have fairly dramatic effects, i.e. they do bring about structural change. But, in terms of their immediate economic impact, they are relatively small and localized; nylons, for example, replaced silk or other stockings but they expanded demand for stockings and did not upset the wider industrial structure. But when a whole cluster of radical and other innovations are linked together in the decline and rise of new industries and services, the consequences are disruptive. This happened in the synthetic materials industry and the semiconductor industry). In the latter, the radical innovations (transistors, integrated circuits, microprocessors) and their incremental improvement and exponentially growing utilization led to the decline, first of radio tubes and then most of the discrete components and sets in use, and on the other hand a rise of wholly new products and services, including the fusion of telecommunications and computing that we now have.

Disruptive versus sustaining innovation

Whilst the distinction between radical and incremental innovations was concerned with how incisive the effect of one step of innovation is with regard to existing skills and knowledge, this distinction focuses on how it affects given occupational, industrial or economic structures (Christensen and Bower, 1996). The motor car e.g., when it came and where it came, over the medium term made horse-drawn carriages and trucks more or less redundant over a period of about 30 years. This meant that occupations such as cartwrights and coachmen and the associated firms declined and more or less disappeared, not to speak of the effect on horses. Conversely, a wholly new population of car manufacturing and maintenance, transport, taxi etc. firms came into being, and in addition a much more developed and extended infrastructure of roads, car parks etc. The quartz and electronic watch or clock is another famous case in point, with the effect it had on the previous mechanical watch manufacture, sales and maintenance structures; this example is presented as a case in Chapter 10. Other more radical innovations were in electronics: the invention of the transistor in the 1950s, the integrated circuit in the 1960s which integrated more transistor functions on one component, and the microprocessor.

Sustaining innovations are those that continue along a technological path already established and allow existing occupational structures, firms and industries to exist and develop further. They may be incremental – but also radical! A prominent example is the Diesel engine: The inventor of the engine, Rudolf Diesel, had conceived this on the basis of the argument that it did not need electrical ignition by a spark as the Otto engine did, that it was thermodynamically more efficient and needed fuel of a lower grade of refinement. The snag was that the timing of the injection of fuel into the piston was problematic, which led to loss of efficiency and rather noxious emissions (the soot which used to come out of older lorries and buses). In the 1970s, Bosch, a firm also specialized in motor electrical fittings, came up with a new Diesel oil injection pump that improved the performance and environment friendliness of the Diesel engine by leaps and bounds, to such an extent that it became much more used in cars. This innovation may be called radical, but it did not upset the extant economic and industrial structures, so that it should be qualified as sustaining.

There are also innovations which are incremental but have a rather disruptive effect. The personal computer in the configuration introduced by IBM in the 1980s did not have radical innovation in the components but led to a disruption in the composition of the industrial landscape, with the decline in mainframe computers and the emergence of new manufacturing and service firms, the most prominent one being Apple.

High and low technology

'High tech' and 'low tech' are very popular characterizations that, however, have to be distinguished from those above. It is common to designate as high tech processes of innovation conducted with a relatively high amount of research and development effort. The OECD, for example, has collected statistics which rate a ratio of R&D effort relative to turnover as high tech when it is above a defined percentage of value added, such as 20 per cent.[2] Now, it has to be noted that such measures are influenced by the organization of the value chain. When an enterprise localizes R&D effort in a separate firm, it by that token brings a high tech firm into being and itself may even become low tech. More aggregate measures for industries and countries are more meaningful, but here again, the international organization of the value chain biases measures. In the value chain of electronic equipment such as computers and telecommunications, although R&D, for example, happens in California or elsewhere in the US, components production and assembly is to a large extent elsewhere, notably in Asian countries. But high tech is of course a sensible concept to typify concentrated and specialized R&D effort as an important factor of production.

However, one must not confuse high tech with radical innovation, or with disruptive innovation. Even when the rate of innovation has to be described as rapid, the innovation may very well be incremental. That does not preclude that it is disruptive; witness the case of Nokia, one of the earlier leaders in mobile communications, which ran into severe difficulties when 'smart phones' came on the market and technical and industrial reorientation did not lead to a sustainable position. However, one may also view the smart phone as a more radical innovation, but then again, it need not be disruptive. All this is to show that any of the mentioned distinctions is difficult to operationalize unambiguously. So, typifying firms, industries, and national economies has to be approached carefully. Recently, a book has made the point that even in developed countries, low tech innovation is much more important than often stylized, and when it is coupled with intensive technical experience embodied in employees of the firm, it does imply high value-added (Hirsch-Kreinsen and Jacobson, 2008).

Changes of a 'technology system' and a 'techno-economic' paradigm

These are far-reaching changes in technology, affecting several branches of the economy, as well as giving rise to entirely new sectors. They are based on a combination of radical and incremental innovations, together with organizational and managerial innovations affecting more than a few companies. An example is the cluster of synthetic materials innovations, petrochemical innovations, and machinery innovations in injection moulding and extrusion. It is often a moot point whether the individual innovations bundled together in a technology system are more radical or incremental, disruptive or sustaining, high or low tech. But together, they may boil down to a more systemic change.

When such changes are together more spectacular, they are known as 'technological revolutions'. These are far-reaching changes, with a major impact on the behaviour of the entire economy. That may take some time, though, which may make the term 'revolution' appear a bit excessive, but this is usual in this academic business: even the 'industrial revolutions' of the past have at least taken decades, whereas the French Revolution took only 4 years, from the storm on the Bastille through the new constitution to the decapitation of King Louis XVI. In other words, the revolutions and paradigm changes take much more time than political revolutions, and by that token they shade into evolutions, but they are pervasive in effect nevertheless.

A change of this kind carries with it many clusters of radical and incremental innovations, and may eventually embody a number of new technology systems. A vital characteristic of this fourth type of technical change is that it has pervasive effects throughout the economy – that is, it not only leads to the emergence of a new range of products, services, systems and industries in its own right, it also affects, directly or indirectly, almost every other branch of the economy. The expression 'technological paradigm' is used because the changes involved go beyond engineering trajectories for specific product or process technologies, and affect the input cost structure and conditions of production and distribution throughout the system. Moreover, once this new technological paradigm is established as the dominant influence on engineers, designers and managers, it becomes a 'technological regime' for several decades. From this perspective, cycles of economic development can be linked to a succession of 'techno-economic paradigms' associated with a characteristic institutional framework, which, however, only emerges after a painful process of structural change.

8.3 Innovation: overview of the major institutions involved

The rise of science-based technology has led to a dramatic change in the nature of the people and institutions involved in technological advance. Through much of the nineteenth century, strong formal education in a science provided an inventor – such as, for example, Thomas Alva Edison – with little or no advantage in problem-solving. By 1900, formal training in chemistry was virtually becoming a requirement for successful inventive effort in the chemical products industries. Indeed, the days when unschooled geniuses such as Edison could make major advances in the electrical technologies were coming to an end, and the major electrical companies were busy staffing their laboratories with university-trained scientists and engineers (Nelson and Rosenberg, 1993).

In general, industrial innovation depends on 'the complex interweaving of basic research', which is concentrated primarily in research institutes and universities, 'and market-induced applied R&D' (Tapon, 1989: 199). However, the integration of basic research with market opportunity does not happen automatically. 'Investments in basic research, while important in seeding possibilities for commercial innovation, will not lead to competitive advantage unless transmitted to and further developed by industry' (Porter, 1990: 80–1). Below, we explain the mechanisms that shape the interplay between basic and industry-specific research. We do so on the basis of a discussion of the major features of the national institutional context that affect national innovation patterns. These are:

- tradition of scientific education
- patterns of basic research funding
- linkages of inventors or firms with research institutions
- degree of commercial orientation of academia
- labour mobility
- venture capital system
- national technology policy.

Most of these features will crop up again in the sections on the specific country explanations. While the first three features affect the stock of knowledge in research institutes, the others affect the flow of knowledge between research institutes and industry. In addition, in the following, we also explain two types of organizational practice that affect the construction of knowledge in industries: inter-firm collaboration and exploitation of foreign technology.

Institutional features affecting the stock of knowledge in research institutes

National tradition of scientific and technical education

A nation's pool of specialized human resources – such as molecular biologists, for example – is created through investments made by individuals seeking to develop their skills. The particular choices of skill development made by individuals are reinforced by social institutions or governments that hope to benefit society or the economy (Porter, 1990). A strong tradition of scientific education endows a country with a base of well-developed institutions devoted to scientific research, which signals to that society's members that scientific research is a worthwhile calling (Locke, 1985). Countries in which it is socially desirable and financially rewarding to pursue a scientific career will tend to produce a greater number of scientists per capita.

However, one must not focus unduly on the education in science of scientists. Industrial innovation has most of all profited from the combination of the practical and experiential with formal education in sciences and research experience. The most pioneering technical entrepreneurs of today are college drop-outs as often as they are trained research scientists or engineers. Bill Gates is not much different from Thomas Alva Edison in type, which demonstrates that, never mind the hype of scientific research, it is tinkering and experimenting which still provides a necessary impetus to innovation. And this is so above all where incremental and non-high tech innovation are concerned, i.e. in the everyday innovation-at-large in a economy. Incremental innovation may, of course, have dramatic effects, even when it is not technical, such as an original distribution model; the effect may be dramatic for a firm and possibly for a whole industry. This again emphasizes the need to distinguish radical, disruptive and high tech innovation. Increasingly, we have economies and societies that have very high tech corners with substantial research and development competence, even down to putting satellites into space and making atomic bombs, but very low tech industries next to these; India is the best example. The opposite applies above all in the central and northern countries of Europe, with rigorous training in engineering from the bottom up linked in careers with science and research training.

Box 8.1 Combining the practical and the academic in technical innovation: Werner Siemens and Johann Georg Halske

Werner Siemens (1816–1892) was one of the leading pioneers and inventors in electrical engineering. Born as the son of a manager of agricultural estates, Siemens joined the Prussian army in the artillery branch because this was known for better technical education, which he wanted to get. As a young career officer, he experimented in his spare time to develop his competence. Serving a sentence (for assisting in a duel) in the fortress of Magdeburg, he made use of the time in prison for galvanization experiments, which led to a patent. In a war with Denmark, he led special operations requiring technical ingenuity, which intensified his relations with higher officers and the governmental nobility. Still an officer, he teamed up with Halske to build up an enterprise, which eventually made him leave the army, endowed with good connections in government, a major financier of communications infrastructure. Halske was a versatile craftsman with academic interests and curiosity, the ideal and overlapping complement to Siemens. Together, they bridged the potential gap between research and development, design in detail and production methods in workshops. Siemens was the inventor of the dynamo and active in the development of sea-bed communication cables, as well as some other aspects of telecommunication and power engineering technologies. Halske advised on innovations and took them to the production stage. With the expansion of the enterprise, Siemens concentrated on general management, the founding of subsidiaries in other countries, and politics. As the enterprise became larger and more bureaucratic, Halske left, a craftsman engineer disgruntled with the new organizational methods. One half of the enterprise, the one focussed on power engineering, was named 'Siemens & Halske' for decades. The Siemens group today is a dominant multinational enterprise in electrical engineering and electronics, next to GEC from the USA, employing 362,000 people world wide.

National funding of basic research

Advances in basic scientific research are not driven by a motive of return on investment, but rather by 'the logic of scientific advance as perceived by academic scientists' (Tapon, 1989: 199). Because of the very long research cycles in sciences like molecular biology, for example, and the enormous costs of laboratory equipment and materials, long-term government support of most fundamental research is a critical factor affecting a country's stock of scientific knowledge (Mowery and Rosenberg, 1993). The manner in which research funding is allocated is also important, as it influences which types of institution (e.g. universities, government laboratories) become the central performers of scientific research.

Linkages with foreign research institutions

The openness of a nation's research institutions to scientific development in other parts of the world can be important for the stock of knowledge. Strategically tapping into the knowledge bases of other countries can help a country's research institutions to develop expertise in areas in which the country lags, thus complementing its existing knowledge base (Porter, 1990; Shan and Hamilton, 1991). Nations vary in the degree to which their research institutions seek to learn from foreign research (Yuan, 1987, cited in Bartholomew, 1997), reflecting differences in historical development of the country's educational institutions. While countries that have been 'early industrializers' (e.g. the UK) have a tendency to focus on domestic invention, 'late industrializers' (e.g. Japan) have a stronger pattern of borrowing and adapting knowledge from other countries (Hampden-Turner and Trompenaars, 1993; Westney, 1993). More recently, therapeutic biotechnology development firms to a considerable extent, regarding knowledge and personnel flows as well as venture capital finance, have become highly internationalized in the sense that they depend on international resources rather than local or national ones (Lange, 2009).

Institutional features affecting the flow of knowledge between research institutions and industry

Degree of commercial orientation of research institutions

In most societies, research institutions and firms have profoundly different missions. While the central goal of universities and research institutes is to create and disseminate knowledge, the principal mandate of firms is to maximize the wealth of shareholders (Swann, 1988; Nelsen, 1991). The degree of cultural distance between academia and industry, however, is rooted in the historical foundations of the educational system unique to each country (see e.g. Mowery and Rosenberg, 1993). A greater commercial orientation in a nation's research institutions translates into a smaller cultural distance between the worlds of academia and industry, which in turn facilitates the flow of knowledge between the two communities. National differences in the commercial orientation of academia, and/or differences in government programmes for technology diffusion have an impact on the extent to which firms collaborate with research institutions (Kenney, 1986; Ergas, 1987).

Labour mobility

Greater movement of individuals between university and industry promotes greater accessibility of firms to the stock of human and technological capital (Ergas, 1987: 201), and greater awareness among academics of commercial markets, thus enhancing the flow of knowledge between research institutions and firms (Swann, 1988). The norms and practices of a nation's research institutions affect the degree to which scientists move between academia and industry. For example, evaluation and promotion systems in universities that allow scientists to pursue contracts in industry can provide an incentive to academics to blend academic and industrial research in their careers, including engaging in industrial consulting (Bartholomew, 1997). Labour mobility between research institutions and firms also reflects the relative 'opportunity cost' of leaving academia for industry (i.e. the potential loss of social prestige or academic standing) as well as the opportunity cost of staying in academia (i.e. the forfeiting of significant financial reward) (Sharp, 1989). How a society confers status on its members – whether according to social position, academic achievement or financial status – thus influences the mobility of scientists between academia and industry.

Availability of venture capital

One option open to scientists is to leave their research institution to start up their own firm. In the field of biotechnology, in particular, start-up companies funded by venture capital serve a particularly important role in diffusing scientific knowledge from research institutions to industry: not only does vital scientific knowledge 'walk out the door' with the academic scientist who establishes the new firm; the new firm also gains an immediate social network of scientists in academia to facilitate ongoing knowledge diffusion (Bartholomew, 1997). The availability of venture capital markets to fund start-up firms varies substantially cross-nationally (Ergas, 1987; Porter, 1990) and is an institutional reflection of a society's degree of individualism and its related view of speculative finance (Lodge, 1990; Hampden-Turner and Trompenaars, 1993).

National technology policy

Nations vary substantially in the underlying orientation of the state towards industry (Lenway and Murtha, 1994). In nations with an individualistic orientation, government is said to assume a limited role in industrial development, allowing the marketplace to regulate competition among firms. That, however, is true to a limited extent only: nowhere outside the former Communist block have subsidies and government contracts been used as extensively in support for innovation as in the USA, notably in defence industries but also aviation, electronics and pharmaceuticals in general. Liberal market economies have never been stingy in subsidizing innovation whilst claiming that they owe it all to efficient markets. In nations with a more collectivist orientation, government takes a direct role, more systematically in different industries, in defining the needs of the community and setting the direction of industrial development to help meet these needs (Lodge, 1990).

Differences in the fundamental orientation of the state also have direct implications for the manner in which technology is diffused from research institutions to industry. Collectivist-orientated states often follow 'diffusion-orientated' innovation policies, in which technology diffusion is considered to be an explicit part of the government's mandate; accordingly, programmes, institutions and structural linkages are established by government expressly for this purpose of facilitating industry's appropriation of new scientific developments (Ergas, 1987; Ostry, 1990). By contrast, individualistic-orientated states leave the flow of knowledge between research institutions and firms to be carried out by market forces.

Organizational practices affecting the stock of knowledge in industry

Inter-firm collaboration

Inter-firm collaboration can be advantageous as a research and development (R&D) strategy because it allows partnering firms 'to realize economies of synergies as a result of pooling resources, production rationalization, risk reduction, and utilization of assets to the efficient scale and scope' (Shan and Hamilton, 1991: 420). Countries vary in the extent to which inter-firm collaboration is a favoured practice, reflecting historically based societal differences in the underlying view of the nature of cooperation and competition (e.g. Hamel et al., 1989; Hampden-Turner and Trompenaars, 1993). The practice of inter-firm cooperation may be further reinforced by a strong government role in coordinating pre-competitive cooperative R&D (Saxonhouse, 1986; Brock, 1989; Westney, 1993). An example of the latter is the organization by the Japanese Ministry of International Trade and Industry (MITI) of research consortia (see Section 8.5 for an extended explanation). Chapter 11 will also explain how industrial networks can aid innovation.

Exploitation of foreign technology

Cross-border R&D alliances, whether among firms, or between firms and research institutions, contain an additional benefit for firms beyond those gained from domestic collaboration. Although a firm may form one or more international cooperative relationships for economic, strategic and other reasons similar to those that drive it to domestic partnerships, an international cooperative venture may provide the firm with access to country-specific advantages embedded in its partners (Shan and Hamilton, 1991: 419). For example, cross-border collaboration can offer biotechnology firms access to the stock of knowledge created by other national systems of biotechnology innovation. Biotechnology in pharmaceuticals may be the most internationalized industry we have.

Firms from different countries vary in how much they strategically source external technology and engage in international R&D activity, reflecting differences in the historical context of economic development (Mansfield, 1988). For example, reliance on foreign technology can be instrumental in late-industrializing economies trying to 'catch up' with economies that industrialized at an earlier date (Hikino and Amsden, 1994). However, in the process of borrowing technology developed by firms from more advanced countries, the late-industrializing country also acquires distinct capabilities in importing and adapting foreign knowledge. This strategy of 'learner' may thus be retained by firms long after the economic 'catch-up' has occurred (Westney, 1993).

The following explanation of the main features of the national innovation systems of the USA, Japan and China, Germany and France illustrates the importance of each of the institutional and organizational features just mentioned, for the specific innovation trajectories in these different countries.

8.4 The American innovation system[3]

The period between 1900 and 1940 witnessed the formation of the structure of the private sector component of the US national innovation system. The turn of the century ushered in the rise of the giant multi-product corporation; this development was supported by industrial research, which ensured the survival of such initiatives. Since federal funding for non-agricultural research was sparse until about 1940, state government support, particularly to universities, provided the primary impetus. Universities rose to the occasion to accommodate and recognize the requirements of industry, agriculture and mining. Although by later standards their research budgets could be seen as minute, to say the least, university research thrived and eventually included collaborations of all sorts with flourishing research departments within private firms.

What distinguishes the US innovation system from its counterparts in other countries? The most obvious trait is its scale: US R&D investment – for most of the post world war era – exceeded the combined investment of all other OECD countries. Another key difference in the innovation system in the US can be seen in the triad structure of industry, universities and the federal government in the performance and funding of research.

Unique to the US innovation system is the extent to which new firms have been behind the commercialization of new technologies in the economy. Development and diffusion of microelectronics, computer hardware and software, biotechnology and robotics: these have all been developed and diffused in the last 40 years by rather small start-up firms – to a much greater extent in the US than in any other country (with the possible exceptions of only Denmark and Taiwan).

What lies behind the contrasts in structure between the US national innovation system and that of other countries? Antitrust statutes in the US importantly affected the structure and performance of the national innovation system. In the late nineteenth century, the increasingly stringent judicial interpretation of the Sherman Antitrust Act escalated the civil prosecution of agreements among firms regarding price and output controls. In the period 1895–1904 (and particularly after 1898), firms seeking to control prices and protect markets reacted to this new legal environment through mergers, particularly horizontal mergers. As the US Justice Department used further interpretations of the Sherman Antitrust Act to prosecute a wider range of firms, corporate America was compelled to greater reliance on industrial research and innovation. Corporate diversification and the use of patents provided firms some manoeuvring room, within the law, to attain or retain market power.

Invention and development of new technologies were not the only core tasks of fledgling corporate research laboratories. These in-house labs were also charged with monitoring the environment for technological threats, and with acquiring new technologies through the purchase of patents or firms. Dupont, for example, can attribute much of its success to acquiring many of its major product and process innovations early on in its development – often based on the advice of its research lab. Similar monitoring roles were played by research facilities at AT&T, General Electric, and Eastman Kodak (although the latter to a lesser extent).

If Sherman Antitrust legislation spurred on the development of US innovation in the early twentieth century, military R&D and procurement contracts were the driving force in the latter half of the century. Since the 1940s, the federal R&D budget has been dominated by military services, the allotment of which fell below 50 per cent of federal R&D obligations in only 3 years during this time. During the early postwar years, this high level of military R&D investment bolstered high-technology industries. In the semiconductor sector, for example, military procurement may have played an even more important role than direct military R&D outlays. Product development in the electronics industry was determined from the outset by the procurement needs of the military and NASA. Such industries subsequently poured profits and overhead from military procurement contracts into company-funded R&D to generate lucrative spillovers for civilian use.

Another factor setting apart innovation in the US from that of Germany or Great Britain, for example, is the parallel way that industrial and academic research developed in the US. Already at the end of the nineteenth century, the pursuit of research – within both US industry and higher education – was recognized as an important professional activity. German industry and academia had set the example, and competitive pressure from the Germans (felt keenly by industry) provided the impetus. How did the two kinds of research become so interrelated? The answer is to be found in the decentralized structure and financial support of the US higher education system, particularly public universities. Public funding of US higher education led the system to grow far beyond that of Great Britain, for example. The nature and politics of public support – state rather than federal funding – created unique advantages for the US system. State funding led to curriculum and research at universities becoming more closely tied into commercial opportunities than could be the case in many European systems. State university systems, attuned to the requirements of the local economy, were able to introduce new programs in a timely fashion in emerging subfields such as engineering, and, to some extent, mining and metallurgy.

Of vital importance to scientific knowledge and problem-solving techniques are the people trained to use them. The pool of technically trained personnel in the US prepared to contend with the rise in scientific know-how, particularly engineers, grew rapidly at the end of the nineteenth century, in part due to the increased number of engineering schools and programs. Although the training of these engineers was rather rudimentary before the Second World War, it met the basic needs of the expanding industrial establishment for technicians trained to cope with the larger body of scientific knowledge. Cutting-edge science would come later. At the time, there were far more technicians than 'scientists'. The diffusion and utilization of advanced scientific and engineering knowledge was supported by the broad-based system of training in the US. Higher education during the early twentieth century, although basic, proved to be more than sufficient to power scientific and engineering development.

A dramatic shift took place from the Second World War onwards. Scientific research, both industrial and academic, was then bolstered by dramatically expanded federal government funding. Postwar federal R&D funding has continued to comprise a substantial fraction of an already impressive national R&D budget. The amount of resources dedicated to R&D since the end of the Second World War is staggering, not only compared with expenditures during other periods in history, but also compared with the investment of other OECD countries. Federal support for university research has led to an immense expansion of academic research, tied into contracts and grants for specific research projects. These are issued, for the most part, by a centralized federal authority, although several other federal agencies, each with their own agendas, have contributed to the huge increases in research demand.

Although federal funds have been especially important to basic research, only 15 per cent of federally funded basic research is currently performed within the federal research establishment. Universities became more important players in basic research during the postwar period – now accounting for a growing share of total US basic research, which stimulates even more collaboration between university and industrial research. This collaboration was well established before 1940, underwent a weakening during the 1950s and 1960s, and has now been restored to prominence. Support of industry for university research can be seen in financial support from industry in establishing on-campus facilities for research with potential commercial value. The spectrum of collaborations is too broad to allow generalizations, and each industry has its own peculiarities regarding the industry/university relationship. Biotechnology provides one example of an extremely close connection between university research and commercial technology. The closeness can be attributed perhaps to the radical nature of biotechnology: scientific breakthroughs in recombinant DNA and genetic engineering techniques are quickly transferred to industry and put into practice.

What other roles did the federal government play in the development of university research? On the supply side, federal actions enlarged the pool of scientific personnel and supported high quality research and teaching by funding acquisition of the necessary physical equipment and facilities. The federal government also fostered the universities' commitment to research, which before the Second World War had a lower priority than teaching. This was done by simultaneously providing funds for education and the support of research within the university community. The US mix of research and teaching in higher education went much further than policies elsewhere in the world. More research is carried out in specialized institutes in Europe and Japan, for example, and in government-run labs.

Despite the shifts in federal government financial support, however, private industry has retained its position as forerunner in research. In 1985, industry performed 73 per cent of total US R&D, and took on more than 50 per cent of the total funding. As mentioned earlier, established firms in the US expanded their R&D greatly in response to the war effort and subsequent Cold War hostilities. Yet, interesting to note is the prominent role played by relatively young industrial firms in developing the postwar US industrial innovation system. These new firms, which pioneered the commercialization of new product technologies such as semiconductors, computers, and biotechnology, presented a new way forward, compared with the pattern in Japan and Western Europe, where new technology development was the province of established firms. What is behind the prominent role taken by new, small firms in the postwar innovation system in the US? One factor is certainly the labour mobility in and out of the large basic research 'incubators' in universities, the government and some private firms. Individuals involved in the development of certain technologies were not adverse to taking their innovations with them and founding firms to pursue commercialization. Biotechnology, microelectronics and computer industries were particularly affected by this pattern. Moreover, within regional agglomerations of high-tech firms the above-mentioned labour mobility had other consequences: channelling technology diffusion and attracting other firms in similar or related industries.

Another important factor behind the success of small, new firms in the US has been the US venture capital market, which played, for example, a particularly important role in establishing many microelectronics firms in the 1950s and 1960s. This sophisticated private financial system also contributed to the growth of the biotechnology and computer industries. Eventually, the supply of venture capital was supplemented by public equity offerings. A relatively permissive intellectual property regime in certain industries (particularly microelectronics and biotechnology) also supported the commercialization of innovations by new firms, thereby promoting technology diffusion and shielding young firms from litigations over innovations that may have had their roots, in part, in the R&D departments of established firms or other research labs. The 1956 consent decree that settled the federal anti-trust suit against AT&T led, among other things, to more liberal licensing and cross-licensing policies for microelectronics. Litigation with regard to biotechnology may have been discouraged by the continuing uncertainty over the nature of intellectual property protection.

Start-up firms benefited importantly also from postwar antitrust policy. Settlement of the AT&T suit in 1956 had two ramifications for new microelectronics firms: first, liberal patent licensing terms set down by the consent decree, and second, prohibitions constraining AT&T from business activities beyond telecommunications. AT&T, with at the time the greatest technological capabilities in microelectronics, was thus blocked from entering into commercial production of microelectronic devices, which paved the way for start-up firms. IBM also lost an antitrust suit in 1956, which mandated liberal licensing of the firm's punch card and reasonable rates for computer patents. Indirectly, major postwar antitrust suits probably supported start-up firms by deterring the established firms from continuing their prewar pursuit of new technology through acquisitions of smaller firms.

A final postwar stimulant for new firms was US military procurement policy, which in the 1950s and 1960s opened the doors, through low marketing and distribution entry barriers, to start-up firms in microelectronics and computers. The possibilities for technological spillovers from military to civilian applications, fuelling the already substantial benefits for such firms, were, in fact, often based on military policy. In contrast to its European counterparts, the US military took a chance on awarding major contracts to firms as yet unproved – by the military or any other market. Such contracts attracted startup firms in industries such as microelectronics. Also firms well-established in civilian markets applied for these contracts, eager to extract any commercial applications from their military R&D efforts.

Box 8.2 Core features of the US innovation system

1 Substantial federal and state level support for university education and research – both basic and commercial.
2 Robust link between research and teaching at universities.
3 Strong research collaboration between universities and industry.
4 Vigorous university–industry labour mobility.
5 Financial support of university research by industry.
6 Substantial civilian spillover resulting from the significant role of military R&D and procurement in a wide variety of sectors, with.
7 Prominent role for small start-up firms.

8.5 Asian innovation systems[4]

The first original Asian innovation system was set up in Japan. The distinctive relationship between government and industry, and the government's pervasive intervention in the economy and with technology strategy were already present in the nineteenth century. Ever since 1868 – the start of the Meiji era[5] – Japanese central government had worked closely with industry in modernizing the Japanese economy and importing foreign technology. The government built and owned plants and factories in industries such as mining, railways machinery and textiles, because it was still difficult for the private sector to finance the required investment and to take risks. In 1873, the Meiji government set up the School of Engineering (Kogakuryo), which was responsible for education in fields such as civil and mechanical engineering, telecommunications, construction, chemistry, mining, metallurgy and shipbuilding. This college produced graduates who later founded many of the major Japanese manufacturing companies.

Japan's higher education has been seen as one of the key factors in the national innovation system. The education system, which had been expanded by the beginning of the twentieth century to include several public and private sector universities and other higher-education institutions, started to supply many trained engineers. From the period between the two world wars, Japan has been among the leading countries in the world in terms of educational opportunity, both at the secondary and higher-education levels (especially in science and engineering). Moreover, Japanese universities have not only helped the private sectors by educating engineers and scientists but also by acting as gatekeepers when overseas techniques were imported into industry, making valuable contributions in introducing, assimilating and implementing advanced technology. In recent years, however, in comparing Japan's postgraduate system of education with that of the USA in the fields of science and engineering, it has been argued that curricula formation in Japan is slow in reflecting the changing nature of science and in introducing an interdisciplinary approach, while financial support for graduate and postdoctoral students in Japan is poor. Potentially, these are significant impediments that may have a long-term detrimental effect on the scientific and technological development of Japanese industry.

Also at the beginning of the twentieth century, several national research institutions were founded. One of the largest and most productive research institutions, established in 1917, was the Institute of Physical and Chemical Research (Rikagaku Kenkyusho, known as Riken). Riken was established with the aim of fostering scientific progress and thereby contributing to industries. Hence, the aim was not purely academic but also practical. Riken was established with roughly half of the funding provided by government and half by the private sector. The Science Council (Gakujutsu Shinkokai, known as Gakushin) was established in 1933 to promote more basic research and, again, both government and private sector provided the funding. Companies also started their own R&D laboratories. While small, in 1923 there were 162 private R&D laboratories affiliated to companies, cooperatives and other private foundations.

Japanese national technology policies between the 1930s and the end of the Second World War were driven mainly by military imperatives. The government retained plants in military-related industries, such as shipbuilding, aircraft, munitions and steel, and in public utilities including telecommunication. The military-owned plants were also a centre of technological development. They hired a large percentage of, at that time still scarce, engineers and imported advanced machinery from abroad. As in the USA, military technology was subsequently transferred to the private sector as the engineers and skilled workers moved from the military plants to the private sector, especially during the disarmament period following the Russo-Japanese War of 1904–05. Also similar to the situation in the USA, the military not only produced goods within its own shipyards and arsenals, but also procured them from the private sector. Since the military, for obvious defence reasons, preferred to procure goods domestically, procurement gave domestic producers in shipbuilding, steel, machines, electrical equipment, and so on, who were under competitive pressure from larger and technically advanced foreign firms, a chance to increase their production and accumulate knowledge through experience.

In terms of industrial composition, food processing and textiles were the largest industries before the turn of the century. By mid-1910, many companies in the metal, machinery, chemical and other heavy industries had begun to grow quickly. Technological progress was an important source of this growth. This technological progress came from indigenous (traditional and domestic) technology and, especially, from technology imported from advanced countries. Indigenous technology was important in the traditional industries but also in providing the opportunity to choose between the technologies available in developed countries, and in adapting and assimilating them to fit domestic conditions. This fact was most notable in the textile industry, the second largest manufacturing industry at the time (next to food processing) and the largest exporting industry before the Second World War.

The role of indigenous technology was limited, however, in modern industries such as metal and machinery, where imported technology played a far greater role. The import of technologies was accompanied by a systematic policy designed to improve these technologies. The method of assimilating and improving on imported technology was mainly some form of 'reverse engineering'. This involved trying to manufacture a product similar to one already available on the world market but without direct foreign investment or transfers of blueprints for product and process design. The widespread use of reverse engineering during the 1950s and 1960s had several major consequences for the Japanese system of innovation. First, Japanese management, engineers and workers grew accustomed to thinking of the entire production process as a system, thinking in an integrated way about product design and process design. This ability to redesign an entire production system has been identified as one of the major sources of Japanese competitive success in industries such as shipbuilding, automobiles and colour television.

Moreover, whereas Japanese firms made few original radical product innovations in these industries, they did introduce many incremental innovations. They also redesigned and reorganized many processes so as to improve productivity and raise quality. In addition, Japanese engineers and managers grew accustomed to the idea of 'using the factory as a laboratory'. The work of the R&D department was very closely related to the work of production engineers and process control, and was often almost indistinguishable. The whole enterprise was involved in a learning and development process, and many ideas for improving the system came from the shop floor. The horizontal linkages between R&D, production and marketing have been pointed to as a most important feature of the Japanese national system of innovation at enterprise level (Freeman, 1988). Hence, rather like the case in Germany, Japanese success in industries such as motor vehicles, steel, semiconductors and machine tools has been based on an integrative approach within large companies far more than on small entrepreneurial firms. In the semiconductor industry, for example, the accumulation of experience through high volumes of production made it possible for Japanese firms to slide along the learning curve and to move quickly from one generation of microchips to the next. Each of these developments at the corporate level was supported by the accumulation of knowledge and technological capability. This, in turn, was underpinned by the practice of sharing experiences by means of staff rotation within the company and by the system of 'lifetime employment' (see Chapter 5).

In these various industries, tacit knowledge was important in the process of manufacturing and development. Tacit knowledge is derived from experience, cannot be codified and is scattered at the forefront of operations, be this in a manufacturing plant or sales department. For this reason, it was necessary for those people engaged in production, sales and R&D to share their knowledge with one another and to learn about the contexts in which their tacit knowledge was being interpreted. This was the reason why firm-specific skills were regarded as crucial in sectors such as automobiles, steel, machine tools and semiconductors. The Japanese management system and corporate organizational structure promote the efficient use of such tacit knowledge and the accumulation of firm-specific skills.

This Japanese approach to the import of technology may be compared and contrasted with the methods used, on the one hand, in the former Soviet Union and, on the other, in less developed countries. The former Soviet Union, too, was engaged in the large-scale development and import of technology in the twentieth century and also used reverse engineering; but in the Soviet system of that time much of the responsibility for diffusion and development rested with central research institutes or project design bureaus. This meant that much of the 'technological learning process' took place there rather than at the enterprise level, and acute problems were experienced in the transfer of technology from the specialized R&D institutes to factory-level management. This weakness was recognized and the institutional arrangements were changed considerably in the 1970s and 1980s to strengthen R&D at enterprise level and to regroup research activities in close relationship with enterprises.

In many less developed countries, on the other hand, the method of technology transfer was very often either through subsidiaries of multinationals or by the import of 'turnkey' plants, designed and constructed by foreign contractors. Neither of these methods is likely to result in an intense process of technology accumulation in the relatively passive recipient enterprise. Dissatisfaction with both of these methods has led, on the one hand, to pressures on multinationals to set up local R&D activities in addition to training. On the other hand, it has led to efforts to 'unpackage' imported technology and to devolve part of the design and development to local enterprises. The Japanese policy of rejecting foreign investment and putting full responsibility for assimilating and improving on imported technology on the enterprise is more likely to lead to 'systems' thinking and to total systems improvement.

Japanese government policies, especially the protection of the domestic market until the early 1970s, played a significant role in Japan's postwar industrial development. Restricting the growing Japanese market, already the second largest in the capitalist economy in the late 1960s, to Japanese firms that were competing intensively among themselves gave a strong incentive to invest in equipment and R&D. In addition, because postwar Japan's Peace Constitution meant that the military was no longer a significant customer to business, industries such as the automobile sector, which had been helped by military procurement before the war but were still in their infancy relative to US and European producers, might have been wiped out were the market opened to foreign competition.

As is the case in most countries, Japan's policies on intellectual property rights were also used to help the indigenous industry. Until the 1970s, the enforcement of the patent system was weak and ineffective to allow the development of domestic industry, which, as mentioned, was largely based on copying foreign technologies. Through the 1980s and 1990s, as Japan's technological ability had attained such a level that there was much to be lost by the infringement of intellectual property, patent law was amended several times in order to strengthen patent protection and enforcement. Japan's patent system is still characterized, however, by 'first to file' and 'pre-grant disclosure' practices. This system implies that firms can quickly acquire the research results of their competitors, and explains why the majority of Japanese producers in, among others, the semiconductor industry, employ the same production techniques while their US counterparts, such as Intel, Motorola and National Semiconductor, adopt different technologies in the production process. In other words, other firms' technology is considered an important source of technological information in Japan. It is argued that Japan's patent system is a 'system for diffusion', in contrast to the US 'system of exclusion'. The Japanese companies' learning process, promoted by spillovers, has been responsible for a continuous process of incremental innovation in the industries mentioned above.

However, the system just described may not necessarily be suited to the new industries, such as biotechnology and information technology (IT), which have experienced rapid growth since the late 1980s. Such industries differ from the traditional ones in not lending themselves as easily to achieving advancements in the technology itself. It has been argued that the rapid advances in science and computer technology initiated a shift in the way new technology is developed (Arora and Gambardella, 1994). While in the past, trial and error, the accumulation of experience, and tacit knowledge played a major role in the process of developing innovations, today one has first to identify the underlying principles governing the behaviour of objects or structures. Hypotheses can then be tested using highly sophisticated instruments and powerful and expensive computers.

For such new technologies, accumulated knowledge or skills become less important, because knowledge and skills are codified in an abstract form and belong to those people who have the advanced and specialized knowledge to understand them. The need for sharing the context in which knowledge is interpreted is also reduced, as is the need for involving the production or sales function in R&D. Rather, it is best if functions are left independent so as to enable researchers to concentrate on their own activities. Under the new system, where technological knowledge can be codified to give it a general meaning, the transaction cost of trading knowledge between different organizations is reduced. In addition, various contractual arrangements can be made (and have, for example, been made between large pharmaceutical companies and bio-venture firms) to transmit knowledge successfully. In this world, since the cost of transferring knowledge is reduced, there is no longer any need for a firm to engage in both development of new technologies and in production or sales. Thus, in the fields of biotechnology and IT, instead of the long-lasting, stable relationships typical of the current inter- and intra-firm organization in Japan, a new type of corporate and industry structure seems to be called for.

When discussing the role of the Japanese government in promoting technological change, one can't leave out the Japanese Ministry of International Trade and Industry (MITI). From the early postwar period onwards, MITI saw as one of its key functions the promotion of the most advanced technologies with the widest world market potential in the long term. In this respect, MITI differed from almost all other analogous ministries and departments in western Europe or North America, which mostly did not see themselves as responsible for long-term technology policies until much later (the 1970s and 1980s). The patent policy just discussed and the protection of the domestic market until the industry was sufficiently developed to cope with foreign competition were part of MITI's industrial policy.

MITI's ability to provide a reasonably accurate identification of the key areas in which to concentrate technological effort and new investment explains its success in restructuring the Japanese economy and orientating the leading firms to a desired course of action. In order to be able to provide good forecasts, MITI established a mode of working that depended on a continuing dialogue on questions of technological development, both with industrial R&D people and with university scientists and technologists. The importance of this national system of forecasting, however, lay in the diffusion and generalization of these expectations through a large number of companies in a great variety of industries. This helped to create a climate where firms would make investments in new products and processes associated with the new technology on a much larger scale than elsewhere in the OECD area.

MITI also initiated technological development programmes. A number of such schemes have been implemented (e.g. the 'Large Scale Projects' programme, the 'Next Generation Projects' programme and the 'Mining and Engineering Technological Research Association' system). During the period 1961–87, 87 such government sponsored 'research consortia' were formed. For MITI, the research consortia were a convenient way to distribute its subsidies in order to promote the technology which MITI (and the participating firms) believed important, most notably semiconductors and computers. MITI also used these research consortia to avoid favouring particular firms and to minimize the cost of supervising the use of subsidies. The role of these research consortia is argued to have declined as more and more collaborative research activities are now carried out by research institutions funded jointly by companies or under inter-company technology agreements.

Moreover, in former times, when the Japanese industry was going through its 'catch-up' phase, in which the technological target was clear and well defined and the players were relatively few well-established large firms with a long history of working closely with government, MITI was able to obtain sufficient information and expertise about the technological field or the capabilities of the companies involved. Nowadays, however, it has become a near impossible task since, in the fields of biotechnology or IT, rapid changes are continually occurring, and small start-up firms are playing major roles. The efficiency of traditional industrial-technology policy is much more limited in these areas. While it is true that the government played a major role in US successes in these fields, this role was mainly limited to supporting the creation of a pool of knowledge and putting in place the necessary infrastructure on which the private sector could build its business, rather than promoting specific commercial projects or companies.

Finally, rather like the German model, the Japanese model of innovation also permits and encourages a long-term view with respect to research, training and investment. Japanese firms easily amass and allocate resources for long-term objectives via the main banking system. In market situations, there would be strong pressures from the capital markets to improve short-term profitability by sacrificing long-term investments. The downside of the dominance of centralized or bank-centred finance is the underdevelopment of capital markets and, as a corollary, a relative lack of venture capital. Venture capital is essential for the establishment of the small entrepreneurial firms that are characteristic of new sectors such as biotechnology. Hence, as suggested, small biotechnology ventures are largely absent in the Japanese industrial environment.

Korean innovation could not be based on as long an historical record of industrialization as Japan. But in its focus on selected industries and products for innovation, in a coordinated way, and in going for the exporting of specific quality products made in large batches, it is close to the Japanese example. Taiwan is quite different, as explained in Chapter 4, but it features a great amount of mobility of engineers with US experience returning to Taiwan to build up new firms and development projects. Here, personnel mobility and international research links are probably the major factor explaining the strong development of a computer industry.

China also appears to have learned from innovation systems in Japan, and it has a great amount of central coordination between industrial policies, universities and research institutes, government-owned and private new firms. When it focuses on an area of innovation, the concentration of resources appears massive. The role of the government is larger than with MITI in Japan. But innovation in China, probably in view of the Maoist heritage and the consequent backwardness, has systematically organized a learning from foreign firms by inviting them in, to found subsidiaries as joint ventures with domestic companies. This allows knowledge flows from foreign input to domestic staff. The major route to promoting innovation capabilities in China, besides massive domestic investment into research facilities, thus seems to be the learning from foreign firms in joint ventures. Likewise, students from China were delegated to study and work abroad massively, probably also relying on re-importing knowledge when they return home. Also, China appears to be more pragmatic about the handling of patents and copyrights than the expected international standards would require.

At this point, it has to be pointed out that the advance of historical China in technical innovation over Europe had been considerable. China has not been a case of technical backwardness at all. Needham (2005) had demonstrated the historical advance of China in all the arts and crafts over the ages, including what was called the 'arts of manufacture' at the time in England, from the invention of gunpowder to silk and china or porcelain.

This sort of innovation was highly experimental and experiential, and the capacities for doing it were highly 'embodied' in the professionals that carried it out. There was also a strong tradition of learning. Where China differed from the occidental countries, was in the lack of a tradition of research for its own sake leading to abstract formal theories. The latter, more technological, kind of advance, combining the empirical quest for truth with the more experiential technical activities, was properly occidental and gave Europe and America an advantage from the late seventeenth century onwards, as science and technical craftsmanship came together.

Now, through the fusion of R&D, industrial policies, research in universities, and learning in joint ventures, China has managed to gain a front position in innovative telecommunications and computer technologies for mass markets in the world. It has thus performed one of the most astounding conversions from a more technical to a more technological regime in the world. It has to be classed, as Japan, as stronger in incremental than in radical innovation. It is definitely high tech in the specific industries mentioned; within its own economy, this conversion probably has to be classed as disruptive since it greatly upset the structures and ways of working in its older industries. It is also somewhat disruptive on an international scale, by the disruptive effects it has had on established manufacturers such as Sony in Japan and Philips in the Netherlands. What all the innovation systems in Asia seem to share is a selective approach to innovation with a view to winning world market shares in the industries selected, a strong role of the government, above all in mainland China, and intensive firm-university and international research and mobility links.

Box 8.3 The core features of the Japanese innovation system

1 Strong government guidance and protection of the domestic industry until the 1970s.
2 Government-sponsored research consortia.
3 Well-established educational system, especially for engineers and scientists.
4 Universities were helpful with introducing, assimilating and implementing imported technology.
5 Development of national research institutions to foster research.
6 A strong role of military R&D and procurement with spillover to civilian areas.
7 Important role for imported technology and reverse engineering.
8 Integrative approach within large companies.

8.6 The German innovation system[6]

Among European states, Germany was a latecomer, in both political and economic terms. In the first third of the nineteenth century, Germany turned to foreign countries, mainly to the UK and Belgium, for new machinery and for skilled workers to bring advanced technology to its industries. This was not easy since Britain at the time restricted the mobility of engineers to other countries. Technical knowledge was also acquired through German visitors, often with encouragement and financial support from the government, and sometimes by means of industrial espionage. Given the backward state of the polity and the economy, the government played a key role in the country's development.

In the eighteenth century, academies of science had been founded in several German states, and scientific research was primarily their task. At that time, many universities were in a poor state and some people called for their abolition. However, some of the states managed to break away from this condition by re-forming their universities or by establishing new ones with a new curriculum. Prominent among these were the universities of Halle and Göttingen. Although the reforms of these universities were important for the further development of the German university system, the origins of the orientation towards research were more widespread. For example, in the chemical community in Germany there were eleven laboratories in 1780, eight of which were located at medical departments and two at mining schools. Moreover, in the late eighteenth century some apothecaries expanded their pharmacies into private institutes that trained pharmacists, manufactured such drugs and chemicals as were traditionally custom-made by the pharmacies, and also engaged in laboratory research. Some of these institutes reached such a high level that their courses were certified by the government to be equivalent to university courses.

In the early nineteenth century, after several reforms, in general, universities became the institutional focus of scientific research in Germany. By the middle of the nineteenth century, the research orientation was firmly established at German universities, following the pioneering model of the newly founded University of Berlin. It was supported by an institutional base, comprising institutes with laboratories for the natural sciences, and specialized libraries for the humanities. University research in Germany rose to a high level, and in some fields (such as medicine, chemistry and physics) ascended to world leadership.

Government funds for the universities increased from 1860 to 1910 by a factor of about five in real terms. This expansion fostered specialization, and many universities created separate departments for natural science. The rise of the German universities took place under the close supervision of state officials. State officials not only pursued a strategy of expanding the Prussian universities, but also of raising their standards further.

Whereas, in the area of science, the German university system accomplished a great deal in the nineteenth century, it did nothing for engineering. In the mind of professors and administrators, engineering lacked the dignity of science and, for this reason, it was not admitted to the university. Some engineering schools had been founded in the eighteenth century to train civil servants for government service: as administrators in mining, civil engineers and architects, or as military engineers and artillery officers.

In the early 1820s, Prussia took the lead in establishing a system of schools to train technicians for private industry. This soon comprised about 20 vocational schools in the provinces providing courses for craftsmen and factory shopmasters. Above the provincial schools, the Technical Institute (*Gewerbeinstitut*) in Berlin offered courses for technicians with the objective of enabling them to set up and manage factories. Most German states quickly followed by establishing polytechnic schools, to some extent also following the French example (see next section).

The vocational schools expanded by offering one or more years of preparatory courses, and most were gradually transformed into secondary schools for general education that differed from the traditional secondary school in Germany, the *Gymnasium*, only by not teaching Latin and Greek, and by stressing mathematics and natural sciences. In the 1870s, their students were admitted to university. In the 1870s, too, the polytechnic schools were elevated to a higher status. They were now called *Technische Hochschulen*, required similar entrance qualifications as the universities, and distinguished their graduates from lesser kinds of engineers by the special designation of *Diplom-Ingenieur.* A further step towards equal status with the universities was achieved in 1899, when the King of Prussia decided in person to give the *Technische Hochschulen* in Prussia the right to grant doctoral degrees. The other states soon followed suit.

As polytechnic schools were upgraded to university level and vocational schools were transformed into secondary schools for general education, a gap opened at the middle level of technical education. Towards the end of the nineteenth century, the states created new technical schools. The basic level of technical training was provided by the traditional apprenticeship. The old craft guilds were abolished in the first half of the nineteenth century but the apprenticeship system lived on with some reforms. Towards the end of the nineteenth century the apprenticeship system was reorganized; chambers of trade were charged with examination.

By the beginning of the twentieth century, Germany had established a sophisticated system of education in scientific, technical and commercial matters, reaching from elementary school to doctoral level. There was a flow of knowledge between universities and *Technische Hochschulen*, as many areas of science such as chemistry were pursued in both, though usually with a greater emphasis on applied science in the latter. Moreover, there were links between the education system and industrial firms, not only through the supply of trained personnel but also through consultancy by professors in engineering and in areas of applied science.

What set this system apart from that of other countries was not only the relatively high standard of research at universities and *Technische Hochschulen*, but also its large size. For example, during the first decade of the twentieth century about 30,000 engineers graduated from colleges and universities in Germany compared to about 21,000 in the USA. Relative to the size of the population this means twice as many in Germany as in the USA. In 1913, there were about ten times more engineering students in Germany than in England and Wales. Akin to the case in Japan, in Germany the bank-based system, which evolved during the period of initial industrialization in the second half of the nineteenth century, provided industry with 'patient capital', allowing a longer-term focus (see Chapter 6 for details). Already in the late nineteenth century, the 'big three' – that is, the Deutsche, Dresdner and the Commerzbank – and firms became closely intertwined. The special ties between the big banks and the large corporations outlived the early years of industrial growth, and remained intact during the Weimar Republic as well as during the time of National Socialism. The creation of the Federal Republic after the Second World War did not endanger the coalition around the universal banking system; it proved its use once again at a time of massive capital shortages, with industrial sectors facing the costs of rebuilding and gaining competitive strength.

At the beginning of the twentieth century, in addition to the universities, the *Technische Hochschulen*, and the academies of science, central government and the federal states financed some 40 to 50 research institutes for specialized research in applied areas such as weather and atmosphere, geography and geology, health, shipbuilding, biology, and so on, some of which had military purposes; most were orientated towards public tasks, such as public health or safety regulation, and some towards supporting technical innovation in the business sector. Some smaller research institutes were financed jointly by the government and the industry. Similarly, the Kaiser Wilhelm Society (which, in 1948, became the Max Planck Society) was financed jointly by industry and the government. Whereas the Kaiser Wilhelm Society had major activities in applied research, and included institutes such as leather research or textile research, after the Second World War, the Max Planck

Society moved back towards basic research, which had brought it international recognition in previous decades.

As in all the countries that were involved in the war, during wartime the German innovation system redirected its activities towards the war effort. Generally, the two world wars had mixed consequences for the German innovation system. German companies lost export markets and patent protection, as well as their daughter companies in foreign countries. In the period of National Socialism the number of students in higher education was reduced drastically whilst vocational education and training took in more people. Moreover, although a large majority of academics tolerated the authoritarian rule of the National Socialists, many scientists and engineers were removed from their posts, most often because they had Jewish roots. Researchers in all fields of scholarship were forced to emigrate, including leaders in their field such as the physicist Albert Einstein and the mathematician John von Neumann. As many émigrés were unwilling, or unable, to return, the National Socialist period had a damaging effect on the quality of German science for more than two decades.

After the Second World War, the basic components of the innovation system were reconstructed: the firms and their laboratories, the schools, the universities and Technische Hochschulen, the Max Planck Society, government research institutes, and so on. In the Western part, the allies introduced a trade union structure that more or less avoided conflicts among specialized trade unions within firms. The Western allies also prohibited R&D for military technology as well as for some areas of civilian technology, including nuclear technology, aeronautics, rocket propulsion, marine propulsion, radar, and remote and automatic control. The key injunctions remained in force until the Federal Republic became a sovereign state in 1955. They effectively wiped out the military and aeronautics industries and in some product groups kept German firms away from the technological front for some time. Before, and before the USA built up its military-industrial complex more massively from 1940 on, Germany was on a par with the USA regarding high tech and radical innovation; it provided the foundations for all the ballistic missile development in the world and had jet engines for aircraft operational from about 1943 on (Sorge and Rothe, 2011). The claim in the varieties of capitalism and the business systems literature (compare Chapter 4) that coordinated market economies or cooperative business systems are not suited for radical innovation, is disproved by pre-1945 Germany and also the pre-1940 USA plus the rest of the Anglo-American complex: these did or do not excel in radical innovation, either.

A major institutional innovation happened after the Second World War: The Fraunhofer Society was in 1949 organized to provide applied research mainly on contract with clients in industry and government. The Fraunhofer Society has close links to universities but about 20 per cent of its budget come from research contracts. Being dependent on contracts, it has a strong orientation towards serving clients. It provides a link between universities and industry, and thus helped to reduce the gap that opened in the German innovation system as the Max Planck Society moved towards basic research.

Since the mid-1970s, the higher-education sector has been neglected in Germany. In particular for the universities, the neglect by government has not only been financial, but also one of governance. Little has been done to install the sort of governance structures that would enable universities to tackle deficiencies in teaching and to adapt with speed and flexibility to new developments in science and technology, in particular such developments that open up new connections between areas that, previously, were distinct and separate from one another. Legislation and social taboo have also played a part, explaining the lag in developing therapeutic biotechnology firms; but a German come-back in this biotechnology example also shows that, when an industry is small and exists in a highly internationalized network of support, a lagging-behind can be redressed (Lange, 2009). In the more traditional areas of mechanical, electrical and civil engineering, however, close collaboration between the technical universities and firms remained strong. That Germany fell behind in radical innovation, is explained by a conjunction of factors: the expulsion of Jews and political opponents from the universities and the research system and the anti-intellectual policies of the Nazis, the ravages of the war and restrictions on postwar high-tech development, which all together after the end of the war led to a focus on 'making useful things' during a long period of severe resource constraints and statutory limitations under the occupation regime.

The creation of better links between industry and the higher-education sector was recognized in the 1980s by federal and state governments as a task for technology policy. Under German law, professors own most intellectual property and generally have long-term relationships with established firms. Universities have thus had little incentive to establish technology transfer labs. Research within the biomedical sciences and other 'pure' research fields has until recently been conducted with minimal attention to possible commercial spin-offs. From the 1980s, state governments have prodded universities to be more sensitive to the needs of regional industry. Most universities and, in some regions, technical and commercial colleges (*Fachhochschulen*) now have a special office for technology transfer.

An official technology policy in the sense of a set of government policies designed to support technical change and to guide its direction has existed at the federal level only since the late 1960s, and at the state level only since the 1980s. Since 1983, the federal government has experimented with support for newly created technology-orientated enterprises.

Box 8.4 The core features of the German innovation system

1. Initially imported technology.
2. Establishment by the government of the academies of science.
3. Private laboratories.
4. High standard of research and education at universities and *Technische Hochschulen*.
5. Excellent vocational training.
6. Specialized research institutes funded by the government.
7. Negative influence of war in terms of prohibitions from carrying out research in certain areas.
8. Applied or contract research carried out by the Fraunhofer Society.
9. Federal support for science parks and small start-ups.
10. Strong industry R&D activity.
11. Link between *Technische Hochschulen* and industry.

The government provided subsidies that helped to strengthen the infrastructure for risk capital. The government also worked with the financial community to introduce measures designed to stimulate the provision of higher-risk investment capital and allow technology firms to undertake the rapid growth trajectories commonly seen in US technology clusters.

Institutional support by the federal government is heavily concentrated on national laboratories and departmental laboratories. Since the 1970s, there have been attempts to improve the links between the national laboratories with industrial technology. Since the 1980s, federal states and some cities have supported science parks to attract new high tech firms to their region or to facilitate the spin-off of new firms from existing organizations. Innovation centres were established, providing space and infrastructure facilities for new science-based firms.

A key factor in the technological strength of any country is the innovation activities of business enterprises. R&D is only a part of these innovation activities, but in many industries it is an essential part. In Germany, about 63 per cent of total national R&D is financed by the business sector, a much higher percentage than in the USA, France, the UK or Italy, but a lower percentage than in Japan, where it is 78 per cent. At the aggregate level, government has not been an important source of funds for R&D performed in the business sector. In 1987, for example, it financed about 12 per cent of all R&D performed by the business sector. About 31 per cent of domestic industrial R&D capability (as measured by R&D employees) is accounted for by the six top spenders: Siemens, Daimler-Benz, the main chemical and pharmaceutical enterprises, Volkswagen and BASF.

To date, German industry has shown a strong technical capability in those areas where it has a long tradition of technological strength. Germany has tended to be strong in complex products, involving complex production processes that depend on skilled and experienced employees on whom responsibility can be devolved. Germany is the undisputed leader in improving and upgrading technology in fields such as chemicals (BASF), machine construction (a welter of mainly medium-sized and smaller firms), motor vehicles (Daimler-Benz, Volkswagen, Audi, BMW, Porsche), electrical and electronic engineering (Siemens). Where radically new areas of technology emerged in the decades after the Second World War – for example, computers, biotechnology and microelectronics – or where, because of the post-Second World War policies of the allied countries German industry had to start anew (as in aircraft), industry developed less technological dynamism.

8.7 The French innovation system[7]

The French system is essentially a creation of the post-Second World War period. The higher education sector, with its dual component (the universities and the Grandes Écoles) dates back to the late eighteenth century and to subsequent developments at given periods of the nineteenth century (the Napoleonic period). But, otherwise, today's institutions have all evolved out of those that were built just after the Liberation from 1945 to 1949, and again from 1958 to 1966. The French national system of innovation consists to a large extent of a set of vertically structured and fairly strongly compartmentalized sectoral subsystems, often working for public markets and involving an alliance between the state and public and/or private business enterprises. The most important subsystems are those that concern electrical power production (conventional and nuclear), telecommunications, aerospace, arms production and electronics. However, the state–enterprise relationship also exists in petroleum, railway equipment and transport systems, civil engineering and marine technology.

Of all sectoral subsystems, the military subsystem of innovation is one of the largest. A large part of the French high tech industry (perhaps really all of it outside the medical sector and pharmaceuticals) has been shaped by the pervasive influence of defence markets and military demand (Chesnais and Serfati, 1990, 1992). This influence did not necessarily have positive outcomes. It has, for example, been argued that the underperformance of the French electronics industry, despite the attention and financial support it has received and against the expectations of its shareholders and governmental supporters, cannot be dissociated from the fact that the military has had priority in setting the industry's R&D and industrial objectives (Serfati, 1991).

Moreover, in instances where new technologies emerge in the defence sector, as in laser technology, the transfer to civilian use has proved a complete failure. The strongly vertical organization of innovation in many sectors has been pointed to as a significant obstacle to the horizontal inter-industry and inter-sectoral transfer of technology. Barriers to inter-industry flows of technology have been further accentuated by a strong secrecy stemming from the important military component of technology production.

The pervasive role of the state in the French economy and innovation system has been explained by the historical weakness of French capitalism, along with the need for state support, and by the important role played by the elite of the Grandes Écoles and the Grands Corps in creating particularly strong links between the state apparatus, the public or quasi-public enterprise sector, and the private industrial and financial sector. By 'corps' is meant a highly trained expert personnel who successfully entered top schools and went to one of the specialized engineering schools. These people, who come from the same schools, to a large extent run the country's major industrial enterprises, the nationalized industries and the public sector. Thus, at the heart of each of the major innovation subsystems is a group of managers, research directors and private office ministerial advisers belonging to the same 'corps'. These people possess a 'lifelong passport' to the highest and best-paid jobs, within a system in which severe business failure almost invariably goes unpunished (Salomon, 1986).

The strong role of the state in science and industry began in 1676 when Colbert founded the French Académie Royale des Sciences with the explicit aim of fostering scientific capacities and fitting them into the machinery of government. Basic science was synonymous with expert science, seeking industrial and military applications. Both the institutional establishment of scientific research and much of manufacturing industry were, from the very beginning, acts of state. Driven by circumstances, the Napoleonic government tried to root science-based innovation in industry. This led in particular to the birth of the country's chemical industry. However, once the impetus of the Napoleonic state-led and state-supported policies had petered out, French private industry did nothing to pursue investment and maintain the ties with research. Hence, from the 1840s onwards, science and industry were divorced. This is made manifest most clearly in the almost total absence of the kind of industrial R&D laboratory that developed from the 1890s onwards in the USA and Germany, and so France occupied a weak position in the 'science push' industries.

By contrast, in sectors where technological development took the form of pragmatic, step-by-step innovations, as in aeronautics and automobiles, French inventors and entrepreneurs were very active. Up to the Second World War, the French automobile industry was the second largest producer in the world. Panhard (today just a military firm, producing tanks) and Peugeot date back to 1890, and Renault to 1899. Michelin produced the first air-tube tyre in 1895. In aviation, too, Frenchmen flying French planes held world records on a par with their US rivals up until the Second World War. Farman and Bréguet were major international exporters of planes, and Gnôme-et-Rhône, Hispano-Suiza and Renault of airplane engines between the two wars.

In general, however, France experienced a slow and uneven development of industrial capacity in the nineteenth century. Industrialization came about in successive bursts on the basis of government-guaranteed and bank consortium-financed demand, notably for railway building (both at home and abroad), ships and arms. The feats of French engineering were principally those of large projects, involving large or very large amounts of capital (e.g. the Suez Canal) and dependent on banks, which were otherwise uninterested in investing. The heart of concentrated French industry was almost from the outset situated in the iron and steel industry, and in products for the railways and the army. In these critical areas, French industrialists went abroad to England and Belgium, and later to Germany, to buy their technology. They even recruited their foremen and skilled operators in these countries.

The legacy of the Napoleonic period, with regard to the organization of teaching and of research in science and technology, proved in time to be an obstacle to the development of science and innovation. When Napoleon undertook the reorganization of French higher education between 1806 and 1811, he largely re-established the centralized structure fashioned in the Ancien Régime in keeping with his increasingly conservative policies in many areas. This structure gave primacy to the training of experts as distinct from researchers and creators.

Box 8.5 Innovation system features specific to France

1. A pervasive element of state and military involvement in the production not just of general scientific and technical knowledge, but often of technology per se in the form of patentable and/or immediately usable products or production processes.
2. A dualist higher education sector (universities versus Grandes Écoles) producing elitist engineers and managers in the Grandes Écoles.
3. The organization and funding of the largest part of fundamental research through a special institution, the National Centre for Scientific Research (CNRS), distinct from the higher-education sector entities, which are funded by the state and governed by scientists in an uneasy relationship with the public authorities.

It was provided in the professional schools, which have come to be known collectively as the Grandes Écoles. The École Polytechnique, for example, was founded in 1794 and provided a grounding in engineering and science.

In contrast to the German *Technische Hochschulen*, the French engineering schools generally lacked the spirit of modern scientific research. Until well into the twentieth century, most of them suffered from parochialism. Though one had to have an extensive and broad mathematical education to be selected for one of the engineering Grandes Écoles, the training and curriculum at each school were designed to train experts, civil servants and managers for a particular ministry. Students at the Grandes Écoles learned the results of science, not the methods of science. They became either abstract mathematicians or production engineers who applied existing knowledge, rather than research engineers, who could make substantial advances in the state of the art. Indeed, while the engineering Grandes Écoles compensate for some of the weaknesses of the university system as far as preserving the level of education is concerned, they do not with respect to the needs of industry (in terms of numbers of trained personnel) and do so less still with respect to long-term basic research. R&D – in particular basic or long-term research – remains weak, and in some instances is still marginal within the engineering schools.

The École Normale Supérieure was initially set up to train the teachers required by the newly established system of secondary education. It passed through a precarious existence during much of the first half of the nineteenth century but was able to build up its research potential and develop its ties with the university in Paris. In the latter part of the century, as a result of the reforms of Pasteur, the École emerged as the best training ground of French scholars and scientists. However, with its 30 science graduates each year, the École Normale represented much too narrow a base on which to build a sound scientific edifice.

The university system, which was abolished by the Revolution and restored in Napoleonic times, was centrally state-controlled and inert, which is also why the state created the specialized Grandes Écoles apart from the universities. Attempts to reform and strengthen the universities took place from the 1880s onwards as part of a wider policy of strengthening through education, the political and social basis of the Third Republic. However, the universities played only a small part in the production of scientific and technical personnel compared with the Grandes Écoles. The provincial universities often found it hard to survive, as Paris attracted both teachers and students, and the competition of the Grandes Écoles attracted a good proportion of students away from the universities. As a result, the universities rarely offered a base for research of any magnitude. Well into the twentieth century, the typical R&D laboratory was of the small personal type that came with the professor's chair. There the professor could pursue his personal inclinations with a few assistants, though the research might not be at the frontiers of scientific advance and the laboratory might be too small, ill equipped and isolated to be efficient.

In some cases, even a scientist of renown might not be lucky enough to have such minimal conditions. Pierre Curie, for instance, had no research funds, no personal laboratory – not even an office. His important work on magnetism was carried out primarily in a corridor. His work with his wife Marie on radium was conducted under extremely adverse conditions. On being proposed for the Légion d'honneur, Pierre Curie wrote to a friend, 'Please be so kind as to thank the Minister, and inform him that I do not feel the slightest need of being decorated, but that I am in the greatest need of a laboratory.' The Paris Radium Institute was established only in 1910, 4 years after Pierre Curie's death (Chesnais, 1993: 199). By 1945, France's industrial base was small and often backward technologically. Moreover, the industrial base (also including the coal and iron mines) and the basic economic infrastructure bore the scars of the two earlier decades of chronic underinvestment, the impact of the slump of the 1930s and the destruction of the war. The state of the industry in 1945 also reflected what have been called the secular Malthusian tendencies on the part of a large proportion of the owners of capital and landed property. More specifically, France has been described as a 'stalemate society' marked by:

- a preference for stability and protection over growth and competition
- a Malthusian fear of overproduction of material goods and of educated people
- the burden of social, religious and political conflict
- the fragmented structure and conservatism of French industry, and
- the domination of agrarian and colonial interests over domestic industrial concerns.

(Hoffman, 1963)

France has had a number of brilliant scientists, but up to 1939 they had generally been almost completely deprived of adequate resources to carry out their research. Between 1945 and 1975, however, large investments in R&D and two phases of intensive science and technology (S&T) institution building took place, explaining a process of growth and enormous transformation. The new innovation system that was built was a 'mission-orientated' type of innovation system in which 'big was beautiful'. From 1945 onwards, a premium has constantly been given to large technology-intensive systems (as in the military area, in electrical power, and in rail transport) or to products that are inherently systemic (e.g. aircraft or space products). As a result, markets are almost always conceived by project leaders as being public. At home these are created through public procurement.

The first phase of institution building took place immediately at the end of the Second World War (1945). In a significant manner it began with the creation of a capacity for R&D and production in nuclear energy, and subsequently for military purposes (lodged in a major agency, the Commissariat à l'Energie, CEA). It also included the reorganization and expansion of the National Centre for Scientific Research (CNRS) and the creation under the Ministry of Post, Telegraph and Telephone of the National Centre for the Study of Telecommunications (CNET). Among the numerical technical agencies also established at the time under the Ministry of Defence, the most important was the National Office of Aeronautical Studies and Research (ONERA), which was given a mandate both for military and civil R&D. The major public agencies in the industries that had just been nationalized in energy and basic infrastructure followed suit.

The most portentous step was to move into nuclear research and production. This was subsequently to lead France into one of the largest nuclear energy production programmes in the world. The building of the CEA's central R&D laboratory and pilot plant capacities at Saclay from 1947 onwards symbolized the start of a transformation of French scientific institutions. In place of the small, poorly equipped laboratories of individual professors that had characterized French science, large scientific resources were brought together in a complex of modern laboratories with teams of researchers and supporting technicians. In a country where no large firm had yet set up a major industrial R&D laboratory based on the US and German model, the building of Saclay was France's first real step into twentieth-century fundamental and applied science.

The CNRS, though founded in 1939 as a belated result of the political interest in science, began to play a role only from 1945 onwards. Through the establishment of numerous laboratories and the research facilities that it administers, the CNRS has, since 1945, provided France with an infrastructure of research institutes similar to that created in Germany after 1911 by the Kaiser Wilhelm Society (today the Max Planck Society). In particular the CNRS has been able to establish and administer laboratories in newer fields of research that could not be placed within the French university structure. Moreover, the CNRS has supported the otherwise very weak university research by, among other things, seconding researchers to university laboratories and by providing the numerous services, assistants and equipment required by scientists, which neither the Ministry of Education nor the university budget had supported adequately.

During the period 1945–58, the production and diffusion of technology were driven almost exclusively by the state, and by innovation capacity lodged principally in nationalized or publicly owned firms. In the second phase of institution building, which took place after de Gaulle's return to power and the setting up of the Fifth Republic (1958–66), innovation continued to be driven by the state. However, policies were enacted to lodge at least a part of the innovative capacity within the industry's national champions. Major institutional decisions in science and technology concerned space research, with the creation in 1959 of a Committee for Space Research. In 1962, under the influence of de Gaulle, a national organization for space research was set up: the National Centre for Space Studies (CNES).

This time, however, public and private firms were involved in the programme from the outset by contracting out a large part of the R&D to the business sector. The same pattern of state–industry relationship, based on procurement and often involving the same firms, was adopted for the arms industry. Military R&D was moved out of the state sector and reorganized on the basis of R&D procurement to industry. The only exception was the military atomic programme, which did not use firm- based R&D procurement.

After 1965, the problems of the French computer and data-processing industries brought about a further development and yet another pattern of state–industry relationships. Faced with the difficulties of the French computer industry and spurred by a US embargo decision, the French government launched a new 'Major Programme' in the field of data processing (le Plan Calcul) and set up a new private data-processing company, which received massive financial aid from the state. The state also set up an Institute for Research into Data-Processing and Automatism (IRIA) and gave further financial assistance to the French components and peripheral equipment firms.

The 1970s and 1980s brought only shifts in emphasis in the area of overall R&D resource allocation and the location of entrepreneurial capacity. Also, the features that were already contained within the system as it had been built in the previous phases became clearer. Two developments warrant special attention. The first has been the consolidation, based on institutions built during the earlier periods, of a large military-industrial complex, which encompasses among other things, parts of the space programme, a part of the activity in telecommunications, and the efforts made to maintain a computer and components industry. The industrial elements of the complex now represent France's most powerful and, at least in appearance, most successful high-tech corporations (in particular, Thomson, Aérospatiale and Matra).

The second novel, but logical, development concerned the steps taken first to build new links between the research capacity accumulated within the public sector and all firms that are ready to take the innovations to market, and later to authorize and even force public research centres to move downstream towards the market and to become 'technological entrepreneurs' in their own right. These changes are far from a full-scale privatization of public sector R&D, but they represent a step in that direction. The status of the R&D laboratories was changed in the 1980s from administrative public institutions to a new generic type of status with some attributes of private law. Under this new status, laboratories have been empowered to establish subsidiaries, acquire shares and seek cooperation around specific projects with scientific and industrial partners in public interest groups (GIP) and scientific groups (GS). These possibilities give the major agencies more incentive to involve themselves in exploiting and marketing their innovations. By the end of the 1980s, however, industrial R&D, or R&D carried out within firms, remained significantly weak. In fact, a group of no more than 150 firms account for the bulk of French R&D. According to a survey, these 150 firms carry out 75 per cent of R&D and receive over 90 per cent of direct government support for R&D. The concentration of R&D by industrial branch is necessarily extremely high. In 1987, eight branches accounted for over 85 per cent of total R&D expenditure: electronics 23.2 per cent; aircraft 17.8 per cent, automobiles 10 per cent; chemicals 10 per cent; pharmaceuticals 7 per cent; energy production 7.2 per cent; data processing 5.2 per cent; and heavy electrical material 4.7 per cent. Industrial branches that account for a significant part of French exports (agriculture and food processing) or still represent fairly important components of French industrial GDP (metallurgy and metal working, textiles, machinery) account for only a very small fraction of industrial R&D. This picture confirms quite logically that, to a large extent, France's innovation system still consists essentially of sectors dominated by public procurement and state funding of technical activities.

8.8 Innovation types under societal effects

A study quoted already in Chapter 7 had compared work organization modes in the countries of the European Union (EU). The same study also established a link between dominant work organization modes and innovation modes. Now, whereas the innovation types initially introduced are widely appreciated and sometimes used, their operationalization in a comparative study across industries and countries is difficult. If we want to get at the intensity of innovation, as a crucial characteristic that we would like to compare and explain more systematically, then ratios of R&D related to turnover or value-added, country by country, are probably not the best idea. They are not only susceptible to accounting differences but also reflect concentration of innovation more than its intensity. As suggested earlier, whether an innovation is more or less intensive (radical rather than incremental, or possibly disruptive rather than sustaining), is not related to R&D concentration. The most radical and disruptive innovations were conducted in small teams. And putting a person on the moon may be a 'great step for mankind' involving huge amounts of money and human effort but it was not a radical innovation, depending on very concentrated incremental engineering in a number fields.

In an approximation of the intensity of innovation, specifically the radical versus incremental quality of innovation, researchers for the EU had done an innovation survey and constructed a rank scale for intensity, with the following ranks:

1 Leaders that are at the forefront of technical change.
2 Modifiers that add modifications to new technology taken over from others.
3 Adopters that take over new technology without creative modification.
4 Non-innovators that use proven and available technology.

The distribution of innovation types per EU country is shown in Table 8.1. We see, above all, a North–South gradient of innovation intensity, with more leaders in the North of Europe and more non-innovators in the South. However, the position of the UK is striking and does not fit this North–South distinction: It has one of the highest non-innovator

Table 8.1 Distribution of innovation modes in 14 EU member nations, 1998–2000

	Leaders	*Modifiers*	*Adopters*	*Noninnovators*	*Total*
Belgium	20	16	14	50	100
Denmark	19	11	14	56	100
Germany	25	25	11	39	100
Greece	13	5	10	72	100
Italy	18	15	4	64	100
Spain	8	5	19	67	100
France	20	10	11	59	100
Luxembourg	24	20	4	52	100
Netherlands	22	16	8	55	100
Portugal	18	16	13	54	100
UK	11	5	16	68	100
Finland	29	10	3	55	100
Sweden	25	14	8	53	100
Austria	20	20	9	51	100

Source: Third Community Innovation Survey (CIS).

percentages in the study, and half the leader percentage of countries at its geographical latitude. On the other hand, we know that in pharmaceuticals, aeronautical engineering and some other high tech industries, it has leading enterprises. On the other hand, research has suggested that the UK has slipped in the league tables for innovation over the years, where 'ordinary' enterprises outside the high tech industries and firms are concerned. We do not want to speculate too much at this point about the exact picture and causes, but suffice it to say that firms in liberal economies may not generate innovativeness on a broader basis. The latter seems to happen in the coordinated market economies and in cooperative business systems; the state-dominated business systems are not inherently doing badly, which is shown by the contrast between France and Spain: France has more than twice as many leaders (Arundel et al., 2007: 18).

A major effect of business systems, on national innovation systems and then innovation intensity, seems to be a polarization effect: cooperative business systems may 'equalize' and generally augment the level of innovation, whereas other business systems, except where there are industrial districts, see the case of Italy, appear to generate a distinction between leaders and non-innovators. That may indeed mean that leaders, or even radical innovators, are brought forth, but the rest remain more detached from these.

The authors of the quoted article now go further, by analysing the relationships between national innovation type scales and types of organizing. They suggest that the innovation intensity is more related to prevalent organizing modes than often suggested and that it is at least as important as relations between firms and external institutes or innovation promoting agencies or policies. On the other hand, they cannot exclude that, through the nature of business systems, internal organizing modes (plus HRM and other institutions) are also related to innovation promoting agencies outside and between firms, which is highly likely given the picture emerging from comparative business systems (see Chapter 4). Also, it is highly likely that cultural patterns such as those promoting individualism or power distance are also related to the encouragement and dispersion of innovative behaviour.

To cut a complex analysis short, here is what the authors say by way of summary: 'The results support the basic conclusion about the positive relation between the use of discretionary learning and firms' capacities for knowledge exploration and innovation' (Arundel et al., 2007: 24). Discretionary learning, the reader will recall from Chapter 7, is inherent to a form of organization with enriched and variable tasks, and it is both encouraged and tolerated by management; workers have discretion in their job performance, and they are expected to learn in using this discretion. On the other hand, Taylorist and lean organization are negatively related to innovation intensity. It is of course impossible to determine from this study whether work organization influences innovativeness or the other way around. But it is important to know that they are associated. And the importance of discretionary learning in innovative enterprises comes out most strongly throughout the analysis.

8.9 Conclusions

The overview of some of the main institutional features of the national innovation systems shows clear institutional differences between countries, leading to different trajectories of innovation. Aside from the differences, there were a few similarities that seem to be required in order for an innovation to function. In one way or another, we found everywhere a link between basic research (carried out at universities or research institutes) and applied or commercial research. Military R&D and procurement has played a substantial role in all countries (except Germany after the Second World War, since it was not allowed to build up a military complex). The importance of spillover from military to civilian technology can be seen from the relatively poorer performance of the German telecommunications and aircraft industries in the postwar period.

The most striking communal feature, however (albeit to different degrees and in different ways), is government support for research and education. Government support, especially in developing the institutional edifice, seems to be a necessary condition in all countries for firms to innovate. This conclusion underlines the point made by Edquist and Johnson (1997) that innovation activities are so uncertain and conflict-ridden that they need institutional support in order to become an important activity. This is not the traditional view of the relationships between institutions and innovations. It is indeed more common to see institutions as entities that introduce stability, even rigidity, into the economy and act as brakes to innovation rather than accelerators. Possibly what explains the relation is that the pooling of resources is crucial for high tech innovation, and the simple fact seems to be that military contracts facilitate this pooling of resources more than commercial propositions. The US system shows that the most spectacular results for high tech and radical innovation are based on a combination of two things which are often thought to be in opposition, but they are not: flexible and risk-prone capital markets for spin-offs and new ventures, together with lavish governmental subsidies and intensive enterprise-university research and development relations.

But the institutional set-up does change over time. Germany and the USA show the clearest and opposed historical shifts: away from radical innovation in Germany post-1945, towards radical innovation in the USA post-1940. Evidently, institutions and culture are not as path-dependent over the long run as often assumed. This also showed in the previous chapters. Institutional rigidity is, in the long run, a threat to technical change and, as a consequence, would make long-run economic development impossible. However, institutions may have both supporting and retarding effects on innovation. The balance between them is clearly different between countries and changes drastically over time. The countries discussed have also shown that a specific institutional set-up can neither permanently support nor retard innovation (i.e. France). This picture confirms that an economy's ability to generate growth depends on its ability to generate technical change, and, at the same time, on its ability to adapt and renew its institutions to support growth and innovation. Within the EU, at least, the clearest factor working for, or associated with, a more widespread rather than isolated innovation propensity, is an institutional and cultural framework which promotes discretionary learning in the wider workforce.

Study questions

1. Explain why, despite globalization, the concept of a 'national' innovation system still makes sense.
2. Explain why institutions and culture matter in an analysis of an innovation system.
3. Explain how history matters in systems of innovation.
4. Explain in what way the anti-trust statutes of the USA have had an effect on the structure and performance of the innovation system.
5. Explain the factors that are argued to have contributed to the prominent role of new, small firms in the postwar US innovation system.

6 Explain how government protection and promotion in Asia helped the indigenous industry.
7 Explain how an emphasis on tacit knowledge may both stimulate and hamper innovation.
8 Explain the features of the German system of innovation that contribute to the German industry's strength in the industries in which it is strong.
9 Explain the features of the innovation system of France that have contributed to an emphasis on large-scale and systemic innovation.

Further reading

Amable, B. (2000) Institutional complementarity and diversity of social systems of innovation and production. *Review of International Political Economy* 7(4), 645–687.

This article uses the concepts of complementarity and hierarchy of institutions to analyse social systems of innovation and production. In doing so it explains why no generalized pattern of convergence towards the same economic model should be expected.

Coriat, B. and Weinstein, O. (2002) Organizations, firms and institutions in the generation of innovation. *Research Policy* 31, 273–290.

This paper develops the innovation system analysis by bringing together the 'institutional' and 'organizational' dimensions of the process of innovation at the firm level. In this way it attempts to make progress towards a more exhaustive and better-articulated representation of the innovation process.

Gambardella, A. and Malerba, F. (eds) (1999) *The Organization of Economic Innovation in Europe*. Cambridge: Cambridge University Press.

The collection of papers in this book explains the organization and dynamics of innovative activities in Europe. The book is one of the few attempts within the literature on industrial economics and innovation to build analytical frameworks that are based on the distinctive features and institutional characteristics of Europe, and especially of the EU.

Mowery, D.C. and Nelson, R.R. (eds) (1999) *Sources of Industrial Leadership: Studies of Seven Industries*. Cambridge: Cambridge University Press.

This book analyses how seven major high-tech industries evolved in the USA, Japan and western Europe. The industries covered are machine tools, organic chemical products, pharmaceuticals, medical devices, computers, semiconductors and software. The emphasis here is on the key factors that supported the emergence of national leadership in each industry, and the reasons behind the shifts when they occurred.

Notes

1 This section is based on Freeman and Perez (1988: 45–47).
2 Information can be found on the website: OECD Directorate for Science, Technology and Industry 7 July, 2011, Economic Analysis and Statistics Division; ISIC Rev. 3 Technology Intensity Definition; Classification of manufacturing industries into categories based on R&D intensities, http://www.oecd.org/sti/ind/48350231.pdf
3 This section draws very much on Mowery and Rosenberg (1993: 29–64).
4 This section draws on Odagiri and Goto (1993: 76–103), Freeman (1988) and Goto (2000).
5 The Meiji era (1868–1911) meant the end of the seclusion of Japan, which was imposed on the country by the Tokugawa government (1603–1868), and the inauguration of a non-feudal central government.
6 This section draws on Porter (1990), Keck (1993), Soskice (1999), Koen (1999) and Casper (2000).
7 This section draws essentially on Chesnais (1993: 192–226).

References

ABPI (Association of the British Pharmaceutical Industry) (2000) *Pharma Facts and Figures: How the Pharmaceutical Industry Contributes to the Health and Wealth of the Nation.* London: ABPI.

Arora, A. and Gambardella, A. (1994) The changing technology of technological change: general and abstract knowledge and the division of innovative labor. *Research Policy* 23, 523–532.

Arundel, A., Lorenz, E., Lundvall, B.-A. and Valeyre, A. (2007) How Europe's economies learn. A comparison of work organization and innovation mode for the EU-15. *Industrial and Corporate Change* 16, 1175–1210.

Bartholomew, S. (1997) National systems of biotechnology innovation: complex interdependence in the global system. *Journal of International Business Studies* 28(1), 24–66.

Brock, M.V. (1989) *Biotechnology in Japan.* London: Routledge.

Casper, S. (2000) Institutional adaptiveness, technology policy, and the diffusion of new business models: the case of German biotechnology. *Organization Studies* 21(5), 887–914.

Chesnais, F. (1993) The French national system of innovation. In Nelson, R. (ed.) *National Innovation Systems.* New York: Oxford University Press, 192–229.

Chesnais, F. and Serfati, C. (1990) L'Industrie d'armement: une locomotive du développement économique français? In Chesnais, F. (ed.) *Compétitivité Internationale et Dépenses Militaires.* Paris: Economica.

Chesnais, F. and Serfati, C. (1992) *L'Armement en France: Genèse, Ampleur et Coûts D'une Industrie.* Paris: Nathan.

Christensen, C.L. and Bower, J.L. (1996) Customer power, strategic investment and the failure of leading firms. *Strategic Management Journal* 17(3), 197–218.

Dosi, G., Pavitt, K. and Soete, L. (1990) *The Economics of Technical Change and International Trade.* New York: New York University Press.

Edquist, C. and Johnson, B. (1997) Institutions and organizations in systems of innovation, in Edquist, C. (ed.) *Systems of Innovation. Technologies, Institutions and Organizations.* London: Pinter.

Ergas, H. (1987) Does technology matter? In Guile, B.R. and Brooks, H. (eds) *Technology and Global Industry: Companies and Nations in the World Economy.* Washington, DC: National Academy Press.

Freeman, C. (1988) Japan: a new national system of innovation? In Dosi, G., Freeman, C., Nelson, R., Silverberg, G. and Soete, L. (eds) *Technical Change and Economic Theory.* London: Pinter.

Freeman, C. and Perez, C. (1988) Structural crises of adjustment: business cycles and investment behaviour. In Dosi, G. Freeman, C., Nelson, R., Silverberg, G. and Soete, L. (eds) *Technical Change and Economic Theory.* London: Pinter.

Goto, A. (2000) Japan's national innovation system: current status and problems. *Oxford Review of Economic Policy* 16(2), 103–113.

Hamel, G., Doz, Y. and Prahalad, C.K. (1989) Collaborate with your competitors – and win. *Harvard Business Review* 67(1), 133–139.

Hampden-Turner, C. and Trompenaars, F. (1993) *The Seven Cultures of Capitalism.* New York: Doubleday.

Hikino, T. and Amsden, A.H. (1994) Staying behind, stumbling back, sneaking back, soaring ahead: late industrialization in historical perspective. In Baumol, W.-J., Nelson, R.R. and Wolff, E.N. (eds) *Convergence of Productivity: Cross-country Studies and Historical Evidence.* New York: Oxford University Press.

Hirsch-Kreinsen, H. and Jacobson, D. (eds) (2008) *Innovation in Low-Tech Firms and Industries.* Cheltenham: Edward Elgar.

Hoffman, S. (1963) Paradoxes of the French political community. In Hoffman, S. (ed.) *In Search of France.* Cambridge MA: Harvard University Press.

Keck, O. (1993) The national system for technical innovation in Germany. In Nelson, R. (ed.) *National Innovation Systems.* New York: Oxford University Press, 115–157.

Kenney, M. (1986) *Biotechnology: The University–Industry Complex.* New Haven, Conn.: Yale University Press.

Koen, C.I. (1999) *Government and the Pharmaceutical Industry: a Comparative Study of Germany and Japan.* Doctoral dissertation. Unpublished manuscript. University of Warwick, Department of Politics and International Studies.

Kogut, B. (1991) Country capabilities and the permeability of borders. *Strategic Management Journal* 12 (Summer/Special Issue), 33–47.

Kogut, B. (1993) Introduction. In Kogut, B. (ed.) *Country Competitiveness: Technology and the Organizing of Work*. New York: Oxford University Press.

Lange, K. (2009) Institutional embeddedness and the strategic leeway of actors: the case of the German therapeutic biotech industry. *Socio-Economic Review* 7(2), 181–207.

Lenway, S.A. and Murtha, T.P. (1994) The state as strategist in international business research literature. *Journal of International Business Studies* 25(3), 513–536.

Locke, R. (1985) The relationship between educational and managerial cultures in Britain and West Germany: a comparative analysis of higher education from an historical perspective. In Joynt, P. and Warner, M. (eds) *Managing in Different Cultures*. Oslo: Universitetsforlaget AS.

Lodge, G.C. (1990) *Comparative Business–Government Relations*. Englewood Cliffs, NJ: Prentice-Hall.

Lundvall, B.-A. (1992) *National Systems of Innovation: Towards a Theory of Innovation and Interactive Learning*. London: Pinter.

Mansfield, E. (1988) The speed and cost of industrial innovation in Japan and the US: external vs internal technology. *Management Science* 34(10), 1157–1168.

Mowery, D.C. and Rosenberg, N. (1993) The US national innovation system. In Nelson, R.R. (ed.) *National Innovation Systems*. Oxford: Oxford University Press.

Needham, J. (2005) *The Grand Titration. Science and Society in East and West*. Abingdon: Routledge.

Nelsen, L.L. (1991) The lifeblood of biotechnology: university–industry technology transfer. In One, R.D. (ed.) *The Business of Biotechnology: From the Bench to the Street*. Boston: Butterworth-Heinemann.

Nelson, R.R. (ed.) (1993) *National Innovation Systems*. Oxford: Oxford University Press.

Nelson, R.R. and Rosenberg, N. (1993) Technical innovation and national systems. In Nelson, R.R. (ed.), *National Innovation Systems*. Oxford: Oxford University Press.

Odagiri, H. and Goto, A. (1993) The Japanese system of innovation: past, present, and future. In Nelson, R.R. (ed.) *National Innovation Systems*. Oxford: Oxford University Press.

Ostry, S. (1990) *Governments and Corporations in a Shrinking World: Trade and Innovation Policies in the United States, Europe and Japan*. London and New York: Council on Foreign Relations Press.

Porter, M. (1990) *The Competitive Advantage of Nations*. New York: Free Press.

Porter, M. and Stern S. (2002) Innovation: location matters. *Sloan Management Review* 42(4), 28–36.

Powell, W.W. and DiMaggio, P.J. (1991) *The New Institutionalism in Organizational Analysis*. Chicago: University of Chicago Press.

Salomon, J.J. (1986) *Le Gaulois, le Cowboy et le Samourai: La Politique Française de la Technologie*. Paris: Economica.

Saxonhouse, G. (1986) Industrial policy and factor markets: biotechnology in Japan and the United States, in Patrick, H. (ed.) *Japan's High Technology Industries*. Seattle: University of Washington Press.

Serfati, C. (1991) *Primauté des technologies militaires, faiblesse des retombées civiles et déclin de compétitivité: le cas the l'industrie électronique française*. Paper presented at the conference on the Social Mastery of Technology, Maison Rhône-Alpes des Sciences de l'Homme, Lyon (September).

Shan, W. and Hamilton, W. (1991) Country-specific advantage and international cooperation. *Strategic Management Journal* 12(6), 419–432.

Sharp, M. (1989) *European Countries in Science-based Competition: the Case of Biotechnology*. DCR Discussion Paper 72. Science Policy Research Unit, University of Sussex.

Soskice, D. (1999) Divergent production regimes: coordinated and uncoordinated market economies in the 1980s and 1990s. In Kitschelt, H., Lange, P., Marks, G. and Stephens, J.D. (eds) *Continuity and Change in Contemporary Capitalism*. Cambridge, US: Cambridge University Press, 101–134.

Sorge, A. and Rothe, K. (2011) The importance of local resource construction in globally integrated and locally non-responsive multinationals: jet engine manufacturers in Germany. In Dörrenbächer, C. and Geppert, M. (eds) *Politics and Power in The Multinational Corporation: The Role of Interests, Identities, and Institutions*. Cambridge: Cambridge University Press, 41–71.

Swann, J.P. (1988) *Academic Scientists and the Pharmaceutical Industry: Cooperative Research in Twentieth-century America*. Baltimore, MD: Johns Hopkins University Press.

Tapon, F. (1989) A transaction cost analysis of innovations in the organization of pharmaceutical R&D. *Journal of Economic Behavior and Organization* 12, 197–213.

Teso, B. (1980) *Technical Change and Economic Policy: the Pharmaceutical Industry.* Paris: OECD.

Westney, D.E. (1993) Country patterns in R&D organization: the US and Japan. In Kogut, B. (ed.) *Country Competitiveness: Technology and the Organizing of Work.* New York: Oxford University Press.

Yuan, R.T. (1987) *Biotechnology in Western Europe.* Discussion Paper. International Trade Administration, US Department of Commerce (April).

9 Multinational corporations: structural, cultural and strategic issues

Learning objectives

By the end of this chapter you will be able to:

- understand the factors leading to the existence of multinational corporations (MNCs)
- reflect on the stages of development and foreign market entry modes of MNCs
- recognize the influence on MNCs of pressures to adapt to local circumstances and to integrate activities worldwide
- critically assess the 'transnational form' as a response to these conflicting pressures
- identify the mechanisms of coordination and control that are used in MNCs
- distinguish between different roles of subsidiaries within the MNC, and relate these roles to the learning capabilities of the MNC
- evaluate the impact of culture and institutions on the management of MNCs
- account for the implications of internationalization on the strategy of a firm
- understand entry mode strategies of MNCs.

Chapter outline

9.1 Introduction

In this chapter we will concentrate on the type of organization that, arguably, deals most intensively with international differences in management and organization: the multinational corporation (MNC). While almost all firms have to deal with international diversity issues more or less frequently, the MNC has to internalize this diversity within its organization in the course of its daily operations. MNCs are not only important as the place where international comparative management is practised; these organizations are also growing in economic importance. International production by MNCs is growing fast, and now spans virtually all countries and industries. In the period 1990–2003 the value of foreign assets held by MNCs has multiplied by five, while in the same period the world gross domestic product increased by only 160 per cent (UNCTAD, 2007). Hence, the MNC is a factor of immense and increasing importance in the world economy.

What is a multinational corporation? This question is not so easy to answer. Of course, in order to be called 'multinational' a firm should engage in business activities in more than one country. The United Nations defines multinational enterprises as 'enterprises that own or control production or service facilities outside the country in which they are based' (United Nations, 1988: 16). The phrase 'own or control' is of importance. It implies that MNCs are actively engaged in international activities. The control mentioned may be based on (partial) ownership, but this is no necessity: foreign expansions may also take the form of contractual arrangements with local firms. On the other hand, foreign investments are not always made with the purpose or effect of gaining control. Some foreign investments are part of a portfolio of non-controlling interests, and are made with the motive of spreading risk. In contrast, foreign direct investment (FDI) is made with the motive of exerting control over the activities financed. Although not all FDI is performed by MNCs, most of it is, and we may say that FDI is an important hallmark of the MNC.

There is no consensus whether the international business activities should be above a minimum level (e.g. 10 per cent of turnover) or of a specific kind (e.g. production and sales as opposed to sales only) before a firm should be called a multinational. The most sensible approach is to assume that MNCs form no homogeneous group, but that these firms can be ranked according to their level of 'multinationality' or 'transnationality'. In the World Investment Reports, published by the United Nations, the transnationality[1] index for the world's largest MNCs is published yearly. This index is the average of three ratios:

1 foreign to total assets
2 foreign to total sales, and
3 foreign to total employment.

(UNCTAD, 2014: web table 28)

When this criterion is applied, the most 'transnational' among the large MNCs are typically those from small home countries and/or producing consumer products like food and beverages, like Nestlé (Switzerland) or ABB (Switzerland and Sweden). This stands to reason, for consumer goods like foods and beverages are more sensitive to cultural and institutional differences than, say, capital goods like machinery. Hence companies active in these sectors need more of a presence in foreign countries if they want to sell there, and for companies from smaller home countries the international market becomes important very quickly, if they want to continue to grow. However, new categories of highly internationalized MNCs also arise, for instance in mining (Xstrata, Switzerland) and telecommunications (Vodafone, UK) (UNCTAD, 2014). Another trend is the rise of multinational corporations from developing and emerging economies. Examples are Cemex (cement, Mexico), Sappi (paper, South Africa) and Petronas (petroleum, Malaysia) (UNCTAD, 2007).

In our discussion of MNCs in this chapter we will first, in the following section, discuss the internationalization processes of MNCs. Subsequently, we will focus on coordination and control within the MNC. After that, we look at knowledge management in the MNC. In the next section of the chapter we will focus in on the ways in which MNCs deal with international diversity. Finally, we will look at aspects of strategy that are unique to MNC.

9.2 The internationalization processes of MNCs

Practically all MNCs started off as companies operating in their home country and have, later, gradually added activities in foreign countries. Exceptions are MNCs that acquired bi-national status at a very early stage of their development (e.g. British-Dutch Shell), and MNCs that are the result of an international merger and have since developed into a new entity (e.g. Swedish-Swiss ABB). Most other MNCs first developed at home, and then started adding international activities. Before discussing the modalities of international expansion and the typical growth paths of MNCs, a preliminary question must be answered: 'Why do MNCs exist at all?' At first sight, this question may seem absurd, so much have MNCs become a fact of life. But from a theoretical point of view that MNCs should exist is not so obvious at all. After all, the previous chapters of this book have been emphasizing the differences between the business environments in different countries. This means that a firm that has experience in one particular country must have a significant disadvantage, vis-à-vis local firms, once it begins operating in another country. There must, then, be advantages that more than offset the disadvantage of not being familiar with the local business environment or the 'liability of foreignness'.

Why do MNCs exist?

Various theories have been developed to explain the existence and continuing growth of MNCs. John Dunning put the most important explanations together in what he called 'the eclectic paradigm' of international investment and production (Dunning, 1993). Dunning focuses on three sets of explanatory factors: ownership factors, location factors and internalization factors.

Starting with the ownership factors, given the 'liability of foreignness' a firm must have certain advantages over local companies if it is to compete successfully in foreign markets. These advantages can be of various kinds. A firm may, for instance, possess specialized technology that cannot easily be bought or developed by local firms. This is true, for instance, of chip-maker Intel. While its chip-making technology is not unique, it is confined to a quite small group of companies, operating worldwide. Another possibility is that a firm may have built up a valuable brand name, which allows it to compete successfully even without superior or hard-to-imitate technology or products. McDonald's is an example of a company that possesses this type of ownership advantage. The company-specific advantage may also be that the firm has certain technological or management skills. Finally, a company may have privileged access to certain raw materials, like bauxite or petroleum. This type of ownership-specific advantage is often of a political nature – that is, it has been granted to the company by the government of the country from which the raw materials originate. All these firm-specific advantages should be difficult and/or costly to create or acquire (otherwise they would not constitute a sustainable advantage), but at the same time they must be relatively easy to transfer to other locations at low cost.

The possession of company-specific advantages is no sufficient explanation for the existence of MNCs. Why would the company that has these advantages not simply put them to use within its home country, and then export its products to foreign markets? For a firm to invest abroad, some location-specific factors must also exist. Location-specific advantages, like firm-specific advantages, can be of many kinds. Historically, an important reason for firms to invest in production facilities abroad was the existence of high import tariffs for finished goods, making it more economical to perform at least part of the production process in the end market. This is an important explanation for the many local assembly plants set up by manufacturing firms before the Second World War. Somewhat comparable is production in foreign countries to minimize transportation costs. Beer brewer Heineken, for example, has production facilities in many countries, to avoid the high transportation costs of a product consisting of 95 per cent of water. Other location-specific advantages may stem from production factors, in particular cheap labour. This is an important reason for overseas investment in labour-intensive industries, like in the apparel industry in Madagascar. Finally, some locations offer a particularly attractive environment for specific types of activity, like the City of London for the financial sector and Silicon Valley in the USA for information technology. These types of location advantage are of a more dynamic nature, since they originate in a historic process of cumulative causation, which gradually makes a particular location attractive for particular activities, mainly because of a concentration of specialized producers and service providers.

However, even the combination of firm-specific advantages and location-specific advantages is insufficient to explain the FDI that makes a company into an MNC. Why would the firm not sell or contract out its specific advantages to a local firm in the country it wishes to enter? The local firm could in that way combine the firm-specific advantages with the location-specific advantages, without being hindered by the 'liability of foreignness'. The explanation put forward in the eclectic paradigm is that markets for firm-specific advantages often fail. Trading technology over a market interface is not impossible, but can be difficult and risky, especially if the technology is very innovative. The buying partner will want to have a deep insight into the technology before deciding about the deal but, in disclosing too much, the selling firm may in fact be giving away the very thing it wants to sell. Protection of intellectual property rights is never very easy, and even less so in the international arena. This is why R&D-intensive firms that expand abroad tend to internalize their international activities. In the case of advertising-intensive firms, the motive is predominantly to avoid the damage to their reputation that would be the result of poor-quality services offered by local representatives, which would decrease the value of the brand (Hennart, 1991).

Internationalization as a learning process

The reasons MNCs exist have been discussed above. Even if there are excellent rationales, however, MNCs do not come about overnight. The main reason for this is the 'liability of foreignness' problem, which can only be overcome by learning. On the basis of a study of the internationalization process of four Swedish firms, Johanson and Wiedersheim-Paul (1975) were the first to stress that internationalization is often a gradual and incremental process. From a purely domestic function with production and sales only in Sweden, these companies first moved into export through independent representatives, then at a certain point in time they decided to set up their own sales subsidiaries in foreign countries, and only after that they moved on to setting up production facilities overseas. This 'establishment chain' shows a gradual increase in the commitment to foreign markets; as the firm learns about these markets, the perceived uncertainty decreases and it commits more resources to them (Johanson and Vahlne, 1977). Not only do companies gradually increase their commitment to foreign markets, they also enter new foreign markets in an incremental way. They start with countries that are similar to their home country in terms of culture, language, institutions, political system, and so on, and only after having successfully established in these countries move on to more dissimilar countries. In this way, they minimize the 'psychic distance' that has to be bridged in their initial steps on the internationalization path, and thus keep the uncertainty they have to deal with within manageable bounds. The initial theory developed by Johanson and Wiedersheim-Paul was based on only a very small number of observations, but later studies have, at least in part, confirmed the gradual stepwise internationalization process (Johanson and Vahlne, 2009). Of course, this general description is not applicable to all firms in all cases. By acquiring existing local firms, MNCs can accelerate their learning process. MNCs can also transfer what is learned from experiences within a particular country to other units operating in the same country, or even to other units operating in other countries. MNCs can sometimes also use their business contacts (buyers and suppliers) as sources of information to expedite learning (Forsgren, 2002). Although such shortcuts are possible, the internationalization process model helps to understand the learning process necessary for the formation and development of an MNC.

Stages of development of MNC organization structures

We will now look at the question of how MNCs organize for the management of the increasing diversity they meet in the internationalization process.

Stopford and Wells (1972) studied the development of the organizational macro structures of US MNCs, focusing on two factors influencing these structures: foreign sales as a percentage of total sales, and foreign product diversity (see Figure 9.1). The macro structure of an MNC reveals the criterion on which the basic grouping of activities within the MNC is based. The first dimension of Stopford and Wells measures the importance of foreign activities, relative to those in the home country. The second dimension can be seen as a proxy for the degree of complexity the MNC meets in managing its international activities. Stopford and Wells describe two distinct paths of development. Most MNCs started with an international unit (a department or a division) taking care of all overseas activities. This is possible only if foreign sales are relatively low and if foreign product diversity is limited. Otherwise it becomes impossible for a single international division or department to manage all foreign activities effectively.

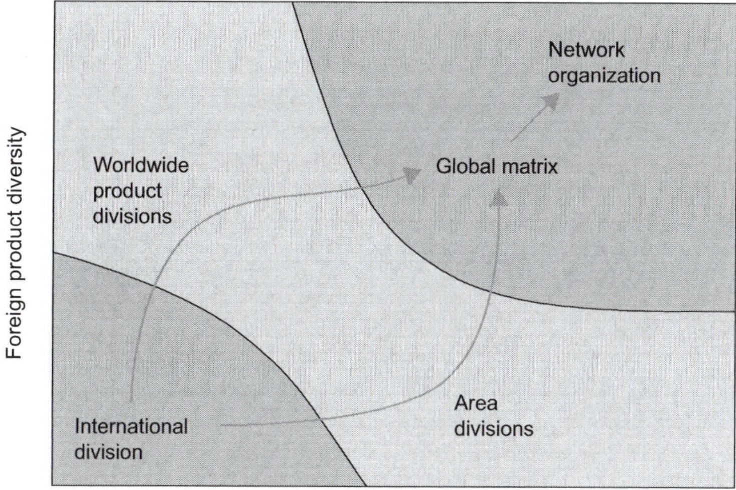

Figure 9.1 Evolution of organizational macro structures of MNCs.

Source: Stopford and Wells (1972).

The direction in which MNCs developed depended on what became the most pressing issue first: the sheer volume of foreign sales or the product diversity of international sales and production. In the first case, the solution was typically to base the organization on geographical divisions. In the second case, the organization would be structured into product divisions, each of which has a worldwide mandate. Each of the two solutions has its advantages and disadvantages. Geographically based divisions have the advantage that all local market know-how is concentrated within a single organizational unit. This allows for flexible adaptation to local circumstances. However, if the MNC produces and sells a range of very different products, it will be difficult for the area-based units to build and maintain all the necessary product and technological expertise. In contrast, worldwide operating product divisions have the advantage of bundling all the expertise concerning a particular class of product and the associated production technologies. However, they will have more difficulty in dealing with country-specific issues.

If both foreign sales and foreign product diversity continue to increase, MNCs need an organizational structure that strikes a balance between the advantages and disadvantages of product-based and area-based divisions. Such a structure can be a matrix structure, in which all major activities are coordinated by both product and area-related managers. This means that a basic classical principle of organization – the unity of command – is abolished. A number of managers in a matrix organization answer to two different hierarchical lines. In a well-balanced matrix these higher managers are equally powerful, meaning that in case of disagreement the parties concerned must discuss and negotiate until agreement is reached. As a result, matrix organizations tend to be cumbersome, in that they entail high coordination costs and may slow down decision-making. We will return to this point later.

Research by Franko (1976) has shown that the typical growth paths of European MNCs are different from those identified by Stopford and Wells in their study of US MNCs. Because of the smaller size of their home-country economies, these MNCs were forced to

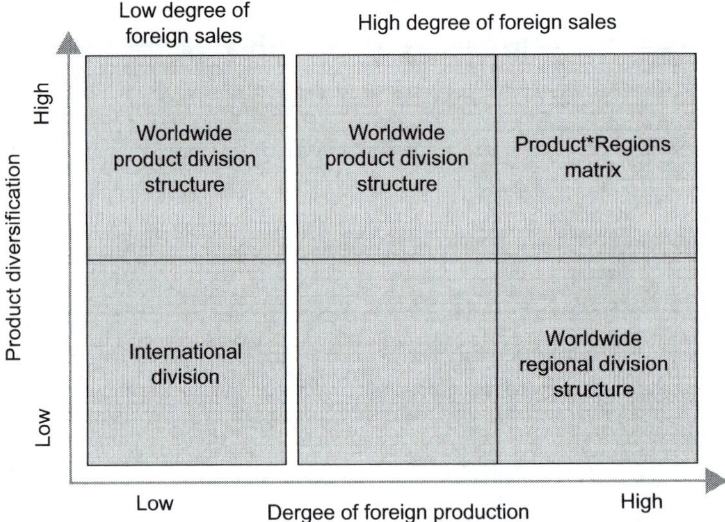

Figure 9.2 Organizational macro structures of MNCs and the relative importance of foreign production.

Source: Egelhoff (1988: 12).

respond to the international dimension of their activities at an earlier stage than was the case for their counterparts in the USA. Also, the cultural and linguistic diversity within Europe prompted the European MNCs to grant their local foreign operations more decision-making power. The result was that, for European MNCs, the geographical division structure was a more important organizational form than for US MNCs. This structure is more likely when, in contrast with US MNCs, no single region (including the home region) dominates the MNC's activities (Daniels and Radebaugh, 2001: 524).

Apart from being based on a biased sample (in that all MNCs studied were of US origin) Stopford and Wells' study is also not completely satisfactory in that they focus on foreign sales as a factor influencing the organizational form of MNCs, but neglect the role of foreign production. Egelhoff (1988) looked not only at the two dimensions distinguished by Stopford and Wells (degree of foreign sales and degree of product diversification), but also added a third factor: the relative importance of foreign production (see Figure 9.2). He found that, with low levels of foreign sales, MNCs opt for either the international division or the worldwide product division structure, depending on the degree of product diversification. This is identical to the findings of Stopford and Wells. If the degree of foreign sales is high, however, the organizational form depends on the relative importance of foreign production. If there is little foreign production, MNCs can continue to function with a worldwide product division structure. If there is much foreign production, MNCs rather opt for divisions based on geographical regions (if the product diversification is low) or for a matrix form (if product diversification is high).

Transnational management

Building on the literature discussed above, and their own research into the structures and strategies of MNCs, Christopher Bartlett and Sumantra Ghoshal (2000) elaborate further

Pressures for global integration

Pressures for local adaptation	Weak	Strong
Strong	Multidomestic	Transnational
Weak	International	Global

Figure 9.3 Bartlett and Ghoshal's typology of MNC strategies and structures.

Source: Bartlett and Ghoshal (2000).

on the management of this type of firm. Their approach centres on the local-versus-global dilemma that all MNCs have to face when deciding where in the organization to vest what sort of decision-making authority. MNCs in their operations have to be adaptive to local circumstances, to the extent that consumer preferences, market structures and government regulations differ between countries. But they also have to integrate activities at a global level if they want to realize economies of scale to the fullest extent possible. Moreover, if the MNC wants to avoid costly duplication of efforts in, say, research and development, it must coordinate and integrate these activities across borders. If the pressures to adapt to local circumstances and to integrate globally are, for the sake of simplicity, assumed to be either high or low, a two-by-two matrix can be drawn in which the four possible MNC strategies proposed by Bartlett and Ghoshal can be positioned (Figure 9.3).

If both the pressures for localizing and for globalizing are weak, the most likely MNC strategy is the international strategy. This is the traditional form of MNCs based in large domestic markets such as the USA. The international activities receive little special attention. Products are typically developed for the domestic market and sold overseas with little or no adaptation. In as far as there is production abroad, this is largely in response to transportation costs or to host-country government policies regarding local content requirements. This form is most adequate for MNCs in certain business-to-business markets, like machinery and equipment manufacturing.

If there are strong pressures for localizing, and weak forces towards global integration, the organizational form predicted is that of the multidomestic firm. This is most fitting in consumer markets, in particular for products that need to be adapted to local tastes, like food and beverages. Local subsidiaries of the MNC act as quasi-independent firms, focusing on their own geographical market, and typically having almost complete freedom in determining their local strategies. The heydays of this type of MNC were in the first half of the twentieth century (Martinez and Jarillo, 1989). In that period, tariff and non-tariff barriers between many countries were still a major factor.

The opposite situation to that benefiting the multidomestic type is that where there are strong forces for globalization and weak forces for local adaptation. The associated type of MNC is the global firm. Here global integration of R&D, design and production dominates at the cost of local adaptation. This form is most likely where economies of scale are intensely important, as in the production of industrial chemicals. According to Martinez and Jarillo (1989), this type of MNC was most prevalent in the period 1950–80.

So far, Bartlett and Ghoshal's description is a variation on the earlier research findings described above. The most interesting contribution made by Bartlett and Ghoshal, however, pertains to the situation in which both those forces driving towards local adaptation and those pressing for global integration are strong. In earlier publications, the matrix form was associated with this situation, but Bartlett and Ghoshal go beyond this structural solution to discuss the mentality that companies need to develop in order to thrive under such demanding conditions. Companies that have the mentality that enables them to simultaneously adapt to local circumstances and to integrate activities across borders are called transnationals. It is important to note that 'transnational' is not just another word for 'matrix structure'. Transnationals will often have matrix-like structures, but that is not the essence of their nature. This lies in the combination of a strategy, a structure and the mentality of the top management of the companies. In the view of Bartlett and Ghoshal, the organizational structure is a dependent rather than an independent variable: if an MNC wants to be a transnational, it first has to change its mentality from the one-size-fits-all thinking characteristic of global management, or from the idea that differences between countries are so fundamental that coordination across national subsidiaries is unfeasible or even undesirable. Some transnationals adopt a formal matrix structure, while others maintain a macro structure centred on either regions or products but dramatically change the way it operates (Westney, 1999). People-orientated coordination mechanisms, such as horizontal communication and the building of a strong corporate culture are seen as more important than the hierarchy or formal rules. Ghoshal and Nohria (1993: 28) refer to 'normative integration' through the 'socialization of managers into a set of shared goals, values, and beliefs that then shape their perspectives and behavior'. However, as Welch and Welch (1997) rightly remark, corporate cultures are difficult to change or to 'manage', and the loss of central control may have negative consequences for the MNC, like increased duplication of effort and dysfunctional inter-unit rivalry. In Section 9.5 we will discuss cultural and institutional factors in the home country of an MNC that may be more or less conducive to adopting the transnational form.

The transnational adapts to local circumstances where necessary, but at the same time achieves a far greater degree of coordination across countries than is the case with the multidomestic company. On top of that, the transnational MNC manages its subsidiaries in such a way that the whole integrated system acquires the flexibility necessary to adapt to changing circumstances, and to allow learning to take place not only between local subsidiaries and headquarters, and vice versa, but also among subsidiaries. We will return to this issue in Section 9.4, on knowledge management in the MNC.

Bartlett and Ghoshal's ideas about the transnational form are not entirely new. In earlier work, 'network organizations' or 'heterarchies' (Hedlund, 1986) have been proposed as organizational forms capable of squaring the circle of local adaptation and global integration. In addition, the importance of the mentality of MNC top management has also been recognized by Perlmutter (1969) in his seminal essay on 'the tortuous evolution' of the multinational company. All in all, there seems to be reason enough to expect something like the transnational form to make headway within the population of MNCs, but what is the empirical evidence?

While we have no historical data that would enable us to gauge the penetration of transnational-like organizational forms, there have been some empirical studies suggesting that the Bartlett and Ghoshal typology rings true. Harzing (2000) gives an extensive overview of typologies of MNCs, together with an indication of the empirical support for each of them. She also tests the Bartlett and Ghoshal typology on data from 166 subsidiaries of 37 MNCs. Overall, she found considerable support for the existence of MNCs with characteristics of the multidomestic, global and transnational type. (The international type of MNC was not included in her study, since it was not as clearly defined as the other types, and had not received much empirical support in earlier studies.) The overall conclusion was that Bartlett and Ghoshal's typology does indeed help to categorize MNCs in groups that share important characteristics. In contrast, Gooderham and Ulset (2002), considering a number of empirical studies, come to the conclusion that although there are signs of increasing lateral coordination and interdependence between subsidiaries of MNCs, prevalence of a crucial aspect of the transnational form, governance through normative integration, has not been established. MNCs employ a multitude of mechanisms for coordinating their internal activities, and it is too simplistic to identify a single mechanism with a particular organizational form.

Below we will look more closely at the mechanisms MNCs use for achieving internal coordination and control. After that we will focus on the relationship between headquarters and subsidiaries within the MNC. First, however, a note of caution with regard to the extent of the simplification of our discussion of macro organizational structures of MNCs is due.

Complex realities

The previous subsection illustrated the complexity of the issue of MNC organizational structures. In reality, this complexity is even far greater than suggested by the discussion above. As a consequence of their historical growth paths, as well as because of growth through foreign acquisitions rather than organic growth, many MNCs display a mixed organizational structure (Daniels and Radebaugh, 2001: 525). Recently acquired subsidiaries often do not fit very well into the existing organizational structure – for instance, because they perform a combination of activities that is uncommon within the MNC. An important issue to keep in mind is that whatever structure the MNC chooses, the international dimension has to be factored in at some point. If the MNC opts for geographical division, then it is very likely that within these divisions there will be departments specializing in the various product categories the MNC carries. Likewise, if the MNC is organized according to product divisions, the responsibility for different geographical areas will be assigned to organizational units within the divisions. Decision-making authority may also be allocated to regional or product-based units depending on the type of decision. For instance, all contacts with local authorities and institutions like labour unions may be delegated to a country or regional manager, while all responsibility for the internal activities of the MNC may be allocated to managers of product-based divisions. An example of such a structural set-up is the Swiss-Swedish producer of power plants and related products, ABB. Finally, for the sake of simplicity, our discussion above neglected the middle-layer structures MNCs often adopt – for example, with some kind of regional headquarters coordinating all product-based divisions within a certain geographic area.

Also, the way in which the forces towards local adaptation and towards global integration work out in a particular MNC and its various units is more complicated than suggested above. Bartlett and Ghoshal (1989) illustrate this with the example of Unilever. At the level of the business unit (e.g. Unilever's detergent business), a balance must be struck between local adaptation and global integration. However, if one looks more closely at the various functions performed within the business unit, like marketing, production or product development, the need for local adaptation and/or global integration may well vary. For instance, the sales function is likely to require more adaptation to local markets than the product development function; we could look even more closely at the particular tasks that are performed within each function in the business unit. Also at this level we are likely to find tasks that need more or less local adaptation and/or global integration. Sales promotion activities are, most of the time, geared specifically to a national market, but in determining the product policy, local managers must coordinate carefully with their colleagues in other countries.

Taking into account this complexity of MNC strategies and structures, we will now look in more detail at the mechanisms MNCs use to coordinate and control their activities.

9.3 Coordination and control within MNCs

In the previous section we discussed the macro structures of MNCs; but the formal macro structure, although important, is but one of the mechanisms MNCs use for organizing their international activities. In this section we will look into the more subtle processes and systems MNCs employ in order to coordinate and control their activities. After that, we will concentrate on the headquarters–subsidiary relationship within MNCs, and discuss the ways in which these relationships are managed.

Coordination and control mechanisms

The terms 'control' and 'coordination' are often used without it being clear whether there is a difference between them. Control can be defined as 'the regulation of activities within an organization so that they are in accord with the expectations established in policies and targets' (Child, 1973: 117). Coordination is 'an enabling process to bring about the appropriate linkages between tasks' (Cray, 1984: 86). Both control and coordination pertain to the direction of efforts towards organizational goals. The concept of 'control' suggests a power difference that is not implied in that of 'coordination' (Harzing, 1999: 9). However, as the two concepts are strongly related, and as coordination/control mechanisms based on power differentials and on other bases in practice coincide, we will use the terms interchangeably.

Synthesizing the literature on control mechanisms, Harzing (1999: 21) distinguishes between direct and indirect mechanisms on the one hand, and personal and impersonal mechanisms on the other. On this basis, she categorizes control mechanisms into four groups (Figure 9.4).

	Personal/cultural (founded on social interaction)	Impersonal/bureaucratic (founded on instrumental artefacts)
Direct/explicit	Personal centralized control	Bureaucratic formalized control
Indirect/implicit	Control by socialization and networks	Output control

Figure 9.4 Four categories of coordination and control mechanisms.

Source: Harzing (1999: 21).

Personal centralized control is based on the organizational hierarchy, and works through supervision and intervention by managers. Bureaucratic formalized control consists of the formulation of rules, procedures and standards for the work activities to be performed in the organization. Output control, in contrast, does not specify work procedures, but plans targets for the organizational units, granting these units a large degree of freedom in deciding how to reach these targets. Control by socialization and networks, finally, is a mixed bag of coordination activities that have as a common characteristic that they are neither hierarchical nor bureaucratic. Mechanisms belonging to this category are the socialization of managers and employees, the informal exchange of information (i.e., not as part of formalized control or reporting procedures), and the formalized lateral relationships between organizational units (but not based on hierarchy, unlike in the case of personal centralized control).

The extent to which these various types of control mechanism are used by MNCs depends on many factors. An important factor is size. Large organizations can rely only to a limited extent on personal centralized control, otherwise the number of managers would be too large and there would be too many layers in the hierarchy. Hence, these large MNCs tend to have a relatively strong emphasis on bureaucratic formalized control. Another factor is the organizational structure, discussed earlier in this chapter. The macro organizational structure can be seen as a schematic rendering of the most important formal authority relations within the MNC. Hence, the structure shows who reports to whom at the top of the MNC, both in the sense of personal supervision and of bureaucratic control. Furthermore, we can assume that in the multidomestic form, the control mechanism used in the relationship between the corporate headquarters and the division will be predominantly of the output control type. Bureaucratic formalized control or personal centralized control would make little sense, as headquarters does not want to interfere in the day-to-day operations of the local subsidiaries. However, the organizational macro structure as such gives few clues as to the mix of control mechanisms used to realize coordination in the organization as a whole (i.e. below the top management level). An exception is the matrix structure. International matrix-like structures are indicated as the structure of choice in situations of high foreign product diversity and high foreign sales (Stopford and Wells, 1972), or in situations where there are strong pressures to localize and strong forces to integrate across borders (Bartlett and Ghoshal, 2000). In this type of situation, and with this kind of macro structure, a strong emphasis on more informal control mechanisms, in particular socialization and networks, is to be expected.

Just as the organizational structure of the MNC can never be based on a single criterion (e.g. product categories or geographical regions), no MNC can achieve the necessary internal coordination with just a single coordination mechanism. The mechanisms should be seen as complements, rather than substitutes (Harzing, 1999: 23). In reality there will always be a mix of control mechanisms, but the balance between the various mechanisms used differs between MNCs and within MNCs at different hierarchical levels. Even at one particular level, different control mechanisms may dominate in different places. For instance, in the relationship between headquarters and some subsidiaries, output control may dominate, while in other subsidiaries a much more direct supervision of the personal centralized type is exerted. This is likely to depend on the roles of the subsidiaries in question within the MNC, a subject we will discuss later in this chapter.

There are several reasons to expect that it is more difficult for an MNC to exert control and realize coordination of its activities than for a firm operating within a single country.

Daniels and Radebaugh (2001: 518) note that four factors cause these greater difficulties, compared to single-country firms:

- greater geographical and cultural distance between units of the MNC;
- greater diversity in the environments (in terms of market conditions, standards, currencies, etc.) in which the MNC works;
- factors that limit the control of MNC headquarters over all the activities of the firm, such as local stockholders, local government regulations, and so on;
- higher degree of uncertainty (e.g. because of a lack of accurate and timely data).

As a result, in the context of the MNC the various control mechanisms meet with a number of specific difficulties. Personal centralized control is made more difficult because local managers may give little support to headquarters interventions, which may easily be seen as ignoring local circumstances and developments. Likewise, bureaucratic formalized control, because of its standardized nature, will often ignore the heterogeneity of the countries in which the MNC operates. The effectiveness of output control is restricted because the limited information flow from subsidiaries to headquarters gives unscrupulous subsidiary managers opportunities for manipulation. Working with socialization and networks is more difficult in MNCs because, for these mechanisms, frequent face-to-face contacts and interactions are essential. Moving around staff in expatriate positions can be a way to promote socialization and the formation of a common organizational culture (although it can also be part of a strategy of centralized personal supervision). However, because of the high cost, the use of this mechanism between headquarters and subsidiaries, as well as among subsidiaries, can only be limited.

Over time, and in conjunction with changing organizational structures, MNCs have started to use a more diverse mix of control mechanisms. Centralized personal control, partly through the use of expatriates, was the dominant coordination mechanism for multidomestic MNCs in the period 1920–1950 (this and the following is based on Martinez and Jarillo, 1989). On top of this, output control (mainly financial performance) was used. Global MNCs (most prominent from 1950–1980) relied more heavily on bureaucratic formalized control in the form of formal planning and budgeting systems. Martinez and Jarillo (1989) observe that these bureaucratic controls were complemented by output control in US MNCs, but more by cultural control (among other things, through the use of expatriates) in Japanese MNCs. As the pressures towards both local adaptation and global integration increased (from 1980), and MNCs moved towards the transnational form, more and more emphasis has been put on the informal control mechanisms belonging to Harzing's (1999) category of socialization and network control. The use of these mechanisms is, however, cumulative: they are used on top of the three other categories of control mechanisms. Hence we can say that from the point of view of organizational control MNCs tending towards Bartlett and Ghoshal's 'transnational' type are very complex organizations.

Headquarters–subsidiary relationships

Christopher Bartlett and Sumantra Ghoshal (1989) make the point that responding simultaneously to pressures of local adaptation and global integration requires more than just a structural solution. More subtle forms of control and organization – like those discussed above under the heading of 'socialization and networks' – are also necessary. Most of all, these authors called for a new mentality, which was seen as necessary in order to achieve the flexibility required. This new mentality not only pertains to the macro structure and the mix of coordination mechanisms used, but also more in general to the relationship between headquarters and subsidiaries.

Bartlett and Ghoshal (1986) observe two dysfunctional 'syndromes' in headquarters–subsidiary relationships in MNCs. The 'UN model' syndrome implies that MNC headquarters' relationships with subsidiaries are based on the assumption that these should be treated in a uniform manner. Subsidiary roles and responsibilities are expressed in the same general terms, planning and control systems are applied uniformly and all subsidiaries typically enjoy the same degree of autonomy. The 'headquarters hierarchy' syndrome points at the tendency in many MNC headquarters to keep all key decisions centralized. The two syndromes are related: because headquarters have the tendency to treat all subsidiaries in the same way, all subsidiaries receive the same low degree of autonomy and play the same restricted role within the MNC (Bartlett and Ghoshal, 1986: 88). By treating their subsidiaries in this uniform way, MNCs deny the possibility that subsidiaries develop in different directions and acquire new capabilities that enable them to play a lead role within their area of competence. The existence of multiple subsidiary roles is one of the essential characteristics of the transnational form.

Building on Bartlett and Ghoshal (1986) and a number of empirical studies, Birkinshaw and Morrison (1995) distinguish between three subsidiary roles (see Table 9.1). *Local implementers* typically operate within a single country. The main responsibility of this type of subsidiary is to adapt global products to the needs of the local market, as far as necessary. Within that local market the subsidiary operates with a certain level of autonomy. *Specialized contributors* have considerable expertise, but in a narrowly defined area. Their activities are strongly intertwined with those of other units of the MNC; hence their autonomy is limited. *Subsidiaries with a world mandate*, finally, have a worldwide (or at least region-wide) responsibility for a product line or certain types of value-adding activity. Thus there is worldwide integration, but the activities are coordinated not by headquarters, but by the subsidiary.

In Table 9.1, a number of dimensions in which the three types of subsidiary differ are indicated. The world mandate subsidiary has the largest strategic autonomy, the local implementer the smallest (all three types score equally in operational autonomy). The

Table 9.1 Roles of MNC subsidiaries

	Local implementer	*Specialized contributor*	*World mandate subsidiary*
Strategic autonomy	low	medium	high
Product dependence on the parent	high	high	low
Inter-affiliate purchases	high	high	low
International dispersion of manufacturing	low	high	medium
International dispersion of downstream activities	low	high	medium
Pressures for national responsiveness	high	medium	low

Source: Adapted from Birkinshaw and Morrison (1995: 748).

'product dependence on the parent' dimension reflects the extent to which the products of the subsidiary are also produced by the parent company. The assumption is that, if this is the case, the subsidiary is more dependent on the parent with regard to these production activities. This dependency is lower for world mandate subsidiaries than for the two other types. Inter-affiliate purchases are products or components that the subsidiary buys from other parts of the MNC. Local implementers and specialized contributors are strongly bound to the MNC by such material flows, world mandate subsidiaries more weakly. International dispersion of manufacturing and of downstream activities shows to what extent the activities performed by the subsidiary also take place at other locations within the MNC. The activities of local implementers tend to be specific to their location, and hence are not replicated elsewhere in the MNC. The activities of specialized contributors are more strongly linked to like operations elsewhere in the world; world mandate subsidiaries fall between these two types in this respect.

It should be borne in mind that the typology is a simplification. As Rugman, Verbeke and Yuan (2011) bring up, subsidiary roles can vary across value chain activities. For instance, a subsidiary may be a specialized contributor in terms of production, but a local implementer in terms of marketing and sales. Also note that Birkinshaw and Morrison's subsidiary typology is based predominantly on operational activities and the exploitation of existing knowledge and capabilities. Later in this chapter we will look at differentiation between subsidiaries in terms of exploration and the development of new knowledge and capabilities.

If we tentatively link the three subsidiary roles with the MNC typology of Bartlett and Ghoshal, a first remark should be that each of the three kinds of subsidiary could be assumed to exist within each of the four types of MNC. However, the description of the subsidiary roles suggests that the local implementer may be assumed to be particularly prominent in international MNCs and multidomestic MNCs. Within the second type of MNC the local implementer will have more autonomy than within the first. The specialized contributor is more likely to be found in the global MNC. The world mandate subsidiary, finally, fits best with the transnational MNC. In this type of MNC the idea that different capabilities may be concentrated in different subsidiaries, and that, consequently, some subsidiaries (rather than headquarters) should have central authority in some fields, is most likely to be accepted.

The issue of differentiation of subsidiary roles within MNCs has been taken up in a study by Ghoshal and Nohria (1993). These authors looked at the pressure to localize and the pressure to globally integrate in the environment of the MNC, and at the internal integration and differentiation in headquarters–subsidiary relationships. A high internal integration means that the MNC intensively uses authority hierarchies, formalized bureaucratic systems and/or socialization mechanisms to achieve a high degree of coordination across its different units. The differentiation dimension pertains to the question of whether the same mix of coordination mechanisms used and/or their intensity differs between subsidiaries, or that MNC headquarters manages all subsidiaries in a uniform way. Putting these two dimensions together, Ghoshal and Nohria (1993) specify four patterns of the overall structuring of headquarters–subsidiary relationships (see Figure 9.5).

Structural uniformity is the pattern in which the structural integration (through hierarchy, bureaucratic means and/or socialization) is strong and uniform throughout the MNC. There is one 'company way' of managing subsidiary relationships. In the differentiated fit variety, different coordination mechanisms are used for different subsidiaries. This is also true for the pattern of integrated variety, but in this case the MNC overlays one

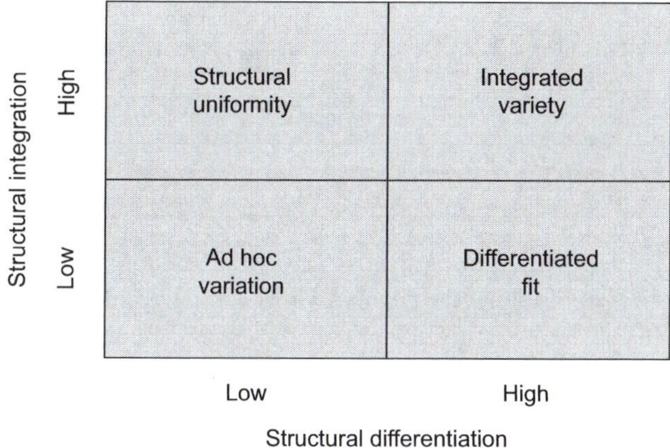

Figure 9.5 Patterns of structuring of headquarters–subsidiary relationships.

Source: Ghoshal and Nohria (1993: 31).

dominant integrative mechanism (which may be of the hierarchical, bureaucratic or socializing kind) for all relationships. Hence, there is more integration of coordination mechanisms than in the previous category. In the case of ad hoc variation, finally, there is neither a dominant coordination mechanism nor a clear pattern of differentiation of coordination mechanisms used across subsidiaries.

Ghoshal and Nohria (1993) predicted that MNCs that matched their pattern of headquarters–subsidiary relationship to their environment would be most successful. The differentiated fit pattern was expected to do best in an environment characterized by high pressures for localizing and weak pressures for globalizing (i.e. calling for a multidomestic approach). The structural uniformity pattern fits best in an environment with strong pressure to globalize and weak pressure to localize (the global approach), and the integrated variety pattern in environments with both strong pressures to localize and to globalize (transnational management). Based on their limited dataset of 41 MNCs the authors came to the conclusion that MNCs that managed their headquarters–subsidiary relationships in a way that fits their environment did indeed perform better than the other MNCs, in terms of return on net assets, growths of these returns and revenue growth. The upshot is that effective MNC management does not only mean that the MNC should have the right macro organizational structure and apply the right mix of coordination mechanisms, but should also be able to differentiate its approach to different kinds of subsidiary. In short, the modern MNC is a differentiated network of units, in which the function of each element to the whole determines the pattern of coordination mechanisms to be used. In the next section we will put this complex picture in a more dynamic light, by focusing on the question of how the internal management of MNCs enables them to learn and develop over time.

9.4 Knowledge management in the MNC

Increasingly, the competitive advantage of companies is seen as residing in their unique sets of competencies and capabilities. As competencies and capabilities can be acquired or copied by competitors, a firm has to work continuously on their further development if it is to remain competitive (Senge, 1990). The concept of the transnational MNC fits very well in this new perspective, as it emphasizes the importance of MNCs' capacity to learn, combining knowledge inputs from all of its dispersed units in flexible ways. In this section, we will discuss the learning MNC in more detail.

Exploitative and explorative learning in the MNC

Looking at the concept of learning, it is first of all important to distinguish between exploitative and explorative learning (March, 1991). Exploitative learning consists of the MNC trying to become better in what it is already capable of doing; its effect is more efficient operation in known fields. The essence of explorative learning is experimentation with new alternatives. The outcome is more uncertain, and may consist of the MNC starting completely new activities. In order to be effective, the MNC must engage in both exploitative and explorative learning, but the balance may differ across companies, industries and time periods. Traditional theories of the MNC, such as Dunning's eclectic paradigm, discussed at the beginning of this chapter, have concentrated predominantly on exploitative learning: the MNC has a particular capability and looks for new locations to better exploit that capability. Hence the emphasis is on the flow of knowledge from headquarters (or the home-country organization) to subsidiaries abroad. However, if we also focus on explorative learning, two-way flow of information and knowledge, both between subsidiaries and headquarters and among subsidiaries, becomes more important. Moreover, a more balanced view of the motives for foreign expansion is due. MNCs not only invest abroad to further exploit their existing capabilities, but also to be able to acquire new knowledge. This type of foreign investment can be called 'knowledge-seeking FDI' (Makino and Inkpen, 2003: 239). This means that the MNC invests in certain countries or regions because it seeks critical capabilities that are bound to those locations (e.g. because they reside in local inter-firm networks). An example is the City of London as an attractor of FDI from knowledge-seeking MNCs in the financial services sector (Nachum, 2003).

Organizing for explorative learning puts different demands on the MNC: 'the distance in time and space between the locus of learning and the locus for the realization of returns is generally greater in the case of exploration than in the case of exploitation, as is the uncertainty' (March, 1991: 85). Hence, it becomes less predictable where in the MNC new knowledge will originate, and where it will be put to use. As a consequence, the MNC also cannot tell which of the many potentially important intra-firm relationships it has to invest in and foster. For the transnational this is a crucial issue, for the capability of the MNC to effectively transfer know-how and capabilities from one unit to another is far from self-evident (Cerny, 1996). Buckley and Carter (1999: 80) observe that 'organizational and cultural barriers internal to the firm become a prime concern when the firm's management is seeking the most effective use of its intangible knowledge assets' ('intangible knowledge assets' referring to know-how and capabilities).

Gupta and Govindarajan (1991) distinguish between four types of subsidiary, in as far as their role in MNC knowledge development is concerned. Some subsidiaries, 'global innovators', serve as the source of knowledge in a particular field for all other parts of the MNC. Other types of subsidiary ('implementers') receive knowledge from headquarters or other subsidiaries and apply it locally, without transferring any knowledge back to other parts of the MNC. 'Integrated players' both give and take, sometimes and in some areas functioning as the source of information, and at other times or in other areas of knowledge as the receptor. 'Local innovators', finally, do develop new knowledge, but this remains specific to their own area of application, and is not shared with other parts of the MNC. Traditionally, MNCs consisted predominantly of foreign subsidiaries acting as implementers and local innovators, the bulk of the innovation coming from the home country organization. This made the demands placed on the MNC organization in terms of communication and coordination relatively easy and predictable. Local innovators and implementers require less communication and coordination than the two other types of subsidiary. Gupta and Govindarajan (1991) predict that global innovators and integrated players will be linked to the rest of the MNC through various integration mechanisms and more intense communication.

Gupta and Govindarajan's typology can conceptually be mapped on that developed by Birkinshaw and Morrison (1995). Global innovators will almost by definition have a world mandate, at least for the field in which they function as a repository of knowledge for the entire MNC. Integrated players will typically be specialized contributors, who have the lead in certain products or services, but depend on inputs from other subsidiaries for other products or services. Birkinshaw and Morrison's local implementers, finally, can be either local innovators (if limited innovation and knowledge development takes place to adapt products or services to the local market), or just implementers.

In a later empirical study, Gupta and Govindarajan (2000) found that coordination mechanisms allowing for rich information transmission (in terms of the informality, openness and density of the communication) positively and significantly influence both the outflow of knowledge from subsidiaries to other parts of the MNC and the inflow into the subsidiary of information from other parts of the MNC (Gupta and Govindarajan, 2000). They found this effect both for formal integrative mechanisms (liaison personnel, task forces, permanent committees) and for more informal corporate socialization mechanisms (job transfers among subsidiaries, and between subsidiaries and headquarters, participation in multi-subsidiary executive programmes, participation in corporate mentoring programmes). These types of coordination mechanism all seem to fall under the rubric of what we have called 'socialization and networks'.

The effect of coordination mechanisms on knowledge sharing is explored in more depth in Noorderhaven and Harzing (2009). Informal social interaction is conducive to both vertical (between headquarters and subsidiaries) and lateral (between subsidiaries) knowledge flows. Formal coordination, in contrast, was found to impede knowledge flows, if anything. This indicates that an MNC that wants to promote internal knowledge flows and learning has little other option than to invest heavily in mechanisms that provide opportunities for face-to-face informal interactions between managers from diverse units in the MNC (headquarters as well as subsidiaries), like international taskforces and international training programmes.

The costs of transnational management

The upshot of the discussion in the previous subsection is that transnational management emphasizing both exploitative and explorative learning requires the MNC to invest in intensive, and hence costly, coordination mechanisms. Moreover, we have seen that a transnational MNC cannot a priori select only a few intra-firm links to invest in. With regard to this second issue, headquarters cannot predict where in the MNC network crucial new knowledge can be developed by what combination of subsidiaries, so all possible links should, in principle, be kept open. This strategy, however, obviously entails costs that can easily become prohibitive. The theoretical number of links varies between network structures. In a 'star structure', one central node is connected to all other nodes, which remain unconnected to each other. In this structure, the number of links is equal to the number of nodes. If an MNC with such an internal structure has *n* subsidiaries, it also has *n* intra-organizational links to maintain. This would be the archetypical international or multidomestic type of MNC, in which only headquarters–subsidiaries relationships are invested in, and links between subsidiaries remain unimportant. The transnational, however, can better be compared with the theoretical structure of the 'fully connected network', in which each node is directly connected to each other node. Here, if *n* is the number of nodes, the number of links becomes (n*(n-1))/2. As an example, take an MNC with 20 local subsidiaries. In a star structure, the number of intra-firm relationships would be 20; but in a fully connected network, the number of links to be maintained would be no less than 190. Clearly the costs of maintaining a network of this size can become a serious competitive disadvantage, at least if the links are to be of the kind that enables the exchange of knowledge that is often difficult to codify.

This brings us to the other point. Transnational MNCs rely relatively much on expensive forms of coordination. Hierarchical coordination and bureaucratic control processes are less important than in the more traditional forms of MNC management. These coordination mechanisms – and the same is true of output control – are not very conducive to the speedy, improvised and high-quality exchange of ideas associated with explorative learning in a differentiated network of MNC units. The knowledge to be exchanged will very often be partly implicit and difficult to codify. As a result the MNC must extensively use coordination mechanisms that allow unstructured information to be exchanged between units in a flexible way. As a result there will be, relatively, much emphasis on coordination through socialization and networks.

This can be clarified with the distinction Thompson (1967) made between various types of interdependence. Thompson distinguished between three types of interdependency (see Figure 9.6). In the case of *pooled interdependence*, two units depend on the inputs from a third unit for their own tasks. However, the two units can function independently from each other. If there is *sequential interdependence*, one unit depends on the inputs from a second unit for the fulfilment of its task, and a third unit in turn is dependent on its own output. *Reciprocal interdependence*, finally, is the term Thompson uses for situations in which units depend on each other's outputs in complex and unpredictable ways.

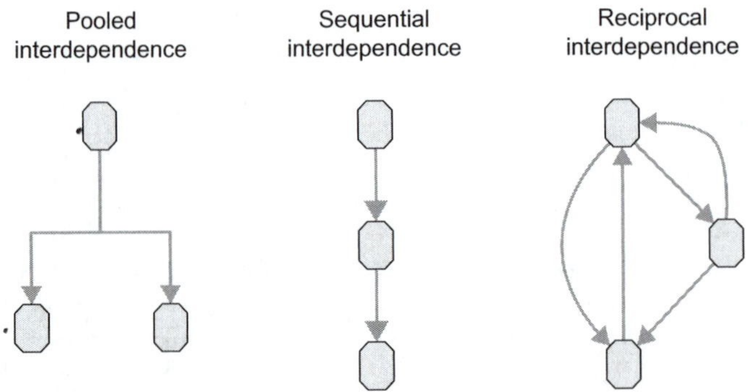

Figure 9.6 Thompson's types of interdependencies.

Source: Based on Thompson (1967).

The three kinds of interdependency can be linked to the types of coordination mechanisms discussed earlier in this chapter. Pooled interdependence exists, for instance, between the subsidiaries of a multidomestic MNC. They are all dependent on headquarters' decisions with regard to targets and budgets, but once these have been decided upon, each subsidiary can go its own way. This type of interdependence can be managed through output control. Sequential interdependence is typical of the relationship between functional departments within a firm. Within an MNC the various production units will often be organized internally along these lines. At the level of the macro structure, MNCs with a global structure create interdependencies between their subsidiaries that often are of a sequential nature, as their activities concentrate on particular elements of the value chain. Sequential interdependence can effectively be managed through bureaucratic formalized control if the issue is of a routine nature, and through hierarchical referral (personal centralized control) if it concerns non-routine issues.

Reciprocal interdependence exists between parties engaged in complex tasks. This is the type of interdependence that at the micro level can be found within departments of units (the following discussion is based on Egelhoff, 1993). If this type of interdependency pertains to routine issues, it can be managed through information systems that allow all parties concerned access to a dynamic and interactive database. If the issue is non-routine, however (as in the case of explorative learning within the MNC), the information that needs to be exchanged and discussed will typically not be the type of standard data one can find in the company's computer systems. Hence, coordination forms that allow for rich, face-to-face information exchange are called for. These are the socialization and networking kinds of coordination mechanism, like task forces consisting of members from different units and/or departments, teams, managers with integrating roles, and so on. It is not possible to unambiguously rank the coordination mechanisms according to their cost. For instance, personal centralized control requires little set-up cost, but the ongoing costs of maintaining this type of coordination are relatively high. For bureaucratic formalized control, it is just the other way around. At any rate, control by socialization and networks can be characterized as high cost, meaning that the management of transnationals as envisaged by Bartlett and Ghoshal (1989) may very well be prohibitively expensive.

9.5 The MNC, culture and institutions

In this section of the chapter we will discuss how the cultural and institutional environments impact on the MNC. In a way, the entire chapter has focused on this issue, for it is mainly because of the cultural and institutional diversity in its environment that the management and organization of MNCs is different from that of large domestically operating firms. In this section we will first look at the question how MNCs are influenced by the culture and institutions of their home country. After that, we will consider how MNCs respond and adapt to cultural and institutional diversity in their environments.

The country-of-origin effect on MNCs

In the globalization literature the MNC is often presented as a harbinger of global practices (Dicken, 1998). However, far from being 'nationless', even the most global MNCs in many respects still seem to be strongly rooted in their country of origin (this section is based on Noorderhaven and Harzing, 2003). Various studies have pointed at this 'country-of-origin' effect. In particular, human resource management practices (Gooderham, Nordhaug and

Ringdal, 1999; Ngo, Turban, Lau and Lui, 1998) and control strategies (Lubatkin, Calori, Very and Veiga, 1998; Harzing and Sorge, 2003) reflect specific influences of the home country of an MNC. Country-of-origin effects can be caused by both the cultural and the institutional specificities of the home country of the MNC. The underlying assumption of the culturalist approach is that individual inhabitants of a country are 'mentally programmed' by the way they were raised by their parents and peers, and by the institutions of the country (Hofstede, 2001). This makes them adopt broad preferences for certain states of affairs that they share with their compatriots. In the institutionalist perspective – for example, the 'business systems' approach (Whitley and Kristensen, 1996), differences in the structures and operations of firms 'clearly stem from variations in dominant social institutions such as the state and the financial system' (Whitley, 1992: 1).

Why would these national factors influence an MNC operating in dozens of countries? A possible explanation is corporate inertia. MNCs may continue to operate in ways attuned to their cultural and institutional home country, but not necessarily to their present multifarious environments. This effect is strengthened by the fact that most MNCs continue to hire country-of-origin nationals for many of their key management positions (Lane, 2000). These managers share the cultural background of their home country, and their perceptions are influenced by the institutional environment in which they grew up and were trained. This is important because the capacity of top managers to think 'geocentrically' is a key factor in a firm's adaptation to its international environment (Perlmutter, 1969: 17).

The question could be asked, however, what country can be assumed to be the country of origin of an MNC? This may be another country than that in which the MNC headquarters are located, as this may have been relocated (e.g., for tax reasons) at a time when the original 'imprint' of the country of origin has already been made. It is also not necessarily the country of ownership, especially not in the case of highly dispersed and internationalized ownership (Almond, 2011). It makes more sense to assume that the country of origin is determined by the 'historical experience and the institutional and ideological legacies of that experience' (Pauly and Reich, 1997: 4). This means that the country in which the MNC originally 'grew up' is most relevant.

While there is mounting evidence that MNCs are indeed subject to a 'country-of-origin effect' (see, e.g., Almond, 2011), there is less clarity about the specifics. What country characteristics cause what types of MNC behaviour, and under which conditions are these effects stronger or weaker? Much work remains to be done. The following sketchy comments mainly serve as a warning that elements of national idiosyncracy can be found even within the actor that is often seen as the herald of globalization: the MNC.

Bartlett and Ghoshal (cited in Birkinshaw and Morrison, 1995: 738) had already recognized the importance of the parent country of origin, and on the basis of their observations noted that socialization was a predominant coordination mechanism in European MNCs, centralization in Japanese MNCs and formalization in US MNCs. Lubatkin et al. (1998), comparing the behaviour of UK and French parent firms after an acquisition, noted that the French companies made more use of expatriate management, and relied more on centralized control than the UK parent companies. More generally, reasoning from a culturalist perspective, Hofstede (2001) opines that differences in power distance and uncertainty avoidance are the most important cultural differences for MNCs (see Chapter 2). Hofstede speculates that MNCs originating in countries with a small power distance will be better able to manage subsidiaries in large power distance cultures than the other way around (Hofstede, 2001: 442). Regarding uncertainty avoidance, Hofstede expects the flexibility to use different degrees of and bases for coordination in different businesses and different parts of the world to be more prevalent in MNCs based in weak uncertainty avoidance countries than in MNCs based in strong uncertainty avoidance cultures (Hofstede, 2001: 444). This suggests that the ability to manage the MNC as a differentiated, but at the same time strongly integrated network of subsidiaries, is at least in part determined by the cultural background of the MNC. Hence, the applicability of the 'transnational solution' may not only depend on industry conditions, but also on the administrative heritage of the MNC.

How do MNCs respond to cultural and institutional diversity?

The decision of an MNC concerning the macro structure most suited to dealing with the institutional and cultural diversity of the environments in which the company is operating can be compared to the 'order penetration point' decision. In deciding where the order penetration point will be located, a firm determines which of its activities will be influenced by market fluctuations, and which not. In mass production, the production process itself is normally scheduled ahead, but the distribution of the final product is determined by demand fluctuations, resulting in an order penetration point between production and distribution. In case of production to order, all or part of the production processes are influenced by the demand fluctuations while, for instance, purchasing activities may be scheduled ahead.

By analogy, we could speak about the 'diversity penetration point' in the MNC. In a multidomestic MNC the main interface between the cultural and institutional diversity in the MNC's various environments and the core of the MNC (i.e. that part of the MNC that does not adapt to the specificities of any of the localities in which it does business – other than that of the home country, see the previous subsection) lies between headquarters and the regional divisions. The regional divisions adapt to the specific demands of their environments, as well as the diversity in the sub-environments they are dealing with. Headquarters guards over the common characteristics and general capabilities of the MNC. In the global MNC the interface between the diverse environments and the MNC is in the relationships between product-based divisions and their subsidiaries in different countries. This means that this intercultural and inter-institutional interface has to be managed in many more intra-firm relationships than in the multidomestic MNC, which will be possible only if the cultural and institutional diversity is smaller or of less relevance. Hence it is no surprise that we see globally integrated MNCs predominantly in industries where local adaptation of the end product or service can be limited.

In the transnational, finally, the situation is more complex. Here there is a diversity interface between the product-based part of the organization and the subsidiaries in different countries. This interface will in many cases be managed in coordination with the region-based part of the MNC (assuming a matrix-like macro organizational structure). On top of this, however, relationships between subsidiaries are also more frequent and important, meaning that cultural and institutional differences will also have to be managed in these relationships. As a consequence, the number of diversity interfaces is again multiplied in comparison with the global MNC. This may be problematic, as the transfer of knowledge across cultural boundaries confronts the MNC with increased complexities (Inkpen, 1998).

Although the findings pertaining to the adaptation of MNC policies to local culture discussed above are far from conclusive, a study by Newman and Nollen (1996) provides some evidence that this type of adaptation does in fact lead to greater effectiveness. These authors studied 176 work units in 18 foreign subsidiaries of a single US corporation, and found that units with practices better fitting the local culture (operationalized along Hofstede's dimensions) performed better than units with less fitting practices. This corresponds to the general trend in the literature that, although the empirical evidence is scarce, consistently points at the importance for MNCs of taking cultural differences into account in their internal management. For instance, Brock, Barry and Thomas (2000) theorize that differences in national culture will affect the planning approaches preferred by headquarters and subsidiaries. Welch and Welch (1997) put forward that national cultural differences will make it more difficult for MNCs to impose parent–company values on their diverse foreign affiliates, hence this favoured coordination mechanism may in fact be difficult to implement. Hofstede (2001: 442) opines that, in particular, power distance differences in which MNC headquarters is influenced by a high power–distance culture, and the subsidiary by a low power–distance culture, lead to problems; the opposite situation would be much easier to deal with. On the other hand, Hofstede expects differences in uncertainty avoidance to be equally problematic, whichever way they go. The conclusion can be drawn that, whereas there are many indications that cultural diversity is indeed an important factor in the management of MNCs, as yet it is difficult to offer specific guidance as to the best way to deal with this diversity.

The situation is not significantly different if we look at institutional differences. The general thrust of the literature is that MNCs need to adapt to local institutional idiosyncracies, but there is a paucity of systematic empirical research (Westney, 1999). Furthermore, there is an overlap between the presumed influence of institutional differences and that of cultural differences. For instance, Hofstede (2001: 443) states that cultural values become (partly) institutionalized in, say, legislation, labour union structures and organizations of stakeholders. In addition, some categories of institution, like the normative component of the institutional profile of a country described by Kostova and Roth (2002: 217) as 'the values, beliefs, norms and assumptions about human nature and human behavior held by the individuals in a given country', seem to be identical to culture. However, institutional environments are assumed to influence MNCs in ways that are different from that ascribed to culture.

Culture enters into the equation through the beliefs and preferences of individuals, predominantly in their roles as managers, employees and other stakeholders of the MNC. The adaptation of the MNC to local institutions is assumed to be a more conscious process. Three mechanisms are usually distinguished (Westney, 1993). Institutions may have a 'coercive' influence, meaning that the MNC is forced by a powerful authority, usually the state, to adapt its organization in a certain way. A second possibility is that the institutional influence is 'normative' – that is, organizational patterns that are deemed to be appropriate within a certain environment are championed (but not coercively prescribed) by, say, professional associations. Third, the influence may be of the 'mimetic' kind, in that the MNC copies organizational features from other companies (local companies or other MNCs) that are seen as successful. In all cases, the MNC adapts its organization to acquire or maintain legitimacy in the perspective of powerful stakeholders, and in this way to increase its chances of survival and success (Xu and Shenkar, 2002). However, this adaptation is restricted to the extent that the MNC also strives for integration across countries and regions (Westney, 1993).

All organizations are subject to institutional influences, but what is typical for the MNC is that it is subject to a variety of different and potentially contradictory influences in the different environments in which it operates (Westney, 1993: 60). At the same time, because of the need for global integration in order to utilize organizational capabilities worldwide, there will be a drive in the MNC towards standardization of structures and processes within the company. As a result the MNC faces a unique institutional complexity, and local subsidiaries are faced with 'institutional duality': they have to maintain legitimacy both in their local environment and within the MNC (Kostova and Roth, 2002: 216). The tension between institutional pressure from the environment and from the MNC is particularly acute within these local subsidiaries. Kostova and Roth show how the extent to which subsidiaries adopt practices institutionalized within the MNC (in their research this was a quality management system) depends, among other things, on the degree of fit between the practice and the local institutional environment.

Some of the other factors influencing the extent of adaptation pertain to the subsidiary–parent relationship. The expectation would be that stronger subsidiaries (in terms of capabilities, value added and influence within the MNC) will have stronger local links with customers and suppliers, and will adapt relatively more to local institutions and less to MNC practices (Rosenzweig and Singh, 1991). However, Kostova and Roth's (2002) findings point in the opposite direction: subsidiaries that seem to be more dependent on the MNC report lower degrees of adaptation to MNC practices. This suggests that much more research is needed in order to unveil the true interplay of institutional influences on the MNC.

The complexity is further increased because the influence of local institutions will vary from situation to situation. For instance, it is likely to depend on the industry in which the MNC operates. For MNCs in service industries, acquiring local legitimacy is essential, because of the intangible nature of services. For this reason the ability to engage in local networks and adaptation to local institutions may be particularly important (Campbell and Verbeke, 1994). Second, MNCs may choose to locate in regions within a country where local institutional pressures are weakest. This is, for instance, the case with many Japanese automobile manufacturing subsidiaries in the USA, which were located in regions where the influence of the traditional automobile labour union was weak or non-existent (Westney, 1993). The influence of state policies may be assumed to vary with the policy credibility of the government in question. When the government is not perceived to be credible in its commitments (e.g. because of past policy changes, or because of its attitude towards business enterprises in general) attempts to influence MNCs will be likely to have only a marginal effect on MNCs (Murtha and Lenway, 1994). This is particularly true if the government's institutional pressure is of the normative, rather than coercive, kind (i.e. requirements do not take the form of formal laws, but rather of informal expectations and demands). Finally, local institutions not only influence the MNC, but this also works the other way around: the introduction by an MNC subsidiary of a new organizational practice in a country may challenge the legitimacy of existing practices, and in this way erode or change local institutions (Westney, 1993). This tendency was also documented by Lane (2000) in a study of the strategies of UK and German MNCs. We will now turn to a discussion of the strategies of MNCs.

9.6 Strategy of the MNC

In this final section of the chapter we will consider aspects of strategy that are unique to MNCs. This is not as easy as it may seem. Self-evidently, strategies of MNCs are strategies that include an internationalization element. Moreover, MNCs must also do the external analysis (e.g., with the help of Porter's five forces framework), take stock of the firm's resources and capabilities, and ponder over the three generic strategies of cost leadership, differentiation and focus (e.g., Peng, 2013). Generally speaking, an MNC's strategy 'refers to choices pertaining to the rate, scope (including degree of diversification) and means (especially entry modes) of international expansion and operations, and to the means of coordinating the multinational corporation' (Martin and Van den Oever, 2013: 333). What is unique to the MNC in this definition is mainly restricted to the international dimension of the expansion and the issue of entry modes. Doz (1980) adds to this another issue that is particular to the MNC. Much more than firms operating in a single country MNCs need to balance two often conflicting forces: the economic imperative of being efficient and effective enough to ensure economic survival, and the political imperative of being acceptable to host country governments.

The issue of the internationalization process of MNCs has been touched upon earlier in this chapter, and was related to the organizational structures of MNCs. In this section we will look at this issue from another angle, and focus on the questions when firms go abroad and how. The *when* question has traditionally been answered by referring to the product cycle, i.e., the idea that products are first introduced and produced in high-income economies, while later production is shifted to low-income economies. The *how* question refers to modes of entry into foreign markets. In considering these questions we will also return to the typology of MNCs developed by Bartlett and Ghoshal (2000).

MNC strategy and internationalization

In 1966 Raymond Vernon published an article in which he presented a new explanation for the phenomena of international trade and production. Previous accounts had been based on comparative statics: production of a product should take place in the economy that had a comparative cost advantage for that specific activity, and international trade was a result of the fact that the optimal location for production could be another place than where the customers were. This explanation ignored the more dynamic aspects of the phenomena of international trade and production, i.e., the fact that a particular product can be produced initially in one country, while production later shifts to other locations.

According to the product cycle theory wealthy, high-labour cost countries have a comparative advantage for the introduction of many types of new products. In these countries customers are discerning and demanding, and willing to pay for new products if these offer specific advantages, in particular the advantage of saving time. For this reason, Vernon (1966) explains, the USA was the country in which labour-saving appliances like home washing machines were first introduced. The fact that high-income markets like the USA are the most attractive locations to launch new products in itself does not mean that production of such new products should also take place there. According to Vernon knowledge can move easily, and entrepreneurs everywhere in the world could in principle come up with new product ideas. This part of Vernon's theory has been strongly criticized for neglecting the difficulty of transmitting knowledge, especially the less codified knowledge that is also necessary for new product development, across national and cultural boundaries and over geographical distances.

Although Vernon underestimated the difficulty of production knowledge transfer, he did acknowledge that location of production of new products in proximity to the customers brings important advantages. According to Vernon (1966) new products in the early stages of their life cycle are not yet standardized, the optimal methods and procedures of production are not yet known, and the product still has to be fine-tuned to the preferences of the customers. This requires swift and effective communication of the producer with customers, suppliers of inputs, and even with competitors. Consequently there are good reasons to start production of a new product in the high-income economy, in the vicinity of the customers and in a sophisticated industrial environment. From a cost perspective this is unlikely to be the optimal location, but it is possible to compromise on cost since in these early stages the price elasticity of demand is low. In this phase demand in other locations is served through production in the main market and exports. Over time, as demand in other high-income economies increases, these exports may partly be replaced by local production, causing a stream of foreign direct investment to these countries.

However, as a product matures, the reasons to locate production close to the customers in the high-income market mentioned above become less decisive. The product becomes standardized, and communication with customers, suppliers and competitors becomes less vitally important. In this stage cost considerations gain weight, and because of the standardization and the increased codification of production processes relocation of production to low-cost countries becomes a viable option. Hence, Vernon (1966) predicts that ultimately production will cease in the high-income economies where the product was originally introduced, and export from low-cost countries to the more developed economies will accelerate.

The product cycle theory is intuitively appealing, and has been immensely influential. However, there is also much ground for criticism. First of all, although ostensibly focusing on products and firms, the theory actually looks at countries (low-income countries versus high-income countries) (Melin, 1992). There is little or no attention to company-specific factors. Moreover, despite the fact that early empirical studies found evidence supporting the product cycle theory at the level of product groups, evidence at the level of individual products was much less convincing (Mullor-Sebastián, 1983). Nowadays, although the general thrust of the theory still seems to have traction, the reality of international productions is considerably more complex than described by Vernon (Tichy, 2011).

In particular, there has been a fragmentation of the value chain that makes obsolete the idea that the production of a complete product moves from one country to the other. In the past quarter century a process of decentralization of production has taken place, while at the same time the boundaries of firms have become increasingly porous (Whitford, 2012). According to Akkermans and Dellaert (2005: 175) 'today, most products and services are delivered through a highly fragmented network of independent and semi-dependent organizations, where nobody is really in charge of the network as a whole'. This fragmentation of the value chain calls for an analysis on a much more detailed level than countries, industries, or even products. If we look at the level of separate value chain activities we see a pattern of dispersion in which advanced economies, relatively rich in R&D and marketing knowledge, concentrate on services and 'intangibles'. Intangibles stands for patents, copyrights, and brand names, but also for difficult to imitate organizational and inter-organizational capabilities (Mudambi, 2008: 700). These activities depend crucially on human creativity, rather than manpower, and they also offer the largest value added. Low-cost countries, less well endowed with R&D and marketing knowledge, or commercial knowledge more generally, focus on lower value adding activities halfway up the value chain, like manufacturing. Because the value added is larger at the beginning and the end of the value chain, Mudambi draws a U-shaped curve, which he calls 'the smile of value creation' (see Figure 9.7).

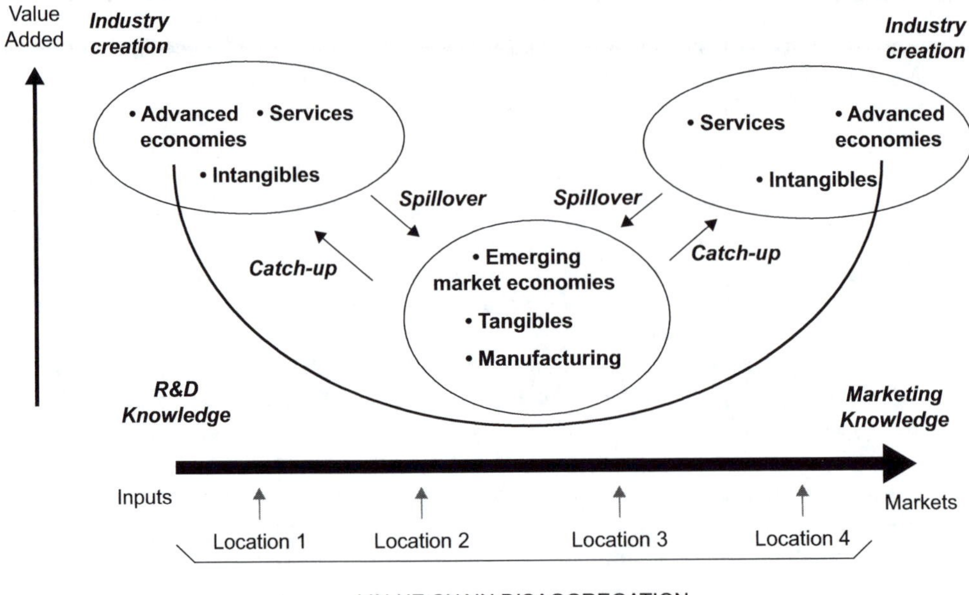

Figure 9.7 The smile of value creation.

Source: Mudambi (2008: 709).

This is a depiction of a dynamic phenomenon, driven by three processes (Mudambi, 2008: 708–709). As producers in emerging economies are operating low value-added activities they are motivated to constantly try to 'catch up' with firms in wealthy economies, e.g., by developing their own brand names or by investing in R&D and design. At the same time firms in these wealthy economies are under competitive pressure to optimize the efficiency of their operations, which causes them to carefully scrutinize their activities, including high value-added activities like marketing and R&D, and to identify and strip out activities that can be standardized and relocated to low-cost countries. This second process leads to 'knowledge spillovers' from rich to emerging economies, and reinforces the catching-up process. Thirdly, and counteracting the first two processes, new products and even industries come into being both based on marketing knowledge and R&D-driven innovation, in a process of 'industry creation'. This third process opens up new opportunities for high-income economies, to compensate for the industrial activities shifting to emerging economies. In spite of the more refined analysis, the picture that emerges from 'the smile of value creation' bears much resemblance to Vernon's product cycle model.

MNC foreign market entry modes

The 'smile of value creation' analysis in the previous sub-section describes how activities and tasks become geographically dispersed. However, this still leaves open the question whether sets of activities across the value chain are internalized within a single firm (vertical integration), or whether some firms concentrate on R&D and marketing, leaving production activities to independent firms in emerging markets. This brings us to the topic of international entry modes. An MNC can choose to perform all activities across the value chain, but then, if it wants to profit from lower production costs in emerging economies, it needs to enter these countries. Conversely, a firm from an emerging economy that invests in a brand name and develops marketing knowledge may also need to establish a presence in high-income countries if it is to compete successfully. In both cases the firm needs to ask itself how it can most successfully build a presence in the other economy: through a wholly owned subsidiary, an equity joint venture, a contractual alliance, through a licence or a franchise, or through international trade (imports and exports of products and components).

There is an immense literature on international entry modes, and this is understandable, for entry mode is 'a key choice that allows firms to strategically tip the balance of costs and benefits in the most favorable manner' (Shaver, 2013: 23). However, maybe because these choices are so complex, this literature has led to an amalgam of insights, but not to a single overarching theoretical framework. We will below first briefly discuss the different international entry modes, and then consider the question what factors influence this choice, with special reference to cultural distance.

Licensing is often the foreign entry mode of choice when the focal firm's advantage consists mainly of process technology. But not all forms of proprietary technology are fit for this mode of entry. The technology in question should be relatively explicit and easy to codify. As codified knowledge can be transferred from one firm to the other relatively easy, this is the type of knowledge that lends itself most readily to licensing agreements. Codified knowledge is often associated with older technologies. This is confirmed by research into the use of licensing, which shows that the probability that a firm uses this entry mode, instead of engaging in own production abroad, is greater the older the technology, the more peripheral it is to the licensing firm's business, the smaller the investment in R&D necessary to develop it has been, and the greater the firm's experience in international licensing (Davidson and McFetridge, 1984). However, some types of knowledge are tacit – that is, non-verbalizable, intuitive and/or not well articulated (Polanyi, 1962). This may, for instance, be know-how with regard to arrangements for the organization of the production process within which the technology to be transferred is to be applied.

Licensing is a low-commitment, low-control mode of foreign country entry. However, both the level of control and the level of resources that need to be committed will in most cases be substantially higher than in the case of exporting. The level of control is higher because various kinds of restriction may be written in the licence agreement. However, the licensing firm also needs to commit more resources, first of all because licensing agreements are complicated contracts and, second, because in many cases a combination of codified and tacit knowledge is needed in order to make the technology transfer work (UNCTAD, 1999). This may mean that the firm has to send some of its own employees to the licensee, at least initially. But the level of risk incurred remains limited. However, there are also some notable disadvantages. The company may become to a certain extent dependent on the local licensee, who may not exert the marketing efforts needed to realize the full potential of the product, or may reduce the consistency of product or service quality. Also, the licensee may use the licence to learn about and eventually 'engineer around' the production technology, and in this way the firm that grants the licence may be opening itself up to a future competitor.

A contractual form of market entry that offers more control is *franchising*. Franchising is a form of licensing of intangible property in combination with assistance over an extended period. Franchising is most often used to transfer the right to use a brand name or trademark, and is primarily used in services and retailing (e.g. McDonald's). In comparison with a licensing contract, franchising offers greater control, while at the same time allowing for rapid international expansion. It is often used in retailing and services, like the fast-food sector, because the firm granting the licence can make use of the local knowledge of the franchisee, which can be an important advantage in consumer markets. A disadvantage is that the control cost can be hefty. As in the case of licensing, the interests of the licensor and licensee can easily diverge. For the firm granting the licence the brand name is often its most important asset, hence it will want to prevent licensees from performing activities that erode the value of this brand name. However, for the licensees any damage to the brand name caused by their actions is, to a large extent, an 'externality' (i.e. they do not bear much of the cost). Thus, if a licensee of an international fast-food chain decides to compromise quality, it bears only a fraction of the costs in terms of the reduced value of the licence, while pocketing all the advantages in terms of lower costs. The only way the licensing firm can avoid this danger is through intensive control.

One step further in the commitment chain is when the MNC decides to enter into a more strategic cooperation with a local company. This can take two general forms: purely contractual or involving equity. In the case of an equity-based cooperation, for our purposes, we will speak of *a joint venture*, while in the case of a purely contractual arrangement we speak of a *strategic alliance*. Both strategic alliances and joint ventures can have various activities as their purpose. Hence, this mode of foreign market entry does not necessarily imply local production, but may also remain confined to marketing and sales arrangements. The difference with the entry modes discussed so far, however, is the degree of commitment from the side of the entering firm. In the forms of market entry discussed so far this commitment remains restricted, and most of the business risk can be said to fall upon the local firm. In strategic alliances and joint ventures, in contrast, the risk is shared between the partners. This risk sharing can be in divergent proportions (in the case of a joint venture, normally as a function of the proportion of equity invested). The fact remains, however, that moving from export, licensing or franchising to an international strategic alliance constitutes a quantum leap on the path of internationalization.

The advantages of both strategic alliances and joint ventures are that, compared with wholly owned subsidiaries (as discussed below), the investments and the risks are reduced. Furthermore, they allow the cooperating companies to combine their strengths, and to learn from each other. An additional advantage for the MNC may be that, compared with some of the other entry modes, they help to create a more 'local' image. The disadvantages are that the MNC has no full control. Related to this, the cooperation may lead to conflicts between the partners. In particular, 50/50 joint ventures are renowned for being conflict-ridden. Furthermore the learning potential mentioned as an advantage of the collaborative entry modes may turn into a disadvantage if the local partner 'outlearns' the MNC to the point that it no longer needs the collaboration and becomes a full-blown competitor. Strategic alliances and joint ventures tend to be unstable; many of these collaborative ventures are discontinued after a relatively short time (Yan and Zeng, 1999). In a sense, in using these entry modes, MNCs can be seen as 'buying options': if the entry succeeds and the local market is attractive enough, the MNC can choose to 'strike the option' by acquiring the joint venture or turning the alliance into a wholly owned subsidiary (Cuypers and Martin, 2007).

Finally, the entry mode requiring the largest commitment and rendering full control is setting up a *wholly owned local subsidiary*. With this entry mode, MNCs have two possibilities: either they start up a new facility from scratch, or they buy an existing local firm. In the first case we speak of 'greenfield' investment, in the second of an acquisition. Acquired companies are sometimes restructured extensively in order to fit into the MNC (e.g. in terms of quality management). If this is the case, the term 'brownfield' is sometimes used, indicating that this is a hybrid mode of entry, with characteristics of both a greenfield investment and an acquisition (Meyer and Estrin, 2001). The advantage of an acquisition or brownfield investment is that local resources – for example, in the form of management know-how – can be incorporated in the MNC. The disadvantage may be that the acquired company often also brings with it numerous local practices and/or inefficiencies that are difficult to reconcile with the MNC's overall policies. A greenfield start-up can be moulded to the MNC's liking to an extent often impossible with acquired companies, because of the sometimes strong resistance to change in existing organizations. The general advantages of wholly owned subsidiaries as modes of foreign market entry are that they offer complete control and that the activities in the target country can be integrated within the global strategy of the MNC to a larger extent than with the other entry modes. The disadvantages are that the resources required are more extensive (since there is no other investor) and hence there is higher risk exposure.

The choice for a particular entry mode may depend on hundreds of factors, which differ between firms, industries, countries and the value chain activities involved. Given the focus of this book we will zoom in on one particular factor: the cultural distance between the home country of a focal MNC and the host country it wishes to enter. Cultural distance is a seminal factor in the foreign market entry mode choice, because it influences both internal and external uncertainty (Slangen and Van Tulder, 2009). This also makes the influence of cultural distance on entry mode choice ambiguous.

Internal or behavioural uncertainty refers to expected or experienced difficulties in dealing with a partner in a foreign country. This type of uncertainty is related to the perceived potential for opportunistic behaviuor by the partner, which is increased when it is more difficult to predict and observe and explain his behaviuor. This condition is aggravated by cultural distance. According to communication theory, dissimilarity between people leads to uncertainty (Gudykunst and Nishida, 1984). Based on this we may assume that in business relations behavioural uncertainty will be higher when dealing with an exchange partner who is more dissimilar, as indicated by a higher cultural distance. Thibaut and Kelly (1959) already observed that people are more confident in predicting the behaviour of culturally similar individuals than that of culturally dissimilar individuals' behaviour, and this has since been confirmed in various studies (Gudykunst, 1983; Simard, 1981). Hence, overall we can predict that when there is a large cultural distance between the home country of the MNC and the country in which it wants to do business, the MNC will try to avoid entry modes that involve intensive and difficult-to-predict interaction with a local partner, i.e., contractual alliances, equity joint ventures and brownfield investments. This means that with a large cultural distance, MNCs will be inclined to either go for arms' length deals like exports or licensing/franchising, or go to the other extreme and make a greenfield investment to establish a wholly owned subsidiary. Within a wholly owned greenfield subsidiary the MNC of course also has to deal with local staff, but here the MNC has the opportunity to exert more hierarchical control, it can select employees who fit its culture, and through internal management procedures it can more easily resolve cultural misunderstandings (Slangen and Van Tulder, 2009). Within the category of wholly owned subsidiaries there is a distinction between greenfield and brownfield investments. A brownfield investment (acquisition of an existing foreign firm) aggravates the internal problems associated with cultural distance. For that reason it is understandable that MNCs tend to make greenfield investments rather than acquisitions if there are high communication barriers between the home country and the host country (Slangen, 2011).

But cultural distance also impacts on the perceived external uncertainty. External uncertainty is associated with the environment in which a company is doing business. A very general concept is that of country risk. Country risk is a general concept of the riskiness of doing business in or with a country, and contains elements reflecting economic and political factors (Cosset and Roy, 1991). Other concepts used in the literature are market risk and political risk. The perceptions of all these types of risk may be influenced by cultural distance. Hence, cultural distance may not only impact on expectations and perceptions of problems with interactions within collaborative ventures or wholly owned subsidiaries, but also on expected risks and transaction costs in dealing with the local environment in the host country. The effect of the increased external uncertainty and risk associated with cultural distance is likely to be a choice for entry modes that enable the MNC to reduce its investment and share risk with a local partner. This expectation is borne out in a number of studies. Hennart and Larimo (1998) and Brouthers and Brouthers (2001) find that if there is a large cultural distance, MNCs tend to prefer joint ventures, rather than wholly owned subsidiaries. Morschett, Schramm-Klein and Swoboda (2010) and Brouthers (2002) find a comparable effect of country risk and investment risk, respectively.

The choice for an equity joint venture merits some special attention. In much of the literature, foreign market entry modes are considered to be different points on a continuum from high to low control, commitment, or risk. However, equity-based and contractual forms are subject to very different logics (Brouthers and Hennart, 2007). In a contractual alliance the terms of the collaboration, including payments, need to be specified ex ante. This is also the case if payments are subject to conditions, because then these conditions need to be formulated before the start of the collaboration. In an equity joint venture, payments are defined as a share of the profits (although there may also be contractually specified payments that are independent of profits). Hence, an equity joint venture allows partners to make some decisions along the way, as the situation in the collaboration develops and uncertainty dissolves. Equity joint ventures are more hierarchical than contractual alliances because they provide the partners with a degree of hierarchical control, e.g., through the board of directors (Kale and Puranam, 2004). Equity joint ventures moreover not only offer the parent firms control through decision powers linked to their equity stakes, but these are also supplemented by a contractual agreement that can be more or less detailed (Fraidin and Lelutiu, 2003). Hence, EJVs offer control over and above what a contractual alliance can offer, while avoiding the full exposure of a wholly owned subsidiary. If the external risk is due to possible discriminatory actions by the local government, having a local joint venture partner may also reduce this risk, as such ventures are less likely to be treated unfavourably than foreign wholly owned subsidiaries (Delios and Henisz, 2000).

9.7 Conclusions

In this chapter we have focused on a very important player in the arena of international comparative management: the multinational corporation. First of all we have considered the question why MNCs exist, and concluded that there must be factors at foreign locations that attract FDI, that in combination with the specific capabilities owned by the MNC lead to opportunities. For a firm to engage in FDI (and so become an MNC) a third factor is also needed: it should be more attractive to perform activities in the foreign country under common ownership than over a market interface (e.g., through exports or licensing). We have also looked at the internationalization of MNCs, and concluded that this is often, but not always, a step-by-step process. As MNCs internationalize further, they also adapt their organizational structure. In doing so they need to find a balance between their receptivity to pressures to adapt to local conditions and pressures to integrate their activities across countries. In case both types of pressures are strong, the MNC may assume the form of a transnational.

The transnational form is more than just an organization structure, it is also characterized by the use of a particular mix of internal control mechanisms and by a mentality. The control mechanisms used by MNCs can be classified into personal centralized control, bureaucratic formalized control, output control and control by socialization and networks. All MNCs employ a mix of control mechanisms, but the composition differs between types of MNCs. The transnational stands out by a relatively intensive use of socialization and networks, an expensive set of control mechanisms. Furthermore, transnationals also distinguish themselves from other types of MNCs by the room they offer to subsidiaries to develop in diverse ways. This is also reflected in the way headquarters–subsidiary relations are given shape.

In today's knowledge-intensive economies, the ability of a firm to learn becomes increasingly important, and this is also true for the MNC. In more traditional models of the MNC, learning and development of new technologies, processes, products and services was first and foremost the prerogative of the home country organization. Knowledge typically flowed from the home country to foreign subsidiaries. Nowadays learning activities become increasingly dispersed within the MNC, and knowledge flows no longer mainly from the home country to foreign locations, but also vice versa, as well as between subsidiaries in different host countries. This increasingly dispersed learning process also has repercussions for the management and internal coordination of the MNC, for while knowledge flows are stimulated by informal coordination mechanism, they are not promoted and sometimes even hindered by more formalized methods of coordination.

Like all organizations, MNCs are influenced by the culture and institutions in their environment. In the case of the MNC there are multiple cultural and institutional environments, but most MNCs are still relatively strongly influenced by their historical home country. This country-of-origin effect is maintained by, among other things, continued prevalence of managers of the historical home country at the top of the organization. But MNCs also need to take into account the culture and institutions of the host countries in which they operate, for reasons of effectiveness as well as legitimacy. MNCs differ in the way in which they deal with this diversity, with some MNCs (e.g., the transnational) allowing the diversity to penetrate deep into the organization, while other MNCs (e.g., the global MNC) restrict internal diversity much more.

Finally we have considered the strategy of MNCs. In many respects the strategy of an MNC is comparable to that of a nationally operating firm, but the international dimension does imply some important differences. First of all, the MNC needs to decide when to expand to what foreign country and with what activities. A classical theory in this respect is the product cycle theory, which predicts that new products will initially be developed and produced in high-income countries. Only later, if the product as well as the production process have become more standardized, and as demand increases, does it become attractive to shift production to low-cost countries. This theory has been dismissed as too coarse for the present-day economy, in which industries and value chains have fragmented.

Still, important elements of product cycle thinking have found their way into 'smile of value creation' theorizing, which predicts that high value added activities like R&D and marketing will mostly be concentrated in high-income countries, and low value added activities like production in low-cost economies. Over time, both upstream (e.g., R&D and design) and downstream (marketing and services) activities may shift to low-cost countries, too. But by that time high-income countries focus on newer products where high margins can still be realized.

The second strategy element typical for MNCs is the choice of foreign market entry. In making this choice MNCs have to balance two types of uncertainty and risk: external risk (connected with the foreign political, economic and market environment) and internal risk (linked to the behaviours of partner firms and foreign managers and employees). External uncertainty drives MNCs to lower commitment modes of entry, like alliances and licensing. Internal risk may lead an MNC to the decision not to work with a local partner, but to set up its own wholly owned subsidiary. If MNCs perceive both high external and internal uncertainty, equity joint ventures may be an attractive mode of entry, since these limit the investment at risk and mitigate the risk of discriminatory actions by the host government, while also offering hierarchical means to curb problems stemming from internal uncertainty.

Study questions

1 Discuss the three conditions leading to the existence of multinational corporations (MNCs). Why is there no need for an MNC to arise if one of the conditions is not present?
2 MNCs historically have tended to develop through a number of stages. Describe these stages, and explain the factors influencing an MNC's progress through successive stages.
3 Describe the types of MNC that arise under varying combinations of weak/strong pressures for local adaptation and for global integration.
4 Describe and critically discuss the 'transnational form' of MNCs.
5 Describe the main mechanisms of coordination and control used in MNCs.
6 Discuss possible roles of subsidiaries in MNCs, in relation to the learning capabilities of the MNC.
7 Discuss how MNCs are influenced by culture and institutions.
8 Make clear how the international dimension impacts upon the strategy of MNCs.
9 Describe the different foreign market entry modes, and explain which factors influence the choice of an MNC for a particular mode.

Further reading

Rugman, A.M., ed. (2008) *The Oxford Handbook of International Business* (2nd edn). New York: Oxford University Press.

An excellent overview of theories of MNCs, the environment of MNCs, and management, organization and strategy issues.

Harzing, A.-W.K. (1999) *Managing the Multinationals: An International Study of Control Mechanisms.* Cheltenham, UK: Edward Elgar.

Although somewhat old by now, this book is still one of the best studies of coordination and control within MNCs.

Dörrenbächer, C. and Geppert, M., eds. (2011). *Politics and Power in the Multinational Corporation: The Role Of Institutions, Interests and Identities.* Cambridge, UK: Cambridge University Press.

A collection of papers focusing on power struggles within MNCs, giving ample attention to headquarters–subsidiary relations. Looks at culture (indicated as national identity) and institutions.

Case: The evolving international structure of Heineken

Case written by N.G. Noorderhaven on the basis of interviews at Heineken corporate headquarters, publicly available information, and Beugelsdijk, Slangen and Van Herpen (2002).

The history of Heineken beer breweries dates back to 1863. The first international expansion consisted of the opening of a brewery in Indonesia in 1931 (at that time, Indonesia was a colony of the Netherlands). In the 1970s Heineken actively used licensing as an instrument of further internationalization, to France, Ireland, Spain and Italy, among other places. At present Heineken is the number three beer brewery in the world, with 165 breweries, 85,000 employees, 250 brands, and active in 178 countries. During its history, Heineken has gone through a series of organizational restructurings to adapt to the growing complexity of its operations and environment. In the 1960s the company was organized into two major groups: Heineken Nederland and Heineken International. The latter was responsible for handling foreign subsidiaries and participations, and international licensing. Heineken Nederland was responsible for the home market as well as for exports (the famous 'green bottles'). Around 1970, as an answer to growing internationalization and diversification, Heineken shifted to a geographical structure, with all domestic operations (beer as well as soft drinks and distilled beverages) remaining in one group, and the international activities coordinated in four regional groupings: Europe, Asia/Australia, Africa and the 'Western Hemisphere'. Around 1983 the company had gradually moved towards a matrix structure with, on the one hand, the operating companies that had increasingly gained independence, and on the other, five regional coordinating directors (the Western Hemisphere being split into the USA, Canada and the Caribbean and South America). A number of functional central staff departments, like Financial and Economic Affairs and Technical Affairs, provided support to the regions, and also tended to be organized along geographic lines (while all being located in the Netherlands). As the functional staff departments could have a strong influence on the operations of the operating companies, there was in practice almost a three-dimensional matrix (see Figure 9.8).

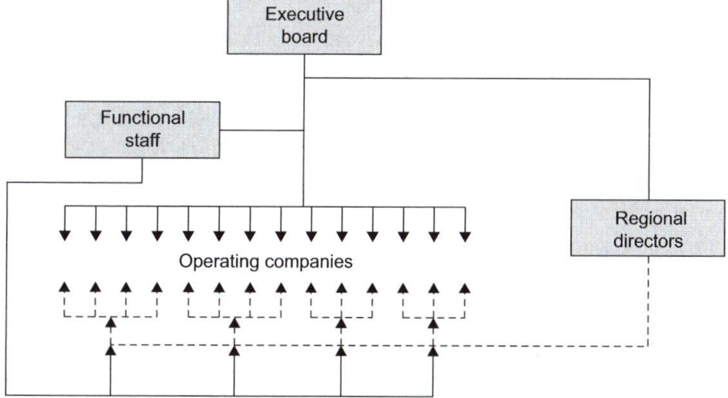

Figure 9.8 Heineken organizational structure around 1983 (simplified).

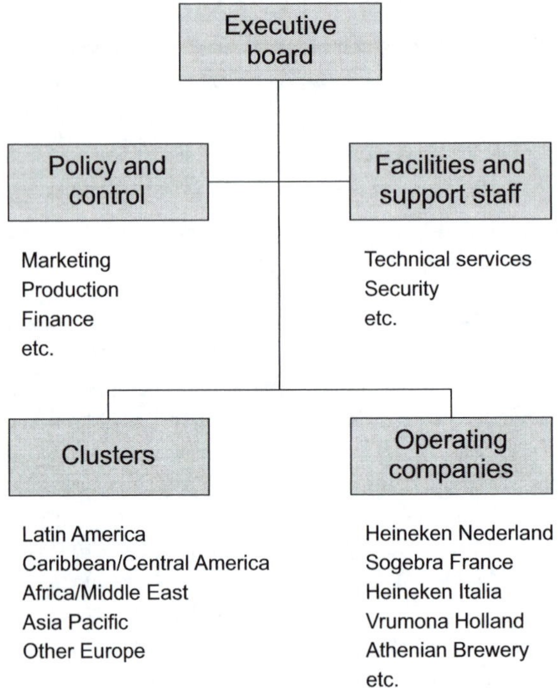

Figure 9.9 Heineken organizational structure around 2003 (simplified).

In the nineties, Heineken became an increasingly decentralized company. This was accelerated when Freddy Heineken stepped down as chairman of the executive board in 1995. His successors, first Gerard van Schaik and subsequently Karel Vuursteen, exerted a much less dominating influence on the company. Compared to the situation in 1983, a substantial part of the corporate staff was decentralized to the level of the regional clusters. The cluster directors were responsible for profit performance in their area, and formed a liaison point between the executive board and the breweries and other plants in their region. These plants functioned as 'quasi-operating companies', meaning that they had a certain degree of autonomy, but not as much as that of the 'real' operating companies (OCs). These OCs reported directly to the executive board. The structure of Heineken around 2003 is depicted graphically in Figure 9.9.

The policy of Heineken was to form an OC if the activities within a certain country or region exceed a certain threshold and came to be of strategic importance. OCs worked within a set of guidelines concerning financial ratios, brand policies, production standards and HRM. In more recent years Heineken has made some more changes to its management structure. Around 2010 the top structure consisted of five regional presidents and five functional chief officers (for strategy, business services, supply chain management, marketing and corporate relations).

Over time, and following strategic steps, like a major acquisition, Heineken has continued to fine tune its organizational structure. The basic principle, however, remained the same, i.e., bringing together at a high management level issues pertaining to the local adaptation and diversity of markets (e.g., positions of brands and distribution systems) and issues pertaining to global integration and optimization of processes (e.g., procurement, supply chain management, technical processes). As Heineken becomes better versed in integrating international activities, the pendulum seems to shift again in the direction of more centralized control. Chief Financial Officer René Hooft Graafland in an interview in 2013 explained how Heineken integrates acquisitions:

> We do better than the previous owners because in many areas we have best practices, for instance the supply chain or how we look at brand portfolios. Apart from that we have a pool of international managers who have seen more than one country.. . . We have done so many integrations by now that we can apply a very structured approach, including a number of principles that we constantly keep in mind.. . . In every integration we do a culture study, in which we compare the local culture of the country and the company with ours. . . . The technical integration should be ready after about six months, things like improvement programs continue much longer.
>
> (http://managementscope.nl/magazine/artikel/748-rene-hooft-graafland-heineken-niet-alleen-sturen-op-cijfers, retrieved July 20, 2014, our translation from Dutch)

It is not easy to find a structure that adequately balances the local and global, and the optimal solution also changes as a result of both changes in the market and internal shifts. An example of the latter was the succession of Freddy Heineken by Gerard van Schaik. The structure that functioned well under Heineken's reign did not do so under Van Schaik, as the latter lacked the personal authority to bring together rivalling executives (Beugelsdijk et al., 2002).

The most recent update in the top management structure took place in 2013, after the acquisition of Asia Pacific Breweries (APB) from Singapore. The CEO of APB, Roland Pirmez, became the new president of the Asia Pacific region. The commercial function was split into marketing and sales, and these two important functional fields were combined with the presidency over the Western European and Central and Eastern European regions, respectively. The aim of Heineken continues to be to think and act both globally and locally. The company is very much aware of the importance of maintaining a strong positive corporate image, and pursues worldwide policies in the fields of employee healthcare and education, terms of employment, and adherence to environmental regulations, and regulations concerning alcohol consumption.

Questions

1 Explain the factors that Heineken must take into account when deciding on its organizational structure.
2 Discuss the advantages and disadvantages of Heineken operating in a decentralized or centralized way.
3 What organizational changes do you expect for Heineken in the future? Will global integration or local adaptation become more important?

Case: Integration of the operations of the London branch of a German bank

Case written by N.G. Noorderhaven on the basis of Moore (2003).

The organization described in this case is the London branch of an unidentified major German bank, headquartered in Frankfurt. The London branch was opened in 1981 and for many years was managed as a quasi-independent operation. Of the 160 staff members, around one third were German, Swiss or Austrian, one-tenth were non-German-speaking foreigners, and the rest were British. In the summer of 1999 the bank started the implementation of a new international matrix structure. Whereas previously most of the contacts between the London branch and headquarters in Frankfurt had been maintained by the general manager of the branch, now individual department heads reported directly to their superiors in Frankfurt. This integrated the activities of the London branch into the overall operations of the bank. This shift brought about considerable tensions in the London branch and, in the process, uncovered fault lines between various categories of employees.

In the first place there were the German expatriates sent to the London branch for a limited period of time by headquarters. These expatriates saw themselves as a bridge between the London branch and headquarters. However, to many other employees they were unfit to play this role, as the assumption was that their main loyalty was with headquarters. A second group of employees was formed by locally hired Germans: employees who, although of German nationality, had been hired directly by the London branch, and hence were not in expatriate positions. These employees emphasized that their nationality did not color their view of the relationship between the branch office and headquarters. A third category of employees, the 'Germanophiles', were those that were not German but had some particular connection to Germany or German culture (e.g., because their spouse was of German origin). Observing the growing tensions between the expatriates and the other groups of employees, the Germanophiles interpreted this as a clash between two parochialisms: that of headquarters, which wanted to impose practices that were supposed to be 'global' but were in reality rooted in Germany, and that of the local staff of the London branch, who resisted any change initiated from abroad. The local UK employees, finally, framed the situation as the imposition of a hostile foreign culture on the London branch.

The overall effect of the restructuring was increased tension and mutual suspicion between employee groups, and resistance to the implementation of the matrix structure. Headquarters, while aware of this resistance, did not recognize the differences between the various groups of employees, except for the general distinction between expatriates and local employees. The resistance against the matrix structure was interpreted in terms of cultural differences between the British and the German. The assumption that all employees of the London branch but the expatriates would be hostile to greater headquarters' interference alienated those groups (locally hired Germans and Germanophiles) who could have functioned as a bridge between headquarters and the branch office. One can speculate to what extent this made the difficulties of implementing the new structure more serious than would have been necessary.

Questions

1 What are plausible reasons for an international bank to switch to an international matrix structure?
2 What could headquarters have done differently in implementing the international matrix structure, in order to minimize resistance from the London branch?

Note

1 Later in this chapter we will use the term 'transnational' to refer to one specific type of MNC. Here we borrow the usage of the term of the United Nations, to refer to all kinds of MNCs.

References

Akkermans, H. and Dellaert, N. (2005) The rediscovery of industrial dynamics: the contribution of system dynamics to supply chain management in a dynamic and fragmented world. *System Dynamics Review* 21(3), 173–186.

Almond, P. (2011) Re-visiting country of origin effects on HRM in multinational corporations. *Human Resource Management Journal* 21(3), 258–271.

Bartlett, C.A. and Ghoshal, S. (1986) Tap your subsidiaries for global reach. *Harvard Business Review* 64, 87–94.

Bartlett, C.A. and Ghoshal, S. (1989) *Transnational Management: Text, Cases, and Readings in Cross-Border Management.* Boston, MA: McGraw-Hill.

Bartlett, C.A. and Ghoshal, S. (2000) *Transnational Management: Text, Cases, and Readings in Cross-Border Management* (3rd edn). Boston, MA: Irwin.

Beugelsdijk, S., Slangen, A. and Van Herpen, M. (2002) Shapes of organizational change: the case of Heineken Inc. *Journal of Organizational Change Management* 15(3), 311–326.

Birkinshaw, J.M. and Morrison, A.J. (1995) Configurations of strategy and structure in subsidiaries of multinational corporations. *Journal of International Business Studies* 26, 729–753.

Brock, D.M., Barry, D. and Thomas, D.C. (2000) 'Your forward is our reverse, your right, our wrong': rethinking multinational planning processes in light of national culture. *International Business Review* 9, 687–701.

Brouthers, K.D. (2002) Institutional, cultural and transaction cost influences on entry mode choice and performance. *Journal of International Business Studies* 33(2), 203–221.

Brouthers, K.D. and Brouthers, L.E. (2001) Explaining the national cultural distance paradox. *Journal of International Business Studies* 32(1), 177–189.

Brouthers, K.D. and Hennart, J.-F. (2007) Boundaries of the firm: insights from international entry mode research. *Journal of Management* 33(3), 395–425.

Buckley, P.J. and Carter, M.J. (1999) Managing cross-border complementary knowledge. *International Studies of Management & Organization* 29(1), 80–104.

Campbell, A.J. and Verbeke, A. (1994) The globalization of service multinationals. *Long Range Planning* 27(2), 95–102.

Cerny, K. (1996) Making local knowledge global. *Harvard Business Review* 74(May/June), 22–38.

Child, J. (1973) Predicting and understanding organization structure. *Administrative Science Quarterly* 17, 168–185.

Cosset, J.-C. and Roy, J. (1991) The determinants of country risk ratings. *Journal of International Business Studies* 22(1), 135–142.

Cray, D. (1984) Control and coordination in multinational corporations. *Journal of International Business Studies* 15 (Fall), 85–98.

Cuypers, I.R.P. and Martin, X. (2007) Joint ventures and real options: an integrated perspective. *Advances in Strategic Management* 24, 103–144.

Daniels, J.D. and Radebaugh, L.H. (2001) *International Business: Environments and Operations* (9th edn). Upper Saddle River, NJ: Prentice-Hall.

Davidson, W.H. and McFetridge, D.G. (1984) International technology transactions and the theory of the firm. *Journal of Industrial Economics* 32, 253–264.

Delios, A. and Henisz, W.J. (2000) Japanese firms' investment strategies in emerging economies. *Academy of Management Journal* 43(3), 305–323.

Dicken, P. (1998) *Global Shift: Transforming the World Economy.* London: Paul Chapman.

Doz, Y.L. (1980) Strategic management in multinational companies. *Sloan Management Review* 21(2), 27–46.

Dunning, J.H. (1993) *Multinational Enterprise and the Global Economy.* Harrow: Addison-Wesley

Egelhoff, W.G. (1988) Strategy and structure in multinational corporations: a revision of the Stopford and Wells model. *Strategic Management Journal* 9, 1–14.

Egelhoff, W.G. (1993) Information-processing theory and the multinational corporation. In Ghoshal, S. and Westney, D.E. (eds) *Organization Theory and the Multinational Corporation.* New York: St Martin's Press, 182–210.

Forsgren, M. (2002) The concept of learning in the Uppsala internationalization process model: a critical review. *International Business Review* 11, 257–277.

Forsgren, M. and Johanson, J. (2010) A dialogue about the Uppsala model of internationalization. In Anderson, U. and Holm, U. (eds). *Managing the Contemporary Multinational: The Role of Headquarters*. Cheltenham: Edward Elgar, 283–304.

Fraidin, S. and Lelutiu, R. (2003). Strategic alliances and corporate control. *Case Western Reserve Law Review* 53, 865–895.

Franko, L.G. (1976) *The European Multinationals: A Renewed Challenge to American and British Big Business*. London: Harper & Row.

Ghoshal, S. and Nohria, N. (1993) Horses for courses: organizational forms for multinational corporations. *Sloan Management Review* 34(2), 23–35.

Gooderham, P.N. and Ulset, S. (2002) 'Beyond the M-form': towards a critical test of the new form. *International Journal of the Economics of Business* 9(1), 117–138.

Gooderham, P.N., Nordhaug, O. and Ringdal, K. (1999) Institutional and rational determinants of organizational practices: human resource management in European firms. *Administrative Science Quarterly* 44, 507–531.

Gudykunst, W.B. (1983) Similarities and differences in perceptions of initial intracultural and intercultural encounters. *The Southern Speech Communication Journal* 49(1), 40–65.

Gudykunst, W.B. and Nishida, T. (1984) Individual and cultural influences on uncertainty reduction. *Communication Monographs* 51(1), 23–36.

Gupta, A.K. and Govindarajan, V. (1991) Knowledge flows and the structure of control within multinational corporations. *Academy of Management Review* 16, 768–792.

Gupta, A.K. and Govindarajan, V. (2000) Knowledge flows within multinational corporations. *Strategic Management Journal* 21, 473–496.

Harzing, A.-W.K. (1999) *Managing the Multinationals: An International Study of Control Mechanisms*. Cheltenham: Edward Elgar.

Harzing, A.-W.K. (2000) An empirical analysis and extension of the Bartlett and Ghoshal typology of multinational companies. *Journal of International Business Studies* 31(1), 101–120.

Harzing, A.-W.K. and Sorge, A. (2003) The relative impact of country-of-origin and universal contingencies on internationalization strategies and corporate control in multinational enterprises: worldwide and European perspectives. *Organization Studies* 24, 187–214.

Hedlund, G. (1986) The hyper-modern MNC – a heterarchy? *Human Resource Management* 25(1), 9–35.

Hennart, J.-F. (1991) The transaction cost theory of the multinational enterprise. In Pitelos, C.N. and Sugden, R. (eds) *The Nature of the Transnational Firm*, London: Routledge.

Hennart, J.-F. (2011) A theoretical assessment of the empirical literature on the impact of multinationality on performance. *Global Strategy Journal* 1(1–2), 135–151.

Hennart, J.-F. and Larimo, J. (1998) The impact of culture on the strategy of multinational enterprises: does national origin affect ownership decisions? *Journal of International Business Studies* 29(3), 515–538.

Hofstede, G. (2001) *Culture's Consequences: Comparing Values, Behaviors, Institutions and Organizations Across Nations* (2nd edn). Thousand Oaks: Sage.

Inkpen, A.C. (1998) Learning and knowledge acquisition through international strategic alliances. *Academy of Management Executive* 12(4), 69–80.

Johanson, J. and Vahlne, J.-E. (1977) The internationalization process of the firm: a model of knowledge development and increasing foreign market commitments. *Journal of International Business Studies* 8, 23–32.

Johanson, J. and Vahlne, J.-E. (2009) The Uppsala internationalization process model revisited: from liability of foreignness to liability of outsidership. *Journal of International Business Studies* 40(9), 1411–1431.

Johanson, J. and Wiedersheim-Paul, F. (1975) The internationalization of the firm: four cases. *Journal of Management Studies* 12, 305–322.

Kale, P. and Puranam, P. (2004) Choosing equity stakes in technology-sourcing relationships: an integrative framework. *California Management Review*, 46(3): 77–99.

Kostova, T. and Roth, K. (2002) Adoption of an organizational practice by subsidiaries of multinational corporations: institutional and relational effects. *Academy of Management Journal* 45, 215–233.

Lane, C. (2000) Understanding the globalization strategies of German and British companies. In Maurice, M. and Sorge, A. (eds) *Embedding Organizations: Societal Analysis of Actors, Organizations and Socio-economic Context.* Amsterdam: John Benjamins, 189–208.

Lubatkin, M., Calori, R., Very P. and Veiga, J.F. (1998) Managing mergers across borders: a two-nation exploration of a nationally bound administrative heritage. *Organization Science* 9, 670–684.

Makino, S. and Inkpen, A.C. (2003) Knowledge seeking FDI and learning across borders. In Easterby-Smith, M. and Lyles, M.A. (eds) *The Blackwell Handbook of Organizational Learning and Knowledge Management.* Oxford: Blackwell, 233–252.

March, J.G. (1991) Exploration and exploitation in organizational learning. *Organization Science* 2(1), 71–87.

Martin, X. and Van den Oever, K. (2013) Progress, maturity or exhaustion? Sources and modes of theorizing on the international strategy–performance relationship (1990–2011). *Advances in International Management* 26, 331–361.

Martinez, J.I. and Jarillo, J.J. (1989) The evolution of research on coordination mechanisms in multinational corporations. *Journal of International Business Studies* 20, 489–514.

Melin, L. (1992) Internationalization as a strategy process. *Strategic Management Journal* 13 (Special Issue Winter), 99–118.

Meyer, K.E. and Estrin, S. (2001) Brownfield entry in emerging markets. *Journal of International Business Studies* 32, 575–584.

Moore, F. (2003) Internal diversity and culture's consequences: branch/head office relations in a German financial MNC. *Management International Review* 43 (Special Issue 2003/2), 95–111.

Morschett, D., Schramm-Klein, H. and Swoboda, B. (2010) Decades of research on market entry modes: what do we really know about external antecedents of market entry mode choice? *Journal of International Management* 16, 60–77.

Mudambi, R. (2008) Location, control and innovation in knowledge-intensive industries. *Journal of Economic Geography* 8, 699–725.

Mullor-Sebastián, A. (1983) The product life cycle theory: empirical evidence. *Journal of International Business Studies* 14(3), 95–105.

Murtha, T.P. and Lenway, S.A. (1994) Country capabilities and the strategic state: how national political institutions affect multinational corporations' strategies. *Strategic Management Journal* 15 (Special Issue Summer), 113–129.

Nachum, L. (2003) Liability of foreigness in global competition? Financial service affiliates in the city of London. *Strategic Management Journal* 24, 1187–1208.

Newman, K.L. and Nollen, S.D. (1996) Culture and congruence: the fit between management practices and national culture. *Journal of International Business Studies* 27, 753–779.

Ngo, H.-Y., Turban, D., Lau, C.-M. and Lui, S.-Y. (1998) Human resource practices and firm performance of multinational corporations: influences of country of origin. *The International Journal of Human Resource Management* 9, 632–652.

Noorderhaven, N.G. and Harzing, A.-W.K. (2003) The 'country-of-origin effect' in multinational corporations: sources, mechanisms and moderating conditions. *Management International Review* 43 (Special Issue 2003/2), 47–66.

Noorderhaven, N.G. and Harzing, A.-W.K. (2009) Knowledge sharing and social interaction within MNEs. *Journal of International Business Studies* 40, 719–741.

Pauly, L.W. and Reich, S. (1997) National structures and multinational corporate behavior: enduring differences in the age of globalization. *International Organization* 51, 1–30.

Peng, M.W. (2013) *Global Strategy.* Mason, Ohio: South-Western.

Perlmutter, H.V. (1969) The tortuous evolution of the multinational company. *Columbia Journal of World Business* (Jan./Feb.), 9–18.

Polanyi, M. (1962) *Personal Knowledge*. London: Routledge.

Rosenzweig, P.M. and Singh, J.V. (1991) Organizational environments and the multinational enterprise. *Academy of Management Review* 16, 340–361.

Rugman, A., Verbeke, A. and Yuan, W. (2011) Re-conceptualizing Bartlett and Ghoshal's classification of national subsidiary roles in the multinational enterprise. *Journal of Management Studies* 48(2), 253–277.

Senge, P.M. (1990) *The Fifth Discipline: the Art and Practice of the Learning Organization*. London: Century Business.

Shaver, J.M. (2013) Do we really need more entry mode studies? *Journal of International Business Studies* 44, 23–27.

Simard, L. (1981) Cross-cultural interaction: potential invisible barriers. *Journal of Social Psychology* 113(2), 171–192.

Slangen, A.H.L. (2011) A communication-based theory of the choice between greenfield and acquisition entry. *Journal of Management Studies* 48(8), 1699–1726.

Slangen, A.H.L. and Van Tulder, R.J.M. (2009) Cultural distance, political risk, or governance quality? Towards a more accurate conceptualization and measurement of external uncertainty in foreign entry mode research. *International Business Review* 18, 276–291.

Stopford, J.M. and Wells, L.T. (1972) *Managing the Multinational Enterprise: Organization of the Firm and Ownership of the Subsidiaries*. London: Longman.

Thibaut, J.W. and Kelly, H.H. (1959) *The Social Psychology of Groups*. New York: Wiley.

Thompson, J. (1967) *Organizations in Action*. New York: McGraw-Hill.

Tichy, G. (2011) Innovation, product life cycle and diffusion: vernon and beyond. In Cooke, P., Asheim, B., Boschma, R., Martin, R., Schwartz, D. and Tödtling, F. (eds) *Handbook of Regional Innovation and Growth*. Cheltenham: Edward Elgar, 67–77.

UNCTAD (1999) *World Investment Report 1999*. United Nations Conference on trade and Development, New York/Geneva: United Nations.

UNCTAD (2007) *The Universe of the Largest Transnational Corporations*. United Nations Conference on Trade and Development, New York/Geneva: United Nations.

UNCTAD (2014) *World Investment Report 2014*. United Nations Conference on Trade and Development, New York/Geneva: United Nations.

United Nations (1988) *Multinational Corporations in World Development*. New York: United Nations.

Vernon, R. (1966) International investment and international trade in the product cycle. *The Quarterly Journal of Economics* 80(2), 190–207.

Welch, D. and Welch, L. (1997) Being flexible and accommodating diversity: the challenge for multinational management. *European Management Journal* 15(6), 677–685.

Westney, D.E. (1993) Institutionalization theory and the multinational corporation. In Ghoshal, S. and Westney, D.E. (eds) *Organization Theory and the Multinational Corporation*. New York: St Martin's Press, 53–76.

Westney, D.E. (1999) Organizational evolution of the multinational enterprise: an organisational sociology perspective. *Management International Review* 39 (Special Issue 1), 55–75.

Whitford, J. (2012) Waltzing, relational work, and the construction (or not) of collaboration in manufacturing industries. *Politics & Society* 40(2), 249–272.

Whitley, R. (1992) Introduction, in Whitley, R. (ed.) *European Business Systems: Firms and Markets in their National Contexts*. London: Sage, 1–3.

Whitley, R. and Kristensen, P.H. (eds) (1996) *The Changing European Firm: Limits to Convergence*. London: Routledge.

Xu, D. and Shenkar, O. (2002) Institutional distance and the multinational enterprise. *Academy of Management Review* 27(4), 608–618.

Yan, A. and Zeng, M. (1999) International joint venture instability: a critique of previous research, a reconceptualization and directions for future research. *Journal of International Business Studies* 30, 397–414.

10 Networks and clusters of economic activity

Sjoerd Beugelsdijk

Learning objectives

By the end of this chapter you will be able to:

- understand why networks and clusters are important for business life
- analyse the positive and negative aspects of the network relationships of firms
- explore how geographical clustering can enhance a firm's competitive position
- critically assess the insights of several theoretical frameworks for understanding the concepts of networks and clusters
- explain why the nature of networks and clusters is context specific, taking a universal approach towards understanding the success of clusters
- assess the argument that institutions are important in industrial districts
- appreciate the difference between the sectoral approach and the cluster approach.

Chapter outline

10.1 Introduction

Over the past 25 years the concepts of networks and clusters have gained popularity in international business in the advanced countries. These concepts refer to a certain kind of strategic cooperation between various organizations, mostly firms. Cooperation is seen as a necessary organizational survival strategy in today's intensely competitive and globalized business environment. Some authors even suggest that cooperation strategies are part of a new industrial order ('alliance capitalism'), in which international competitiveness depends on the continuous collaboration of firms with external sources of knowledge (Best, 1990; Dunning, 1997; Dicken, 1998; Porter, 1998). In spite of its current popularity, the idea of inter-organizational cooperation is, of course, not new. For example, it is well known that the UK cotton industry of the late nineteenth century derived much of its competitiveness from the well-developed cooperation of producers with suppliers of machines and transport facilities (Lazonick, 1992).

What *is* new, however, is both the aim and the complexity of modern cooperative efforts. Often, these are aimed at the collaborative research and development (R&D) needed for the realization of innovations, that is, new products, services and processes. In many cases, the technology-based aim of these cooperative strategies involves a complex inter-play of different parties (e.g. firms, universities and private research institutes), providing each other with complementary knowledge. This type of cooperation has led to the emergence of different types of network and geographically concentrated clusters of economic activity.

While it is hard to give a definition of networks and clusters that encompasses all variants of economic cooperation, in general, networks can be seen as chains of competitors, suppliers, customers and/or knowledge institutes with the aim of creating value added. Clusters could then be seen as constituting a subgroup of networks, in that they have a clear geographical dimension. There are, for example, many cross-border networks of firms operating in the field of semiconductors (e.g. cooperation between Toshiba, Hitachi and AT&T). Simultaneously, however, there are some geographically concentrated clusters in this branch of activity. Well-known examples of such regional clusters in semiconductors are Silicon Valley in California and Cambridge in the UK.

The increasing popularity of networks and clusters in international business explains the inclusion of this subject in this book. Both management and policy-makers are interested in the power of network-and cluster-type relationships for increasing the international competitiveness of companies and entire sectors. In order to provide you with a good grasp of the fundamentals of networks and clusters, this chapter discusses network theory and, subsequently, the concept of clusters. The case at the end of the chapter will help you to test your knowledge of networks and clusters in a comparative setting. It requires you to take a comparative view and combine the insights generated in this chapter with the insights discussed in previous chapters.

The chapter starts with a brief examination of the drivers of networking and clustering – that is, the increasing need for innovation and specialization. Next, the fundamentals of an important theory of forms of governance, transaction cost theory, are discussed, as networking can be perceived as a hybrid form of governance.

Subsequently, the chapter stresses the geographical dimension of inter-firm cooperation. In this context, concepts such as industrial districts and Porter's cluster approach are introduced. The chapter ends with an overview of the different dimensions of networking and clustering that can be identified in practice. Finally, in the spirit of this book the question is explored to what extent clusters in different regions are comparable. The conclusion is that clusters can be compared on a number of common dimensions, but to understand their success we need to have fine-grained knowledge of local conditions, including culture and institutions.

The chapter shows that networks and clusters are not only important carriers of business life, but are also complex inter-organizational structures with many different faces, because they are rooted in different societal structures. This means that there is also an important international-comparative dimension to clusters and networks.

10.2 Balancing competition and cooperation

The emergence of networks and clusters as important vehicles in business life can be related to trends that have been going on in the world economy for some time. These developments include, in particular, globalization, technological developments and changes in market demand (Dicken, 1998). Through the combined effect of these trends, market rivalry has not only intensified, but has also changed character. As explained in the introduction, globalization refers to the phenomenon of an increasing number of economic relations in today's world economy. Due to the liberalization of world trade, the opening of previously sheltered economies (e.g. eastern Europe and China) and the resulting increase in foreign direct investments (FDIs), more and more and different types of relationships between parties in the market place are emerging. The phenomenon of globalization seems to induce integration of activities that are geographically dispersed with no company or country being able to operate in a totally independent manner. This new global context forces companies to change their competition strategies in the market.

Besides globalization, there is a tendency for an accelerating pace of technological development. In particular, developments in the information and communication technologies (ICTs) have caused a reduction in transportation costs for people, goods, services and information (Dicken, 1998). Although these 'space-shrinking technologies' have resulted in cost reductions, simultaneously the R&D needed to develop new technologies has become more expensive. The latter is caused by the fact that, nowadays, most innovations are realized by combining separate complex technologies ('crossroads technologies'); modern examples are mechatronics and biochemistry.

Another important market development is the change of preferences at the demand side of the economy. Contractors and consumers both place heavier demands on the quality of the products and services they buy. As a result, products and services have to be tailored to the individual customers' requirements. This process of 'customization', which started in the capital goods industry, has also penetrated the market for consumer goods. An example of the changing pattern of demand can be found in the automobile industry. Because the demand for automobiles has matured, producers have to supply a far greater variety of vehicle types than they did previously. In this way, they hope to create new markets and attract new customers.

These trends in the world economy have resulted in the paradoxical situation that firms have to cooperate in order to remain competitive. Success stories of clusters, in which competition and cooperation co-exist with an innovating economy, show that firms are able to resolve the paradox. An illustration of this can be found in the Italian region of Emilia Romagna, where firms producing ceramic tiles are cooperating in the field of purchasing and research on materials, while, at the same time, competing aggressively with each other in the marketplace (Pyke, 1995).

The idea that competition and cooperation should go hand in hand can be found in several recent contributions in the literature too. According to Enright (1996), for instance, firms should not ask themselves whether to compete or to cooperate, but rather on what dimensions to compete and cooperate. This question involves a trade-off between access to more resources versus potential loss of firm-specific knowledge to competitors.

Related to such arguments is Audretsch and Thurik's point (1997) that a fundamental shift has taken place from a 'managed economy' with homogeneous mass production as the central issue towards a so-called 'entrepreneurial economy'. In this kind of economy, the competitiveness of companies is primarily based on entrepreneurship, heterogeneity and innovativeness. Here, competition and cooperation are not substitutes any more, but rather complements.

Not all firms in all countries are equally good at cooperating and, partly based on cultural and institutional features, in some countries entrepreneurship and innovativeness are more prevalent than in others. Indeed, the type and intensity of cooperation, as well as the ways in which cooperation and innovation are successfully achieved, differ between countries. In Germany, for example, entrepreneurship and innovation in the biotechnology sector only developed after significant government involvement and adaptation of the institutions at the sector level. The Japanese keiretsu, on the other hand, are a different type of inter-organizational cooperation that developed in response to the lack of efficiently functioning institutions after the Second World War, combined with market-distorting government policies. The case at the end of this chapter is a further illustration of these arguments.

10.3 Networks from a theoretical perspective

To explore the issue of networking and clustering from a theoretical point of view, both the insights derived from transaction cost economics and network theories are discussed here. Transaction costs theory offers an economic perspective on networking, whereas network theories perceive the network type of cooperation more as a societal activity than a purely economic outcome based on costs and benefits.

Transaction cost theory

The choice of market, hierarchy or hybrid forms

Coase (1937) and, particularly, Williamson (1975, 1985) have developed transaction cost economics. The focus of these authors is on the organization of economic transactions between parties. They do not take the neoclassical notion of a representative firm as their unit of analysis. Instead, they take transactions between economic actors as the analytical starting point. According to Williamson (1985), 'a transaction occurs when a good or service is transferred across a technologically separable interface. One stage of activity terminates and another begins.' When economic parties execute transactions, they meet transaction costs – that is, the costs of information and communication needed to find, negotiate, agree upon and monitor contracts. As an example, just think of the marketing costs a producer has to incur in order to attract new customers.

In general, these costs may be divided into three categories: contact costs, contract costs and control costs (Nooteboom, 1999). Costs of contact and contract may appear in the phase before doing business (ex ante), while control costs may arise when parties have carried out transactions and one of the parties is, say, cheating (ex post). The main argument of transaction cost economics is that parties will look for the most efficient governance structure to coordinate their transactions. Ultimately, they will choose that mode of governance in which the sum of both transaction costs and production costs is minimized.

In his first book, Williamson (1975) follows Coase (1937) and only sees market and hierarchy (merger) as alternative governance structures. In his later work (1985), however, he replaces this dichotomy by a continuum on which 'hybrid forms' (cooperative forms such as networks and clusters) are positioned between the poles of market and hierarchy. The efficiency of each of these governance structures depends on the properties of human behaviour as well as on the characteristics (dimensions) of transactions.

The assumptions of transaction cost theory regarding human behaviour are 'bounded rationality' and 'opportunism'. Bounded rationality means that individuals have restricted cognitive capabilities so that their behaviour can be seen as 'intendedly rational but only limitedly so' (Simon, 1961). Opportunism is a form of strategic behaviour and reflects the incentive of individuals to cheat if this will improve their position. In consequence, Williamson (1975) defines opportunism as 'self-interest seeking with guile'. Both the bounded rationality and the opportunism of individuals cause costs in executing transactions. The height of these transaction costs is determined by three dimensions of transactions – that is, their asset specificity, uncertainty and frequency.

The first dimension of a transaction is its asset specificity, or the degree to which the transaction has to be supported by investments in special assets, which have no or little use outside the transaction. These investments create a relationship of dependency between the transaction partners. A classic example of a transaction-specific investment is a mould a supplier develops for a customer to use to press the coachwork of a special model of car (Nooteboom, 1999). The second dimension is the frequency of a transaction, referring to the question of how often it takes place. The last dimension, the uncertainty surrounding transactions, is inherent in economic activities, since human behaviour is assumed to follow rules of bounded rationality.

Why markets and hierarchies are not always efficient

When the degree of asset specificity, the frequency and the uncertainty of a transaction are all relatively low, transaction cost theory predicts that the market is the most efficient governance structure to coordinate transactions. In this case, the transaction costs for parties are low because the price mechanism can efficiently coordinate their transactions. However, when transactions are characterized by high asset specificity, frequency and uncertainty, the market is no longer efficient. At that moment, internalization of the transaction in a hierarchy (i.e. an organization governed by authority) involves reduced transaction costs for the partners. For the less extreme, intermediate cases, hybrid forms between market and hierarchy are suitable alternatives (Williamson, 1991).

As suggested, in countries such as Japan (the keiretsu) and Korea (the Chaebol), these hybrid governance forms, such as networks, emerged as a reaction to the business environment in which the firms operate. Supplier networks, like the one around the Japanese firm Toyota, developed in reaction to the domestic environment after the Second World War and a specific combination of government policies. By forming its own supplier network, Toyota gained an advantage over competitors in the USA because it was relieved of two major transaction costs: costs linked to internalization and costs associated with decomposed subcontracting. In addition, successful networks like Toyota's develop intra-group understandings that lead to significant reductions in both inter-firm coordination costs and direct production costs per unit of output (Edwards and Samimi, 1997).

In general, it has been suggested that 'hybrid vertical inter-firm relations' might be more efficient than market and hierarchy (Noorderhaven, 1994). In this light, seven in-depth case studies among Dutch companies indicate that, since the 1980s, the number of inter-firm relationships has grown compared with the strategic alternatives of market and hierarchy, and that the competitive positioning of the cooperating firms has been strengthened (Commandeur, 1994). On the basis of an analysis of surveys among about 700 firms in the Dutch province of Brabant in the period 1987–1992, a significant positive correlation was found between innovation results and the joint R&D efforts of suppliers and users (Oerlemans, 1996). The conclusion from this finding is that cooperating firms can use knowledge from their environment more efficiently than firms innovating in isolation. The problem with this conclusion, however, is that not all national institutional environments allow equally for cooperation and, further, that not all national cultures are equally prone to adopt cooperative business practices.

The latter indicates clearly that the purely economic view of cooperation offered by transaction cost economics is incomplete. The transaction cost approach has been criticized, moreover, for being too rigid, mechanical and pessimistic, reducing cooperation to only a static cost–benefit problem. In reality, as suggested, cooperation is also a societal phenomenon through which different parties complement each other and can over time develop trust relationships. This crucial role of trust is central in the network embeddedness approach.

Network embeddedness

The concept of embeddedness was introduced by Karl Polanyi in his classic book *The Great Transformation* (1944). He describes the anarchy in nineteenth-century England when the social foundations of the economy for a short period crumbled. Polanyi finds it unrealistic to assume that economic actors act separately from society. Economic action without the societal element would be only the 'bare bones'. A famous and more recent contribution in this respect is Granovetter's 1985 paper. In this paper, the author explores to what extent economic action is embedded in the structures of social relations in modern industrial society. He discusses two strands of literature that are related to the issue of social structure and economic action. First the Benthamian approach, which assumes rational, utility-maximizing individuals that are not, or are only slightly, affected by social relations. Second, the new institutional economics, personified by Williamson, argues that behaviour and institutions can best be understood as resulting from the pursuit of self-interest by rational, more or less atomized individuals.

Granovetter argues that social relationships, rather than generalized morality (what he calls the over-socialized conception) or institutional arrangements like contract or authority structures (the under-socialized conception), are mainly responsible for the production of trust in economic life.

Granovetter notes (1985: 485) that both under- and over-socialized views share the same conception of human action regarding atomized actors. He notes that, in the under-socialized account, atomization results from the narrow utilitarian pursuit of self-interest and, in the over-socialized account, from the fact that behavioural patterns have been internalized and ongoing social relations have thus only peripheral effects on behaviour. In other words, the fact that the internalized rules of behaviour are social in origin does not differentiate this argument decisively from a utilitarian one.

Granovetter opposes the view of individuals as atomistic actors. A fruitful analysis of human action requires us to avoid the atomization implicit in the theoretical extremes of under- and over-socialized conceptions. Actors do not behave or decide as atoms outside a social context, nor do they adhere slavishly to a script written for them by the particular intersection of social categories that they happen to occupy. Their attempts at purposive action are instead embedded in concrete, ongoing systems of societal relations (Granovetter, 1985). Granovetter's concept of embeddedness has been widely recognized and is now also seen as one of the standard theories on firms and their behaviour. Other researchers have taken his concept of embeddedness further. Zukin and DiMaggio (1990) distinguish four different kinds of embeddedness:

1 Cognitive embeddedness refers to the ways in which rational economic action is limited by uncertainty, complexity and the costs of information.
2 Political embeddedness observes that economic action is always carried out in a greater political context.
3 Structural embeddedness refers to the fact that economic exchange always takes place in a larger social structure of ongoing interpersonal relations. It focuses on the social embeddedness of economic action.
4 Finally, cultural embeddedness observes that economic assumptions, rules and rationality are limited and shaped by culture. Collective understandings and norms shape economic strategies and goals.

It is obvious that all these four forms of embeddedness are interrelated. The structural embeddedness perspective is closely related to the network approach discussed earlier. Uzzi is explicit about the embeddedness perspective:

> Whereas neo-classical accounts focus predominantly on asocial and price-determined allocative mechanisms, the structural embeddedness approach emphasizes how social networks achieve outcomes that may equal or even surpass market alternatives.
>
> (Uzzi, 1996: 682)

Trust

A crucial component in the cultural embeddedness perspective is trust, of which different types have been identified (Nooteboom, 2002). First there is the distinction between macro sources, which apply apart from any specific exchange relation, and micro sources arising from specific relations. Whereas the former arise from the institutional environment of laws, norms, and standards, the latter is personalized and therefore yields 'thick' trust. Building on this macro-micro distinction, Nooteboom distinguishes between two other types of trust. The following table is taken from Nooteboom (2002) and summarizes insights from the literature.

Table 10.1 Sources of cooperation

	Macro	*Micro*
Egotistic	Sanctions from some authority (the law, God, Leviathan, dictator, organization), contractual obligation	Material advantage or self-interest: shadow of the future, reputation
Altruistic	Ethics: values, social norms of proper conduct, moral obligation, sense of duty	Bonds of friendship, kinship; habituation, empathy

Source: Nooteboom (2002).

Numerous typologies of trust exist at the micro level. One of the most commonly accepted typologies of trust besides the distinction macro (generalized)/ micro (personal-individual) is calculus-based trust, knowledge-based trust and identification-based trust (Nooteboom, 2002). Calculus-based trust has to do with the fear for the consequences of not doing what one promised to do. In this case the shadow of the future is dark enough to create pressure to do what has been promised and not behave opportunistically. Knowledge-based trust is grounded in the predictability of the other's behaviour. This may be experience based or established through reputation. Identification-based trust, finally, is based on the perceived similarity between partners yielding empathy and trust. In this case the bond of friendship is an important vehicle for the creation of trust.

Nooteboom (2002) argues that trust is based on both rational reasons and psychological causes. The first arising from a rational evaluation of the trustee's trustworthiness. This can be based on knowledge of the trustee inferred from reputation, records, norms and standards, or one's own experience. A psychological cause is empathy. This is the ability to share another person's feelings and emotions as if they were one's own, thereby understanding motives of action of the other. Empathy affects both one's own trustworthiness, in the willingness to make sacrifices for others, and one's trust, in the tolerance of behaviour that deviates from expectations. One will more easily help someone when one can identify with his or her needs. 'One can more easily forgive someone's breach of trust when one can identify with the lack of competence or the motive that caused it. Since one can identify with the other, one may sympathize with his or her action, seeing perhaps that this action was in fact a just response to one's own previous actions' (Nooteboom, 2002: 81).

Trust is fundamentally related to networks. Through the role of reputation, social networks can serve as a basis for trust. Burt and Knez (1995) show that what they call 'third party gossip' amplifies both the positive and the negative in relationships, because it makes actors more certain of their trust (or distrust) in one another. Trust affects the strength of a relationship. Trusting relationships may develop inside a (closed) network, in which actors build up a reputation of trustworthiness that becomes important information for others in that same network.

At the personal-individual level, trust is regarded as a property of individuals or characteristic of interpersonal relationships. But at the organizational level firms may also develop trust through ongoing interactions between their (top) managers, which establish and reinforce norms of equity (Gulati, 1998). The importance of trust for economic transactions has been stressed extensively. These studies can also be seen as a critique or extension of Williamson's (1975, 1985) transaction cost theory as discusses in the previous section. Informal, personal connections between and across organizations play an important role in determining the way these firms cooperate and compete (Ring and Van de Ven, 1992).

Disadvantages of being embedded

Embeddedness not only creates advantages such as high trust. There are negative elements as well. Maintaining social ties generates costs, but the social relations of an actor in a network also create obligations towards the other network members (implicit contracts). The necessary condition for a dense social network is trust. A crucial element of trust is reciprocity, and reciprocity creates obligations. Therefore, the positive side of being embedded in a network is the advantages of transacting with less transaction cost. The negative side of being a member – the other side of the trust coin – is the obligational side. These obligations expose an actor to the danger of 'free riding' by other members of his network on his own resources. Hence, cosy inter-group relationships can give rise to the problem of free riding (Portes and Sensenbrenner, 1993).

The second negative aspect of high levels of embeddedness is the fact that a dense network and the accompanying community norms can place constraints on individual behaviour. Membership of a tightly knit or dense social network can subject one to restrictive social regulations and sanctions, and limit individual action. All kinds of levelling pressures keep members in the same situation as their peers, and strong collective norms and very 'solid' communities may restrict the cognitive scope of individuals (Portes and Sensenbrenner, 1993; Meyerson, 1994; Brown, 1998); or, as Woolcock puts it, using social capital as a key characteristic of embeddedness:

> high levels of social capital [and trust] can be 'positive' in that it gives group members access to privileged 'flexible' resources and psychological support while lowering the risks of malfeasance and transactions costs, but may be 'negative' in that it also places high particularistic demands on group members, thereby restricting individual expression and advancement, permits free riding on community resources; and negates, in those groups with a long history of marginalization through coercive non-market mechanisms the belief in the possibility of advancement through individual effort.
>
> (Woolcock, 1998)

Embeddedness may therefore reduce adaptive capacity. This may imply the danger of lock-in effects and path dependency. These lock-in effects may be strengthened by processes of cognitive dissonance in tight groups (Meyerson, 1994; Rabin, 1998). Individuals that make up a dense network tend to develop a commitment to one another and to their group. Information that disturbs the consensus of the group's perception of reality is likely to be rejected. Woolcock (1998) uses the term amoral familism to describe the presence of social integration within a group but no linkages outside this group. In his view, amoral familism undermines the efficiency of all forms of economic exchange by increasing transaction costs. On the other hand, there is amoral individualism. In this case, there is no familial or generalized trust at all and only narrow self-interested individuals exist. Individuals are not embedded in a cohesive social network. A theoretical approach like transaction cost economics fits very well in this view. In this theory there is no room for social networks and trust relationships that are based on anything beyond immediate reciprocity.

If embeddedness has both positive and negative effects, the question arises as to whether there is an optimal level of embeddedness. Optimal in the sense that firms can benefit from the advantages of being embedded, but do not suffer from the disadvantages. In a study of the apparel industry in New York it has been shown that there is a U-shaped pattern between the likelihood of failure of a firm and the degree of embeddedness, which implies that there is indeed an optimal degree of embeddedness. In a study of the banking sector, similar results were found (Uzzi, 1996, 1999). Firms are more likely to secure loans and receive lower interest rates on loans if their network of bank ties has a mix of embedded ties and arm's-length ties. Embeddedness seems to yield positive results up to a certain threshold (see Figure 10.1). Hence, the positive effects of being a member of a network are based on the same mechanisms that cause the negative effects.

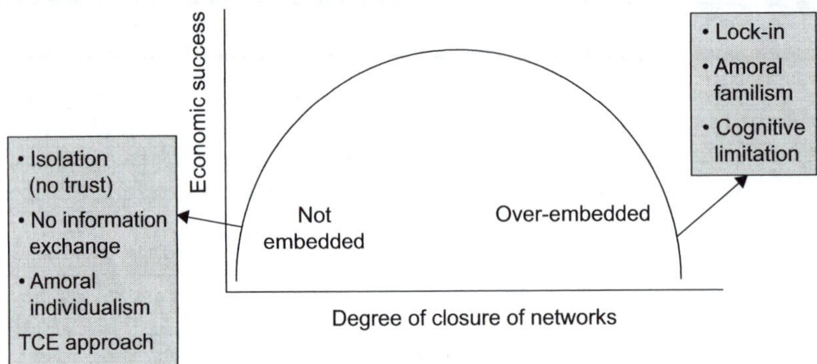

Figure 10.1 Economic success and degree of network closure.

10.4 From networks to clusters

Until now, we have considered networks of economic activity as sets of relationships, without paying attention to the spatial dimension. Many networks are, indeed, not bound to a certain location. Just think of the network of shoe manufacturer Nike. At Nike's headquarters in Oregon, USA, there are only 900 employees. The rest of this company's activities are performed by a close network of suppliers that perform parts of the production process (e.g. laces, plastic, heels) all over the world. Besides such a-spatial, international networks, however, many networks are localized in a certain place; they are geographically concentrated and may contribute to a large extent to regional economic development. Despite all tendencies that point to the decay of distance, in the end, all economic actions have to be located somewhere. As is the case with networks, several concepts are used to denote these spatially concentrated networks.

In the next section, some of the most important notions in this respect are discussed. Subsequently, attention is paid to industrial districts, and Porter's conceptualization of clusters. The main message of all these approaches is that being part of a geographically concentrated network may enhance a firm's competitive position.

Industrial districts

How firms benefit from geographical clustering

The historical roots of the cluster concept can be found in the literature on 'industrial districts'. The notion of industrial districts goes back to Alfred Marshall, who presented an economic analysis of the location of industries. In his handbook *Principles of Economics* (1890), Marshall explains the development of geographically concentrated clusters, which he calls 'industrial districts', by three factors: specialized labour, dedicated intermediate inputs and knowledge spillovers. Firms are attracted to a particular location by a labour market with highly skilled workers. These workers not only possess specialized technical skills, but also knowledge about people and their activities in the industrial district. Next, location near a pool of specialized intermediate inputs provides advantages to a firm. In this way, the firm can obtain equipment, tools, technologies and services from supporting industries. Moreover, firms can absorb knowledge spillovers in an industrial district, because it is easier to realize information exchange within the same location than over great distances.

The various benefits of regional concentration are external to the particular firms ('external economies'), but internal to the industrial district as a whole. Marshall argues that the achievement of these benefits depends on the existence of close social relationships between firms, creating an 'industrial atmosphere' within the district. It is clear that such an atmosphere favours the learning and innovation process of the firms in the region:

> Good work is rightly appreciated, inventions and improvements in machinery, in processes and the general organization of the business have their merits promptly discussed: if one man starts a new idea, it is taken up by others and combined with suggestions of their own; and thus becomes the source of further new ideas.
>
> (Marshall, 1890 (1947 edition): 225)

The importance of institutions in industrial districts

Marshall left most of his ideas on industrial districts undeveloped. However, over the last 25 years, his analysis has played an important role in explaining the economic success of clusters of small firms in the north of Italy (Pyke, 1995). In the region of Emilia Romagna, for example, clusters producing machine tools, ceramic tiles, knitting and footwear can be found. Although around three quarters of the manufacturing workers are employed in firms with 100 or fewer employees, the region has developed from one of the poorest in Italy to one of the richest in Europe. The success of the clusters in northern Italy attracted the interest of policy-makers and researchers (see Box 10.1).

Box 10.1 Industrial districts in northern Italy

Generally, northern Italy is seen as a set of industrial districts par excellence. In contrast to the poor south, the Mezzogiorno, the northern part of Italy, has shown high growth rates based on network structures in such artisan sectors as textiles, clothing, leather, shoes and ceramics. Santa Croce, for example, a town between Florence and Pisa, is a breeding place for production and innovation in high-quality leather manufacturing (Amin and Thrift, 1994). At the beginning of the 1990s, 300 small- and medium-sized firms specializing in tanning cooperated with 200 suppliers of raw leather. In spite of the gradually approaching maturity of the worldwide leather market, this network proved to be very stable and less vulnerable to cyclical movements than stand-alone firms in the sector. As reasons for this stability, Amin and Thrift (1994) point to four factors related to the embeddedness of the leather producers in Santa Croce.

To start with, the agglomeration in the field of leather encouraged the growth of complementary firms in paint, chemicals and marketing. Next, by cooperating, the firms were able to reap scale and scope economies, leading to efficiency gains and process innovations. Furthermore, semi-public organizations, such as local chambers of commerce, municipal bodies and local training centres, played a supporting role in Santa Croce. Finally, the close ties between the firms were not only maintained for economic reasons. The entrepreneurs also met each other in civic associations and at social occasions throughout the town. Interestingly, it was the Communist Party that helped to create this atmosphere of collectivity among the local entrepreneurs, thus also facilitating cooperation in the economic field.

Clusters of small firms in other countries were also identified and studied. Well-known examples of such so-called 'Marshallian industrial districts' are Jutland (Denmark), the Basque country (Spain), Baden-Württemberg (Germany), Toyota City (Japan), Sinos Valley (Brazil), Daegu (Korea), Silicon Glen (Scotland), Flanders Language Valley (Belgium) and Silicon Valley (California). In the analysis of these success stories, however, the researchers place more emphasis on the role of institutions than did Marshall (You and Wilkinson, 1994). In addition to inter-firm linkages, linkages with institutions, such as trade associations, research institutes and government agencies, can also be important factors in explaining the success of industrial districts.

Further research on industrial districts was stimulated by Piore and Sabel. In their book *The Second Industrial Divide* (1984), these authors identify fundamental shifts in the social organization of production and exchange in industrial economies. They argue that, since the 1970s, the system of mass production has been in crisis. An indication of the possible end of this period of 'Fordism' is the emergence of networks of small firms. The firms in a network can acquire competitive advantage by using their flexibility to specialize in niche markets. By cooperating with firms and institutions they can benefit from cost advantages ('collaboration economies'). Because cooperation is facilitated by face-to-face contact and local institutions, the emerging cluster will often be situated in one region.

Industrial districts: exhibiting a mix of competition and cooperation

In the 1990s the concept of 'industrial districts' benefited from renewed interest thanks to Krugman's work (1991). In his contribution, the original ideas of Marshall (1890) are formalized and brought up to date. Krugman stresses the importance of large-scale firms, with increasing returns to scale for the emergence of a cluster at a particular location. These firms will attract supplier firms in order to lower transportation costs and they will stimulate the development of a local pool of skilled labour around these firms. Through the exchange of specialized inputs, services and labour, the firms within the cluster learn from each other continuously. In this way, they can profit through 'agglomeration economies'. The author thus views geographic clustering of production as a means for firms to create sustainable competitive advantage, even in a world economy that is becoming more and more closely integrated.

Other authors (Best, 1990; You and Wilkinson, 1994) in the 1990s see the key to understanding the success of an industrial district in the particular mix of competition and cooperation among its firms. The firms in an industrial district are specialized, but complement each other through cooperation in the field of product design or manufacturing. At the same time, the firms have to compete in the product market with other firms supplying similar products and services in the district. The cooperative aspects of inter-firm relationships help the firms to overcome their disadvantage of small size, while the competitive aspects provide them with the flexibility that large, integrated firms often do not possess. A balance between competition and cooperation thus seems crucial for the functioning of industrial districts. Reviewing the various contributions in the literature, Rabellotti (1998) concludes that an industrial district can be identified by four stylized facts:

1 proximity – a group of geographically concentrated and specialized small- and medium-sized enterprises (SMEs)
2 common behaviour – a common behavioural code as the various actors are linked by the same cultural and social background
3 linkages – a set of linkages between firms based on the exchange of goods, services, labour and information

4 institutions – a network of public and private local institutions supporting the various actors in the cluster.

Porter's concept of clusters

How firms derive competitive advantage from their embeddedness in clusters

Undoubtedly, Porter's book, *The Competitive Advantage of Nations* (1990), has made the most influential contribution in the field of clustering. Porter is interested in why only certain countries generate many firms that become successful international competitors in one or more industries. For his research on the competitive advantage of nations Porter has carried out case studies in ten different countries (including Germany, Japan and the USA). In his analysis, Porter focuses on the individual firm and its position in the structure of a particular cluster of firms. He suggests that domestic competition continuously creates pressures on firms to innovate. In his view, firms and their linkages of competition and cooperation with other organizations are the key to the competitive advantage of these firms, but also to that of the whole nation. Porter argues, then, that these innovative firms derive competitive advantage from their place within a group of four sets of factors (determinants), which he calls the 'diamond'. These factors are as follows.

1 Factor conditions. This determinant refers to a nation's position with regard to factors of production. Competitive advantage is not so much created by basic factors (cheap unskilled labour, natural resources, etc.), but rather by advanced factors, which have to be upgraded constantly (e.g. highly skilled labour and a modern infrastructure).
2 Demand conditions. The nature of home market demand for a product or service influences the success of a firm in international markets. This depends on the relative size and growth of the home market, the quality of demand and the presence of mechanisms transmitting domestic preferences to foreign markets.
3 Related and supporting industries. These play an important role in the ability of firms to compete internationally. The existence of industries that provide firms with inputs for the innovation process stimulates competition and cooperation. Often, the exchange of these inputs is facilitated by geographical proximity.
4 Firm strategy, structure and rivalry. Differences in national economic structure, organizational culture, institutions (e.g. the capital market) and history contribute to national competitive success. These conditions determine how firms are created, organized and managed, as well as how intense the domestic rivalry is.

The determinants of the diamond reinforce each other and together create the national environment in which firms operate. If this context is dynamic and challenging, nations will ultimately succeed in one or more industries, since firms are stimulated to upgrade their advantages over time.

Porter also mentions two additional factors that play a role in national competitive advantage.

5 Chance events. Chance factors can cause shifts in a nation's competitive position and include elements such as major technological changes, shifts in exchange rates or input prices, and important political developments.

6 The government. Governments play an important role in influencing the dynamics between the four determinants of the diamond through regulations related to business, policies towards the physical and educational infrastructure, and so on.

The value chain approach to clustering

Porter's view on clusters is based on his earlier publication, *Competitive Advantage* (Porter, 1985), in which he uses the concept of 'value' to analyse the competitive position of a firm. Porter argues that a firm can be seen as a value chain – that is, the collection of activities that are performed to design, produce, market, deliver and support a product that creates value for the buyers. Each of these activities can contribute to lower costs for the firm, and creates a basis for product differentiation. The firm's value chain is embedded in a larger stream of activities, which is called the 'value system'. The value system includes suppliers, delivering products and services to the firm, and various channels. On its way to the buyer the product passes through the value chains of these channels, which perform additional activities for the firm (such as distribution activities).

Thus creating and sustaining competitive advantage not only depends on the firm's value chain, but also on the question of how the firm fits into the overall value system. As a result, clusters of competitive industries emerge, providing primary goods (end products), machinery for production, specialized inputs and associated services. According to Porter, these clusters of related and supporting industries are crucial for competitive success. An important element of Porter's value chain approach to clustering is its emphasis on the end use of products. Consequently, Porter distinguishes 16 possible clusters in terms of the final products that result from them, divided up as follows:

1 Upstream clusters: materials/metals, semiconductors/computers, forest products, and petroleum/chemicals.
2 Supportive clusters: transportation, energy, office, telecommunications, defence, and other multiple business services.
3 Downstream clusters: food/beverages, housing/household, leisure, healthcare, textile/clothing, and personal affairs.

Porter considers the performance of products made in a cluster on the world market as a main indicator of its competitiveness. By including only the more competitive half of all clusters in a country, one can draft a 'cluster chart', which can be used to make a comparison of the relative specialization patterns between countries. This relatively simple idea of clusters has had considerable influence on researchers and policy-makers over the years. In various countries (the USA, the Netherlands, Italy, Denmark, Sweden and Finland) the diamond and value chain analyses have been used as a framework to analyse the competitiveness of (parts of) the national economy.

How both horizontal and vertical linkages play a role in clusters

In his recent works, Porter (1997, 1998) emphasizes that the cluster approach offers an alternative to the traditional sectoral approach. The latter approach takes sectors (industries) as the units of analysis and deals only with horizontal relationships and competitive interdependence (i.e. relationships between direct competitors in the same product market). The cluster approach focuses on horizontal relationships too, but also on vertical relationships and synergetic interdependence between suppliers, main producers and users.

Table 10.2 The sectoral approach versus the cluster approach

Sectors	*Clusters*
Focus on one or a few end-product industries	Comprise customers, suppliers, service providers and specialized institutions
Participants are direct or indirect competitors	Include related industries sharing technology, information, inputs, customers and channels
Hesitancy to cooperate with competitors	Most participants are not direct competitors, but share common needs and constraints
Dialogue with governments often aimed at subsidies, protection and limiting competition	Wide scope for improvements on areas of common concern, improving productivity and raising competition
Less pay-off to investments	Induce investments by both the private and the public sectors
Risk of dulling local competition	Forums for a more constructive and a more efficient business-government dialogue

Source: Porter (1997).

Thus the cluster approach cuts through the classical division in sectors and provides a new way of looking at the economy (see Table 10.2). In addition to his earlier thoughts on clustering, Porter (1998) pays extensive attention to the link between clusters and competitive advantage in his book, *On Competition*. He argues that clusters stimulate the competitiveness of firms and nations in three different manners. First, participating in a cluster allows firms to operate more productively. They have a better access to the means needed for carrying out their activities – such as technology, information, inputs, customers and channels – than they would have when operating in isolation. Second, this easier access will not only enhance the participants' productivity, but also their ability to innovate. Third, an existing cluster may provide a sound base for new business formation, as the relationships and institutions within the cluster will confront entrepreneurs with lower barriers of entry than elsewhere.

In summary, with the help of different concepts (the diamond, the value chain, the value system), Porter stresses the importance of clusters in creating and sustaining competitive advantage, not only for individual firms, but also for a nation as a whole.

10.5 Comparing regional clusters

Given the success and positive effects of networking and clusters, it comes as no surprise that local, regional and national governments all over the world have tried to mimic the success of well-known clusters such as Silicon Valley (see Box 10.2 for the case of Baden-Württemberg in Germany). Perhaps the most famous example of regional clustering, is Silicon Valley within California's Santa Clara Country. In this micro-electronics cluster, companies produce semiconductors and computer chips which are sold worldwide to other component or system manufacturers. Often, the combination of competition and cooperation among its firms is seen as the success factor for Silicon Valley's successful economic performance (Saxenian, 1994). What, however, can we really learn from such success stories of regional clustering? Can successes such as Silicon Valley be re-created elsewhere?

Box 10.2 The engineering cluster in Baden-Württemberg

A traditional case of clustering can be found in the German region of Baden-Württemberg (B-W). This region is widely seen as one of the biggest industrial success stories within Europe over the past 30 years. The region contributes a great deal to Germany's image as a renowned car- and machinery-producing nation. The region's success is based on the presence of an engineering cluster deeply rooted in the economy. Leading firms, including Daimler-Benz, Bosch, Audi and IBM, cooperate fruitfully with small supplier firms (*Mittelstand*) in the field of automotive, electronics and mechanical engineering. A number of knowledge institutes (universities, polytechnics, basic and applied research institutes, as well as technology transfer centres) provide work with these firms under research contracts. What is often forgotten, however, is that B-W has less employment in large plants and enterprises than the German average.

The literature has put forward several factors to explain B-W's success. First of all, the importance of history has been emphasized. The tradition of clustering within B-W can be traced back to pre-industrial crafts (Cooke et al., 1995; Hassink, 1997) and often poor soil, which forced people to earn a living outside farming and think of new products and techniques. Thus, there has been a fruitful base on which to build. Interestingly, this industrial tradition has proved to be advantageous even in modern times. Technical pragmatism in the crafts was seamlessly linked with university engineering. The region's recent specialization in multimedia has its roots in the engineering cluster, and B-W has had an active cluster policy for years. The regional state has been proactive in promoting cooperation between 'state, industry and science' for a long time. Many state-sponsored programmes have been designed to help market parties in the process of clustering. Examples are the formation of a technology transfer system ('Steinbeis-Stiftung') and financial aid to firms wishing to cooperate. But this cluster is not an industrial district because the enterprises in it have a wide industrial spread and many different products. What they share is a common network with education, training, research and technology transfer establishments.

Within it, however, B-W has an industrial district in one part of the region: in and around Tuttlingen, there are over one hundred firms making surgery instruments and other medical equipment. These have their own craft occupation to regulate, and their links with local training establishments. The emergence of the present district is particularly interesting: it was a district of cutlery makers that ran into competitiveness problems with the customs union in Germany, after 1834; it collectively re-specialized in something new at the time: surgical instruments such as scalpels. This in due course proved more lucrative, with more customized production and therefore higher profit margins.

The possibility of learning by looking abroad ('learning-by-comparing') is a matter of degree, and depends on several contingencies. These contingencies can be seen as preconditions that affect whether the foundations of a cluster in one place can be transferred to another. These contingencies relate to, among others, the degree of uniqueness, the complexity, the scale of change an initiative involves, as well as the proximity of institutions and values of the areas compared (Rose, 1993; Hospers and Beugelsdijk, 2002). The contingencies help understand why attempts to create a cluster in a new place will be a success or failure. We now deal with the uniqueness of the regional structure and the regional culture.

Uniqueness of regional structure

The well-known examples of regional clusters are complex in that they do not have a simple cause-and-effect structure. Trying to copy one of the 'best practices' such as Silicon Valley can involve a large change within the economic structure of a country. Often, these clusters have structural assets that are not always available in areas that want to copy them. Examples are the presence of a long tradition in particular economic activities (crafts in both Baden-Württemberg and Emilia-Romagna) or the availability of a specialized 'stock' of human capital (Silicon Valley). In developing high-tech clusters governments often ignore the question of whether the preconditions for such clusters are present in a region. The risk of ignoring these structural contingencies is that clusters may end as 'cathedrals in the desert' (Hassink, 1992). In their book on the most significant high-tech areas in the world economy, Castells and Hall (1994) show that starting new clusters from scratch (*ex nihilo*) is very difficult. Generally, the costs of such a policy are high and, if successful, the clusters will need a long time before they are embedded in their environment.

Two examples of failed attempts to recreate clusters are Akademgorodok (Russia), and the Mezzogiorno (Italy). Inspired by a visit to Silicon Valley in the late 1950s Khrushchev and his advisors wanted to create their own high-tech area, resulting in Akademgorodok, a place in Siberia (Josephson, 1997). Although this 'City of Science' still exists, it has had severe problems surviving due to its lack of embeddedness in the region. A similar case can be found in southern Italy (Mezzogiorno). The dominant role of national policy-makers in setting the priorities and dividing the resources was one of the main reasons why policies towards this region failed in the 1970s. The national government's ignorance of regional specificities resulted in a construction of industrial complexes that did not fit into the existing structure of southern Italy (Leonardi, 1995). The existence of these 'cathedrals in the desert' shows that every region's economic structure is unique and should be taken into account. It is, however, not just those specificities in the regional economic structure that help explain why in some areas clusters are successful and in others they are not. Increasingly, the importance of soft elements related to culture, institutions and trust are recognized as key success factors.

Uniqueness of regional culture and institutions

Institutions and values are both related to the fundamental cultural characteristics of an area. They refer to the 'soft' factors in a community such as its customs, norms, political ideologies, and conventions, including the degree of trust. Together with the structural economic features of an area, this cultural dimension is highly relevant in explaining the success of regional clusters. This was already recognized by Alfred Marshall (1890). The achievement of agglomeration benefits in the process of regional clustering is by no means an economic regularity. In Marshall's view, the realization of these benefits also depended on the existence of close social relationships within an industrial district creating an 'industrial atmosphere'. In regions like Emilia-Romagna ('Third Italy'), a culture could develop in which citizens were willing to cooperate – up to today. It was this centuries-old tradition of cooperation that has been put forward as one of the explanatory factors for the good performance of this region (Di Giovanna, 1996). Similar social aspects are part of the explanation of the Silicon Valley's success (Saxenian, 1994). Here, interdependencies between engineers are based not only on 'input–output' relations, but also on close contacts leading to social capital and trust which helps share knowledge, and develop new technologies which would be hampered if it could only be done based on formal contracts.

One aspect of the regional culture and institutions is the political culture and system. The relevance of political culture is especially visible in the cases of Emilia-Romagna and Silicon Valley. Whereas in the first case the left-wing government headed by the communist party has heavily intervened by providing social services and establishing business service centers, in the latter case the regional government has mainly taken a liberal, laissez-faire approach. In both cases, however, these political specificities are likely to have contributed to the regions' economic success (Cooke and Morgan, 1998; Saxenian, 1994). As mentioned in Box 10.2, this also holds for German Baden-Württemberg where the *Land* government has had a relatively autonomous position (e.g. in tax, research and technology policy), which can be traced back to the historically grown federal political system of Germany. The Christian-democratic *Land* government in Baden-Württemberg has been pro-active in promoting regional development, particularly in the field of training, education and marketing of the region to attract investment (Cooke, 1996).

10.6 Conclusions

In this chapter we have identified globalization, technological developments and changes in market demand as trends in the world economy that have not only intensified competition, but have also changed its character. The competitiveness of firms has become increasingly dependent on their ability to innovate and cooperate with other parties in innovative clusters. As a result, firms have to find a balance between competition, on the one hand, and cooperation on the other. The notion of networking and clustering has been studied by several authors over time.

Transaction cost considers networks as alternatives to markets and hierarchies. Additionally, network theory conceptualizes networks as separate forms of economic coordination in which social and institutional factors play an important role. The spatial dimension of cooperation is emphasized in literature on industrial districts, as well as Porter's work on clustering.

The approaches of networking and clustering essentially try to combine several dimensions of clusters. In fact, the ideas discussed in this literature only differ to the extent that they stress one or more dimensions of (spatial) cooperation in particular. By combining the several views, a multidimensional cluster approach arises that can take into account the pluriformity of networks and clusters in business life. Moreover, by combining the insights of authors working in transaction cost economics, the network theory, the industrial district tradition, the ideas of Porter and the innovative milieux literature, the following dimensions for defining clusters can be derived.

1 A horizontal dimension: linkages between firms that perform similar activities and that are direct competitors outside the cluster on the product market.
2 A vertical dimension: (innovative) cooperation between synergetic interdependent firms (suppliers, main producers and users) in a value chain.
3 A geographical dimension: a concentration of economic activities in a region with the presence of a skilled labour pool and firms providing specialized inputs to other firms.

4 An institutional dimension: a cluster as a cooperative in which, apart from firms, several institutions (e.g. knowledge institutes) are involved.

The geographical concentration of networks and the development of clusters is not a universal process. Although the essence of cooperation and competition is the same all over the world, the way firms organize themselves, and the role of local and national governments, is context-specific. In many cases the reasons for a cluster's success is derived from a unique regional economic structure or a unique (regional) culture.

Case: Innovation in the Swiss watch industry

A well-known and often cited example of an innovative milieu is the Swiss watch industry (Camagni, 1991; Weder and Grubel, 1993). In the 1970s this industry met with severe problems due to increasing competition from cheap Japanese watches. Based on artisan production dating back to the seventeenth century, the Swiss Jura d'Arc had developed an international reputation for watch-making, machine tools and micro-electronics ('Swiss made' still stands for high quality). The industrial district was part of a watch and clock-making region that was truly international, stretching into France (the mountains close to the Alps) and Germany (the Black Forest) alike. Looking back at the economic history of the Swiss watch history in the 1970s, one may say that the local parties working in the watch industry more or less became victims of the so-called 'Icarus paradox': due to their centuries-long success, they lost the connection to the worldwide trend of micro-electronics that had also invaded the world of watch manufacturing. The Japanese, though, only beat the Swiss to the first watch with an integrated circuit by a narrow margin, but they were able to introduce and market it on a wider scale, faster. The result was a delayed reaction to the Japanese threat: most Swiss watch-makers reacted only when the market for traditional watches had already collapsed. The region more or less fell into the trap of 'institutional lock-in' due to over-embedded relationships between local firms and institutions. Consequently, the number of workers in the Swiss watch industry decreased from 90,000 in 1970 to 33,000 in 1985. Now, what happens in an industrial crisis: will firms tighten up their ranks and collaborate more, or will everyone under threat 'go it alone', to save one's own firm rather than working together?

Interestingly, thanks to the relationships between the local parties in the Jura d'Arc, the region was able to recover from this crisis. The close ties between local firms and institutions now proved to be an advantage: they facilitated collective learning and innovative action. Here, the notion of an innovative milieu really came to the fore. With the help of local government, business associations and research centres, plans were developed on how to turn the tide, while building on unique local factors. The result of this collective search for regional renewal was twofold. On the one hand, in combating the Japanese competitors the focus still remained partly on producing expensive quality watches. On the other hand, the region's industry associations also decided to develop cheap but trendy watches under the brand name Swatch (Swiss watch). This established a wholly new brand of watches with particularly colourful exterior and look. In terms of price these new devices aimed to rival the watches made in Japan, and through their fashionable Swatch brand, they had a unique selling point. In particular this last strategy turned out to be a fruitful approach. Swatch as a 'new combination' of traditional Swiss quality and trendy marketing was soon a popular concept that contributed to the revival of the local watch industry. Note that this meant investing in the brand as a collective resource. The Swiss watch-making firms could still profit from being part of a close network of formal and informal institutions in the Jura d'Arc. They remained part of an innovative milieu by fostering the ingrained collective organization of the firms. It is also noteworthy that the district had already brought forth a new specialized firm for the development and production of electronic components for watches and clocks, Intersil, in 1967. This firm grew in the area and was only later moved from Geneva to California. The district, rather than crumbling under global competition, was becoming technologically more complex. There were also further technological developments instigated in the – international – region: for the precision fanatics keen to have the most exact time of day and never having to re-set the watch, watches could be linked to national laboratories which measured and kept an official standard time.

But this is not the end of the story, yet! After electronic quartz watches had become the state of the art in the industry, another turn came, which was to many unexpected, but the 'old hands' in the industry had already speculated about the return of the mechanical watch. This is precisely what happened, starting in the 1990s. From a museum piece, the mechanical watch turned into a luxury item, costing a thousand euros or more! Manufacturing techniques in mechanical engineering had also evolved, making more precise and reliable clockworks and movements feasible, even for watches. High precision mechanical clocks, notably in the form of navy chronometers, had always been possible but more costly and too large to wear on an arm-wrist. Now, firms started offering high precision watches that sometimes even made a point of displaying the interior mechanics, as a luxury of sophistication based on tradition. Again, a new firm had emerged to develop and make the technical core of the watches, as something that required substantial investment in sophisticated machinery, an investment that would have overburdened individual watch-makers. And again, the industrial district had reasserted itself, bringing up a new fashion that linked up with the older mechanical tradition. Since the new mechanical luxury watches fetched enormous prices, the earnings from these watches even outpaced earnings from the sale of electronic quartz watches. Anyone who had predicted that in the 1980s would have met with disbelief. All this was researched by Raffaelli (2013). It goes to show that, never mind the wide-spread idea that industrial districts in due time crumble under global competition, the opposite is true: if and when a district revitalizes itself, due to the ongoing cooperation of participant firms and their investment in new collective resources, the district can be kept alive and kicking.

Study questions

1. Explain why networks and clusters are important for business life.
2. Discuss how geographical clustering can enhance a firm's competitive position.
3. Assess the explanatory power of the concept of 'cultural embeddedness'.
4. Discuss how industrial districts exhibit a mix of cooperation and competition.
5. In recent years, firms that are part of the Japanese keiretsu and the Korean Chaebol have been argued to experience deteriorating performance precisely because they are part of a network. Use network theory to explain these negative side-effects.
6. Silicon Valley is a successful example of an innovative cluster of firms. Use the knowledge introduced in this chapter to explain why and under what conditions, or why not, governments should try to emulate the Silicon Valley story.

Further reading

Ebers, M. (1997) *The Formation of Inter-Organizational Networks.* Oxford: Oxford University Press.

This book includes excellent papers that all focus on the recent trend among organizations to form networks with competing organizations. Most of the theory presented also applies to networks among non-competing organizations.

Faust, K. and Wasserman, S. (1999) *Social Network Analysis: Methods and Applications.* Cambridge: Cambridge University Press.

For the diehards among you, this book is highly recommended for those wishing to carry out quantitative analysis on networks.

Murphy, J.T. (2002) Networks, trust, and innovation in Tanzania's manufacturing sector. *World Development* 30(4), 591–619.

Excellent article, which explores the societal dimension of innovation for a group of manufacturers in Mwanza and Tanzania.

Parrilli, M.D. (2001) *The social roots of successful economic policies: the cases of the third Italy and Nicaragua.* L'institute Discussion Paper 18, Institute for Industrial Development Policy: Ferrara, Italy, www.linstitute.org/papers/.

On the basis of an analysis of the districts of the third Italy and of Nicaragua's clusters, this paper shows that the difficulty that policy-makers have in replicating successful stories in developing contexts stems from a neglect of the 'real society that exists behind the market' that surrounds the local production system.

References

Amin, A. and Thrift, N. (eds) (1994) *Globalization, Institutions and Regional Development in Europe.* Oxford: Oxford University Press.

Audretsch, D.B. and Thurik, A.R. (1997) *Sources of Growth: The Entrepreneurial versus the Managed Economy.* Discussion paper. Rotterdam: Tinbergen Institute.

Best, M. (1990) *The New Competition: Institutions of Industrial Restructuring.* Cambridge, MA: Harvard University Press.

Brown, T.F. (1998) *Theoretical Perspectives on Social Capital. Working paper. Program for Comparative and International Development.* Baltimore: Johns Hopkins University.

Burt, R. and Knez M. (1995) Kinds of third-party effects on trust. *Rationality and Society* 7(3), 255–292.

Camagni, R. (1991) *Innovation Networks: Spatial Perspectives*, London: Belhaven.

Castells, M. and Hall, P. (1994) *Technopoles of the World: The Making of Twenty-First-Century Industrial Complexes.* London: Routledge.

Coase, R.H. (1937) The nature of the firm. *Economica* 4, 386–405.

Commandeur, H.R. (1994) *Strategische Samenwerking in Netwerkperspectief: Een The- Oretisch Netwerk voor Industriële Ondernemingen.* Alblasserdam: Haveka.

Cooke, P. (1996) The new wave of regional innovation networks: analysis, characteristics and strategy. *Small Business Economics* 8, 159–171.

Cooke, P. and Morgan, K. (1998) *The Associational Economy: Firms, Regions and Innovation.* Oxford: Oxford University Press.

Cooke, P., Morgan, K. and Price, A. (1995) The future of the Mittelstand: collaboration versus competition. In O' Doherty, D.P. (ed.) *Globalization, Networking and Small Firm Innovation.* London: Graham & Trotman.

Davies, H., Leung, T.K.P., Luk, S.T.K. and Wong, Y.-H. (1995) The benefits of guanxi: the value of relationships in developing the Chinese market. *Industrial Marketing Management* 24, 207–214.

Di Giovanna, S. (1996) Industrial districts and regional economic development: a regulation approach. *Regional Studies* 30, 373–386.

Dicken, P. (1998) *Global Shift: Transforming the World Economy* (3rd edn). London: Chapman Publishing.

Dunning, J.H. (1997) *Alliance Capitalism and Global Business.* London: Routledge.

Edwards, C.T. and Samimi, R. (1997) Japanese interfirm networks: exploring the seminal sources of their success. *Journal of Management Studies* 34(4), 489–510.

Enright, M.J. (1996) Regional clusters and economic development: a research agenda. In Staber, U.H., Schaefer, N.V. and Sharma, B. (eds) *Business Networks: Prospects for Regional Development.* Berlin: Walter De Gruyter.

Granovetter, M. (1973) The strength of weak ties. *American Journal of Sociology* 78, 1360–1380.

Granovetter, M. (1985) Economic action and social structure: the problem of embed- dedness. *American Journal of Sociology* 91, 481–510.

Gulati, R. (1998) Alliances and networks. *Strategic Management Journal* 19(4), 293–317.

Hassink, R. (1992) *Regional Innovation Policy. Case-Studies from the Ruhr Area, Baden- Württemberg and the North East of England.* Utrecht: Faculty of Geographical Sciences, Utrecht University.

Hassink, R. (1997) What distinguishes 'good' from 'bad' industrial agglomerations? *Erdkunde* 51, 2–11.

Hospers, G.J. and Beugelsdijk, S. (2002) Regional cluster policies, learning from comparing? *Kyklos* 55(3), 381–402.

Josephson, P.R. (1997) *New Atlantis Revisited. Akademgorodok, the Siberian City of Science.* Princeton: Princeton University Press.

Krugman, P.R. (1991) *Geography and Trade.* Cambridge, MA: MIT Press.

Lazonick, W. (1992) *Organization and Technology in Capitalist Development.* Aldershot: Edward Elgar.

Leonardi, R. (1995) Regional development in Italy, social capital and the Mezzogiorno. *Oxford Review of Economic Policy* 11, 165–179.

Marshall, A. (1890, 1947 edn) *Principles of Economics.* London: Macmillan.

Meyerson, E.M. (1994) Human capital, social capital and compensation: the relative contribution of social contacts to managers' incomes. *Acta Sociologica* 37, 383–399.

Noorderhaven, N.G. (1994) Transaction cost analysis and the explanation of hybrid vertical interfirm relations. *Review of Political Economy* 6, 19–36.

Nooteboom, B. (1999) *Interfirm Alliances: Analysis and Design.* London: Routledge.

Nooteboom, B. (2002) *Trust.* Cheltenham, UK: Edward Elgar.

Oerlemans, L.A.G. (1996) *De Ingebedde Onderneming: Innoveren in Industriële Netwerken.* Tilburg: Tilburg University Press.

Park, S.H. and Luo, Y. (2001) Guanxi and organizational dynamics: organizational networking in Chinese firms. *Strategic Management Journal* 22, 455–477.

Piore, M.J. and Sabel, C.F. (1984) *The Second Industrial Divide: Possibilities for Prosperity.* New York: Basic Books.

Polanyi, K. (1944) *The Great Transformation.* New York: Rinehart.

Porter, M.E. (1985) *Competitive Advantage: Creating and Sustaining Superior Performance.* New York: Free Press.

Porter, M.E. (1990) *The Competitive Advantage of Nations.* New York: Free Press.

Porter, M.E. (1997) *Knowledge-based Clusters and National Competitive Advantage.* Presentation to Technopolis, Ottawa, 12 September.

Porter, M.E. (1998) *On Competition.* Cambridge, MA: Harvard University Press.

Portes, A. and Sensenbrenner, J. (1993) Embeddedness and immigration: notes on the social determinants of economic action. *American Journal of Sociology* 98(6), 1320–1350.

Pyke, F. (1995) Endogenous development in a global context: the scope for industrial districts. In O'Doherty, D.P. (ed.) *Globalisation, Networking and Small Firm Innovation.* London: Graham & Trotman.

Rabellotti, R. (1998) Collective effects in Italian and Mexican footwear industrial clus-ters. *Small Business Economics* 10, 243–262.

Rabin, M. (1998) Psychology and economics. *Journal of Economic Literature* 36, 11–46.

Raffaelli, R. (2013) Industry and industrial change in a mature field: the re-emergence of the Swiss watch industry. Boston College: PhD thesis.

Ring, P.S. and Van de Ven, A. (1992) Structuring cooperative relationships between organizations. *Strategic Management Journal* 13, 483–498.

Rose, R. (1993) *Lesson-Drawing in Public Policy. A Guide to Learning across Time and Space.* Chatham: Chatham House Publishers.

Saxenian, A.L. (1994) *Regional Advantage: Culture and Competition in Silicon Valley and Route 128.* Cambridge, Massachusetts: Harvard University Press.

Simon, H.A. (1961) *Administrative Behavior.* New York: Macmillan Press.

Smith, R.P. and Van de Ven, A. (1992) Structuring cooperative relationships between organizations. *Strategic Management Journal* 13(7), 483–498.

Tsang, E.W.K. (1998) Can guanxi be a source of sustained competitive advantage for doing business in China? *Academy of Management Executive* 12(2), 64–73.

Uzzi, B. (1996) The sources and consequences of embeddedness for the economic performance of organizations: the network effect. *American Sociological Review* 61, 674–698.

Uzzi, B. (1997) Social structure and competition in interfirm networks: the paradox of embeddedness. *Administrative Science Quarterly* 42, 35–67.

Uzzi, B. (1999) Embeddedness in the making of financial capital: how social relations and networks benefit firms seeking financing. *American Sociological Review* 64, 481–505.

Weder, R. and Grubel, H.G. (1993) The new growth theory and Coasean economics: institutions to capture externalities. *Weltwirtschaftliches Archiv* 488–513.

Williamson, O.E. (1975) *Markets and Hierarchies: Analysis and Antitrust Implications.* New York: Free Press.

Williamson, O.E. (1985) *The Economic Institutions of Capitalism.* New York: Free Press.

Williamson, O.E. (1991) Comparative economic organization: the analysis of discrete structural alternatives. *Administrative Science Quarterly* 36, 269–296.

Woolcock, M. (1998) Social capital and economic development: toward a theoretical synthesis and policy framework. *Theory and Society* 27, 151–208.

Xin, K.R. and Pearce, J.L. (1996) Guanxi: connections as substitutes for formal institutional support. *Academy of Management Journal* 39(6), 1641–1658.

You, J. and Wilkinson, F. (1994) Competition and cooperation: towards understanding industrial districts. *Review of Political Economy* 6, 259–278.

Zukin, S. and DiMaggio, P. (eds) (1990) *Structures of Capital: the Social Organization of the Economy.* Cambridge: Cambridge University Press.

11 Globalization: interdependencies, harmonization and societal specificity

Learning objectives

By the end of this chapter you will be able to:

- explain the complementarity of three core societal institutions – the systems of corporate governance, competence generation/personnel management and industrial relations
- understand the need to distinguish between different levels of analysis when tracing the impact of globalization forces
- analyse interdependencies, harmonization, translation and strategic sorting effects
- explain why and how resilience often prevails against convergence, by a more detailed analysis using the mentioned effects
- appraise whether institutional theory is sufficiently powerful to analyse the impact of globalization pressures
- evaluate the role of cultural characteristics in explaining change at the societal, organization and management levels
- reflect on the supposed link between globalization and MNCs.

Chapter outline

11.1 Introduction

The different opinions on the consequences of global forces form the starting point of this chapter. As we explained in the first chapter, the globalization literature exhibits divergent opinions on the consequences of globalization, which can be summarized in four possible scenarios.

1 Convergence towards the Anglo-American neoliberal market system (i.e. Dore, 1996; Streeten, 1996; Streeck, 1997).
2 Greater specialization of national models in accordance with domestic institutional and cultural characteristics (Vitols, 2001; Sorge, 2003).
3 Incremental adaptation of the domestic institutional context in a largely path-dependent manner (i.e. Whitley, 1994; Casper, 2000).
4 Hybridization with change in a path-deviant manner (i.e. Whitley, 1999; Lane, 2000).

These scenarios do not directly mention culture, but cultural developments tend to be related to institutional ones, and the debate on cultural convergence or divergence uses similar notions. In Chapter 4, we developed some theoretical concepts, which can help us understand institutional change as a result of global pressures. We argued that, in order to understand the impact of globalization, we need to study how social institutions are complementary to one another, in the sense that one institution functions better because some other particular institutions or forms of organization are present (Amable, 2000). Hence, when analysing the effects of global pressures, we have to explain how a destabilizing effect of change reacts with the resilience of cultural and institutional elements of the social system, and how change and resilience not only conflict but lead to a new synthesis.

This chapter uses the dynamic concepts, explained in Chapter 4, to analyse further the directions of change in the relevant managerial fields that have been studied in this book. From the outset, a caveat is in order. The manifold studies shown and discussed in this book together have one major nasty flaw: they have focused on different things, they have used different empirical operationalizations, they have dealt with different countries and different periods in time. Researchers have had specific findings in terms of concepts, operationalizations, place and time, but they have used highly general concepts (convergence, hybridization, etc.) to build theory. In a way that cannot help but confuse readers, they have uncomfortably combined specific empirical results with general theoretical frames in which the whole world is the stage and the sky the limit. In view of this predicament, our warning is that there simply does not exist a general theory that is corroborated in detail, on what the general upshot of globalization is.

But there is something that can be offered to make sense of various findings. Effects can be defined that are like a conceptual tool-kit. Such effects work differently for different substantive themes, periods and places. But they also work together in combination, which is a challenge for the sophisticated analyst. Let us go through them one by one.

(1) What we have seen, notably in the chapter and cases on multinational enterprises, points to a development towards increasing **interdependencies** between enterprises in different countries. Multinational enterprises, international supply and value generation chains, the rapid development of international financial markets, and of supranational regulatory regimes, all attest to such interdependencies. They have clearly interrelated actors and markets, and this tendency looks rather stable. This is despite the recent tendency of electorates and governments to revive more national and even nationalist concerns. We could see this in the EU and its member countries and also in Russia, the United States, China, Japan and South America. Chinese assertiveness, the politics of Vladimir Putin, the Tea Party movement in the USA, nationalist election results in the UK, France or Hungary,

are all shades of the same phenomenon. Nationalist reactions, which have become stronger notably as a consequence of the world financial crisis, grapple with interdependencies that have come to be addressed as problems. But they have not found a way of doing away with them. This shows us that interdependencies are unchangingly important, even when they do not lead to assimilation or harmonization of culture and institutions. Interdependencies may deepen, although tendencies back to national autonomy and specificity are strong. We cannot conclude that the former leads to the latter. A world that has coherence in the sense of 'coming together' within interdependencies, does not necessarily 'unite' in converging on more similar culture and institutions.

(2) The next effect is one of establishing and spreading a number of practices, rules, codes of practice and regulatory schemes that are undoubtedly supranational or transnational. They may, though, have an origin in a specific country and in this way a societal effect in the background. Examples from different chapters in the book are: Taylorism, group work, lean production, industrial districts of different varieties, liberal coordination by competitive markets, government control of the economy, diversified quality production, codes of governance, and many more. All such conceptualized practices have had a societal origin which explains their original nature: the USA, Japan, Northern Italy, England, absolutist France and then the Soviet Union and China, Germany, Anglo-American law systems. At the same time, they were transferred from their origin to other places, becoming generic concepts to some extent imagined to be generic models. International rule-making and definition of 'best practice' drove this transfer. This is an effect we can call **assimilation or harmonization**, to avoid the more laden term of convergence because this has been used to denote more sweeping tendencies and it carries the risk of overgeneralizaton.

(3) Assimilation, however, only allows us to characterize the surface of institutions or of culture in more internationally mobile parts of the population and labour force. We observe that every time that an institutionalized practice is transferred from one place to another, its nature, meaning and spread, the interests behind it and the purpose they serve, changes. The practice which was stylized in general practical literature changes form and meaning as it is integrated into new locations. Societal effects are important in this transfer to explain what adaptation takes place; the phenomenon of shifting forms and meanings was particularly addressed by researchers who emphasized the **reinterpretation** and **translation** of practices into new contexts, which are inherent to transfer. The emic approach to cultural comparison outlined in Chapter 3 has supplied the methodology and concepts for studying this effect in minute detail. Also, researchers emphasizing piecemeal and path-dependent adaptation have given this effect a lot of attention.

(4) However, not every practice that becomes decontextualized and recommended for transfer, succeeds in every new destination. A more general (culturally or institutionally) comparative scheme (such as comparisons of values by Hofstede and others, VoC and BSys), allows us to make rough predictions about what practice might fit under which context, and the changes and adaptations that are likely and recommendable. The details of adoption, adaptation or failure are best understood using the emic approach. There is yet another effect which addresses an important ingredient of cross-national differences. This may be called the **strategic sorting of organizational contingencies, by region or nation**. This addresses the tendency, with international competition and the international division of labour, for enterprises in specific sub-industries, stages in the value chain of products and services, modes of operations management or generic strategies, to cluster in particular societies or regions. Production of high value and luxury cars has become dominated by Germany, production of a number of customized investment goods by

Germany and Switzerland, microprocessors and general software products come from the west coast of the USA, personal computers and other popular IT and consumer electronics equipment from East Asia. This strategic sorting of enterprises by nations is often neglected by researchers who work with cruder standard industrial classifications devoid of strategic significance. It is not based on natural advantage or pure cost advantages, but on advantages developed over time, in the institutions generating resources (Chapters 5, 6, 7, 8 and 10).

The fourth effect is probably the most radical one, and it points to not only persisting but potentially increasing divergence between countries. Why should there be any reason, within standard organization theory including the strategy literature, for enterprise organization and the generation of productive resources to be assimilated between countries, if different countries specialize in different value generation processes? This effect follows from interdependencies (the first effect) just as much as the second one, of harmonization and assimilation; it is simply in addition dependent on a regional or national clustering of productive activities, whereas the second effect is clearest when there is no strategic sorting by regions or nations. The third effect is one that tempers the working of the second and the fourth effect, insisting as it does on the embeddedness of every practice and inevitable continuity.

There is of course another possibility: nothing much changes. This, however, would not be an effect of something specific but simple inertia. Now, in a changing world there is always something that changes. At an aggregate level, lack of change is more likely, but with regard to specific arrangements, there tend to be combinations of change and inertia. When we define the range of a research question, this definition more or less determines the answer about the weight of change and inertia within the combination in which they are invariably associated. Conscious that the weighting of change and inertia thus is a methodological artefact, we will refrain from sweeping characterizations as we start the overview and only very carefully advance to broader characterizations.

This is the way, then, that the sum total of the book should be remembered and applied. Sweeping statements about how the world of organizing and managing is advancing in a more global age, are of little value because they are too sweeping. We made an attempt at the disaggregated treatment of different effects. This allows more precise and adapted explanation, research and practical recommendation. Even an extremely globalized industry such as freight shipping requires the combined analysis of effects: how can we otherwise explain that bulk carriers around the world have officers from the country of the owner, seamen from the Philippines, and registration and a flag of Panama, Liberia or Greece? We add Greece because the country even has an article in its constitution forbidding taxation of international shipping companies. But we present a more nuanced case, of civil aviation, after this chapter, to allow and encourage the combined study of effects and the application of most of the theories and methodologies in this book.

In the subsequent sections, we will home in on two fields that were governed by opposed basic assumption of dominant effects: corporate governance and human resources. Corporate governance was assumed to be increasingly governed by international financial markets and new internationalized standards of accounting and governance, and by codes of conduct; human resources on the other hand had been shown to be rather sticky, staying more within national traditions and linking up more firmly with everything that has made societies different in the past. We focus on the USA and the UK on the one hand and on Japan and Germany on the other. Again, we will show that the picture is more nuanced, pointing to commonalities between different spaces and institutional domains within societal contexts. This reinforces some messages from earlier chapters in a more pointed way.

11.2 Corporate governance

Two main models of corporate governance were discussed in Chapter 6: the 'outsider', or the Anglo-American system, and the 'insider' model, like the German and Japanese systems. The distinction between the two systems is often made in terms of whether the banks play a dominant role or whether the stock market is the main locus of monitoring and control. The take-over mechanism is at the heart of the Anglo-American open market model of corporate governance. Any party can bid for the control rights of a listed company by accumulating a large enough ownership stake. The building blocks of the insider-based system of corporate governance in Germany and Japan are the important role played by the banks as large creditors and large parent firms, and the high degree of interlocking shareholdings. In contrast to UK and US views of the firm as a property of owners, who are the sole 'residual claimants', German and Japanese corporate governance has drawn fewer distinctions between the private rights of owners and social or political obligations in the context of social groups or society.

In the context of the globalization debate, neoclassical orthodoxy has claimed that one or the other corporate governance model is economically superior and that, over time, we should see convergence towards this model of 'best practice'. The shareholder or outsider model was heavily criticized in the early 1990s for its tendencies to under-invest and to focus on short-term results (Porter, 1990). But in the 1990s and up to the financial crisis of 2007+, the majority view was that the shareholder model will prevail due to the globalization of capital markets and the growing power of institutional investors. The argument is that, since international capital markets are increasingly dominated by diversified portfolio investors (such as mutual funds and pension funds) seeking higher returns, companies must adopt the shareholder model or be starved of the external capital needed to invest and survive (Lazonick and O'Sullivan, 2000, cited in Vitols, 2001).

The question now is: has the stakeholder model of corporate governance been changing towards the shareholder model as a result of globalization pressures? In order to answer this question, it is useful to look at the developments of four major interrelated and complementary categories of the German and Japanese corporate governance systems:

1 formal legal and regulatory changes
2 changes in the structure of corporate ownership
3 growth of the stock market, and
4 emergence of a market for corporate control.

(Coffee, 2001)

Taken in isolation, one aspect of a system, such as stable shareholding arrangements in Germany and Japan, may appear arbitrary. There is widespread agreement in the literature that changes in one of these categories would affect the others (Nowak, 2001). One school of thought holds that law affects the economic system (La Porta et al., 1997; Roe, 1997), while another argues that law and regulation are likely to be a result of the economic system (Easterbrook, 1997). In any case, the assumptions of dialectical relationships between systemic elements and the tendency for institutional coherence imply that when change in one of the aforementioned categories occurs, we should expect change in another.

The most important regulatory changes in Germany and Japan were in company law and financial regulation. In the 1990s, to increase the attractiveness of German capital markets, German legislators initiated the Second and Third Laws for the Promotion of

Financial Markets. The Second Law (in 1994) set up an Anglo-American-style Federal Securities Supervisory Office (*Bundesaufsichtsamt für Wertpapierhandel*) and imposed the first formal German prohibition of insider trading. The Third Law (passed in 1997) liberalized restrictions on mutual funds and venture capital companies, and allowed more liberal listing requirements, to try to encourage more German and foreign companies to list on the German stock exchanges, and also to expand the access to capital of small and medium-sized enterprises (Schaede, 1999; Nowak, 2001; Vitols, 2001).

A significant reform of German company law was effected through the Law for Corporate Control and Transparency in Large Companies (KonTraG), which modifies the Joint Stock Company Law 1965 (Aktiengesetz). The law was a response of the Kohl government to a number of major failures of supervisory boards to control boards of management. The primary goals of the KonTraG, which became effective in May 1998, were to improve the monitoring effectiveness of German supervisory boards and corporate disclosure to the investors. In addition, the legal liability of the management board in the case of dishonest or fraudulent behaviour was also tightened. In order to provide management with proper performance-based incentives, the KonTraG also simplified the use of stock option programmes through share buy-backs and capital increases, allowing German companies to adopt 'typical' Anglo-American practices (Nowak, 2001).

Although these reforms have led to a somewhat more liquid and transparent stock exchange for the largest German companies (particularly the largest 30 companies in the Deutscher Aktienindex, or DAX), most significant are the elements of continuity that remain. The vast majority of German companies are not listed on the stock exchange, remain embedded in 'relational networks', including their local banks, and continue to receive their external finance mainly in the form of bank loans. The most important banking group – especially for the vast *Mittelstand* (small and medium-sized companies) – remained the publicly owned municipal savings bank sector (*Sparkassen*), which continued to account for more than half of all banking system assets in Germany, in addition to the cooperative banks (Vitols, 2001: 348).

Small- and medium-sized enterprise (SME) owners have been criticized for avoiding listing in order to prevent any dilution of their control and for their unwillingness to reveal profitability. Such SMEs have not made much use of share capital as a means of fulfilling their growing financing needs, despite reforms aimed at making it easier for them to do so (the 1986 introduction of a Second Market (*geregelter Markt*) and the 1994 Law on Small Public Companies (*Gesetz über kleine Aktiengesellschaften*). The SMEs, on the other hand, argued that there remain barriers to listing. For example, continuing credit institutions – in effect, banks – must be involved in the first segment of trading (i.e. issuing shares). As the banks are concerned about their reputation, they are thought to be careful about dealing with new entrepreneurs (Vitols and Woolcock, 1997). Despite regulatory changes, the majority of German firms (but also other European firms operating within the Rhineland model) did not show a preference for market-based transactions. By the end of the 1990s, the number of German and other European (with the exception of UK) corporations that issued tradable shares remained small. In the EU, on average 64.3 per cent of trading volume was accounted for by 13 firms; for Germany, this was 85.5 per cent by 35 companies; for the UK, in contrast, this was 59.9 per cent by 102 firms and 51.4 per cent by 113 firms on the NYSE (DAI 1999). In general, the concentration of stock trading in a few companies remained higher in Rhineland countries than in Anglo-American countries. Table 11.1 confirms this picture by showing the differences in the degree of liquidity and depth of financial markets between the two models. There are still substantial differences in the ratio

Table 11.1 Stock market capitalization (market value as a percentage of GDP)

	1995	*2000*	*2005*	*2010*
Germany	23	67	44	44
Japan	69	54	104	75
UK	122	147	134	137
USA	93	135	135	119

Source: The World Bank, compiled by Bijlsma and Zwart (2013).

of capitalization to GNP between the USA and the UK on one hand and Germany and Japan on the other. Even in 2010, German and Japanese stock markets remained minor players in comparison to the US and UK markets.

Deregulation of the financial markets in Japan started from the late 1970s. Important measures were the easing of restrictions in 1979 and 1981 on the issuing of unsecured straight and convertible bonds and approval in the mid-1980s for banks to issue convertible bonds (Koen, 2000). After the bad loans crisis of 1996, the Japanese government implemented further deregulatory measures to foster the restructuring of the financial sector and to revitalize financial markets.[1] From 1997 onwards, Japan embarked on a stepwise reform of its general accounting rules, including, among others things, the adoption of market value reporting, as opposed to the current book value reporting, for all securities holdings in March 2001, and the adoption of market value estimation of cross-held shares in March 2002. In 1998, the Foreign Exchange Law was revised, which resulted in a complete liberalization of cross-border transactions. Foreign investments into Japan became legally unrestricted, although many informal restrictions on corporate take-over remain. In 1998, too, a new Financial Holding Company Law allowed bank holding companies, and, in 1999, brokerage commissions were deregulated. Rather like in Germany, Japan reformed corporate law in 1997, and introduced stock options, share buybacks and holding companies.

At a first glance, it seems that regulatory change in Japan did succeed in creating a deeper capital market with a high number of listings. The volume of share trading in the Japanese capital markets is not concentrated in only a few firms – as in the other Rhineland-model countries – but spread over a more or less similar number of firms, as in the USA and the UK. From the late 1970s onwards, large Japanese corporations started to make greater use of the bond and securities markets, issuing convertible bonds and other equity-linked debt instruments. The change in the pattern of corporate financing was accelerated in the mid-1980s, when the Japanese economy experienced a huge and steady rise in stock prices following the Plaza Accord of October 1985. Prices on the Tokyo Stock Exchange increased two-and-a-half times between 1985 and 1989. Bond issuance in the domestic market, which was mainly composed of convertible bonds, grew sharply from 1986 onwards (Miyajima, 1998). Table 11.1, on the other hand, shows that market capitalization as a percentage of GDP, while somewhat higher than in Germany, still points to a relatively illiquid and thin market in comparison with that of the USA and the UK. This conclusion is supported by a Bank of Japan study which argues that, to date, the changes to Japan's financial system in the 1990s have not produced a striking increase in financial transactions via capital markets. According to Japanese flow of funds accounts, the percentage of bank loans in the financial liabilities of non-financial businesses remained virtually unchanged from 38.9 per cent at the end of 1990 to 38.8 per cent at the end of 1999. During the same period, the percentage of shares, equities and securities increased from

38.9 per cent to 43.1 per cent (Baba and Hisada, 2002). More recently (2013) the percentage of bank loans of non-financial businesses has decreased to 27 per cent, but this is still way above the corresponding figure of 6 per cent for US firms (Bank of Japan, 2014).

Like Germany, Japan has a large SME sector, which is not listed and is embedded in 'relational networks' including local banks. The SME sector accounts for more than 99 per cent of all Japanese firms and contributes to about 70 per cent of employment (Economist Intelligence Unit, 2010). In terms of shipment value, the SME manufacturing subsector accounts for about 51 per cent of the total and nearly 50 per cent of the productivity of its industry as a whole (Owualah, 1999). In the 1970s, as the large firms tapped alternative sources of funds in the capital markets, commercial banks began to provide funding to SME companies. Commercial banks, in conjunction with regional, long-term credit and trust banks, are now the dominant source of finance for SMEs in Japan. At the end of the 1990s, 77 per cent of financing for plant, equipment and long-term operating funds for SMEs was provided by commercial, regional and trust banks (Owualah, 1999). It was argued that if the relationships between banks and these borrowers were to weaken, a large number of businesses might be forced into bankruptcy; their performance will deteriorate if they cannot secure financial assistance (Baba and Hisada, 2002). And indeed, in the recent recession lending to SMEs by banks has sharply declined, and the Japanese government had to step in with an Emergency Guarantee Program. Nevertheless, the SME sector has remained vulnerable (Economist Intelligence Unit, 2010).

Despite regulatory changes to revitalize the market mechanism, Table 11.2 shows that owner–company relations in the Rhineland model toward the end of the 1990s were still most often characterized by one or more large shareholders with a strategic (rather than pure share value maximization) motivation for ownership. A total of 90 per cent of listed companies in Germany had a shareholder with at least a 10 per cent stake in the company. The types of investor likely to have strategic interests – enterprises and banks – together held 52 per cent of shares (or 42 per cent and 10 per cent, respectively). Enterprises generally pursue strategic business interests. Large German banks have tended to view their shareholdings as a mechanism for protecting their loans and strengthening their business relationships with companies, rather than as a direct source of income. The ownership types having smaller shareholdings – investment funds, pension funds/insurance companies and households – accounted for only 35 per cent of total shareholdings of the large German companies (or 8 per cent, 12 per cent and 15 per cent respectively). There are, to be sure, differences between Japanese and German SMEs: Germany has more SMEs that sell their own products independently, whereas Japan has more that are integrated into subcontracting networks of the keiretsu groups.

Table 11.2 Structure of ownership (percentage of outstanding corporate equity held by sectors, 1998)

	USA	*UK*	*Germany*	*Japan*
Households	49	21	15	24
Non-financial firms	–	1	42	24.1
Banks	6	1	10	22
Insurance enterprises and pension funds	28	50	12	11
Investment funds and other financial institutions	13	17	8	2.2
Non residents	5	9	9	9.8

Source: Rebérioux (2002: 114): *Tokyo Stock Exchange Fact Book 1999*, for Japan.

The Rhineland system is thus characterized by concentrated ownership by actors pursuing a mix of financial and strategic goals (Vitols, 2001: 343). Hence, despite the tendency for the German financial model to adopt features of the Anglo-American model of finance, a critical distinction has remained: the majority of the German firms continue to have stable, long-term shareholdership, protecting firms from the short-termism of Anglo-American capitalism.

Despite the changes, many fundamental aspects of German company law have been preserved. Neither the dual-board system nor the principle of employee board representation were abolished. There was some political questioning of parity codetermination around the turn of the century, but this has subsided and died more or less completely with the financial crisis, after which parties from right to left, together with the unions and the employers, started to extol the virtues of the 'social market economy' again. The basic principle of the Joint Stock Company Law of 1965 – that neither shareholders, top managers, nor employees should exert unilateral control of the company – has remained intact (Vitols, 2001: 347). That employee representation is safeguarded also means that the concentration of ownership rights, which is a core feature of the Rhineland model, will also persist. This conclusion is supported by a study by Pedersen and Thomsen (1999), in which the impact of employee board representation on ownership structure is tested. The study found that employee representation stimulates the creation of countervailing power (i.e. a concentration of ownership rights) to ensure that owner interests are represented on the board.

As in Germany, and despite signs of change, share ownership has remained institutionalized in Japan. In this respect, Table 11.2 shows that, at the end of the 1990s, the major and stable shareholders were financial institutions and industrial corporations. While the accounting change is said to have induced the sale of cross-shareholdings among affiliated firms, it is hard to find strong evidence for this claim. In order to mitigate the impact of stock price movements on their profits, many Japanese firms and banks would have started to reduce their stockholdings in other firms (Yoshikawa and Phan, 2001). A survey of 2426 companies in 1999, however, showed that 42 per cent of outstanding shares were still considered stable, and 16 per cent were believed to be cross-held (Schaede, 1999). In the late 1990s, the large horizontal keiretsu still held, on average, some 18 per cent of all outstanding shares within their group. More recent data show that especially as a result of attempts by the Japanese government to revitalise the economy, capital inflows have driven up foreign ownership, to a record high of 28 per cent of all stocks in 2013.[2] At the same time 'stable shareholdings' and reciprocal holdings declined (Yoshikawa and McGuire, 2008). However, notwithstanding these changes in the ownership structure, the typical characteristics of business groups with cross-ownership have remained a central characteristic of the Japanese economy (Ahmadjian, 2006). It therefore seems that, as in Germany, there is in the Japanese system a mixture of change and continuity. Indeed, the importance of the pattern in the rise of foreign ownership and the decline in cross-shareholding is that it is not evenly distributed. The impact of the change in ownership pattern is greater in some firms than in others.

The literature has argued that the biggest step that could be taken to radically change the distribution of ownership of financial assets, or the distribution of assets between categories, is to promote US- and UK-style pension funds and mutual funds by creating tax incentives for employers and employees to defer compensation (Vitols, 2001: 348).[3] Such a proposal was made by the nascent mutual fund industry in Germany but, due to opposition from the insurance industry, this was dropped (Vitols, 2001: 348). Thus, although the

Table 11.3 Financial assets of institutional investors* (as % of GDP)

	1992	*1995*	*1999*	*2005*	*2010*
Germany	34,0	45,3	76,8	117,1	120,9
Denmark	55,7	65,1	98,0	172,9	231,1
Norway	36,4	42,4	53,9	54,8	68,3
Sweden	88,8	102,9	137,8	132,9	145,5
Japan**	78,0	89,3	100,5	101,0	102,0
UK	131,3	164,0	226,7	198,0	221,0
USA	127,2	151,9	207,3	176,9	191,8

*Insurance companies, investment companies, pension funds and other forms of institutional saving.

**Japan 2005 and 2010 excluding investment funds.

Sources: 1992–1999 compiled from OECD (2001); 2005 and 2010 from OECD (2013).
OECD (2001). Recent trends: Institutional Investors Statistican Yearbook, retrieved from: http://www.oecd.org/finance/financial-markets/2444676.pdf, August 28, 2014.
OECD (2013). OECD Institutional Investors Statistics 2013, retrieved from: http://dx.doi.org/10.1787/instinv-2013-en, August 28, 2014.

financial markets have been somewhat liberalized, the increase in the relative importance of the type of institutional investor dominant in the UK and the USA (i.e. pension funds and mutual funds) is limited. Table 11.3 confirms this picture; it shows that despite the gradual increase in financial assets (as a percentage of GDP) of institutional investors in different countries, Germany and Japan, as well as other Rhineland-model countries, are lagging far behind the USA and the UK. In addition, the composition of the portfolios of institutional investors in Germany and Japan, the prototype countries of the Rhineland model, still shows a preference for bonds and loans, as opposed to a preference for shares in the Anglo-American countries. Pension reform in Japan includes the introduction of an Anglo-American style (that is, a 401(k)-type) pension scheme, from 1 October, 2001. This reform, it was hoped, would bring about the participation of households in the capital markets in Japan. Participation in this defined-contribution scheme is compulsory and includes the investment into bonds and investment trusts, for example. Members have to select the type of investment themselves. However, in the period 2000–2011 there has hardly been an increase in stock ownership of Japanese households, and Japanese households hold their financial still mainly in bank deposits (Von Richthofen, 2012).

The Japanese government is faced with a very serious pension fund shortfall in future decades. In the hope of reducing the severity of this situation, the government is expanding the investment opportunities available to the population. It is hoped that this scheme will gradually encourage private investors to include shares in their long-term financial planning, thus increasing the volume of capital flowing to the stock market. Up to now, Japanese households' operations in the stock markets have been on a relatively small scale. Japanese private investors are known to be risk averse, and to attach greater importance to the safety and liquidity of their capital than to its profitability. At the end of 2000, for example, Japanese households held more than half of their financial assets in cash and deposits with credit institutions (Deutsche Bank Research, 29 October 2001). The extended downturn in the Japanese stock markets, combined with the risk averseness of the population, makes it highly likely that most households will go for bonds instead of shares to set up their pension schemes.

A law reform that is thought to enable and stimulate the unwinding of the complex 'web' of cross-shareholdings in Germany was the tax reform enacted in 2000, especially the amended article 8b of corporate tax law, which states that public companies' capital gains on the sale of shareholdings were generally to be tax-free as of 1 January 2002 (Deutsche Bank Research, 7 February 2002). It had been argued that the 'web' of cross-shareholdings and *Konzerne* had partly been maintained by a stiff tax of over 40 per cent on the sale of shares by corporations (Schaede, 2000). However, the small number of large listed public companies, combined with the fact that in some of the sectors in which German companies are among the most competitive in the world, the prevailing ownership structures are highly concentrated (automotives, telecoms, post and insurance), suggest that the number of large-scale transactions as a corollary of the tax law reform is unlikely to be high. Moreover, while companies from sectors such as utilities, steel-making and electrical engineering are looking to divest business and subsidiaries that no longer form part of their core activities, these divestments are sometimes part of reciprocal activities. In addition, these companies were looking to use the proceeds from these divestments to acquire shareholdings and companies in their core business, thus preserving the pattern of concentrated ownership (Deutsche Bank Research, 7 February 2002).

Similarly, the corporate tax reform in Japan was argued to enable companies to reorganize around their holding companies by way of either 'spinning off' or 'spinning in'. Holding companies were said increasingly to be used to spin off and separate unprofitable business units (i.e. divisions, departments and subsidiaries) from profitable ones so that not only tax advantages could be gained, but also the non-competitive units could be disposed of in the M&A market (Ozawa, 2003). At the same time, however, there seems to have been a 'Japanized', or culturally specific, way in which the new holding structure has begun to be used, a way in which some parent companies are merely avoiding their announced lay-off plans for corporate restructuring by creating new, unlisted subsidiaries and hiving workers off the parent's books.[4] Finally, while take-overs were becoming part of economic normality in Germany and Japan,[5] Anglo-American style 'hostile' take-overs following public bids have remained rare (Deutsche Bank Research, 7 February 2002).[6] The history of German industry reveals only very few cases of hostile take-overs, some of which either led to a consensus in the final stages of the dispute or failed outright.[7]

Box 11.1 Corporate greed on trial

In April 2004, the *Economist* reported on the most spectacular trial in German corporate history. The trial concerned extra bonuses paid to senior managers of Mannesmann after the take-over of Mannesmann by Vodafone in February 2000. Six former Mannesmann officials, including Josef Ackermann, then the chief executive of Deutsche Bank and chairman of the supervisory board of Mannesmann, were indicted of committing a breach of trust in accepting bonuses worth 57 million euros. German penal law is strict in handling cases of 'disloyalty' (*Untreue*), meaning any self-interested action not conforming with the interest of the organization. The prosecutors argued that supporting a take-over for a bonus represented disloyalty to the organization including its shareholders of the time. The German public saw this as corporate greed on trial. The prosecutors suggested that the bonuses were bribes to secure the biggest hostile take-over in history (*Economist*, 3 April 2004, Kultur clash, 63). Although the accused were not convicted, the trial left a lasting ugly taste in the mouth of Germans 'savouring' anything that followed in the corporate world, notably the financial crisis and how technically bankrupt banks and enterprises were rescued, with the leading managers often still earning bonuses on the basis of pre-crash 'performance'. Interestingly, in the Mannesmann affair one of the persons indicted as a member of the supervisory board (Zwickel) but not convicted, was the head of the metalworkers' union (IG Metall) at the time. His predecessor (Steinkühler), formerly a leading light in industrial relations and popular with the political left, had earlier achieved being convicted, for insider trading as a member of a supervisory board. Codetermination thus not only prevents but also spreads corporate greed.

In Japan, there has been reluctance on the part of the Japanese business community, and society as a whole, to engage in take-overs even between Japanese companies. The Japanese business community still attaches great value to the traditional Japanese management style bearing regard to a long-term perspective, stable employment and protection against corporate raids.[8] The major institutional reason for the absence of hostile take-overs in the form of public bids in both countries is the complex ownership structures of many large companies, which put up barriers to transfers of control, thus providing incentives for the management of the target company and bidder, as well as controlling and influencing shareholders on both sides to seek a consensus.

To sum up, while there have been formal legal and regulatory changes in Germany and Japan, these only had a modest impact on:

- the structure of ownership
- growth of the stock market, and
- patterns of corporate control.

What we have seen thus demonstrates the working of a limited harmonization effect, in that a number of statutory and other measures were taken to move in the direction of liberal capitalism. However, these measures were specific and limited, they were to some extent reversed and they did not change anything about the differences between liberal and coordinated economies. But what we saw in addition is that reinterpretation and translation of measures to fit them into an existing ensemble of institutions and culture are very much in evidence, as actors notably in Japan attribute meanings to new measures that accord with established interests and predispositions. As a consequence important differences between financial systems remain, but the crude distinction between bank-based and market-based systems increasingly becomes too simplistic (Allen, Chui and Maddaloni, 2004). We can also see that some interdependencies were at work, but the question is whether these were as structurally economic as the discourse has pretended, or more political. It is also curious that the rising public debt in the economic downturn after the bursting of the Japanese asset price bubble in 1997, which has endured at least until 2013, was financed through domestic bonds. By comparison, the USA have financed their massive public indebtedness mainly from abroad, above all China. But it is also true that Japan has had substantial foreign direct investment into other countries in East Asia, as well as an increasing inflow of foreign investments in Japanese stocks, particularly since the most recent crisis.

11.3 The personnel and employment relations systems

'Patient capital' in Germany and Japan enables a different set of coalitions between capital and labour than is feasible in the UK and US systems. Insulation from shareholder pressure to maximize returns, even at the expense of cutting labour costs and employment, exhibits a strong 'institutional interlock' with the system of lifetime and stable employment, in-company training, seniority-based wages and promotion (in Japan), a relatively low stratification of rewards, and the social perception of the firm as a community (Dore, 1994). As such, the system of corporate governance is embedded in the systems of employment relations and human resources. The complementarity of these institutions requires us to move beyond the analysis of change in a single institutional domain. Since each institutional complex depends for its viability on the others, serious erosion tendencies in one complex will, in the longer run, produce erosion tendencies in the other two. This section, therefore, analyses the dialectics of change in the systems of industrial relations and human resources.

Germany

The German system of employment relations is a vital part of the German system of diversified quality production (see Chapter 7, on operations management), both in its capacity for securing social peace and through its relation with the quality and stability of labour (Streeck, 1991). The most important features of the system in these respects are the relatively centralized and coordinated form of collective bargaining, and the integration of labour at the enterprise level through codetermination mechanisms, together with the intertwining of functions between unions at regional and central levels and works councils in the enterprise. At the enterprise level, relatively high levels of employment security, secured through codetermination mechanisms, combined with patient capital, which allows for long-term strategies, have provided management with the incentive to invest in high levels of skill training and internal promotion. Bargaining within industries has been credited with considerable advantages for both labour and management: a high coverage rate and a relatively egalitarian wage distribution, promoting solidarity and union strength; social peace and the predictability of wage demand have enabled employers to combine the payment of relatively high wages with constant rises in labour productivity (Lane, 2000: 212).

Box 11.2 Vital features of the German personnel and industrial relations system

- A relatively centralized and coordinated form of collective bargaining
- Codetermination mechanisms
- Clear separation of functions between unions and works councils
- High levels of employment security.

Despite the challenges in recent years, from external political and economic changes, the most important pillars of the industrial relations system have proved their resilience. While there has been some decentralization of bargaining, with works councils assuming more influence over negotiations so as to better match bargaining outcomes to the economic performance of firms, regionalized negotiations are still prevalent (Begin, 1997: 181).

Moreover, hardship clauses, permitting an employer to avoid an industry agreement, still have to be authorized centrally (Hassel and Schulten, 1998). In general, social partnership is still valued by most employers because the social peace it creates affords the stability, predictability and cooperation needed for the German production model. This is particularly true in the many firms where export activity remains more important than production in foreign subsidiaries (Lane, 2000), but also in the internationalizing firms. This is no mean feat, given that Germany has been shaken by the effects of unification in 1990, in a different way but to an extent not dissimilar to Russia and China. The destruction of most of East Germany's manufacturing through sudden equalization of wages in East and West, and the restructuring of the East German economy by massive public transfers, to the tune of about 150 billion euros a year for decades, has implied massive consequences in East and West that are often forgotten today. Nowhere else in the world was a formerly centralized communist country of 16 million inhabitants changed into a part of a dominant capitalist country within about 5 years, without developments approaching sharp disaffection and turmoil but increasing levels of welfare despite rising social inequality. Between 1990 and 2002, Germany had more to contend with at home than managing globalization. Given the economic and political problems in liberal and state-dominated business systems, the relative stability and growth in Germany are truly breath-taking. One of the consequences, though, of the way that unification was managed, was a sustained lowering of the national standards of living (real wages), public debt increases until 2003, and severe measures to control the public debt and regain competitiveness. Probably no other country in the world could have done that.

It has been argued that the internationalization of German firms would facilitate the erosion of organizational regulation and interest representation (Streeck, 1997). There has been evidence in support of this fear. In some sectors, such as the car and electrical engineering industries, the development of transnational production chains has forced works councils into concession bargaining. However, concessions remain more the exception than the rule in industry-wide bargaining (Jackson, 1997) and have involved mainly working time flexibility (Lane, 2000). Internationalization did result in weakened competencies of plant-level codetermination by bringing centralization of strategic decision-making at the industrial group level. Plant management within large internationalized German firms, which are the traditional negotiating partners of the works councils, has been losing competencies in strategic decisions (Streeck, 1995). However, works councils can use a variety of options to coordinate across enterprises and bypass negotiations with partners who lack 'sovereignty'.[9] But on the other hand, in the mid-2000s German multinational enterprises started cutting back foreign investment more than went abroad. The reason was that some disenchantment about unplanned infrastructural, competence, coordination and cost problems came together with the rediscovery of production advantages at home (predictable administration, workers skills, better infrastructure, better unit labour costs/productivity).

In addition, as already indicated, labour's representation on supervisory boards remains unquestioned, thus supporting the stakeholder 'mentality' and impeding the adoption of Anglo-American style hire-and-fire policies. Share options are used in some German firms as a management incentive, but because one-sided decision-making is limited, they tend to be targeted at groups rather than individuals (Casper, 2000), or are available to all employees, not just managerial ones, as at VW (Lane, 2000: 220). In general, German workers continue to be among the highest paid, as well as the socially most secure in the developed world. The realization that the viability of the German production policy continues to depend on its core workforce is argued to still have a hold on most German management (Lane, 2000).

Although Germany was preoccupied by domestic (re-unification) problems until 2002, the crisis it entered in 2002 because of the latter and the ensuing reforms put internationalization very much on the agenda, and this had already started in towards the end of the 1990s. Interdependencies became abundantly clear, with the attempts to regain competitiveness under wage restraint and with the new Euro currency regime. Strategic sorting is therefore more in evidence, although assimilation of more liberal policies and reinterpretation are also visible. The unique advance in exports growth and competitiveness after the financial crisis, which was identical in Sweden, a country outside the Euro but with 'managed' currency exchange rates, attests to a strategic sorting effect.

Japan

Rather like Germany, Japan's system of industrial relations plays an important role in its production strategy. Unlike in Germany, however, and with very few exceptions (e.g. the Seamen's Union), Japanese unions are enterprise unions, each representing the employees of a different firm and organizing both blue- and white-collar employees; also dissimilar to the situation in Germany, Japanese corporate law is based on the unitary board system. Hence, employee participation, or codetermination, is not adopted in Japan. Despite the structural dependence on the firm, however, Japanese unions have had a considerable stake in, and have fought hard to defend, two core institutions of the Japanese human resource system: lifetime employment and seniority-based pay and promotion (Lincoln, 1993).[10] These institutions have been credited by both management and labour with major advantages. Management views them as a way to secure labour peace and retain skilled workers. For the unions they were ways to stave off management's tendency to lay workers off in order to adjust labour costs and to beat the threat of an inflated cost of living in the early postwar period (Ornatowski, 1998).

Box 11.3 Vital features of the Japanese personnel and industrial relations system

- Seniority-based wages
- Lifetime employment.

More than in Germany, lifetime employment is an important part of Japanese management practice because it reduces the significant commitment problems associated with firm-based private-sector training. In the unitary education system of Japan, the state focuses on the provision of general education, leaving firms to organize and invest in their own firm-specific technical training (Nishida and Redding, 1992). Lifetime employment provides incentives for workers to stay with the company that trains them, which, in turn, makes it safe for the firm to invest heavily in skills without fear of workers absconding with these skills to other firms (Thelen and Kume, 1999). As in Germany, this practice is linked to the nature of corporate governance in Japan, which is less subject to short-term financial disciplines and tends to put off radical restructuring of industrial activities and to avoid taking drastic measures if at all possible (Nohara, 1999).

Unlike in Germany, however, lifetime employment is not protected by codetermination rights in Japan, but is firmly grounded in legal precedents set by the Japanese court, which has made it almost impossible for employers to terminate or lay off their regular-status employees without the employees' or their unions' consent (Morishima, 1995). Also dissimilar to the situation in Germany, lifetime employment has always applied to the core full-time workers or the 'insiders' only in the biggest companies,[11] representing probably never more than one-third of the entire workforce,[12] and declining to about 20 per cent more recently (Ono, 2010). Moreover, while the Japanese lifetime employment rule means long-term stable employment, it has never excluded massive dismissal.[13] The system has also always been seen as a flexible one in which only about 20 per cent of all employees serve continuously at the same company from youth until the age of 60. Intra-group transfers, temporary and permanent – in a sense a sub-system of the lifetime employment system – help corporate groups shift the workforce, yet avoid laying off their core employees and are responsible for much of the system's inherent flexibility.[14] Similarly, the current growth of part-time and temporary employment as a response to the downturn and the need for firms to cut costs, is at the same time a means of maintaining the security and benefits accorded to core workers (Coe, Johns and Ward, 2011). It is seen as a flexible strategy aimed at sustaining a relatively rigid and costly commitment to lifetime employment of the core (Osawa and Kingston, 1996).

Rather like in Germany, and despite the challenges to the system in recent years, patterns of change and resilience are closely interwoven. As a result of the ongoing recession, there have been pressures for change in lifetime employment and in the seniority system in particular. In order to cut labour costs, large Japanese companies have shed an increasing amount of their labour force. Well-known examples are Nissan, which has closed five car plants and shed 21,000 jobs to stave off bankruptcy; Nippon Steel, which shed 40 per cent of its 10,000 white-collar workers between 1993 and 1997; Sony, which got rid of 17,000 jobs; and NEC which disposed of 15,000.[15] Such dramatic cuts explain the plethora of articles in the popular business press that predict the demise of lifetime employment.

However, the fact that the Japanese lifetime employment system has always been limited to a small proportion of the workforce, combined with the diversity of practices that have always been used by Japanese corporations to cut labour costs in times of distress, demands caution when examining, and making bold statements about so-called dramatic changes to the system. In general, a lot of Japanese firms still tend to rely on traditional responses to negative situations (Tanisaka and Ohtake, 2003). These include a reduction in working hours and overtime payment for currently employed full-time core workers; an increase in 'service overtime' (overtime without pay); less employment for new graduates; and an increase in *shukko* (temporary transfers between firms) and *tenseki* (transfers to another company, or change of long-term employment), both of which effectively reallocate workers within the internal labour market (Mroczkowski and Hanaoka, 1997; Sato, 1999; Fujiki et al., 2001; Genda, 2003). Overall job mobility in Japan remains much lower than in most other advanced economies, particularly the US (Ono, 2010). Moreover, many of the current job cuts are argued to have been designed to minimize job losses in Japan and to maximize those elsewhere; some of them are said to be part of early-retirement programmes[16]; and others affect the peripheral rather than the core workforce.[17]

Moreover, labour shedding via dismissals and calls for voluntary retirement, which happens increasingly during the ongoing recession, is still considered the very last resort for Japanese firms in streamlining their structures, and to be a measure that only these firms in critical condition would resort to (Tanisaka and Ohtake, 2003). Indeed, while most Japanese firms have adopted a mandatory retirement system with the age of 60 as the common retirement age, the system at the same time functions to secure employment for full-time regular workers until the mandatory retirement age (Sato, 1999). It seems more appropriate, then, to see the new conditions of employment as modifications of the lifetime employment system, not a contradiction of it (Kono and Clegg, 2001). Until now, the basic structure of the Japanese employment system has remained intact. Lifetime employment of the core is retained – not only because it is a protected right, but also because of the heightened dependence on stable and predictable relationships with labour at the plant level, in the context of tightly coupled production networks and the demands of producing at high quality on a just-in-time basis (see Ono, 2010).

Similarly, while a few major Japanese employers have made the choice to modify the rules regarding seniority-based pay and promotion,[18] this is far from being a modal practice. In the early 1990s, the recession and the emphasis on the creation of new technological resources in Japan induced large Japanese companies to renew their incentive mechanisms, particularly their wage systems. Some firms have introduced a lump-sum salary that is renegotiated annually and depends to a large extent on individual performance and on the performance of the employing organization. By linking employee compensation to both kinds of performance, employers expect that wage levels will be more flexible in response to changes in individual performance and the economic prosperity of the firm (Morishima, 1995). The new system is also intended to provide incentives for employees to increase their productivity and commitment to the goals of their employing organization, as well as to encourage autonomy and individual creativity, particularly among white-collar workers, whose productivity is considered rather mediocre, even if this development means sacrificing some of the benefits of cooperation (Nohara, 1999). Most importantly, the reforms are seen as essential to maintaining the stability of long-term employment.

The combined review of both employment and seniority systems could probably best be understood as an attempt to recover the 'lost' balance between jobs, ability and wages. Technological developments in the past decade have outstripped the skills of experienced workers, and the need to fill the gap has unleashed fierce competition among firms for promising young workers because of their adaptability to new technology. Younger employees, however, are increasingly less tolerant of the principle of equality of results and patiently waiting for the promotion implied by the traditional seniority system (Ornatowski, 1998). Older workers, on the other hand, are highly paid as a result of seniority-based wage components but do not possess the skills necessary to do the new sophisticated jobs (Sato, 1999). Reforms of the wage system have thus been motivated by attempts to achieve advantage in competition with other firms over the most desirable young workers, as well as by a desire to make it less costly for firms to retain older workers. However, partly as a result of the system's enterprise-orientated incentives, the new human resource practices are diffusing only slowly in Japan (Jacoby, 1995).

Again, we see a mixture of effects, and this time the interdependencies effect is large, as actors responded to the crisis Japan has lived under since 1997; industrial restructuring also involving foreign direct investment and domestic cut-backs is visible. There also has been some assimilation of more liberal personnel policies, although tempered with a large measure of reinterpretation and translation. We could also see that interdependencies have worked to effect some strategic sorting, as formerly strong industries in consumer electronics started to leave Japan. But on the whole, continuity of practices is very strong, as is the relative nationalism of Japan, in the restriction of inward capital and human resources mobility. Much as Japan has considered itself as exceptional, in this respect it is no exception. Despite radical changes over the years in China, it has become similarly open in the outside direction but also in control of inward investments and movements.

11.4 Conclusions

In general, the effects of the new practices on German and Japanese organization and management are proof of resilience and small-step adaptation. The corporate governance system has been most affected. However, in this case, it could also be argued that the most radical changes at the institutional level, while showing tendencies to convergence towards the Anglo-American model, revitalize the existing model far more than producing path-deviant change. Changes in financial regulations and corporate law in Germany and Japan have not produced any clear movement towards equity-centred systems of corporate finance and an outsider model of corporate governance. Ownership still tends to be concentrated and stable, and there is not much of a market in corporate control. Instead, control over companies is held by a majority of stakeholders. The traditional stakeholder 'mentality' and reality still prevail in both countries.

The stakeholder mentality of the insider model – which requires broad consensus – helps to explain why the employment relations and human resource systems of both countries, while experiencing reform, still rest on the pillars of enduring social partnership and employment security. Moreover, the correlation between culture and labour market institutions, which is identified in the research of Nickel and Layard (1997), underlines that these pillars are not likely to change in the near future. In Chapters 2 and 3 we have seen how culture and institutions are historically embedded and intertwined with societal arrangements. This amalgamation is extremely resistant to planned as well as unplanned change. In addition, it seems unlikely that major stakeholders, such as the unions, will accept the dilution of established rights. In both countries, the unions are strengthened in their positions by the fact that the current features of the systems of corporate governance, employment relations and human resources jointly support the production model of internationally competitive domestic industries. This is a clear strategic sorting effect. As the USA, the UK and France became deindustrialized, new industrial countries gained ground and the coordinated or cooperative economies (Germany, Sweden, Switzerland, Austria) shifted to strategies of diversified quality production. The preservation of these production models depends on the combined availability of long-term, patient capital; social peace and partnership between capital, management and labour; highly skilled labour; and a network of long-term and cooperative relationships. These requirements are irreconcilable with Anglo-American-style capitalism, which emphasizes short-termism in managerial strategy and relationships, and instant hire-and-fire practices. Hence, we would argue that far more than leading to the demise of the existing German and Japanese systems, by injecting a healthy dose of competition at all levels, reforms, even though they are path deviant, will help to remodel and improve them. This would be an argument in favour of some assimilation but more on the surface, with strong reinterpretation and translation effects, and a healthy dose of strategic sorting.

When large German companies, such as Hoechst, Bayer and BASF, have restructured their organizations, this was less an expression of organizational hybridization, as Lane claims (2000), than of 'greater specialization in national industrial profiles' (Vitols, 2001: 360; Sorge, 2003). Unable to enter new growth fields (i.e. biotechnology),[19] which require more radical innovation, these three companies disposed of their pharmaceuticals subsidiaries. Initially, all three companies relocated their innovative activities in pharmaceuticals to the USA, either through the establishment of new research facilities there or through the acquisition of existing firms (particularly in the biotechnology area). More recently, however, it seems that German companies are simply disappearing from the pharmaceutical industry. Hoechst disappeared as a German pharma company by merging with the French Rhône-Poulenc, with the new company's headquarters (Aventis) in France. BASF has sold all of its pharmaceutical operations to a US company. Bayer was also argued to have increased its focus on core competencies, and a there was a preference towards maintaining chemicals activities and selling off pharmaceuticals (Vitols, 2001). But later, it reinvented itself as a pharma company again, merging with Schering and jettisoning the chemical activities into Lanxess. Far more than hybridization, what is happening in this industry points to further specialization and strategic sorting. The firm that kept most consistently to the chemicals and derived products is BASF, and this also turned out to have the most sustained success. Different from the older pharma firms, Germany has also seen a rapid growth of successful makers of generic drugs such as Hexal and Ratiopharm.

Further specialization does not occur at the level of societal institutions, however. Rather, as indicated, we have discussed some evidence of path-deviant change at that level. In fact, it seems that path-deviant reforms in Germany and Japan, which allow for Anglo-American-style management practices, contributed to intensified specialization at the industrial level. For example, the tax reform in Germany, which was expected to lead to the unwinding of cross-holdings, rather than doing so, in general stimulated the divestment of non-core activities. Similarly, in Japan, in order to attract young employees, some companies bypassed the institutionalized seniority-based wage system and implemented Anglo-American-style remuneration packages that are performance-based. However, rather than diluting the entire system, these measures, at the same time, enabled these companies to preserve lifetime employment, which is one of the cornerstones of the Japanese production model. This model has a comparative advantage in the so-called medium-tech sectors characterized by incremental innovation and large firm-specific human capital investments.

In general, there is more evidence of path dependency and resilience than of hybridization or path-deviant change at the organization and management level. This finding can perhaps best be explained by the dynamics of bargaining processes within the insider or stakeholder model, which strive to obtain an equilibrium situation between diverging interests and acquired rights, including those of labour. While it is true that regulatory reform shows tendencies that could be perceived as path-deviant in both Germany and Japan, its effects point to the wish to preserve and revitalize the current model. These findings again support the starting point of this chapter: the choice of a particular level of analysis, to a large extent, determines the type of evidence one obtains and, thus, the argument that one is able to defend. When the research focus is on societal institutions, one can find evidence that points to path-deviant change and hybridization. When looking at the level of the firm, though, there is evidence of incremental adaptation and path dependency as well as further specialization of the industrial profile. All this boils down to strong assimilation and reinterpretation effects, and non-negligible evidence for strategic sorting.

An aspect of the findings that may or may not be surprising is that effects do not appear to be different for corporate governance and for competence generation/human resources/employment relations. The societal effect that relates the different resource spaces to one another, notably the link between operations systems and the organizational space on the one hand and strategies on the other, links the effects across different spaces and systems. This means that although corporate governance was felt to be a unifying force for the world, it has turned out to be less than that. Different sorts of actors, different sorts of interests and different perceptions or predispositions have made for different mixtures of change and resilience in the details. Even the adoption of corporate codes of governance, as we saw in Chapter 6, could not dispense with culture as an explanatory factor.

There is no evidence in support of a sweeping convergence argument within institutional or societal frameworks. Similarly, within the cultural framework, there is no evidence in support of the convergence argument. Research that focuses on cultural analysis – whether from the etic or emic viewpoints – finds considerable differences between cultures and these differences seem to be path dependent. Perhaps an important proof of this argument is that the country scores on Hofstede's national cultural dimensions, which were calculated on the basis of a dataset from the 1980s, are still valid, at least in as far as relative positions of countries are concerned, and used widely in today's research.

Additional evidence in this direction comes from a study by Inglehart and Baker (2000). These authors tested the thesis that economic development is linked with systematic changes in basic values. Their research was informed by modernization theorists from Karl Marx (1867) to Daniel Bell (1973, 1976), who argued that economic development brings pervasive cultural changes. It was also based on research by scholars such as Max Weber ([1904] 1958) and Samuel Huntington (1993, 1996), who claimed that cultural values are an enduring and autonomous influence on society. Using data from the three waves of the World Values Surveys, which include 65 societies and 75 per cent of the world's population, Inglehart and Baker found evidence of both massive cultural change and the persistence of distinctive cultural traditions. Economic development was found to be associated with shifts away from absolute norms and values, towards values that are increasingly rational, tolerant, trusting and participatory. Cultural change, however, was found to be path dependent. The broad cultural heritage of a society – Protestant, Roman Catholic, Orthodox, Muslim, Confucian or Communist – was found to leave an imprint on values that endure despite modernization. Moreover, the differences between the values held by members of different religions within given societies were found to be much smaller than are cross-national differences. Once established, such cross-cultural differences are argued to become part of a national culture transmitted by educational institutions and mass media. Hence, while there is some talk of global communications and worldwide cultural standardization, as in McDonaldization and Coca-Colonization, the basic systems of national values endure in the midst of change.

This argument provides us with further confirmation that societal institutions, while surely experiencing change, are not converging and will not converge in the future. And this may very well go together with increasing interdependencies, as we saw. Since national culture relates to societal institutions, full convergence at the institutional level would imply convergence of cultural traditions. Following Inglehart and Baker's study, since the latter is not happening, full institutional convergence will not take place, either.

The question about convergence was inadequate to start with, as we now see. For contrary to the usual tacit assumption, internationalization is not only a force for assimilation and harmonization; it is also an important trigger for increasing diversity, and this works through the strategic sorting effect which has often been overlooked. Whereas the translation effect moderates assimilation and harmonization and conserves existing culture and institutions, the strategic sorting effect is productive of societal diversity. It does not come out when we control for contingencies in cross-national comparisons; but when we look at the changes in whole populations of organizations in different countries and their strategies, as we did in the French and German machine-tool industry case, then this sorting appears (see the Case at the end of Chapter 7). Another comparison that revealed it earlier, was an Anglo-German comparison of the introduction of microelectronics into the products in a number of industries: whereas in Britain the introduction was more related to structural changes, from 'older' industries to new ones and high-tech, in Germany microelectronics were more used to modernize existing types of products and improve the competitive position of firms in traditional industries, without the structural ruptures one could observe in Britain (Sorge et al., 1989).

A final important question to answer is 'What does all of this imply for the management of multinational companies (MNCs)?' If the world political economy becomes globalized, as some argue, then multinationals should gradually be losing their national characters, and converging in their fundamental strategies and operations. This fits with Theodore Levitt's 1983 paper in favour of the global company. He argued that the global company will outperform the multinational company by concentrating 'on what everyone wants rather than worrying about the details of what everyone thinks they might like' (1983: 2). Nowadays, however, an increasing amount of research talks about the 'myth of globalization' and the fact that most of the largest companies operate in only one of the three dominant clusters – the EU, Japan and North America (Rugman, 2001) – and not on a global scale. It is argued that globalization is misunderstood – it does not mean, and has never done so, a single world market with free trade, and it is merely an ideal (Rugman, 2012).

Moreover, in a study on retail companies, Rugman and Girod (2003) argue that the likelihood that a (retail) firm will act globally is determined to a great extent by the size of its primary market. A total of 83 per cent of their study's domestic-only firms come from the USA, a fact that the authors attribute to the size of the US market. They explain that most US firms do not have to go abroad to generate sufficient growth. The bi-regional MNCs, by contrast, come mainly from small European nations and have larger sales in North America than in Europe. Rugman and Girod argue that this was a strategic choice carried out through acquisitions since the 1960s. They write that these companies acted as locals as much as possible, not using European names in North America. The conclusion drawn from this study is that, while the retail industry is becoming more international and there is an overall need for firms to expand abroad in order to generate new growth, this is not global activity. Most of the international activity is within the local home region of the retail MNC. Hence, Rugman advises managers not to buy in to the globalization myth but rather to concentrate on building strategies that create advantage in their major regional markets (Rugman, 2001).

Additional confirmation of the absence of global companies, and the absence of global pressures leading to convergence, can be found in a study of German, Japanese and US multinationals (Pauly and Reich, 1997). This study shows that German, Japanese and US MNCs continue to diverge fairly systematically in their internal governance and long-term financing structures, in their approaches to research and development (R&D), as well as in the location of core R&D facilities, and in their overseas investment and intra-firm trading strategies. Consistent with the line of thinking in this book and, especially, with Chapter 9 on MNCs, the study shows that durable national institutions and distinctive ideological traditions still seem to shape and channel crucial corporate decisions. Indeed, the evidence of this study suggests 'a logical chain that begins deep in the idiosyncratic national histories that lie behind durable domestic institutions and ideologies and extends directly to the structures of corporate governance and long-term corporate financing' (Pauly and Reich, 1997: 23). Those structures, it is argued, in turn appear plausibly linked to continuing diversity in the corporate foundations of national innovation systems. The latter is precisely what we concluded from Chapter 8 on national innovation systems, and what we have repeated at the beginning of this chapter.

To sum up, there is no truly global political economy with truly global corporations emerging, acting as the sinews of convergence in the world economy. It is clear that the globalization template upon which much current theoretical and policy debate rests remains weak. Although the world has been 'coming together' within interdependencies – despite this, because of resilience and reinterpretation when assimilation does take place, and because of this, through strategic sorting effects – convergence is not happening on a broader front. It does happen with regard to specific phenomena, but these are usually related to opposite effects. We have offered the tools for working out how this precisely works for which enterprises, industries and countries. The next chapter offers an integrative case for practising these tools, combining knowledge from the different chapters. As we finish this edition, the world has moved from an enthusiasm about economic and political liberalization to ideas about 'pluricentralism' and to resurgent nationalism or sectarianism. Anything else would have been highly surprising. There is a regular pattern of societal aggregation in larger empires leading to overextension and resurgent nationalism and regionalism.[20] These insights and tendencies should reinforce the interest in comparative international management.

Study questions

1 Explain the complementarity of three societal spaces – systems of corporate governance, competence generation/personnel management and employment relations.
2 Give examples of the four internationalization effects mentioned in the beginning, and discuss them.
3 Why is it essential to distinguish between different levels of analysis when analysing the impact of globalization forces?
4 Analyse the effect of the so-called globalization forces on the following societal systems in Germany and Japan: corporate governance, competence generation/personnel management and employment relations.
5 Discuss the viability of path-deviant change in organization and management in German and Japanese corporations, using harmonization and translation effects.
6 Is it possible to characterize institutional change in different national cases, using standard BSys and VoC concepts?
7 Evaluate the role of cultural characteristics in explaining change at the societal, organization and management levels.
8 Explain how the MNC fits into the picture of internationalization, especially to what extent it drives globalization.

Further reading

Govindarajan, V. and Gupta, A. (2000) Analysis of the emerging global arena. *European Management Journal* 18(3), 274–84.

In contrast to mainstream opinion nowadays, and despite all evidence to the contrary, both authors maintain the claim that globalization is one of the main issues facing companies today. They claim that twin forces – that is, ideological change and technology revolution – underline the existence of globalization.

Pauly, L.W. and Reich, S. (1997) National structures and multinational corporate behavior: enduring differences in the age of globalization. *International Organization* 51(1), 1–30.

This article focuses on German, Japanese and American MNCs, and examines whether they are losing their national characters, and are converging in their fundamental strategies and operations as a result of globalization. The article shows that MNCs continue to diverge fairly systematically and that durable national institutions and distinctive ideological traditions still seem to shape and channel crucial corporate decisions.

Ruigrok, W. and Van Tulder, R. (1995) *The Logic of International Restructuring*. London: Routledge.

This book offers an integrated and interdisciplinary framework to analyse the dynamics of the international economy. The authors explain in a very clear way that the nationality of companies continues to be a decisive factor in today's supposedly 'borderless' economy.

Case: Global outsourcing: divergence or convergence?

There tended to be a prejudice in the debate over 'outsourcing': that all new industrial countries such as India have to offer is cheap labour and a telecommunications link. Just look, they say, at the extent of the high-end research and development (R&D) work being undertaken in India. Yet by the crude measure of patents earned by the Indian subsidiaries of multinational firms, a significant amount of innovation now stems from India. In 2003, Intel's Indian subsidiary filed 63 patents. Its president, Ketan Sampat, says that the 1,500 IT professionals employed by the firm in R&D in Bangalore are engaged in 'engineering challenges as complex as any other project on the planet'. They use the fastest supercomputer in India (ranked as the 109th most powerful computer in the world) and are divided into four product-design divisions covering ultra-wideband radio, enterprise processors, mobile and wireless chip-sets, and communications.

For Intel, which has a similar-sized R&D operation in Israel, and smaller facilities in Russia and China, the attractions of Bangalore are simple: the best climate in India and 'very smart people', who are technically well-educated and speak good English. D.B. Inamdar, the senior civil servant in the provincial government's IT Department, says that some 140,000 IT professionals now work in Bangalore – about 20,000 more than in Silicon Valley. Some 50 colleges produce 40,000 more each year. Intel's approach is to hire and train college graduates, supplementing them with about 100 senior engineers, mostly (like Mr Sampat) returning expatriates. Intel and others also point to the congenial 'ecosystem' developed as technology companies have clustered in Bangalore.

For SAP, a German software firm, the appeal of the Bangalore ecosystem includes the presence of its customers, its global partners and, crucially, some 3,000 engineers trained in SAP software on the books of Indian IT services such as Wipor, Infosys and Tata Consultancy Services. SAP has 850 staff in Bangalore, a number likely to grow by 500 this year, but can, with a local phone call, quickly add qualified engineers for particular projects.

Wipro's boss, Vivek Paul, says that R&D is becoming 'like the movies'. Firms, like film studios, are increasingly unwilling to keep expensive teams together between projects. For Wipro, providing firms with an alternative to doing R&D with permanent in-house teams has become a big business, accounting for one third of its $1 billion in annual revenues, and employing 6,500 people. It is probably the world's biggest R&D services firm. Its customers include all the big telecoms-equipment vendors (except Germany's Siemens). Its smallest commitment to any of these clients is 300 people. Elaborate procedures protect the customer's intellectual property, including mandatory 'cooling-off' periods for engineers between clients, and sometimes a right of veto on their redeployment. The corollary is that the breadth of industry knowledge is part of the sales pitch.

The approach, says Mr Paul, varies from micro-management by the customer, who takes on Wipro engineers virtually as members of his own staff, to 'total product ownership' – the handing over to Wipro of a mature product and all its global development and maintenance requirements, such as adaptation for a particular market. This allows customers to redeploy their own engineers to the next big thing.

Sarnoff's Mr Cherukuri calls this the 'globalisation of innovation' – continuing the erosion in the past 20 years of the old model of corporate R&D, dominated by the big firms with big budgets able to erect big barriers to entry to their markets. This is part of a broader trend, prompted partly by a rising number of entrepreneurial innovators and growing amounts of venture capital to finance them, towards a more 'dispersed' model of R&D. Now, the internet has removed geographic barriers to using far-flung talent, and the popping of the dot-com bubble 'has spread innovation off-shore'. The dispersal is becoming global.[21]

Questions

1 Explain which effects 'outsourcing' in innovation demonstrates, in the present case.
2 Is Bangalore an industrial district?
3 Discuss economic, cultural and institutional reasons for the emergence of Bangalore as the phenomenon that it has become.
4 Look at the names of companies mentioned as having subsidiaries in Bangalore. Now, imagine that you are responsible for software for flight management systems in Rockwell Collins, the market leader in aviation electronics in the USA. Would you consider relocating the function to Bangalore?

Notes

1 A complete schedule of financial system reform is available at the Ministry of Finance (MOF) website at www.mof.go.jp.
2 *Financial Times*, 23 June, 2013.
3 A large proportion of US shares is held in 401(k) pension plans. These are financed from employee – and frequently also employer – contributions. The contributions are paid from income before tax, and the accumulated assets only become liable to tax when the capital is disbursed. The name is taken from section 401(k) of the 1978 US Internal Revenue Code.
4 *Economist*, 'The way Enron hid debts' (2002).
5 Following the Financial Holding Companies Law of 1998, in order to improve the long-term health of the bank system, a move towards mega-mergers among the largest banks took place.
6 'Hostile' here means directed against the interests of the target company's management.
7 Until the UK company Vodafone acquired Mannesmann AG in 2000, a German company had never been acquired in a hostile take-over.
8 *Nikkei Weekly*, 20 September 1999: 3.
9 See Jackson (1997) for an extended discussion of these options.
10 Seniority-based pay and promotion is a system or practice that emphasizes the number of years of service, or age and educational background, in determining pay and promotion.
11 The group of so-called more 'peripheral' workers, or 'outsiders', usually includes women, youths and older workers.
12 Japan Institute of Labor, 'The labor situation in Japan, 2002/2003', 22; *Economist*, 18 November 1999, 'The worm turns'; 23 August 2001, 'An alternative to cocker spaniels'.
13 *Japan Labor Bulletin*, Mid- and long-term prospects for Japanese-style employment practices, 33(8), 1 August 1994.
14 *Japan Labor Bulletin*, 'The labor situation in Japan 2002/2003', 22.
15 *Economist*, 9 October 1997, 'On a roll'; 18 November 1999, 'The worm turns'; 23 August 2001, 'An alterna- tive to cocker spaniels'.
16 *Japan Labor Bulletin*, September 2003, 4.
17 *Economist*, 9 October 1997, 'On a roll'; 23 August 2001, 'An alternative to cocker spaniels'.

18 In 1999, Matsushita changed its seniority-based wage system for its 11,000 managers. This behaviour was followed by some other big companies; i.e. by Fujitsu, Fuji Xerox, Asahi Glass, Asahi Breweries, Kansai Electric and Itochu Corporation (*Economist*, 20 May 1999, 'Putting the bounce back into Matsushita').

19 See Casper (2000) for an extended explanation of incremental adaptation in a largely path-dependent way in German biotechnology companies.

20 Sorge (2005) showed this for the formation of society in Germany, but the argument is worth a tentative generalization.

21 Extracts from 'Innovative India', © *The Economist* Newspaper Limited, London, (3 April 2004).

References

Ahmadjian, C. (2006) Japanese business groups: continuity in the face of change. In Chang, S.-J. (ed.), *Business groups in East Asia: Financial Crisis, Restructuring, and New Growth*. Oxford, UK: Oxford University Press, 29–51.

Allen, F., Chui, M.K.F. and Maddaloni, A. (2004) Financial systems in Europe, the USA, and Asia. *Oxford Review of Economic Policy* 20(4), 490–508.

Amable, B. (2000) Institutional complementarity and diversity of social systems of innovation and production. *Review of Political Economy* 7(4), 645–687.

Baba, N. and Hisada, T. (2002) *Japan's Financial System: Its Perspective and the Authorities' Role in Redesigning and Administrating the System*. Tokyo: Bank of Japan, Institute for Monetary and Economic Studies. Discussion Paper No. 02- E-1.

Bank of Japan (2014) *Flow of funds – Overview of Japan, US and the Euro area*. http://www.boj.or.jp/en/statistics/sj/sjhiq.pdf, retrieved on 29 August 2014.

Begin, J.P. (1997) *Dynamic Human Resource Systems: Cross-National Comparisons*. Berlin: Walter de Gruyter.

Bell, D. (1973) *The Coming of Post-industrial Society*. New York: Basic Books.

Bell, D. (1976) *The Cultural Contradictions of Capitalism*. New York: Basic Books.

Bijlsma, M.J. and Zwart, G.T.J. (2013) *The changing landscape of financial markets in Europe, the United States and Japan*. Bruegel Working Paper 2013/02, Brussels: Bruegel.

Casper, S. (2000) Institutional adaptiveness, technology policy, and the diffusion of new business models: the case of German biotechnology. *Organization Studies* 21(5), 887–914.

Coe, N.M., Johns, J. and Ward, K. (2011) Transforming the Japanese labour market: deregulation and the rise of temporary staffing. *Regional Studies* 45(8), 1091–1106.

Coffee, J.C. (2001) *The rise of dispersed ownership*. Columbia Law School Working Paper, No. 182.

DAI (1999) *DAI Factbook 1999*. Frankfurt am Main: Deutsches Aktieninstitut.

Deeg, R. and Perez, S. (1998) *International capital mobility and domestic institutions: corporate finance and governance in four European cases*. Paper presented at the 1998 Annual Meeting of the American Political Science Association, Boston, 3–6 September.

Deutsche Bank Research (2001) Japan's investors becoming less risk-averse? *Frankfurter Voice*, 29 October.

Deutsche Bank Research (2002) Corporate takeovers in Germany and their regulation. *Frankfurt Voice*, 7 February.

Dore, R. (1994) *Financial Structures, Motivation and Efficiency*. Unpublished manuscript. London: London School of Economics.

Dore, R. (1996) Convergence in whose interest? In Berger, S. and Dore, R. (eds), *National Diversity and Global Capitalism*. New York: Cornell University Press.

Easterbrook, F. (1997) International corporate differences: markets or law? *Journal of Applied Corporate Finance* 9(4).

Economist Intelligence Unit (2010) *SMEs in Japan: A New Growth Driver?* London: Economist Intelligence Unit.

Fujiki, H., Kuroda Nakada, S. and Tachibanaki, T. (2001) Structural issues in the Japanese labour market: an era of variety, equity, and efficiency or an era of bipolarization? *Monetary and Economic Studies* (Special Edition), February.

Genda, Y. (2003) Dangers facing businessmen in their 20s and 30s who work for large companies. *Japan Labour Bulletin*, 7 February.

Hassel, A. and Schulten, T. (1998) Globalization and the future of central collective bargaining: the example of the German metal industry. *Economy and Society* 27(4), 486–522.

Huntington, S.P. (1993) The clash of civilizations? *Foreign Affairs* 72(3), 22–49.

Huntington, S.P. (1996) *The Clash of Civilizations and the Remaking of World Order*. New York: Simon & Schuster.

Inglehart, R. and Baker, W.E. (2000) Modernization, cultural change, and the persistence of traditional values. *American Sociological Review* 65, 19–51.

Jackson, G. (1997) *Corporate governance in Germany and Japan: developments within national and international contexts*. Draft paper. Cologne: Max Planck Institut für Gesellschaftsforschung.

Jacoby, S.M. (1995) Recent organizational developments in Japan. *British Journal of Industrial Relations* 23(4), 645–650.

Koen, C. (2000) *The Japanese main ban model: evidence of the pressures for change*. Unpublished paper. Tilburg: Tilburg University.

Kono, T. and Clegg, S. (2001) *Trends in Japanese Management*. Houndsmills, Basingstoke: Palgrave.

Lane, C. (2000) Globalization and the German model of capitalism – erosion or survival? *British Journal of Sociology* 51(2), 207–234.

La Porta, R., Lopez-de-Silanes, F., Shleifer, A. and Vishny, R. (1997) Legal determinants of external finance. *Journal of Finance* 52, 1131–1150.

Lazonick, W. and O'Sullivan, M. (2000) Maximizing shareholder value: a new ideology for corporate governance. *Economy and Society* 29 (February), 13–35.

Levitt, T. (1983) The globalization of markets. *Harvard Business Review* 61 (May/June), 92–102.

Lincoln, J.R. (1993) *Work Organization in Japan and the United States*. Oxford: Oxford University Press, 54–74.

Marx, K. (1867) *Das Kapital: Kritik der Politischen Ökonomie*. Vol. 1. Hamburg: O. Meissner.

Miyajima, H. (1998) The impact of deregulation on corporate governance and finance. In Carlile, L.E. and Tilton, M.C. (eds) *Is Japan Really Changing its Ways*? Washington, DC: Brookings Institution Press.

Morishima, M (1995). Embedding HRM in a social context. *British Journal of Industrial Relations* 33(4), 617–637.

Mroczkowski, T. and Hanaoka, M. (1997) Effective rightsizing strategies in Japan and America: is there a convergence of employment practices? *Academy of Management Executive* 11(2), 57–67.

Nickel, S. and Layard, R. (1997) *Labour market institutions and economic performance*. Discussion paper series 23. Oxford: Centre for Economic Performance.

Nishida, J.M. and Redding, S.G. (1992) Firm development and diversification strategies as products of economic cultures: the Japanese and Hong Kong textile industries. In Whitley, R. (ed.) *European Business Systems, Firms and Markets in their National Contexts*, 241–267.

Nohara, H. (1999) Human resource management in Japanese firms undergoing transition. In Dirks, D., Huchet, J.-F. and Ribault, T. (eds) *Japanese Management in the Low Growth Era*, Berlin: Springer, 243–262.

Nowak, E. (2001) Recent developments in German capital markets and corporate governance. *Journal of Applied Corporate Finance* 14(3), 35–48.

OECD (2001) *Recent Trends: Institutional Investors Statistical Yearbook*. OECD.

OECD (2013) OECD Institutional Investors Statistics 2013.

Ono, H. (2010) Lifetime employment in Japan: Concepts and measurements. *Journal of the Japanese and International Economies* 24(1), 1–27.

Owualah, S.I. (1999) Banking crisis, reforms, and the availability of credit to Japanese small and medium enterprises. *Asian Survey* XXXIX(4), July/August.

Ornatowski, G.K. (1998) The end of Japanese-style human resource management? *Sloan Management Review*, Cambridge 39(3), 73–84.

Osawa, M. and Kingston, J. (1996) Flexibility and inspiration: restructuring and the Japanese labour market. *Japan Labour Bulletin* 35(1).

Ozawa, T. (2003) Japan in an institutional quagmire: international business to the rescue? *Journal of International Management* 9, 219–35.

Pauly, L.W. and Reich, S. (1997) National structures and multinational corporate behavior: enduring differences in the age of globalization. *International Organization* 51(1), 1–30.

Pedersen, T. and Thomsen, S. (1999) Business systems and corporate governance. *International Studies of Management and Organization* 29(2), 43–59.

Porter, M. (1990) *The Competitive Advantage of Nations.* New York: Free Press.

Rebérioux, A. (2002) European style of corporate governance at the crossroads: the role of worker involvement. *Journal of Common Market Studies* 40(1), 111–134.

Richthofen, P. von (2012) *Overview of Japanese capital markets.* Paper presented at the Equity-Based Insurance Guarantees Conference, Tokyo.

Roe, M. (1997) The political roots of American corporate finance. *Journal of Applied Corporate Finance* 9(4).

Rugman, A. (2001) *The Myth of Global Strategy.* AIB Newsletter, second quarter, 11–14.

Rugman, A. (2012) *The End of Globalization: Why Global Strategy is a Myth and How to Profit From the Realities of Regional Markets.* London: Random House.

Rugman, A. and Girod, S. (2003) Retail multinationals and globalizations: the evidence is regional. *European Management Journal* 21(1), 24–37.

Sato, A. (1999) Employment and treatment of middle-aged and older white-collar employees after the bubble. *Japan Labour Bulletin* 38(6), June.

Schaede, U. (1999) *The Japanese Financial System: from Postwar to the New Millenium.* Harvard Business School Case Study 9–700–049. Boston: Harvard Business School Publishing.

Schaede, U. (2000) *The German Financial System in 2000.* Harvard Business School Case Study 9–700–135. Boston: Harvard Business School Publishing.

Sorge, A. (2003) Cross-national differences in human resources and organization. In Harzing, A.-W. and Van Ruisseveldt, J. (eds) *Human Resource Management* (2nd edn). London: Sage.

Sorge, A. (2005) *The Global and the Local: Understanding the Dialectics of Internationalization.* Oxford University Press, 2005. (Paperback version 2006).

Sorge, A., Campbell, A. and Warner, M. (1989) *Microelectronic Product Applications in Great Britain and West Germany: Strategies, Competence and Training.* Aldershot: Gower Press.

Streeck, W. (1991) On the institutional conditions of diversified quality production. In Matzner, E. and Streeck, W. (eds) *Beyond Keynesianism.* Aldershot: Edward Elgar, 21–61.

Streeck, W. (1995) *Industrial democracy beyond co-determination?* Paper presented at the Conference on Worker's Participation in Europe: Institutions, Industrial Relations and Technology, Centro di Studio Economici Sociali e Sindacali (CESOS), Rome, 9–10 November.

Streeck, W. (1997) German capitalism: does it exist? Can it survive? In Crouch, C. and Streeck, W. (eds) *Political Economy of Modern Capitalism.* London: Sage.

Streeten, P. (1996) Free and managed trade. In Berger, S. and Dore, R. (eds) *National Diversity and Global Capitalism.* New York: Cornell University Press.

Tanisaka, N. and Ohtake, F. (2003) Impact of labour shedding on stock prices. *Japan Labour Bulletin*, January, 6.

Thelen, K. and Kume, I. (1999) The effects of globalization on labour revisited: lessons from Germany and Japan. *Politics and Society* 27(4), 477–505.

Vitols, S. (2001) Varieties of corporate governance: comparing Germany and the UK. In Hall, P.A. and Soskice, D. (eds) *Varieties of Capitalism: The Institutional Foundations of Comparative Advantage.* Oxford: Oxford University Press.

Vitols, S. and Woolcock, S. (1997) *Developments in the German and British Corporate Governance Systems.* Discussion paper. Workshop on Corporate Governance in Britain and Germany, Berlin, WZB.

Weber, M. [1904] (1958) *The Protestant Ethic and the Spirit of Capitalism.* Translated by T. Parsons. Reprint, New York: Charles Scribner's Sons.

Whitley, R. (1994) Dominant forms of organization in market economies. *Organization Studies* 15(2), 153–82.

Whitley, R. (1999) *How and why are international firms different? The consequences of cross-border managerial coordination for firm characteristics and behavior.* Paper presented at the 15th EGOS colloquium, University of Warwick, 4–6 July.

Yoshikawa, T. and McGuire, J. (2008) Change and continuity in Japanese corporate governance. *Asia Pacific Journal of Management* 25, 5–24.

Yoshikawa, T. and Phan, P.H. (2001) Alternative corporate governance systems in Japanese firms: implications for a shift to stockholder-centered corporate governance. *Asia Pacific Journal of Management* 18, 183–205.

12 Integrative case

Airlines – a global industry and exemplary enterprises

Outline

Introduction
The industry: history, regulation and business models
History
The postwar international order
Deregulation and new business models
Types of airlines
The value chain and internationalization
KLM
Southwest Airlines
China Southern Airlines
Lufthansa Group
Study questions
Further reading
Notes
References

Introduction

This integrative case is to allow you to bring all the combined knowledge in this book, from various chapters, to bear on specific explanations:

1 Explain what happens in an enterprise, by referring to its cultural and institutional embeddedness.
2 Compare enterprises across countries, to see which comparative findings in the book make sense in this industry.
3 Relate comparative findings on airlines to global, national and local regulation, and to business models including internationalization strategies.

In fact, we present a two-level case: civil aviation is an industry case, and in this industry case, we have four airlines as cases. These were selected to stand for different institutional and cultural settings, and also for different business models and strategies. There have also been changes of regulation and of business models over time. The beauty of the industry is that it appeals to people because they will mostly have flight travel experience, and both teachers and students can themselves expand the cases, by collecting additional material. The industry association, IATA (International Air Transport Association) offers statistics and other information on its website, and so do the individual airlines discussed here. Teachers and students can also themselves generate new cases of other airlines. In a manner of speaking, the sky is the limit!

Another beauty of civil aviation is that in one way, it is a very global industry, not only for the reason that aircraft fly around the globe, which makes the airlines interested in foreign destinations as places for subsidiaries or alliances, and as places in which competitors reside. There is also a lot of supranational regulation, probably more than in any other industry. Yet, at the same time, national and local regulation and resources of support are strong. The industry case thus in no way casts a prejudice on the famous, more superficial issue of whether global effects and internationalization are more important than national or local factors. It is precisely their combination that is worth the attention. Furthermore, civil aviation is a service industry, which attracts attention to an industry that is not in manufacturing, where most of the comparative studies discussed in this book were carried out. Let us see how findings are often generated in manufacturing work for services. On the other hand, as we shall see, the value chain does not feature clear distinctions between aeronautical engineering and aviation, so that the link with manufacturing is still there.

Another idea in the construction of this industry case and the individual airline cases, suggested by 'integrative' in the title, is the following: Often, cases are written in order to get students to apply specific theories that help to solve a particular question. The assumption is that a specific theory should be applied to solve a particular problem. Our idea goes further. Some explanatory and practical problems are 'systemic', i.e. they have ramifications across thematic areas and across levels of analysis, so that the student or the practitioner needs to engineer a combination of theories in order to arrive at a satisfactory explanation or solution.

The industry: history, regulation and business models

History

Air travel became a more regular and extensive business in the 1920s and 1930s. There was demand to overcome distance faster, notably when it was not bridged by other means of transportation, to do this without compromising on the luxury of first class sea travel if possible, and to appeal to a sense of adventure without compromising too much on safety. There were two main types of freight: people and mail. Pioneering mail services went from one end of the USA to the other, and from one continent to another. People were transported over distances short and long alike. Characteristic long distance routes were, for example, across the Atlantic. There was one variety, by sea-plane, which took off and landed on the water. Another variety was the airship, which was propeller-driven, but the lift came from hydrogen stored in a massive cigar-shaped tank, and the speed was slow. This alternative vanished more or less completely after the disastrous accident with the Hindenburg at Lakehurst in 1937. Colonial countries were keen to reduce the time of travel between the mother country and the colonies and started state-run airlines for this purpose. The national airline started first (in 1919) and still operating under this name and trademark, is KLM (Koninklijke Luchtvaart Maatschappij) in the Netherlands, which featured a long distance line to Indonesia. Some South American, African and Asian airlines were initiated by airlines from North America and Europe.

Almost from the start, air transport was international, which makes functional sense because the point in air travel is to cover longer distances more quickly. In a spirit of gentlemanly cooperation that governed at the time, it was not difficult to get landing and overflight rights in other countries; these were often colonized countries, and independent countries generally welcomed being connected by air. This atmosphere changed somewhat with the beginning of the Second World War, when even civil planes from enemy nations risked being shot at. Air travel started to operate in an ambiguous zone between rivalry and camaraderie between airlines that were mainly state-controlled or 'flag carriers', i.e., dependent on or regulated by governments. In awareness of this situation and in view of the need to set up a more formal scheme of international air travel regulation, the USA and her allies took the initiative, through the Chicago convention of 1944 when the war was still going on, to draw up a charter in the form of a treaty to which further countries could accede. Under this charter the International Civil Aviation Organization (ICAO) was founded, an authority of supranational government dependent on the member states and operating as an agency of the United Nations, to regulate and provide a number of standardized technical, juridical and administrative means (navigation aids, air traffic control, air safety, etc.). Air transport therefore became an internationally regulated industry, soon (about 20 years) after coming into existence. An international industry association, of which airlines could become members, IATA (International Air Transport Association) was likewise founded; this had an even longer history, starting in Geneva linked with the League of Nations, then moving to Havanna in Cuba and then to Montréal in Canada, from which a sizeable part including the headquarters moved back to Geneva in Switzerland.

The postwar international order

The fundamental principle of the Chicago convention and ICAO was that nation states reciprocally gave each other's airlines 'freedoms of the air': landing and take-off, dropping and taking on board passengers for international trips, overflight and cabotage (the right of an airline from another country to fly passengers from one destination to another within a country). Reciprocity was fundamental throughout: what was granted to airline A from country A by country B, also had to be granted to airline B from country B by country A. Throughout the early history of civil aviation, price competition, costs and lacking profitability have been problems. Pilots and other staff were often enthusiasts or idealists who wanted to fly, whatever the salary. There were waves of concentration to reduce cut-throat competition. There was a tendency of institutionally safeguarding satisfactory returns, supported by both airlines and governments. Emerging from the Second World War and into the new order under the Chicago convention, the internationally organized industry entered into a regime of international cartelization, which was formative and probably necessary to allow the initial growth of the market and of airlines. It made civil aviation a more commonplace, regular, safe and comfortable mode of (long) distance travel. Whereas until the beginning of the 1960s, sea travel was still commonplace, it was subsequently greatly reduced in relative importance. Cartelization was carried out by IATA, the world-wide industry association, and this prescribed not only prices but service standards. This cartelization was not only tolerated but driven by the USA; the market in and to/from the USA was divided into an international part serviced by only two firms (Pan American and Trans World Airways) and a domestic one, with enterprises such as United, Eastern, Delta, Northwest, Braniff and others. In Europe, national flag carriers emerged, supported by governments but also, through the Chicago principle of reciprocity, always competing on international routes with at least one airline from the respective other country. The upshot is that there were guaranteed prices, but there was always competition in an – at least – duopoly.

One of the few prominent exceptions today, forgotten during the postwar period, is that between 1945 and 1956 and in practice a bit longer, German air space was hardly subject to the Chicago principle of reciprocity. Since flying planes was forbidden to Germans, airlines of the powers of occupation (Air France, British European, Pan American) and neighbouring countries (Scandinavian Airlines System, Swissair, KLM) liberally carved up the West German domestic and international market, also putting in stops in Germany to fly passengers from one domestic destination to another.

With travel to foreign holiday destinations becoming more attractive, a new type of airline emerged that was under the Chicago and IATA regulation separate from the classical airlines. These were the 'charter' airlines which offered full plane capacity to tour organizers, at negotiable prices. The classical airlines had guaranteed prices but could not fill seats by varying prices; the charter airlines could liberally fill seats but could not penetrate the more lucrative segment of scheduled flights. This segment of the air travel market was therefore more liberal, free of IATA price-setting. As economists would immediately suspect, the difference in prices and regulation was to become an 'imbalance' that led to decades of wrangling between different types of airlines. The details of this protracted and complex wrangling eventually led to a radical change of international regulation, to a new type of IATA and a further differentiation of airline types.

Deregulation and new business models

This was not a change in one fell swoop but happened over about a decade. Try to visualize the business situation in the late 1970s. One thing is that the difference between IATA and charter prices was being eroded by way of arrangements like APEX and Super-APEX which committed passengers to booked flights and offered price reductions for such conditions as putting a week-end between departure and return. The classical carriers were confronted by the problem of how to move passengers from a more provincial place such as Remscheid in Germany (not unimportant industrially) to a place like Pittsburgh, Pennsylvania in the USA, on a business trip to a client firm. Conventionally, airlines coped with such demand by offering flights with stops en route, to drop passengers at different destinations. By the rules following from the Chicago convention, a flight of a foreign airline with stops en route in the USA would not have allowed the airline to pick up passengers at, say, Boston to drop them at Pittsburgh. That made extended connections with stops en route uneconomical, for between the first and the next destinations in the foreign country, the plane would become increasingly empty.

Confronted with such problems consequent to regulation – regulation that was also in aid of competition by imposing the principle of reciprocity – airlines started operating code shares and alliances. A shared code means that one airline in part charters seats on board flights of a different airline. It is useful in particular when an airline sharing the code can connect passengers from its own flights more easily. The pioneers of code sharing were Dutch KLM and Northwest in the USA, two airlines with a shared problem: a focus on a limited number of home airports, Amsterdam for KLM and mainly Minneapolis-St.Paul for Northwest. But the first alliance that was world-wide rather than bilateral, came about in 1997 through the combination of forces by United from the USA, Lufthansa from

Germany, Thai, Air Canada and SAS. This STAR Alliance is still the largest alliance in aviation and today has 27 members operating a fleet of 4,450 planes. Forming or entering an alliance allows an airline to organize connecting flight networks more easily. This makes it possible to fill seats better without going against rules and arrangements following the Chicago convention, simply by using the network of flights offered by a partner airline. The idea of making alliances to create hub-and-spoke networks of flights the world over, was claimed by or credited to, heads of both Lufthansa and SAS, but the idea was a development on an initial idea from KLM, as we saw. Both Lufthansa and SAS, based on the regional spread of population in their main area of intake, were more or less compelled to work out a way of guiding the home clientele through hubs anyway, where many foreign and even more intercontinental destinations were concerned. Quickly, other airlines imitated the practice and formed the rivalling alliance networks Sky Team and Oneworld. Each alliance consists of potent airlines in different continents that together can form a worldwide network of connections through hub-and-spoke systems. It is clear that such interconnected systems require a great deal of meticulous planning, technical and administrative efficiency, to make passengers from a less prominent place arrive comfortably in a distant and similarly less spectacular destination (e.g. from Düsseldorf to Pittsburgh), without too many delays and without losing their luggage en route.

Other innovations were complementary to this way of filling seats on planes, such as new reservation and pricing systems. In Europe, British Airways was the pioneer in such revenue management systems in the 1980s, allowing a marketing of flights in close tune with customer demand and giving the ability to charge more when demand was high. British Airways was also a first mover in introducing a new class of service, Club Class between First and Economy, given that a gap was opening between First and an Economy class increasingly filled by stingy super-savers. Other airlines more or less copied this new class division, and they have over time added new types of division to match the potential demand for relative luxury (from legroom and privacy up to meals) or status distinctions with the price and the service supply. You can directly explore the variety of reservation systems by visiting websites of airlines.

Pervasive deregulation was necessary for all this to happen. This started more seriously in the later 1970s, and over time it completely changed the role of IATA, doing away with the cartel role and leaving mainly two other roles: those of a lobby at different levels of government, and of a consultancy, to train employees in member airlines, with regard to specialized techniques and skills that an efficient airline requires. Interestingly, in the consultancy role, IATA considers its main competitor to be one of its members, Lufthansa.

One area of the airline business has been less affected by deregulation, though. When an airport is filled to capacity, it is not easily possible to generate new capacity where it is required immediately. Now, take-off and landing slots at busy airports are not given according to a strictly liberal principle. If they were, they would be auctioned. However, auctioning never happens. Very often, take-off and landing slots are attributed by, more or less, committees dominated by established interests traditionally connected with an airport. It would not be far-fetched to say that in order to get more slots at London Heathrow, you more or less have to buy an airline that does have slots. Lufthansa, for example, had done this by buying British Midland, but it was not economically lucrative because BM continued making losses, so that it was sold again to – guess who? – British Airways, the most potent local competitor, as it happens.[1] Furthermore, although the offer of flights has been considerably broadened in the European Union so that a rather free competition between EU airlines has come about, more internationally, access of airlines to a country is still governed by the old Chicago principle of reciprocity. In addition, there are numerous ways of loading the dice of competition, and all manners of favours to give to local champions (flag carriers). This is most visible in the Arabian peninsula, which is not only richly endowed in oil but lies more or less right in the centre of the aviation world: from any airport in the Arabian peninsula, most other important airports in the world are within a circumference of under 15,000 km, which happens to be the range of current main very long range aircraft (Boeing 777 and 787, Airbus 380 and 350). So, Dubai, Abu Dhabi and other airports on this peninsula and in its vicinity have started competing as hubs for the whole world.

Types of airlines

But next to this grand world of diversified carriers offering networked long, medium and short haul services, implying enterprises of great complexity with different sorts of planes, an entirely different aviation world has arisen, also due to deregulation: a world of simplified point-to-point flights, often 'with no frills', geared to the economical customer, often travelling for private motives such as seeing friends or having a holiday. Such operations can be more standardized, do not involve the movement of passengers and luggage between flights that have to connect, and they are usually carried out using only one or two types of plane. Standardization and simplification reduce overhead costs, and further measures to cut variable costs have also been taken (restriction of services, reduction of wage costs, going against collective bargaining with unions or works councils). The pioneer of this business model was Southwest in the USA, and it has had many followers, the other earlier ones arising with headquarters in the UK and Ireland (Easyjet, Ryanair). Today, although they have become a new type of airline with its own business model geared to cost leadership, they have also become potent competitors for the networked carriers.

As a result, there are currently the following main types of airlines[2]:

- full service network carriers
- low cost carriers
- holiday carriers (formerly called charter airlines)
- regional carriers (sometimes linked with network carriers)
- traditional freight carriers
- integrators
- hybrid carriers.

Here, we concentrate on the main passenger airlines (who also carry freight in the belly of the plane and often have specific freight divisions). We therefore disregard the last three types, and also the regional and the holiday carriers.

A director of IATA remarked: 'isn't it funny that hosts of people make money on aviation, except the airlines!' It is indeed true that all of the main US airlines have at different times gone into bankruptcy and were continued and re-launched based on 'Chapter 11' regulation. Most of the European network carriers have experienced problems of profitability. Even in the haven of liberal capitalism, full service carriers have had severe problems of profitability, deregulation and concentration notwithstanding. On the other hand, the new low cost carriers have mostly been much more profitable. Some Middle Eastern and Asian network carriers have apparently proved profitable, but accounting for profits and support is a problem. Companies like Emirates benefit from very low tax rates, easy access to finance, governments willing to spend in infrastructure, and very restrictive regulations regarding labour unions, not to speak of Western export subsidies if it comes to buying aircraft. The world of aviation continues to puzzle the observer, riddled as it is by differentiation into types and the persistence of local and national factors, next to a more liberal world order governed by supranational regulation.

The value chain and internationalization

An interesting fact is the composition of the value chain around airlines. Flying passengers from one point to another requires a great amount and diversity of inputs, the usual ones being capital (above all planes) and workers: pilots and cabin staff, ground service personnel, sales and administrative employees, technicians for maintenance, repair and overhaul (MRO), and many others, down to cooks for preparing in-flight meals. Now, many services can be bought from other firms and often are. Likewise, planes can be owned or leased. Civil aviation is a very technical business requiring a lot of training for many personnel; the main capital equipment, planes, comes from an industry which is classed as 'high technology', meaning that making planes requires research and development to a degree which is significantly above the average for manufacturing. However, and this is not known by many people although everyone in and around aviation knows it, even aircraft manufacturers hardly make money by developing and making planes, but more by selling spare parts and MRO.

MRO, like the licensing of planes, is subject to stringent regulation and is very demanding, in view of the priority of safety. A plane and an engine are typically expected to have a life of 20–25 years, without an accident due to malfunctioning. There is a system of checks, from the A check by pilots before any flight down to the D check about every 4 years, when the whole plane is more or less taken apart and every part and component is examined, tested and often replaced. Checks can be made by the manufacturer (of the plane or the engine), specialized and licensed service firms, or by the airline itself when it has a licence. An airline thus has a lot of decision choices with regard to the different services, of the 'make-or-buy' type. Some airlines are 'lean' and buy in or contract out; others provide the service in-house. Some airlines 'integrate backwards' or diversify the services they offer on the market; others run a lean operation.

The most integrated and also the largest airline in the world is nowadays often forgotten; this was Aeroflot, the Soviet monopoly flag carrier. Aeroflot was not only the largest airline in the world but also an annexe of the Soviet air force, with their substantial transport capability; it also operated and organized more or less anything to do with airport and navigation facilities, a *kombinat* in the truest sense of communist industrial organization. The state also told Aeroflot which planes to buy. This did not at all imply technological backwardness; the Tupolev 104 entered service more or less at the same time as the French Caravelle and the British Comet, the first civil planes driven by jet engines, then clearly in advance of the Americans.

Historically significant cases of forward integration by aircraft manufacturers were those of Boeing in the 1930s (in the USA) and Junkers (in Germany) in the 1920s. Boeing had owned United, and Junkers had started civil aviation services, hoping to beat the competition by reserving the use of their planes – thought to be superior – to their own civil aviation division or company. The arrangement did not prove beneficial; in the USA it was outlawed but also the start of Douglas's rise to a dominant position as a plane manufacturer; the plane that the others could buy – the DC3 – was superior to the Boeing 247! However, in the postwar period government owners of flag carriers in Europe did enforce the buying of domestically developed and produced planes on their firms. That was also to some extent a history of failures which detracted from the viability of some carriers, manufacturers or government budgets. The most notable cases were British European Airways and British Overseas Air Corporation (later united into British Airways) because of the BAC Trident, the Concord and the VC10, and Air France and Air Inter because of the Concorde[3] and the Mercure. Nowadays airlines are mostly free to buy planes as they think fit, but there are also exceptions that we shall mention, which have a distinctive economic rationale.

Where internationalization is concerned, there are clear patterns in aviation: in large national markets such as the USA, concentration of firms has been very important, leading to integrated enterprises and trademarks even when mergers rather than acquisitions occurred, and when the former domestic airlines have 'swallowed' or killed the former exclusively international airlines. Within the European Union, although airlines can now operate freely across borders, mergers or acquisitions that kept trademarks and subsidiary enterprises were dominant; the scarcity value of slots at overloaded airports is one main reason. Examples are the Lufthansa Group, Air France-KLM and British Airways-Iberia. Across other national boundaries, the formation of alliances has been predominant. In the former Soviet Union, not only the union was dissolved but also the monopoly carrier gave way to a series of competing airlines. In China, something similar happened but not quite, as we shall see below.

In the following sections we will zoom in on four airlines: KLM, Southwest, China Southern, and Lufthansa. Southwest is the pioneer of the low-cost model, and exemplifies the type of company that increasingly forms a threat to the established legacy carriers. Two such legacy carriers are KLM and Lufthansa. KLM is an example of a successful entrepreneurial firm within the old regulations, profiting from a lack of efficiency of its rivals. Lufthansa offers the example of a flag carrier with a big home market, but which had to catch up after having been set at a disadvantage for historical reasons, and which has become the most multinational enterprise in the business. China Southern, finally, is the most dynamic airline in the most dynamic aviation market in the world; it illustrates the changing landscape of civil aviation in China.

KLM[4]

KLM (short for Koninklijke Luchtvaart Maatschappij – Royal Air Traffic Company) was founded in 1919 by aeronautic pioneer Albert Plesman. It is the oldest airline in the world still operating under its original name. True to the spirit of its founder, KLM has indeed proved itself a pioneering airline throughout its history. For instance, in 1929 KLM started a scheduled service to Indonesia, which was until the outbreak of the Second World War the longest scheduled flight in the world. In 1991 KLM was the first European airline to introduce a customer loyalty program. The pioneering alliance with Northwest, initiated in 1993, has already been mentioned in the general description of the industry. KLM was also the first airline in the world to offer self-service kiosks for transfer passengers. Finally, with the formation of the Air France–KLM Group in 2004 these two airlines were trailblazers for the formation of like groups built around British Airways and Lufthansa.

At the time of the merger with Air France in 2004, KLM was the tenth largest airline in the world. That is an amazing accomplishment, given the small home market. How did KLM succeed to punch so much above its weight? One could say that KLM has been able to turn its disadvantage into an advantage. Many flag carriers were soothed by the relatively comfortable duopolies on many routes that were the outcome of bilateral agreements concerning landing rights, and lacked incentives to be as efficient as possible. Having no strong home market, KLM needed to lure away customers from other airlines' turfs, if it wanted to grow. The strategy of KLM became to 'steal' customers from other European airlines, by seducing them to fly to their final destination via its hub airport Schiphol Amsterdam, instead of through their national carrier's network. This means that in many cases KLM had an operational disadvantage, as it needed to make more (expensive) take-offs and landings. Moreover, to seduce customers in foreign markets, the airline needed to offer competitive prices. This is possible only by having a very strict cost control over operations, and by being able to respond swiftly to moves made by competitors. As a result KLM became an airline with an organizational culture characterized, according to its own employees, by being dynamic, commercial, entrepreneurial, pragmatic, and even opportunistic. In line with this positive self-image, the trade journal *Air Transport World* nominated KLM the 'Airline of the Year' in 1985.

Based on this strategy KLM became a big airline in a small country. The company has also profited from the Open Skies agreement between the Netherlands and the USA in 1992. This enabled the Dutch carrier to reap the fullest benefits from its joint venture with Northwest Airlines. This alliance, started as a 20 per cent minority share in Northwest in 1989, had a tumultuous history in terms of governance (with Northwest accusing KLM of secretly trying to gain control over it), but always remained very profitable to both partners. Having a link, through Northwest, to hundreds of destinations in North America, was a formidable boost to KLM's strategy. Northwest at that time was the sixth largest airline of the USA, with hubs in Minneapolis, Detroit and Memphis, and strong on both the domestic and the Pacific market. *Business Week* (19 February 1995) called the KLM-Northwest joint venture 'the first successful model of the strategic tie-ups that every airline covets . . . KLM and Northwest are skirting legal and cultural constraints that have stymied other airborne alliances and are pooling resources in the closest thing to a merger their industry has seen'.

This agility to stretch the envelope by playing the regulatory system could be seen as the most important strategic competence of KLM. However, in the period 1987–1997 the European Union in three steps abolished all restrictions to airlines in its internal market, and in 2008 an Open Skies agreement between the EU and the USA was concluded. This liberalization proved to be a game changer. KLM came under increasing competitive pressure, for two reasons. For one, the liberalization opened the door to low cost providers like Ryanair and Easyjet. These companies became very active in KLM's (already small) home market, offering direct flights to many European destinations from Amsterdam and other Dutch airports. Moreover, the various liberalization measures brought about a wave of consolidation in air transportation, which traditionally had been a very fragmented industry. For relatively small players, like KLM, there seemed to be no other option than to link up with other airlines. Sabena (Belgium) and Swissair are examples of airlines that could no longer compete as independent companies.

From 1990 onwards the search for one or more strong partners became a central element in KLM's strategy. On several occasions the company tried to come to an agreement with British Airways, but each time these attempts stalled because KLM wanted to have a bigger say in combined operations than BA would allow. KLM also tried to put together its own alliance network with SAS, Swissair and Austrian Airlines, under the codename Alcazar, but this attempt failed, too. Finally, a collaboration with Alitalia was announced in 1998.

This combination would start as a joint venture, but would gradually evolve to something close to a full merger. With hindsight it may be said that the difficulties and dangers of this strategy have been underestimated. Alitalia was a notoriously inefficient airline (which optimistically was interpreted by KLM as offering plenty of room for improvement). The combination also brought together companies from two very different cultures. The possible impact of this was somewhat pushed under the carpet by KLM CEO Leo van Wijk: 'If there is one thing I have learned during my long career at KLM it is that as long as you speak the business's language with each other you will always come to an agreement' (quoted in Jagersma, 2003: 330, our translation from Dutch). In reality however, the language gap was not so easy to bridge, as hardly any Dutchmen spoke Italian, and many Italians spoke poor English. Moreover, the political landscape in Italy was complex, and this ultimately led to the downfall of the combination. The new Malpensa airport near Milano was to be an important hub in the combined KLM-Alitalia network, but the development of this hub was undermined because the old airport of Milano was not closed down, as originally planned, and the infrastructure around Malpensa continuously lagged behind. Not believing any more in a positive outcome, KLM broke off the collaboration, leading to a successful damage claim of Alitalia.

In 2000 KLM stood alone again, and started to look for a partner even more franticly. During a few years, negotiations went on and off with British Airways and Air France simultaneously, and in May 2004 a merger with Air France was established. The French state at that time still had majority ownership of flag carrier Air France, but in the 10 years under first Christian Blanc and later Jean-Cyril Spinetta it had made a remarkable shift from the 'sick man' among European airlines to a successful and profit-making company. According to *Air Transport World* (Anonymous, 2005a: 26) 'Jean-Cyril Spinetta . . . awoke Europe's sleeping airline giant when he took the helm in 1997 and guided it firmly to the top of the industry'. According to Spinetta the two agreed that both Air France and KLM were 'middleweight champions in a heavyweight contest. In an increasingly global industry, we needed to get critical mass' (Anonymous, 2005b: 76).

The two airlines formed a new holding company that has the ownership of the two airlines, and these continued to operate quasi-independently. At the time of the merger, Air France–KLM was the largest airline group in the world in terms of passenger-miles. The merged company was headed by a Strategic Management Committee in which Air France and KLM each had four seats (with a casting vote for CEO Jean-Cyril Spinetta). This equality was in marked contrast with the relative weight in terms of shareholdings (approximately 80–20) and operational size (approximately 2:1). The Air France–KLM combination can be characterized as an acquisition that was managed as a collaboration between equals. The slogan of the combination was 'one group, two airlines, three businesses', underlining the continued own identity of Air France and KLM as operators. The three businesses were passengers, cargo and maintenance. The combination became a central player in the Skyteam alliance, and operated strong trans-Atlantic alliances with Delta Airlines (that had swallowed Northwest in 2008).

At the basis of this friendly merger was a deep understanding between the two CEOs, Spinetta and Van Wijk. Self-evidently, a merger bringing together companies from two culturally very different countries like France and the Netherlands poses some challenges. On top of that, the company cultures were seen to be very different, with KLM acting like a cowboy in the eyes of many Air France managers, and Air France still having characteristics of a state-owned company according to KLM managers. A culture assessment performed in February 2004 pointed at marked differences in decision-making style (with

KLM striving for consensus, and Air France being more hierarchical); time orientation (KLM more short-term, Air France more long-term oriented); and working style (KLM focusing on processes; Air France more on outcomes). But top management did not want to pay too much attention to culture, fearing that this would only increase the perceived differences.

Notwithstanding these differences the combination was successful, with Air France–KLM outperforming most of their competitors in the period 2004–2008. With the credit crisis setting in, however, the downside that the merger model followed became more visible. The integration between the two operating airlines had deliberately been slow and partial, but this also meant that cost synergies were not realized to the full extent. From 2009 onwards the group has gone from one cost-cutting exercise to another, with so far only limited success. Interestingly, the cultural differences, which had not been played up during the good years, also did not seem to be a real impediment when the going got tough, possibly because by then the companies were sufficiently used to each other.

Southwest Airlines[5]

Whereas KLM was a pioneer of the airline industry in general, Southwest has become famous as being the pioneer of the low-cost model. Southwest Airlines was established in 1967, and after a judicial battle for permission to fly, started operations from Dallas, and originally served only destinations in Texas. Today it is the largest domestic carrier in the USA, with about 45,000 employees and 550 planes, all of the Boeing 737 type.

The early legal struggles show that life for a newcomer like Southwest was not easy in the late 1960s and early 1970s, but this changed when President Carter signed the Airline Deregulation Act in October 1978. The deregulation provided the level playing field on which Southwest could excel. Herb Kelleher, the founder, was an outsider to the industry, and based the new company on an original set of ideas (although he heavily borrowed from Pacific Southwest Airlines, a company that operated until 1988). Rather than competing head-on with established carriers, Kelleher positioned Southwest as a company that could create a new market segment. Southwest offered an alternative to the car, offering faster transportation for the same price. All the same, Southwest and the many copycats that came in its wake do also form a threat to the established legacy carriers.

The business model of Southwest is based on a number of principles that were radically different from those of the established carriers at the time. First of all, Southwest works with a simple fare structure and, of course, low fares. Southwest's average one-way fare in 2012 was a bit under $150. A low fare can only be offered when operations are very efficient, and that was where most of the other characteristics of Southwest were geared to. The composition of the fleet, consisting of aircraft of only one type, allows for economies in maintenance and crew training. Instead of using travel agents, Southwest sells tickets directly to the customers, first mainly over the phone and since 1995 over the internet. Southwest was one of the first airlines to have a website. In order to save on high airport charges Southwest operates mainly from secondary airports. Southwest realized a higher aircraft utilization than traditional carriers, among other things because of a very short turnaround time at the gate: 15 instead of 45 minutes. As a result, its planes could make 10 flights a day, twice the industry average. The service provided by Southwest was point-to-point, i.e., no interlinking and connections that lead to complex planning and baggage systems. The focus was on transportation, without too many frills in terms of meals, drinks, etc. Part of the no-frills philosophy is also ticketless travel, and the use of plastic, reusable boarding passes. Finally, Southwest has been strong in avoiding the cyclical investment trap that plagues the industry, with all airlines typically ordering new aircraft in good times, which become operational when the market is already in a downturn. The strategy of Southwest has been to invest anti-cyclically, ordering aircraft when the market is slow, hence being able to negotiate very good conditions with the aircraft producer, Boeing. The effect has also been a controlled growth trajectory over the years.

One final but crucial element of Southwest's model consists of the employee policies. This is vital, because although the summary of the main cost-saving elements of Southwest's business model may give the impression of austere service provision, Southwest employees went out of their way to make flights enjoyable experiences. This is not feasible without good employee relations, and hence in contrast with what one might expect, Southwest is not necessarily a low-wage company, and it has never resisted unionization; in fact 82 per cent of employees are union members. Because it was a new start-up, salaries at Southwest were initially lower than those at traditional airlines, but as it is a policy of the company not to fire employees, the employee body is slowly ageing, adding to the costs. Moreover, the fact that Southwest in many years was the only airline making a profit caused unions to ask for wage increases, while many other companies went through restructuring accompanied by wage cuts. As a result Southwest today pays higher salaries to pilots and cabin crew members than the industry average for comparable positions. Southwest has also installed generous employee ownership schemes, with the effect that the company at present is 10 per cent employee-owned.

While the attention to good labour relations and the rising salary costs to a certain extent compromise the low-cost nature of Southwest, the upside is that labour productivity at Southwest is very high. Moreover, the company has been able to nurture a very characteristic culture, the 'Southwest Spirit', which has been instrumental to offering the passengers a pleasant experience. Southwest cultivates friendliness and a sense of humour, leading sometimes to very unorthodox examples of customer service. For instance, the example is known of a gate agent who volunteered to look after a dog of a departing customer for 2 weeks. Flight attendants regularly engage in all kinds of practical jokes and make hilarious flight announcements. This spirit is carefully cultivated, as is apparent from a quote from Southwest founder Herb Kelleher:

> It's just a lot of people taking pride in what they're doing . . . You have to recognize that people are still the most important. How you treat them determines how they treat people on the outside . . . I give people the license to be themselves and motivate others in that way. We give people the opportunity to be a maverick. You don't have to fit in a constraining model at work – you can have a good time.
>
> (quoted in Inkpen, 2013: 8)

The key to a policy that gives so much freedom to act to employees at all levels is a very careful selection process. In this process, Southwest singles out prospective employees with the right personality and attitude, rather than a specific education. 'We can change skill levels through training. We can't change attitude' (Kelleher, quoted in Teagarden, 2008: 8). Essential to the philosophy of Southwest is the notion that if you want employees to treat customers with care, concern and respect, the company has to treat them in the same way.

The success of Southwest ever since its founding has been tremendous. But the question may be asked whether the formula can also be maintained now iconic leader Herb Kelleher is no longer at the helm (he stepped down as CEO in 2008 and was succeeded by Gary Keller). Southwest is no longer the underdog, but has become a big company. The 2010 acquisition of AirTran also poses challenges, as this firm needs to be integrated without losing the unique Southwest spirit, and the acquisition also added foreign destinations to Southwest's network, a breach of one of the principles of the company. Adding international destinations brings more complexity to the operations, among other things in the reservation system. Labour unrest resulting in steep wage hikes in 2004 may be a sign that things have changed at Southwest. And it is now Southwest's turn, as an established incumbent, to be challenged by new entrants like JetBlue and Spirit, which have eroded Southwest's position in established profitable niches. What will be a viable strategy for the future?

The website *Aspire Aviation* (http://www.aspireaviation.com/2012/02/06/southwest-airlines-faces-challenges-in-airtran-integration/, retrieved on 20 July, 2014) already sees signs of a 'paradigm shift' at Southwest. The airline is trying to become more attractive to the business traveller, with new destinations in the Northeast, including congested airports the company shunned in the past. With the move to become more oriented towards business travel also the point-to-point nature of the operations is diluted as connectivity becomes more important, with for instance Philadelphia coming to resemble a hub airport for Southwest. But even though the emphasis now is on increasing revenue, according to *Aspire Aviation* Southwest cannot ignore its rising costs. Sooner or later it will have to confront its employees, as major competing airlines that have gone through Chapter 11 proceedings have been able to shed labour costs. Moreover, the sacrosanct policy of free check-in luggage may have to be abandoned.

All these signs suggest that the North American airline industry landscape is still subject to important forces for change, and it will be interesting to see how Southwest will navigate these evolving conditions.

China Southern Airlines

This airline is the largest and most dynamic one in China. It is, arguably, also the most 'occidentalized' airline in China and for this reason enables us to examine the working of a Chinese 'societal effect' particularly well.[6] Civil aviation in China after the Second World War was much like in the Soviet Union, where Aeroflot was a state monopoly line with quasi-govermental functions, involvement in the infrastructure of aviation and a distinctive military connection. This was also what Lufthansa had come to be under the Nazis. The Chinese airline was then called CAAC (Civil Aviation Administration of China). In 1987, the government of the People's Republic of China decided to split up this public enterprise and administration, generating a number of airlines that became joint-stock enterprises. Their organizational roots were in the operating divisions of CAAC. After an initial wave of privatizations that produced literally dozens of new airlines, a subsequent wave of concentration by take-over reduced the numbers considerably, again. With the economic reforms and development in China, air travel was opened up to rapidly increasing numbers of people, both internationally and domestically.

The principle of division applied to CAAC was to some extent regional; every one of the major airlines emerging had a regional focus that could also include several regions. They also had hubs in particular regions, and all of the larger airlines emerging served both, the international market and a number of domestic routes. The fleets were accordingly mixed, including long-range and medium-range aircraft. The airlines that emerged as the most important ones, after mergers, were:

- Air China
- China Southern
- China Eastern.

Longer established Chinese airlines in the international market were, in addition, Cathay Pacific in Hong Kong and Chinese Airways in Taiwan. Notably Cathay Pacific had made a name for itself by excellent service, winning a number of prizes. With the reverting of Hong Kong from British rule to the Chinese government in 1999, Cathay Pacific thus became a Chinese airline under the same state but governed by a somewhat different politico-economic system.

The other three large airlines after the wave of concentration were rather comparable in size, with China Southern coming out as the largest airline not only in China but also in Asia, in terms of passengers carried and the size of the fleet. Air China was most focussed on Peking as a hub but also other larger cities; it joined the Star Alliance and is visible in most parts of the world. Both China Eastern and China Southern, however, joined the Sky Team alliance, joining Delta in the USA and Air France-KLM. Cross-holdings of shares are not uncommon between Chinese airlines, so that competition does have its limits. Air China has a mutual cross-ownership of a quarter of equity capital with Cathay Pacific in Hong Kong. Cathay Pacific is a member of the Oneworld alliance, and has been one for at least traditional reasons (the old colonial link with British Airways and Quantas in Australia). This significant cross-ownership is apparently not hampered by the membership in different alliances, Star Alliance for Air China and Oneworld for Cathay Pacific. So far, the important airlines in China are all full service carriers with hubs-and-spokes operations and membership in alliances. Whilst Sky Team has both China Eastern and China Southern, Oneworld (dominated by the old colonial axis from Britain to Australia) is missing in mainland China. There are also regional carriers, but no significant low-cost airline has emerged so far; Asia outside China, though, does have low-cost airlines.

An interesting corporate governance incident occurred in 2007: the media had published in 2006 that the Chinese government intended selling large parts of its majority in the shares of China Eastern; a consortium of Singapore Airlines, Emirates and Japan Airlines, and Singapore Airlines and Temasek Holdings were together on the way to doing the transaction with the Chinese government. But Cathay Pacific tried to block the transaction by bidding for shares, which meant a take-over battle in China, though not as dramatic as would have happened in Anglo-American countries. The China National Aviation Corporation (successor to the CAAC) also became involved, as did Air China. The result was that even a sale of 25 per cent of the shares to foreign interests was judged detrimental to national interests, and ownership remained in China, with a cross-holding by Air China which is also linked by cross-holding to Cathay Pacific.

China Southern, however, featured a more visible exposure to the Western capital markets; it listed at both the New York and the Hong Kong stock exchanges and raised capital there, even before listing at the Shanghai stock exchange. This was quite distinctive. Significantly, too, the headquarters of this airline and one of its major hubs are in Guangzhou. This is an area of about 12 million inhabitants not far from Hong Kong in the Canton

(Guangdong) province, on the estuary of the Pearl River. In the same larger area there is also Shenzhen, another boom town of 10 million inhabitants, which had been developed as a free trade zone after the end of the 1970s, with different laws and regulations of economic governance. This was China's first major experimental step into the creation of capitalist institutions, a sort of new Hong Kong within the People's Republic. The expansion of the airline has so far been the most significant one in China. It is not by accident that its headquarters are in the earliest and most remarkable growth area outside Hong Kong.

The fleet currently numbers 464 planes and 50 more are ordered. Like the other major Chinese carriers, this airline has a mixture of Boeing and Airbus planes. For the medium-range routes, there is a balanced mixture of Airbus 320–200 (114 planes) and Boeing 737–800 (112 planes). Similarly, the airline has ordered both, the Airbus 380 and the Boeing 787 (the 'dreamliner') for long distances. Characteristically, both former Soviet and Chinese airlines have been using planes from Western manufacturers, particularly the Chinese and particularly for foreign routes. But acquisition of planes should not be imagined as purely commercial endeavours in China. It is quite apparent that the airlines, in a coordinated way and under the auspices of the government, have been negotiating with the manufacturers, not only about the selling prices but also the commitment of these manufacturers to opening production subsidiaries in, or outsourcing production to, China. Through coordinated negotiations about the ordering of hundreds of planes from Chinese airlines, Airbus was led to open a final assembly plant for the Airbus 320, the most frequently sold model, in China. Further investments followed suit. Acquisition of planes abroad is clearly set within centrally coordinated negotiations about investment of their manufacturers into manufacturing and service facilities in China. When a decision or transaction in the aerospace industry or aviation is announced in the press, it is habitual that the accompanying picture not only shows representatives of companies but also higher politicians. Furthermore, both the expansion of Chinese enterprises internationally and the policy for allowing direct investment of foreign multinationals in China, are governed by the principle of learning and technology transfer; forming joint ventures facilitates this. In 1990, Chinese Southern started an aircraft maintenance joint venture together with Hutchison-Whampoa (from Hong Kong) and Lockheed, the US aircraft manufacturer – though not of civil planes any more – at Guangzhou. China Eastern did something similar, with MTU from Germany for jet engine MRO.

The main hubs of the airline are at Peking, Guangzou, Chongqing and Ürümqi, with many other focus airports. Where code shares are concerned, China Southern not only has them with Sky Team members but also others, notably with prominent Star Alliance members such as United, Thai and Asiana. Doing code shares with airlines outside an alliance is not uncommon in the business, but it appears to be particularly prevalent on Asian routes, including routes from Europe to Australia.

Lufthansa[7] Group

The name translates into English as Air Hansa; the Hanseatic League was a medieval confederation of towns and territories in the Holy Roman Empire and beyond, allied to organize peaceful trade among the members principalities and towns. The brand symbol on the tailplane of the company's aircraft has over all the years been the crane bird which, in older mythology, symbolized endurance and loyalty. A company then called 'Luft Hansa' was founded in 1925, by the merger of the two larger civil aviation firms that were suffering losses. Its network soon became international, and it had pioneering operations in postal services to Brazil via West Africa, also establishing subsidiaries in South America, one of which today is Avianca, the Colombian airline. Luft Hansa made a name for itself by pioneering instrument flight along routes in Europe, as a way of making services regular despite the weather and in the night. A legendary chief of operations of the time was Carl August von Gablenz, a man with a military, technical and pilot background, and he very much pushed the instrument flight programme, against some controversy in the company and in the public because of the risks involved. As chief of operations, he also himself explored a new route to China over the Pamir mountains on a very adventurous flight – without paying passengers. Von Gablenz 'died with his boots on', in a flight accident in 1942,[8] something that has not happened to airline board members since.

Before and during the Second World War, Lufthansa was harnessed to the Nazis' efforts to make Germany a leading nation in aviation. Göring, a top Nazi, was a former First World War fighter ace and became minister of aviation, heading the new air force and civil aviation plus the aeronautical industry all in one. The head of the board of management of Lufthansa (LH), Erhard Milch,[9] became a general and secretary of state of the new air ministry after 1933. Planes bought by Lufthansa also had to be suited to military transport purposes. In the war, the airline became a transport and MRO arm of the air force. Much as it still flew civil routes until the bitter end of the war, it had been militarized beyond recognition and many aircrew were shot down whilst supplying and relieving troops over such dangerous places as the Mediterranean or Stalingrad. At the end of the war, there was nothing left of the company's assets, no planes, no workshops, no money; the company was dissolved. Both military and civil aviation were out of the question for Germans for 10 years. That was the time when airlines of neighbouring countries and the powers of occupation established themselves in an airspace that was, in West Germany, a very open market, except for German airlines.

Despite the war experience and the Nazi association, LH had become so much established as a trademark and a national symbol, that even in East Germany, when German aviation became possible again, the Communists immediately came up with the name and trademark again. Two Lufthansas were re-founded, one in the West and one in the East. The dispute about the label was settled, amazingly, by a court in Belgrade which held that the name was the property of the West German government since the East German one had symbolically severed all relations with the former German *Reich*. But the early period was difficult; entirely new planes had to be bought, there were new air traffic control methods and standards, and suitable pilots were lacking. The first generation of long distance captains was American, with salaries more than three times as high as those for German captains.

But in organizational culture, LH at first linked up with the pre-war tradition to some extent. An engineering enthusiasm and perfectionism permeated the organization, not only in the MRO services. Braunburg (1980) mentions that technical knowledge was instilled in the cockpit staff more than in comparable American airlines; he himself reports being chased around the plane, as a younger co-pilot on flights to South America, by the captain, with the task of finding and identifying specific valves or switches, just for the exercise. There was also initially some maintenance of the gruff and surly treatment known from the air force, called the 'tone of the barracks square' in Germany. More recently, though, it appears to have acquired an organization culture marked by a sense of purpose, flexibility, consideration and identification with the company (Sackmann, 2004: 73–94).

To what extent this cohesiveness can be maintained now that the airline is moving routes and staff outside the network connections, into a subsidiary (Germanwings) which is closer to the low cost business model, remains to be seen.

LH soon established itself in the market again, with governmental subsidies. But the market in Germany was initially as open and competitive as nowhere else, and the foreign competition had enjoyed a head start and 10 years' advance. LH tried to join up again with pre-war standards of reliability and sought to add quality of on-board service. Probably the most distinguished figure in the company during the earlier years was Reinhardt Abraham, board member and head of engineering after 1972. He was said to have given shape to the new fleet of jet planes, at the time by a focus on buying Boeing planes. The initial Boeing 737, probably the world's most successful plane ever, with of course a lot of modifications in successive generations, was developed on the basis of a LH specification and co-development activity, under Abraham's regime.

One of the earlier business problems was that, just at the time that the company had bought piston-engined and propeller-driven Lockheed Super Constellation and Super Star planes for long distances, PANAM and others massively invested into the new long-range jet aircraft (Boeing 707 and DC 8). That substantially changed the terms of competition on the North Atlantic route, the most important one at the time, cutting flight times in half. LH had to follow suit, so that the investment into the propeller planes just bought became difficult to earn back. The company appears to have learned that rejuvenation of the fleet has to be made lucrative, which can be helped by increasing the re-sale value of aircraft through painstaking MRO, which again increases the power of the MRO services in the organization. Furthermore, since there is little money to be earned by making planes but more by selling licensed spare parts and by MRO, LH gladly went for this lucrative niche and internalized MRO as far as possible. Later, Lufthansa Technik, as a division, offered MRO to anyone who came. It has consistently had higher profit margins in MRO than in passenger transport. For example, in 2009, Lufthansa Technik, the engineering division, generated 30 per cent of the operating results of the company, on the basis of only 10 per cent of its turnover. This development led to a fifth place in the league table for MRO in the world, higher than any other airline; the front positions are taken by Asian specialized MRO companies. One of the latest important moves following this business model was the foundation of N3, a joint venture with Rolls-Royce Aero Engines for MRO of Rolls-Royce Trent engines, a greenfield site in Arnstadt in East Germany. The Trent is in the class of engines with the greatest size and thrust, offered for planes such as the Airbus 380 and the Boeing 777 and 787.

At the top of the company, it is significant that after 1991, the chairmen of the board of management have been aeronautical engineers (and former heads of Lufthansa Technik) for 20 years, Jürgen Weber first and then Wolfgang Mayrhuber. These have led and marked the rise of the company to a leading position in the world. The airline has also put across an image of technical fanaticism in its in-flight magazine, which has had reports on technical change in aircraft, engines, air traffic control and airports, which is not found in any other airline's magazines. These focus on the attractions of destinations more exclusively. The most significant piece in this tradition was a lead article in 1983 about rivets, as a magnificently diverse and ever evolving queen of fastening techniques in aircraft manufacturing. To the *connaisseur*, it was riveting . . .

Marketing has not been a traditional strength of the company; it has lagged behind British Airways in the introduction and sophistication of seat pricing and reservation systems. One of the reasons was that pricing and reservation were decentralized, which impeded the procurement of the best systems. Before the start of the Star Alliance, the company was in considerable difficulty (Lehrer, 2006). But after that, its profitability improved considerably. However, it remained ridden with logistical problems due to the decentralized spread of business areas and population in Germany. Whilst Germany had an airport called Central Airport in the 1930s (Berlin-Tempelhof), the industrial and commercial pre-eminence of Berlin vanished after 1945, and West Germany was at a loss to define a main hub until the later 1950s, when Frankfurt-on-the-Main grew into this role. However, LH for a long time has not had a clear centre and headquarters; technical services were centred on Hamburg, flight services on Frankfurt, and commercial functions on Cologne. Over time, Frankfurt became more important, as a hub and company centre, but in the 1990s, the new Munich airport also developed into a hub role, following the grown industrial importance of Bavaria. Intercontinental flights also became more frequent in Düsseldorf, in the country's main industrial area but only 300 km north of Frankfurt. In the 1980s, competition from KLM became more important; apart from its own connections, KLM also used Eurowings, a German regional carrier, to ferry passengers from all over Germany to Amsterdam and deliver them to KLM's long-distance connections (see the KLM case above).

At that time, LH became very sensitive about competition from neighbouring countries. Like no other country in Europe, Germany has 11 neighbouring countries and lies right in the middle of competitive hubs: Amsterdam, Brussels, Zürich, Vienna and Copenhagen. As it happened, the flag carriers of Belgium, Switzerland and Austria drifted into difficulties in the 2000s; this was maybe predictable for Sabena in Belgium[10] but certainly not for Swissair which had an excellent reputation for quality of service and reliability. But smaller companies in smaller countries could not develop sufficiently extended hub-and-spoke networks because they did not have the scale of operations. For full service network carriers, the threshold of competitiveness had been rising. LH was very much afraid lest other larger airlines in Europe should play the KLM/Eurowings game. They not only bought Eurowings to reduce the flow of passengers going via Amsterdam, but also Swissair (renamed Swiss after bankruptcy) and the successor of Sabena (Brussels Airlines) when these went bankrupt, and Austrian AUA just before its difficulties became more virulent. In Italy, LH founded Air Dolomiti as a wholly owned subsidiary to ferry passengers from Italy to Munich for further connections; Italy had been plagued by a malfunctioning flag carrier for years (see the KLM case).

Today, LH Group has become the most multinational airline group in the world where nationality of the different components (wholly owned subsidiaries) is concerned. Swiss, Brussels Airlines, Air Dolomiti and Austrian are the main foreign subsidiaries and operate under their own trademarks; but they are integrated into the route system, planning, flight codes and group functions of LH. Since LH for reasons of its dispersed home market has to use hubs more than competing airlines in Europe anyway, and the hub airports have less non-changing passengers than e.g. London and Paris, LH gave Brussels, Zürich and Vienna the functions of a hub in its own network. Thus, LH connections to Africa started to be routed through the new Brussels hub using Brussels Airlines, and other Southern or Middle Eastern connections via Zürich using Swiss. This brought Swiss back to profitability in no time and Brussels followed suit. Austrian remained more problematical but seems to be improving, but LH also abolished an extremely generous collective agreement (automatic wage increases) in Austrian radically. It has also been building up a subsidiary closer to the low cost business model, Germanwings, to fly routes that do not connect hubs and have fewer passengers with connecting flights. LH hubs now include Frankfurt,

Munich, Zürich, Vienna, Brussels, and to a minor extent Düsseldorf. The centre of Germanwings' operations is at Cologne-Bonn.

LH Group now has about 120,000 employees and one of the larger fleets in the world, with over 600 planes, but more than half of them fly under other trademarks or subsidiaries mentioned above. 200 planes are presently ordered from manufacturers, but old ones are also due to be phased out as a function of demand. Efficiency is, in view of this diversity and the need to coordinate different subsidiaries and operations across five major hubs, a demanding challenge. But in 2013 the Group had a better earnings development than British Airways-Iberia, and a much better one than Air France-KLM.

Study questions

1 Assess the regulatory and economic international context of civil aviation. Analyse and compare forces working towards cross-national assimilation and harmonization, with the forces working towards specific and different business models and strategies.
2 For each airline discussed above: analyse the economic rationale of the business model and the strategy, the mode of internationalization and organizational characteristics.
3 Again for each airline discussed above: show what in the behaviour or policies of the airline is clearly rooted in established national cultures and institutions.
4 Again for each airline discussed above: is there something in the behaviour and policies of the airline which strikes you as going against national culture and institutions? How can the deviation conceivably be explained?
5 How do cultural and institutional factors relate to one another, in the comparative analysis of the airlines you just did?
6 Look at the overall evolution of civil aviation regulation and airline business models and modes of organizing since the end of the Second World War. Are airlines becoming more alike, or different? In the diversity that you see, which role is played by countries in which the airlines are embedded?

This work can be extended indefinitely, because there are many more airlines in the world, and using search engines, you can retrieve a lot of information about them. The industry association, IATA, also has a website which leads on to a great deal of information, some of which is free and some of which can be ordered (www.iata.org/).

Further reading

Abeyratne, R.I.R. (2001) *Aviation Trends in the New Millenium.* Aldershot: Ashgate.

For anyone who likes to dig deeper into civil aviation, this is a detailed and informative treatment of commercial and liability issues, and developments of aviation in the different world regions. It is particularly detailed about regulative and juridical questions.

Notes

1 Any reflections on 'level playing fields' in a 'liberal market economy'?
2 Deutsches Zentrum für Luftund Raumfahrt e.V. 2008, Analyses of the European air transport market. Airline business models. Cologne: DLR. See http://www.dlr.de/fw
3 The different spelling is no mistake. In Britain, the name of the plane finished without an e, in France with one.

4 This case was written on the basis of Noorderhaven, Kroon and Timmers (2010); Jagersma (2003); observations and interviews at Air France – KLM; and the KLM website (http://www.klm.com/corporate/en/).

5 Case written on the basis of Inkpen (2013); Jagersma (2003); Lawton (2003); Teagarden (2008); and the Southwest Airlines website (http://www.southwest.com).

6 Research on Chinese airlines is hard to find. We rely on information on websites: [en.wikipedia.org/wiki/List_of *airlines*_in_China] is a good entry, and on China Southern, [en.wikipedia.org/wiki/China_Southern_Airlines] has detailed information.

7 Much of what is reported is owed to a knowledgeable and very personal history of the company by Rudolf Braunburg (1980) *Kranich in der Sonne. Die Geschichte der Lufthansa.* Frankfurt a.M.: Fischer. Braunburg had been one of the first postwar pilots.

8 In a way both similar and dissimilar to Albert Plesman in KLM and Herb Kelleher in Southwest, von Gablenz became a folk hero. The company headquarters of Lufthansa after the Second World War was for many years in a street in Cologne duly named after him. When LH moved its headquarters, the street name moved with it!

9 Milch was the most prominent Nazi government member who was also a son of a Jewish father – which did not make him a Jew by Jewish but one by Nazi standards. Queried by higher party members how he could permit a Jew to lead the air ministry and Lufthansa together, Göring is supposed to have replied: 'It is up to me to decide who is a Jew'. Milch was considered an energetic and capable organizer.

10 A joke among passengers was that Sabena is the abbreviation for 'such a bad experience never again'.

References

Anonymous (2005a) Air France-KLM Group ATW Airline Achievement awards. *Air Transport World* 42(2), 26–27.

Anonymous (2005b) Award winners optimistic, realistic. *Air Transport World* 42(4), 76–78.

Braunburg, R. (1980) *Kranich in der Sonne. Die Geschichte der Lufthansa.* Frankfurt a.M.: Fischer.

Business Week (1995) Flying high at KLM. *Business Week International* cover story. BloomBergBusinessWeek Business Week Archives. Online. Available HTTP: <http://www.businessweek.com/stories/1995-02-19/flying-high-at-klm-intl-dot-edition>, retrieved on 23 August, 2014.

Inkpen, A. (2013) *Southwest Airlines.* Thunderbird School of Global Management case A09-13-0008.

Jagersma, P.K. (2003) *KLM – Waarheen Vliegt Gij?* Heemstede: Holland Business Publications.

Lawton, T.C. (2003) Managing proactively in turbulent times: Insights from the low-fare airline business. *Irish Journal of Management* 24(1), 173–193.

Lehrer, M. (2006) German industrial strategies in turbulence: corporate governance and managerial hierarchies in Lufthansa. *Industry and Innovation* 4 (1), 115–140.

Noorderhaven, N.G., Kroon, D.P. and Timmers, A.D. (2010) KLM na de fusie met Air France: Cultuurverandering in het perifere gezichtsveld. Digitaal Cahier for J. Boonstra, *Leiders in cultuurverandering; Hoe Nederlandse organisaties succesvol hun cultuur veranderen en strategische vernieuwing realiseren.* Stichting Management Studies, Den Haag.

Sackmann, S. (2004) *Erfolgsfaktor Unternehmenskultur.* Wiesbaden: Gabler.

Teagarden, M.B. (2008) *Creating the Future at Southwest Airlines.* Thunderbird School of Global Management case A09-08-0014.

Index

Note: Page numbers followed by 'f' refer to figures and followed by 't' refer to tables.

C

H

Y

Z